PRESENT-DAY PSYCHOLOGY

PRESENT-DAY PSYCHOLOGY

*An Original Survey of Departments,
Branches, Methods, and Phases, Including
Clinical and Dynamic Psychology*

&

Edited by A. A. ROBACK

*With the Collaboration of Forty Experts
in the Various Fields*

PHILOSOPHICAL LIBRARY
NEW YORK

Printed in the United States of America

Table of Contents

PART I

TOPICAL DEPARTMENTS

Part II

BRANCHES

PART III

DYNAMIC AND CLINICAL PSYCHOLOGY

PREFACE

Anthologies and collective surveys have never been so plentiful as they are today. Sometimes one questions whether the avalanche of such over-all digests is a healthy sign for science and literature, whether it does not encourage a tendency to take the easy road and to depend on the judgment of editors rather than on one's own discernment. While the present editor is inclined to see the danger in such a disproportion of actual science as compared with fragmentary and not properly sifted, occasionally even ill-assimilated, reports, there is this to be said on behalf of the survey, viz., that it does fill a need in our age of specialization and rapid progress in the sciences, with many thousands at work on research. No man can possibly master more than a segment of his science, and unless he wishes to become wholly absorbed in his own little area, he must look to some conspectus which would bring all the results together.

Although the present survey is perhaps the most comprehensive in psychology, thus far, outside of an encyclopedia, it is by no means exhaustive, and was not intended as such. It will be gratifying if the result should be considered as representative not of a single trend, no matter how influential or prestige-laden, but affording us a fair view of all trends and topics.

Even the academic research worker scarcely realizes what is involved in a publication consisting of forty contributions, with each of the collaborators accustomed to produce in his own individual style. Aside from the fact that the productive investigator is not keen on writing general summaries, there is the matter of individual differences, of school angles, of methodological approach.

When a few contributors are invited to collaborate, the task is comparatively easy, but as the number increases, the difficulties multiply. The present work has necessitated the writing of nearly 700 letters; and, of course, some telegrams and long distance calls may be taken for granted. In the first place, this is not a case of "many are called but few are chosen." Usually the person qualified as a contributor to a symposium is engaged in research of his own, which he is loath to leave. Even the average psychologist has little leisure time, and those who have gained prominence do not rest on their laurels. Often, the time set turns out to be too short notice, and with the best of intentions, the prospective contributor must beg off. Emergencies, trips abroad, illness, etc. are the cause of interruptions and sometimes the abandonment of the task. The chapter on neurology was assigned to five different men before it was finally completed. An interesting booklet could be written on the individual differences of contributors. How prompt and meticulous some are, and how dilatory others! While one contributor will send his Ms. by airmail special delivery to meet the deadline, another must be reminded again and again that he is delaying the publication. Small wonder that the volume is a year late in appearing, but then perhaps, too, the editor was too sanguine in his calculations, and should have expected something of the sort.

Only in one instance was it necessary to return an excellent paper by one of the foremost linguistic scholars of today, because he had misunderstood the scope of the work and produced an essay on a single specialized subject. After casting about for a substitute in vain, I found it more expedient to tackle the chapter myself.

In every case contributors are wholly responsible for the content of their chapters after following the editorial directives. Revision concerned the style or diction (particularly in chapters written by newcomers to the United States) and in contexts where the sense was not clear, the writers were asked to rephrase the passage. One chapter, alone, the most controversial of all, required the exchange of at least a score of letters.

An effort was made to include some of the European view-points and recent achievements in psychology through foreign contributions, but with very limited success. Naturally Germany and Austria are to some extent represented by recent arrivals from those countries. We have one British collaborator, but contacts with others, in France and in Switzerland, did not materialize. At best, such contributors could have handled only parts of a topic or branch.

The dedication to a German psychologist who is almost un-known in the United States should not be regarded as a whim or fancy on the part of the editor. At the time Kurt Huber's name was mentioned in my HISTORY OF AMERICAN PSYCHOLOGY, *I had not yet been able to ascertain whether the man was merely a rebel against Hitler, toward the latter part of the Nazi war, or a genuine fighter for liberty. My recent inquiries of the Rector of the University of Munich, brought little information except for the address of Professor Huber's widow, but I have since found* Huber zum Gedächtnis *which appeared in 1947 (Regensburg: Habbel); and it is my considered opinion that the scientific and philosophical contributions of this rare spirit should be made known to the English-speaking world. He was not yet 50 when the Nazi executioner severed his head. His last days were spent in writing bracing letters and serene verse to his wife and young son.*

The most heartening thing about my quest was learning that Mrs. Klara Huber was residing on . . . KURT HUBER *Strasse in Gräfelfing. And what has become of the many Hitler streets, avenues, boulevards, terraces, parks, etc.? This time the mills of the gods were not so slow in the grinding.*

The sad news of Dr. William E. Galt's sudden death just as the volume was to go to press poignantly brings to mind the painstakingness and considerateness of our lamented colleague, whose chapters on attention and memory have considerably enriched this symposium.

PRESENT-DAY PSYCHOLOGY

In this arduous labor, my pleasant relations with all of the contributors have somewhat lessened the burden and suspense. I feel indebted to my co-workers for their splendid coöperation; and it is my belief that many a student and instructor will be beholden to them who have given generously of their time and energy in order to help consolidate the gains of their science.

A. A. ROBACK

Cambridge, Mass.
Feb. 20, 1955

PART I

Topical Departments

INTRODUCTION

The present work is the outgrowth of the editor's *History of American Psychology*. If it is possible for one man to cover the gradual development of a science during three centuries, diachronically treated, the synchronic purview of psychology during the past quarter-century is beyond the powers of even the most prodigious surveyor, for he would have to be conversant with the progress of every special field from neurology to statistics.

It would, of course, have been ideal if such an individual could be found; for the volume would then have achieved a measure of unity which no collaboration could ever hope to attain, but under the circumstances, the next best thing was to press into service a number of experts each to tell the story of a chosen field or parcel.

This is an age of anthologies and symposia. Both have their merits and faults. The anthologist's task is comparatively easy. He has but to examine a number of works on a given topic and to choose what he considers appropriate for his purpose. He can take as much or as little as he sees fit, once he has obtained permission. On the other hand, anthologies are a matter of scissors and paste, and while in *belles-lettres,* they have always occupied an honored place, because there *variety of form* is an object in itself, in science, *per contra* the anthology often is a short-cut both for editor and reader. The scientific worker, after all, does not need a digest to guide him. He can by a little effort make his own selections, and the multiplication of scientific anthologies does not bespeak a healthy development; for it means gathering material from, say, a score of books and articles and bringing it out in one volume. All duplication leads to waste, so far as actual scientific production is concerned.

COMPILATION IS NOT COLLABORATION

The collective volume, in the sense of a symposium, possesses the obvious merit of bringing something new to the storehouse of knowledge. Everyone contributing has been intrusted with a task, and all are working toward a goal as conceived by the editor. In a small degree, the symposium may be likened to an orchestra concert as compared with that furnished by the "disc jockey", as he is jocularly called. Canned music of a high type may, and often does, give greater thrills than an indifferent regular performance, especially where the programme is unimpressive, but other things equal, collective effort called forth by spontaneity is more fruitful of results.

The symposium, however, is not without its handicaps. In the first place, it is not always that an editor can select the contributors. It is becoming more and more difficult to find an eminent scientist who is free to accept an assignment unless the deadline set is many months away. Even then, one cannot be sure that certain incidents or mishaps will not intervene to nullify the promise. Supposing, however, all collaborators eventually deliver their chapter, there is the further snag of lack of uniformity; for no matter how specific the directives might be, individual differences will enter considerably in the interpretation as well as in the execution of the specifications. Some are prone to treat the material as a sort of bibliographical survey, citing authors but devoting little space to the elaboration of the findings; others, again, will deal largely with their own investigations, thus narrowing the area to a small strip. Occasionally, too, someone approaches his task as if it were an encyclopedic assignment. It is unnecessary to dwell on the amount of work entailed in the editing of a large collective work which often requires the rewriting of whole passages, and a great amount of revision after extensive correspondence. Even then, uniformity and mechanical regularization have not been achieved. But, perhaps, this shortcoming is not so serious as it is generally believed. Possibly rigid standardization has been overstressed, and a whiff of variety is at times refreshing.

It would have been ideal, if each department or field could have been treated against an historical background, where the chief figures in that field for the past half century all received their due, and yet where special emphasis is laid on the more recent research. This expectation is borne out in some of the chapters only.

Several remarks must be made now on the plan of this work. In the first place, it will be observed by the reader that the volume is divided into five parts: (a) departments, (b) fields, (c) clinical and dynamic phases, (d) methods, (e) borderlands. The traditional classification has been adhered to because, after all, it is the simplest and most satisfactory in that it is known to all and does not purport to place psychology into a narrow physicalistic framework. Even if sensations and perceptions were to be viewed as coming under one head, there is sufficient difference between them to warrant their being taken up in separate chapters. Despite the moves to reduce all sensation and perception to discriminative reactions, the very innovators often sense that they are leaving a gap, which the terminology of Hull, Tolman, and the Russian Pavlovians cannot bridge. It is certainly better to keep the old label and enumerate the contents, both old and recent, than to discard it for something which at once commits us to a behavioristic position.

There can scarcely be any disputing as to the fields. Some may wonder why this or that field is included. My aim has been to be comprehensive and catholic. Everything which is under investigation and of psychological import should find a place in a general symposium. Of the traditional branches, differential psychology has of late been regarded as a sort of adjunct, in each case, to the individual departments. It would certainly be very difficult to condense even the most important findings of differential psychology in a single chapter.

Clinical and dynamic psychology are treated together and in a separate division largely because of convenience. This area has grown to such an extent as to overshadow the other fields.

What used to be called abnormal psychology is now incorporated in a larger stretch with new appointments. Dynamic psychology is more than a field. It is a special phase of psychology which runs through all human nature. Hence the amount of space allotted to this division is not disproportionate.

The two chapters under the caption of Methods may seem out of place. Certainly a division labeled Methods should include a good deal more, but neither integrative psychology nor statistics would fit into a classification of branches. They deal rather with methods of application.

Under borderlands and humanistics are grouped those topics which are not sufficiently advanced or extensive to be regarded as full branches, and have not been treated as such in general textbooks. Such developments are comparatively recent. In some instances, as the psychology of religion, the psychology of values etc., the subject-matter transcends the general framework.

The present work purports to cover not only the main departments and fields but also such often inaccessible areas as are usually neglected. In a sense, this symposium is calculated to make amends for the gaps all too frequently occurring in similar collections. From their constitution, one might have thought that all psychology consisted of learning or projective testing or depth analysis. And because some points of view and treatments preponderate, all further attempts to treat psychology collectively tend to perpetuate this somewhat narrow approach, objectivistic as it may be. The net result is that certain topics are almost taboo, at least for the time being, until the lopsidedness reveals itself when experimentalists begin to take stock of their life achievements and ask themselves whether psychology as a comprehensive discipline can afford to omit from its purview all that does not squeeze into a physicalistic mould. Learning has opened up new vistas, but why must we give up other lines of investigation?

Physicalism in psychology has fortunately been somewhat curbed by the advent of psychoanalysis and even Gestalt psychology, but it has found it expedient to espouse at least Freud's teaching, in order to make an ally out of a foe. Such a form of strategy is more political than scientific. It tends to make of two very influential schools a power group so as to control the whole theatre of inquiry. Since nothing succeeds like success, and nothing by the same token, is apt to produce failure like neglect, we are running the hazard of losing a considerable amount of information and enlightenment because of a partisan compact, powerful by virtue of its position and academic facilities.

That must not be. We ought not to throw overboard topics like emotion, e.g., only because there is a trend at present in that direction. Let us remember that trends also come and go, that operationism has not yet proved itself as the arbiter of what is matter for psychological investigation any more than behaviorism or reflexology has. *

If, therefore, some chapters are not as lengthy as they might have been expected while others, generally treated very briefly, if at all, are elaborate, it is largely due to the method of procedure outlined above, viz., to balance things and not to heed the decisions of the mighty, for they might be biased, perhaps just as biased as the editor of this collective volume.

---

*It is indeed gratifying to note that P. W. Bridgman, the original proponent of operationism in all science, which has had such a vogue in anti-mentalistic circles and laboratories, wishes us now (*Scientific Monthly,* July, 1954, vol. 79) to gain "mastery of the microscopic world of introspection." The slow pendulum is beginning to move in the other direction.

CHAPTER I

RECENT FINDINGS IN GENERAL NEUROLOGY

JOSEPH G. KEEGAN, S.J., Ph.D.

Chairman, Dept. of Psychology, Fordham University

EDITORIAL NOTE

Whether it was due to Freud's declaration of the independence of the mental or to the growing specialization in psychology proper, neurology is no longer regarded as a branch of psychology (cf. the label "physiological psychology") as in the days of the pioneers. Yet we cannot disregard the fact that it is more intricately connected with it than physics, chemistry, or even biology. And the laboratories still eagerly seek to explain and interpret the mental in terms of the neurological; indeed, there is a special hankering for physiological linkage among the para-Freudians. Freud himself more than once would drop a hint as to the physical basis of his dynamic principles ("perhaps by transforming freely mobile into bound energy"). Many still look to neurologists as their guiding stars in their especially behavioristic (operational) explorations. If neurology, therefore, is not an integral part of psychology, it is its closest neighbor.

Dr. Joseph G. Keegan, who has kindly undertaken to do this first chapter in our collective work, was a lecturer in biology at Canisius College before embarking on his psychological studies. After an apprenticeship under Sir Cyril Burt at the University of London, he concentrated in physiological psychology at Yale University, where he received his doctorate, after which he resumed his teaching at Fordham University where he is currently Chairman of the Psychological Department. He is also a member of several learned societies both in the United States and abroad.

From Dr. Keegan's summary we learn, for one thing, that the issues in neurology have not been settled with any greater finality than those in psychology, and that the former is sometimes dependent on psychological research for further orientation.

In the extensive amount of research pertaining to the broad field designated as neurophysiology, there is increasing evidence that psychologists must extend their horizons so as to include biochemistry as well as neuro-anatomy and electrophysiology. Hence, in undertaking to present a resumé of recent findings one must carefully delimit boundaries. In the present chapter attention is directed only to those recent studies that investigate or attempt to elucidate general neurological function. No effort will be made to include the sense organs and the major emphasis will be on the following four aspects of neurological research: (a) localization of function with particular reference to distinctions between old and new brain; (b) epithalamus and emotions; (c) neural relations in behavior called abnormal; (d) findings gleaned from lobotomy and lobectomy.

Effect of Cerebral Lesions

In several recent surveys[10, 18] attention continues to be directed to functional aspects of larger brain divisions as well as to those of more minute specific areas. It has been noted, for instance, by Cloake[10] that such higher functions as orientation, body schema as well as a speech and intellectual function can be maintained quite well by one hemisphere even when that one had not been the normally dominant one. The functions that seem to be tied to their hemisphere, as it were, and incapable of being transferred to the other hemisphere are the sensory and motor (Rolandic) functions and the hemisphere's visual half field. But it is pointed out that the diencephalon, especially the hypothalamus is of great importance in the maintenance of consciousness and the functions referred to as those of the highest level.[1] In a slightly different context, Klebanoff *et al.*,[18] emphasize that much recent work with the brain-injured child may indicate even more generalized cerebral localization of function in children.

11

In an effort to test "equipotentiality" of cortical function in rats, Pickett[25] investigated the blinded animal's retention and relearning of a maze habit. The habit in question was controlled solely by somesthetic stimuli. Lesions in the posterior areas of the cortex attaining in extent up to 41.6 per cent had no effect on the learned habit. Within the range of lesions (8.8 to 41.6 per cent) contrary to expectation on the basis of Lashley's work, there was no relation between extent of posterior lesion and retention, post-operatively. On elevated mazes sensori-motor lesions produced uncoördinated running but there was again no relation between extent of the lesion (ranging from 5.7 to 38.1 per cent) and the deficit due to motor incoördination. In the alley maze, sensori-motor lesions averaging 23 per cent did not produce deficit significantly greater than posterior lesions of about the same amount (23.6 per cent). But there was a high positive correlation between deficit and extent of sensori-motor lesion.

Rosner[30] also working with rats, found that lesions of the neocortex amounting to less than 15 per cent of total cortex produced no impairment in performance on two types of mazes that had been previously learned. With lesions that amounted to more than 20 per cent of neocortex there were signs of refusal to perform.

Also comparable lesions of older cortex produced significantly poorer post-operative performance than lesions of neocortex.[2] Harlow and his co-workers[16] and Leary et al.,[21] studied the effects of anterior and posterior cortical lesions in monkeys. Stereotypy was noted by the latter workers in monkeys having frontal lesions. In the former study the posterior lesion animals performed as well as the normal animals on problems of the delayed response type. But monkeys with frontal injuries performed more poorly on the same task. For discrimination problems the results were reversed: in these, frontal-lesion animals and normal animals exceeded the level of performance manifested by the posterior-lesion monkeys. As a result of this work at the Wisconsin laboratories, the authors stress the complementary features of "frontal and posterior syndrome" and discount an hypothesis of equipotentiality in the associative cortex.

Stewart and Ades[34] on the basis of earlier experimentation as well as that reported in the article under consideration, conclude that "spontaneous reorganization" can occur in the central nervous system. Specifically, they think this occurrence can account for the fact that a learned auditory habit is retained without retraining trials, if the superior temporal gyri are ablated in two stages. Provided a period of seven days or more is allowed to elapse between the two operations, they found that a conditioned avoidance response to sound was retained. With prefrontal lobectomy performed before the two-stage ablation in the temporal lobe the habit was lost after the final ablation regardless of the time interval between the two-stage temporal ablation; consequently any such "reorganization" within the temporal lobe and its connections would presuppose intact prefrontal lobes and anterior commissure and corpus callosum too, according to these authors.

RECLASSIFICATION OF CORTICAL AREAS

Rosvold and Pribram [31] point out that both human and animal evidence has suggested a division of frontal lobes into (a) lateral granular and transitional cortex[3] that are involved in certain forms of problem solving behavior, and (b) medial granular and agranular cortex, that are involved in emotional expression. Consequently, they undertook to explore further the comparative physiological relevance of these regions by comparing the behavior of baboons with lesions in these respective areas. Daily ratings of characteristic emotional expression and level of performance on delayed response tests were determined. Preoperative tests furnished data for dividing nine animals into approximately equated groups, one control and two experimental or operated groups. These latter had bilateral ablations of the lateral-frontal and medial-frontal regions respectively. Postoperatively the lateral-frontal animals were unable to perform beyond chance on the delayed-response type of test and could not be retrained, whereas the medial-frontal animals showed little or no deficit or could be retrained if deficit occurred. However, as judged by the daily ratings, there were no consistent intergroup differences in emotional expression.

Recently Pribram and Maclean[27] used the method of strychnine neuronography to explore the interconnections between the limbic and extralimbic cortex of the medial and basal aspects of the cerebral hemispheres. On the basis of their careful explorations they describe the following six regional systems:

(a) *Fronto-temporal*: there was a firing pattern[4] common to the posterior orbital, anterior insular, temporal polar and peri-amygdaloid areas; (b) *Medial occipito-temporal;* findings revealed a new two-way relationship between the limbic areas of the medial temporal cortex and regions of medial occipital and medial temporal extralimbic cortex; (c) *Medial parieto-occipital*: connections here are with the hippocampus; (d) *Medial fronto-parietal*: they report a previously unrecognized amount of firing of the medial cortex from the superior frontal area; (e) *Medial frontal*: this region is delineated by firing pattern common to strychninization of the limbic cortex of the subcallosal and medial orbital areas and the extralimbic cortex of the ventromedial frontal polar area; (f) *Hippocampus*: though no reciprocal connections between the hippocampus and other regions are established, there was an interesting unidirectional firing of these regions.

Crucial to any cortical division on the basis of neuronographic findings, in the view of these authors are the thalamocortical systems which make available to the cortex information from extracortical structures. They point out also that, in development, the organization of the extra-limbic cortex may be influenced by the adjacent phylogenetically older limbic cortex. At any rate their results indicate that, for the medial and basal cortex, the inter-relationship between limbic and extra-limbic cortex provides a basis of distinction. They call attention to the fact that four of the regions they identify bridge grossly defined hemispheric lobes, namely the fronto-temporal, medial occipito-temporal, medial parieto-occipital and medial fronto-parietal regions.

EXPERIMENTATION ON MONKEYS

An investigation of the effects of cortical ablation on learned discrimination is that of Riopelle *et al.*,[29] reporting from the Wisconsin laboratories on their work with monkeys. They used animals that had received a great amount of preoperative training on a variety of visual discrimination tasks and divided the animals into four groups as follows: (a) a visual group or animals with bilateral ablation of the prestriate areas; (b) a frontal group of animals that had extensive unilateral decortication and frontal lobe ablation on opposite sides; (c) a posterior group which resembled the second group except that the contralateral area ablated was a region between the intraparietal and lunate sulci; (d) a control group of unoperated animals. One outcome was that there were no differences between any of the operated groups and the normal animals on simple discrimination. However, the posterior group was notably inferior to the others in pattern discrimination and mirror-image pattern discrimination. On serial discrimination tests both frontal and posterior groups proved inferior.

Meyer, Harlow, and Ades[23] also working in the Wisconsin laboratories, noted little impairment in performance of monkeys on delayed response and oddity problems after bilateral ablation of the prestriate areas. Evaluating their own results in relation to some of Lashley's[20] earlier work, the authors hypothesize that differences in experimental findings are due to differing amounts of previous training on the type of problem employed. They think that habits applicable to a particular problem may be lost but that those applicable to the solution of a class of problems remain after pre-occipital ablation. In this connection, it is notable that the oddity problem seemingly is a sensitive indicator where large unilateral ablations are concerned. Contralateral ablation either of frontal or posterior areas enhances the effect but unlike other learning tasks the oddity problem shows up deficiencies even after training on a series of problems of the same class.

Warren and Harlow[36] used three groups of monkeys to compare learning ability as influenced by frontal and parieto-temporo-occipital lesions respectively. The learning tasks involved visual discrimination and the three groups included a normal unoperated group as well as groups representing frontal lesions and lesions in the parieto-temporo-occipital areas respectively. They found that the frontal and posterior groups were inferior to the normal group on problems involving color-pattern, form-pattern and size-pattern discrimination. There were no significant intergroup differences in object discrimination. In a comparable investigation, Blum[5] used monkeys with frontal cortex ablations to study the effects on delayed response to auditory and visual cues, as well as upon an auditory discrimination problem. Lesions involved dorsal, midlateral, or ventrolateral areas of the granular layer of the frontal cortex; and in some animals all these parts were ablated. The severer deficiencies were shown by the animals having midlateral lesions while the performance of animals having dorsal and ventro-lateral lesion was only slightly deficient. The author sought an explanation in terms of a general perceptual loss since the impairment found did not appear to be related to any particular sense modality.

CRUCIAL INFERENCES

Also working with monkeys, Wade[35] studied the comparative effects of prefrontal lobectomy and lobotomy and found that "intellectual function" was not impaired in several other tests, but on the delayed response test there was impairment.

Differentially, lobectomy increased reactivity whereas lobotomy caused its reduction.[5] Impairment of delayed reaction was about equal following both of these operations but a form of operation involving circumsection did not affect delayed response, although it did introduce some instability in a conditioned discrimination response. Pribram *et al.*,[26] employing baboons ablated dorsolateral frontal cortex in one group and ventrolateral cortex in another.

For both groups the ablations were bilateral. Before ablation

16

training was given in visual discrimination and delayed response performance. It was notable that postoperatively there was greater performance impairment on both tasks for the animals with dorsolateral ablations. The important inference from this study was that much of the previously observed behavioral effect of frontal ablation in other research was predominantly associated with deficit in the dorsolateral area.

Prefrontal lobotomy has also been studied in relation to the social behavior of monkeys. Brody and Rosvold[8] set up in these animals a dominance hierarchy marked by aggressive attacks directed downward in the hierarchical order. Prefrontal lobotomy upset this order and this social change was evidently associated with loss of their learned avoidance responses on the part of operated animals previously in the lower ranges of the dominance hierarchy. There resulted in effect both upwardly directed aggression and upward movement in the hierarchy.

After cerebral operations performed on human patients to relieve epileptic seizures, Forgays[11] observed that there were delayed intellectual and aphasic as well as sensory and motor defects.[6] The delayed effects usually manifested themselves about two days after operation and spontaneous recovery occurred usually in about a month. In the group of 50 patients, all major portions of the cortex were variously represented. In an additional report Forgays[12] states that the delayed disturbances were manifest following frontal plus parietal as well as following bilateral parietal lesions. But the effects were less noticeable after bilateral parietal lesions. No significant impairment followed bilateral frontal, bilateral occipital or anterior cerebellar lesions.

EPITHALAMUS AND EMOTION

There has been a great deal of interest in recent years in the possibility of assigning to parts of the forebrain such as the olfactory brain or rhinencephalon a rôle in emotional behavior. Though their discussions revolve largely about the morphology or anatomy of the rhinencephalon, Pribram and Kruger[26a] have presented a fundamental analysis, especially of the relevant fore-brain structures that are not typical neocortex. They assemble and integrate the histological and electro-physiological data that render plausible a distinction of three systems within the rhinencephalic formations: a) those having direct connections with the olfactory bulb (olfactory tubercle, area of the diagonal band, prepyriform cortex, cortico-medial nuclei of the amygdala); b) those having direct connections with the former or first system but not with the olfactory bulb (subcallosal and fronto-temporal transitional cortex, septal nuclei and basolateral nuclei of amygdaloid complex); c) those having direct connection with the second system but not with the olfactory bulb or with the first system (Ammon's formation, retrosplenial and cingulate transitional cortex).

In addition there are afferent connections from the septal nuclei and amygdaloid complex to the epithalamus and anterior hypothalamus. The third system, besides being related to the anterior thalamus via the fornix and septal nuclei, is also connected with the posterior hypothalamus via the fornix. The point to be stressed functionally is that some of these formations have been shown to be affected electro-physiologically not only by olfactory but also by non-olfactory stimuli. There is evidence too, that stimulation of structures in the first and second, and to some extent of those in the third system results in respiratory, vascular and gross motor changes. The point is made that these allo- and juxtallo-cortical formations of the rhinencephalon cannot be designated as uniquely olfactory. Could it be that stimulation that "arouses" the organism to produce electrical activity of isocortex, induces electrical hypersynchrony in Ammon's formation? Although the authors do not favor the substitution of "visceral" for "rhinal" in designating the functions common to these parts of the brain, they do think the relation of these structures with peripheral structures contrasts with the organizational discreteness of afferent and efferent projection systems in relation to neocortex.

Anand and Brobech[1] produced electrolytic lesions bilaterally in the amygdaloid nuclei of rats and noted no change in food intake despite a decrease in spontaneous activity. The animals failed to develop any savageness. Similar effects were observed in cats except that food intake remained normal, provided the lesions did not affect the lateral hypothalamus.

Lindsley et al.,[22] in 1950, had reported an investigation correlating behavioral and EEG changes following chronic brain lesions in the general region of the subthalamus and hypothalamus. In 1952, French, Amerongen, and Magoun[13] showed that in the monkey, as well as in the cat, a region comprising the midbrain tegmentum, subthalamus, hypothalamus and medial portion of the thalamus functions as a unit in response to peripheral stimulation. At any rate potentials were evoked as a result of peripheral stimulation of the somatic as well as auditory, visual, and even visceral systems. In addition to the potentials recorded, they observed signs of such behavioral reactions as arousal, wakefulness, attention, and awareness of stimulation. In a second study, French and Magoun[14] using nine monkeys made extensive lesions in the central cephalic portion of the brain stem and reported that, although complete destruction was fatal, lesser lesions resulted in akinesis and hypersomnolence. The hypersynchronous EEG potentials that were prevalent were not responsive to sensory stimulation.

EMOTIONAL REACTIVITY UPON SEPTAL LESION

Reference has already been made to the Rosvold and Pribram[31] statement that medial granular and agranular cortex of the frontal lobes may be involved in emotional expression. Their own results in the study cited did not successfully clarify the situation in regard to emotional behavior or its control. But well known are the general patterns produced in animals by Sherringtonian decerebration which has involved transections at the brain stem. Another approach to the analysis of the neural factors involved in emotional expression has sought to clarify the rôle of subcortical mechanisms. An approach of equal interest would be furnished in the anatomical availability to experimental lesion of the septal region of the forebrain. This would be an approach in terms of an analysis of paleo-cortical function. For the caudal portion of the septal region is the massive fornix column which receives fibers originating in the hippocampus and has extensive efferent connections with the thalamus and hypothalamus.

Brady and Nauta[7] investigated the behavioral changes exhibited by albino rats with surgical lesions in the septal forebrain region. They divided 30 animals into an unoperated control group of six animals and two operated groups. One of these latter groups (18 animals) constituted the "septal" and the other (6 animals) a "cingulate" group. The lesions of the latter were in the cingulate cortex. Pre- and post-operative data were collected on all animals relative to: a) the acquisition and retention of a conditional emotional response of the "fear" or "anxiety" type; b) magnitude of the startle response; and c) general emotional activity as reflected in ratings on a seven-item rating scale.

Seemingly there were gross and dramatic changes in behavior on the part of the animals that had received lesions in the septal region. The changes involved a striking picture of alertness with limbs rigidly extended and eyes attentively following the movements of any observer approaching the cage. There was an explosive startle reaction to the sudden presentation of an auditory stimulus. The authors report significant increase in both emotional reactivity and startle response postoperatively in the animals having septal lesions. It was also found that such lesions diminished the strength of the previously conditioned "fear" responses, although they did not appear to affect the acquisition of such a response. The magnitude of the changes in behavior of the "septal" animals was roughly commensurate with the extent of injury to the fornix column, a finding which suggests the importance of this paleocortical fiber bundle in neural transmission involved in affective behavior. The failure of such changes to appear following lesions of the cingulate cortex is of great interest, but one must note that the experiment leaves open the question whether the effects of septal lesion are due to interruption of septodiencephalic connections or interference with the massive hippocampal hypothalamic discharge pathway.

The effects of diencephalic stimulation in rats were studied by Chiles[9]. In an effort to delineate further the rôle of the brainstem reticular formation and other subcortical structures stressed by Lindsley *et al.*,[22] as well as by other investigators, the author sought further behavioral correlates of disturbances in the so-called subcortical "activating system". It should be recalled that Lindsley and his associates, for instance, noted EEG characteristics resembling those of sleep following lesions in this system. On the other hand, thalamic stimulation *via* implanted electrodes was found to produce an alert behavioral attitude.

In the present study of Chiles, the aim was to note on a quantitative measure of performance the differential effects issuing from stimulation of various nuclei in the subcortical activating system. Six cats were trained on a bar-pressing response and electrodes were then implanted as follows: in the posterior hypothalamus in one animal; in the ventromedial thalamic nucleus in four animals, and in the centrum medianum of the thalamus in the sixth animal. Since the animals responded more slowly and with greater variability under stimulation for all electrode placements, it was concluded that stimulation of the diencephalon serves as a distractive influence on the rate of responding. Such a conclusion is taken to be more conformable to the view that increased emotion produces more variable behavior but not a higher level of performance. The conclusion would thus be out of line with Lindsley's suggestion that the emotional level is related to activity of the midbrain activating system.

RESULTS IN PSYCHOLOGY AND BRAIN INJURY

Sheer[32] reported for schizophrenic patients with frontal lobe operations an immediate postoperative loss on psychomotor tests of the type claimed to involve attention but test performance returned them to preoperative level by 12 months after the operation. Thirty patients were divided into three groups of ten each according to the operative procedure : venous ligation, orbital, and superior cortical ablations. The superior ablation subgroup and four cases in the venous ligation group with more extensive posterior operations showed more decrement and took longer to reach preoperative level than did the others.

Smith[33] found no effect on learning or on bilateral transfer of learning in a mirror drawing test on the part of human subjects after complete or nearly complete corpus callosum transection. Results on learning and bilateral transfer of learning of a stylus maze were not consistent. Altschule, Siegel, and Henneman[2] report that blood glutathione level of untreated manic-depressive, involutional, and schizophrenic patients as well as that of some seven neurotic patients was in or below the normal range. Subsequent to shock therapy the level rose and the rise was more notable in those having lowest levels initially. It must be noted, of course, that in other studies similar efforts to relate phospholipids and cholesterol concentration to various types of psychotic disorders have been unrewarding as far as positive results are concerned. However, of some interest are the findings of Papez and Bateman[24] who studied cytochemical nerve cell changes either of biopsies at time of prefrontal lobotomy or immediately after death in schizophrenics.

They noted the presence of inclusion bodies which appeared to increase in count and in size with the severity of the disease. They were of the opinion that staining characteristics of such bodies suggested presence of phospholipids and ribonucleic acid. Like that of certain animal viruses the activity of the inclusion bodies may be a proteolytic one.

Intensive study of persons suffering brain injuries of various types has been continued by Teuber and his group in New York. A recent study by Battersby, Teuber, and Bender[4] reports test data on 80 World War II veterans with frontal or occipital brain injuries. Control subjects suffered from wounds involving peripheral nerve injuries. The tests were a modification of the Maier String Problem, Weigl Test and Gottschaldt figures. In the problem-solving behavior probed by the Maier String Problem test both frontal and parieto-occipital brain-injured showed remarkably little disruption of problem-solving behavior. Time for solution was longer for some subjects but the group differences were not statistically significant. For the "normals", scores on the problem-solving test correlated better with perception of hidden contours (Gottschaldt figures) than with sorting (Weigl test). But neither of these correlations met significance in the brain injured. Nor was there any clear differentiation between frontal and parieto-occipital brain injured in these respects. These results are hard to interpret in terms of any assumed priority of the frontal lobes in the process of integration.

In a survey covering evaluation of postoperative work adjustment on the part of 116 schizophrenic patients, Greenblatt and Solomon[15] compare the therapeutic gains due to three types of lobotomy. There was a five-year follow-up on patients who received prefrontal lobotomy. In comparing relative therapeutic efficacy of the several operations, bimedial lobotomy, bilateral lobotomy and unilateral lobotomy, respectively, the authors claim evidence showed bimedial lobotomy was superior in the treatment of chronic schizophrenics. The outstanding indicia of improvement were increased initiative and ability to form object relationships, increased work capacity, and recession of psychotic symptoms. On psychological tests, the chief gains appeared in tests of abstractive capacity, a finding that may seem to contradict the results in other studies of the sequelae of psychosurgery. However, it could be that the contradiction is mostly superficial in that the schizophrenics in this study were chronic and therefore preoperative efficiency must have been poor on such functions as abstract thinking. At any rate, one of the points made by Klebanoff et al.,[18] in the survey mentioned earlier, was that patients whose preoperative test performance was not markedly disturbed are the ones who show impairment in such functions as abstract thinking, memory, and learning ability.

In a report on 339 leucotomized patients, Kostic[19] claims that prefrontal lobotomy produces better results with those patients in whom pre-operative personality was better. But duration of illness and age of the patient were not factors significant for the outcome. The benefits from the operation were about as satisfactory in different forms of schizophrenia as in cases of psychoneurosis. Though using fewer subjects, Johnson and Ehrenberg[17] divided their patients into two general groupings related to reaction types. Those maintaining a basic integration of the self constituted one grouping and those suffering from marked schizophrenic disorganization were placed in a second grouping. Of the former 82 per cent were found to be symptom-free and discharged from the hospital, whereas only eight per cent of the disorganized group was regarded as freed from the psychosis, although an additional ten per cent was returned to the community.

In a careful study of fifteen cases receiving bilateral prefrontal lobotomy, Raskin, Strassman, and Van Winkle[28] present findings on the immediate neuropathology that ensues. In their series none of the lobotomy wounds remained quiescent, but the cutting of brain tissues starts a chain of histopathological events. Beginning with edema, hemorrhage, and necrosis, in the surgical field, the process continues to include organization of newly formed capillaries and proliferation of fibroblastic cells. The thalamus showed numerous cystic formations in one case examined five years after operation. With more specific reference to the thalamus, Bateman and Papez[3] examined histologically the thalamic nuclei in 12 cases of dementia praecox, paranoid type. The degenerative changes they noted would be presumably related to the accompanying psychosis, since there was no question here of lobotomy. All cases showed chronic lesions of nerve cells. Cortical changes were more severe, showing cell destruction and loss of dendrite and axon processes.

Bonner, Cobb, Sweet, and White[6] discuss the results of several types of frontal lobe surgery in operations undertaken for the relief of pain. Operations were unilateral and bilateral lobotomy and orbital gyrectomy. Following bilateral lobotomy (6 patients) the consistent personality changes noted were deterioration of behavior and impairment of judgment. These were most

24

severe immediately after the operation but abated with the passage of time. After bilateral lower quadrant lobotomy (9 patients) the most notable feature observed as resultant was apathy, which did not abate with passage of time. Following unilateral lobotomy (19 patients) there ensued a slight flattening of affect, inappropriate affect, and decrease in amount of spontaneous speech. One is rather forcibly impressed that apparently patients lobotomized for pain suffer greater mental or personality change than do those lobotomized for psychosis. It is essential to stress the possible superficiality of comparative judgments in this context but the above hardly accords with the finding of Kostic[19] already mentioned that lobotomy produces better results with patients whose preoperative personality showed better organization.

SUMMATION

The studies, both animal and human, on localization of function continue to show the great need of careful intercomparison of a) tests employed, and b) specific cortical areas affected by lesion or ablation. Certainly, clearly defined pictures of impairment are not yet available; and one cannot refrain from expressing the regret that generalizations expressed in earlier decades were premature, if asserted or interpreted as plausible or accepted doctrine. As generalizations formulated in the interests of hypothesis testing they have, of course, been extremely productive, as is now evident. But lurking in many former accounts has been the assumption that such generalizations may have already been tested theory. It has taken a long time to discover otherwise.

There is some evidence that loss of frontal lobe cortex produces stereotypy of behavior and interferences with performance of the delayed-response variety. On the other hand, posterior lesions rather than frontal injury produce a lessening of discrimination performance. Equipotentiality is not favored by such findings. Of additional significance are results indicating possibility of reorganization in other cortical areas provided prefrontal cortex is intact.

Of great interest but difficult to evaluate fully in the present state of knowledge are certain findings indicating possible behavioral as well as structural (architectonic) differences between lateral and medial portions of the frontal lobes. The latter may be concerned with emotional, the former with problem-solving behavior.

There has been continued interest in the use of the oddity-problem with primates and some support for its sensitivity as a technique in instances of cortical loss wherein other measures fail to show any differences. With particular reference to the function of pre-striate occipital cortex there is the added suggestion that the specificity or generality of the habit being studied may be the significant variable to assist in reconciliation of many of the discrepancies of outcome in different accounts of experimentation. The habits lost may be those that are applicable to a particular problem. Another contribution of note in the research touching frontal lobe function is that deficits reported for such ablations may be related to lesions in the dorsolateral area rather than to the lobe as a whole.

In terms of the research reported there has been considerable interest in attempts to clarify the rôle of various brain regions in emotional expression. An anatomical and electrophysiological clarification has been one definite result but one still looks for behavioral and psychological confirmation with reference to rhinencephalic structures and their contribution. The septal region has received increased attention and there are indications that this and related paleocortical areas play an important part in emotional expression. Such results as are available warrant caution in assigning too prominent a rôle to the midbrain activating system. However, it would appear that some kind of general statement is possible with reference to the function of septal region and amygdaloid complex in this context. It looks as though the hypothalamus is related to these structures in some such way as the dorsal thalamus is related to the isocortex.

Though psychosurgery is no longer a recent development, it continues to evoke interest and research in regard to its consequences. One finds within this interest an increased effort to differentiate among various types of brain surgery. The differentiation is not simply lobotomy versus lobectory, although that dichotomy is very evident. There is, however, a further effort to distinguish by their sequelae the operations performed predominantly on orbital or medial areas as well as those performed unilaterally and bilaterally, respectively. A final emphasis is that which aims to explore the relevancy of previous intellectual ability, emotional status, and personality organization for an adequate evaluation of the effects of surgery.

FOOTNOTES

[1] In a very brief but important contribution to theory Stanley Cobb points out the basic confusion of localizing in any strict sense a temporal sequence or process such as consciousness. Looking at consciousness as the function of an integrated nervous system in action (rather than as a function of the brain or some brain area) he quotes from an article published by Hughlings Jackson in 1887 to clarify the sense in which brain centers can be regarded as physical bases of mind. Jackson had enumerated three general positions: a) mind acts through the nervous system to produce physical effects; b) activities of the highest nervous centers and mental states are one and the same thing or different aspects of one thing; c) states of consciousness are utterly different from nervous states of the highest centers, but occur correlatively to the latter and without mutual interference. The position outlined under c) was the one accepted by Jackson.

Holding that one must still choose between Jackson's three theories, Cobb asserts that most modern neurologists would take a position somewhat akin to the second, *viz.*, some form of a double-aspect theory. Furthermore, Cobb does not agree with Jackson that consciousness and mind are synonymous. In this context it may be added that, accepting Cobb's definition of consciousness as "awareness of environment and of self," it would be difficult to equate it with the totality of mental functioning. There is great merit also in pointing out, as Cobb does, that consciousness is a variable state with many degrees. He thus furnishes a realistic and possible specifiable sense in which to speak of the cortical "localizations" of various discriminative mechanisms of consciousness. So one can speak more in accord with the facts of observation and need not be tempted to deny any localization because extensive cortical removals fail to render the patient totally unconscious. (The reference is to: Cobb, S. "Consciousness and Cerebral Localization," which appeared in *Epilepsia*, Third Series, 1952, vol. I.) In the opinion of this reviewer the three theories offered by Hughlings Jackson do not precisely exhaust the possibilities, for they do not include the unification of neural and mental states that would prevail in a union conatural as well as dynamic.

[2] It should be noted, of course, that such comparability is frankly inexact. Lesions of the older or paleocortex and of the neocortex respectively may be comparable as to the amount of tissue destroyed but more important

than amount is the consideration of what functions are subsumed. In all mammals the entire cerebrum constitutes a mantle or covering which has developed to such physical proportions that its hemispheres enclose and conceal some structures that are telencephalic as well as underlying diencephalic and midbrain parts. But the telencephalon itself contains some structures that are phylogenetically "old," as, for instance, the *substantia nigra* as well as the *corpus striatum.* In the phylogenetic process, the corpus striatum is considered to have relinquished some of its functions to the ever-developing cerebral hemispheres. The distinction of grades of "newness" is difficult and classifications of brain regions as "new" or "old" are especially complicated in reference to the pallium or mantle. It suffices to state, however, that "neocortex" designates cortical formations that have passed through developmental stages to reach a six-layered stage. Older formations are called "allocortex." The general situation might be clarified somewhat by referring to considerations about a specific region. In a very informative paper dealing with the morphology and function of the "olfactory brain" or rhinencephalon Karl Pribram and Lawrence Kruger point out that in reptiles the entire forebrain is still "dominated" by olfactory connections. Such neural components are recognizable in submammalian vertebrates and even in mammals can be distinguished, but "newer" formations have been added. They indicate the phases of phylogenetic development together with examples pertinent to the olfactory brain. In order of appearance in the mammalian brain there is first the archipallium and for this they instance the hippocampus. For the paleopallium or intermediate phase they cite olfactory lobe and probably the septal region. The newest development would be the neopallium. Admitting the difficulties arising from the existence of intermediate conditions, (e.g., cortex resembling neocortex but lacking six layers clearly defined) these same authors think the general distinction between paleo- and archicortex can be sustained, but suggest that certain newer transitional formations be classified with adjacent older cortex rather than with the rest of the neocortex. For a detailed discussion of such classificatory problems in respect to the rhinencephalon reference should be made to Pribram, K. H. and Kruger, L., Functions of the "Olfactory Brain." *Annals of the New York Academy of Sciences,* March 24, 1954, vol. 58, Article 2, pp. 109-138.

[3] Such distinctions are made on the basis of the cellular components of the cortical area in question. Pribram and Kruger in the same article to which reference was made in note 2 above, attempt to correlate the genetic and the cytological indices for distinctions between paleo- and neocortex. As they point out, agreement among cytoarchitectonicists is not always present, but on the whole it appears best to reserve the term neocortex for that showing six layers. The layers, beginning with the outermost, usually include a plexiform layer, several distinct layers of pyramidal cells, and an innermost layer of spindle cells. However, there are differences in relative prominence of the several layers from one brain region to another and such differences were taken into account by Brodmann in his "mapping" of cortical areas. Furthermore, certain cortical regions appearing to develop in a similar fashion, possess fewer layers (two or five rather than six) and are thus like neocortex developmentally, but different by the criterion of their architectonics. Transitional cortex is the designation preferred for these by Pribram. In brief, fully developed cortex would be neocortex or granular cortex; allocortex would be agranular and cortex showing some degree of lamination—say, two layers of cell components would be transitional.

4 Among the methods of exploration of functional relationships between nerve cells and nerve centers are the classical histological studies of pathways, and particularly the study of specially stained preparations to determine the interconnections involved. By all such methods conclusions are inferences that nerve impulses or neural discharges traverse the pathways specified. The preparations are not living cells or tissue. The improved methods for electrical and chemical stimulation and the development of recording techniques have made available more direct ways of tracing (in terms of amplitude, duration, and frequency) the actual firing or impulse discharge associated with neural activity. Whether spontaneous or activated through appropriately controlled stimulation, such firing patterns can be studied through the recording of the electrical potentials generated by active nerve tissue. The application of strychnine to a limited area of cortex leads to heightened sensitivity, e.g., hyperesthesia in a sensory area, and diffusion or irradiation of neural activity in functionally related areas. Electrical methods of recording the irradiated potentials are thus part of the procedure in strychnine neuronography.

5 Results such as these continue to be a source of puzzlement. But the possibility cannot be overlooked that the differences may be functions of greater and less tissue reorganization following lobectomy and lobotomy respectively. In this respect lobotomy, the less severe of the two surgical procedures, could be conceived as producing its definitive sequel more immediately. Following lobectomy, on the other hand, formation of scar tissue could serve as a source of excitation, at least for a period of time subsequent to operation.

6 The "cortical insult" referred to in Forgays' (11) article would be, of course, the actual brain-tissue damage inflicted in the operations upon the cortex of epileptic patients. The operative procedure or surgery in itself constitutes an insult or assault on the involved and surrounding tissue. It is usually considered that such local results outlast in duration the general effects of surgery referred to as "shock." On the other hand, they probably do not remain to constitute part of the final pattern designated as deficit due to removal of neural tissue (lobectomy) or severance of fibers (lobotomy).

REFERENCES AND BIBLIOGRAPHY

1 Anand, B. K., and Brobeck, J. R., Food intake and spontaneous activity of rats with lesions in the amygdaloid nuclei. *J. Neurophysiol.*, 1952, *15*, 421-430.

2 Altschule, M. D., Siegel, E. P. and Henneman, D. H., Blood glutathione level in mental disease before and after treatment. *Arch. Neurol. & Psychiat.*, 1952, *67*, 64-68.

3 Bateman, J. F. and Papez, J. W., Significance of the thalamus in psychoses. *J. Clin. & Exp. Psychopath.*, 1951, *12*, 89-103.

4 Battersby, W. S., Teuber, H. L., and Bender, M. B., Problem-solving behavior in men with frontal or occipital brain injuries. *J. Psychol.* 1953, *35*, 329-351.

5 Blum, R. A., Effects of subtotal lesions of frontal granular cortex on delayed reaction in monkeys. *Arch. Neurol. & Psychiat.*, 1952, *67*, 375-386.

6 Bonner, F., Cobb, S., Sweet, W. H. and White, J. C. Frontal lobe surgery in the treatment of pain. *Psychosom. Med.*, 1952, *14*, 382-405.

7 Brady, J. V. and Nauta, W. J. H., Subcortical mechanisms in emotional behavior: affective changes following septal forebrain lesions in the albino rat. *J. comp. physiol. Psychol.* 1953, *46*, 339-346.

8 Brody, E. B. and Rosvold, H. E., Influence of prefrontal lobotomy on social interaction in a monkey group. *Psychosom. Med.*, 1952, *14*, 406-415.

9 Chiles, W. D., Performance during stimulation of the diencephalic activating system. *J. comp. physiol. Psychol.*, 1954, *47*, 412-415.

10 Cloake, P., Some aspects of cortical function. *Brain*, 1952, *75*, 273-291.

11 Forgays, D. G., Reversible disturbances of function in man following cortical insult. *J. comp. physiol. Psychol.*, 1952, *45*, 209-215.

12 Forgays, D. G., Reversible disturbances of function in rats following cortical insult. *J. comp. physiol. Psychol.*, 1952, *45*, 216-225.

13 French, J. D., Amerongen, F. K. and Magoun, H. W., An activating system in brain stem of monkey. *Arch. Neurol. & Psychiat.*, 1952, *68*, 577-590.

14 French, J. D. and Magoun, H. W., Effects of chronic lesions in central cephalic brain stems of monkeys. *Arch. Neurol. & Psychiat.*, 1952, *68*, 591-604.

15 Greenblatt, M. and Solomon, H., Survey of nine years of lobotomy investigations. *Amer. J. Psychiat.*, 1952, *109*, 262-265.

16 Harlow, H. F., Davis, R. T., Settlage, P. H. and Meyer, D. R., Analysis of frontal and posterior association syndromes in brain-damaged monkeys. *J. comp. physiol. Psychol.*, 1952, *45*, 419-429.

17 Johnson, O. and Ehrenberg, R., The correlation of lobotomy results with basic reaction types. *Amer. J. Psychiat.*, 1952, *108*, 817-829.

18 Klebanoff, S., Singer, J. L. and Wilensky, H., Psychological consequences of brain lesions and ablations. *Psychol. Bull.*, 1954, *51*, 1-41.

19 Kostic, S., Experiences and results in prefrontal lobotomy: a clinical study of 339 leucotomized patients. *J. ment. Sci.*, 1953, *99*, 786-795.

20 Lashley, K. S., The mechanisms of vision: XVIII. Effects of destroying the visual "associative areas" of the monkey. *Genet. Psychol. Monogra.*, 1948, *37*, 107-166.

21 Leary, R. W., Harlow, H. F., Settlage, P. H. and Greenwood, D. D., Performance on double-alternation problems by normal and brain-injured monkeys. *J. comp. physiol. Psychol.*, 1952, *45*, 576-584.

22 Lindsley, D. B., Schreiner, L. H., Knowles, W. B. and Magoun, H. W., Behavioral and EEG changes following chronic brain stem lesions in the cat. *EEG Clin. Neurophysiol.*, 1950, *2*, 483-498.

23 Meyer, D. R., Harlow, H. F., and Ades, H. W., Retention of delayed responses and proficiency in oddity problems by monkeys with preoccipital ablations. *Amer. J. Psychol.*, 1951, *64*, 391-396.

24 Papez, J. W. and Bateman, J. F., Changes in nervous tissues and study of living organisms in mental disease. *J. nerv. ment. Disease*, 1951, *114*, 400-412.

25 Pickett, J. M., Non-equipotential cortical function in maze learning, (Abstract) *Amer. Psychologist*, 1951, *6*, 270.

26 Pribram, K. H., Mishkin, M., Rosvold, H. E., and Kaplan, S. J., Effects on delayed-response performance of lesions of dorsolateral and ventromedial frontal cortex of baboons. *J. comp. physiol. Psychol.* 1952, *45*, 565-575.

26a Pribram, K. H. and Kruger, L. Functions of the "olfactory brain." *Ann. N.Y. Acad. Sci.*, 1954, *58*, 109-138.

27 Pribram, K. H. and Maclean, P. D., Neuronographic analysis of medial and basal cerebral cortex. II Monkey. *J. Neurophysiol.*, 1954, *16*, 324-340.

[28] Raskin, N., Strassman, G., and Van Winkle, C. C., Neuropathologic lesions following lobotomy: a study of fifteen cases of bilateral prefrontal lobotomy. *Amer. J. Psychiat.*, 1953, *109*, 808-816.

[29] Riopelle, A. J., Harlow, H. F., Settlage, P. H. and Ades, H. W., Performance of normal and operated monkeys on visual learning tests. *J. comp. physiol. Psychol.*, 1951, *44*, 283-289.

[30] Rosner, B. S., Effects of cortical lesions on maze retention by the rat. *J. comp. physiol. Psychol.*, 1953, *46*, 56-60.

[31] Rosvold, H. E., and Pribram, K. H., The effects of combined lesions of lateral granular and transitional cortex compared with the effects of combined lesions of medial granular and agranular cortex of the frontal lobes of baboons. (Abstract) *Amer. Psychologist*, 1951, *6*, 271.

[32] Sheer, D. E., The effect of frontal lobe operations on the attention process. (Abstract) *Amer. Psychologist*, 1952, *6*, 261.

[33] Smith, K. U., Experimental analysis of the associative mechanism of the human brain in learning functions. *J. comp. physiol. Psychol.*, 1952, *45*, 66-72.

[34] Stewart, J. W. and Ades, H. W., The time factor in reintegration of a learned habit lost after temporal lobe lesions in the monkey, (Macaca mulatta). *J. comp. physiol. Psychol.*, 1951, *44*, 479-486.

[35] Wade, M., Behavioral effects of prefrontal lobectomy, lobotomy, and circumsection in the monkey (Macaca mulatta). *J. comp. Neurol.*, 1952, *96*, 179-207.

[36] Warren, J. M. and Harlow, H. F., Learned discrimination performance by monkeys after prolonged post-operative recovery from large cortical lesions. *J. Comp. physiol. Psychol.*, 1952, 45, 119-126.

CHAPTER II

ISSUES AND RESULTS IN SENSORY PSYCHOLOGY

P. RATOOSH, PH.D.
Assistant Professor of Psychology
The Ohio State University

EDITORIAL NOTE

Whether we call them receptors or sense organs, the psychological experience which they mediate must be regarded as the very foundation of our science. Physiologists have often shown their partiality by discarding the terms "senses" and "sensation." It has become fashionable as a result of logical positivism seeping into psychology to do away with every term which savors of the least subjectivism. A recent letter from one of the foremost psychologists in America to the editor of this volume contains the following sentence: "One almost never hears the word sensation nowadays, for the same problems are stated and worked on and solved, and the word behavior comes in. The transformation equations that modern positivism has made clear are used, and this is an alternative language." To which we may reply, "Yes, it is true that we can test sensation through discrimination methods, but what about the sensory experience itself? In other words, of what use is the equation here, and the alternative term, except as a game which affords one some gratification?"

For this reason, the senses are not evicted from their rightful domain. It is only a pity that more space could not be allotted to this ever-growing department which is intrenched in physiology, and is more of a comparative study than a self-contained topic.

Dr. Philburn Ratoosh, who has contributed the chapter on the senses, is a graduate of Yale, taking his doctorate at Columbia University. He has taught at Columbia University and the University of Wisconsin and is at present Assistant Professor at The Ohio State University. He has given courses on the physiology of the sense organs both in the psychology and physiology departments.

GENERAL INTRODUCTION

The initial effect of an environmental change on an organism occurs in one or more sense organs. Here begin the internal events that lead to the adaptation of an organism to its environment.

CLASSIFICATION

The receptor organs can be classified on the basis of the kind of energy to which they are sensitive. For example, senses like touch and hearing, on this basis, are mechanoreceptors. Sherrington suggested a classification depending on whether the receptor gives information about immediate external environment, internal environment, distant environment or bodily position. The receptors Sherrington classed respectively as exteroceptors, interoceptors, teleceptors and proprioceptors.

Some properties of receptors are specific to a particular system and derived from characteristics of that system. We should expect the visual mechanism, for example, to manifest properties that depend on the chemical nature of the photosensitive substance in a rod or a cone, and the aural apparatus to have characteristics derived from the complex mechanical structure of the middle ear. Other properties of receptors, however, are general properties of nerve elements. Phenomena like absolute threshold, latency, limits of sensitivity, differential threshold and adaptation can be discussed with regard to any sensory system.

THE SENSORY NERVES

The best place to look in attempting to describe phenomena common to all the sense modalities is the sensory nerves. The receptors themselves differ widely, responding as they do to different kinds of physical energy. Likewise neural impulses initiated in the different receptors terminate in different structures in cortical sensory areas.

Since all stimuli initiating activity in receptors are transformed

35

into impulses in sensory nerves, we must seek to find the means of encoding information about the environment that sensory nerves employ. It has been demonstrated experimentally by Lucas and Adrian, and others, that the magnitude of response of a nerve fiber to a stimulus above threshold and the speed of conduction of the impulse depend on the particular fiber and on its condition and not on the magnitude of the stimulus. This principle—the all-or-none law—restricts the dimensionality of encoding that a fiber can utilize. A single fiber can transmit information about time—the onset or cessation of a stimulus—or about the amount of stimulation—this is encoded in the frequency of impulses in the fiber. The particular fiber, or the number of fibers, stimulated produce another kind of information. Finally, information may be conveyed in the temporal arrangement of the arrival of impulses in a cortical area from various fibers, *i.e.,* fibers by firing asynchronously may convey information by the degree of asynchrony. Thus, conceivably, the pattern of arrival of impulses at some point in the nervous system contains a fourth kind of information. Modulator and volley theories utilize this principle.

MÜLLER & SHERRINGTON

In 1840 Johannes Müller formulated a doctrine that has assumed prime importance in sensory physiology. Arguing against the philosophical realism of his day, Müller asserted that sensations are produced by conditions of nerves and not directly by states of the external world, that the specific sensation produced is determined by the nature of the sensory system excited and that each nerve is capable of being excited only by a particular class of stimuli. Sherrington in his classical *The Integrative Action of the Nervous System* defined the function of a receptor as the lowering of threshold for one kind of stimulus—the "adequate" stimulus—and raising of the threshold for others.

Application of Müller's principle to the sense modalities gives us the place theories of the senses. For example, in a receptor organ some cells may be sensitive to the low end of the stimulus continuum, some to the middle range, and others to the high end. Since each of these groups synapse with different sensory nerves, information about the stimulus quality is conveyed by which fibers are activated. These theories, then, explain sensitivity to a range of the adequate stimulus in terms of the selective sensitivity of groups of receptors.

COMMON GROUND OF PHYSIOLOGY AND PSYCHOLOGY

The sensory mechanisms are objects of investigation of both physiology and psychology. Although researchers in each of these areas often work in the other, a distinction can be made between the two modes of investigation. The psychologist *qua* psychologist studies sensory mechanisms by making inferences from behavior. Through a training procedure or set of instructions, the sensory psychologist employs the organism's response as an indicator of sense organ activity. The physiologist, on the other hand, makes more direct measurement at some level of the sensory system.

These two approaches are coördinate and, at best, complement each other. Occasionally, however, apparently contradictory conclusions are drawn from the employment of these two equally valid techniques. When a psychophysical experiment yields a result that is not corroborated by physiological data in the same area, then the physiological technique cannot be adequate. This is so because psychophysical techniques reflect the end product of the sensory system.

Information contained at a particular level of a sensory system cannot exceed the information contained at any more peripheral level of that system. To expect otherwise is tantamount to the assertion that a level of the sensory system itself can add information about the environment that the receptor did not receive. We may compare this situation with the problem of translating a passage from one language to another. In the translation some information may be lost. But the translated passage can never contain *more* information than the original.

THRESHOLD MEASUREMENTS

The most fruitful data in sensory psychology have been obtained in threshold measurements. The concept threshold requires elucidation. The threshold is a point on a stimulus continuum that divides the continuum into two response categories. In Stevens' words,[1] "The threshold is the value that divides the continuum of stimuli into two classes: those to which the organism reacts and those to which it does not." A stimulus to which the organism does not respond is below threshold at that time, and thus any reference to responses to subliminal stimuli is meaningless. For a modern discussion of techniques for threshold measurement, see Graham.[2]

The wide disparity in the amount known about the different sense modalities is striking. There is a tremendous number of research papers published in vision and hearing, a paucity of publications relating to smell and taste and an almost complete dearth of research about the labyrinthine system.

The chief reason for this variation is not hard to find. It is not related to interest or importance very directly. On the contrary, interest in an area is often generated and developed by a few active workers.

The direction and amount of research in sensory psychology is to a large degree determined by the ease and precision of control of stimuli. And control of stimuli obviously requires knowing what the stimuli are. Clearly in those modalities such as smell and taste where the stimuli are not understood extensive basic research is precluded.

The stimulus for labyrinthine activity is known and controllable. The difficulty here is the difficulty of stimulating that system without stimulating other modalities.

VISION

PHOTOCHEMISTRY

The most primitive level of explanation of responses to visual stimuli is in the photochemistry of the rod or the cone. From about 1920 to his death in 1947 Selig Hecht[3] developed a theory of vision that probably summarized more data than any other proposed account. Hecht's theory describes events only in the single sense cell. It contains no terms referring to possible interactions among a number of cells.

In each rod or cone there is a photosensitive substance that breaks down into two or more components in the presence of light. This reaction moreover is reversible. Hecht's basic assumption concerns the rate of decomposition, that it is an increasing function of luminance and that it decreases in time with constant exposure, *i.e.,* in light adaptation.

From a differential equation describing the rate of decomposition Hecht was able to describe three sets of data (under somewhat specialized conditions) relating to brightness discrimination, visual acuity, and flicker.

Wald and Clark,[4] in a study of human dark adaptation, demonstrated that Hecht's paradigm is too simple. Wald and Clark found that dark adaptation curves following a long ex-

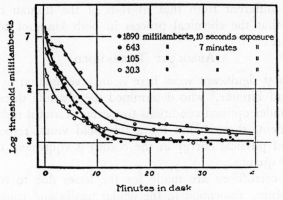

Fig. 1. Dark adaptation curves following exposures to various luminances and durations. From Wald and Clark.[4]

posure to a low luminance are different from those following a short exposure to a high luminance. As shown in Fig. 1 the dark adaptation curve following exposure to 30.3 millilamberts for seven minutes crosses the curve following exposure to 1890 millilamberts for 10 seconds.

In previous work on retinal pigments Wald had shown that rhodopsin, the rod substance, decomposes and recombines in a way similar to the following:

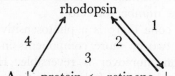

$$\text{vitamin A} + \text{protein} \leftarrow \text{retinene} + \text{protein}$$

A short exposure to a high luminance causes a large breakdown of rhodopsin (reaction 1) but recombination via reaction 2 is rapid so that recovery is swift. A long exposure to a low luminance causes a steady state to be attained, and recovery here depends on the synthesis of rhodopsin from vitamin A — a slow process.

Hartline and McDonald[5] reported a similar crossing of dark adaptation curves in the eye of the horseshoe crab (*Limulus*).

Although the sensitive substance in the eye of *Limulus* is certainly different from that in rods of the human eye, this suggests that the chemical process in both kinds of cells may be similar.

Absolute Threshold

The most significant work here is an investigation by Hecht, Shlaer and Pirenne,[6] who determined the absolute threshold of the eye under optimal conditions for seeing. Careful radiometric measurements showed that for a threshold visual response the amount of physical energy at the cornea is equivalent to fewer than 150 quanta.

When corrections are made for the losses due to reflection at the cornea, absorption in the ocular media and transmission at the retina, the figure is reduced to five to 14 quanta absorbed by rods. The number of rods in the area involved is so much greater than this that it is extremely unlikely under these conditions that any rod absorbs more than one quantum. This leads to the startling conclusion that a rod is activated by a single quantum. Since it can respond to the smallest amount of energy that can be delivered, it is as sensitive as it can become. Thus the concept threshold applied to the rod becomes meaningless.

The significance of this result for biological variation in general lies in the fact that, at least at the threshold, the variability in response is determined to a far greater degree by the variability in the stimulus than by the variability of the organism.

Temporal Effects. The Bunsen-Roscoe law of photochemistry was first applied to and verified for the human eye in 1885 by Bloch, who found that for short flashes the product of luminance times exposure time is constant for a constant visual effect—It=c.

Graham and Margaria[7] have shown that the critical duration, the duration in which Bloch's law is valid, is a function of the size of the stimulated region, being smaller for large areas.

Hartline[8] has demonstrated the law to be valid (at least for short durations) in the single optic nerve fiber of the king-crab (*Limulus*).

Spatial Effects. Ricco in 1877 suggested a simple relation between area and luminance for a threshold effect in the fovea. He proposed that the product of the two is constant for a threshold effect—AI=k. Graham, Brown and Mote[9] investigated the relation over a wide range of areas. They proposed a theory based on the supposition that the excitatory effect of an elemental area is inversely proportional to some power of its distance from the center of a stimulated region. Integrating excitatory effects from all elements of area gives the total excitatory effect at the center.

This theoretical notion indeed predicts Ricco's law but only for small areas—the only range in which it holds. For larger areas the theory is consistent with other suggested relations.

Piper had suggested the relation, $A^{1/2}I = c$, and Löhle, who demonstrated experimentally that Ricco's law holds for small areas, showed that for large areas the threshold luminance is independent of area—$I = A^0I = c$.

Graham, Brown and Mote[9] succeeded in demonstrating that the relation between area and luminance for a threshold effect cannot be described by a power function $A^kI = c$, where k is a constant.

ACUITY

The visual angle of the thinnest visible line on a white background viewed under optimal conditions is about 0.5 seconds. (This is less than the width of a wire 3/32 inches in thickness seen at a distance of half a mile.) The diameter of a foveal cone is about thirty times this value. The involuntary movements of the eye during fixation have an amplitude averaging about one minute of arc.

Hecht and Mintz[10] calculated the effect of diffraction at the pupil when the finest perceptible line is presented to the eye and concluded that the blurring of the image produced by diffraction decreases the illumination of the row of cones in the center of the shadow from that of an adjacent row by an amount very nearly equal to the differential threshold. They therefore concluded that the limit of visual acuity is set by the difference threshold.

Another study casts doubt on this interpretation: Senders[11] by presenting lines in intermittent light above the critical fusion frequency found that visual acuity is superior to what would be predicted from the application of brightness discrimination results to the Talbot brightness.

The significance for acuity of the small eye movements (physiological nystagmus) during fixation has been dramatically demonstrated by Riggs and Ratliff,[12] who, by cementing a mirror on a contact lens on the viewing eye, succeeded in keeping an image stationary regardless of eye movements. The effect of this ingenious arrangement is to cause lines ordinarily visible to disappear after a few seconds of viewing. This indicates that the normal eye movements are essential for maintenance of high acuity by preventing local retinal adaptation.

INTERACTION

In the discussion of visual resolution no mention has been made of the length of lines employed. That thin lines are visible only when they attain a critical length implies that a retinal effect is summating—that some interaction process is taking place.

Much the same kind of interaction is displayed in a number of phenomena. In a brightness discrimination study Ratoosh and Graham[13] found that, even when all stimuli are restricted to the rod-free area of the fovea, the difference threshold decreases as the test-field increases in size.

Beitel[14] obtained a similar result for the absolute threshold. He found that the threshold for a small foveal region is diminished by the presence of a nearby area when the luminance of the latter is of the same order of magnitude as the threshold of the former. He further found the effect to increase as the separation decreases.

A like effect has been obtained in flicker by Creed and Ruch,[15] who observed that the critical fusion frequency of a small, foveal field is raised when a large, illuminated area is made to surround the flickering field.

In the frog eye Hartline[16] has reported that the discharge of impulses in a single optic nerve fiber increases when the retinal area illuminated increases. This summation of excitation is a result of the summation of activity in convergent pathways to a ganglion cell.

The results of Ratoosh and Graham, of Beitel and of Creed and Ruch cannot be explained in this manner. In the rod-free area of the human fovea no convergent pathways exist. There is a one-to-one relation between cone and optic nerve fiber in this area. There are, it is true, lateral connections in the human fovea—amacrine and horizontal cells are found there. These may provide the means by which spatial summation occurs. But it is not likely that the difficulty can be resolved in this manner. Hartline,[17] in a later study, found that in the *Limulus* eye, where there are neither convergent pathways nor lateral connections, the discharge of impulses in a single optic fiber can be made to decrease when retinal cells adjacent to the illuminated cell are illuminated.

The above results can be summarized in a consistent manner even if the interacting mechanism is unknown.

Consider two points in a small foveal region. A small increase in retinal illuminance at one of the points apparently has two consequences: it increases the excitation at the point illuminated and decreases the excitation at the nearby point, this decrease becoming smaller as the distance between the points increase. This much Hartline has found experimentally in the *Limulus* eye.

To rationalize the results of Ratoosh and Graham, Beitel and Creed and Ruch, we shall have to make an assumption about threshold. Let us assume: (1) that, for the detection of a difference between two retinal illuminances in the same retinal region presented at successive times, the ratio of the smaller excitation to the larger must exceed a critical value; (2) that the excitation in a region is a negatively accelerated, monotonically increasing function of the illuminance of that region; and (3) the excitation in a retinal region is a decreasing function of the size of the illuminated region nearby.

Assumptions (1) and (2) imply that the differential threshold is a monotonically increasing function of the background luminance. Thus, if the background luminance is increased by a constant amount, the resulting increase in excitation will depend on the absolute value of the background luminance, being smaller for larger values. Therefore, for a constant ratio of excitations a greater threshold difference will be required at high background luminances. This conclusion is in accord with all of the data of brightness discrimination.

Assumptions (1) and (3) predict Beitel's finding that the threshold for a small, foveal field is reduced by the presence of a dim, nearby area. These assumptions also lead to Ratoosh and Graham's result that brightness discrimination improves when the size of the background field is increased. The results of Creed and Ruch, that a surround for a foveal flickering field raises the critical fusion frequency, are also described if the threshold detection of flicker is held to require a constant ratio of excitation in the light period to excitation in the dark period.

Whatever the mechanism the effect of the depression is to enhance contrast. Consider a circular, retinal region at high luminance with a very large, dim background. In the brightly illuminated area the depression of excitation is greatest at the center and there is a gradient of excitation from the center to the periphery, which therefore appears brightest. In the background the depression is greatest in the area adjacent to the circle—this area therefore appears dimmest.

COLOR VISION

Dichromatism of the central fovea was first reported in 1894 by König. Hartridge[18] has demonstrated that the same kind of dichromatism exists outside foveal areas when the stimulus is small. Thus, Hartridge believes, this dichromatism is not caused by the absence of rods.

Hsia and Graham[19] have recently redetermined the luminosity curve of the dark adapted foveal cones. They find that sensitivity is at a maximum at 550 mμ and that abrupt changes in the curve's direction occur near 460 mμ and 600 mμ. Also their subjects showed higher luminosity values in the blue than the standard CIE luminosity curve.

Hurvich and Jameson[20] in another determination of foveal sensitivity confirm all three of these results. In addition they report[21, 22] that when the eye is adapted to chromatic fields, the luminosity curve is altered so that sensitivity to the range of stimuli similar to the adapting stimulus is diminished. When white light is used in the adapting field, the luminosity curve for a 1° foveal area shows a slight change, similar to a Purkinje shift, with a change from light to dark adaptation.

These results deny the validity of theories of color vision that attribute chromaticity and luminosity to different mechanisms.

HEARING

ABSOLUTE THRESHOLD

The relation between absolute threshold and the frequency of pure-tone stimuli is well known. The minimum threshold is found at about 3000 cycles per second. At this frequency Wilska found that the extent of movement of the tympanic membrane is less than 10^{-9} centimeter, less than one-tenth of the diameter of a hydrogen atom. Bekesy[23] made a further calculation to determine the movement of the basilar membrane in response to a threshold stimulus and found this value one one-hundredth again as small—10^{-11} centimeter.

PITCH

Stevens and Volkmann,[24] using a fractionation procedure, developed a pitch scale that relates pitch to frequency. Stevens,

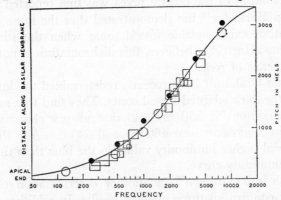

Fig. 2. The relation between pitch location on the basilar membrane and the pitch scale. From Stevens and Volkmann.[24]

Davis and Lurie[25] by recording action potentials from the acoustic nerve of guinea pig determined the region of the basilar membrane maximally stimulated by various frequencies. It is possible to make a comparison between these studies. As may be seen in Fig. 2 these functions are almost identical if pitch in mels and distance from the apical end of the basilar membrane are plotted along the same axes. The curve represents the function relating pitch and frequency, and the circles and rectangles represent points of stimulation on the basilar membrane for various frequencies.

Stevens and Volkmann conclude from this coincidence that pure tones an equal number of mels apart stimulate equally distant points on the basilar membrane. Furthermore a subject who follows instructions to set one tone so that it has half the pitch of another makes an adjustment in frequency such that it maximally stimulates a point on the basilar membrane half way between the point maximally stimulated by the higher tone and the apical end of the basilar membrane.

In 1935 Stevens[26] performed an experiment to investigate the relation between pitch and intensity for various frequencies. His data, all from one subject, indicated that pitch of high tones increases with intensity while pitch of low tones decreases with intensity. In 1951 Morgan, Garner and Galambos[27] repeated this study with a large number of subjects and found the changes in pitch with intensity to be very slight for the average subject but to be in the direction found by Stevens. A few subjects, however, showed large changes in pitch of the order of Stevens' subject.

We find here a sensory function that displays wide individual differences. A large-scale study of this function remains to be done.

LOUDNESS

From data of Fletcher and Munson obtained by a fractionation procedure Stevens and Davis[28] developed a loudness scale. Loudness as a function of intensity with frequency as a parameter is shown in Fig. 3. This figure shows that in general loudness increases more rapidly with intensity the lower the frequency. For example if a subject reported that he heard a 1000 cycle per second tone and 100 cycle per second tone at the same loudness and then the intensities of the two tones are reduced

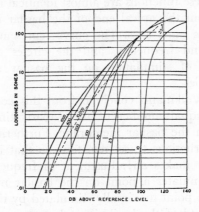

Fig. 3. The loudness function. From Stevens and Davis.[28]

equally, he will report the 1000 cycle per second tone as louder than the 100 cycle per second tone, whereas if the intensities are increased equally, he will report the 100 cycle per second tone as louder.

NEUROPHYSIOLOGY

Action potentials from single units of the auditory system in cat were recorded by Galambos and Davis.[29] Each of their isolated units displayed a range of sensitivity, but each had a frequency to which it was most sensitive. Frequencies near the most sensitive frequency elicited a response only when the intensity of stimulation was increased. The response areas of the units —intensities and frequencies that excited a few of the units—are shown in Fig. 4.

In addition to response areas Galambos and Davis[30] showed in a later investigation that some single units possess inhibitory areas. They demonstrated that a discharge excited in a unit by a tone may be depressed by the addition of another tone. This

48

inhibition bears a close resemblance to the depression of excitation occurring in the retina particularly if frequency in audition is held to be analogous to retinal location in vision.

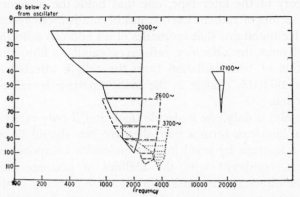

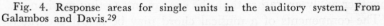

Fig. 4. Response areas for single units in the auditory system. From Galambos and Davis.[29]

The discovery reconciles the pitch discrimination capacity of the human ear with Gray's principle that a pure tone activates a number of fibers sensitive to frequencies close to the frequency of the stimulus but activates maximally only those fibers whose sensitivity is greatest at the frequency of the stimulus.

(Galambos and Davis first supposed that the units from which they were recording action potentials were single fibers of the auditory nerve. Later microscopic examination of the auditory nerve led them to suspect that they had recorded not from first order neurons but from cell bodies of second order neurons,[31] so that the inhibition observed occurs postsynaptically.)

SMELL

Necessary and sufficient physical or chemical properties of stimuli that give rise to olfactory responses are still unknown. Apparently volatility of a substance is necessary for an olfactory response, since studies initiated by E. H. Weber in 1847 indicated that no odor sensations result from filling that nasal cavity with a normally odorous liquid.

Theories of the nature of the olfactory stimulus are of two types: those that assert the stimulus to be chemical and those that assert it to be physical.

A theory of the later type, one that holds the olfactory cells to be detectors of radiant energy, has been advanced recently by Beck.[32] He maintains that molecules of an odorous substance are adsorbed onto the olfactory cells in a capillary film, that the distribution of heat radiation from the cells is affected by the film, and that this change in the cooling pattern is the stimulus for olfaction.

If the film is only one molecule thick and if only molecules of the same kind can form a film, then subjects should be able to analyze a mixture by smell into its molecular components. This prediction, consistent with the abilities of perfume chemists, places the olfactory mechanism in the same category as the ear, another analyzer, rather than the eye, an integrating mechanism. (The components of a musical chord may be heard accurately but the components of a mixture of colored lights cannot be seen). If this view is correct, then the attempts to classify odors are as futile as the attempt to find a small number of tones, mixtures of which can match any pure tone.

That certain optical isomers, which in a pure state have the same infrared spectrum, differ in odor has been cited as a chief argument against the theory. But Posvic[32a] suggests that it is unlikely that those pairs of isomers reported as differing in smell were in pure form and that the differences in smell can be attributed to traces of impurities.

TASTE

The greatest recent progress in taste has been made not in the psychology of gustation but in its neurophysiology. It is becoming increasingly recognized, following Börnstein's suggestion,[33] that the relation between taste and somesthetic sensation is far closer than that between taste and smell. Consequently it would be expected that cortical representation of taste is adjacent not to that of smell, as has been widely held, but to a somatosensory area.

This is in agreement with a study of Patton, Ruch, and Walker,[34] who showed that in monkey bilateral lesions in the arcuate nucleus, where somesthetic fibers from the face synapse, increase the animal's threshold for a quinine concentration in water by a factor of 100.

The long-held belief in the existence of distinct, primary taste qualities has received physiological confirmation in Pfaffmann's study[35] recording action potentials for single fibers of the gustatory nerve in cat. Pfaffmann found fibers that responded only to acid, some that responded to acid and a solution of sodium chloride and some that responded to acid and quinine. He found none that responded to a sugar solution.

Degree of certainty varies with regard to the chemical properties of stimuli for the primary taste qualities. There is greatest agreement about the significance of the hydrogen ion for sour. But even here the question is far from settled. Undoubtedly, the sourness of acids is a function of pH and degree of dissociation but not of these variables alone. Saliva, acting as a buffer, increases the pH of acids held in the mouth.

Anions, Cl^-, Br^-, I^-, NO_3^- $SO_4^=$, appear to be the chief stimuli for salt, but the cations also play a role since the chlorides of lithium, potassium and sodium have slightly different tastes.

For sweet and bitter the story is still less clear. Many sugars and alcohols are sweet, but so are some salts of beryllium and lead. The alkaloids are bitter, but some ammonium and magnesium salts are also. No common properties of sweet or of bitter stimuli have as yet been established.

Contrary to the widely-held belief that deprivation increases the taste sensitivity to nutrients required, Meyer[36] found that thresholds for salt, bitter and sweet remain constant in human beings throughout a 34 hour period of food deprivation.

THE LABYRINTHINE MECHANISM

The vestibular system is the only sense modality that has been studied as much in response to inadequate stimulation as it has in response to its adequate stimulus. The reason is obvious. It is much easier to syringe the ears with water than to rotate an experimental subject bodily. Responses of motion are forthcoming in either case. Moreover adequate stimulation of necessity gives rise to other sensations, notably kinesthetic ones.

In discussions of this mechanism the statement is often made that the labyrinthine system is *without sensations*. It is then pointed out that this is consistent with the fact that the system has no cortical representation. It is easy to believe that, as in the case of many other fictions about behavior, the anatomical "fact" preceded the behavioral opinion. Gerebtzoff[37] found a cortical response to rotation in cat. Penfield and Rasmussen[38] report that stimulation of the temporal cortex produces sensations of movement of the whole body in space.

Gernandt,[39] in an electrophysiological investigation of single units in the vestibular nerve of cat, found that the majority of units investigated showed an increased discharge over spontaneous activity in response to rotation toward the recording side and a decreased discharge below the spontaneous rate in response to rotation toward the opposite side, but a few units whose response to rotation was a complete inhibition of neural activity. This inhibitory effect, found in the visual, auditory, and vestibular systems, appears to be a general phenomenon in the neurophysiology of sensory systems.

THE SKIN SENSES

Specific receptors for pressure that do not respond to thermal stimulation, and specific receptors for warmth or cold that do not respond to mechanical stimulation are known to exist. But recently a class of duplex receptors has been discovered.

In experiments on cats Hensel and Zotterman[40] recorded action potentials from the lingual nerve while cooling areas on the tip of the tongue. Large spikes appeared only when the area stimulated contained mechanoreceptors. The appearance and termination of the spikes follow the onset and cessation of the cooling so closely that the possibility of a secondary mechanical effect's being responsible for the spike is unlikely.

In another study Hensel and Zotterman[41] recording from cold fibers in the lingual nerve of dogs and cats investigated Weber's idea, still widely held, that thermal receptors respond only to changes in temperature. They found that cooling the tongue below 23°C. results in action potentials from the cold fibers in the lingual nerve; these persist more than one hour at nearly constant frequency while temperature remains constant. When the tongue is rewarmed, impulses cease immediately. Interestingly, this is an example of a sensory system that is active without *receiving* external physical energy.

Hardy, Goodell and Wolff[42] found that on the blackened skin of the forehead and of the back of the hand the pain threshold to thermal radiation is inversely proportional to skin temperature between 15°C. and 45°C. They show that if the skin is warmed slowly the threshold for pain is reached at 44.9°C. They conclude also that at any rate of heating the skin must attain this temperature before pain is felt. It is not clear, however, from their results either that the pain threshold could not be reached at a lower threshold if the rate of heating is high or that pain would not be felt if the skin were heated at a high rate beyond that temperature.

The function of the sense cells in the ampullae of Lorenzini in the dogfish has been investigated by Sand.[43] Using electrophysiological techniques he observed that the neural discharge rate from the cells in the ampullae increases in response to slight cooling and decreases or even ceases in response to warming. This effect is another example of the general inhibitory phenomenon mentioned above in the discussion of the vestibular system.

THE WEBER-FECHNER LAW

No mention has as yet been made of the Weber-Fechner law. This function was proposed by the physiologist Weber, who in 1834 on the basis of experiments on the minimum detectable differences in weights in the hand, concluded that the minimum increase in weight that can be felt is proportional to the weight in the hand before the extra weight is added. Fechner later developed this relation, and what has become known as the Weber-Fechner law—that the ratio of the minimum detectable difference in magnitude divided by the reference magnitude, $\Delta I/I$ is constant—was believed to be a general law with the constant taking on different values for different sense modalities. Helmholtz showed that the relation does not hold for vision, and no one has ever been able to find an aspect of a sense modality in which it does hold. But the Weber-Fechner law is an example of a proposition that, having great intuitive appeal, is held long after it is shown to be false or, at most, true for only a small part of the data to which it purports to apply.

FOOTNOTES

[1] Stevens, S. S. Mathematics, measurement, and psychophysics. In *A handbook of experimental psychology* (Ed., S. S. Stevens). New York: John Wiley, 1951.

[2] Graham, C. H. Behavior, perception and the psychophysical methods. *Psychol. Rev.*, 1950, 57, 108-120.

[3] Hecht, S. Rods, cones, and the chemical basis of vision. *Physiol. Rev.*, 1937, 17, 239-290.

[4] Wald, G. and Clark, A. B. Visual adaptation and chemistry of the rods. *J. gen. Physiol.*, 1937, 21, 93-105.

[5] Hartline, H. K. and McDonald, P. R. Light and dark adaptation of single photoreceptor elements in the eye of Limulus. *J. cell. comp. Physiol.*, 1947, 30, 225-253.

[6] Hecht, S., Shlaer, S. and Pirenne, M. H. Energy, quanta, and vision. *J. gen. Physiol.*, 1942, 25, 819-840.

[7] Graham, C. H. and Margaria, R. Area and the intensity-time relation in the peripheral retina. *Amer. J. Physiol.*, 1935, 113, 299-305.

[8] Hartline, H. K. The nerve messages in the fibers of the visual pathway. *J. opt. Soc. Amer.*, 1940, 30, 239-247.

[9] Graham, C. H., Brown, R. H. and Mote, F. A., Jr. The relation of size of stimulus and intensity in the human eye: I. Intensity thresholds for white light. *J. exp. Psychol.*, 1939, 24, 555-573.

[10] Hecht, S. and Mintz, E. V. The visibility of single lines at various illuminations and the retinal basis of visual resolution. *J. gen. Physiol.*, 1939, 22, 593-612.

[11] Senders, V. L. Visual resolution with periodically interrupted light. *J. exp. Psychol.*, 1949, 39, 453-465.

[12] Riggs, L. A. and Ratliff, F. The effects of counteracting the normal movements of the eye. *J. opt. Soc. Amer.*, 1952, 42, 872-873.

[13] Ratoosh, P. and Graham, C. H. Areal effects in foveal brightness discrimination. *J. exp. Psychol.*, 1951, 42, 367-375.

[14] Beitel, R. J., Jr. Inhibition of threshold excitation in the human eye. *J. gen. Psychol.*, 1936, *14*, 31-61.

[15] Creed, R. A. and Ruch, T. C. Regional variations in sensitivity to flicker. *J. Physiol.*, 1932, *74*, 407-423.

[16] Hartline, H. K. The effects of spatial summation in the retina on the excitation of the fibers of the optic nerve. *Amer. J. Physiol.*, 1940, *130*, 700-711.

[17] Hartline, H. K. Inhibition of activity of visual receptors by illuminating nearby retinal areas in the *Limulus* eye. *Fed. Proc.*, 1949, *8*, 69.

[18] Hartridge, H. The change from trichromatic to dichromatic vision in the human retina. *Nature*, 1945, *155*, 657-662.

[19] Hsia, Y. and Graham, C. H. Spectral sensitivity of the cones in the dark adapted human eye. *Proc. nat. Acad. Sci.*, 1952, *38*, 80-85.

[20] Hurvich, L. M. and Jameson, D. Spectral sensitivity of the fovea. I. Neutral adaptation. *J. opt. Soc. Amer.*, 1953, *43*, 485-494.

[21] Jameson, D. and Hurvich, L. M. Spectral sensitivity of the fovea. II. Dependence on chromatic adaptation. *J. opt. Soc. Amer.*, 1953, *43*, 552-559.

[22] Hurvich, L. M. and Jameson, D. Spectral sensitivity of the fovea. III. Heterochromatic brightness and chromatic adaptation. *J. opt. Soc. Amer.*, 1954, *44*, 213-222.

[23] Békésy, G. von and Rosenblith, W. A. The mechanical properties of the ear. In S. S. Stevens (Ed.), *Handbook of experimental psychology.* New York: John Wiley, 1951.

[24] Stevens, S. S. and Volkmann, J. The relation of pitch to frequency: A revised scale. *Amer. J. Psychol.*, 1940, *53*, 329-353.

[25] Stevens, S. S., Davis, H. and Lurie, M. H. The localization of pitch perception on the basilar membrane. *J. gen. Psychol.*, 1935, *13*, 297-315.

[26] Stevens, S. S. The relation of pitch to intensity. *J. acoust. Soc. Amer.*, 1935, *6*, 150-154.

[27] Morgan, C. T., Garner, W. R. and Galambos, R. Pitch and intensity. *J. acoust. Soc. Amer.*, 1951, *23*, 658-663.

[28] Stevens, S. S. and Davis, H. *Hearing.* New York: Wiley, 1938.

[29] Galambos, R. and Davis, H. The response of single auditory-nerve fibers to acoustic stimulation. *J. Neurophysiol.*, 1943, *6*, 39-58.

[30] Galambos, R. and Davis, H. Inhibition of activity in single auditory nerve fibers by acoustic stimulation. *J. Neurophysiol.*, 1944, 7, 287-303.

[31] Galambos, R. and Davis, H. Action potentials from single auditory-nerve fibers? *Science*, 1948, *108*, 513.

[32] Beck, L. H. Osmics: Olfaction. In O. Glasser (Ed.), *Medical physics.* Chicago: Year Book Publishers.

[32a] Posvic, H. The odors of optical isomers. *Science*, 1953, *118*, 358-359.

[33] Börnstein, W. S. Cortical representation of taste in man and monkey. I. Functional and anatomical relations of taste, olfaction, and somatic sensibility. *Yale J. Biol. Med.*, 1940, *12*, 719-736.

[34] Patton, H. D., Ruch, T. C. and Walker, A. E. Experimental hypogeusia from Horsley-Clarke lesions of the thalamus in *Macaca mulatta. J. Neurophysiol.*, 1944, 7, 171-184.

[35] Pfaffmann, C. Gustatory afferent impulses. *J. cell. comp. Physiol.*, 1941, *17*, 243-258.

[36] Meyer, D. R. The stability of human gustatory sensitivity during changes in time of food deprivation. *J. comp. physiol. Psychol.*, 1952, *45*, 373-376.

37 Gerebtzoff, M.-A. Des effets de la stimulation labyrinthique sur l'activité électrique de l'écorce cérébrale. *Compt. rend. Soc. Biol.,* 1939, *131,* 807-813.

38 Penfield, W. and Rasmussen, T. *The cerebral cortex of man.* New York: Macmillan, 1950.

39 Gernandt, B. Response of mammalian vestibular neurons to horizontal rotation and caloric stimulation. *J. Neurophysiol.,* 1949, *12,* 173-184.

40 Hensel, H. and Zotterman, Y. The response of mechanoreceptors to thermal stimulation. *J. Physiol.,* 1951, *115,* 16-24.

41 Hensel, H. and Zotterman, Y. The response of the cold receptors to constant cooling. *Acta Physiol. Scand.,* 1951, *22,* 96-105.

42 Hardy, J. D., Goodell, H. and Wolff, H. G. The influence of skin temperature upon the pain threshold as evoked by thermal radiation. *Science,* 1951, *114,* 149-150.

43 Sand, A. The function of the ampullae of Lorenzini, with some observations on the effect of temperature on sensory rhythms. *Proc. roy. Soc. B.,* 1938, *125,* 524-553.

Thanks are due to the editors of the *American Journal of Psychology* and the *Journal of Neurophysiology,* as well as to John Wiley Sons, for their courtesy in connection with the use of illustrations appearing in this chapter.

CHAPTER III

CURRENT THEORETICAL APPROACHES TO PERCEPTION

PAUL BAKAN, PH.D.

Assistant Professor of Psychology, Michigan State College

EDITORIAL NOTE

Probably there is no other department of psychology that has developed as fruitfully as perception. In certain quarters it has become customary to treat perception as a stage of sensation. While it may be regarded as an extension of the more elementary processes, there can be no doubt that the transformation through experiences of the past and the core of meaning which attaches to it bring perception into a different category.

Perception as a study has traveled far since the days of Kant and his successor, Herbart. It has become the source-target of Gestalt psychology. It has figured in every other system with a phenomenological background. It has, of course, always been at the root of learning, and has offered a challenge to physiological theory, but lately the social and clinical approaches have thrown a good deal of light on the subject, and even the world wars have not been without their quota of information. Not least intriguing is the linking of personality with perception, so that the one becomes a function of the other.

Dr. Paul Bakan, formerly research associate in the department of psychology at the University of Illinois, and a member of the faculty of Michigan State College, has accumulated the results of various workers in the field, and has brought the subject of perception up to date, seeking a modus vivendi *among the welter of theories. Whether opposed factions can strike a compromise is doubtful, but to have at least a summary of the latest crisscrossing trends is itself of great service, especially when we consider that perception is the gravitating center of gravity for diverse researches, and the borderland between subjectivism and objectivism in psychology.*

CURRENT THEORETICAL APPROACHES
TO PERCEPTION

Psychology is beset by a group of concepts such as learning, motivation, and perception, each of which, when reified, misconstrues the holistic nature of organismic activity. Such reification often leads to serious problems of definition, and to definitions of questionable utility. This, in turn, leads to the postulation of various *kinds* of perception (7) or various *kinds* of learning (40).

In the case of perception (and also learning) there is no unanimity concerning the number of kinds involved; nor is it always clearly known whether the breakdown into different kinds of perception is dictated by the facts of perception, or whether it is the result of different assumptions about the nature of the stimulus. Gibson (13), for example, offers a list of four kinds of perception: 1) perception as discrimination, 2) perception of objects and events, 3) perception of meanings and values, and 4) perception of ambiguous or equivocal stimulation. These four kinds of perception are then consolidated to yield two kinds of perception, namely, "literal" perception, a combination of the first two, and "schematic" perception, a combination of the other two. With the specification of these two types of perception, the stage is set for Gibson's suggestion that two separate theories might be needed to account for the two types of perception.

The breakdown of perception into two types such as literal and schematic, or structural and functional, or externally determined and internally determined, or non-projective and projective is common practice today. Such a breakdown must lead to questions about the relative importance of each type, or the way in which the two types interact. Within this orientation, the major issue in perceptual theory begins to parallel somewhat the perennial heredity-environment issue. It would be unfortunate if we had to look forward to the endless dispute which usually follows when conceptual dichotomies are taken as anything but analytic devices.

In the context of the heredity-environment problem one may ask whether "heredity" ever exists independently of an "environment," and similarly, does "externally" determined perception exist independently of "internally" determined perception. It appears more likely that the apparently different kinds of perception really represent the results of different analytic approaches to the problem of perception; and the difference in analytic approaches is in turn a function of different beliefs concerning the nature of the stimulus. Experimentally it is possible to emphasize one or the other "kinds" of perception. For example, in the classical psychophysical experiment attempts are made to keep set, motivation, attitude, and other internal factors from varying. Such selective gathering of data tends to emphasize the importance of external stimulus variables in perception. However, it is important to recognize that keeping the internal variables constant is not the same as eliminating them. The effects of motivational and attitudinal factors, where such factors have been allowed to vary, have been demonstrated.

In the following exposition of some theoretical and conceptual trends in perception, it may be noted that differences in theoretical formulations of perception are to a considerable extent influenced by the conceptual balance which various theorists strike between the external and internal factors. An attempt will be made to show that the theoretical formulation developed is determined by the theorists' conception of the constitution of the stimulus.

Psychophysical Approaches

Graham (15, 16) has suggested a broad use of the psychophysical method as the most appropriate strategy for the explication of functional relationships in the field of perception. Arguing that there have been many theorists but little adequate theory in the field, he suggests that a body of quantitative relationships is necessary to define and explain the field of perception. For Graham the basic data of perception consist of response frequencies as they relate to variations in specified aspects of stimuli and specified conditions of the organism. Data collected by means of psychophysical methods, and formulated in stimulus-response terms are to provide the body of quantitative relationships required for the explanation of perception. The use of psychophysics does not imply any particular theoretical commitment. No rules are provided for the kind of variable selected, the definition of the stimulus, or the definition of the response. It is assumed that these are problems for the individual theorist or experimenter.

Gibson's approach (12) is a good example of the use of psychophysics in studying perception. Gibson's program calls for an analysis of space into the basic phenomenal variables of which it is composed. This type of analysis leads to a conception of the stimulus in terms of surface, edge, and shape. Since it is assumed that the phenomenal characteristics of the perceived world are a function of the distribution and sequence of energies on the retina, the problem is to relate the properties of the physical world to the properties of experience as reported by the observer. The following statements represent Gibson's statement of the basic principles of his psychophysical formulation (12):

"1) The elementary impressions of a visual world are those of surface and edge.

2) There is always some variable in stimulation which corresponds to a property of the spatial world.

3) The stimulus variable within the retinal image to which a property of visual space corresponds need be only a correlate of that property, not a copy of it.

4) The inhomogeneities of the retinal image can be analyzed by the methods of number theory and modern geometry into a set of variables analogous to the variables of physical energy.

5) The problem of how we perceive the visual world

can be divided into two problems to be considered separately, first the perception of the substantial or spatial world, and, second, the perception of the world of useful and significant things to which we ordinarily attend."

The perceptual dichotomy discussed earlier is suggested in the fifth principle above. It is assumed (second principle) that the properties of the "literal" visual world approach an exact correspondence with variables of physical stimulation. In contrast to this there is the world of "schematic" perception where meanings act upon perceptions to select or modify spatial properties. The determinants of the schematic world are the personality and culture of the perceiver. The schematic aspects of perception are not explicitly dealt with in the framework of Gibson's psychophysical formulation.

Helson's theory of the adaptation level (19, 20) is an outgrowth of traditional psychophysical research which failed to demonstrate fixed correlations between stimulus energies and sensory quality. In this theory the concept of the effective stimulus is expanded to include not only the physical stimuli in the situation, but also the residual effects of previous stimuli. It is assumed that sensory judgments are made with reference to the physical stimulus attended to, all other stimuli in the situation, and the effects of previous stimuli of the same class as the stimulus being judged. All effects of stimulation, past and present, are pooled to form a single level with respect to a given class of stimuli. This is the adaptation level. The location of the adaptation level on some stimulus continuum determines how other stimuli on the same continuum are judged or perceived or evaluated. Stimuli at the adaptation level are perceived as neutral, and stimuli below the adaptation level are responded to in a manner opposite to stimuli above the adaptation level. In judging weights, for example, judgments of light and heavy are determined by whether the weight is below or above the adaptation level for the class of stimuli being judged. The adaptation level may be expressed quantitatively if the stimuli can be quantified or translated to a numerical scale. This formulation is not limited to sensory judgments but can be applied to judgments about any stimulus dimension. Wherever the concept of frame of reference is applicable it is theoretically possible to define it in terms of the adaptation level. Thus the concept of frame of reference can be given mathematical expression. It should be noted that the delineation of stimulus classes is required in order to make use of the concept of adaptation level. The delineation and quantification of stimulus classes, however, is the function of the investigator and in the final analysis may be a function of certain a priori modes of constituting the stimulus.

PERCEPTION AND THE BRAIN

Tolman (39) has argued that some sort of brain model is implicit in most theories of perception. He has urged that these models be made explicit by perceptual theorists. Of the modern perceptual theorists, Köhler and Wallach (26) and Hebb (18) have been most explicit in the presentation of brain models.

Köhler and Wallach conceive of the brain as a volume conductor, where the excitations of specific nerve cells are relatively unimportant. In keeping with the general belief in psychophysical isomorphism, it is argued that the basis of perception is the occurrence of electrical currents in the occipital cortex. These currents are aroused by visual excitation. The flow of the currents in the neighborhood of the excitation increases the resistance of the tissue through which it flows. This increase in resistance, called satiation, results in changes of current flow, which result in perceptual changes. This brain model has deductive implications for a variety of perceptual phenomena including figural after-effects, figure-ground reversals, illusions, thresholds, autokinetic effect, apparent motion, and depth perception. This type of model also has implications for modalities other than the visual.

Köhler and his associates (24, 25) have obtained what they believe to be the cortical correlates of perception. They have demonstrated relationships between visual and auditory perceptions and the occurrence and pattern of direct currents in the cortex. This is considered further confirmation of the theory of psychophysical isomorphism. The verification and extension of these findings would be of great significance in understanding psychophysiological relations.

Hebb (18) rejects the type of field theory proposed by Köhler and Wallach (26). He argues that this type of theory does not deal adequately with central factors such as attention, expectancy, and attitude. And it leaves too little room for the factor of experience. Hebb proposes an alternative brain model which is designed to deal with the problems of perception, learning, and those central processes exemplified by attention and expectancy. In the context of this model a particular perception depends on the excitation of particular cells at some point in the central nervous system. The following statements quoted from the introduction to Hebb's book (18) indicate the nature of the brain model formulated.

> "Any frequently repeated particular stimulation will lead to the slow development of a 'cell-assembly,' a diffuse structure comprising cells in the cortex and diencephalon, . . . capable of acting briefly as a closed system. . . . A series of such events constitutes a 'phase-sequence'—the thought process. Each assembly action may be aroused by a preceding assembly, by a sensory event, or normally by both. . . . The theory is evidently a form of connectionism . . . though it does not deal in direct connections between afferent and efferent pathways. . . . The connections serve rather to establish autonomous central activities which then are basis of further learning."

This brain model has some rather important implications for perceptual theory since it emphasizes the close relationship between learning and perception.

THE STATE OF THE ORGANISM AND PERCEPTION

Traditionally, perceptual theorists have accepted the view that visual and auditory perception depends primarily on exteroceptive stimulation. This has resulted in an experimental and theoretical emphasis on the distance receptors, with neglect of other organismic factors. However, there is a considerable body of evidence which indicates that such perception is not completely determined by exteroceptive sensory factors. Percepts that are apparently visual or auditory may be in part determined by organismic factors other than the visual and auditory receptors. This possibility has been recognized by various theorists (14, 17, 23, 32, 38, 43) and it has recently been incorporated as the central notion in the sensory-tonic theory being developed by Werner and Wapner (41, 42).

The sensory-tonic theory is an organismic theory which attempts to overcome the limitations of purely sensory interpretation of perception. The basic hypothesis is that organismic states are an essential part of perception. Since sensory stimulation affects muscle tonus and since muscle tonus affects perception, any stimulus is necessarily sensory-tonic. Furthermore, there is functional equivalence between sensory and muscular factors with respect to a perceptual end product. For example, the perception of verticality, may be affected equivalently by visual stimulation and by muscular stimulation on one side of the body.

A related construct is that of vicariousness or vicarious channelization, meaning that available sensory-tonic energy may be released either through muscular activity of movement, or through perceptual activity. Thus the introduction of motor involvement just before looking at pictures may decrease the amount of perceptual movement as measured by verbal responses to pictorial material.

Another construct of the sensory-tonic theory is equilibrium. It is assumed that the organism tends to establish a steady state or body equilibrium. Stimuli may or may not interfere with this equilibrium. The notion of equilibrium can be illustrated with reference to the perceived vertical. When the body is erect, a perpendicular rod is perceived as vertical because its stimuli do not disturb the body equilibrium. If the body is tilted or if some extraneous stimulation is applied to one side, it is assumed that a change in equilibrium is induced. Then the perpendicular rod would not be "in tune" with the new equilibrium state and it will be necessary to shift the rod into an objectively tilted position in order for it to be "in tune" with the new equilibrium and therefore seem as vertical. In this framework the perceptual properties of an object are a function of the way in which stimuli coming from the object will affect the existing sensory-tonic state of the organism.

LEARNING AND PERCEPTION

The relationship between learning and perception has long been recognized by perceptual theorists and has made its mark on the vocabulary and thinking of psychology. Witness the influence of concepts as unconscious inference, apperceptive mass, and determining tendency in the past, and trace and context more contemporarily. Recently there has been a renaissance of interest in the relationship between learning and perception. This is part of the broader trend in which the so-called internal factors in perception are emphasized.

The most fundamental treatment of the problem is that proposed by Hebb (18). He is concerned, not only with the effect of learning on perception, but with the more basic problem of perceptual learning. According to Hebb the learning of apparently simple perceptions is a slow process taking place in childhood. This slow process involves motor as well as sensory factors. Hebb distinguishes three properties of a perceived figure, 1) a primitive sensorily determined unity, 2) a non-sensory unity, and 3) an identity. The primitive unity refers to the unity and segregation from the background which is a direct product of the sensory excitation pattern and the inherited characteristics of the nervous system on which it acts. This represents a more or less nativistic component of perception. The non-sensory unity is one in which the boundaries of the figure are not fixed by gradients of luminosity in the visual field, but are affected by experience. Thus the unity of the foreground of an unbroken landscape depends on more than a sensory delineation of figure and ground. Identity is the third property of a perceived figure. It refers to the properties of association inherent in a perception. A figure has identity when it is seen as similar to some figures and dissimilar to others. The object that has identity is capable of being associated readily with other objects or with some action. Identity generally depends on prolonged experience with an object of perception.

Some recent theories of the relationship between learning and perception emphasize cues and the integration of cues in perception. Boring (4) and Brunswik (8, 9) both start with the observation that perception is characterized by constancy and is not determined exclusively by projections on the retina. Both of these theorists invoke the notion of cues to account for the discrepancy. In the case of size perception, for example, Boring distinguishes between the core of the perception which is the size of the retinal projection of the object, and the context of the perception. The context consists of other sensory data as well as knowledge about the perceived object. The core and context are then integrated in some way to make possible the correspondence of perceptions to real objects. Brunswik (8, 9), assuming an explicit functionalist position, sees the task of the perceiving organism to be the "achievement" of real objects in perception. The perceptual reaction is said to be governed by a set of more or less implicit hypotheses concerning the correspondence between stimulus cues and distant objects. Previous experience is important in determining these hypotheses. The hypotheses may have different degrees of subjective certainty. They interact in some way to effect a compromise which tends to achieve a high degree of probable success for the organism.

A series of perceptual demonstrations developed by Ames has

dramatized some of the features of the relationship between learning and perception (10, 27). These demonstrations show that where there is a possibility of ambiguity in a perceptual situation, the ambiguity is resolved in such a way that the observer's previous experience with similar perceptual objects determines what is perceived. For example, an oak leaf presented in an alley with cues of size and distance ambiguous, is seen as of a given size and at a given distance depending on the observer's preconception of how big an oak leaf should be. Likewise, a geometrically distorted room with "normally" appearing windows, linoleum, and hanging objects is seen as a geometrically normal room with right angles between floor and ceiling.

Cantril and his co-workers (10, 22, 27) have attempted to extend the results of these demonstrations to perception in general. Some of the points made by Lawrence (27) with reference to the Ames demonstrations can be generalized to all perception. It is claimed that perceptions are based not on one phenomenon, but on the statistical average used as presumptions by the observer. These statistical averages are based on a great many past experiences. Perceptions result from a swift and unconscious weighing by the mind of a large number of indications or cues. This point of view is similar to that of Brunswik in its emphasis on the functional nature of perception. For example, Ittelson (22) sees perceptual constancy behavior as an attempt to create and maintain a world which deviates as little as possible from the world of past experience, since this attempt offers the observer the best opportunity for effective and successful action.

PERSONALITY FACTORS AND PERCEPTION

In recent years there has been a tendency for personality theorists and social psychologists to look to the field of perception for help in their understanding of behavior. The assumptions underlying this approach are 1) that an individual's behavior depends on his perception of the world and 2) that the

way an individual perceives the world depends upon his behavior. This rediscovery of perception has also had a beneficial
effect on "traditional" perception psychology by emphasizing
factors in perception which have been largely neglected, if not
in principle, then at least in the workaday world of perception
psychologists.

It is hardly necessary to belabor the point that the "same"
external stimulus does not always appear the same to all perceiv-
ers. The importance of this fact is recognized by those theorists
interested in the relationship between internal factors such as
learning or personality and perception. For example, Bruner
(5) has written that the "internal motive state changes the
probabilities of occurrence of alternate mediating processes for
the same external stimulus." The experimental results generally
support the notion that perception may be influenced by drives,
social values, interests, beliefs, expectancies, frustrations, attitudes, defenses, and the like (3, 5, 6, 34, 36, 44). The problem
is not whether or not these experiments are touching upon
important facts, but rather the problem lies in the area of interpretation and integration of these facts. There seems to be no
general agreement among theorists as to what these experimental
results mean. As Postman (34) has pointed out there has been
in this area a diversity of theoretical interpretations ranging
all the way from the fitting of brain models to orthodox psychoanalytic theory. Perhaps the difficulty lies in the fact that in
combining the concepts from various areas of relative ignorance
we are in effect multiplying the area of ignorance that can be
observed at a given time. Knowing little enough about needs
or defenses, what can we know about the effects of needs or defenses on perception? Recognition of this problem is shown in
the following quotation from Postman (34):

"To the extent that the process variables have remained
unidentified, the constructs used in the interpretation
of the data are apt to be on shaky operational ground
and have an unwarranted amount of surplus meaning.
It is now clear for example that concepts like 'perceptual

defense' and 'perceptual vigilance' were inadequately defined and implied too much precisely because they were not anchored in specifiable manipulations of the organism."

Despite the lack of theoretical rigor, the accomplishments growing out of a new way of looking at perceptual problems have been of great significance. No future theory of behavior can afford to ignore the personality variables in perception.

SOME OTHER APPROACHES TO PERCEPTION

Though an attempt has been made to present an account of contemporary theoretical trends in the field of perception, space limitations have prevented the presentation of all theoretical formulations or more than a very cursory examination of those views which are presented. A more exhaustive treatment should consider some of the approaches making use of mathematics and mathematical models. Among the mathematical approaches are Luneburg's (28) formulation of the problem of space perception in terms of non-Euclidean geometry, the models of Rashevsky (35) and Pitts and McCulloch (33) which may have deductive implications in the study of perception, and recent developments in information theory (11, 21, 30, 37) which promise to have considerable application in the study of perception.

Other approaches to the problem of perception include Berlyne's attempts to incorporate perceptual constructs into Hullian behavior theory (2), Michotte's experiments purporting to show that certain modes of perceptual experience such as causality and substantiality are primitive and phenomenally given (29), the work of Kohler (23) on conditioned perception, the important theoretical account of the sensory order proposed by Hayek (17), and Motokawa's demonstrations of retinal induction effects in visual perception (31).

The Basic Problem in Perceptual Theory

It should be quite apparent by now that in the realm of perceptual theorizing there is anything but uniformity. Theories and gropings toward theories vary in scope, complexity, and level of analysis and the experimental work dictated by the various points of view shows considerable variation. In view of this diversity, can a least common denominator be found around which the problem of perceptual theory can be organized?

An event becomes a problem within a particular theoretical context when the occurrence of that event can be said to be at variance with a theoretical assumption, implicit or explicit. Thus, if it is assumed that all horses are white, the occurrence of a black horse becomes an event requiring explanation. Similarly, if there are grounds to believe that the up-down orientation of the perceived world should correspond to the up-down orientation of the image of the world on the retina, then there exists the problem of explaining why the world appears right-side-up. The problem of explaining size-constancy arises if we have grounds to believe that the perceived size of an object should correspond to the size of its retinal projection, i. e. if there are grounds to believe that it should appear smaller with increasing distance from the observer.

It should be noted that the beliefs or assumptions that determine which events require explanation may be arbitrary. The different beliefs entertained by theorists determine the phenomena with which their theories attempt to deal. Current perceptual theorists do not seem to be greatly concerned with explaining why the world is perceived right-side-up despite an upside-down retinal image. Hardly anyone today believes that the up-down orientation of the world should correspond to the up-down orientation of the retinal image. But there are theorists who are concerned with explaining why the apparent size of an object does not decrease with distance in proportion to the decrease in the size of its retinal image. They still entertain seriously the belief that perceived size should correspond to the size of the retinal image. On the other hand, it may just as easily be argued that the correspondence is not between the perceived size of an object and the size of its retinal projection, but between the perceived size of an object and the *total* stimulation on the retina. This would include the retinal projection of the object whose size is being apprehended and also the projection of other objects in the visual field. Such an approach in terms of the relationship between the phenomenal world and the total retinal stimulation is essentially that taken by Gibson (12).

If it is assumed in a theory that all visual perception is determined by the distribution of stimulation on the retina, then the theory does not have to explain this assumption. It is primarily concerned with functional relationships between retinal stimulation and visual perception. Within this context the effect of non-retinal stimulation on visual perception becomes a problem in the same sense that an upright appearing world is a problem in the context of a theory which assumes that the up-down orientation of the visual world should be the same as the up-down orientation of the vertical image. On the other hand, a theory in which it is assumed that visual perception is not determined by retinal stimulation alone but also by the condition of the rest of the organism does not have to explain this assumption but can turn its attention to the explication of functional relationships between states of the organism and visual perception. This is essentially the approach taken by Werner and Wapner (41, 42).

A broad interpretation of organismic states may lead to the assumption that states of the organism characterized by needs, values, and previous experience can also influence visual perception. Such an assumption leads to an interest in functional relationships between need, value, and experience variables on visual perception. This broad interpretation of the stimulus complex determining visual perception results in approaches like those of Bruner (5), and the "new look" theorists (3).

Thus it is apparent that the different "kinds" of perception referred to earlier in this paper result from different beliefs held by various perceptual theorists concerning the constitution of the stimulus for perception, rather than from basically different kinds of perception. The apparent differences between "kinds" of perception are due to a situation in which different aspects of the total stimulus field are varied while other aspects are controlled in accordance with the beliefs about the determinants of perception held by the investigator.

The argument developed here need not be limited to visual perception, but may be applied to all other aspects of perception. Furthermore, the essential point about the importance of the belief of the scientist need not be limited to the field of perception but may be extended to encompass psychology as a whole.

Clearly the beliefs entertained by the investigator can determine the complexion of a theoretical formulation. These beliefs determine what the scientist regards as the events requiring explanation, what he regards as stimulus, and what he regards as response. Bakan (1) has emphasized the importance of the psychological processes of the investigator in an experimental situation; he has suggested that an analysis of the psychological operations of the scientist must be taken into account in any thoroughgoing operational analysis of an experimental situation.

It has been suggested that the beliefs of the scientist determine the way in which he constitutes the stimulus. An attempt has been made to show how the conceptual constitution of the stimulus varies in different theoretical formulations. The scientist should therefore recognize the limitations inherent in a theoretical system in which the stimulus is an important concept and in which it must be defined, either implicitly or explicitly. For the definition of the stimulus in any theoretical context is influenced by certain assumptions made by the theorist concerning what aspect of a total situation is the stimulus. The scientist constitutes a conceptual stimulus with which he hopes to approximate a "real" stimulus. But his "stimulus" is a construct and not an entity.

REFERENCES

[1] Bakan, D. Learning and the scientific enterprise. *Psychol. Rev.*, 1953, *60*, 45-49.

[2] Berlyne, D. E. Attention, perception, and behavior theory. *Psychol. Rev.*, 1951, *58*, 137-146.

[3] Blake, R. R., and Ramsey, G. V. (eds.) *Perception: an approach to personality*, New York: Ronald, 1951.

[4] Boring, E. G. The perception of objects. *Amer. J. Phys.*, 1946, *14*, 99-107.

[5] Bruner, J. S. Personality dynamics and the process of perceiving. In *Perception: an approach to personality*. (Blake, R. R. and Ramsey, G. V. eds.) New York: Ronald, 1951.

[6] Bruner, J. S. and Goodman, C. C. Value and need as organizing factors in perception. *J. Abnorm. Soc. Psychol.*, 1947, *42*, 33-44.

[7] Brunswik, E. Discussion: remarks on functionalism in perception. *J. Personal.*, 1949, *18*, 56-65.

[8] Brunswik, E. *Systematic and representative designs of psychological experiments*. Berkeley: Univer. Calif. Press, 1947.

[9] Brunswik, E. The conceptual framework of psychology. *Int. Encycl. Unif. Sci.*, Vol. 1, No. 10, Chicago : Univer. of Chicago Press, 1952.

[10] Cantril, H., Ames, A., Hastorf, A. H., and Ittelson, W. H. Psychology and scientific research. *Science*, 1949, *110*, 461-464, 491-497, 517-522.

[11] Garner, W. R. and Hake, H. W. The amount of information in absolute judgments. *Psychol. Rev.*, 1951, *58*, 446-459.

[12] Gibson, J. J. *The perception of the visual world*. Boston: Houghton Miflin Co., 1950.

[13] Gibson, J. J. Theories of perception. In *Current trends in psychological theory*. Pittsburgh: Univers. of Pittsburgh Press, 1951, 85-110.

[14] Goldstein, K. *The organism*. New York: American Book Co., 1939.

[15] Graham, C. H. Behavior, perception, and psychophysical methods. *Psychol. Rev.*, 1950, *57*, 108-120.

[16] Graham, C. H. Visual Perception. In *Handbook of experimental psychology*. (S. S. Stevens, Ed.) New York: Wiley, 1951.

[17] Hayek, F. A. *The sensory order*. Chicago: Univer. of Chicago Press, 1952.

[18] Hebb, D. O. *The organization of behavior*. New York: Wiley, 1949.

[19] Helson, H. Adaptation-level as frame of reference for prediction of psychophysical data. *Amer. J. Psychol.*, 1947, *60*, 1-29.

[20] Helson, H. Adaptation-level as a basis for a quantitative theory of frames of reference. *Psychol. Rev.*, 1948, *55*, 297-313.

[21] Hochberg, J. and McAllister, E. A quantitative approach to figural "goodness". *J. Exp. Psychol.*, 1953, *46*, 361-364.

[22] Ittelson, W. H. The constancies in perceptual theory. *Psychol. Rev.*, 1951, *58*, 285-294.

[23] Kohler, I. *Aufbau und Wandlungen der Wahrnehmungswelt*. Vienna: Rudolph M. Rohrer, 1951.

[24] Köhler, W. and Held, R. The cortical correlate of pattern vision. *Science*, 1949, *110*, 414-419.

[25] Köhler, W., Held, R. and O'Connell, D. N. An investigation of cortical currents. *Proc. Amer. Philos. Soc.*, 1952, *96*, 290-330.

[26] Köhler, W. and Wallach, H. Figural after-effects. *Proc. Amer. Philos. Soc.*, 1944, *88*, 269-357.

27 Lawrence, M. *Studies in human behavior*. Princeton: Princeton Univers. Press, 1949.

28 Luneburg, R. K. *Mathematical analysis of binocular vision*. Princeton: Princeton Univ. Press, 1947.

29 Michotte, A. *La perception de la causalité*. Louvain: L'Institute Superieur de la Philosophie. 1946.

30 Miller, G. A. What is information measurement? *Amer. Psychol.*, 1953, *8*, 3-11.

31 Motokawa, K. Field of retinal induction and optical illusion. *J. Neuphysiol.*, 1950, *13*, 413-426.

32 Murphy, G. and Hochberg, J. Perceptual development: some tentative hypotheses. *Psychol. Rev.*, 1951, *58*, 332-349.

33 Pitts, W. and McCulloch, W. S. How we know universals. *Bull. Math. Biophys.*, 1942, *7*, 301-322.

34 Postman, L. Perception, motivation and behavior. *J. Personal.*, 1953, *22*, 17-31.

35 Rashevsky, N. *Mathematical biophysics*. Chicago: Univers. of Chicago Press. rev. ed. 1948.

36 Schafer, R. and Murphy, G. The role of autism in a visual figure-ground relationship. *J. Exp. Psychol.*, 1943, *32*, 335-343.

37 Shannon, C. E. and Weaver, W. *The mathematical theory of communication*. Urbana: Univer. of Illinois Press, 1949.

38 Sperry, R. W. Neurology and the mind-brain problem. *Amer. Scientist*, 1952, *40*, 291-312.

39 Tolman, E. C. Discussion. *J. Personal.*, 1949, *18*, 48-50.

40 Tolman, E. C. There is more than one kind of learning. *Psychol Rev.*, 1949, *56*, 144-155.

41 Werner, H. and Wapner, S. Sensory-tonic field theory in perception. *J. Personal.*, 1949, *18*, 88-107.

42 Werner, H. and Wapner, S. Toward a general theory of perception. *Psychol. Rev.*, 1952, *59*, 324-338.

43 Witkin, H. A. Perception of the upright when the direction of the force acting on the body is changed. *J. Exp. Psychol.*, 1950, *40*, 93-106.

44 Witkin, H. A. et al. *Personality through perception*. New York: Harper, 1954.

Chapter IV

THE COGNITIVE PROCESSES

Theodore F. Karwoski

Director, Psychological Laboratory, Dartmouth College

EDITORIAL NOTE

The higher thought processes, as they have been traditionally called, are an outgrowth of perception, but there is much else involved. Animal psychologists have attempted to study these in mice and rats as well as in primates. Behaviorism tried to supply a non-mentalistic base, and operationists are continuing the machine approach. Soviet reflexologists have been ready to tackle some of the thought problems as at least one speaker at the 1954 International Congress of Psychology, held at Montreal, has indicated, but it is evident that much of the mechanical approach consists of nibbling; for thinking cannot be properly understood except in mental terms.

While in the United States, the thought processes have been treated sporadically and cavalierly, they present a central issue in England. Both Oxford and Cambridge have shown interest in this sphere. In his Clayton Memorial Lecture on "Thinking," Sir Frederic Bartlett submits the following view of thinking.

> *Thinking proper is a process of filling up gaps by a succession of different steps which have an inherent order of sequence. Its outstanding or defining character, is that at each step the number, and, often less clearly, the order of successive steps offer a progressive limitation of freedom, until at some stage before the issue is reached, the subsequent steps become completely objectified in the sense that they are the same for all thinkers.*

Dr. Theodore Karwoski, as Director of the Dartmouth Psychological Laboratory, has had ample opportunity to study such problems empirically. Dr. Karwoski is the co-author of Psychology.

INTRODUCTION

The Cognitive Processes concern those functions through which we obtain knowledge of the world. Sensation, perception, memory and thinking are the classical subject matter of cognition. Reality as we know it is mediated through the cognitive processes. These processes are apprehended in different forms such as sensations, percepts, images, thoughts and ideas. In general they have the common quality of being for us the representations of reality. Many of these mental contents can be observed by introspection. There are, however, some which are not observable, such as bare thoughts unsupported by mental images. The aim of this chapter is to analyze cognition in terms of the *symbolic process* in order to organize cognitive material and at the same time to point up critical issues.

What is the most generic or the most common function performed by cognitions? An obvious answer is that they give us knowledge about the world and events. Mental phenomena refer to something other than themselves, to stimuli in the external world, in which one's own body is a part, or they refer to other mental events. In other words cognitive processes perform a *symbolic function*. Philosophically this is a reasonable generalization, but psychologically it is difficult to be explicit as to just what is symbolically happening in experience. Moreover, the word symbol used in this broad sense is confusing because the word has been specifically defined by psychologists. Thus symbols and signs are sharply distinguished although they both perform a symbolic function. The only psychological concepts which are sufficiently broad to cover the cognitive processes are "awareness of" or "consciousness of," but these words mean too many things. They are the end results in experience for which we wish to know the particulars. In this kind of dilemma perhaps the best approach is to examine what psychologists have to offer concerning the symbolic function of the main categories of cognition: sensation, perception, memory and thinking.

The symbolic processes in sensation and perception. For convenience these four categories of cognition may be separated into two groups: sensation and perception on the one hand and memory and thinking on the other. Sensations and perceptions are said to be objective because we experience them as if they are independent and external to us. Their symbolic function is said to be "stimulus bound" or closely related to the stimulus situation as it is presented to us. As such sensations become "signs".* Thus shadows on an object are a sign of its solidity and clearness may be a sign of its distance. Signs may signal events in which case they are called "signals." Thus the sound of a locomotive precedes the appearance of a train; a smile suggests good will. Memory and thinking, on the other hand, are subjective. The symbolic function is initiated and experienced by the individual within himself. Ideas, thoughts and memories are examples. The person or "interpreter" supplies his own signs. (21) Such signs are called *symbols*. According to Susanne Langer (17) "Signs announce their object; whereas symbols lead us to conceive their objects." Thus the steeple is a sign of a church but the symbol of religion.

Let us consider the symbolic implications of sensation and perception first. Sensations are symbolic in that they are the signs for the various kinds of energy which bombard the organism. We do not experience these energies as such, but each form of energy is normally *invariably correlated* with a kind of sensation. Thus light, sound, taste, smell and touch are the signs of electromagnetic waves, air waves, chemical, gaseous and mechanical energies. From these sensations the qualities of experience are derived. Sensations are psychophysical correlates; whenever we are stimulated by a light wave length of 750mu, we always experience the same sensation, namely that of red. Psychophysical correlates are innately given and so do not

* Psychologists use the word cue synonymously with sign. It is better to use one or the other in order to avoid confusion between signs, cues and clues.

have to be explained. Since the function of sensation is to supply information about objects, rather than energies, the sensation in effect is a sign of itself. Another way of saying this is that sensations are the primary or natural signs of experience. The issue is not as clear as presented here. Light can be experienced by stimuli other than the normally adequate electromagnetic energy. Pressing the eyeball elicits light but not as efficiently as in ordinary vision. Years ago Hering pointed out that color sensation can be modified by memory. He introduced the concept of memory color. Katz (13) has developed this distinction in his conception of surface or object color versus film color which corresponds to the color of the psychophysics.

The notion that sensations are the signs of energies which effect the organism through the sense organs opened an area of research which is known as psychophysics. Psychophysics seeks correlations between the physical properties of the stimulus and sensory experience. Important correlations have been discovered in vision and audition but there is still much to be done in the modalities of taste, smell and touch. (29)

Sensations are also signs in a more practical sense. Unlike the scientist the layman uses signs to obtain the meaning of things and events. When sensations are used as signs of objects and occurrences the process is known as perceiving. Thus the smell of lilac may be a sign of the lilac in bloom; tastes are signs of food, etc. There are sensory signs of distance and direction by which we locate objects which emit sounds. The psychologist experiments by excluding suspected signs until one is found which eliminates the capacity to localize the object. Perception may be defined as the utilization of sensations as signs in order to get at their meanings. Sensations as signs which mean things are usually learned by experience although there may be signs of distance and direction which are innate or instinctive.

In defining the stimulus, these two levels of sensation as a sign must be distinguished. As a natural sign the stimulus always refers to the physical energy stimulating the organism.

As a sign of percepts or objects the stimulus is commonly called the "stimulus situation" or "stimulus object." In this sense a slap on the back is said to be a stimulus. In the first sense stimuli refer to what the world does to us directly; in the second sense there is an additional function of what we do to the world in reacting to its forces. This is a difference between sensing and perceiving.

Perception has raised important problems which are still active issues. One concerns the hundred year old controversy between the so-called nativists and empiricists. How much of perception is psychophysical, innately given, and how much is added by learning? During the course of the controversy empiricists practically reduced perception to learning. But there was always the underlying uncertainty which was adequately expressed by Gestalt psychologists who asked,—How is it that the world looks all of one piece and corresponds so nicely with objective reality? Can all this be an inference from piece meal learning? Another lively issue raised by perception is involved in a basic difference of opinion between phenomenologists and behaviorists. In spite of the ambitious research of the behaviorists, many psychologists cannot accept the quality of muscular contraction as equivalent to the texture of perceived experience.

In a careful analysis of phenomenal space perception, Gibson (6) sets limits to the achievements of learning. His analysis is based on the conceptions of psychophysics as applied to larger units than the traditional sensory data of psychophysics. Light energy gradients are ordered in the retinal image. These ordinal relations or gradients correspond to texture, slant and edges in the objective world. Sharp changes in energy distribution give contour. These gradients yield a natural solid world directly. To Gibson the retinal stimulus distribution and distal (phenomenal) objects are strictly correlated. Consequently space perception is innately given in the same way that sensations are "stimulus bound."

There is the big problem of the poverty of perceptual awareness in infants. The genetic development of perception from childhood to maturity supports the view that perception is an accomplishment of laborious learning. Gibson does not deny the role of learning. Learning helps, but inevitably the world becomes structured in terms of basic psychophysical correlates of perception. But well-attested facts show that our visual perceptions are modified if not distorted by various sets or attitudes which we bring to the situation. To account for such facts Gibson distinguished between what he calls *literal* and *schematic* perception. Literal perception is the real psychophysical perception which is innately determined and rigid. Schematic perceptions, on the other hand, are judgments about objects and things that are added to or attached to the basic correlates. In the world of significant things, where there is some ambiguity because there are too many things to attend to at once, where certain things are selected while others are neglected, we exercise our judgment. Being uncertain we schematize.

The distinction between literal and schematic perception has implications concerning the symbolic function of perception. The signs of the literal world are innately given. There is no problem on the phenomenological level of what these signs refer to or indicate. The signs stand for themselves. In the schematic world the signs are indirect and indeterminate. They are called signs or clues depending on the degree of conscious awareness of their significance. Signs fuse with their objects; clues are separable from their referents like symbols. By signs we perceive, by clues we infer.

Under the notion of schematic perception we can say that the sign or clue indicates something other than itself. Consider the situation where an object is in front of another and partly covers it. This is called the clue (sign) of interposition. In this case the fact of the interposition can be either a clue or sign. The clue of interposition leads to the logical deduction that one object is separated from the other. Perceptually we do not infer logically at all. In perception sign and referent are inseparable.

PRESENT-DAY PSYCHOLOGY

This is also true of clues in the act of perceiving but clues can be logically isolated whereas signs are not. Signs are scientifically isolated by experiments which eliminate all factors except the suspected sign.

In schematic perception clues from without or from within, such as attitudes and suggestions are apt to be prominent but in the act of perceiving they look just as real as literal perception. The signs, and clues of "schematic" perception do not carry tags by which they can be distinguished from "literal" perception. Perhaps the tags are present but we have not discovered them. The fact that individuals differ in the ease with which they respond to signs of perception is a lead. Some subjects need more time than others to obtain typical illusions, including stereoscopic fusion. There may be more time variance in schematic than in literal perception. This notion suggests a continuum on which the signs of literal and schematic perception and the symbols of thought may be ordered.

Perceiving as a way of thinking. The concept of schematic perception opens for consideration the general role of the influence of perception on memory and thinking. In fact, recent studies in perception have furnished new evidence that perceiving is not unlike the process of judging in the form of rapid weighing of information.

A group of social psychologists have concerned themselves with the effect of social and personality factors on perception. They have attempted to measure changes in perception due to the influence of social suggestion, needs such as hungers, achievements, and personal values on presented stimuli. They have exposed stimuli for very short periods, used reversible figures or one way or another worked with reduced stimuli. In the main their results support the thesis that social and personality dynamics are important variables in perception. An objection has been raised against the use of reduced stimuli on the ground that at best such experiments concern imperception rather than perception. But the fact remains that the effects are perceived as if they were real. Furthermore, in real-life situations stimuli are often ambiguous; therefore, their studies are not altogether artificial. Two leaders of this movement, Bruner (4) and Postman (25), have independently synthesized these results in the form of a cognitive theory which they call an expectancy or hypothesis theory of perception. The following is a statement of Bruner's theory with Miller's variation in the second paragraph.

"The stronger the hypothesis, the more will ambiguous information be suitable for confirming hypotheses. This implies, in short, that personality and motivational and experiential factors, having a maximum effect upon the kind of hypotheses adopted, will therefore have a maximum effect upon the emergence of perception in situations where information is ambiguous. In other words the personality of the individual enters more and more into the perception as ambiguity or his ignorance increases. It is probable that a better way to state this is in the reverse, which is that the greater the ambiguity existing and the greater the ignorance, then the more it is necessary for the organism to create a strong hypothesis in order to maintain its equilibrium, its homeostasis, and to relieve it from anxiety concerning the potential threat which develops from its ignorance." (20, p. 277)

Ames and his colleagues working in perception with tridimensional exhibits came to conclusions which are similar to those of Bruner and Postman. Ames speaks of an assumptive world. In facing a perceptual situation certain assumptions about it are aroused. The elicited presumption is a statistical probability from past experience. In a sense we can "perceive probability." This weighing of probabilities takes place swiftly and unconsciously (19).

Although both the Ames group and Bruner-Postman theorize from the cognition, where the hypotheses and presumptions presumably reside, their data indicates, that the hypotheses are triggered by external signs or clues. Thus playing cards which have been colored unconventionally (hearts in black, spades in red, etc.) are exposed tachistoscopically from very short exposures to longer ones in order to determine the changes in perception with increasing information as the stimuli are exposed longer. Subjects tend to see the cards in their known colors much longer than they should if perception were the only variable. Likewise in their experiments on the role of values in perception (valued coins being seen larger, valued words being perceived sooner, etc.) external stimulus clues consistent with an individual's preferences or values determine the percept. Their experiments intending to show that personal values or internal stimuli influence perceptual thresholds were less successful but the evidence from other sources adequately supports the hypothesis. In the Ames demonstrations the signs of perception are so arranged that they are in conflict and what one sees is the best hypothesis set up by the cues. In one experiment, however, that of Hastorf (7) specific meanings were implanted in the subject before observation. The observers were given the task of adjusting a circle of light so that it looked to be the same distance away as a target. When they were told this circle was a ping-pong ball, they made different settings than when told it was a billiard ball.

Assumptions and hypotheses raise the problem of *knowing* and *seeing* (3). Knowing is in the province of thinking. Ordinarily we say thinking is carried on by symbols and not signs. *Signs of perception give meaning by becoming the thing they mean.* The signs of distance and depth are *seen* in three dimensions; tri-dimensionality is not merely logically inferred. Knowing that railway tracks are equi-distant, having a symbol of equi-distance in our minds, we look at the tracks and in fact we see them equally spaced. At another moment the tracks seem to converge. We have here a case where both signs and symbols are operating at the same time. When the sign of retinal size is dominant we see convergence; when the symbol of known equality is in control the tracks look parallel. Mere knowing cannot ordinarily produce a percept. That is the way the symbols in thinking operate, otherwise we would be subject to hallucinations all the time. However, evidence does suggest that when a symbol is supported by various clues in the environment which are congruent with it, the symbol can fuse with these equivalent signs or clues at the expense of the sign of retinal size. In this way knowing is seeing.

In 1709 Bishop Berkeley made the astonishing proposal that muscular cues of convergence and accommodation are the primary signs of distance and depth. How can such diverse things as muscular contractions be translated into the texture of vision? Nevertheless Berkeley opened a door which has had revolutionary effects on psychology. In recent times the muscle cues or signs have lost their primacy in space perception. Convergence and accommodation have limited application and require the support of visual signs. Consequently the so-called secondary or monocular signs of vision have grown in importance. Now Werner and Wapner (31) have proposed a sensory-tonic theory of perception, which is based on evidence that muscle tonus as an index of states of equilibria affects perception. The theory is also concerned with resolving the paradox "of interaction between sensory events and events such as motor activity, drives and other characteristics of organic states." An example of the experiments is the task of adjusting a rod in a dark room so that it appears vertical. "Under electrical stimulation of the right neck muscle it was tilted more to the left. Auditory stimulation functions in an analogous way. . . ." Tilting the body to one side shifts the vertical to the other. The authors are also working on changes in complex stimuli caused by the equilibrating tendencies of the organism. The new idea is the notion of *equivalence* between sensory and muscular factors in particular and organismic factors in general. This theory suggests that body equilibria and disequilibria may be signs of characteristic changes in perception.

The "assumptions" of Ames and the "hypotheses" of Bruner and Postman equate perception with thinking. However, the signs and symbols involved are not those of rational thought which can be delayed and manipulated. They act swiftly and unconsciously. We might say they are "perceived thinking" or "projected thoughts" since they are translated into perceptions. This body of knowledge is filling a gap which psychologists have neglected until recently. Perception was mainly exploited for sensory signs of distance and depth; thinking was mainly confined to studies of reasoning and problem solving. The tendency to look at perceiving as thinking and thinking as perceiving bridges the gap between the specific techniques and knowledge of experimental psychologists and those of clinical and social psychologists. The work of Werner and Wapner points in the same direction. Werner (31), who showed the generality and importance of "physiognomic" qualities in perception, hopes to explain the projected perceptions obtained by *projective techniques* and in natural physiognomic perceptions. Life demands that we make daily quick appraisals of things, people and events. We take our chances, make our judgments and pass on. To act intuitively on minor issues makes life less exhausting. Therefore, it is necessary to emphasize that an important phase of the problem of thinking and reasoning is the category of perceptual thinking. When thinking is seen, it is difficult not to believe. Like the Gestaltists the motivational psychologists are impressed with the fact that the world is of one piece, in spite of diversities. Does not the need for constancy of the environment and definiteness of objects have something to do with its actualization? (27)

Primitive generalization in behavior. In perception and learning we deal with a relatively concrete situation—here and now —which we can see and manipulate. When we enter the field of thinking we find an overloaded mechanism. All that has been learned and perceived in the past is potentially there. In thinking there is another dimension—time. This time is not confined to one's life span—it extends to historical time which is acquired by learning. Man has been called the time-binding animal. (14).

Fortunately much of this overloading is unconscious most of the time, which lends the mind a sort of a constant background or environment which maintains a condition of minimal tension. When we think the material is activated toward some end state or goal; tension is reduced and the process comes to a minimal state of excitation, to begin all over again. The process is started by some disturbances which we do not fully understand, but which are known as "determining tendencies," mental sets and tasks. The process is selective and self-directing.

The approach to the thought process through introspection reached a limit at the turn of the century. To progress further, psychologists have turned to objective studies of thinking behavior. One reason for this shift was the discovery that humans can arrive at solutions such as deriving concepts and yet be unable to describe how they managed it. Much of the evidence on the nature of the cognitive processes comes from studies which were not intended to get at cognition directly. We have already covered the point in human perception which led to a theory of hypothesis in perceiving. As psychologists found that their data showed results which were due to unobservable variables they tended to posit "intervening" variables between stimulus and response. Thus the conditioned reflex led to positing the intervening variable of "expectancy" or "anticipation." Some times these intervening variables are interpreted cognitively. Tolman, working on the learning of animals, went so far as to posit "mental maps" in rats to account for behaviors which to him were not otherwise understandable. Krechevski (15) has contributed the idea that rats utilize hypotheses at "choice points" in learning mazes. Tolman's theory is known as the sign-significate theory of learning. (28) Another prominent theory of learning, the reenforcement theory of Hull, which was originally formulated without benefit of cognitive processes, has recently been modified by one of his students in terms of a major intervening variable which is called the *"mediating process."* Osgood (23) conceives of the mediating process as one of stimulus and response, but his logic can easily be translated into stimulus-sensory relations. The mediation process is symbolic. Responses which are not made to the object directly but become conditioned to the object by secondary conditioning can become symbols of the object by generalization. Thus the spoor of a deer is not the deer, but the spoor points to the deer. The response to the spoor is not the response to the actual deer but it is part of the context of the total response leading to the response to the deer. On the basis of partial identity the response to the spoor becomes a sign for the response to the deer itself. Afterwards the organism can stimulate itself by such signs. In this way words become signs. Therefore a stimulus pattern which is not the object is a sign of the object if it evokes a mediating reaction which is a fractional part of the previously evoked behavior of the object. Osgood does not object to calling these signs thoughts or ideas, but he prefers to think of them in terms of evoked responses.

Two categories which are useful for conceptualization are that of "equivalent stimuli" and "concept formation." Because these two processes are apparently similar some psychologists have proposed that there is a relation of identity between them. On the level of equivalent stimuli the simplest organisms perform like humans on the highest cognitive level known to us— concept formation. The problem here is the broad one of how the organism can *generalize* from experience. Under equivalent stimuli it will be convenient to subsume similar phenomena such as "stimulus generalization" and "stimulus transposition."

Stimulus generalization. Pavlov and his colleague Anrep performed the original experiments on the sense of touch and pitch in animals. Anrep (1) conditioned dogs to a vibratory stimulus applied to the body. The place of conditioning was on the thigh which was designated as O. After that, without further reenforcement, the following positions were tested and the amount of saliva flow measured. No. 1 on the hind paw, No. 2 on the pelvis, No. 3 on the middle of the trunk, No. 4 on the shoulder, No. 5 on the foreleg, No. 6 on the front paw. The secretion was recorded for 30 seconds during which stimulation lasted.

Number of place stimulated	1	0	2	3	4	5	6
Secretion	33	53	45	39	23	21	19

Bass and Hull (2) repeated this experiment on humans measuring the amount of psychogalvanic deflection. Hovland (10) used a similar technique except that the conditioned stimulus was sound. The results of these two studies yielded stimulus generalization gradients which were similar in shape. It should be pointed out that in these studies the gradients were based on the means for many subjects for the tested positions. The individual readings differed considerably. However, the tendency was lawful and not random. Stimulus generalization in humans is similar to that of the lower animals.

Transposition. The concept of transposition is similar to stimulus generalization except that it is the *relationship* between stimuli that is generalized. Chicks are conditioned to eat from the larger of two disks. After the habit is established the experimenter removes the smaller disk and replaces it with a disk which is larger than the conditioned disk. Will the creatures now respond to the disk they were originally conditioned to? What happens is that the chicks go to the now larger disk. The implication is that the chicks respond to the relative size and not to the absolute size of the disks. The results are limited to a range of size difference. If a very large disk is introduced, the chicks respond to the originally conditioned disk. An example of transposition from common experience is that notes transposed to different keys sound alike to us. Transposition of this primitive nature bears superficial resemblance to transposition in learning where the animal transposes the object in the environment to arrangements which aid in solving a problem. Thus an ape moves boxes under a banana hanging from the ceiling.

Equivalent stimuli. Rats are conditioned to jump to a platform marked by a certain shape such as a triangle, but not to jump to the shape of a cross. Then other shapes are substituted in place of the triangle. Those shapes to which the rat jumps are said to be equivalent to the rat. In this manner such questions can be tested as: Can a rat abstract shape? or what are the significant aspects of the phenomenal world of the rat?

Concept formation. A typical procedure is to show a person various shapes, each one accompanied by a nonsense word, by saying "this is dax." Another form may be "lep," etc. Then are presented many shapes which have the property of lep and dax. The subject is supposed to become able to distinguish dax and lep. After many presentations he can often pass a test made up of new shapes, but fail in stating a generalization defining the class of dax and lep. It is difficult to conceive of a rat succeeding on a problem of concept formation which requires deliberation in terms of similarities and differences with each presentation of a stimulus. Man can delay his symbols indefinitely; therefore, he can deliberate. However, much of the process in concept formation takes place unconsciously even in man. The animal, on the other hand, can carry a symbol for only a short time and so must react compulsively.

On the surface of observed performance it might seem that there is a continuum from simple to complex: stimulus generalization, transposition, equivalent stimuli, concept formation. The idea is suggestive and is seriously entertained by some psychologists, other psychologists have noted that animals with brain damage generalize more than normal animals. In retests generalization diminishes in decorticated animals indicating that the animals profited from experience. "It is illogical to suppose that a partially decorticated rat utilizes higher levels of behavior than a normal one." (30) Lashley has summarized the research in this area in the following words.

"In contrast to . . . a view of intellectual functions as composites of simpler neurological processes, there is some reason for believing that generalization is one of the primitive, basic functions of organized nervous tissue. For example, the transposition of reactions along a stimulus dimension has been found in all organisms which are capable of differential response. That is, when the animal is trained to choose the larger or brighter of two objects and is then confronted with a still larger or brighter he chooses on the basis of relative size or brightness. Such generalizations, transpositional responses, are universal, from insects to primates. They persist in the rat after total destruction of the striated cortex and thus seem to be as primitive as is discrimination." (18, p. 202-3)

There is no satisfactory explanation of the different forms of primitive generalization. The problem has bearing on the cognitive processes not only because of superficial resemblances between these simple forms of generalization and cognitive ones but because there is the further problem of how these phenomena can be explained neurologically. In all cases localized areas in the brain are stimulated. Then new stimuli evoke the original response. It is problems like these which have encouraged so-called field theories of cortical and mental activity. (33) Obviously the nature of neurological explanation has bearing on conceptions of the cognitive processes.

Simple generalization in thinking. Although primitive generalization cannot be identified with cognitive analogues it is true that in cognition there are simple forms of behavior which are embarrassing to a conception of the cognitive processes being eminently rational. Moreover, there is the problem of primitive thinking. It is a strange coincidence that nervous generalization and conscious generalization appear so similar in performance. Since we do not fully understand either form of generalization the problem remains as an interesting one for speculation. One approach to understanding the nature of primitive thinking has been the genetic one of studying the development of age norms in thinking.

Piaget's (24) studies of children which show widespread generalization in thinking should be recalled. Especially his concepts of ego-centric, syncretic, animistic and justaposition thinking. If a star and moon are seen together and the child is asked what causes the moon or vice versa he is likely to say that the star made it because it is near it. Werner (32) emphasizes the tendency in children and primitive people to think in global or "holophrastic" ways. Most adults often indulge in such forms of analogizing. Without our metaphors and similes communication would be different and probably impoverished. This general problem may be captioned as the problem of similarity and difference.

Dennis (5) investigated animistic thinking in college graduates and undergraduates in a university. The questions asked whether various inanimate objects were alive. The people were required to give serious answers. Forty-five percent of those questioned stated that one or more of the objects was living. The objects which were most often reported alive were the lighted match, the sun and the ocean. The following are samples of the strange replies to the concept of ocean.

"Living because it is constantly maintaining life. Movement is characteristic of it, and life is brought forth by it." "Living. It has moods and is temperamental just like many human beings." "Living—it moves and makes noise and is powerful and changing. Sometimes calm, sometimes stormy. We cannot control it." "Living, continually in motion, changing, etc."

Are these replies poetic or literal? One cannot be sure from this preliminary study. Certainly it is easy for man to stretch his analogies across wide gaps of difference. Is it easier to note similarities rather than differences or do we prefer similars to differences? The writer (12) once presented elementary psychology students with a series of couplets such as bat-ball, chimney-house, etc. The subjects were asked to respond to these pairs of words spontaneously as either similar or different. The reaction time of the responses was measured. The results showed that, everything being equal, the students gave predominantly "similar" responses and the reaction time was significantly lower for "similar" responses than for "different" responses. Introspective reports from subjects who responded to the spoken words with a visual image showed one way in which the judgment was made. When the two words were visualized as a unit the response was "similar" whereas if the units were not related into a whole the response was "different". Thus for the couplet cage-lion, some who imaged the lion in the cage said "similar"; others who imaged the lion outside of the cage responded with the word "different". It does seem that for various complicated reasons there is less resistance to judging similarities than differences. Is this another facet of the organism's need for conformity and inter-relatedness of events? (27)

The conditioned reflex model has bearing on the problem of similarity and differentiation. The model has more generality if similarity is bracketed with primitive generalization and differentiation with concept formation. Mowrer and Lamoreaux (22) have noted that there seem to be two phases in conditioning proper. Only later in the process of conditioning are the responses differentiated. The second stage is discriminative learning. This interpretation of conditioning as a two phase process, suggests that differentiation is a higher level process, more specific to the situation, than the first over-generalized stage. In the two kinds of conditioning—classical and instrumental—the two phases are relatively isolated.

Ideation. Psychologists have accepted concept formation as the experimental model for studying the higher mental processes in thinking. We need to note similarities and often the essential similarities are grasped quickly enough for sudden, insightful solutions. Sensing broad similarities is natural and easy for the organism. It is when similarities must be weighed against differences that higher mental processes are necessary. In concept formation the selection of a similarity factor is a tentative hypothesis, which is checked against each stimulus and finally verified for the entire assortment of stimuli. Sensing similarities starts the process; it is finished by discriminating. The process can take place unconsciously. In invention, persistence in working on the task is an important factor. Concept formation is easiest with concrete objects as the material than with abstract notions. Heidbreder (9) did a concept formation experiment which was disguised as a rote memory test. Her subjects were required to derive three concepts while seemingly only memorizing. She found that concepts for concrete objects were easier than for spatial and number relations. The most difficult was the concept of number.

Thinking has been approached indirectly through perception

and learning in situations where the stimuli are presented to the subject. Distinct from these is thinking as ideation, where the environment plays practically no role. The material of ideation is free of the constraints of the physical environment. These materials are, therefore, called symbols, rather than signs, because mental symbols stand for or represent things, as words stand for objects. Symbols have been called "substitute signs". There is much more freedom in symbol thinking than in sign thinking (perception). Symbols do not normally coalesce with their referents as signs do in perception. Therefore, symbols can be delayed from their referents indefinitely. If one asks a child what red is, the child may search the room for some time and then point to a red object. Symbols of thought are free of space and time relations and can be displaced at will. Thus one can imagine water flowing up hill. Moreover, symbols can be preserved in words and made stable by definition. All these properties give mental symbols a flexibility that accounts for man's superior achievements. Science developed with man's capacity to use symbols to refer to other symbols in the form of mathematical equations. Mathematical symbols are not only economical in organizing knowledge but they are not encumbered with common sense associations. Language is man's unique symbolic property but there are limitations to its value. Language can mold one's thinking so that one may feel that he is thinking whereas he is really "talking off the top of his head." Words can acquire the rigidity of percepts; the process is called reification. The general semanticists have studied extensively the dangers of thinking in words. Hayakawa (8) writes, "The first of the principles governing symbols is this: The symbol is not the thing symbolized; the word is not the thing; the map is not the territory it stands for."

The above treatment of mental symbols as discrete things, on the analogy of the way we use language symbols, has the appeal of simplicity. It leads readily to the notion that mental symbols can be arranged in different ways, suggesting infinite possibilities of patterning as a basis for imagination. This conception is roughly correct; it is oversimplified in view of the known complexities of mental processes and brain mechanisms. We have seen that stimuli are not too specific in their effects on the brain. Stimuli generalize, are transposable and have equivalences. All these properties are due to the way the nervous system works. Analogous properties are present in ideation. There are other complications which were not explored such as the role of context in perception and frame of reference in ideation. The specific event is influenced by contextual surroundings. Nor have the important effects of desire and emotion on ideation been considered. There was a time when it was thought that the symbol was carried by a memory image, which made it reasonable to think that mental symbols were relatively discrete things in the mind. The imageless thought controversy (11, 34) has largely discounted the idea that thoughts are carried by images. Thought processes apparently can take place without any introspective signs of their presence, except, perhaps a general feeling of tension.

The symbolic process in therapy. The symbolic processes have received much attention in practical applications such as mental therapy and more recently Cybernetics or the theory of communicating information. Before therapy is briefly discussed a summary of what has already been stated is in order. The sensation is a sign of itself. In the experience of living or the attainment of the meaning of objects, sensations become signs of things and events. They also serve as signals which indicate things are going to happen. In nature, signals are paired with the events they indicate; clouds-rain, spoor-deer, etc. In space perception Gibson proposed the extension of innate signs of space to include gradients such as texture, slant and edge. The meaning of objects is obtained by experience with them. Schematic perception concerns the knowledge of objects. The signs or clues of schematic perception, whether they are sensations, memories or related attitudes tend to fuse and become part of the percept. Thus schematic percepts are hypotheses about a situation. The peculiar property of perception is that the hypothesis is perceived unless the hypothesis is altogether incongruent with the given signs or clues. As far as verity of perception is concerned literal and schematic perception are often undistinguishable. In ideation the symbols are normally separate from the objects they stand for. In perception the signal, as a sign of expectancy, is more like a symbol in its time relations than a sign. Thus we have a continuum in terms of fusion or relative detachability of the associated events. The meaning of sensation and literal perception is directly given; in schematic perception we have learned clues; and in memory and ideation we use learned symbols. This continuum suggests an underlying time variable.

The nature of the cognitive processes is important to students of mental therapy. General Semantics (14), Rogers' client-centered therapy (26) and psychoanalysis all have made specific contributions to our knowledge of the symbolic processes. General semantics is primarily concerned with the malfunctions in the use of symbols in every day living but it also has its therapeutic implications. General semantics emphasizes the conscious symbols of thinking or linguistics. It shows how symbols tend to slip from their referents, which leads to poor communication and understanding. There is the danger of reification of words and the tendency for words to generalize beyond their specific meaning so that the words become relatively meaningless. All these factors promote a loss of contact with reality and engender feelings of inadequacy and insecurity. Therapy consists in regaining contact with reality by training in the proper use of symbols. General semantics implies that words as symbols of communication often have zero validity to the communicant.

Rogers uses the so-called permissive technique in therapy. The neurotic does not perceive the world nor himself as others do. When given opportunities to talk about himself and his problems before a sympathetic person who is the symbol of the outside world, the patient gradually changes on his own accord. Strong judgments and reactions tend to diminish, and problems seem less important and threatening as they are talked about. A kind of self correction takes place as one reviews one's self in the presence of another. A condition is reached where the patient's perceptions are changed. The environment looks different and the patient's perception of himself is from a new point of view. The process seems to be one of detaching fixed signs and clues from one's perceptions and replacing them with signs and clues which provide more realistic perceptions. In this sense it is said that the patient's perceptions are modified with therapy. Perhaps the notion that this form of therapy is based on changing one's perceptions is an overstatement. A real change in the literal sense of the term perception would mean that the patient has acquired another form of rigidity which follows from the way signs function in perception. Certainly some change in perception takes place but more valuable are the changes in the use of symbols, which are more flexible and tentative. Nevertheless, the notion of changing perceptions is a new twist in the approach to therapy.

Psychoanalysis has introduced the concept of the unconscious symbol. Such symbols stand for repressed desires of which the individual is unconscious. Kubie (16) has particularly interested himself in the problem of the symbol. The human organism has two symbolic functions: language and neurosis. In speech we use a symbol for things we are conscious of; in neurosis for things we are unaware of. A symbol can serve both conscious and unconscious needs. Thus eating serves not only the biological needs, as shown in compulsive eating. Practically everything that the child does can have a dual symbolic function: things that the child is aware of and at the same time of things it is not aware of. Dream symbols are common examples. The unconscious symbols are the forms by which man expresses his psychological tensions which he is unwilling or unable to face. It is the symbolic process of self deception. The capacity to use symbols is identical in both language and neurosis; the symbols differ only in the quality of being conscious or unconscious. We recognize the difference by the purpose the unconscious symbol serves. The aim of therapy is to discover this purpose of unconscious symbols and bring it to conscious awareness. The interesting fact about symbols revealed by psycho-analysis is their dual function.

The dichotomy of conscious and unconscious symbolic processes is immanent in all signs and symbols. It is necessary for the symbolic process to function automatically for thought to progress efficiently. The child learns to walk and talk in a stumbling fashion but with learning, sign and referent, word and thought becomes automatized. In this sense signs and symbols function unconsciously in habits and in ready modes of thought in order to minimize the organism's expenditure of energy. In the area of thinking James referred to such unconscious symbols as the "fringe of consciousness" because they are in some measure accessible to introspection. In habits and in thinking, signs, symbols and their referents are reduced to mere figments or suggestions of themselves. The process is similar to shorthand. The psychoanalytic concept of the unconscious symbol is different from such reduction of cues and short circuiting. The symbol, in analysis, is unconscious in a positive sense. The organism actively represses the symbol from directly entering consciousness so its effects are experienced as if without a cause. Since repression does not eliminate symbolic reference together with the symbol, the organism must invent a cause or supply a symbol compatible with the felt experience. The various inventions for the unknown cause constitute the neurotic symptoms. The unconscious symbol of psychoanalysis is different in form and purpose than the symbol of marginal or fringe awareness.

Summary and conclusion. The purpose of this chapter is to envisage the cognitive processes as unified in some form of a continuum and in doing so to point up significant issues in the psychology of cognition. The unifying principle used is the concept of the symbolic process. The symbolic process was reduced to signs and symbols. Therefore, sensation, perception, memory or learning, and thinking were analyzed in terms of the nature of the signs or symbols in these areas. The symbolic process in psychoanalysis was brought in because in this area the symbols are dual in nature and unconscious. Thus a conceptual system for envisaging all the cognitive processes was attempted in terms of the symbolic properties of signs and symbols. Suggestions leading to a time continuum on which signs and symbols could be ordered were offered very tentatively. The cognitive processes are basically symbolic in nature. The problem, then, is how to think of sensations, percepts and thoughts as symbols having special properties adequate to the known differences in sensing, perceiving, and thinking. In this chapter this way of thinking about cognition was presented as a frame work for some important problems in cognition.

BIBLIOGRAPHY

[1] Anrep, G. V. The irradiation of conditioned reflexes. *Proc. roy. Soc.,* 1923, *B94,* 404-25.

[2] Bass, M. J., and Hull, C. L. The irradiation of tactile conditioned reflexes in man. *J. comp. Psychol.,* 1934, *17,* 47-65.

[3] Boring, E. G. Visual perception as invariance. *Psychol. Rev.,* 1952, *59,* 141-48.

[4] Bruner, J. S. Personality dynamics and the process of perceiving. Chapter 5 in Blake, R. R., and Ramsey, G. V. (Eds.) *Perception: an approach to personality.* New York, Ronald, 1951.

[5] Dennis, W. Animistic thinking among college and university students. *Scient. Mon.,* 1953, *76,* No. 4, 247-9, page 249.

[6] Gibson, J. J. *The perception of the visual world.* Boston: Houghton Mifflin, 1950.

[7] Hastorf, A. The influence of suggestion on the relationship between stimulus size and perceived size. *J. Psychol.,* 1950, *50,* 195-217.

[8] Hayakawa, S. I. *Language in thought and action.* New York: Harcourt-Brace, 1949, page 31.

[9] Heidbreder, E. The attainment of concepts. *J. gen. Psychol.,* 1946, *35,* 173-223.

[10] Hovland, C. I. The generalization of conditioned responses with varying frequencies of tone. *J. gen. Psychol.,* 1937, *17,* 125-48.

[11] Humphrey, G. *Thinking: An introduction to experimental psychology.* London: Oxford University Press, 1951.

[12] Karwoski, T. F., and Schachter, J. Psychological studies in semantics: III Reaction times for similarity and difference. *J. soc. Psychol.,* 1948, *28,* 103-20.

[13] Katz, D. *The world of color.* London: Kegan Paul, Trench Trubner, 1935.

[14] Korzybski, A. *Science and sanity.* Lancaster, Pa.: Science Press, 1933.

[15] Krechevski, I. Brain Mechanisms and "hypotheses." *J. comp. Psychol.,* 1935, *19,* 425-468.

[16] Kubie, L. S. The relationship of symbolic function in language formation and in neurosis. In von Foerster (Ed.) *Cybernetics*. New York: John Macy Jr. Foundation, 1951.

[17] Langer, S. *Philosophy in a new key*. Cambridge, Mass.: Harvard University Press, 1942, page 61.

[18] Lashley, K. The problem of cerebral organization in vision. Biological Symposia, 1942, 7, (Visual Mechanisms) 301-22, page 302-3.

[19] Lawrence, M. *Studies in human behavior*. Princeton: Princeton University Press, 1949.

[20] Miller, J. G. Unconscious process and perception. Chapter 9 in Blake, R. R. and Ramsey, G. V. (Eds.) *Perception: an approach to personality*. New York: Ronald, 1951.

[21] Morris, C. W. *Signs, language and behavior*. New York : Prentice-Hall, 1946.

[22] Mowrer, O. W. and Lamoreaux, R. R. Conditioning and conditionality. *Psychol. Rev.*, 1951, *58*, 196-212.

[23] Osgood, C. E. *Method and theory in experimental psychology*. New York: Oxford Press, 1953.

[24] Piaget, J. *Judgment and reasoning in the child*. New York: Harcourt, Brace, 1928.

[25] Postman, L. Toward a general theory of cognition. In Rohrer, J. H., and Sherif, M. (Eds.) *Social psychology at the crossroads*. New York: Harper, 1951.

[26] Rogers, C. R. Perceptual reorganization in client centered therapy. Chapter 11 in Blake, R. R., and Ramsey, G. V., (Eds.) *Perception: an approach to personality*. New York: Ronald, 1951.

[27] Stagner, R. and Karwoski, T. *Psychology*. New York: McGraw-Hill, 1952.

[28] Tolman, E. C. *Purposive behavior in animals and men*. New York: Appleton-Century-Crofts, 1932.

[29] Troland, L. T. *The principles of psychophysiology. II. Sensation*. New York: Van Nostrand, 1930.

[30] Wapner, S. The differential effects of cortical injury and retesting on equivalence reactions in the rat. *Psychol. Monog.*, 1944, *57*, No. 262, I-59, page 49.

[31] Werner, H. and Wapner, S. Toward a general theory of perception. *Psychol. Rev.*, 1952, *54*, 324-38, page 326.

[32] Werner, H. *Comparative psychology of mental development*. New York: Harpers, 1940.

[33] Wertheimer, M. *Productive thinking*. New York: Harpers, 1945.

[34] Woodworth, R. S. *Experimental psychology*. New York: Henry Holt, 1938.

Chapter V

RECENT VIEWS ON ATTENTION

William E. Galt †
Research Associate and Secretary, The Lifwynn Foundation

EDITORIAL NOTE

As new topics come up in the course of research, some of the old departments are apt to be pushed in the background, or absorbed in some new constellation. Attention, as one of the foundations of psychology, has been especially let down of late. It can, of course, be approached from an objectivistic avenue, but consciousness is its warp and woof. "The degree of consciousness" is the definition found in the textbooks of yesteryear, and Titchener would make the treatment of consciousness the touchstone of the writer's psychological affiliation. William James's chapter on attention in his classic work is full of insights which must have been thrilling for students half a century ago, and are not without value today. In human learning, at least, attention is still the chief feature. To speak of it in terms of selectivity or to explain it on the basis of Münsterberg's action theory or McDougall's drainage theory is not enough.

Attention has its behavioristic side of course, and through controlled observation, much could be inferred as to the mental state of the observed, but the experience of attending per se *has its place in any study of the mind; and gradations of attention from the listless to the rapt state have not been done justice to in the literature.*

Dr. William E. Galt, whose Vita *will be reserved for the following chapter has done well to connect attention and memory, although attention is the prop of perception even in greater measure. The references to Dr. Trigant Burrow's concepts of cotention and ditention are particularly appropriate, inasmuch as they appear to be built around experimental evidence.*

† Deceased.

104

PRESENT-DAY PSYCHOLOGY

phase in the total experimentation. They dealt for the most
part with the complication experiment and with the range

INTRODUCTION

The phenomena of attention and memory have been closely
interwoven throughout their historical development. This interrelationship was early noted by psychologists, and it has remained of significance despite marked alterations of views in
regard to the attentive and memory processes themselves.[1] It
has been generally held that attention affects memory at two
points: 1) at the time the impression is first received (registration), and 2) at the time of reproduction (recall). It is commonly recognized that unnoticed events can not be reproduced,
that attention to the stimulus is the essential condition for its
later recall, and that the effectiveness of retention reflects the
degree of attention during the registration of the impression.
Furthermore, at the time of reproduction attention selects which
of the many possible associates of a previous impression shall
become effective.

There is the further parallel that both attention and memory
were subjected to experimental psychological methods of study
in the last half of the 19th Century. Wundt and his students
began their investigation of attention in the early sixties, and
Ebbinghaus his intensive study of memory in 1879. These more
or less parallel developments were milestones in the history of
psychology since they represent initial efforts to apply laboratory techniques in an approach to the "higher mental processes."
A summary of the findings and developmental trends in these
two related fields will be presented separately in the following
pages.

EARLY EXPERIMENTAL STUDIES

The studies on attention in Wundt's laboratory received their
maximal emphasis in the nineties and represented an important

phase in the total experimentation. They dealt for the most part with the complication experiment, and with the range, and fluctuation of attention—classical problems which continued to be investigated in the newly established laboratories in this country and abroad by students of Wundt. Of these students Titchener was most influential in carrying forward and developing experimental investigations of attention. He regarded attention as one of the three fundamental issues upon which any system of psychology must be based. In line with the psychology of content or the structural viewpoint emphasized by Wundt, Titchener defined attention as attributive clearness and as serving a selective function in determining the focus of consciousness. He says: "In the last resort, and in its simplest terms, attention is identical with sensory clearness."[65] He numbered among his students such well-known investigators of attention as Pillsbury and Dallenbach. During the first three decades of the new century many experimental studies on this subject came from Titchener's laboratory and from those of his students. Dallenbach[15] established and differentiated various types of clearness. Geissler[24] examined the definable steps or levels of clearness involved in attention. Other subjects investigated were conditions of attention—range, degree, prior entry, distraction and distribution, etc.

It was found that attention characteristically shifts from point to point when the individual is in process of examining objects. In other words, the attentive adjustment is not fixed and rigid. Just as the environment is constantly changing in various ways, the function that keeps the organism in touch with changing conditions must be sensitive and responsive to these changes. Experiments showed that, though capable of very rapid shifts, attention is a unitary process in that two conflicting activities cannot be attended to at the same time. When *simultaneous* attention is demanded by both activities, the response breaks down.[2]

During this period further work was being done on the two types of attention first differentiated by Wundt as active and passive (later called voluntary and involuntary),[3] and on the characteristics of a stimulus which enhance its attentional value. It was established that change, strength, size, repetition, striking quality and definite form were stimulus properties that operate spontaneously to capture involuntary attention. The principles determining voluntary attention were usually stated in terms of conscious will, of social pressure or of momentary interest. Naturally these findings were quickly assimilated in such applied fields as education and advertising. Methods for the measurement of attention involving the presentation of simultaneous disparate activities, of alternating disparate activities, and of liminal stimuli[4] were developed and perfected.

INFLUENCE OF FUNCTIONAL VIEWPOINT

The viewpoint characterizing the laboratories in which attention was first studied experimentally was definitely one of structuralism. But other orientations soon came to influence the course of development in this field. Existing more or less contemporaneously with the content or structural emphasis in psychology, although strictly a minority or opposition party in the heyday of the new experimental psychology, was the "act" or functional viewpoint in respect to behavior. At the risk of being a little disreputable, the advocates of this orientation withstood both the appealing simplicity of the associationistic, atomistic psychology and the blandishments of precise and rigidly controlled experimental methods constructed in accordance with these premises.[5] The functional interpretation was backed by less experimental work but was more credible from the point of view of everyday experience. Regarding the mind as a succession of acts rather than as a procession of mental impressions or qualities, it assigned to attention the rôle of selectivity. In line with the etymology of the word,[6] James[(36)] described attention in terms of the anticipatory adjustment of the organism. He looked upon this adjustment as involving both a sensorial component and an ideational preparation which co-existed in all concrete attentive acts. When Behaviorism came along it was quick to seize upon the functional interpretation of attention and to divest it of all ideational connotations. While Watson himself ignored the topic altogether, other Behaviorists reduced attention to a reflex adjustment to incoming stimuli, to implicit speech, or to a muscular (and glandular) set of the organism in respect to an object.[50] Thus attention for these objectivists became reduced to motor set and assumed minor significance in the framework of their psychology. However, there were those who adhered to the less constricted viewpoint of the functionalists. This was especially true in France where Ribot[53] emphasized the causal relationship between emotion and attention, and Binet[5] viewed it as an adaptive process of the organism, determining the direction of thought.

PERIOD OF RELATIVE NEGLECT

For approximately a quarter-century—from the early twenties to the middle forties—there was a conspicuous loss of interest in the topic of attention. This is reflected in the fact that regular summaries of the topic in *The Psychological Bulletin* were discontinued, and fewer and fewer abstracts appear under this heading in *Psychological Abstracts*. This circumstance is partly explained by the fact that attention has not been a crucial problem for the prevailing modern psychologies, and has for the most part been largely ignored by them. As we have seen, Behaviorists either make no mention of attention or reduce it to reflex motor set. Gestalt psychology explains the selective process in terms of figure and ground, and discards attention entirely. Hartmann says: "Gestalt theorists make the concept of attention superfluous by denying to it the three grand functions which it was traditionally supposed to discharge, viz., that of synthesizer, for it is not justifiable by observation; that of threshold-determiner, for it is the gestalt which establishes the threshold; and that of a term denoting clearness, for changes of clearness also involve changes of the gestalt."[30]

The neglect of the subject of attention by major movements in psychology was further complicated by the fact that the closely related field of *mental* (or *preparatory*) *set* was being rapidly developed. Pascal[50] notes that early antecedents of the concept grew out of problems relating to experiments in reaction time and weight lifting. From its inception, then, mental set was closely interrelated with the organism's discriminatory behavior. Thorndike and Woodworth were influential in the specification and application of the concept. Mental set was correlated by different investigators with central and with peripheral processes, and was looked upon as the selective factor determining response. A considerable number of psychologists felt that the concept adequately covered the phenomena of attention, and many research projects in sensory discrimination and other areas of behavior where the attention factor is vital, were subsumed under the new rubric. It is not surprising, therefore, that beginning with the 1920's there was a marked decrease in emphasis on attention as reflected in the experimental literature, and the space allotted to the subject in psychology text-books.[7]

Here and there, however, among the ranks of psychologists or investigators in related fields there were those who felt that the concept of attention should be retained, and that it demanded a more fundamental, dynamic position in the field of man's behavior than was entailed in correlating it with such discrete factors as sensory clearness or motor set. The contribution of these students has been to advance broader, more integrative concepts which give to attention a greater significance in its relation to the organism as a whole. In a recent book, Dollard and Miller follow an early lead of Binet[5] in stressing the importance of attention in directing thought processes. They say: "The crucial consideration . . . is that thoughts can be manipulated to exactly the extent to which attention responses can be directed and concentrated."[16] We have already seen that Ribot[53] early identified attention with emotional states, and recently Murphy[49] has emphasized the importance of inner needs or motivational factors in the process. Nina Bull[8] looks upon attitude in its physiological meaning as basic in attention and emotion. On the basis of her experimental studies she suggests that emotion and attention "can, and should, be studied together in their relation to each other as parts of one operation."[7]

BURROW'S CONCEPTS

In the phylobiological researches of Burrow and his associates, attention occupies a central position. (Chap. XII[11]). Looking upon it as a bionomic process through which the organism is brought into contact with the objects and conditions that surround it, Burrow emphasizes the fact that "attention originally represented far more a coördination of the organism *with* the object than the directing of its interest *at* the object." (p. 116[9]). As has been emphasized by students of developmental psychology, this *participation with* is considerably more characteristic of the orientation of the child than of the adult. Phylogenetically, too, it marks a primitive, total type of organism-environment interaction. Burrow holds that the more specialized, projective process of attention, whereby the organism stands opposite the object or image and focuses upon it mentally, developed concomitantly with man's increasing use of sign, symbol and language. Furthermore, this advance in man's separation from his environment and his objectification of it, though essential to his development, was accompanied by features that were definitely detrimental to coördinated functioning, especially as it related to social contact and communication. As man came more and more to stand apart from the objects and conditions of his physical and social environment, to "know" them predominantly through the abstract word or symbol rather than through the direct physiological response of the total organism, a divisive, partitive element entered into the function of attention that largely interrupted organism-environment rapport. Total goal orientation, with its absorption in the object or task, tended to be intercepted and attention was largely diverted to the affect-laden image of the self and its secret gain. Intensive and extended studies of individuals in social groups have shown that this subjective image-involvement, with its concomitant affective blurring of the object or condition, is characteristic of the habitual response of the "normal" individual no less than of the neurotic, and is a basic factor underlying interrelational hostility and conflict.

Burrow, then, differentiates two types of attention—the direct, effective, participating relationship of man to his physical and social environment (cotention), and his self-reflexive, affective and divisive interrelational adjustments (ditention). Since attention is found to be largely a physiological function involving muscular, vasomotor and neural patterns, Burrow and his associates were able to develop a method for differentiating between the internal patterns of response accompanying cotention and those accompanying ditention. It was found that the consistent application of a technique which focused on the physiological stress occurring in the ocular area—an area playing such a prominent rôle in attention—resulted in the gradual reabsorption of affectively projected images of oneself and others, and in the increasing reëstablishment of a cotentive adaptation with its more effective interrelational adjustment.

A further aspect of Burrow's investigation of attention has been the instrumental measurement of differences in physiological function in the two adaptational modes—cotention and ditention. These recent studies have been directed chiefly toward determining patterns of eye-movements,[13] of respiration[10] and of the brain-wave activity[12] that consistently differentiate the two types of attention. A recent book[11] contains the detailed results of this experimentation. In brief, it was found that the two basic attitudes of the organism were accompanied by consistently different physiological patterns in these three areas of function.[8]

Numerous investigators have shown that eye-movements, respiration and patterns of cortical activity are significantly related to attention, emotion, and such symbolic processes as thinking and imagination. ([61, 37, 35]) By further clarifying the significance of attention in the adaptive process and demarcating the difference in patterns of physiological function accompanying different adaptive constellations, Burrow has contributed to a widened, organismic view of the processes underlying human behavior and its individual and social disorders.

ATTENTION LINKED WITH PERCEPTION

Today attention (attending) is quite generally considered to precede and to be an integral component in perception.[9] It is often referred to as a *pre*-perceptive attitude or adjustment of the organism, largely determining the perceptual response. Psychologists have recently been much interested in the study of perception and have demonstrated that a host of individually and socially motivating factors—tissue needs, autistic desires and interests, group prejudices and socially systematized attitudes —influence and at times determine what is perceived. A view of attention which regards it as a pre-perceptive attitude would, it appears, place the emphasis upon attention as being the portion of the total perceptual process in which such motivational factors play a dominant rôle.

In a recent book, Hebb[31] speaks out forcefully for the need of psychologists to recognize explicitly the importance of attention, and to deal with the facts consistently. He looks upon attention as the process that produces the selectivity of a response and describes it as "a central facilitation of a perceptual activity." He refers to the electroencephalographic findings indicating that all parts of the brain are continually active so that any incoming excitation must be superimposed upon an already existing excitation. He points out that this fact is in agreement with the assumption of a central neural factor that brings about modification in the action of a stimulus, and that "the theoretical problem now is to discover the rules by which it operates." He goes on to say that "the problem is after all the problem of attention, and seen best in the activity of the whole animal."[31, p. 102]

Berlyne[4] also expresses the renewed trend of interest in the subject. He speaks of the importance of attention for applied psychology and psychopathology, and feels that behavior theory can no longer ignore it. Like Hebb and other recent investigators, he conceives of attention as an integral part of the perceptual function and, by suggesting that it "be regarded as the *momentary effective reaction-potential of the perceptual response,"* attempts to bring the concept into Hull's system of behavior theory.

CORTICAL LOCALIZATION

Little has been said as yet about the cerebral localization of attention. The trend in psychology in the past several decades has been away from the view that attention or other intellectual functions can be localized in rather specific areas of the cortex. There is some evidence, however, that suggests that the prefrontal brain areas are significantly correlated with the attentive function.

In delayed response experiments with monkeys Jacobsen and others[32, 33, 34] have demonstrated that bilateral ablation of the prefrontal brain areas results in the animal's inability to sustain delayed orientation, while this ability is not disturbed by damage to other brain areas. This fact was first interpreted as evidence that memory is localized in this cortical region. However, later results tend to show that the function disturbed in "prefrontal" monkeys is not memory but attention. The operated animals are restless, and their difficulty is in noting where the food is placed rather than in a lapse of memory during the delay period. Experiments which reduced the operated animal's distractibility or abolished interfering stimuli, such as the administration of light sedatives[66] or the extinguishing of lights in the experimental room during the period of delay,[42] led to successful performance, as did also procedures which forced attention to the task, e.g., pre-delay reinforcement.[20] Recent studies of schizophrenic patients after undergoing frontal lobe operations contribute similar evidence.[59] Additional investigations with monkeys also show that disturbances in attention result from extirpation of prefrontal areas. For example, while all simple discriminations can still be learned, a considerably larger number of errors are made, and this is particularly true in complex discriminations, involving antagonistic cues.[29, 67]

Other extirpation and stimulation experiments have brought to light the presence in the frontal lobe of an adversive area in close association with a suppressor band. It is suggested by Ruch[56] that this complex may represent the neural substrate of attention and that the "adversive movements" have the function of directing the sense organs and the body as a whole toward a stimulus object, thus constituting a motor aspect of the process. The suppression of general motor activity and the orientation of eyes and body to a specific stimulus is characteristic of attention, as is also the suppression of cortical activity which appears to be brought about through projection fibres from this same area.

SUMMARY

In summarizing the developments during the past half century in the field of attention we may say that there have occurred many alterations in concepts and emphasis. The period under review opened with the topic holding a key position in psychological thinking and experimentation since in the Wundtian and Titchenerian systems it determined what would occupy focal clearness in consciousness. With the shift in emphasis from sensory elements and the content of consciousness to figure-ground relationships and the response systems of the organism, there came about among academic psychologists a de-emphasis upon the importance of attention and a general neglect of it. The subject, however, continued to be dealt with in such applied fields as education, advertising, and psychopathology where its practical importance could not be ignored. This disparaging trend has now been reversed. During recent years the concept has been made meaningful in relation to the adaptive response of the organism. Attention has been looked upon as an internal steering process; as an adjustment of the whole organism to the environmental situation, rather than as a selective response of specific sense organs. Contrasting patterns of attention have been delineated, and the significance of these patterns for vital problems in individual and social behavior indicated. There has been the effort to define attention in objective, operational terms, and this must be regarded as a significant development provided that in so doing the concept is not again robbed of its essential meaning as an active process in perception that is anticipatory and purposive.

FOR FOOTNOTES AND BIBLIOGRAPHY SEE END OF CHAPTER VI.

CHAPTER VI

TRENDS IN THE STUDY OF MEMORY

WILLIAM E. GALT

Research Associate and Secretary, The Lifwynn Foundation

EDITORIAL NOTE

To many, if not most of the younger experimentalists today, memory is the forgotten topic in psychology. Since Ebbinghaus performed his pioneer experiments, investigator upon investigator, largely in the laboratories of G. E. Müller, Schumann and Pilzecker, have cultivated that area. F. C. Bartlett's Remembering *seems to be the last important work on the subject and, excelling the ponderous German reports, it takes an empirical stand, in the line of British tradition, with an eye for what is practical and accessible. The theoretical is not ignored but not viewed as a goal.*

In American textbooks, memory seems to have capitulated to learning, i.e., it has fallen from its independent status and become a satellite of a larger incorporated territory, filled with mazes and cages. This streamlining may have its uses, where there is a closer coöperation among researchers from different fields, but in order that this tendency does not run away with itself, it seems advisable to detach memory from the learning train and overhaul it separately, and that is what Dr. Galt has done.

Dr. Galt, who received his bachelor's, master's and doctor's degrees at Columbia University, has been associated with The Lifwynn Foundation, Westport, Connecticut, since 1927, and since 1939 (with an intermission) has been director of the psychological laboratory in that institution. Between 1942 and 1946, he served as aviation psychologist with the U. S. Army Air Forces. In addition to a number of articles, Dr. Galt has published Phyloanalysis: A Study in the Group or Phyletic Method of Behaviour Analysis (*London,* 1933) *and has edited* Science and Man's Behavior, The Contribution of Phylobiology (*New York,* 1953). *The latter is a posthumous volume by Dr. Trigant Burrow, late Scientific Director of The Lifwynn Foundation.* Dr. Galt died suddenly on February 5, 1955.

APPLICATION OF EXPERIMENTAL METHOD

Prior to Ebbinghaus, memory had been thought of as a faculty or agency rather than as a function or process susceptible to measure. While there was much armchair philosophizing about learning and forgetting and the supposed dichotomy that existed between them, there was as yet no thinking along quantitative lines. Through his development of nonsense syllable material for learning, and his learning, saving and prompting methods for testing retention, Ebbinghaus[17] applied quantitative methods of study to both learning and forgetting. Although Ebbinghaus worked exclusively with himself as subject, his studies were so well conceived and controlled that his findings have been verified to a remarkable degree by later workers in the field. He stimulated a great amount of psychological research through delineating many problems in remembering, and his concepts and the extension of his methods occupied memory investigators for the next quarter century or more.

Ebbinghaus' initial studies emphasized the enormous amount of forgetting that occurs within the first minutes after material is learned. Although the absolute amount forgotten was a function of the type of material with which he worked (nonsense syllables), the general form of the curve of forgetting has been corroborated in countless studies. Ebbinghaus worked with such problems as the differential rate of forgetting, the memory span, the influence of over-learning, the best distribution of practice, backward and remote associations.

After the publication of his results on memory in 1885 Ebbinghaus turned his attention to other psychological problems and G. E. Müller[45] succeeded him as the foremost exponent of the experimental method in the field. Müller improved and standardized the nonsense syllable technique and introduced the method of paired associates. He also developed such concepts as reinforcement, associative, terminal and retroactive inhibition to explain the mechanical interaction of associations. Müller and Pilzecker[46] were the first to show experimentally that interpolated activity affects the retention of previously learned material, and thus to challenge the earlier supposition that progressive forgetting was a direct function of the passage of time. This finding opened up the whole field of retroactive and proactive inhibition which was to occupy experimental investigators for many years to come. It raised the question of the necessity of a "setting" or consolidation period if material was to be remembered—a concept later strengthened by Jenkins and Dallenbach's[38] work on the effect of sleep on retention, by studies of amnesias resulting from head injury,[57] and by observations of the memory defects occurring after shock therapies.[43]

The association doctrine was very much to the fore at the time experimental interest developed in memory, and naturally greatly influenced evolving concepts in respect to this function. According to the associationistic viewpoint, all mental life can be explained as an organization of sensory impressions resulting from the stimulation of the sense organs by the various stimuli that impinge upon them. Mental complexes were elaborated from these impressions through the association of ideas. A mechanical view of memory fitted easily into this ideational system. Memory was effective when an impression or complex idea was firmly associated with another impression or idea so that the occurrence of one called forth the other. A good memory was thought to consist of an infinite number of discrete and more or less rigid associations. These ideas dominated the thinking and the experiments on memory conducted by Ebbinghaus, as they had dominated the work of Wundt and his students in respect to attention. They also considerably influenced Müller although he broke away from strict associationism to the extent of saying that the *interaction* among the aroused associations was important in determining the emerging idea or memory. Müller also required his subject to give introspective reports, and thus established the fact that, in the process of memorizing, the subject does not receive material passively, but that he is active—grouping the material, hearing it in rhythmical form, establishing meanings, etc.

The Behavioristic view of memory is in general accordance with associationistic ideology but with emphasis on physiological rather than "mental" components. It regarded memory as resultant upon relatively fixed, low resistance pathways connecting afferent sensory impulses with efferent motor responses. All mental or experiential elements are eliminated. Watson[69] says that memory "is any exhibition of manual, verbal or visceral organization put on prior to the time of the test." As can be readily seen, this is not a concept that would lead to new developments in this field. Roback[54] early called attention to the fact that the Behaviorist treatment of memory was merely a begging of the question.

EARLY FUNCTIONAL INFLUENCE

Of lesser experimental vigor but almost parallel in time with Ebbinghaus' studies there was developing in France a functional emphasis which held that at least some memories are not rigidly retained but are unstable and undergo changes as the result of emotional factors. Such concepts were greatly reinforced by the testimony studies carried out by Stern,[60] by Binet,[6] and by Münsterberg.[48] The startling fact growing out of these investigations was the marked unreliability of recall, and the distortion brought about by such extra-associational factors as suggestion, prejudice, personal advantage, and other affectively motivated trends.

Also there was a growing dissatisfaction with the exclusive use of material as remote from everyday experience as nonsense syllables. Many psychologists felt that the laws established for the rote-memory of nonsense syllables were too narrow a base on which to build an understanding of the function in its total aspect. As Cameron has pointed out, the very difficulty which workers with nonsense syllables experienced in selecting material devoid of prior associations, of rhythm or of other qualities enhancing learning and retention was a strong indication that memory was not a passive process dependent upon discrete associational connections but that it was an active response that organized its data into meaningful patterns.

THE GESTALT CONTRIBUTION

With the emergence of the Gestalt School there was increased emphasis upon the active nature of the remembering process but, at the same time, specific nuances of interpretation were added. In considering the changes that occur in memory images with decreasing clearness, Wulf,[71] for instance, found that the common feature in all changes is in the direction of a more familiar configuration or a "better gestalt." It was emphasized that the total situation at the time of learning (the organization of the field) is an important factor in bringing about the changes that take place in what is remembered. The problems of retention and forgetting are viewed in terms of the logical relevance and structural properties of the memorized material.

Although adhering to Gestalt principles, a slightly different treatment is given to memory by Lewin and his followers. Emphasizing the dynamic interplay of forces, they hold that memory, like other psychic events, must be understood in terms of psychic "tension-systems" set up by the needs or intentions of the organism. In line with this hypothesis is the experimental finding of Zeigarnik[72] and many later investigators that material relating to interrupted tasks (undischarged tension-systems) is better retained than that relating to completed tasks (discharged tension-systems).[10]

ADDITIONAL DEVELOPMENTS

Bartlett's[3] studies made explicit many aspects of the developing trend in the interpretation of memory. Through the serial reproduction of legends, studied over a period of years, he supplied concrete evidence to uphold his view that memory of an incident does not depend merely on static, unchanging traces. More importantly it depends upon attitudes at the time of recall and is an imaginative reconstruction using a small core of detail which is actually remembered. Many later studies have emphasized the influence of existing attitudes within the individual upon material remembered. To mention but a few, Watson and Hartmann,[70] and Edwards[18, 19] showed that the political frame of reference of a person largely determined the kind of material that he remembered; Clark[14] found that the two sex-groups remembered differently a story dealing with a struggle for status between a man and a woman.

William James's characteristic remark that we learn to swim in the winter and ice-skate in the summer is a provocative statement of a memory phenomenon that has received much experimental substantiation. Customarily explained by the assumption that error tendencies weaken more rapidly than correct responses, this phenomenon is closely related to the whole problem of reminiscence pioneered by Ballard's[2] investigations with children.[11] Although not primarily an experimentalist himself, James conducted one investigation in the field of memory that is historically significant. Using himself as subject, he ran a series of tests to determine the effect of practice in memorizing certain kinds of poetry upon memory for poetry in general. The results led him to conclude that general retention cannot be improved by training; that, in the strict sense, there is no such thing as general memory training. Many psychological investigations were initiated to verify and extend James's finding, and these "transfer of training" studies brought about a profound alteration in educational procedures.

Thorndike's[64] "law of effect" also represented a departure from the more mechanical explanation of learning and retention in terms of the factors of frequency and recency. Briefly, the law holds that of the responses made to a situation, those accompanied or followed by a satisfying state are "stamped in" while those accompanied or followed by discomfort will be "stamped out." In this law there is reflected Spencer's "pleasure-pain" theory of learning and Freud's view that emotions are important in determining what is forgotten and what is remembered. This trend, already anticipated by earlier investigators, led to a spate of experimental studies on the remembrance of material associated with pleasant and unpleasant sensory impressions and life-experiences. Much of this research was undertaken by psychologists in the hope of refuting a specific aspect of psychoanalytic formulations. There was much confusing evidence from the earlier of these investigations resulting from such factors as faulty assumptions and methodology, laboratory artificiality, and prejudice for or against Freud.[22] But although in the more recent, better conceived and controlled experiments the results favor the view that material connected with a pleasant affective tone is better retained than that associated with an unpleasant tone,[26] no causal relationship could be established. The intensity of the emotional factor was of importance, and often proved of more significance than its pleasant or unpleasant quality. Individual differences also were great. There can be little doubt, however, that the results of these studies showed the influence of emotion on memory.

Freud's Dynamic Concepts

Freud, of course, was champion of a dynamic view of memory in which affective forces were the determining factors. In Freud's formulations we have the extreme antithesis of the view of memory as the passive retention of material which fades away with the passage of time. For him, time lapse *per se* has little effect upon the retention of experiences. Rather, forgetting is due to an active process of repression which prevents material unacceptable to the ego from emerging into consciousness. Freud bolstered his viewpoint with a wealth of clinical material as well as examples from everyday life—slips of the tongue and pen, incidental or faulty acts and other "mistakes".[22]

In general, the investigations of the various amnesias, and of the effect of drugs and hypnosis on memory have served to strengthen Freud's emphasis on dynamic, motivational factors in forgetting. Hypnotic drugs were used with considerable success with soldiers in World War II to reactivate traumatic memories which were inaccessible to the conscious recall of the patient. Furthermore, this reactivation appears to be brought about not through a change in the personality of the patient but through a temporary removal of inhibitions (repression).[41] In the experimental setting of the psychological laboratory Zeller[73] has demonstrated an analogue of the Freudian theory of repression. The restoration of memory for periods of amnesia has been accomplished through hypnosis even where the memory disturbance occurs as an apparent result of head trauma.[27]

So far we have been considering disturbances in retention characterized by the repression or forgetting of specific materials or events. In rare cases, however, it appears that emotional factors can be of importance in impairing the function of recall quite generally. Syz[62] reports a dramatic case in which a complete loss of retention for current data occurred as the apparent consequence of a fall resulting in a brain concussion. Intelligence was not impaired and memory for events before the head injury was good. But as of the date of the accident all memory registration ceased completely. After a period of some three years in which there was little spontaneous improvement, the function of recall was progressively and permanently restored through combined hypnotic and analytic treatment. Personality difficulties were uncovered which gave substance to the view that the complete inability to recall current happenings served unconsciously as a defense against threatening problems of a moral nature. The case clearly demonstrates that the function of recall may be practically abolished for several years while the capacity for it remains intact as shown by its reinstatement through appropriate psychotherapeutic measures. It seems reasonable to conclude, then, that while Freud's position that nothing ever experienced is completely forgotten is undoubtedly extreme, he has nevertheless established a framework for the understanding of memory phenomena that were previously inexplicable.

Freud[22] raised a problem in regard to memory which had formerly received little attention—the problem of childhood amnesia. He questioned why memory should lag behind all other psychic activities, especially since the conditions favoring registration and reproduction are at a peak during childhood years. No one who has been intimately associated with young children and noted the interest and absorption with which they apply themselves to new material, and the ease and fidelity with which they absorb and reproduce it, will doubt that the problem is a significant one. It appears to the author, however, that Freud's explanation that childhood memories are lost in the suppression from consciousness of infantile sexuality, like his concept of infantile sexuality itself,[23] is on too narrow a base. Schachtel's[58] recent article takes a broader viewpoint. He believes that childhood amnesia results from the later development of conceptual and conventional memory schemata unsuitable to accommodate the organismic, unified nature of childhood experience, rather than from the action of a "censor" repressing early sexual experiences. In developing the difference in modes of experiencing between the infant and the adult, Schachtel mentions that the objectification of the environment and the consciousness of the "I" or self both develop relatively late in childhood. This viewpoint relates interestingly to the formulations of Trigant Burrow[9, pp. 251-271] who emphasizes the striking difference between the phyloörganismic behavior-patterns of adult and child. Certainly the discrete, partitive and projective orientation characteristic of the adult (the *'I'-persona* in Burrow's terminology) is sufficiently different from the total, participating experiences of infancy and early childhood to explain the inability of adult consciousness to assimilate and retain them.

LOCALIZATION OF PHYSIOLOGICAL SUBSTRATE

It is fairly well agreed that the physiological substrate of memory consists of some type of central trace or engram set up during the learning period. But there is little agreement in regard to the nature and location of the structural alteration. Many concepts have been advanced, but conflicting evidence and a lack of definite knowledge as to how the brain functions has prevented the development of a unified view. Early experimentalists (associationists) were inclined to a mechanical interpretation. They postulated that changes occurred in discrete nerve fibres or at synaptic points with lowered resistances as learning progressed, and with increased resistances as a result of disuse. More recent investigators hold that memory traces are not confined to specific neural fibres or localized patterns but are in some way organized into far-flung configurations of cortical response. It has been suggested that the reverberatory neural after-effects of a sensory occurrence provide a temporary physiological basis of memory of the stimulus, and that this is later reinforced by some more permanent structural change.[31]

As mentioned earlier, the newer trend in psychology negates the view that memory or other intellectual functions can be localized in specific cortical areas. Some authorities recognize practically no localization of memory but maintain that it is a function of the cortex as a whole.[28] Lashley's[40] view is that while different cortical areas have relatively specific memory functions, these functions are not organized in accordance with customary memory tests. He suggests that we may find localization of general memory factors but not of specific memories. Teitelbaum[63] also posits primary focal areas for different memory functions but says that because of the interdependence of these functions particular memory losses do not occur with the destruction of these specific areas.

While the majority of current views deny any strict cortical localization of the memory function, there exists some contradictory evidence. For example, Penfield[51] found that by stimulating the temporal lobes of epileptic patients he could elicit specific memories of earlier experience. His interpretation is that "whenever a normal person is paying conscious attention to something, he is simultaneously recording it in the temporal cortex of each hemisphere," and that the cortical patterns in this area store the details of earlier experiences. This theory seems to be contradicted by the results of human brain damage which show that large portions of the temporal lobes can be destroyed without loss of particular memories. Whatever the final interpretation of these findings may be, it is undoubtedly true that the temporal lobes embody an important center for the organization of memory experiences. Monkeys with both temporal lobes removed are badly deteriorated animals that appear to have forgotten previous training. A specific memory defect, visual agnosia or the loss of ability to recognize familiar objects by sight, has also been found in monkeys with temporal lobe lesions.[39]

Summary

A static view of memory regarding it as a storehouse of unchanging engrams set up by such mechanical factors as frequency and recency of stimulations has given way to a dynamic interpretation which stresses such factors as meaningfulness, organization of the learned materials, and the emotional needs and strivings of the learner. It has been well established that memory is reconstructive, not reduplicative; that it consists of a core of experience which is patterned and repatterned in accordance with individual wishes, personality structure and the prevailing social and cultural pressures. The importance of such factors is minimal in the traditional laboratory experiment dealing with the rote memorization of discrete, meaningless material (e.g., nonsense syllables); it is maximal in the setting of everyday life where incoming experiences can be organized into meaningful wholes and where they carry emotional or affective significance for the experiencing individual.

Concepts regarding memory have, then, like those concerning attention, undergone fundamental changes during the past half century. But despite the altered views in respect to each, the two functions continue to be regarded as inseparably interconnected.

FOOTNOTES

[1] For example, Pillsbury (1911) says: "Wherever we turn in the consideration of the memory problem . . . we find that we cannot account for memory even superficially unless we consider its connection with attention. Whether it be learning or retention, recall or recognition, the key to the effectiveness of the process and even to its nature is to be found in attention." (52) So differently oriented an investigator as Margaret Floy Wash-

burn (1916) comments: "Not the simultaneous experiencing of two objects, but simultaneous attention to them, forms a tendency to recall." (68) And in a recent article (1953) Ralph Gerard states: "Recall is a matter of attention, a selecting or rejecting of particular memory traces." (25)

2 Later studies have shown that although distracting stimuli not directly conflicting with the stimuli being attended to (not in the same sense modality) may not cause a lowering of performance, they do necessitate increased energy output on the part of the organism and thus reduce efficiency. (21)

3 A third type is usually added today. It is called habitual attention and, like involuntary attention, requires no conscious effort. Habitual attention is arrived at only after a phase of voluntary effort, or practice. It is closely related to individual drives, interests and attitudes.

4 The work with liminal stimuli brought into focus the involuntary fluctuations in clearness that can be readily observed when attention is concentrated on a faint stimulus. No matter in what sense modality one is experimenting, there occur variations in which the intensity of the stimulus appears to wax and wane. The time sequences of these fluctuations range from a fraction of a second to several seconds. They vary with the individual, with the sense modality, and with the conditions of the experiment. Many hypotheses have been advanced to account for these fluctuations but their cause is still not definitely determined. They are usually regarded as being related to changes in the efficiency of the sensory mechanisms.

5 Although Münsterberg was far from being classifiable as a member of the functional school, it is related that after listening, at an early psychological meeting, to a lengthy discourse on the exactness, the strict controls and the scientific validity of the experimental psychology of the Wundtian tradition, he remarked with his characteristic daring: "Ja, es ist exakt, aber es nützt nichts!"

6 Attention is derived from L. *attendere,* pp. *attentus,* to stretch forward.

7 In the last decade the pendulum has begun to swing the other way and there has been a definite increase of interest in the subject. Recent psychological texts, for example those by Munn (47) and Ruch (55), give considerable space to attention and emphasize the importance of the attending process in steering behavioral responses.

8 In cotention, the breathing is slower and deeper, the eyes are steadier and more centered, and there is an alteration in the brain-wave pattern, consisting of a reduction in alpha percentage and a general diminution in cortical potential, which is most marked in the parietal or motor area.

9 Munn says: "Attending and perceiving are in some respect indistinguishable. What one psychologist discusses as fluctuation of attention, another discusses as fluctuation of perception. . . . In all such cases the end product is the same, whether considered from the aspect of attending or that of perceiving." (47, p. 397.)

10 Recent evidence indicates that the Zeigarnik effect (remembering uncompleted tasks better than completed ones) applies only to memory for tasks performed under conditions that are emotionally non-stressful. Although individual differences are large, it has been found that the opposite trend occurs where non-completion of the experimental tasks threatens self-esteem, or in other ways is of stressful emotional meaning to the subject. In such cases it would seem that the tendency to suppress ego-threatening memories enters in, and that this trend is stronger than the Zeigarnik ef-

fect, thus giving the recall advantage to the completed rather than the uncompleted task.

[11] Some factors which favor reminiscence have been determined although the conditions under which it occurs are not completely known. In order to secure reminiscence the material must, of course, be incompletely learned. The determination to recall and the meaningfulness of the material are factors which favor reminiscence. The phenomenon is usually explained in terms of better organization of the learned material, and of the disappearance of the temporary factors of fatigue and satiation which favor inferior performance directly after learning drill. These same factors operate in giving superior recall scores for learning by distributed practice rather than by massed practice.

GENERAL REFERENCES

Boring, E. G., *A History of Experimental Psychology*. New York: Century, 1929, pp. xvi + 699.

Cameron, D. E., Remembering. New York: *Nerv. & Ment. Dis. Monog.* (72), 1947, pp. 110.

Flugel, J. C., *A Hundred Years of Psychology, 1833-1933*. New York: Macmillan, 1934, pp. 384.

McGeogh, J. A., Memory. *Psychol. Bul.*, 1928, *25*, 513-549.

Murphy, G., *An Historical Introduction to Modern Psychology*. (Second ed.) New York: Harcourt, Brace, 1930, pp. xvii + 470.

Rapaport, D., *Emotions and Memory*. Baltimore: Williams & Wilkins, 1942, pp. ix + 282.

Roback, A. A., *History of American Psychology*. New York: Library Publishers, 1952, pp. xiv + 426.

Stevens, S. S. (Ed.), *Handbook of Experimental Psychology*. New York: Wiley, 1951, pp. xi + 1436.

Williams, R. D., and Knox, G. W., A survey of dynamic principles governing memory. *J. Gen. Psychol.*, 1944, 30, 167-179.

Woodworth, R. S., *Contemporary Schools of Psychology*. New York: Ronald Press, 1931, pp. vi + 232.

SPECIFIC REFERENCES

[1] Alper, T. G., The interrupted task method in studies of selective recall: a reëvaluation of some recent experiments. *Psychol. Rev.*, 1952, *59*, 71-88.

[2] Ballard, P. B., Oblivescence and reminiscence. *Brit. J. Psychol. Monog. Suppl.*, *1*, No. 2, 1913, pp. 82.

[3] Bartlett, F. C., *Remembering: A Study in Experimental and Social Psychology*. Cambridge: Cambridge Univ. Press, 1932, pp. x + 317.

[4] Berlyne, D. E., Attention, perception and behavior theory. *Psychol. Rev.*, 1951, *58*, 127-146.

[5] Binet, A., Attention et adaptation. *L'Année Psychol.*, 1899, 6, 246-404.

[6] ——Le bilan de la psychologie en 1910. *L'Année Psychol.*, 1911, *17*, V-XI.

[7] Bull, N., A sequence concept of attitude. *J. Psychol.*, 1946, *22*, p. 172.

[8] Bull, N., The Attitude Theory of Emotion. New York: *Nerv. & Ment. Dis. Monog.*, 1951, *81*, pp. xvii + 159.

[9] Burrow, T., *The Biology of Human Conflict*. New York: Macmillan, 1937, pp. XXIX + 435.

[10] —— Kymograph records of neuromuscular (respiratory) patterns in relation to behavior disorders. *Psychosomat. Med.*, 1941, *3*, 174-186.

[11] —— *Science and Man's Behavior: The Contribution of Phylobiology.* Ed. by W. E. Galt. New York: Philosophical Library, 1953, pp. xii + 576.

[12] Burrow, T., and Galt, W. E., Electroencephalographic recordings of varying aspects of attention in relation to behavior. *J. Gen. Psychol.*, 1945, *32*, 269-288.

[13] Burrow, T., and Syz, H., Two modes of social adaptation and their concomitants in ocular movements. *J. Abn. & Soc. Psychol.*, 1949, *44*, 191-211.

[14] Clark, K. B., Some factors influencing the remembering of prose materials. *Arch. Psychol.*, 1940, No. 253.

[15] Dallenbach, K. M., Attributive vs. cognitive clearness. *J. Exp. Psychol.*, 1920, *3*, 183-230.

[16] Dollard, J., and Miller, N. E., *Personality and Psychotherapy: An Analysis in Terms of Learning, Thinking and Culture.* New York: McGraw-Hill, 1950, p. 449.

[17] Ebbinghaus, H., *Memory: A Contribution to Experimental Psychology.* Trans. Ruger, H. A., and Busenius, C. E. New York: Teachers College, 1913, pp. 123.

[18] Edwards, A. L., Political frames of reference as a factor influencing recognition. *J. Abn. & Soc. Psychol.*, 1941, *36*, 34-50.

[19] —— The retention of affective experiences—a criticism and restatement of the problem. *Psychol. Rev.*, 1942, *49*, 45-53.

[20] Finan, J. L., Delayed response with pre-delay re-enforcement in monkeys after the removal of the frontal lobes. *Amer. J. Psychol.*, 1942, *55*, 202-214.

[21] Freeman, G. L., Changes in tension-pattern and total energy expenditure during adaptation to "distracting" stimuli. *Amer. J. Psychol.*, 1939, *52*, 354-360.

[22] Freud, S., Psychopathology of everyday life. In: *The Basic Writings of Sigmund Freud.* Ed. by A. A. Brill, New York: Modern Library, 1938, pp. 33-178.

[23] Galt, W. E., Note on the psychoanalytic concept of "polymorphous perverse." *Amer. J. Orthopsychiat.*, 1941, XI, 535-539.

[24] Geissler, L. R., The measurement of attention. *Amer. J. Psychol.*, 1909, XX, 473-529.

[25] Gerard, R. W., What is memory? *Sci. Amer.*, 1953, *189*, p. 126.

[26] Gilbert, G. M., The new status of experimental studies on the relationship of feeling to memory. *Psychol. Bull.*, 1938, *35*, 26-35.

[27] Gillespie, R. D., Amnesia. *Arch. Neur. & Psychiat.*, 1937, *37*, 748-764.

[28] Goldstein, K., The mental changes due to frontal lobe damage. *J. Psychol.*, 1944, *17*, 187-208.

[29] Harlow, H. F., and Dagnon, J., Problem solution by monkeys following bilateral removal of the prefrontal areas. I. The discrimination and discrimination-reversal problems. *J. Exp. Psychol.*, 1943, *32*, 351-356.

[30] Hartmann, G. W., *Gestalt Psychology.* New York: Ronald Press, 1935, p. 279.

31 Hebb, D. O., *The Organization of Behavior.* New York: Wiley, 1949, pp. xix + 335.

32 Jacobsen, C. F., Studies of cerebral function in primates. I. The functions of the frontal association areas in monkeys. *Comp. Psychol. Monog.,* 1936, *13,* No. 63, 3-60.

33 Jacobsen, C. F., and Elder, J. H., Studies of cerebral function in primates. II. The effect of temporal lobe lesions on delayed response in monkeys. *Comp. Psychol. Monog.,* 1936, *13,* No. 63, 61-65.

34 Jacobsen, C. F., and Haslerud, G. M., Studies of cerebral function in primates. III. The effect of motor and premotor area lesions on delayed response in monkeys. *Comp. Psychol. Monog.,* 1936, *13,* No. 63, 66-68.

35 Jacobson, E., Electrophysiology of mental activities. *Amer. J. Psychol.,* 1932, *44,* 677-694.

36 James, W., *The Principles of Psychology.* New York: Holt. (2 vols.)

37 Jasper, H. H., and Cruikshank, R. M., Electro-encephalography. II. Visual stimulation and the after-image as affecting the occipital alpha rhythm. *J. Gen. Psychol.,* 1937, *17,* 29-48.

38 Jenkins, J. G., and Dallenbach, K. M., Oblivescence during sleep and waking. *Amer. J. Psychol.,* 1924, *35,* 605-612.

39 Klüver, H., and Bucy, P. C., "Psychic blindness" and other symptoms following bilateral temporal lobectomy in rhesus monkeys. *Amer. J. Physiol.,* 1937, *119,* 352-353.

40 Lashley, K. S., Functional determinants of cerebral localization. *Arch. Neur. & Psychiat.,* 1937, *38,* 371-387.

41 Lindemann, E., Psychological changes in normal and abnormal individuals under the influence of sodium amytal. *Amer. J. Psychiat.,* 1932, *11,* 1083-1091.

42 Malmo, R. B., Interference factors in delayed response in monkeys after removal of frontal lobes. *J. Neurophysiol.,* 1942, *5,* 295-308.

43 Melton, A. W., Chapter on learning in Annual Review of Psychology. Stanford, California: *Annual Reviews,* 1950, *1,* pp. 9-30.

44 Meltzer, H., The present status of experimental studies on the relationship of feeling to memory. *Psychol. Rev.,* 1930, *37,* 124-139.

45 Müller, G. E., *Zur Analyse der Gedächtnistätigkeit und des Vorstellungsverlaufes.* (3 vols.) Leipzig: Barth, 1911-1917, pp. 403, 597, 682.

46 Müller, G. E., and Pilzecker, A., Experimentelle Beiträge zur Lehre vom Gedächtnis. *Ztschr. f. Psychol. & Physiol. d. Sinnes.,* 1900, *1,* 174-198.

47 Munn, N. L., *Psychology. The Fundamentals of Human Adjustment.* (Second ed.) New York: Houghton, Mifflin, 1951, pp. 385-399.

48 Münsterberg, H., *On The Witness Stand.* New York: *Boardman,* 1923.

49 Murphy, G., *Personality: A Biosocial Approach to Origins and Structure.* New York: Harper, 1947, pp. 350-351.

50 Pascal, F. C., The trend in theories of attention. *Psychol. Rev.,* 1941, *48,* 383-403.

51 Penfield, W., Memory mechanisms. *Arch. Neur. & Psychiat.,* 1952, *67,* 178-198.

52 Pillsbury, W. B., *Attention.* New York : Macmillan, 1908, pp. 147-148.

53 Ribot, Th., *The Psychology of Attention.* Chicago: Open Court Pub. Co., 1911.

54 Roback, A. A., *Behaviorism and Psychology.* Cambridge: University Book Store, 1923, pp. 68-69.

55 Ruch, F. L., *Psychology and Life*. (Fourth ed.) New York: Scott, Foresman, 1953, pp. 236-253.

56 Ruch, T. C., Chapter 5 in *Handbook of Experimental Psychology*. New York: John Wiley & Sons, 1951, pp. 175-176.

57 Russell, W. R., Amnesia following head injuries. *Lancet*, 1935, 2, 762.

58 Schachtel, E. G., On memory and childhood amnesia. *Psychiatry*, 1947, 10, 1-26.

59 Sheer, D. E., The effect of frontal lobe operations on the attention process. *Amer. J. Psychol.*, 1951, 6, 261. (Abstract)

60 Stern, W., The psychology of testimony. *J. Abn. & Soc. Psychol.*, 1939, 34, 3-20.

61 Strongin, E. I., Bull, N., and Korchin, B., Visual efficiency during experimentally induced emotional states. *J. Psychol.*, 1941, 12, 3-6.

62 Syz, H., Recovery from loss of mnemic retention after head trauma. *J. Gen. Psychol.*, 1937, 17, 355-387.

63 Teitelbaum, H. A., The principle of primary and associated disturbances of the higher cortical functions as applied to temporal lobe lesions. *J. Nerv. & Ment. Dis.*, 1942, 96, 261-273.

64 Thorndike, E. L., The law of effect. *Amer. J. Psychol.*, 1927, 39, 212-222.

65 Titchener, E. B., *A Text-Book of Psychology*. New York: Macmillan, 1910, p. 267.

66 Wade, M., The effect of sedatives upon delayed responses in monkeys following removal of the prefrontal lobes. *J. Neurophysiol.*, 1947, 10, 57-61.

67 Warden, C. J., Barrera, S. E., and Galt, W. E., The effect of unilateral and bilateral frontal lobe extirpation on the behavior of monkeys. *J. Comp. Psychol.*, 1942, 34, 149-171.

68 Washburn, M. F., *Movement and Mental Imagery*. Boston: Houghton, Mifflin, 1916, p. 34.

69 Watson, J. B., *Behaviorism*. New York: People's Inst. Pub. Co., 1924, p. 212.

70 Watson, W. S., and Hartmann, G. W., The rigidity of a basic attitudinal frame. *J. Abn. & Soc. Psychol.*, 1939, 34, 314-335.

71 Wulf, F, Ueber die Veränderung von Vorstellungen. (Gedächtnis und Gestalt) *Psychol. Forsch.*, 1922, I, 333-373.

72 Zeigarnik, B., Das Behalten erledigter und unerledigter Handlungen. *Psychol. Forsch.*, 1927, 9, 1-85.

73 Zeller, A. F., An experimental analogue of repression. II. The effect of individual failure and success on memory measured by relearning. *J. Exp. Psychol.*, 1950, 40, 411-422.

CHAPTER VII

THE STATUS OF EMOTION IN CONTEMPORARY PSYCHOLOGY

MAGDA ARNOLD, Ph.D.

Professor of Psychology, Loyola University

EDITORIAL NOTE

Although the affects have been regarded not only as the mainsprings of action, as they were wont to be dubbed in the older textbooks, but actually have become the basis of all motivation and the underlying factors of neurosis, indeed the central issue in all depth psychology, there appears to be a movement afoot to ease this department out of psychology. This might be a vigorous resurgence of the tendency found in James, Lange, and Sergi to minimize, or even to nullify, the rôle of the emotive consciousness by placing all the emphasis on the sensory experience of what is going on in the body (vascular, muscular, organic)—a tendency intensified by the demands of objectivistic theory, equating even James's slight mentalistic residue with some motor expression.

It is because of this effort on the part of anti-mentalistic psychologists that so much space was allowed to Dr. Magda Arnold, who has covered the ground extensively in her critique of recent treatments of emotion. Thus, and thus only, can such undermining attempts be challenged and countervailed. It is easy to wave aside phenomena by implying that they do not exist, or at any rate are a phase of something else which has loomed large more recently. The question is: what validity do the arguments possess? Dr. Arnold makes a careful analysis of them and shows up their weakness, and even if her own point of view should turn out just as vulnerable, she has performed a service.

Dr. Magda Arnold taught at the University of Toronto, Wellesley College, and Bryn Mawr College. At present, she is Professor in the Department of Psychology at Loyola University in Chicago. She is co-author of The Human Person *(New York, 1954) and has just completed a work entitled* Emotion and Personality.

136

The present stand of psychologists is curiously ambiguous on the topic of emotion. As an area of research and theory, it has practically disappeared from academic psychology. In the last three volumes of the *Annual Review of Psychology* there is no chapter on emotion, and neither is it covered under Personality or similar topics. At the same time, physiologists and medical men show great interest in the connection between life situations, emotions, and bodily disease (Wolff, 1951). Clinical and experimental studies are reported on aggression, frustration, anxiety but without any indication as to how these phenomena are related to emotion and certainly without a theory which would integrate them. Moreover, the interest of clinicians and educators in various forms of emotion remains unabated and even the layman is asking himself anxiously whether the insecurity of our time, its anxieties and frustrations, will allow him to salvage his emotional integrity. It seems that everybody is interested but the psychologist. In fact, it almost looks as if the devotee of pure science were leaving this particular field to the expert in applied science, refusing him the tools which research and theory could provide. Take in addition the popular guides to happiness and emotional security which dispense recipes for dealing with any and all emotional problems and a picture emerges which is rather unique in modern science.

APPROACHES TO SUBJECT

The reasons for this chaotic condition are many. There have been at least three professional approaches to the problem of emotion which have given different and indeed conflicting results, and no theory has been offered to reconcile them. Experimental psychologists, for instance, have shown that emotions disturb goal-directed actions, that they break up efficient habit patterns and force regression to random responses. Biologists, on the other hand, have pointed out that emotions have an emergency function, are therefore useful for the organism. Finally, clinicians have insisted that emotion in the form of love and aggression is the prime mover of human activity and the necessary condition for normal human development.

These results are contradictory only as long as we see emotion as a unitary function so that all emotions are assumed to have the same mechanism and must produce the same effect. If we were to conceive that different emotions might have different effects, it would seem plausible that some emotions might break up habit patterns but others might not; that some might be useful for specific purposes, fight or flight, and that others might not only be useful but indispensable for personality development as a whole. Hence contradictions will either remain or be resolved depending on our theoretical views.

Not only are there conflicting opinions as to the rôle played by emotion in the economy of the living being, the very status of the phenomenon, its causes, conditions and mechanism, are still in question. To the unsophisticated, emotion is an experience *sui generis,* never to be confused with a non-emotional state; the psychologist is not so sure. There is general agreement that during emotion we experience a bodily upset which is very noticeable when the emotion becomes intense. But there is disagreement when it comes to explaining how an unemotional experience gives rise to emotional experience and bodily upset, that is, how perception arouses emotion. There is the further question how emotion as an experience is related to the bodily disturbance noticed during emotion: does emotion give rise to the bodily disturbance, or does the bodily upset give rise to emotion? In the first case, emotion is assumed to be an experience *sui generis,* in the second, emotion would be the sensory perception of bodily changes, as William James and Carl Lange pleaded many years ago.

The neuro-physiological mechanism proposed for emotion will obviously differ depending on our view of what is cause and what effect. In either case, the mechanism must be inferred from our knowledge of neural functioning. Our blueprint may be either schematic and general, giving a possible way of functioning, or it may be specific and detailed, suggesting definite neural pathways.

Obviously, the reconciliation of conflicting results from experimental and clinical findings depends on our theoretical position, but so does the psychological sequence of events in emotion as well as the proposed neurophysiological mechanism. Therefore the greater part of this necessarily restricted survey will be devoted to theories of emotion rather than research findings, though such findings will be mentioned where they are crucial for theory.[1]

The various theoretical approaches deal with different aspects of the problem as one after another came to be emphasized in the developing science of psychology. Neurophysiological theory, beginning from William James' theory of emotion, reflects the concern of the young science with finding some physical basis of emotion. As soon as the individual came to be seen as acting on his own instead of as experimental subject, psychological theorists (McDougall and Freud) concentrated on instincts as the driving forces of human nature. Conflict theories, from Dewey to Madison Bentley, tried to explain the genesis of emotion as the clash of opposing tendencies. Still later, emotion became simply a release of energy (Duffy) or a motor attitude (Bull). The purposive character of emotion was stressed in motivational theories (Leeper), its action character by behavioristic theories (Watson, Skinner, Hull). The existentialist reaction (Sartre) saw emotion as a meaningful human activity, while the neo-scholastic functional approach (Michotte, Gemelli, Arnold and Gasson) considers emotion as the reaction of a person to something that affects him. Some of these varied aspects of emotion were emphasized only by one theory and theorist, others proved more enduring and have given rise to many theories, each attempting to complete the preliminary explanations of its predecessors. This has been the case particularly for the neurophysiological approach where recent findings required a new integration.

In the Twenties, the period from which our survey will start,

Cannon had just announced his Emergency and Thalamic Theory of emotion, which claimed to give a neurophysiological explanation better fitted to available facts than the James-Lange theory. The resulting controversy takes us right into the thick of the struggle.

Neurophysiological theories

William James (1884, 1893, 1894,) and Carl Lange at almost the same time (1885) had said that the "cold" perception of an object will arouse an emotion by producing various visceral (for Lange, circulatory) changes which incite to action and are perceived as an emotional state. The bodily state causes the felt emotion: we are afraid because we run. But what causes the bodily upset and why does a given situation arouse sometimes fear, sometimes anger (and sometimes, we may add, no emotion)? James answers:

> The same bear may truly enough excite us to either fight or flight according as he suggests an overpowering "idea" of his killing us, or one of our killing him. But in either case the question remains: Does the emotional excitement which follows the idea follow it immediately, or secondarily and as a consequence of the "diffuse wave" of impulses aroused? (1894, p. 518.)

For James, of course, the emotion follows the diffuse wave of impulses. But this explanation glosses over the fact that the "idea" of the bear killing us or of our killing him is rather different from the mere perception of a bear apart from his designs upon us. We have not simply a cold perception or idea, we judge intuitively that the bear means us harm and estimate whether to meet it by fight or flight. If there were no difference between a "cold" perception and such an estimate of the bear's design upon us, it would be difficult to explain how a perception can arouse an emotion at one time and not at another. To call upon the law of association, as James does in later explanations, is of little advantage. Association does not account for the experiencing of an emotion on the first encounter with an object (according to Hebb, 1946b, chimpanzees show fear the first time they see a snake, or the model of a human or chimpanzee head), nor does it account for a particular kind of emotion (fear or anger) when the object may have been connected with other emotions before.

Walter B. Cannon (1927, 1931) refuted James' position by pointing out that emotion is reported by experimental subjects before peripheral changes are perceived; that injury or disease might abolish all bodily sensations, yet the patients reported that they felt emotions as they did before. In these cases, there were no sensations from viscera or blood vessels, hence there should have been no emotion if the James-Lange theory were correct. For Cannon, the only alternative was a central organ of emotion, the thalamus, which adds an emotional *quale* to incoming sensory impulses in their course through the thalamus to the cortex. Ordinarily, this emotional coloring of sensations is not perceived because the cortex inhibits thalamic discharge. When emotional stimulation is intense (in startle) the excitation breaks through this inhibition and is perceived. At the same time, the thalamus activates the sympathetic nervous system which produces various visceral changes. In other emotional situations, conditioned response processes are aroused in the cortex, which determine the direction of response (fight or flight) and release the appropriate thalamic pattern. When released, the thalamus discharges its specific pattern upward to the cortex (emotional awareness) and downward to the periphery (emotional expression). Thus emotion is always a release from cortical inhibition. Cannon based his view of cortical inhibition primarily on the fact that decorticated animals show violent rage when they come out of the anaesthetic, tied, as they are, to the animal board. Since it is assumed that rage cannot be felt without the cortex, it was called sham rage; and since it was thought to be an exaggerated rage reaction, it was assumed to be the result of release from cortical inhibition.

But it is known that normal animals also show rage under the same conditions. Moreover, if a normal cat is enraged it may not be safely handled for hours, while a decorticated cat can be handled with impunity. Unless it can be shown that rage is more intense and more lasting in decorticated animals, rage cannot be called a release phenomenon.

Bard (1934) found later that animals still show rage if not only cortex but thalamus is removed, so that only the posterior part of the hypothalamus is left. Hence it has been accepted as a fact that the hypothalamus is necessary for integrated emotional expression. If the hypothalamus is removed also, the integrated rage pattern fails to develop. But such experiments prove at most that the hypothalamus is necessary for the expression of rage, they do not prove that either thalamus or hypothalamus generates rage (or any other emotion) nor do they prove that the cortex normally inhibits the thalamus. Masserman showed that convincingly in a series of ingenious experiments. He stimulated the hypothalamus in normally active cats by means of implanted bipolar electrodes, and obtained a convincing picture of extreme rage with hissing, spitting, unsheathing of claws. But the normal activity of the animal was hardly disturbed by this hypothalamic storm. Masserman reports that the cat would continue lapping milk, grooming itself or even purring though it showed all the symptoms ordinarily associated with rage. He concludes, therefore,

> that the behavior induced by hypothalamic stimulation was mechanical, stereotyped and stimulus-bound and no more demonstrated the presence of a pervasive affect than the mechanical closure of a person's fist by a stimulus applied to his median nerve would indicate that the person to whom the hand belonged was enraged and preparing to engage in fisticuffs. (1950, p. 45.)

Both Bard and Masserman also obtained behavior that resembled the flight reaction in fear, Bard in cats after removal of cortex and thalamus, in response to airblast, and Masserman by hypothalamic stimulation of intact cats. But the fear pattern also was different from its counterpart in normal animals. Instead of strenuous attempts at escape as seen in frightened animals, these cats merely had fits of aimless and precipitate running. Masserman concludes that

despite the dramatic (but deceptive) emotional mimetic response produced by stimulation of this region, the hypothalamus apparently plays no significant rôle in the affective or conative experience of fear or rage. (1942, p. 635.)

Since there is no evidence that the thalamus generates emotion or induces emotional experience either, Cannon's thalamic theory must be taken as a speculative inference from the fact that there is a hypothalamic effector station for emotional expression. It hinges on the possibility that the thalamus may add "emotional coloring" to all incoming sensations, to be later sorted out by cortical conditioning. How specific emotions could develop from such unassorted affect is difficult to explain. On the other hand, if specific effector patterns for fear or rage or any other emotion are genetically determined, the picture becomes even more complicated. In that case, some generalized "affect" would have to be added to incoming sensory impulses, while specific patterns would be activated as soon as cortical inhibition is removed. Since we do not feel generalized affect but fear or anger or love, the specific pattern would have to send impulses to the cortex as well as to the autonomic effectors. This is but a negligible refinement of the James-Lange theory. In both theories, emotional experiences occur after relays from effector patterns arrive in the cortex: for James and Lange, they are relays from muscles and viscera, for Cannon, they are relays from the hypothalamic effector station.

For many later theorists, Cannon's thalamic theory seemed no great improvement over the James-Lange theory. Newman *et al*, for instance, point out that the emotional excitation has to run the whole gamut from perception to peripheral changes and finally to action so that no one structure is more involved than any other. They say:

Cortical, thalamic, organic, and peripheral conditions are all necessary. Of utmost importance is the interpretation of the situation, an insightful response which determines whether or not the emotional pattern will be complete and therefore whether peripheral conditions shall function in emotion or in some non-emotional response. In short, the emotion is a configurational response concerned with the process of resolving tension toward a particular goal. (Newman, *et al,* 1930, p. 326.)

These writers agree that many factors are integrated in an emotional response, and Cannon would not contradict them. But Newman *et al* would insist that the whole sequence is necessary for emotion, while Cannon would maintain that the circuit cortex-thalamus (hypothalamus)-cortex is necessary for emotional experience while the pathways to the periphery are not. For emotional expression, however, only the hypothalamus with its peripheral effectors would be necessary on Cannon's theory.

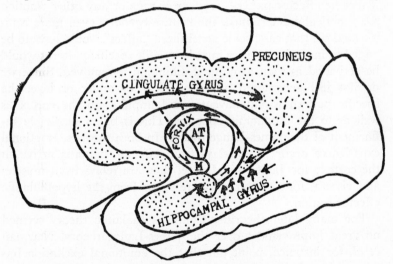

Fig. 1 (From: Paul D. McLean, Psychosomatic disease and the "visceral brain." Psychosom. Med. 1949, *11,* 338-353. p. 340.)

The shaded area of cortex represents what was formerly known as the limbic lobe of Broca and subsequently termed the rhinencephalon. It corresponds to the structures which represent Papez' "mechanism of emotion."

AT — anterior thalamic nucleus.

M — mammillary body in hypothalamus.

Papez' "mechanism of emotion." (1937) Later theorists continue this preoccupation with the sequence perception-emotion-bodily upset. Papez, for instance, sketched a "mechanism of emotion" in a brilliant exposition of the brain as a vast interconnected system which essentially serves three different kinds of integration: the stream of perceiving comes from various sense receptors through the sensory nuclei of the thalamus to the sensory areas of the cortex; the stream of integrative thought branches off in the thalamus via the dorsomedial nuclei to the frontal lobes; and the stream of feeling branches off in the thalamus to go via the mammillary bodies in the hypothalamus to the anterior thalamic nuclei and the cingular cortex. This stream of feeling also receives a current from the cortical area around the hippocampus which arrives in the mammillary bodies via the fornix. Sensory impulses to the cortex connect with relays going to the hypothalamus where they receive their emotional coloring. Emotion is perceived when these relays arrive in the cingular gyrus. But emotion can also be built up in the hippocampal gyrus, the impulses be relayed to the hypothalamus to receive their emotional coloring, and then experienced as emotion when relays from the hypothalamus arrive in the gyrus cinguli. (Fig. 1.)

Thus the hypothalamus becomes again an "organ of emotion", though Papez insists that it is merely one relay station in a total circuit. If the emotional *quale* is added in the hypothalamus, the question immediately arises: How can the hypothalamus decide what emotions to add? The stimulus does not inevitably produce fear or anger or love, yet emotional coloring is added to the stream of sensations before it has arrived in the cortex to result in perception. Since there is no mention of specific patterns of emotion, as there is in Cannon's theory, it is unclear how that generalized affect is sorted out to be perceived as specific emotions like fear, anger, love.

The same difficulty recurs in another form when we turn to the *expression* of emotion. Emotional expression may be incited cortically (from hippocampal gyrus) or by incoming sensations from the sensory nuclei in the thalamus. In the second case, the expressive mechanism would be activated before the three divisions of the stream of sensory impulses have arrived in the cortex. Admittedly, Papez was more concerned with establishing a mechanism of emotional *experience* than with describing the mechanism of emotional *expression*. The logic of his own system would require that the stream of sensory impulses, integrated by the thought process, provided with coloring by the emotive process, should be perceived *on arrival in the cortex* and so give rise to emotional expression. Emotional expression which starts before the object is perceived, before sensations are integrated and organized, and before they are felt as affectively toned, is a logical impossibility.

Papez quotes both anatomical and clinical evidence in support of his theory. It seems clear on anatomical grounds that there is a connected circuit of the kind required. Clinically, it has been found that injury or disease involving the areas included in Papez' "mechanism of emotion" either increases the patient's excitement, irritability or anger, or makes him apathetic. The great merit of Papez' theory of emotion is his suggestion of a specific brain mechanism mediating emotional experience which makes it possible to test the hypothesis. On the basis of evidence collected thus far, there is little doubt that the circuit from hippocampus to hypothalamus to anterior thalamus and gyrus cinguli is involved in emotional experience and expression. What is doubtful is the rôle of the hypothalamus as a receptor organ for emotion which determines the emotional quality of incoming sensory impulses.

D. O. Hebb's theory of emotion. (1946, 1949) The mechanism of emotion may also be explained as a sequence of events in the brain without specifying the location of such circuits. James, Cannon and Papez had assumed that emotion is a psychological experience though they disagreed as to its nature. For James, emotion is a sensation-complex, for Cannon and Papez, an experience *sui generis*. Hebb, however, does not acknowledge that emotion refers to some experience at all. He defines emotion as "the neural process that is inferred from and causes emotional behavior, with no reference to consciousness." (1949, p. 148.) Since Hebb believes that explanations may be either psychological or neurological but not both, he chooses the more basic neuro-physiological explanation:

> Though it has been tried before now, an explanation cannot be half neural anatomy and half consciousness. They are different levels in a logical hierarchy. A problem recognized at one level can be resolved by recourse to a more fundamental set of conceptions, but an hypothesis cannot well comprise two levels, take in two universes of discourse at the same time. (1949, p. 3)

But as a matter of fact, explanations which are restricted to the next lower level of a hierarchy will not explain the level in which the theorist is primarily interested. Problems of war and peace cannot be explained by pointing to the personal conflicts of individual members of the warring nations. The mammalian digestive system cannot be explained by the digestive processes in cells. Unless the function of the digestive tract is described and explained, an explanation on the level of cell function would never even hint at the fact that food must be eaten and go through stomach and intestines before cells can be nourished.

Moreover, as psychologists we must reconcile ourselves to the cold fact that we must use terms which refer to human experience if we want to be understood. If we insist on neurological explanations, they must be retranslated later or they cannot be applied to human behavior. This is a predicament familiar to behaviorists and Hebb does not escape it. It is never a choice between two kinds of explanations. The psychological interpretation is obligatory, though by itself not sufficient. While a higher level cannot be reduced to the next lower level, our understanding of the higher level may be completed by a knowledge of its roots.

Hebb chooses a neurological explanation in preference to a psychological explanation because "writers on the topic of emotion insist that there is no characteristic conscious event that can be called an emotion." (1946, p. 101.) The writers he quotes

(Dashiell, Duffy, Dunlap, Harlow and Stagner, Landis, Lashley, Young,) are either neo-behaviorists who deny conscious states by definition, or psychologists who deny that emotion has any status at all (Duffy, 1934). But emotions are facts of common experience. Even an objective psychologist like Knight Dunlap says:

> When the plain man speaks of fear, rage or grief, he apparently has reference to some facts—moreover, to facts which are, or can be experienced (and experience is an occurrence, and an undisputed fact). (1928, p. 151.)

Experience is something lived through *of which we are aware.* Hebb recognizes that awareness is somehow involved when he says:

> Psychologists agree that there is no special conscious quale of an emotion; but this *does not imply that there is no awareness of a tendency toward a certain kind of action,* any more than the experimental failure to find specific patterns of muscular action is a denial that a frightened person may run away, or that an angry one may strike. . . . *How such awarenesses are to be explained psychologically I do not pretend to know; but it is clear that they exist.* (1946a, p. 103.) (My italics.)

Thus an awareness seems to exist which the plain man calls fear, rage, grief, etc. If the psychologist refuses to call this awareness a conscious emotional state he must be prejudiced against using such a concept in his theory—which, of course, is the case with behaviorists.

The psychologists quoted by Hebb also insist that there is no recognizable emotional pattern. Yet Hebb found that there is an intuitive recognition of chimpanzee emotion which allows prediction, if "frankly anthropomorphic concepts of emotion" are used by the observer. In contrast, an objective description of behavior patterns resulted in an "almost endless series of specific acts in which no order or meaning could be found". (1946a, p. 88.) Such an intuitive recognition cannot well be "the inference that one of these postulated (neurophysiological) states exists in the subject", as Hebb says. This inference is not intuitive but depends on the reasoned proposition that emotion is a neurophysiological state. One of the caretakers in the colony, for instance, said of the chimpanzee, Bimba, that she is "quick to resent slights", that she "gets mad over nothing at all", observations which Hebb says are apt and accurate. Such a recognition surely is based on the man's own experience of slights and irritations, not on an inference grounded in something completely unknown to him. The only reason why anthropomorphic terms make it possible to recognize emotions is the fact that they refer to some human experience which is recognized in other human beings and can be used to recognize animal emotions as well.

If an observer is able to recognize a given behavior pattern as belonging to one and the same emotion in spite of individual variations and in spite of variations in different situations, he must do it by referring certain responses to something he knows which unifies them into a variable pattern. He cannot refer these responses to a hypothetical neuro-physiological state because he does not know that state nor does he know what responses such a state could induce. If it were possible to work out the pattern by reasoned inferences, then it could have been done from the objective descriptions of behavior patterns.

When Hebb refuses to define emotion in experiential terms, he turns his back on concepts which have served as a basis for recognizing emotions—in favor of a hypothetical neural process which could never contribute to the recognition or description of the phenomenon. Hypothetical constructs are useful and sometimes indispensable when they substitute for an inferred process which cannot be observed. But to substitute such constructs for an experiential fact is of doubtful value.

But let us see how Hebb describes the neural processes which he equates with psychological activities including emotions:

Any frequently repeated particular stimulation will lead to the slow development of a "cell-assembly", a diffuse structure comprising cells in the cortex and diencephalon (and also, perhaps, in the basal ganglia of the cerebrum), capable of acting briefly as a closed system, delivering facilitation to other such systems and usually having a specific motor facilitation. A series of such events constitutes a "phase sequence"—the thought process. Each assembly action may be aroused by a preceding assembly, by a sensory event, or—normally—by both. The central facilitation from one of these activities on the next is the prototype of "attention".

It is proposed also that there is an alternate, "intrinsic" organization, occurring in sleep and in infancy, which consists of hypersynchrony in the firing of cortical cells. But besides these two forms of cortical organization *there may be disorganization.* It is assumed that the assembly depends completely on a very delicate timing which might be disturbed by metabolic changes as well as by sensory events that do not accord with the pre-existent central process. When this is transient, it is called *emotional disturbance;* when chronic, neurosis or psychosis. (1949, p. xix.) (italics added.)

Thus emotional disturbance is cortical disorganization of phase sequences organized into cell-assemblies. The phase sequence (which may be a perception, a thought, an image or a concept,) is fleeting and continually needs new sensory content to maintain its organization. Hebb says:

. . . some phase sequences are more firmly established than others: that is, more capable of perpetuating themselves. The level of stimulation from sense organs affects the persistence, and a phase sequence may perpetuate itself by raising this level, as when one knits his brows and pinches himself to stay awake. (1949, p. 222.)

These phase sequences can be disturbed in various ways. Hebb analyzes fear as an example of disturbing emotions and concludes:

The immediate source of fear is a disruption of a coördination, principally acquired, in the timing of cellular activities in the cerebrum. The disruption may be due to conflict, a sensory deficit or constitutional change. With disruption there at once occur processes tending to restore the integration of cerebral activities; in fear these include either liminal or subliminal activation of processes determining avoidance. Optimally avoidance tends toward completely averting the cerebral disruption, and at this stage avoidance without fear would be said to occur. (1946b, p. 271.)

Since the phase sequence needs ever new content to maintain its organization and to endure, sensory events are needed to provide it.

But sensory events should not support the phase sequence too strongly, so that it runs its course immediately and cannot continue to dominate association-area activity. The well-developed phase sequence depends, for a continued existence, on repeated checks from the environment. Hence . . . the preoccupation with what is new but not too new, with the mildly frustrating or the mildly fear-provoking. (1949, p. 233.)

If emotional disturbance is a disruption of cerebral organization, pleasant emotions are its continued growth and development:

Pleasure is not the activity of particular structures in the nervous system, and not even a particular kind of pattern of cerebral organization, but fundamentally a directed *growth* or *development in cerebral organization*. It is thus necessarily a transient state of affairs in which a conflict is being reduced, an incipient organization being dissipated, or a new synthesis in assembly action being achieved. . . . (1949, p. 232.)

Thus emotions are either developing phase sequences or disrupted phase sequences; some emotions are pleasant, some disturbing.

But there is a serious flaw in this explanation. Throughout, the neuro-physiological account depends on concealed psychological causation. *Conflict,* for instance, could disturb cortical organization only if the two phase sequences constituting the conflict had a different frequency. If a boy is disturbed because he cannot decide whether to go to Harvard or to Yale, can it be assumed that the neural impulses of the Harvard phase sequence and those of the Yale phase sequence have a different timing?—According to Hebb, *sensory deficit* arouses disturbance (fear of darkness) because of the expectancy that stimulation will be continued. And expectancy (or attention) is central facilitation of phase sequences. But why should the non-arrival of facilitated phase sequences result in disruption instead of in resumption of the "intrinsic organization" of sleep? Such an explanation cannot account for the fact that some human beings sleep at nightfall while others are afraid in the dark. *Avoidance,* like conflict, is not a neuro-physiological concept (which illustrates our contention that psychological terms cannot be avoided even in a neuro-physiological explanation). Phase sequences either have coördinated frequencies or they do not; they cannot foresee a future disruption, therefore cannot activate "processes determining avoidance." The thinking human being can and does foresee danger and tries to avoid it, but his performance cannot be credited to cell assemblies which by definition can only initiate nerve impulses at certain frequencies, and to phase sequences which can only relay them. As a noted neurologist put it:

> The most that can be claimed for neuronal circuits is that they integrate the ceaseless flow of afferent impulses from the different receptive fields. They are the refining machinery of sense data, and, as Head proposed, provide a new construction which is presented to consciousness, but they do not and cannot provide conceptual knowledge as such, nor include any appreciation of the universal as such. (Walshe, 1952, p. 13.)

We may admire Hebb's attempt to construct a consistent system in which central neuronal activity by its own laws of functioning will do everything the human being was thought to do, but we cannot call it successful. His hope was that this theory would rid us

> once and for all of the little man inside the skull who approves of some sensory events relayed to him by the nervous system, disapproves of others, and guides behavior accordingly; who encourages stimulation of the afferents from the genitalia in his crafty and teleological aim to perpetuate the species, and who for the same purpose becomes violent when C fibers are stimulated or when he foresees that they are going to be. By some such approach as the one suggested, it may become possible to understand the directedness and order in behavior, and the variability of motivation, as produced by neural functioning alone. (1949, p. 234.)

But it seems that the rôle of the little man has been taken over by the brain with its cell assemblies and phase sequences which now act on their own, just the way Hebb describes. Whatever the fashion in psychological explanations, human beings do approve or disapprove, not of sensory events but of things, ideas, or people. Human beings may encourage or refuse sexual stimulation, they may intend to have children or refuse to do so. Cerebral organization serves such human decisions but cannot make them. To ascribe the "directedness and order" of human actions to the laws of neural functioning really is animistic and anthropomorphic, while talking about human beings in terms of human experience is merely appropriate.

Exclusive concentration on neural mechanisms will never give an intelligible account of human experience. For the plain man, emotion is an easily recognizable experience: it has an object (he is angry at or afraid of *something*) and he has a particular reaction to it (he is angry, afraid) which shows all over (his muscles tense, he trembles). So far, psychologists seem to have disregarded the object-subject relationship as well as the subject's experience, to concentrate on the "all-over" bodily effects and their neurological mechanism. Since emotion is a fact of experience which is used to good advantage in the recognition and description of emotion both in man and animal, it is up to the psychologist to explain it in intelligible terms, that is in terms which refer to human experience and behavior. As Hebb himself says:

> Whatever the anthropomorphic terminology may seem to imply about conscious states . . . it provides *an intelligible and practical guide to behavior.* (Hebb, 1946a, p. 88.) (Hebb's italics.)

Arnold's Excitatory Theory. (Arnold, 1945, 1951) starts out from the fact that we experience well differentiated emotions, and argues that such felt differences cannot be an illusion. She reviews Cannon's emergency theory and recent physiological evidence and comes to the conclusion that fear is characterized primarily by excitation of the sympathetic nervous system, while anger primarily represents parasympathetic excitation.[2] If that is the case, then it stands to reason that these two branches of the autonomic nervous system would have separate cortical connections which could be traced to establish cortical and subcortical circuits activated in different emotions.

Since emotions are not aroused by every perception, there must be something which distinguishes an "emotional" perception from a "cold" perception. An object can be perceived either as it is, objectively, apart from any reference to the observer, or it can be perceived as affecting him in some particular way. The second kind of perception really includes a judgment that the object is beneficial or harmful, suitable or unsuitable for the subject. This judgment cannot be reasoned but must be immediate and intuitive, for animals and infants seem to be able to make it. Only after something is judged dangerous, harmless or beneficial in this intuitive way, will there be felt a tendency away from it or toward it—and this felt tendency is the emotional experience (of fear, anger or love). Since it is a *real* tendency which is felt (i.e. a beginning movement) it will result in real bodily changes. These are sensed in turn and often also judged in their effect upon us: What does this tremor, this racing heart, mean to us? This secondary estimate is definitely reasoning and often rationalization and may lead to organ neurosis.

Obviously, this treatment of emotion implies that it is considered neither as a complex of sensations nor incipient movements but as an experience *sui generis*. It includes the estimate of the object, the felt tendency and the physiological changes, though the only *necessary* factor is the intuitive estimate. (This would, for example, allow for so-called "unconscious" emotions.) If the interpretation of the situation determines what kind of emotion is felt and whether emotion is felt at all, it is obvious that such a judgment, however immediate and intuitive, requires a functioning cortex. Not only is the cortex necessary for the estimate of the situation, there must be cortical *excitation* of the aroused (and felt) tendency toward the object, which must be relayed to autonomic effectors before bodily changes can appear.

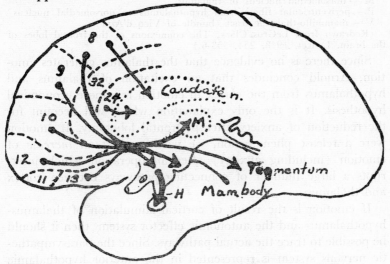

Fig. 2A. Main pathways from frontal lobe.

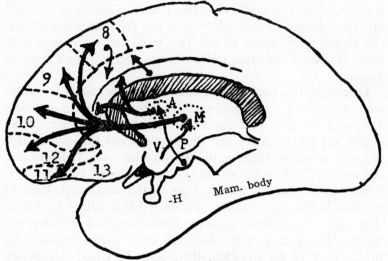

FIG. 2B. Main pathways to frontal lobe.

A — anterior nucleus of thalamus
H — hypophysis, posterior lobe innervated from supraoptic nucleus of thalamus
M — dorsomedial nucleus of thalamus
P — periventricular fibers from hypothalamus to dorsomedial nucleus
V — mammillo-thalamic tract (bundle of Vicq d'Azyr)
(Redrawn from LeGros Clark, The connexions of the frontal lobes of the brain. Lancet, 1948, 254, 353-6.)

Since there is no evidence that the thalamus generates emotion, Arnold concludes that an excitation of thalamus and hypothalamus from the cortex in emotion is a more economical hypothesis. It is the only explanation which will account for the reduction of anxiety after prefrontal lobotomy. If emotion were a release phenomenon, we would expect an *increase* of emotion (including anxiety) after an operation which interrupts a large number of connecting pathways between cortex and thalamus.

If emotion is the result of cortical stimulation of thalamus-hypothalamus and the autonomic effector system, then it should be possible to trace the actual pathways. Since the parasympathetic nervous system is represented in the anterior hypothalamic nuclei which have connections with the anterior thalamic nuclei and the cingular gyrus (cf. Fig. 2 A, B.) Arnold suggests that this circuit is activated in anger. The sympathetic nervous system is represented in the posterior hypothalamus, connected through the dorsomedial thalamic nuclei with the frontal lobe and is active during fear. Since these are two-way connections, from cortex to hypothalamus as well as from hypothalamus to cortex, this circuit is normally activated from the cortex during emotion. When it is activated from the hypothalamus (as in Masserman's stimulation experiments) there is evidently emotional expression without emotional experience—which substantiates the view that cortical activity is necessary in the intuitive estimate of the situation before emotional experience can occur.

After prefrontal lobotomy, the dorsomedial nucleus of the thalamus completely degenerates. This would mean that anxiety is reduced because the excitation of sympathetic effectors is now prevented and with it a prolongation and intensification of the emotion. After lobotomy, the patients still feel fear but their continued apprehension has disappeared and with it the physiological effects of fear. The even more recent removal of the dorsomedial nuclei (thalamotomy) by Spiegel *et al* (1951) seems to provide additional evidence, for it has the same effect as lobotomy in reducing anxiety but does not seem to produce the defect in initiative and integrated thinking shown in nonpsychotic patients after lobotomy (Rylander, 1948). It is further significant that assaultive patients who had not improved after lobotomy or removal of dorsomedial nuclei, were calmed when the anterior thalamic nuclei were removed as well, the very nuclei which according to this theory are excited during anger.[2]

This theory recognizes emotion as a specific psychological phenomenon, hence claims that the necessary condition for its arousal is a psychological appraisal of the situation. At the same time, it specifies the mechanism which is active during emotion. What remains to be done, perhaps, is a more careful description of the intuitive estimate which arouses emotion to show whether it could really be considered a separate factor in perception.

Instinct Theories of Emotion

For the theorists who follow James and Lange, the sequence beginning from the physiological changes after perception to the full-fledged action will take the lion's share in the description of the phenomenon called *emotion*. When emotion is not a specific phenomenon but a complex of bodily sensations and reactions, then the important factor to be investigated is the bodily upset. Now it is possible to see these violent changes, this bodily upset as physiological means to some end but that requires the admission of some organismic purpose, be it ascribed to chance selection or to the wisdom of the body. Since emotions disturb homeostasis, the physiological changes must be a preparation for some action which will eventually restore it. Hence psychologists from James onward have investigated the relation of emotional changes to instinctive action.

W. McDougall. (1933) Both McDougall and Freud follow this lead. Biologically oriented, they are inclined to equate organismic purpose with human purpose. For both of them emotion has also psychological aspects, but these are strictly subordinate to instinctive urges.

For McDougall as for William James, the distinctive quality of an emotion is determined by the bodily changes, therefore the emotion must follow the bodily upset. But McDougall insists that it is impossible to accept the James-Lange theory in its extreme form. To explain the bodily changes, it is necessary to refer back to the innate drive or instinct which arouses them. An emotional situation arouses an instinct which is felt as an emotion and at the same time is expressed in peripheral changes which urge to action and end in action. Thus every instinct is felt as an emotion, and there is no emotion without its coördinated instinct.

The instinct is aroused by a sensation complex "that has significance for the animal." Objects or situations which do not arouse the instinct naturally, arouse it by association. Of course, this explanation like that explaining emotion as aroused "by conditioning", is simply an admission of ignorance. Anything can become associated with or conditioned to anything else but there must always be a first occasion on which the instinct is aroused by its natural or unconditioned stimulus. But a fear of something unfamiliar cannot be aroused by a situation which naturally calls out an instinct, for not all unfamiliar objects arouse fear. On the other hand, to suppose that fear is aroused by associating the unknown object with some previously feared thing will not do either, for such associations as exist may have been pleasant. (Hebb, 1946b, found, for instance, that chimpanzees would be afraid of a familiar attendant if he was dressed slightly differently.)

Thus McDougall's explanation that the bodily pattern is associated with an instinct does not satisfactorily account for the arousal either of the emotion or the instinct. However, McDougall's expedient makes it possible for him to say that emotions are useful for the organism, for they are but the experience of the instinct in action. But by the same token, McDougall does not account for the fact that emotions sometimes disturb ongoing action, unless his concept of emotion as "excitement" is used to explain the overflow of excitation from the somatic into the autonomic system. Explaining emotion as excitement, McDougall is then forced to say that emotion evaporates if the action is often repeated. To account for emotions which contradict this assumption (a mother's love becomes stronger rather than weaker the more actively she cares for her child) McDougall has to introduce "sentiments" having a separate neural structure, which organize many different emotions around one central object. But sentiments are only assumed to organize emotions, not to change them. If repeated actions weaken the emotion, they should do so whether or not this emotion is included in a sentiment.

Freud and the psychoanalytic theory of emotion. As we saw in McDougall's theory, a so-called "mentalistic" outlook does not prevent a psychologist from seeing emotion as a complex of bodily changes which are felt as excitement. Neither does such an outlook guarantee that the arousal of emotion will be looked for in the psychological import of the situation. This is illustrated again in Freud's views on emotion.

Like McDougall, Freud claims that the sexual instinct moves to action and is experienced as an affect; unlike McDougall, he claims that the *libido is the only driving force,* together with its twin and counterpart, aggression. These opposite poles, he says, are found in all sentient beings which move between growth and decay, life and death throughout their span of existence. Affect (or emotion) is a quantity of psychic energy which must be discharged. When this discharge is prevented, there is a disturbance which is experienced as another affect—anxiety. According to his earliest views (before 1900) anxiety is "a subcortical deflection of somatic sexual excitation." Thus emotion is the experience either of an energy discharge, or of its deflection. This implies a discharge theory of love and aggression, and a conflict theory of anxiety. This view is actually preserved in substance throughout the many later modifications of his theory.

In his later formulations (after 1900) Freud considers affect as a motor or secretory function, set in action by ideas in the unconscious. The pleasure principle uses autonomic innervations as discharge channels for instinctual tensions, while the reality principle governs such discharge over the motor system. Affect becomes a pleasurable alternative to action, to be indulged in when action is impossible—hence it has value as a safety valve when tension is too high. The obvious objections—that emotion often occurs before action becomes imperative and that instinctual actions are accompanied by strong emotion—have been pointed out by analysts recently (Jacobson, Rapaport). These authors conclude that a discharge or safety-valve theory of affect is inadequate.

In his mature formulations (1926) Freud dealt particularly with anxiety. Now as in his earlier years, anxiety plays a unique rôle. Though it is the ego which experiences all affects, the ego finally learns to set one affect in motion (anxiety) instead of merely suffering emotions. As to the origin of anxiety, Freud traces it back to the birth trauma.[3] During evolutionary development, the bodily reaction to the trauma of birth has finally traced a neural groove, as it were, which is later activated by any danger situation. But the ego does not have to wait passively until danger arouses this pattern in an overwhelming anxiety attack. The ego can anticipate danger, apprehend it, and so arouse slight anxiety, a mere anxiety signal, which makes it possible to escape the real danger. In this way, Freud says, the ego can now dominate instinctual forces: controlled by the pleasure principle, they will withdraw from pain. However, it is the ego itself which feels the painful anxiety aroused by the imagined danger situation, and the ego which suffers when instinctual demands are obstructed.

At any rate, Freud assigns one origin to fear and anxiety and another to love and aggression. Anxiety is newly aroused every time the ego perceives danger, whether that danger is actually present or merely expected. Love and aggression remain discharge phenomena (affect charges) of instinctual drives. Anxiety is still a product of conflict as it was in his first formulation, but now the conflict is between the ego and any situation which threatens it while his first formulation implied that it was a conflict between the libido and an obstruction, which results in a transformation of libido into anxiety. But even in his later formulations danger really represents a barrier to the libido. Whether the immediate danger is external or internal, anxiety always means an inhibition of libidinal gratification. Hence Freud feels justified in continuing to hold that anxiety is converted libido but also his later conception that anxiety is "the universal reaction to the situation of danger." In his mature work on *The Problem of Anxiety,* he says:

> It is undeniable that in abstinence, in perverted interference with the normal discharge of sexual excitation, or in the diverting of the latter from its psychic elaboration, anxiety arises directly out of libido; that is to say,

there is brought about that state of helplessness of the ego in the face of excessive tension arising from ungratified need which results, as in birth, in the development of anxiety, so that there is again a possibility, which although obvious is of no great consequence, that it is precisely the excess of unutilized libido that finds its discharge in the form of anxiety. (1936, p. 81.)

At the same time, true anxiety is the reaction to a real external danger, newly aroused each time a dangerous situation is perceived or apprehended. Love and aggression, on the other hand, are active continually, they cathect objects, discard them, take objects belonging to another drive and can even change their instinctual aim. In this way, Freud's formulation gives a different status to different emotions, a division which is justified only on his assumption that love and aggression are coördinated to the sexual instinct while fear and anxiety are reactions to its obstruction. To common human experience, anger is newly aroused in response to obstruction just as is fear. And fear can become enduring anxiety in the same way as anger can become enduring hostility. For a phenomenological analysis, there is no such difference between the two emotions. That Freud himself has never felt quite easy over this division is shown by his often expressed doubts and his attempt to salvage anxiety as converted libido. If he could have done so, all emotions would have acquired the same status, they would all have become expressions of the instinctual drive.

Later analysts have developed one or the other aspect of the Freudian view, though none of them can be said to have worked out a consistent theory. *Fenichel* (1945), for instance, proposed that increased ego-mastery in genetic development results in a change in the character of the affect. While id-impulses reigned, emotion was their expression; hence affect was a discharge of drive tension:

Affects are originally archaic discharge syndromes that supplant voluntary actions under certain exciting conditions. Now the growing ego learns to "tame" affects and

to use them for its own anicipating purposes. (1945,
p. 43.)

Fenichel simply substitutes a conflict theory of emotion for
a discharge theory. But a conflict theory cannot deal with pleasant emotions, nor can it account for emotions as yet untamed.
Fenichel claims that emotion breaks through such taming only
when ego-control fails, hence full emotional expression represents a regression to an earlier stage, before ego-mastery was
complete. This, however, could only be applied to anxiety and
anger, the typical conflict emotions. It can obviously not be
held that the full expression of sexual emotion is a throwback
to an archaic and infantile stage.

Later on, Jacobson (1951) criticized both the discharge and
the safety-valve theory of emotion and pointed out

that not only all normal ego functions but particularly
direct instinct gratifications, such as the sexual act or
eating, are accompanied by intensive affective expressions.

She suggests that affect is the experience of either increase
or decrease of drive tension. The tensions may either be *within*
the id (sexual emotion and rage) or ego (fear and object interest); they may be *between ego and id* (fear of id-impulses,
shame, disgust,) but they may also be *between ego and superego*
(guilt-feelings, depression).

Thus Jacobson's theory implies that emotion is really increasing or decreasing excitation. While it is true that psychological processes are never stationary and must either increase
or decrease in intensity, it is by no means certain that every
increase or decrease in drive tension is an emotion or, for that
matter, that emotion is the experience of an instinctual drive.
Hunger, for instance, is not generally accepted as an emotion.
It may give rise to irritability or a genuine emotional state, but
often does not (for instance in a man like Gandhi who fasts for
a purpose). Decreased hunger will result in a feeling of relief,
but that again is not usually considered an emotion.

Rapaport (1953) recognizes various deficiencies of later theories and proposes to extend Freud's theory in such a way that the fruits of his earlier as well as his later insights will be combined into a systematic theory. He points out that the various emotions have inborn patterns of discharge and originally act as a safety valve for drive tension when the drive object is out of reach. At this stage, genetically the earliest, emotional experience is the "affect-charge" of the drive. The drive must reach a certain intensity before it goes into action. Gradually, the growing ego is able to delay both the expression of affect and the action. This is done by various measures of defense which result in part-drives with their own affects. New affect channels are created and derived motives use these affects as safety-valve. Thus a hierarchy of motives (drives) and affects is established together with the developing ego-structure. The ego which originally endured affects now can control them. Massive emotional outbursts still happen, either as result of weakened ego-control or as "regression in the service of the ego." Since emotional expression may arouse tension (anxiety) in turn, emotions may themselves become motives of defence.

Unfortunately, such a combination of theories blurs the distinctions Freud took such pains to establish. For Freud, anxiety never was the experienced affect-charge of a drive, nor the safety valve for drive tension. It was precisely because he could not assume an anxiety drive that Freud first suggested that anxiety must be converted libido (hence the deflected expression of a drive). Only after long search and uncertainty was he finally forced to the conclusion that anxiety must be the *response* to drive-obstruction, not its converted expression.

Rapaport uses the language of energetics for all affects, even anxiety. Freud's careful analysis of anxiety is forgotten as is his insight that a perceived external danger, later internalized, is the necessary and sufficient condition for the arousal of this particular emotion. Rapaport neglects the special status of anxiety when he speaks of the early discharge character of emotion. But his explanation of the later "taming" of affects refers to anxiety practically exclusively; imagined or expected annoyances or sexual pleasures may give id-satisfaction but can hardly be said to control id-impulses. Thus he assumes a developmental sequence which applies to emotion in general, but actually speaks first of one kind of emotion (love/aggression) and then of another (anxiety and related affects).

In summary it can be said that psychoanalytic theories of emotion are inclined to concentrate on the drive-tension aspect, hence imply that emotion is the experience of autonomic excitation, as contrasted with action which engages the motor system. For those emotions which are a direct expression of a drive (an affect charge) psychoanalytic formulations seem to follow the James-Lange theory. For anxiety, which Freud had reduced in principle to a fear of external danger, the perception of some danger is the necessary antecedent. Hence fear is newly aroused as the result of an estimate of danger, while love and aggression represent the sporadic awareness of a continuous drive. Later psychoanalytic theorists have not realized this fundamental dichotomy in Freud's treatment of emotions and so have either combined where combination is not possible (Fenichel, Rapaport,) or they have tried to reduce all emotions to one or other member of the dichotomy (Jacobson).

CONFLICT THEORIES OF EMOTION

Among academic psychologists the tendency has similarly been to concentrate on the sequence of bodily upset and motor action, even when their interest was focused on the psychological aspect of emotion rather than its physiological mechanism. The conflict theory of emotion, dating back to the last years of the 19th century when Dewey formulated it, was well established in the Twenties. Its great attraction, no doubt, was the ease with which the arousal of emotion could be explained. The bodily upset seemed a convenient proof that emotion was the result of some obstruction of goal-directed action, hence in itself disturbing. Either the James-Lange theory or the thalamic theory could be used with equal facility to explain the mechanism of emotional disturbance as a result of conflict. While Dewey espoused the

James-Lange theory, later conflict theorists used the thalamic theory which permitted the notion that the cortex could be disturbed in its function by a conflictful situation so that thalamic excitation could break through cortical inhibition.

While *Paulhan* (1930) considered emotion as the result of a simple arrest of motor tendencies which resulted in an overflow of excitation, *Hodge* (1935) thought emotion is aroused when higher brain centers cannot initiate an appropriate response to the situation, or when such response is not successful. For him, "emotional reactions are inversely proportional to the ability of the higher centers of the brain to meet a given situation." *Darrow* (1935) distinguished between excited emotions (rage, fear,) and emotions without excitement (sorrow, remorse, embarrassment, amusement). Only the excited emotions are hypothalamic phenomena. They occur when a serious external threat produces a conflict of impulses in the cortex (functional decortication) which releases the hypothalamic centers. The other emotions are the result of a psychological interpretation of the situation.

As both Darrow and Dewey have seen, a conflict theory cannot account for all emotions. But there are other psychologists who make conflict a criterion of emotion in such a way that they either neglect any emotion which is not the result of a conflict, or doubt its status as an emotion. *Madison Bentley* (1924) for instance, who considers that emotion is the reaction to a predicament, doubts whether joy is a real emotion because it is hard to conceive of a joyful predicament. *Howard* (1928) for whom emotion is a confused and disturbed state, thinks that it has no value at all but represents a defect in human nature; he implies that constructive or creative emotions probably are not emotional in nature.

A conflict theory of emotion is an incomplete theory because it can only account for some emotions but not for all. Neither psychoanalytic theory nor a conflict theory can resolve the dichotomy, nor are they altogether successful in evading a solution.

ENERGY RELEASE THEORY (E. DUFFY, 1934)

Eventually, it became clear to some theorists that emotion as a disturbance, or an awareness of drives, a complex of sensations or an ill-defined behavior pattern did not deserve separate status as a psychological phenomenon. Meyer (1933) and Duffy (1934, 1951,) in short succession suggested that emotion had been little more than a chapter heading which should be superseded by more basic categories now that psychology had come of age and no more needed to depend on common sense categories.

Duffy pointed out that the energy released in human behavior had so far been conceived as specific to the various channels of release. Hence separate driving forces were postulated to correspond to these channels: drives, instincts, motives, emotions. The common factor in all these concepts is a *release* of energy and its *direction* toward specific objects. Hence Duffy suggests that the term "emotion" should be discarded altogether and be replaced by classifying behavior according to the degree of energy mobilization and direction. She says:

> The degree of energy mobilization . . . is the extent of release of the stored energy of the organism through metabolic activity in the tissues. This appears to occur in a continuum, from a low point during deep sleep to a high point during frantic effort or excitement . . . (1951, p. 32.)

There is no doubt that energy mobilization and direction can be inferred in every emotion. But there is also no doubt that the same can be said of every other psychological or even physiological process.

To analyze behavior, we must make distinctions. The obvious divisions are those which are given by immediate experience: sense perception is different from thinking and both are different from wanting or striving. Degrees of energy mobilization cannot be readily differentiated either in experience or by observation: extreme effort and emotional excitement, for instance, may have the same measurable energy output, but as experienced, effort is laborious while excitement is not. Hence the conditions of energy release are diametrically opposed and will have to be taken into account in our prediction of behavior. Where Duffy assumes a continuum of energy expenditure, to be measured by physiological indices, there are genuine qualitative differences, even in this example. There are also qualitative differences between various emotions which do not correspond to quantitative differences in energy output: fear, love and anger may have the same degree of excitation but the energy expenditure does not necessarily vary concomitantly; love and anger may have the same degree and direction of energy release, but nobody would confuse them.

When we remember Hebb's finding that objective description of emotional responses (which certainly included intensity and direction) yielded a meaningless pattern useless for prediction, we are bound to conclude that common experience which has always distinguished emotion from other behavior patterns, should not be discarded unless we have something better to put in its place.

ATTITUDE THEORY OF EMOTION (NINA BULL, 1951.)

In contrast of Duffy, Nina Bull reports that there are objectively distinct behavior patterns in different emotions produced hypnotically. She suggests that the distinction between emotional experience and emotional expression is but a crude approximation to a whole series of changes: the individual reacts to an emotional stimulus with a preparatory motor attitude which gives rise to feeling as well as to action. "We feel angry as a result of *readiness* to strike, and feel afraid as a result of *readiness* to run away. . . ." (1951, p. 6.) This readiness includes a neural disposition which arouses an *actual motor attitude* when activated. As soon as the motor attitude is aroused, it is felt as an orientation toward or away from something, that is as emotional experience.

The "neural disposition" implies some definite brain structure activated during emotion. Nina Bull accepts Papez' theory of emotion which implies that one brain mechanism activates all types of emotion, hence it is not clear how the various motor patterns become differentiated. Moreover, there is no indication how the neural disposition is activated. What selects the motor attitude of anger rather than of fear? It cannot be the stimulus because the stimulus does not always arouse an emotion and if it does it may not always arouse the same emotion. The question how a cold perception turns into an emotion, or, to use Bull's terms, how a cold perception activates a neural disposition so that a specific motor attitude is aroused, is left unanswered. The emotional situation is evaluated only after the motor attitude has risen to awareness, hence has no part in this activation.

While the careful distinction between neural disposition, motor attitude and action is a genuine contribution, and the substitution of a "readiness to act" for overt action is a much-appreciated refinement of the James-Lange theory, the attitude theory of emotion suffers from all the other deficiencies of the older view. In addition, the theory assumes that the motor attitude rises into awareness as felt emotion but also that this mental component is needed "to whip the motor process into shape and give it point" (1951, p. 10) otherwise, the motor attitude may merely be felt as vague suspense, excitement, restlessness. If the "readiness to strike" is felt as anger rather than any other emotion because the motor pattern is specific to begin with, no mental component is needed to whip it into shape. If it is not felt as anger unless there is "a clear-cut mental attitude . . . to give the sense of aim and purpose", there is no guarantee that the motor attitude arouses the mental attitude, in fact, we would expect exactly the opposite.

MOTIVATIONAL THEORY (LEEPER, 1948).

After this all-time low, when emotion was denied even the status of a chapter heading, or was made to trail in the wake of a motor attitude, the theory of emotion found a defender in R. Leeper who tried to restore it to its rightful place in the life of the human being and animal. Perhaps he realized that emotion was bound to be suspect as long as psychologists saw it only as a disturber of the peace. At any rate, he insisted that emotion is itself purposeful, that fear does induce to flight, anger to attack.

In a spirited criticism of the concept of emotion as disorganized and disorganizing, Leeper points out that organization of one process always implies some disorganization, namely that of interfering processes. Emotion itself is always organized: viscerally, because the visceral changes are favorable for behavior consistent with the emotion; behaviorally, because emotional action is organized toward fight or flight or a friendly approach; experientially, because attention is concentrated on the object of emotion.

Leeper admits that emotional organization may not always be useful to the person (e.g. in stage fright which is organized toward withdrawing from the situation). But the term organization means simply harmonious function of the parts concerned in the emotional process without implying harmonious functioning in the organism as a whole. However, extreme emotion (terror, extreme rage) may disorganize emotional action; but Leeper insists that a process should be assessed according to its normal rather than its excessive effects (e.g. excessive salt intake has different effects from the effects of a balanced diet including normal amounts of salt).

Thus all emotions, as long as they do not become excessive, have an organization which is directed and sustained. Hence

emotional processes operate primarily as motives. It means that they are processes which arouse, sustain and direct activity. (1948, p. 17.)

As motives, emotions are aroused in a psychological situation:

. . . it is quite a possible hypothesis that the perception of the emotion-producing situation produces the emotional process (which may have a conscious aspect to it, and which may produce also an autonomic discharge, either directly or via some subcortical centers, and which may then be reinforced or supported by widespread bodily changes). And it is quite a possible hypothesis that this emotional process . . . then operates to motivate behavior. (1948, p. 18.)

Hence the interpretation of the situation arouses both emotional experience and behavior which motivates action. Leeper points out that this explanation is usually rejected by psychologists as naïve common sense because of the supposedly unsound assumption of mind interacting with body which is implied in it. He makes the obvious point that such interaction is implied also when the James-Lange or thalamic theories are given as explanation of emotional experience. We might point out in addition that such interaction could be implied even in the simple statement that the driver steps on the brake because he sees a red light. But on the modern assumption that the human being is a psychosomatic unit instead of the possessor of two separate entities, mind and body, there can be no objection to assuming a connection between experience and behavior.

Leeper's insistence on emotion as facilitating appropriate action has been timely and constructive. However, a theory of emotion must also indicate the relation of emotion as an organized process to the larger organization of the personality as a whole. Non-emotional goal-directed action is determined by the person. But goal-directed action induced by emotion carries the person along and can be resisted only with difficulty. What still needs to be explained is the relation of emotional action with its curiously compelling character to other goals important for the person as a whole.

P. T. Young (1949) answers Leeper's criticism by pointing out that Leeper himself distinguishes between emotions which are organized and organize (emotions of normal intensity) and emotions which disorganize (excessive emotions). Hence emotions cannot always be organized. Young's objection seems to be legitimate and can be answered only if disorganization is explained as the physiological effect of emotion on action. As Arnold (1945) has pointed out, extreme rage results in massive muscular contractions, hence makes for incoördination. And terror paralyzes because intense sympathetic stimulation interferes with muscular contractions. Thus emotion urges to action (is organized in a certain direction) but its physiological concomitants may disorganize behavior, that is, make effective action impossible.

For Young himself, an emotion is

> an acute affective disturbance within the individual as a whole, arising from psychological situations and manifest in conscious experience, behavior, and especially through bodily changes which are regulated by the autonomic nervous system. (1949, p. 189.)

Emotional upsets are the result of motivated action. "In every emotional upset some motivating factor is thwarted, or satisfied, or excites the individual" (1943, p. 392). And a motive is any factor which arouses, sustains, or changes bodily activity. At best, an emotional upset seems to be a sign that there is overt action which has been aroused in some way.

Emotional upsets are only one of a number of affective processes among which Young includes feelings of pleasantness or unpleasantness, moods, attitudes, interests, organic aches, hunger, thirst, fatigue. These processes are not necessarily disturbances (e.g. feelings of pleasantness, a cheerful mood), do not have to be aroused by psychological situations (e.g. hunger or thirst), do not necessarily accompany motivated action (e.g. organic aches), and do not obviously excite the autonomic nervous system (e.g. interests). Hence the distinguishing marks of emotion do not fit these processes. Young includes them under "affective" phenomena together with emotion because they have a polarity not found among other psychological processes. Such a polarity is undoubtedly present in pleasantness-unpleasantness, interest-aversion and the like. But organic aches have no such polarity, neither do emotions.

Young's view makes of emotion an incident in motivated action, satisfying, disturbing, exciting, but cannot account for emotion which occurs without overt action. His theory provides no criterion by which affective phenomena can be distinguished from other psychological activities. In its very breadth of scope, his theory demonstrates the problems encountered by a comprehensive theory of emotion rather than their possible solution.

BEHAVIORISTIC FORMULATIONS

Logically enough, behaviorists of all persuasions consider emotion as an aspect of instinctive behavior. From Watson to Skinner and Hull, emotion is a modification of drive. For Watson, emotion is

> a hereditary "pattern reaction" involving profound changes of the bodily mechanism as a whole, but particularly of the visceral and glandular system. (1919, p. 195.)

This is aroused in the case of anger, fear and "love" by specific stimulus situations (restraint, loud sounds, stroking). Gradually the instinctive pattern becomes modified in the course of development. In the adult, it is only recognized as facilitation or inhibition of response:

> Apparently the hereditary pattern as a whole gets broken up. At any rate, it largely disappears (the parts never disappear) except under unusual conditions, and there can be noted only a reinforcement or inhibition of the habit and instinctive . . . activities taking place at the moment. (1919, p. 197.)

Skinner and Hull are fairly close to Watson in their formulations. For Skinner (1938), emotion represents changes in reflex strength; for Hull (1943), the concept of emotion is neither used nor defined but is subsumed under increases and decreases in drive strength.

For Tolman (1932), feelings and emotions are "immanent determinants of behavior", which occur in sequence:

> (a) sign-gestalt expectations of resulting physiological goods and bads as "promised" and "threatened" by the immediate stimulus-situations; (b) incipient movements and visceral activities resulting, in physiological fashion, from the release of these sign-gestalt-expectations; and (c) resultant organic and kinaesthetic stimulations, (1932, p. 264.)

Interestingly enough, the sign-Gestalt expectations of promised "goods" and threatened "bads" is a fairly close equivalent of the intuitive estimate of the situation which we have discussed before. For Tolman, the situation is estimated and so induces to incipient action which produces sensory consequences. The only stage left out in the sequence is the awareness of attraction and repulsion, an omission which is to be expected in a behavioristic account. For Tolman, (as for William James)

> The emotion, as "conscious feeling", is but the complex of resultant organic and kinesthetic "sensations", which enter "conscious awareness". (1932, p. 266.)

In so far as behavioristic formulations assume that emotion is a change in drive strength (Watson, Skinner, Hull,) they suffer from the same disadvantages as does Duffy's concept. The observed variation in drive strength does not reliably distinguish emotional from non-emotional behavior, or one emotion from the other. Tolman's theory supplements the James-Lange theory by accounting for the emotion-producing quality of some perceptions, but does not escape the objections raised against the older theory that emotion is felt before physiological changes can be sensed.

EXISTENTIALIST NOTIONS

Sartre's theory of emotion. (1948.) Jean-Paul Sartre criticizes psychological theories of emotion tellingly by pointing out that they neglect the human experience and human significance of emotion in their zeal for concrete and if possible "objective" facts. Emotion is a way of experiencing reality. Since we as human beings are aware of this experience and can reflect upon it, the objective approach discards the most valuable evidence. For Sartre,

> the emotion signifies, in its own way, the whole of consciousness or, if we put ourselves on the existential level, of human reality. . . . That being so, it is impossible to consider emotion as a psycho-physiological disorder. It has its essence, its particular structures, its laws of appearing, and its signification. It cannot come to human reality *from the outside*. On the contrary, it is man who *assumes* his emotions, and consequently emotion is an organized form of human existence. (1948, p. 18.) (Sartre's italics.)

Sartre sees the signification of emotion in the unique relationship to external reality which it indicates. For him, emotion always has an object-reference:

> Emotional consciousness is, at first, consciousness *of* the world. . . . It is evident . . . that the man who is afraid is afraid *of* something. Even if it is a matter of one of those indefinite anxieties which one experiences in the dark, in a sinister and deserted passageway etc., one is afraid *of* certain aspects of the night, of the world. (1948, p. 51.) (Sartre's italics.)

As long as the emotion lasts, it maintains that focus on the object. It is an unreflective awareness of the object, not an awareness that the subject has an emotion. For Sartre, emotion occurs when the world becomes too difficult. When all ways to action are barred yet we must act, we transform the world by magic. This transformation of the real world into a world of magic is made possible by emotion. Action which had become impossible now becomes unnecessary.

> Flight is a fainting which is enacted; it is a magical behavior which consists of denying the dangerous object

with our whole body by subverting the vectorial structure of the space we live in by abruptly creating a potential direction on the *other side*. It is a way of forgetting it, of denying it. (1948, p. 63.) (Sartre's italics.)

Sartre uses the same principle to analyze joy. Here the magical transformation becomes necessary because the possession of something we love can never be instantaneous or complete. Joy is an attempt to make it so.

> Joy is a magical behavior which tends by incantation to realize the possession of the desired object as instantaneous totality. This behavior is accompanied by the certainty that the possession will be realized sooner or later, but it seeks to anticipate this possession. (p. 69.)

Thus emotion sets up "a magical world by using the body as a means of incantation." At the same time, the physiological disturbance testifies to the sincerity with which the magical belief is held. Emotion originates in a "spontaneous and lived degradation of consciousness in the face of the world." (1948, p. 77.) Consciousness endows the world with magical qualities as a last resort, when it becomes impossible to cope with reality. As a result consciousness sinks to a lower level of awareness, into passivity. In its passivity, it is taken captive. Objects first attract it, then trap it. Once consciousness is enmeshed in emotion, the emotion tends to perpetuate itself.

Emotions enmesh consciousness and overwhelm it because the magical quality they confer upon the world seems to be enduring:

> The horrible is now within the thing, at the heart of the thing. It is its affective texture; it is constitutive of it ... The horrible is not only the present state of the thing; it is threatened for the future; it spreads itself over the whole future and darkens it; it is the revelation of the meaning of the world. (1948, pp. 80-81.)

According to Sartre, this magical quality is an aspect of the world which penetrates all our relations with reality. It is not only conferred by emotion, it is given in reality itself. In fact, only because there really is magic in the world can emotion seize upon it, diffuse it or concentrate it on a given object.

Thus Sartre posits a world of instruments for action which is strictly deterministic, and another world of magic which "acts upon consciousness immediately," offers no instruments for action and can only be combatted by "absolute and massive modifications of the world" in emotion. Hence emotion is

> The return of consciousness to the magical attitude, one of the great attitudes which are essential to it, with appearance of the correlative world, the magical world. (1948, p. 33.)

In his insistence that emotion can only be understood as a special relationship of the human being to the external world, Sartre's theory represents a much-needed corrective. There is no doubt that any emotion refers to an object and clings to it as long as it remains an emotion. It is also true that emotional awareness is unreflective, immediate, object-bound. Nevertheless, it remains a reaction to the object, therefore is active.

Not all emotions are reactions to difficulties—this would be another version of a conflict theory of emotion. Nor does emotion deny its object. If it did, not only the need for action but the need for emotion would be over, for Sartre admitted that emotion continually refers back to the object and clings to it. If flight is "a fainting which is enacted" and fainting is an effective denial of the object, as Sartre says, then fainting is also the end of emotion. Emotion does urge to action: fear induces to flight, anger to attack, love to approach. To explain such action away by interpreting it as a denial of the object is to do violence to the very experience, the very awareness to which Sartre appeals in his analysis.

If emotion is not necessarily the reaction to overwhelming difficulties, then consciousness is not necessarily passive. Since emotion itself signifies "the whole of consciousness, of human reality", it is merely poetic license to speak of consciousness as being passive, degraded to a lower level when this same consciousness had to be active in establishing a magic world. The compelling character of emotion is sufficiently explained by the apparent permanence of the harmful, the horrible, the enjoyable aspects. To support it further by calling it a magical attitude is to label without explaining. It may be magic that anything in the world can have significance for us, can aim at us personally, so to speak. But it is so only if we assume that living beings are unrelated and isolated monads living in an alien and fragmented world.

It is interesting to reflect that Sartre's approach is the exact opposite of the behavioristic account. While behaviorists ignore human experience and awareness, Sartre makes consciousness explain itself and even posit itself. At both extremes, the system must be maintained by anthropomorphic interpretations. For the behaviorist, the brain or an assumed drive or reflex reserve, initiates, selects, and directs action. For the existentialist, consciousness acts or is passive, confers qualities upon objects, and existence upon itself. In the pursuit of both extremes it is overlooked that it is the human being who acts, that he does not create either himself or his consciousness, but neither does he act out his drives automatically.

FUNCTIONAL THEORIES

There are some theories of emotion which seem to take the middle road. *Michotte* (1950) for instance reports an interesting experiment which is relevant to his theory of emotion.

Two upright colored rectangles, A and B, moving along a slot, were shown to the subjects. The rectangles moved at various speeds, with each other, toward or away from each other. In describing these movements, the observers very rarely gave a purely objective description, for instance "A pushes B forward". Rather,

> they often had an obvious tendency to complete these
> indications by comparisons . . . which implied emotional

states, attitudes, tendencies attributed to the objects. (1950, p. 115.)

The subject would say "It is as though B was afraid when A approached, and ran off", or "A joins B, they fall out, have a quarrel, and B goes off by himself" or again "It is like a cat coming up to a mouse and suddenly springing on it and carrying it off." In general Michotte found that rapid movement of the rectangles toward each other was interpreted as violence or anger; movement in the same direction, as flight; a slow approach as gentleness; slow movement in the same direction after contact as "going together"—to a hideout or a lovers' rendez-vous.

Though each subject is strictly an observer, he evidently has the impulse to see the two rectangles as affecting each other in some way. He seems to judge from his own experience that a situation which affects someone (even a rectangle) personally must be emotional in character. Michotte points out that this functional connection between subject-object becomes much clearer when the observer's own movements are involved, when he approaches or withdraws, pushes or is being pushed. Here he is no more merely an observer, he is the agent, and the movements appear no longer the expression of an emotion, they become one of its constituents.

For Michotte, emotion is a functional connection between subject and object, established by a reaction of the person.

It is *I* who repels, who embraces, who avoids, etc. For the observer the reactions which he witnesses are conveyed by an object distinct from himself; it is that person whom he sees over there who goes toward the other and shakes his hand. In the case of the agent, on the other hand, the action is not that of another person, nor is it properly speaking the action of his own body (as a thing); it is *himself* who acts in such a way toward such and such a person or thing or who feels this affective reaction for this person or thing. (1950, p. 124.)

The other person's movement (e.g. an assailant hitting him) is similarly interpreted as being caused by the other and affecting himself.

Thus emotion depends on an immediate estimate of the function of the object in relation to the subject. It is a felt functional connection. Michotte points out that such an estimate is possible to animals as well. In man, however, there is an additional factor,

> for he is not merely a being which "feels", but also one which "thinks", and "knows", so the emotions he experiences usually have an intellectual aspect. Onto the felt connection is superimposed the knowledge of the *abstract* relation implied in that connection. A man "feels" himself attracted or repelled by an object, and at the same time he "is aware" of the attraction or repulsion, he knows it is happening. (1950, p. 126.)

For Michotte, the "functional connection" between object and subject is established by an intuitive judgment which may be supplemented by reflection but is not itself reflective; hence emotion is possible to animals as much as to human beings.

Gemelli (1949) who has done considerable experimental work on the physiology and psychology of emotion during the last thirty years, has recently worked out a consistent theoretical formulation from a very similar point of view.

He first distinguishes feeling from emotion by suggesting that feelings should be called "objective" because they seem to adhere to the object, while emotions are "subjective feelings" since they involve the person as a whole. Objective feelings are always a reaction to some sensation (e.g. feelings of hunger, thirst, well-being, discomfort, anguish, lightness, strength, etc.), are elementary and primitive and cannot be further defined. Emotions or "subjective feelings" are produced when the subject "considers a situation or an object or a person in relation to himself." (1949, p. 207.)

To illustrate the difference between objective and subjective feelings, Gemelli quotes some introspective reports of which I will quote only one:

> The sound was sweet and pleasant; but this pleasure gave way quickly to another pleasure which was more subtle. The sound evoked in me the memory of a particular incident in my recent vacation during which I heard this music; and I felt my soul pervaded with joy. (1949, p. 211.)

The two types of feeling have a distinctive character:

> While the objective feelings, or affective sensations are related to sensory stimuli as such, and are commonly considered as qualities of the sensation itself, the so-called subjective feelings which can also be initiated by a sensation are largely dependent on another content of consciousness, a memory evoked by the sensation, an idea or even a perception or an image. (1949, p. 210.)

Both objective and subjective feelings are regulators of action. There is an intimate relation between feelings and action tendencies (instincts) so that they can both be "produced conjointly—a sensation being sufficient to touch off the entire biological complex of which they both are part." (1949, p. 300.) In someone who is fond of sweets, for instance, the sight of candy immediately touches off an objective feeling of pleasure "and the awakened pleasure stimulates him to react by helping himself. . . ." (1949, p. 300.) In the same way, subjective feelings or emotions are joined to instinctive tendencies which aim at the satisfaction of organismic needs or evaluate objects, situations and people. Though feelings regulate actions by making us aware of action tendencies aroused by various objects, these action tendencies may not always urge to the most effective action, neither may the action toward which they urge always be in the best interest of the person as a whole.

Therefore the feeling reaction must be complemented by an intellectual evaluation of the situation. The action finally decided upon may either implement the felt tendency or be contrary to it. Hence feelings are only one element of action.

The action tendencies themselves (often called instincts) are evoked when the object is seen as affecting the person:

> A knife seen by the subject does not by itself alone awaken any biological complex; it is purely an object of perception. But if the subject in perceiving such an object, has also knowledge that it has a dark significance, because of the special circumstances in which he sees it, so that it constitutes a menace, immediately there will occur in him a movement of repulsion, with a general feeling of disgust, resulting in the still more general feeling known as fear. (1949, p. 305.)

It seems that for Gemelli there is always an objective feeling which is then followed by the emotion proper (the subjective feeling). This is an interesting suggestion which, however, would have to be substantiated by closer analysis. The transition from objective to subjective feeling seems to require a change of regard which may occur in some emotions but need not occur in all.

The action tendency is organized as a neurological pattern, an inherited predisposition which is activated when a situation is perceived as desirable, menacing, annoying. Gemelli mentions that this is the same "neural predisposition" which is postulated by Nina Bull in her attitude theory of emotion. However, it is important to realize that Gemelli's theory provides for an activation of this predisposition by a *psychological* reaction, an estimate of the situation in relation to the subject, while for Nina Bull the psychological reaction follows the activated motor attitude. Gemelli holds that the estimate of the situation arouses the motor attitude and at the same time first the objective, then the subjective feeling. Hence Nina Bull sees her analysis as a refinement of the James-Lange theory, while Gemelli points out that emotion must be understood from a functional point of view, as the result of a perceived special relationship between object and subject which also arouses the appropriate action tendency.

Following the same lead, *Arnold and Gasson* (1954) recently suggested that emotion is the *felt tendency toward or away from an object*. It is aroused when the object is seen as affecting the person either beneficially or harmfully. This estimate of the object resulting in a felt attraction and repulsion, completes sense perception. The object perceived is also judged to be suitable or unsuitable and is accordingly approached or avoided. Action is initiated by the felt action tendency and completed (in human beings) by a choice of reasonable actions.

Arnold and Gasson show that *the tendency toward* things and persons (love) is basic, for such objects in the external world can complete and satisfy the subject. The *tendency away* from something is an attempt to preserve the integrity of the subject, or to preserve the things needed for his continuing integrity. Hence fear, aversion, dislike, is a response secondary to love because it is the response to something which threatens the subject or the things he loves. Emotion can thus be classified as positive and negative.

All organismic functions, perceptual and appetitive (emotive) have degrees of impulsion: When there is enough light, we see effortlessly; but in dim light we peer, we make an effort to see. In the same way, we feel an easy attraction to something which is available, but we long and strive for the same thing when it is out of reach. Hence emotions can also be distinguished according to their degree of impulsion as those which simply tend toward their objects and those which contend against difficulties. As examples of the first kind are listed love, desire (i.e. simple wanting), joy and delight; hate, aversion, sorrow or sadness. Contending emotions are: fear, which urges us to a strenuous effort to escape; anger which urges us to attack the obstacle to a cherished goal; longing or striving which urges us to make every effort to attain our goal; desperation which rails against the obstacles that forever keep us from the goal.

Such action tendencies are called "instincts" only when they urge towards objects the possession of which is imperative either for the preservation of the individual (e.g. food) or of the species (mate). But all these tendencies do depend on innate neural patterns which are activated as soon as the relationship of object to subject is perceived. Since felt tendencies urge the subject toward or away from things in the external world, emotions must influence action. But action does not depend only on emotion which is based on the intuitive unreasoned estimate of the situation. With human beings, action depends also on a reasoned evaluation of the goal and the available and effective means to it. Hence emotions may sometimes facilitate and sometimes hinder reasonable action. Biologically, emotions are useful because they facilitate the action to which they urge. In animals, they are reliable guides to action in a normal environment. In human beings, they often hinder reasonable actions which are neither attractive nor immediately rewarding.

In human beings, emotions must be educated. If they are aroused as the result of an estimate that something is desirable or undesirable, it should be possible to train this estimate. That this can be done is shown, for instance, in the development of various food likes and dislikes which can be acquired accidentally but can also be trained. Since long-range goals are established by the person and often have aspects which are not immediately attractive (e.g. learning a language) these felt tendencies toward something desirable and away from something undesirable must be brought under the control of the person if they are to be a help rather than a hindrance in personality integration.

Finally, Arnold and Gasson distinguish feelings from emotions by pointing out that feelings are reactions to the way in which an object affects organismic functioning, while emotions are immediate reactions to the way in which it affects the person. In Gemelli's example, for instance, hearing a pleasant sound means smooth auditory functioning which is experienced as pleasantness. When the sound reminds the subject of some joyful incident, he reacts to that incident as it affects him as a person, hence the feeling is swallowed up in emotion. According to this view, however, the only feelings recognized are pleasantness-unpleasantness, while Gemelli lists feelings of strength, lightness, anguish, etc. in addition.

Our survey has shown that some theories of emotion emphasize one aspect at the price of another. If that happens, the theory becomes one-sided. In general, the triad *emotional experience, expression* (bodily changes) and *action* must be covered to give a balanced theory. If one aspect is unduly emphasized we fall into an extreme position. A balanced theory must explain the nature of emotional experience and its differentiation from unemotional experience; the mechanism mediating bodily changes; and emotion as a factor in goal-directed action. There are other problems which must be solved before a theory will be complete: the sequence from perception to emotion, i.e. how is emotion aroused; the relationship of various kinds of emotion, and the relation of emotion to other affective processes; and the significance of emotion for personality integration.

Though the scope of a theory of emotion is wide, present-day experimental and clinical resources are similarly extensive. Hence it is not too optimistic to hope for an early integration of such findings which will be the basis of an adequate theory of emotion.

FOOTNOTES

[1] Surveys which are experimentally oriented can be found in: Harry Helson (ed.), 1951, *Theoretical foundations of psychology*, Chapter on Feeling and Emotion by J. G. Beebe-Center; S. S. Stevens (ed.) 1951, *Handbook of experimental psychology*, Chapter on Emotion, by D. B. Lindsley. There are earlier surveys by Hunt (1939 and 1941), Lund (1939), Ruckmick (1936) and Young (1942), while an exhaustive treatment of theories of feeling and emotion by Gardiner, Metcalf and Beebe-Center dates back to 1937. The two symposium volumes on Feelings and Emotions edited by Martin L. Reymert (1928 and 1950) provide a good cross-section of the field.

[2] Recent experimental work seems to have confirmed that anger and fear are accompanied by different physiological states. Wolff (1951) reported that anger resulted in reddening and swelling of the mucous membrane in the gastric fistula of a patient observed for many years. At

PRESENT-DAY PSYCHOLOGY

the same time, motility and gastric acidity increased. Wolff listed similar changes in the mucosa of nose, colon, and vagina during anger and resentment in many other patients. Fear produced the opposite effects (pale mucosa, decreased gastric secretion and motility). Milhorat and Diethelm (1947) reported that an adrenalin-like substance could be found in the blood during anxiety without tension (fear) while an acetylcholine-like substance was found during resentment (anger). When the emotional state was one of mixed anxiety and tension (worry) both substances were present.

3 While Freud insists that anxiety is the response to an objective danger which was first aroused during birth, he sharply repudiates Rank's attempt to trace childhood phobias directly to the birth trauma. For him, fear or anxiety is always aroused by actual danger. Birth is merely the first occasion of danger, which has resulted in a psycho-physiological disposition to anxiety. Every later danger situation activates the disposition because it is a repetition of the earlier danger. (1936, pp. 71-79.)

REFERENCES

1 Arnold, Magda B. Physiological differentiation of emotional states. *Psych. Rev.*, 1945, *52*, 35-48.

2 —— An excitatory theory of emotion. In: *Feelings and Emotions.* Martin L. Reymert, (Ed.) New York, McGraw-Hill, 1950.

3 Arnold, Magda B., and Gasson, J. A. Feelings and emotions as dynamic factors in personality integration. In: *The Human Person,* M. B. Arnold and J. A. Gasson, (Ed.) New York: Ronald Press, 1954.

4 Bard, Philip. The neuro-humoral basis of emotional reactions. In: *Handbook of general experimental psychology.* C. Murchison (Ed.) Worcester, Mass.: Clark Univ. Press, 1934.

5 Bentley, Madison. *The field of psychology,* 1924.

6 Bull, Nina. The attitude theory of emotion. *Nerv. Ment. Dis. Monogr.* New York: Copyright by Smith Ely Jeliffe Trust, Carel Goldschmidt, Trustee, Coolidge Foundation, 1951.

7 Cannon, W. B. The James-Lange theory of emotion. *Am. J. Psych.,* 1927, *39*, 106-124.

8 —— Again the James-Lange and the thalamic theories of emotion. *Psych. Rev.,* 1931, *38*, 281-295.

9 Darrow, C. W. Emotion as relative functional decortication: the role of conflict. *Psych. Rev.,* 1935, *42*, 566-578.

10 Dunlap, Knight. Emotion as a dynamic background. In: *Feelings and emotions.* Martin L. Reymert (Ed.) Worcester, Mass.: Clark Univ. Press, 1928.

11 Duffy, Elizabeth. Emotion: an example of the need for reorientation in psychology. *Psych. Rev.,* 1934, *41*, 184-198.

12 —— The concept of energy mobilization. *Psych. Rev.,* 1951, *58*, 30-40.

13 Fenichel, O. *The psychoanalytic theory of neurosis.* New York: W. W. Norton & Co., 1945.

14 Freud, Sigmund. *The problem of anxiety.* Tr. H. A. Bunker. New York: Psychoanalytic Quarterly Press and W. W. Norton & Co., 1936.

[15] Gardiner, H. M., Metcalf, R. C., and Beebe-Center, J. G. *Feeling and emotion.* New York: American Book Co., 1937.

[16] Gemelli, Agostino. Orienting concepts in the study of affective states. *J. Nerv. Ment. Dis.*, 1949, *110*, Pt. I, 198-214, Pt. II, 299-314.

[17] Hebb, D. O. Emotion in man and animal: an analysis of the intuitive processes of recognition. *Psych. Rev.*, 1946a, *53*, 88-106.

[18] —— On the nature of fear. *Psych. Rev.*, 1946b, *53*, 259-276.

[19] —— *The organization of behavior.* New York: John Wiley & Sons, 1949.

[20] Helson, Harry, (Ed.) *Theoretical foundations of psychology.* New York, Van Nostrand, 1951.

[21] Hodge, F. A. The emotions in a new role. *Psych. Rev.*, 1935, *42*, 555-565.

[22] Howard, D. T. A functional theory of the emotions. In: *Feelings and emotions.* Martin L. Reymert (Ed.) Worcester, Mass.: Clark Univ. Press, 1928.

[23] Hull, Clark L. *Principles of behavior.* New York: D. Appleton-Century Co., 1943.

[24] Hunt, W. A. A critical review of current approaches to affectivity. *Psych. Bull.*, 1939, *36*, 807-828.

[25] —— Recent developments in the field of emotion. *Psych. Bull.*, 1941, *38*, 249-276.

[26] Jacobson, Edith. The psychoanalytic theory of affects. (1951) Ms. (Abstract under the title: Problems in the psychoanalytic theory of affects. *Psychoanal. Quarterly*, 1952, *21*, 459-460.)

[27] James, William. The physical basis of emotion. *Psych. Rev.*, 1894, *1*, 516-529.

[28] Leeper, R. W. A motivational theory of emotion to replace "emotion as disorganized response." *Psych. Rev.*, 1948, *55*, 5-21.

[29] Lund, F. H. *Emotions: their psychological, physiological and educative implications.* New York: Ronald Press, 1939.

[30] McDougall, William. *The energies of men.* New York: Chas. Scribner's Sons, 1933.

[31] Masserman, J. H. The hypothalamus in psychiatry. *Am. J. Psychiat.*, 1942, *98*, 633-637.

[32] —— A biodynamic psychoanalytic approach to the problems of feeling and emotion. In: *Feelings and emotions.* Martin L. Reymert, (Ed.) New York: McGraw-Hill, 1950.

[33] Meyer, Max F. That whale among the fishes—the theory of emotions. *Psych. Rev.*, 1933, *40*, 242-300.

[34] Michotte, Albert E. The emotions regarded as functional connections. In: *Feelings and emotions.* Martin L. Reymert (Ed.) New York: McGraw-Hill, 1950.

[35] Milhorat, A. T., and Diethelm, C. Substances in blood of patients during emotional states. Effect on the isolated rabbit intestine. *Federation Proc.*, 1947, *6*, 165-166.

[36] Newman, E. B., Perkins, F. T., and Wheeler, R. H. Cannon's theory of emotion: a critique. *Psych. Rev.*, 1930, *37*, 305-326.

37 Papez, J. W. A proposed mechanism of emotion. *Arch. Neur. & Psychiat.*, 1937, *38*, 725-743.

38 Paulhan, F. *The laws of feeling.* Tr. C. K. Ogden. New York: Harcourt, Brace & Co., 1930.

39 Rapaport, David. *On the psychoanalytic theory of affects.* Ms. 1953.

40 Reymert, Martin L. (Ed.) *Feelings and emotions.* The Wittenberg Symposium. Worcester, Mass.: Clark Univ. Press, 1928.

41 Reymert, Martin L. *Feelings and emotions.* The Mooseheart Symposium. New York: McGraw-Hill, 1950.

42 Ruckmick, C. A. *Psychology of feeling and emotion.* New York: McGraw-Hill, 1936.

43 Rylander, Gosta. Personality analysis before and after frontal lobotomy. In: The frontal lobes. *Res. Publ. Ass. f. Res. Nerv. Ment. Dis.* Baltimore: Williams & Wilkins Co., 1948.

44 Sartre, Jean-Paul. *The emotions. Outline of a theory.* Tr. Bernard Frechtman. New York: Philos. Library, 1948.

45 Spiegel, E. A., Wycis, H. T., Freed, H., and Orchinik, C. The central mechanism of the emotions. *Am. J. Psychiat.*, 1951, *108*, 426-432.

46 Skinner, B. F. *The behavior of organisms.* New York: Appleton-Century, 1938.

47 Stevens, S. S. (Ed.) *Handbook of experimental psychology.* New York: John Wiley & Sons, 1951.

48 Tolman, E. C. *Purposive behavior in animals and man.* New York: Century Co., 1932.

49 Watson, J. B. *Psychology from the standpoint of a behaviorist.* Philadelphia, J. B. Lippincott Co., 1919.

50 Wolff, H. G. Life situations, emotions, and bodily disease. In: *Feelings and emotions.* Martin L. Reymert (Ed.) New York: McGraw-Hill, 1950.

51 Walshe, F. M. R. Thoughts upon the equation of mind with brain. *Brain*, 1953, *76*, 1-18.

52 Young, P. T. *Emotion in man and animal.* New York: John Wiley & Sons, 1943.

53 —— Emotion as a disorganized response—a reply to Professor Leeper. *Psych. Rev.*, 1949, *56*, 184-191.

CHAPTER VIII

PERSONALITY STUDY
AT CROSSROADS

A. A. ROBACK, Ph.D.
Chairman, Dept. of Psychology, Emerson College

EDITORIAL NOTE

Personality seems to be the cynosure of most workers in the human expanse. It is a comparatively recent department, and the concept has not had time to become stale or outmoded. Because of its many components, it may serve as a kaleidoscope, changing from position to position. If every department in psychology possesses some fascination, then personality has a special allure, because it furnishes the balance sheet as it relates to us as total individuals.

Because of its vast reach, it has become a sort of psychological octopus and can no longer be treated both comprehensively and succinctly. A certain selection of topics must be made. Hence the writer has discussed the chief points of view at the present time and has included also such questions as the criterion of personality, *precisely because it is never so much as mentioned elsewhere.*

A. A. Roback, a graduate of McGill University, has received his doctorate at Harvard University. The author of a score or more of volumes on a variety of subjects and about 1800 articles and reviews in numerous periodicals (some of his writings have been translated into German, Spanish, Swedish, Flemish, Hebrew and Russian) Dr. Roback has specialized along the lines of personality. He has taught at a number of universities, including Harvard and Massachusetts Institute of Technology. His most recent works are Personality in Theory and Practice *(Cambridge, 1950) and an enlarged edition of his earlier* Psychology of Character *(London, 1952),* A History of American Psychology *(New York, 1952) and* Destiny and Motivation in Language *(Cambridge, 1954). In his psychological writings, he has been a consistent opponent of the stimulus-response and other mechanistic schools.*

Personality

Personality is something the meaning of which we all know until we are asked to define it, or to put it somewhat differently, everyone appears to have a clear idea of it but the psychologist. Perhaps it is because the man in the street just takes the article for granted. Possibly he is singling out some one phase of it, while the psychologist takes a deeper view, but one of the most interesting features of this study is that it is only within the past generation that it has found a place in textbooks. The topic of personality was generally found discussed in philosophical treatises. Its psychological counterpart was the *self,* to which William James devoted a classical chapter in his *Principles of Psychology* and the briefer course.

At present, we not only handle the self, as well as personality, but in addition, we manage to introduce the ego in a psychoanalytic garb, leaving the *organism* for a biological approach and the *individual* to the sociologist. Not that the psychologist is precluded from using all these terms, so long as he changes the frame of reference.

In general one might say that self is more private than the personality which, even if we don't accept the social-stimulus theory, still, as its etymology implies, bears a social face. It is more what we appear to others than to ourselves. The self is what we mean to ourselves, and because so much of it is hidden from the world, it may offer greater difficulty. The ego, which in psychoanalytic parlance is the intermediary between the id and the superego, i.e., the realistic principle, partakes of both the self and the personality. Normally all three develop *pari passu,* but frequently, there is an overdevelopment of the one at the expense of the other.

Personality differs from all other departments of psychology in that it is not a function or process like sensation or perception or imagination. It is not even a very complex process, although in *Psychological Abstracts,* it is placed under that rubric. Even intelligence, although not a process either, nevertheless stands for a number of operations involved in perceiving, judging, reasoning, etc. But what functions does personality perform? It would appear to resemble a general mould consisting of lesser moulds which we call traits and attitudes and from which there spring more or less uniform acts, i.e., such as will be brought about by similar conditions. In other words personality is an *organization*. Roback has defined it as "the integrated organization of all the cognitive, affective, conative and physical characteristics of an individual as it manifests itself in focal distinctness and carrying a meaning to others."* There are other definitions aplenty, from the purely personalistic to the interpersonal and behavioristic, but it is not necessary to list them here, as they will be found in the same author's *Personality in Theory and Practice.*

LATE RECOGNITION IN PSYCHOLOGY

It was largely due to the older view of sticking to introspection alone that personality received practically no space in textbooks, while most of the discussions of this subject appear in philosophical treatises, or in psychological works written primarily by philosophers. Once, however, the first symposium on personality was published (Roback, 1925) followed by R. G. Gordon's *Personality*, in 1926, A. A. Roback's *Psychology of Character* and his *Bibliography of Character and Personality*, together with Valentine's *Psychology of Personality*, in 1927, and the launching of *Character and Personality*, by Robert Saudek, with the coöperation of A. A. Roback, the whole field opened up for scores of psychologists, who, in order to make up for the long neglect, began to fill the bag with a vast assortment of odds and ends. In one bibliography subsidized and published by the National Research Council, we find not only a number of dictionaries listed but articles in German on frog reactions, on psychogalvanic reflexes, the skin of the cat, and the like. Ap-

* This definition has been accepted in *Warren's Dictionary of Psychology*, prior to the addition of the phrase "and carrying a meaning".

parently the two assistants copied the German titles without knowing the meaning of the words, and dumped all in the bag.

Too Many Cooks

More than a quarter of a century has elapsed since then. Personality has been studied by representatives of the various schools, behaviorists, operationists, organismists, gestaltists, psychoanalysts, hormists, and factorial theorists, not to speak of the cultural anthropologists and sociologists. They have all made certain contributions, but they are all inclined, like the blind, in the fable, who were examining the elephant, to reach their final conclusion as to the nature of the elephant on the basis of some particular part which they happened to explore. Thus the behaviorist is certain that personality is just a name for a collection of conditioned habits, and his successor, the operationist, is sure that personality is the result of operant conditioning. We should not be surprised to hear some day that the more ambitious cybernetic group will claim for their gigantic robots a goodly portion of personality.

The dynamic approach is seen in Kurt Lewin's field system, in G. W. Allport's functional autonomy, and in H. A. Murray's thematic exploration, but above all it is evident in all depth treatments, whether it be Freud's, Jung's, Adler's, or Rank's. The unconscious, in the broader sense than either Freud or Jung takes it, has become a stamping ground for all projective theorists; and since clinical psychology must needs look to psychoanalysis, on the one hand, and tests, on the other, it almost goes without saying that, with the army of clinical psychologists which steadily grows in number, the topic is subjected to an extensive and rigorous workout, but personality seems to be playing a game of hide-and-seek with them.

In all this hurrying and scurrying to get "results", the constitutional factor is mainly ignored, and those who take stock in genes and heredity are regarded by the overwhelming majority of social and clinical workers as old-fogeys. Kretschmer's type schema is ridiculed; Sheldon, because he is too voluble and doesn't know enough to keep opinions to himself, is being rated as a publicist, and with the forces united from the various camps to make this a push-button world, with no regard for innate tendencies and spontaneous moves countervailing external stimuli, the psychologist who, while accepting the weight of the environment, nevertheless is not ready to give up the biological orientation is regarded as a back number, an anachronism of 1904, *anno* 1954, but there are unmistakable signs of the pendulum starting in the opposite direction, as we shall see presently.

Why is it that there is so much dissension among psychologists as to the nature of personality? The answer to that lies in the variety of personalities who are studying personality, and above all—perhaps something that has not been expressed in print before, the types of teachers the students of personality have had during their graduate days at the university. There may be other reasons also but the teacher influence looms large with the majority of psychologists. At one time, during the controversies between Cornell and Harvard, "laboratory atmosphere" was an oft-repeated phrase used to account for different results in investigations carried out presumably under the same conditions. At that time, the implication was that a certain amount of guidance in one direction or another on the part of the director or his assistant would color the methodology and certainly the conclusions.

We need not go so far as to inject innuendo in explaining present-day disagreements, but the influence of the instructor who has standing will weigh heavily with most fledgelings, unless they nurse a personal grudge against him (and even that is no guarantee) or are fortunate in possessing an independent mind, something uncommon even in the academic world. This in itself is an investigation which should have been carried out on a large scale, and it can be done more readily than many other projects which are being undertaken thanks to large grants. The problem is: to what extent will workers in various controversial fields be shown to deviate in their point of view from those under whose tutelage they have come over a period of years, especially if a paternal attachment had been formed. If the paternal bond seems ruled out by Freudian theory, then for the sake of the research, let us call it a relationship of nepotism.

In *Personality in Theory and Practice,* the author has likened the exploration of personality to the approach to an enormous castle with moats and turrets and parapets, subterranean passages, all of which cannot be reached through one avenue. Contemporary prosoponologists* have realized this only too well, hence they have made a dash for several avenues all at once, and one can imagine with what results. To a number of them, it must appear that the more handles to the pot of personality, the more content it possesses and the safer it is to manipulate, but here safety lies not in numbers, and not even in number (quantitation) but in a clear-cut conception of what we are trying to find, and a divestment of all personal influences in our pursuit of knowledge. I know very well that the chief appeal will be to experimentation, but accepting that recommendation whole-heartedly, the final conclusion is only as valid as its weakest link, and where things are taken for granted to begin with, the results can be only as they are. I have yet to see a large investigation being carried on for a number of years in some phase of psychology and the results showing a conclusion entirely contrary to the hypothesis which initiated the whole series of experiments.

Let us not forget that at each step in our venture there are pitfalls and stumbling blocks. There are several strata, and if we should happen to be lucky with one layer, we can still lose our way in the second, or wander in the third. The fact that we came out somewhere, holding in the palm of our hand some explanation, does not yet mean that we have anything substantial. It only means that the "beggar is never out of his

---

* The term "personologist" is a hybrid, and therefore the Greek *prosôpon* (from which doubtless the Latin, *persona,* is derived) suggests itself as the base for our technical word.

road", and if we beg the question, we are sure to come out right in our own eyes at least.

Personality is simply a name for (a) a number of components (b) organized in a special manner and (c) operating in such a way as to bring certain results, favorable or unfavorable. The components alone do not spell personality. Even the organization is insufficient for that purpose. It is the dynamic working of this whole organization which finally counts. We must, however, begin with the ingredients. And it is here that the first divergence takes place. Naturally, if psychologists differ as to the materials selected, the rift will become greater and greater until they are found not to speak the same language.

Personality is so comprehensive that it may take in every psychophysical process, and indeed at times one wonders whether writers on the subject have not made personality synonymous with psychology. Textbooks on personality, as a rule, start with reflexes and end up with psychoanalysis and cultural anthropology. The principle seems to be that the bigger the textbook, the better, and therefore the greater sales expectation. That point of view is something we must combat. Unless we select, our material will be a hodge-podge, and we shall not see the trees for the forest. In a city, there are pebbles, bits of paper strewn around, puddles on a rainy day, and a thousand and one other such things. They have their place in conversation or in reports. Even a banana peel may have its significance in causing the accidental death of an important man or woman, but would such odds and ends figure in the description of a city? Would one not rather describe the public buildings, and the streets, the parks, and surroundings by which the place is known. Similarly should we not endeavor to find in personality those crucial constituents without which the whole concept would be nugatory?

STRUCTURE

We shall all agree, no matter what our pet theory or school, that personality develops in childhood and adolescence, but as to the determinants, it is a different story. For the behaviorist, personality reduces to a system of habits and no more. Psychoanalysts pin practically all on the pregenital development of the libido—Oedipus fixation, oral and anal hangovers (such as weaning and toilet experiences in the first years of life). Imitation and cultural traditions inculcated by the elders play a very important part among many psychologists of today as accounting for the development of a certain personality. To judge from their works, particularly those steeped in cultural anthropology, one would think that a whole people is envious, jealous, suspicious, generous, arrogant, frustrated, aggressive, submissive or lazy. Cultural anthropologists have gone out to primitive places in order to enlarge our vistas, but when they have returned, they seem to judge us, the more or less civilized, by primitive standards. It is a measure similar to the methods of animal psychologists who put generations of rats through their paces and then apply the conclusions gained from these experiments to the most complex human situations. But "a man's a man for a' that", and for all we know, the animal psychologist does not know what the rat's little brain is about, when certain goals are attained. The rat may be "reasoning" from his angle and not as the experimenter thinks he should be on the basis of some theory.

DETERMINANTS

The great problem in personality research is to be sure where the work begins. Personality unlike sensation, perception, or memory, is not approachable through direct experiments. If we wish to gain some conclusion as to the amount of forgetting we do after a specified interval, or whether we can remember logical facts as well as performances, we need but arrange a series of experiments, but while we can presumably test personality through a thousand and one different methods, we may yet be far from grasping its core and nature for the very reason that it is so complex, that it has developed so slowly over a period of years, for every individual, and that we are at sea as to how much weight to put on the countless steps.

Thus when the initial impacts are sought, it is possible to attach importance to the very experience of birth (Freud, Rank) or even to the intra-uterine pressures.

For all we know, some psychologist may wish to start the environmental chain of influences with the moment of conception. Speculation can be just as rife here. Then there follow the long array of Freudian pregenital complexes which are said to powerfully affect the personality of the child for all time, and the social and family attitudes make more dents in the personality. The heredity factor has during all this probing been neglected or at least slighted; yet it may well be that 60-80% (differing with the individual) of the personality is already predisposed by the genes which the child inherits. But the biological factor offers too simple a solution and does not allow for the play of ingenuity which all the other theories require. Also it is not popular in an electronic world which seeks results to suit our convenience and comfort. It is, however, questionable whether the pure environmentalist can get better results than the moderate hereditarian—and I have never come across an absolute hereditarian.

On Traits

Let us take another turn. We are anxious to discover the unit of personality, and it looks as if the trait would answer the purpose, but that would imply a belief in biological determinism which is anathema for the cartel composed of behaviorists, sociologists, anthropologists, and operationists, hence the trait is regarded merely as a superficial label for a series of acts, which, to the casual observer, fall into a certain pattern. This view probably started with Dewey but especially was Thorndike its spokesman; the whole Columbia school was saturated with it, and since New Haven is within commuting distance, it pervaded the halls of Yale too, with its recent stress on mechanical behavior and operationism which seeped into Harvard via engineering interests. Some very creditable work has been done along these lines but in what fields? In personality? No, in animal psychology, in sensation, in learning; and so gratified are many with the results in the limited regions—that they are willing to swallow the applications to personality study, by shutting their eyes to the fact that they have only imbibed the liquid. The substance cannot be negotiated when it comes to personality. It is for this reason that the chapter dealing with personality in B. F. Skinner's *Science and Human Behavior,* which is calculated to demonstrate once and for all how operationism can explain everything, is called the "Self", and that it is surprisingly or disappointingly meagre—a scant eleven pages in which it is evident that the author does not feel at home and would like to get out of that region as soon as possible.

Why is the habit a better unit of personality? Is it because it lends itself more readily to conditioning or to reinforcement? But no one makes the claim that traits cannot be modified through either internal effort or external pressure. And a trait suggests a systematized unity around a motivating force, whereas a habit suggests only a stimulus-response relation entirely unattached and motivated only through the particular conditioning. The trait presupposes a something from within which modifies the effect of the conditioning. The habit might just as well apply to an object like wood, paper, a stone, e.g. which is worn away by friction.

In the treatment of personality we see then that at every step there is a possible bifurcation. Those who believe they are taking the middle course come under the ban of the pure conditionists who because they are operating on a physicalistic basis identify themselves as the exclusively scientific psychologists. But they are scientists only in their own experimental domain. Where their particular brand of experimentation will not extend, they become speculative, without admitting it, and perform legerdemain, without being aware of it. Hence it is that by far the majority of these scientists shy away from personality research, leaving the field open to psychoanalysts and clinical psychologists who dominate the scene through sheer numbers and professional influence.

It is high time that this bias were exposed; and that can be done only by bringing together all the *non-sequiturs* and question-begging of the various behavioristic schools. Luckily, the pretentious claims of the conditionists have not impressed many of the British psychologists and an authoritative voice is still heard now and then in protest against the move to smother the personality in a welter of habits, responses, and the like. To this point we shall revert later.

The road to personality understanding is filled with all sorts of pilgrims, from the most positivistic negativists (if I may use this oxymoron) i.e., those who on the strength of their rabbit or mice experiments reach a positivistic conclusion that personality is but a name for an organized series of responses, to the animist of Neo-Scholasticism. These extremes were with us all the time, but personality soon became the cynosure of anthropologists, sociologists, clinicians, and psychoanalysts and, of course, more recently factorial analysts, until it began to be pulled in all directions, There are, of course, the personalists who establish a point of view rather than results, and are primarily philosophers. While the others start with fragments, endeavoring to build up a personality, the personalists start with it and deduce from it a number of interrelated facts.

In the brief compass of a chapter it would not be feasible to elaborate on the various personality slants, but several of the prevailing trends should receive some treatment. Not all these trends are isolated and independent. There is sometimes an overlap, a common use of material and a resorting to the same methods. A rather detailed chart could be drawn showing alliances and secessions, agreements and differences, sources of information, data exploited, methods used, etc.

SIX LARGE DIVISIONS

In general it may be said that the study of personality is now in charge of the conditionists, the culturists, the inter-personalists, the clinicians (including the psychoanalysts), bio-geneticists and constitutionalists, and the factorialists. There is a great deal of give and take among some of these schools, as we shall see, yet much depends on what stress is being laid, whether it is just frequency of reinforcement, or experiences in the earliest childhood, or situations at any given time, or the interplay of individuals, or that which we bring from our own. A good deal too hinges upon the introduction or omission of purpose and value.

It would be possible to introduce also the literary prosopo-nologist, i.e., the student (who may be a psychologist of note) with a penchant for gaining insight from characters in fiction and from biography. To one writer, at least, it would seem that not enough of this exploration is done. Would it not be more sensible to make our generalizations about personality from the lives of outstanding individuals than out of the reactions of rats and pigeons? And would not Shakespeare, Dostoyevsky, Tolstoy, Balzac, Victor Hugo, De Maupassant, Proust, Hardy and others who served in the capacity of divers be apt to come up with valuable observations? Were psychologists to turn their eyes to literature, they would ponder a bit before translating their animal results into conclusions on human personality.

OPERATIONISM SLURS PERSONALITY

Strange to say, although the word "behavior" is about the most frequently used term in psychology, "behaviorism" is no longer popular; operationism takes its place, and operant be-havior with its reinforcements replaces the conditioned reflex. For the operationist, the "self is simply a device for representing a functionally unified system of responses organized around a discriminative stimulus" (Skinner) while "traits are certain conditions of reinforcement and deprivation." But that defini-tion of the self would fit any electronic robot such as we are developing today. Is there really no difference between a *golem* and the human being so far as personality goes?

Skinner opines that "we can predict and control response more readily than a trait." What he means is that traits are not necessary for reinforcements. Perhaps it would be better for the operationist if there were none, but since we know that traits do exist, just as properties in objects exist, it would behoove us to reckon with them. In rejoinder to the above quotation, one might well reply that we can predict and control a response more readily when we know something about the trait of the individual we are about to control. If we approach a generous man for a contribution to a worthy cause, we would need to do less cajoling or pleading than in the case of a skinflint, and if we are certain that he is a "tough customer", stubborn as a mule, we leave him severely alone, unless we wanted to make a special study of the man or are dedicated to a mission. Think of how much time and misery we could have saved ourselves, if we had been better acquainted with the traits of those we were to deal with.

Let us not be deceived by the self-complacent statement about the merely verbal existence of the self. It is by no means new. David Hume, over 200 years ago, had already voiced the same expression. "For my part", he wrote in his *Treatise of Human Nature,* "when I enter most intimately into what I call *myself,* I always stumble on some particular perception or other, of heat or cold, light or shade, love or hatred, pain or pleasure. I can never catch *myself* at any time without a perception". Hume was arguing chiefly against the notion of a self as a substance. The fact is that whenever we are conscious of some task, some purpose, some anxiety, we invariably think of the self which gives it its special force. Task or purpose or fear or pain without the *I* or *me* is rather colorless. The circumstance that we are not always aware of the self does not necessarily mean that it does not exist in the mental structure. And even if it should be simply a Kantian synthetic unity of apperception, it is still an *operant,* an entity which functions significantly in the personality and, as was previously intimated, it is the *inner* phase of the personality.

CULTURE AND PERSONALITY

There is something either provocative or alluring about the study of personality. It is always invaded by outside sciences. The anthropologist deals with cultures. Personality is a tiny fragment of the unit which occupies his attention, yet he seems to have a lien on it. Anthropology is a species of sociology, hence the anthropologist and the sociologist have made common cause, and "the environment" is their Eldorado. Franz Boas was the man who led the rebellion against the biogenetic conception of personality which seeks to explain individual differences on the basis of genes. In this way, he may be regarded as the great ally of the conditionists, from the Simon-pure behaviorists to the operationists. But all sociologists are environment-involved. If sociology deals with the milieu, then everything pertaining to man (or beast for that matter) must come under that purview. Did not Gabriel Tarde, even before Boas, trace all human action back to imitation? If imitation governed all our behavior, we should scarcely be expected to develop as anything but a society of apes. Imitation is, of course, one factor in the growth of the child, and 'keeping up with the Joneses' is without doubt an extension of this general tendency into adult life, but is it pure imitation alone? Is there not also a tendency to *outdo* the Joneses and a wish to become the model for others to imitate?

R. Linton, (1945) who may be considered Boas's successor at Columbia, while naturally loyal to the anthropological principle, nevertheless is frank enough to see the obstacles. Linton has no difficulty in accounting for basic personality type in a society i.e., common personality elements of the society as a whole, nor is he at a loss to explain status personalities, like configurational responses from different social levels or of the opposed sexes, but what will one do with individual differences or personality norms, as he calls them? The overzealous attitude of Boas and most of his disciples in denying or at least minimizing these individual differences in order to bolster their view is mentioned by Linton who is one of the most open-minded of anthropologists. He can at least see both sides, even if he still leans toward his own after reviewing the various possibilities. "The innate qualities of the individual will influence strongly the sort of experience which he derives from this interaction with the environment. . . . However it is also obvious that two children of equal intelligence or strength may derive quite different experience from different situations." But he does appear to be more flexible than his colleagues when he concludes that "there seems to be abundant evidence that neither innate abilities nor environment can be regarded as constantly dominant in personality formation" (Linton, 1945, pp. 132-133). Yet he seems to hesitate in ascribing much to physiological structure, and is content with leaving the issue open until we learn more about the *modus operandi* of the relationship.

Linton, who is of course steeped in the postulates of his science and the doctrine of his Columbia school, is nevertheless not only an ex-field worker. He is a thinker, too, and therefore one of the most critical of present-day anthropologists. He, for one, admits that personalities are configurations of a unique sort, one which has no close parallel at the level of physical phenomena. Moreover, he even adverts to the consistency of overt behavior. "The individual's repetition of similar responses to similar stimuli, in those cases when such responses are complex and obviously not instinctual can only be accounted for on the assumption that experience is, in some way, organized and perpetuated. Unfortunately observed behavior is often susceptible of more than one psychological interpretation." (p. 85) He even recognizes that "to add to the confusion, most of the attempts to describe personality involve the use of terms drawn from the more familiar field of physical phenomena and scarcely applicable to psychological ones."

All anthropologists, however, are chary about invoking innate factors to account for individual differences. Personality to them is only a chip of the cultural block, and what cannot be explained by means of the cultural pattern is treated with the *status* or *subcultural* dye, and, of course, the individual becomes the product of his social milieu, sex, economic stratum, of what has happened to him in early childhood, due to his objective environment or contacts with members of the family and others.

The majority of humdrum individuals who follow the crowd may find a place in this scheme but the atypical or deviant members are apt to give the anthropologist some trouble. "The causes of such aberrant personalities are still imperfectly understood. They unquestionably derive in part from accidents of early environment and experience" Linton tells us. "In how far still other, genetically determined factors may be involved we are still unable to say." Would it not be legitimate to transpose the degree of certainty and uncertainty in the two statements? These accidents are simply assumed; heredity and genes are facts.

Linton has also hit the nail on the head in his less professional mood, when he speaks of the lack of psychological training among anthropologists. Citing his own case as a field worker, he admits that he did not know what to look for. We can also imagine that groups belonging to a vastly different culture will not reveal themselves, and that their behavior is apt to be misunderstood and therefore misinterpreted. A whole tribe is put down as jealous, or suspicious, or aggressive or meek, and that is ascribed to their system of upbringing. In addition the psychoanalytic dynamisms are enlisted in order to give weight to these early experiences, but that is piling one assumption upon another in order to bolster the cultural doctrine.

Thus Kluckhohn and Leighton (1947) see in the Navaho character, anal-erotic traits, which Freud had associated with orderliness, thrift, and stubbornness. The minute ritualism, toilet training, in which the excrements are concealed, and the fear which is basic in Navaho religion are to be taken as evidence of the validity of the theory. E. H. Erikson (1945) studied the Sioux and the Yurok tribes and found the former belligerent although generous, while the latter who were sedentary, compared with the roaming buffalo-hunters, enjoyed fishing and the peaceful arts, and were economical and acquisitive. The Saulteaux, a branch of the Algonkians were found to be (A. I. Hallowell, 1940) ambivalent in that they are on the surface coöperative, patient, law-abiding and peaceful, sharing their surplus food, yet guilty of unformalized covert aggression, often implemented through so-called witchcraft and sorcery. Under such conditions, anxiety is rife, and a paranoid state is often in evidence. Dorothy Eggan (1943) described the Hopi Indian as hospitable and friendly with a generous spirit, but still displaying marks of maladjustment; and friction amongst them is quite common, and "the worst is anxiously and habitually anticipated." Mrs. Eggan is one of the few contemporary anthropologists who do not trace this trait to experience in infancy, for Hopi society is such that many of the Freudian postulates do not apply altogether. Children are brought up in the most unrestrained manner, and many elders are regarded as fathers and mothers by the Hopi children. Economic factors as well as acculturation difficulties are seen by this writer as the causes of such maladjustment.

Geza Róheim's investigations (1932) have been confirmatory of Freudian principles in the interpretation of primitive cultures. Kardiner, in several studies with collaborators (1944, 1945) e.g., in that on Alorese culture which, according to him, is built around the proposition that life is a difficult struggle, with most of our neighbors, particularly women, untrustworthy and therefore likely to thwart our best-laid plans, thinks that these are bound to develop a type of personality which is anxious, suspicious, frustrated and lackadaisical. The historical circumstance is supposedly the requirement of the women to work in the fields to the neglect of the babies after a couple of weeks' nursing, the result being that the children remain hungry and uncomfortable and develop tensions unrelieved by the parental image, which the child in other cultures might form in early months.

Margaret Mead (1954) who had studied the culture of the Manus in New Guinea over 25 years ago and has revisited them after a quarter-century has discovered a different personality type of the younger generation in that the Manus then were a disagreeable, greedy and quarrelsome people, while now after conquest by the Germans had taught them contentment in peace, and missionaries indoctrinated them with ideas of brotherly love, just as the Australians inculcated into them the rudiments of law and justice, they have become relaxed and happy.

Enough has been cited to bring before the reader the methods and results of cultural anthropologists, with and without psychoanalytic attachments. All seize upon some one environmental accident (historical, economic, geographical) and make the culture contingent upon the consequences for the individual, who is a mere wave in the cultural sea. One might imagine that all individuals are alike because they have had a similar upbringing. It is obvious that these anthropologists starting with a certain premise must arrive at a particular conclusion, and where their science deals with the group, the individual is slurred only as an object conforming to the dimensions of the mould in which it is cast. To this extent the culturist supports a species of Platonism.

I have no way of testing the field data supplied by anthropologists, but there is one group ubiquitous and putatively well known that I am familiar with through its chief languages, literature, lore, and life, and the amazing ignorance betrayed in scientific circles in regard to that people makes me wonder how much validity can be ascribed to the field facts colored by theory, in the case of remote aborigines. How many times have we read in serious studies that Jews were clannish or inclined to capitalism or rebellious, or overambitious, or averse to manual labor, timid, unfit for war or self-defence, loud, unruly, and so on *ad libitum*? Of course theories were framed galore as to how they got that way, e.g., being a minority group, they were persecuted, hence they sought to overcompensate through shrewdness and the acquisition of wealth. Hence all Jewish children hear nothing at home but harangues on money, and begin to think in terms of money, and, as I have read recently, all Jewish humor turns around that topic! If the Jews are not heavy drinkers, it is, we are told, because of the ceremonial wine drinking on the Sabbath and Festivals! Famous scientists will tell us that Jews do not exist in science, yet in the next clause or sentence they will maintain that Jewish scientists come to the fore because they have faith in each other. In my youth I have written a satire "Anthropology as She is Wrote", with considerable documentation, but the gallery of ludicrous stereotypes in scientific books which has collected since bids well to make that satire seem altogether too sober.

For one thing, one might gather that the individual is but a mode of the group, and the group culture is a function of some accident perpetuated through habit. It does not occur to the anthropologist that not all things which happen are accidents, and that every group is composed of typical and atypical individuals, and that many personality traits are altogether apart from rather than a part of culture, and that it would be more to the purpose to make longitudinal studies of the family history first, after which environmental gleanings might be incorporated in order to produce the full picture.

In the case of the Dionne quintuplets where the culture has been absolutely the same, and where nurse and governess, physicians and guardians, have done their utmost to equalize their attitude toward each of the children, individual differences are still found, and are usually explained by the environmentalist as resulting from some trifling incident, like the inadvertent raising of someone's voice in the one case and not in the other. When we realize how much an individual, yes even a small child, can endure without its personality becoming warped, often rather the reverse, we can only snicker at such fanciful reasons. It has been objected that we do not yet know how the genes work in specific cases. But at least we do know that they are at work. Why are they admitted in the case of physical characteristics and not when it is a question of mental traits? But as for the numerous circumstantial incidents that are supposed to have formed the personality of the individual, it is assumed first that they occurred, and then a theory, usually a very intricate one, is created to show how the events shaped the life of the child and later adult. We may admire the ingenuity, but is the procedure scientific?

INTERPERSONALISM

Close to the cultural slant on personality is that of interpersonalism. It does not take much acumen to sense that this view reduces the rôle of personality and makes it one among many stations, the journey ending somewhere in the territory of sociology. Personality is no longer a unit for itself but a relationship. This is essentially a social conception. Hence, no wonder that it was in sociology and social psychology that the foundations were laid for this new structure. Cooley and Mead, and probably Dewey, had been among the masons, but it was reserved for the genial Harry Stack Sullivan to put up a psychiatric scaffolding and thus give it a chance to rear itself, on a wider site. It may surprise many readers to learn that Karl Marx was the patron saint of interpersonalism, for it was he who defined the individual person as "a point of intersection of social relations," and this probably is at the root of all communism, in that the person is but a point not to be considered for and by itself.

In his posthumous work, *The Interpersonal Theory of Psychiatry* (1953) Sullivan develops a system which is based on both observation and speculation. He is strong in framing definitions, and leading us from one conclusion to another, he almost convinces us that things are as he states them. His style, reminiscent of Georg Groddeck's, is informal (the book consisting of a series of lectures and notebook material) and the language is simple, although the ideas are rather complex, forming chains with many links jutting in various directions.

Sullivan develops his system in terms of needs and tensions, dynamisms and patterns, using a similar method to Freud's although differing in the underlying postulates, such as the triangle relationship of infancy. He may be called a psychoanalyst or depth psychologist, but of the para-Freudian variety. The psychic world which he builds up for the infant, child, adolescent and adult is constituted of relationships arising out of physical wants and their satisfactions, and the anxiety which intervenes when things go awry.

Personality begins, according to Sullivan, with the double personification of the "mothering one" into a good mother and a bad mother, depending upon the amount of satisfaction it receives in the form of food or tenderness. Another and more important insight comes later when the child begins to recognize a good-me, a bad-me, and a not-me, making up the self-system. Good-me is formed around experiences in which "satisfactions have been enhanced by rewarding increments of tenderness" as a result of the mothering one's appreciation of the infant's progress. In bad-me, there is a setting of anxiety induced by the mothering one or some other elder, while a not-me personification results from a condition of intense anxiety and is found in schizophrenia with its manifestations of dissociated behavior. In normal people, it may show itself in dreams.

Throughout his lectures, Sullivan leads up to the argument that self is a product of interpersonal relations; and being a detailist, *par excellence,* he dwells on every possible move of the infant and the mothering one as something significant in the development of the former's personality. Let us assume that the infant is impressed and reacts to every situation. The question is to what extent this event really does make a dent, to what extent some children will be unsusceptible to or will be able to overcome the discomfiture which to others may become a serious involvement, and this, again, brings us to the problem of biological equipment.

In her introduction to *The Interpersonal Theory of Psychiatry,* Mabel Blake Cohen makes it clear that "Sullivan's conclusions are based in part on inference and in part on his clinical observations, especially schizophrenics, since much of their psychotic experience partakes of the nature of experience in early infancy" and that workers with infants tend to confirm Sullivan's conclusions. Perhaps the observations are what they confirm, rather than the etiological conclusions.

Sullivan has given us a well-thought out system. Surely his contribution to psychiatry is undeniable, but to point out the significance of interpersonal relations for psychiatry is not the same as proving that personality consists of nothing but interpersonal relations. That these relations enter in is a principle which is almost obvious. No individual lives in a vacuum. We may concede, too, that most infants act alike under given conditions. That does not mean, however, that the reverberations in the future will be alike. Even if all infants are rapacious and unreasonable, it may very well be that some of them will become great humanitarians without experiences in infancy having been the causes.

If we were to apply the same procedure to the physical world, we might wish to speak not of an electron or proton but of "interparticularism"; for there, too, each particle is constantly being affected by the others, often violently, but we do take a substantive view of these particles, although they are systems of relations. In the matter of the person or self, there is infinitely greater reason for so doing because we are directly aware of this entity, and are conscious of its division in case of neurosis, and integration when we recover.

Leary and Freedman (1951) have attempted to work out a scheme whereby the interpersonal mechanisms could be scored and applied to interaction in a group. Personality is envisaged as revealed on three levels, public, conscious, and private, each to be assessed through different methods.

Interaction and Situationalism

There is much in common between interpersonalism and interaction as a theory, since both stress acts and relations in the structure of personality. This whole conception, which stems from sociology, would naturally minimize the part that the individual plays and bring to bear the innumerable situations between a system of need-dispositions and drives on the one hand and social objects on the other. The school, intrenched in the Harvard Social Relations Department, and drawing upon psychoanalysis, has become influential for several reasons, which need not be gone into at present.

In *Toward a General Theory of Interaction,* T. Parsons and E. A. Shils act as hosts to psychologists and anthropologists with the purpose in view of establishing a basis for coöperation in social science, which to them would include psychology. We are particularly interested in the chapter "Personality as a System of Action", which at once gives us some link as to the direction. Here we are introduced to a very elaborate terminology and intricate theories, abstractly formulated. According to the above-named authors, the "personality system is an organized set of primary and complex need-dispositions which are related to one another in a hierarchical way". This system contains not only need-dispositions of a physical nature but such as are relative to social objects. We must also look for rôle expectations and value-standard components. The relation between the actor and object may be *universalistic,* when the object falls into a general category, aligned with other objects, or *particularistic* when it stands in a particular relation to the ego. The presentation is heavy with technical terms like "ascription achievement", "collectivity orientation alternative", and smacks of a scholasticism which is strong on definition and classification but weak on offering samples of reality. Many of the definitions are couched in such language as to make it difficult to grasp their meaning. To take one illustration, "Motivation (or motives) in this last sense may be conceived as denoting certain more or less innate systems of orientations involving cognition of and cathectic attachment to certain means and goal objects and certain more or less implicit and unconscious 'plans' of action aimed at the acquisition of cathected relationships to goal objects" (p. 111).

At any rate, one is gratified to note "more or less innate factors" are conceded to operate in motivation, but that is about as far as the concession goes. As for the rest, we have but a series of formalistically expressed situations between actor and environment, from early infancy, against a psychoanalytic background, such as the special mechanisms of defence repression and rationalization to projection. Not once do we meet the self or personality as a living unit, conscious as a being, aside from the various rôles played. And yet such an ego is often tacitly assumed by the writers, in making the distinction between *ego* (not in the Freudian topographical sense) and the *alter*.

Classification is the foundation of science, yet it can be so overdone as to cause confusion. We can take any phenomenon or event, and place it in a large number of different categories in some kind of continuum in each case. We can talk of a book as a visually-perceived or, in the case of the educated blind, a tactually-perceived object, or as an author-reader set of relations. The chief question is: What purpose does it serve? Perhaps a librarian will build up a system in which such a relationship will fit in, but that is only because of his special involvement or bias, and if sociologists choose to make of personality a system of social action, then again it is because they happen to have chosen sociology for their field. Let them by all means tackle the social factors in personality, but why must they tinker with the psychological core, which it is their fancy to whittle away with the sociological knife?

That our personalities are moulded by events and situations and other personalities goes without saying. A mere chance happening, such as meeting someone who either lights up or blights our life means far more than many of the situations in early childhood which have lately been made into a fetish by psychologist, sociologist and anthropologist.

Albert Schweitzer in his *Memories of Youth* has this to say about how his life was shaped.

As I look back upon my youth, I realize how important to me were the help, understanding, and courage, the gentleness and wisdom so many people gave me. These men and women entered into my life and became powers within me. But they never knew it. Nor did I perceive the real significance of their help at the time.

One wonders, however, whether his infantile relations to his mother were any different from those of other children to theirs. Indeed, one wonders whether, had the denizens of gangdom met the same people he did during his formative years, their life would have been even a faint approximation to his, apart from the intellectual differences.

I cannot help being puzzled at the countless constructs that are being invented by social scientists and psychologists while neglecting the incidents and episodes of real life, as found in history and biography. They drop the known and knowable and chase the unknown and, in most instances, the unknowable, in true romantic fashion.

The individual from the fetal period on is subject to many thousands of experiences and influences. Ellsworth Huntington has even gone so far as to consider the season of birth (temperature) as an important factor; and for all we know, the sun spots and transits of certain planets at the time of birth may be of some account, as astrologers insist, but we are quite content to deal with those influences which may in some sense be checked; and the hereditary plus such situational causes as can be reasonably traced and related to the individual would seem to be sufficient for our purpose. An idio-empirical shock (A. A. Roback, 1950) e.g., stumbling upon the body of a murdered parent would mean a good deal more for a child than the scolding of a nurse or a slap by the mother. As G. W. Allport (1953) puts it, "no one varies it [his behavior] in ways that are not already his." Is it sensible to suppose that all could stand the horrors of war and the atrocities of international gangsterism equally well, were it not for varying parental attitudes, and food and toilet habits imposed on the infant?

PSYCHOANALYTIC TREATMENT OF PERSONALITY

The psychoanalytic interpretation of personality is so widely known and has been so universally discussed that it would be repeating something that every reader by this time has seen and heard too often. The present writer has dealt with it more than once, but particularly in his *Psychology of Character* (1952 edition). Because of its emphasis on infantile experiences, and therefore at bottom environmentalism, although the constitutional has not been overtly denied, it offers a vast assortment of dynamisms, and a still larger variety of fittings, so that we can always find our way out of the maze of theory.

It may be anticipated that those who join hands with psychoanalysis will not rest content with merely accepting. It will not be long before they will wish to give a new twist to the discipline which they have espoused. They will seek to reform it or, at least, make it more acceptable in keeping with the *Zeitgeist*. Since operationism is looked up to as *the* scientific method, aligned with physicalism, efforts will naturally be made to operationize psychoanalytic dynamisms. In that event, it would be necessary to find not only the 'why', in terms of unconscious motivation, but the 'how' of the 'why'. The whole dynamic system will be tested in either a biological or physiological crucible, depending upon the provenance of the tester; but Freud, it will be recalled, despite his thorough grounding in physiology, would have none of it in his sphere of jurisdiction. The psychic should be able to take care of its own problems without seeking support from some other science, which would naturally confuse the picture by introducing its own parameters and postulates. The new allies (largely para-Freudians) are intent upon 'dignifying' psychoanalysis by applying their own scientific categories and even quantitative standards.

We are entering the period of model-seeking. Whether this has been suggested by cybernetics and its robots, the new 'need' is working off its tension in symposia, experiments, and confabs. D. Rapaport (1951) affirms that "the conceptual model implicit to psychoanalysis is sufficiently broad and flexible to embrace on the one hand those realms of psychological phenomena which other models effectively conceptualize, and on the other those realms which have remained intractable to them."

Some like Hebb(1951) require a neurological model and when "neurologically based theory can be enlarged to fit in the Freudian and Lewinian ideas, modified as necessary, our understanding both of personality and of apparently less complex phenomena should be greatly increased" (p. 52). Rapaport, on the other hand, adheres to the psychological model inherent in the psychoanalytic system.

The operational approach to psychoanalysis is exemplified by Blum and Miller's (1951) investigation of the 'oral character' as employed by Freud. The experimenters undertook a difficult job to test a simple hypothetical trait. For, in the first place, they had to make sure that their subjects were of the oral type. Children in the latency period were selected for the purpose. First it was necessary to establish what the 'oral character' really is, and what traits it encompasses. Among the components of this type are listed such things as (a) interest in food (b) need for approval and affection (c) dependency (d) concern over parting with supplies as against receiving (e) need to be ingratiating (f) social isolation (g) inability to divide loyalties (h) suggestibility (i) depressive tendencies (j) non-tolerance of boredom. Teacher ratings, time sampling, sociometrics, and projective tests were applied against the actual findings in experiments to probe the 11 components enumerated. The hypothesis of orality is, of course, originally Freudian, but a number of writers have added facets of their own, and the investigators leaned heavily on Fromm's clinical picture, which is scarcely more than speculative based on common sense such as "since they need many hands to feel secure, they have to be loyal to numerous people. . . . Since they cannot say 'no', they love to say 'yes' to everything and everybody, and the resulting paralysis of their critical abilities makes them increasingly dependent on others."

Blum and Miller have shown considerable resourcefulness in planning and executing this extensive investigation on 18 pupils, both boys and girls, but the harvest is not plentiful. "The resulting correlations lent strong support to hypotheses dealing with (a) extreme interest in food, and (b) social isolation. Fair support was given (a) need of liking and approval, (b) concern over giving and receiving, and (c) boredom tolerance." All the other hypotheses were either unsupported or equivocal, yet the authors are satisfied that the over-all results held promise "for the investigation of psychoanalysis by traditional techniques."

It is precisely because the hypotheses were so many and because the methods, elaborate and ingenious enough, were not necessarily applicable to the hypotheses, that we cannot be certain as to what was really tested, whether other causes may not have been responsible for the results submitted.

A PERSONALISTIC VIEW

To the average psychologist, personality is only a name given to a collection of processes operating as a system. Think away memory, sensation, imagination, perception, emotion, etc. and no residue is left which you can call the person. Hence the dispensableness of the term 'personality' for all positivists, not that they can actually do without employing it, in their daily intercourse, but scientifically they are bent on making short shrift of the concept.

At the other extreme of the prism, there is the psychologist who thinks of the person as the only real entity through which all else is reflected. Nearly all personalists are philosophers with an idealistic background, but some psychologists are affiliated with the personalistic movement, in that they regard personality as central to psychology, and as a totality rather than a congeries to be analyzed piecemeal.

The first English presentation of personalism is probably that of F. A. Rauch, who held that "the person is not only the centre of man but also the centre of nature" (Rauch, 1840). It would seem as if the person, according to Rauch, lends meaning to the scattered fragments of nature, unites them in a coherent whole. A second important representative of personalism was G. T. Ladd for whom the "development of mind can only be regarded as the progressive manifestation in consciousness of the life of a real being which . . . proceeds to unfold powers that are *sui generis* according to laws of its own" (Ladd 1892, p. 53).

Personalism did not crystallize into a school until B. P. Bowne intrenched himself at Boston University with a long line of students and fortified his reputation in philosophy through a series of large works displaying acumen and wide learning. The Western outpost is found in the University of Southern California, thanks to the zeal of R. T. Flewelling. In France, personalism took shape under the deft hands of Charles Renouvier, friend of William James, but as a *psychological* field of inquiry it was first cultivated by William Stern, in Germany whose *Studien zur Personwissenschaft* marked a turning point in the whole conception, for Stern, although a philosopher too, as what German-trained psychologist is not, could stand his ground as firmly as any laboratory psychologist; and it is well to note that Heinz Werner, partial to personalism, is a former student of Stern's while G. W. Allport, probably the most influential of the school, somewhat modified, and removed from the metaphysical wing, has also studied in Stern's psychological institute. Among the other psychologists who take up a personalistic position are Gardner Murphy (1951), who stresses the person as a whole rather than any particular psychological act, which must be envisaged as "the act of a whole person", and, in a restricted sense, the present writer may be added to that group.

Gordon Allport (1953) has formulated the criteria of an adequate theory of personality as follows:

(1) Human personality is centered in the organism rather than in society.

(2) The organism is filled, not empty.

(3) Motivation is not to be understood in terms of earlier forces but is to be interpreted as "normally a fact of present structure and function."

(4) Its units of analysis must be capable of living syntheses.

(5) Self-consciousness must enter in although it is not to be relied on exclusively.

Allport's critique of both philosophical personalism and psychological positivism (or mechanism, I should call it) is both sound and comprehensive. So far as the former is concerned, the slurring of social influences on the individual is pointed out, as a defect, as is the too great stress placed upon consciousness. The self can be an agent and yet not always be an individual known to the individual himself.

There can be various grades of psychological personalism from the self-psychology of Mary Calkins to perhaps such as approve of an inferred self, and set up an *integrative* personality as our model, rather than an *integrated* personality (E. R. Hilgard 1949). Personalism is at a disadvantage because it is generally linked with religious and/or mystical tendencies. It is opposed by all physicalistic disciplines because (a) the person or self is something which is not found in the animal laboratory, and therefore does not permit of a continuum among the species, (b) it cannot be directly experimented upon. It is opposed by sociologists and cultural anthropologists who start out by attributing all personality development to the environment. Psychoanalysis is averse to it because it places no premium on the early years of infancy, and because it underrates the rôle of the unconscious. Hence personalism has powerful foes; and if it can still hold its own, it is because there is something fundamental about the *experience* which cannot be conjured away. There is nothing mystical or awesome about it. Certainly we are not born with full-blown personalities. They grow, but the same sun, rain, and wind will produce different effects in different seed. A personalist does not necessarily believe in a soul, but he does take cognizance of the fact that a normal human is aware of his experiences, his goals, his standing with others and is constantly comparing himself with others, even if the process is only marginal. In Cartesian fashion we might say, "I judge myself in relation to others, therefore I am a person." An idiot, on this view, would not be a personality. Animals have no personalities. A psychotic, despite the derangement, can still be a personality, allowing for the deficit.

A personalist is not likely to ascribe all changes in an individual's traits to a reverberation of the distant past that needs to be covered up, as the reaction formation would imply, or to some new social setting which imposes the changes. A youth may have become punctual whereas in the past he had been happy-go-lucky because he "came to his senses", because he reasoned out the ill consequences of his lateness and decided to turn over a new leaf. An overthrifty person could realize after some discussion or reflection that "you can't take it with you", that the dime saved is not worth the pains or the privation, or the loss of prestige. Why is this not a sufficient reason for the change? In other words, reasoning need not be rationalization in the Freudian sense, and the social impulse in an individual is not necessarily a cultural steer in the anthropological sense, or an institutional sanction in the sociological frame of reference. There is such a thing as enlightenment which does not always surge up from the dark depths of the unconscious. There can be such a thing as spontaneity in the individual, as well as a degree of independence, both deriving from the organic structure with its interplay of genes, in so many permutations and combinations, affecting the cognitive, emotional, and conative phases of man.

FACTORIAL ANALYSIS AND PERSONALITY

In a statistical era, one may expect an approach to personality which takes into account the correlations of variables, regardless of the type of variable. The labelling is done only after such items as trait-components have been subjected to rigid analysis through factorial treatment. Categories are arranged in this fashion the importance of which will depend on the weighting obtained. C. E. Spearman, at London University, trained a number of psychologists who dedicated themselves to such explorations through mathematical means. Thus, the number and kinds of drives could be established through the administration of a variety of tests, factorially treated. Although the representatives of this school are not committed to hereditarianism, they are at least not given to making of personality an environmental machine.

R. B. Cattell recognizes environmental influences, but innate and congenital (acquired while *in utero*) characteristics are not explained away. In his *Introduction to Personality Study* (1950) as well as in his larger work (*Personality: A Systematic Theoretical and Factual Study,* 1950) he tried to accord nature and nurture their respective due. From internal correlation, he deduces twelve (eventually omitting one and adding two other) primary personality factors, in contrasted pairs, such as *cyclothymia-schizothymia, dominance-submissiveness, urgency-melancholy, anxious emotionality-rigid poise,* etc. In the later version, he discards *neurasthenia-vigorous character* and introduces pairs like *sophistication vs. simplicity* and *bohemian unconcern vs. conventionalized practicality.*

Another product of the London School who has made personality his special subject is H. J. Eysenck, who has already published three books bearing the word 'personality' in the title. Eysenck favors such unpopular views in America as constitutional typology, and is inclined to see more in heredity than the bulk of American psychologists would countenance and is eager to show up the biased interpretation of experimental results in terms of environmentalism, citing the British psychiatrist E. Slater whose denunciation of the "notion that one should accept as true that which has convenient practical applications" so common in psychological circles, especially in the United States, is as sharp a rebuke as we have read in a long time— and well-merited.

On the basis of extensive tests on monozygotic and dizygotic twins (Eysenck and Prell, 1951), Eysenck concludes

> that heredity plays a very strong part in the determination of personality differences and that psychology can-

not go on making the easy and implicit assumption, which is inherent in both psychoanalysis and behaviorism, that environment is the only major variable determining individual differences. This belief which has acquired a mystical and almost religious fervor in the USSR is also widespread in democratic countries, for reasons which as Pastore has pointed out, may not be entirely apolitical. (1952 in *Annual Review of Psychology*, ed. by C. F. Stone, vol. 3, p. 161.)

One other observation by Eysenck shows us where he stands as regards tests and ratings with which our journals are filled these days. After discussing the results obtained in the Michigan study of the prediction of success in the Veterans Administration training programme in clinical psychology, his conclusion is that the final results are a devastating comment on and criticism of the clinical methods of interviewing and projective testing current in most applied personality work. It was found that "the most efficient clinical predictions in terms of both validity and economy of data are those based only on the matters contained in the credentials file and in the objective test profiles".

Constitutional School

We finally come to the constitutional view of personality with which the present writer identifies himself, and which at the present time is the most unpopular, for one thing, because it is the oldest, dating in its embryonic stage from the time of Hippocrates, who centered personality in the humors. No one now talks about the humors except in a historical context. There have been a few who traced the personality make-up to the endocrine glands (L. Berman) but the constitutionalist in psychology is not committed to any hormone theory. He believes, with K. S. Lashley (1947) that "if the same kinds of structural differences are found to occur among individuals of a single species, they justify the inference of genetic determination of corresponding individual differences" and that "some of the more conspicuous structural differences have been shown to be hereditary" (p. 325).

Lashley goes still further and puts his expert finger on the sore spot of environmentalism when he points out that

> Discussions of heredity and environment have tended to regard the nervous system, if it is considered at all, as a vaguely remote organ, essentially similar in all individuals and largely moulded by experience. Even the limited evidence at hand, however, shows that individuals start life with brains differing enormously in structure; unlike in number, size, and arrangement of neurons as well as in grosser features. The variations in cells and tracts must have functional significance. (p. 333)

It is somewhat strange that although Lashley has been extensively quoted when he was regarded as an ally of behaviorism, his critique of environmentalism, which brings him into the opposing camp, seems to fall on shut eyes and deaf ears. All the more reason to cite such passages and expect some response.

Does a constitutionalist deny the effect of environment in the development of the individual? By no means. He merely discounts the alleged potency of some of the experiences, and maintains that different individuals, in accordance with their neural organization, will react to and absorb these experiences in different ways. To say that in every case, the lack of sufficient food or affection in early childhood will bring on the subsequent mental ills is to make out of a casino roulette an oracle. No doubt a number of children need a full supply; others can get along with less, and, even if they miss it at the time, will learn to adjust or turn to other satisfactions, not necessarily fantasies. Why must we assume that all are born with the same affective strength, with maximum cravings? This question holds even if we accede to all of the Freudian dynamisms. Compensation is a central dynamism because it mediates so many others, yet the extent of compensation and its direction must needs vary with diverse constitutions. If different kinds of material (iron, steel, wood, paper, cloth) will be affected differently by, say, climatic conditions, why must we suppose that the most delicate of all organized substances, the nervous system in man will react with absolute uniformity for millions of individuals, given the same conditions? It seems altogether too elementary to even ask it, but so ingrained is the environmentalist doctrine in academic and professional circles that it is accepted implicitly.

OBJECTIONS TO TYPOLOGY

Since all typologies are based on constitutional considerations, whether it is the primary and secondary-function classes (Gross) or the introvert-extravert dichotomy (Jung) or the organo-systemic schemata of Sigaud and Kretschmer, or somatotypy (Sheldon), there is a wide opposition to any theory which groups individuals according to their build or appearance. Of course, the outcry is that we all have a little bit of everything and that pure types are a fiction, and furthermore, as two sociological authors (Gerth and Mills, 1953) write: "They do not succeed in isolating, or in making fine enough distinctions among the various elements of the total character structure ... the results are gross and generally unrevealing. . . . There are other ways to explain any correlations which might exist between types of constitutions and temperamental or personal traits" (p. 40).

What these and other critics do not seem to appreciate is that the type only indicates a tendency in one direction or another, that it is a convenient mode of labelling without making a full report on a person. That it will be only a stepping-stone to a further study goes without saying. It enables us to first place our acquaintance so that we might know how to approach him. As for the causal basis of the relationship, e. g., stoutness with the cyclic and extraverted type, there is no dearth of theories, e. g., MacAuliffe's colloidal view of the human organism, whose aggregate of molecules are in constant oscillation between compression and dispersion, solidification and liquefaction, so that the round type is composed of cells which are extremely hydrophilic with great surface tension and osmotic pressure necessitating great expenditure of energy and demanding a dynamic sweep. Gross's explanation of the primary and secondary function types is based on the physiological theory of reverberation of the nerve. And may we not eventually find radioactive differences in the cells among individuals? Why is it more incumbent upon the constitutionalist to go into all the intricacies of physiological chemistry and physics than upon the environmentalist who often is not even burdened with the task of proving correlations?

The constitutional point of view is direct, straightforward and free from complicating factors that are closer to the imagination than to reason. It is more widespread than is generally supposed, but its powerful counterpositions (sociology, psychoanalysis, reflexology, operationism, and cultural anthropology) tend to occlude it; and what makes it worse is that while the latter are more or less organized in an environmentalist front, those who are underscoring the endogenous factors in personality are not disposed to band together or to make propaganda. The reports on twins brought up in separate foster homes have favored the constitutional and bio-hereditary schools, but the conclusions are not exploited by their representatives. If the odds are against the constitutional conception of personality, it is largely the result of sociological and psychoanalytic influences abetted by behavioristic postulates—all of these answering the hopes and wishes of the average educated person to transform man through working on his past experiences—deconditioning, in other words. The opposite point of view is regarded as fatalistic, but that is far from the truth. Hereditary tendencies may perhaps more easily be modified than repressed past experiences (many of them only conjectured, dreamed up) can be dissolved or resolved.

THE STRATIFICATION OF PERSONALITY

There is yet another angle to this large field, which has been cultivated almost wholly in Germany, where it is called *Persön-*

lichkeitsschichtung. The concept is not new although the Germans seem to think that it has originated with them, hence it has practically turned into a movement. N. Hartmann even receives credit for providing the philosophical basis for the stratification of personality (1923) in that he "sees the world as a compound of interrelated layers of different modes of existence. These layers are the inorganic, organic, and mental . . . not segregated from one another but . . . interdependent and interacting" (A. R. Gilbert, 1951). There is nothing novel or astounding in this. Mark Hopkins, way back in 1878, "explains the steps which lead up to man from such properties as gravitation and cohesion through chemical affinity and vegetable life" (Roback, 1952, p. 85). And is not William James's division of the self into a "material me", a "social me", and a "spiritual me" a stratification? Indeed, wherever we turn, we notice bipartite and tripartite divisions, whether it is the typologists, or Freud with his topographical id, ego, and superego, or McDougall with his instincts, sentiments, and character, or Lewin's spheres of personality. Even the early French systems of Ribot and Paulhan suggested something of a hierarchy of elements, and contemporary factorial analysis points to the same general conception of something central interlinked with subsidiaries, and the Russian Pavlovians—do they not now speak of "first-signal" and "second-signal" conditioning? And is this not a species of stratification? And do we not also make much of the *phenotype* and the *genotype* or *manifest* and *latent* personality in our discussions? Stratification is no new concept, although it may be that the present-day school has the horizontal zone in mind like geological strata, whereas many of the past divisions could have been meridional strips, although not necessarily so.

The two features, however, which stand out in this new German concentration are (a) the search for an anatomical source, which was not difficult to find, viz., the old brain and the new brain, the former governing the vegetative and affective processes while the latter is the font of the cognitive-volitional stratum (b) the particular stress on organization and consolidation on an incorporative scale, and not on an associative and coöperative plan. The lower layer supports the upper layer which, normally, and on a mature level, controls it. There is no isolation of strata. They each have their function, but within the domain of the large whole. Even this new direction is not so new to any student of physiological psychology. McDougall in his primer of physiological psychology, which appeared just about fifty years ago, gave us a lucid account of the relation between the neural and the psychic on the various levels of the brain and cord, as it was known then.

As for the number of layers, these will differ with the various psychologists. E. Rothacker recognizes five layers: the vital, the vegetative, the affective, the aspirational, and the personal—all governed by the ego, who both pilots and is being carried as is the captain in the case of boat and waters. P. Lersch, on the other hand, speaks of but two layers, the *endothymic* and *personal,* the former serving as a vital commissary for the ego-ruling figure, implied by the latter.

Maladjustments and neuroses will arise when there is friction between the layers, and the greater the discord, the more serious the trouble. The ego-centre must then seek to smooth over the difficulty and is diverted from its mapped-out goal. Sometimes the ego-centre is not equal to the task, and the layers not only jam one another, but overrun the ego-centre.

We can apply the concept even to space and time. Heiss does not mention space, perhaps because of the tridimensional appearing to us as an integrated unit, but he does make much of time, the past, present, and future. No doubt children live mostly in the present. Youth directs its thought to the future, and advanced age looks back to years gone by.

> *Of the past the old man's thoughts were*
> *And the maiden's of the future.*

We can in a trice change the tense of our thoughts. Here there is no problem whatever. But our affective overload *can* play havoc with our memory, and our time-sense then is out of kilter. As Pierre Janet (1925) has related, we can have memories that are too real—bringing extra vividness to events which happened a long time ago, just as repression drives the memories out altogether from the conscious sphere into the unconscious reservoir.

PERSONALITY STUDIES IN FRENCH

Since we have taken up some of the recent German views on personality, it might be expected that contributions in French would also be included in our survey, especially as the French psychologists have had occasion to complain that we practically ignore their writings. There may be some truth in this plaint, and one of the reasons is that French psychology is still interwoven with philosophy in many of the higher institutions in France, Belgium, and Switzerland which weakens its position so far as their American colleagues are concerned who look upon philosophy as a sort of secular theology, with certain metaphysical terms taking the place of "God". Secondly, however, the French books on personality and character do not seem to make much headway. The French bull *"plus ça change, plus c'est la même chose"* is quite apropos here. The advances are made in the form of astute observations and applications to history and literature, but the framework appears to have changed not at all. No wonder Pierre Janet, in his well-rounded and lucid lectures on personality at the Sorbonne (*L'Évolution psychologique de la personnalité*) informs us that "I am a bit terrified by programmes" (p. 536).

The Germans, on the other hand, just thrive on programmes, schemata, systems, etc., and through their complex word-formation have been able to coin impressive terms which serve as keys to something apparently novel and architectonic, while the French employ a few common words which sound like a very ordinary phrase or statement. The critical student will discount the pretentiousness of the German discovery and see in the French material more than meets the eye, but after all even scientists are so constituted that they will give more credit to the complex, as against the simple, the abstract as against the concrete homely illustrations of everyday life. Then, too, the Germans utilize more names, make more moves on an ideational chessboard, so to speak, aside from being better organizers and propagandists, and thus they can gain the ears of the world, even now after the decline of German psychology.

After this *excursus,* it may be explained that this is not the place for dealing with national contributions. The French writers have been comprehensively treated in the author's *Psychology of Character,* a number of years ago. Truth to tell, the French have not brought out many books and articles on the subject in the last two decades. While American psychological periodicals fairly bristle with papers on personality, at least with the word in the title, such are few and far between in the French philosophical and psychological periodicals.

CRITIQUE OF JANET

Of treatises, that of Janet mentioned above and published twenty-five years ago is still the most important on the subject. Its merit consists in the flashes of insight and range of experience which the author covers. But the systematization is scarcely adequate. Even his definition of personality as an internal structure (Janet uses the word *"travail"* apparently as we might say colloquially "affair") and not merely an external series of actions, words and processes of all sorts, for the purpose of unification and differentiation as regards the corporal, social, and temporal. Now does this definition satisfy us? Is "of all kinds" any better than "etc." And do we have personality for the purpose of unifying and differentiating? And again, the corporal, social, and temporal do not make a continuum, unless you explain these words in such a manner as to wish to substitute other terms. Here Janet has not, in advanced age, abandoned his old philosophical *métier.* The corporal, in Janet's sense, refers to the psychophysiological elements which are the base of personality; the social includes the affective elements (emotions, sentiments, temperament) while the temporal, curiously enough, deals with the abnormal, since we are susceptible to changes in time. Each of the parts is developed with clarity and garnished with unusual illustrations from Janet's own rich experience, but the handle, which the Germans polish with such great care, is somewhat crude.

Janet is not sanguine as to the predictability of human action. In the reflexes, the sensations, memory, perception, we could go by laws, but in the case of personality "there is in this account—the account in time, something incomprehensible, altogether original, which is not found in the other relations. Personality has thus become distinct because one has introduced time. ... We arrive at a point where the personality of individuals is not a question of science, [but] where it is a question of history." And how does Janet proceed to fill in the gap? He must needs appeal to imagination. Here Janet, who would like to be, if not a pure behaviorist, then at least a physicalist, must pathetically resort to an intuitionism which would shock all operationists. It may have been due to the fact that he detested programmes and systems, leaning toward an objective psychology, that Pierre Janet, although the most important French psychologist of his day, left no school in France. In this respect he fared better in the United States. Of his thousands of students, there is scarcely one who has identified himself with Janet's special doctrines. Most of the contemporary psychologists no doubt have been influenced by him, but not enough to be professionally conscious of the fact.

Variety Without Novelty

There is no dearth of books in French on personality, character, the self, and allied topics. For the most part they are brief treatises, written in a popular style, and selective rather than comprehensive. There are brilliant literary productions like Ramon Fernandez' *De la Personnalité* (1928) in which the literary viewpoint is ranged against the academic, or Emile Peillaube's *Caractère et Personnalité* (1935), bringing to the fore the Catholic personality model, tinctured, of course, with theology. There is N. Braunshausen's *L'Étude expérimentale du Caractère* (1937) which gives a survey of the personality testing programme; and although published in Belgium, it may be considered close to the French treatment. O. Lemarie in his *Essai sur la Personne* (1936) complains that the failure in the present-day picture of personality is the lack of method. It is his belief, at least, that the humdrum analytic and static approach should become dynamic and evolutional in order to catch the essentials of character. Lemarie also takes up a spiritual position, no matter what the method, and leads the discussion right up to considerations of the personality of God.

One may turn to the personality studies by R. LeSenne (*Le Mensonge et le Caractère,* 1930) and particularly his *Traité de Caractérologie* (1945) which belongs to the more solid works in French, or one may cite J. Toulemonde's book *La Caractérologie* (1951) which concerns itself mainly with types, and particularly those he labels *confiant* and *méfiant,* i.e., the confiding and the suspicious, corresponding to the extravert and introvert dichotomy, or to A. Burloud's *Le Caractère* which bases its thesis on the elementary tendencies plus dispositions and acquired factors. Burloud defines the elementary tendency as a "distinct principle of activity, a dynamic temporal and plurivalent form, which registers directly or indirectly through an image, a judgment, or a movement" (p. 18). Burloud comes close to McDougall in his stress of conation, purpose, and will, even if he never mentions his name, but he manages to include a good deal of his French predecessors and endeavors to combine their classification with that of Heymans and Wiersma and others.

LeSenne, like most continental psychologists, takes *character* to mean that which has a congenital foundation and is permanent, while *personality* is more inclusive and takes in all the acquired tendencies, as well. The *I,* on the other hand, is the active centre which unites the two. The arrangement is likened to a piano (character), the composition (personality), and the pianist (the *I*). Certainly that is not in line with the presentation of this chapter, but it is typical of European theorists.

As for the rest, LeSenne develops a characterology based on the Dutch account of Heymans and Wiersma, and since out of their factors of emotivity, activity, and primary or secondary function, as the case may be, they had built up eight classes or types,* he elaborates on them by delineating each in great detail, drawing on literature and biography, with which he is unusually familiar. A list of ninety questions in the original Dutch investigation has been examined for correlations so that a certain quantitative approach or treatment has been attempted. The classification is superior to the older ones of Ribot, Malapert, Paulhan, and other French characterologists of the early century, but it is still just a descriptive study of types, interesting enough, but not sufficiently dynamic.

In a sense, much of the material corresponds to that in W. H. Sheldon's books, where there are also type combinations galore, but there, the physical measurements, at least, afford us a firmer and safer beachhead. One of the most instructive portions of LeSenne's treatise is the psychological character sketch, or as it is called "idiograph," of Alfred de Vigny.

If we may include the French Swiss here, then W. Boven's textbook *La Science du Caractère* (Lausanne, 1931) should be noted. If we follow the author's premises, then the book is systematically constructed. Boven speaks of character as if it were an all-embracing article synonymous with the individual. He starts with an elementary or primary layer of *dispositions,* largely vegetative and motor, which might include needs (well-being), sympathy, tidiness, then he goes on to a second layer, which is more complicated that he designates *traits,* like honesty, pretense, miserliness. These are resultants or secondary, in that past experiences might have had their effect on the individual; and finally there is the third layer consisting of cognitive qualities. These are called *lineaments,* comprehending imagination, memory, reflection, etc. He is not averse to accepting Freudian mechanisms like repression (but is mistaken when he makes this a

* For a full discussion of Heymans and Wiersma's work, see Roback's *The Psychology of Character,* chapter 14.

conscious process, and apparently confuses *repression* with *suppression*). However he will have nothing to do with the libido theory of psycho analysis, which he considers a mystification.

The French waver between the sensory and the motor, between a mentalistic and a behavioristic point of view, and so they are apt to come to a compromise. The term *idées-forces* has been popular with them since Fouillée's time, and Janet has been impelled to talk of psychology as the science of conduct (*conduite*) in order to include the mental, which, as he believed, would have been impossible had he defined it as the science of behavior (*comportement*).

Of present-day psychologists in France, D. Lagache, perhaps, is the most cosmopolitan and, in a sense, the successor of Janet, even if on a much smaller scale; for he has made it his business to reach out for new conceptions in other countries, and has acquired a great deal of experience in the clinical field. He is thus conversant with psychoanalysis and at the same time has more than a bowing acquaintance with the claims of molar behaviorism and totality theories like those propounded by gestalt psychology. Like Janet he would not put his eggs in one basket, and yet while he distributes them, there are not enough in any one place to afford an adequate meal to satisfy our scientific hunger.

In espousing psychoanalysis, he has, of course, started where Janet left off, but it may be that he has too many irons in the fire to forge the longed-for instrument. His own brand of psychoanalysis comports with what we should call para-Freudianism, for he believes in the totality aspect of man, thus approaching Franz Alexander. He makes more of the ego than Freud ever did; and moral conduct, to him, is not to be ignored in the overall treatment of patients. The "you" is stressed in the "we" relationship between any two people, which is reminiscent of J. Mark Baldwin's *socius*, and approaches the interpersonalism of the sociologists and H. S. Sullivan among the psychiatrists. Lagache is still moving in a French orbit as his gaze is directed elsewhere. Thus French tradition is blended with Viennese, German and American extracts.

DIALECTIC PERSONALISM

Perhaps E. Mounier who died in the prime of life after the publication of his fourteenth book should be accorded some space here because of his influence as a personalist especially through his journal, *Esprit*. Mounier figures more as an apostle or prophet than a psychologist or even philosopher. He shuns the systematic and inspires through his germinal ideas couched in figurative language. The strangest part of his philosophy is that it is born of the union of Christianity and—of all things—Marxism, so that we might call him a socialistic personalist, minus the materialism. Nor does he rest there. He is even willing to cull wisdom from Hitler, as when he approvingly quotes "given a certain problem any decision, even an incorrect decision, is better than none" (*Qu'est ce que le Personnalisme?* 1946). We are inclined to think nevertheless that the world would be better off if criminal maniacs took their orders from their keepers and were barred from making their own decisions. Since Mounier's sphere is sociological and religious, one might infer that his personalism, dialectically enough, runs close to interpersonalism.

CRITERION OF PERSONALITY

We must yet advert to one important issue which so far only the present writer has made an attempt to thresh out, and that is the criterion of personality. In his *Personality in Theory and Practice,* (Roback, 1950) the question is asked "Do we place value on personality outside of the instructiveness that attaches to it as a study, or is it no different in this respect than, let us say, the field of colloids in chemistry or topology in mathematics? There are no criteria there. We merely derive data and collate them into a system. Is personality no different from topics in the physical and natural sciences? It would seem as if most psychologists revel in the thought that this is so—a hangover from the days when their predecessors were bent on elevating psychology to the level of a natural science." (p. 278)

We are far removed from that period. Psychology needs no support from other quarters and can stand on its own feet. It can exercise its own prerogatives. Its problems are partly of a general scientific nature, and partly specific, peculiar to its subject-matter. Personality is, in a sense, the goal of psychology. It is the house, while psychology is only a congeries of bricks, tiles, shingles, slabs, mortar, etc. The mason-psychologists might tell us: 'we have acquitted ourselves well in constructing this house. Anything beyond that is outside our jurisdiction.' I am of the opinion—and hope there are others who share it—that we must have a criterion by which personalities might be judged. Not a few will, if pressed on that point, transfer this function to the realm of character. They will argue that evaluation does not come up for consideration here. There are no good or bad personalities, but well-adjusted or poorly-adjusted personalities.

Adjustment No Criterion

That I contend is a rather restricted view, inadequate on several counts. (1) It lacks perspective, dealing, as it does, with the individual at a certain period only—a purely temporal standard. Its short-range policy is evident when we compare a well-adjusted Babbitt or bounder with a poorly-adjusted saint. (2) The full meaning of adjustment has long been in question. Is it possible to be inwardly adjusted without being outwardly adjusted, and vice versa? (3) Should a well-adjusted individual, for some reason, perhaps in another milieu, become maladjusted, would that argue for a complete drop in the evaluation?

By examining our own attitudes to great personalities, we shall see that in every case, from the vantage point of posterity, it is the beneficent *influence which they have exercised on others and the world at large that counts*. Nothing else is of equal value: neither intelligence, nor charm, nor jolliness, nor artistry, organizing ability, skill—in short, personality will not be valuable unless there has been a positive human relationship with others. It is in this direction that some of the future work on personality should be deflected, otherwise we are scurrying around like ants without realizing what the whole bustle is for.

In this connection, the *adequacy valence* of personality must also be taken up. To begin with, it must be apparent that although personality consists of hundreds of ingredients, its essence or nucleus, like a carefully arranged bouquet of flowers, would contain but very few items. The peak of the pyramid does not allow too much space, even though "there is always room for one more." It is not necessary to fix the number at this juncture. We might reason as follows: Personality is made up of four departments of characteristics: (a) the physical, (b) the cognitive, (c) the affective, and (d) the conative or volitional. Each of these large divisions (artificial, to be sure, from an operational angle, nevertheless analytically indispensable) must yield its quota to the composition of a human personality. It stands to reason, then, that the core of personality, in its highest form, will also be represented by each of these divisions. Our task is now to discover the most important or *basic* element in each of these classes and group them together as constituting the *adequacy valence*.

In brief it may be said that (a) out of the cognitive sphere we take *insight* as the most important factor (b) out of the affective, *sentiment* recommends itself, and out of the volitional layer, *independence* or *courage* stands out. This triad with the less important physical factor of *animatedness* should represent a true picture of an adequate personality. These three items (animatedness is but subordinate) are worth more than perhaps 99 others on which we spend a fortune and years of labor measuring. And as a corollary it may be stated that no one can have been a good influence in the lives of a great many individuals without possessing insight, sentiment, and independence in a large measure.

REFERENCES

1 Allport, G. W. *Personality; A psychological Interpretation*. New York: Holt, 1937.

2 Angyal, Andras. A theoretical model for personality studies. *Journal of Personality*, 1951, vol. 20.

3 Blum, G. S. and D. R. Miller. Exploring the psychoanalytic theory of the "Oral Character". *Journal of Personality*, 1952, vol. 21.

4 Child, I. L. Personality, In: *Annual Review of Psychology*, 1954, vol. 5.

5 Eggan, D. The general problem of Hopi adjustment. *The American Anthropologist*, 1943, vol. 45.

6 Erikson, E. H. *The psychoanalytic study of the child*. New York: Intern. Univ. Press, 1945.

7 Eysenck, H. J. Personality, In: *Annual Review of Psychology*, 1952, vol. 3.

8 —— *The Structure of Human Personality*. London: Methuen, 1953.

9 Feifel, Herman. Ego structure and mental deterioration. *Journal of Personality*, 1951, vol. 20.

10 Gilbert, A. R. Recent Theories of Stratification of Personality. *The Journal of Psychology*, 1951, vol. 33.

11 Hallowell, A. I. Aggression in Saulteaux society, *Psychiatry*, 1940.

12 Hebb, D. O. The role of neurological ideas in psychiatry. *Journal of Personality*, 1951, vol. 20.

13 Janet, Pierre. On memories which are too real. In: *Problems of Personality* (Ed. by A. A. Roback). London: Kegan Paul, 1925.

14 Kardiner, A. *et al. The psychological frontiers of society*. New York: Columbia University Press, 1945.

15 Krech, David and Klein, G. S. The problem of pesonality and its theory. *Journal of Personality*, 1951, vol. 20.

16 Lashley, K. S. Structural variation in the nervous system in relation to behavior. *Psychol. Rev.*, 1947, vol. 54.

17 Leary, T. F., Freedman, M. B., Ossorio, A. G. and Coffey, H. S. The interpersonal dimension of personality. *Journal of Personality*, 1951, vol. 20.

18 Lersch, Ph. *Aufbau des Charakters*. Leipzig, 1938.

19 Leighton, D. and Kluckhohn, C. *The Navaho*. Cambridge: Harvard University Press, 1946.

20 Linton, R. *The cultural background of personality*. New York: Appleton-Century, 1945.

21 MacKinnon, D. W. Personality. In: *Annual Review of Psychology*, 1952, vol. 3.

22 Miller, D. R. and Blum, G. S. Exploring the psychoanalytic theory of the "Oral Character." *Journal of Personality*, 1951, vol. 20.

23 Murray, H. A. and Kluckhohn, C. (ed.) *Personality in Nature, Society and Culture*. New York: Knopf, 1949.

24 Ossorio, A. G., Freedman, M. B., Leary, T. F. and Coffey, H. S. The interpersonal dimension of personality. *Journal of Personality*, 1951, vol. 20.

24 a Parsons, T. and Shils, E. A. *Toward a General Theory of Interaction*. Cambridge: Harvard U. Press, 1951.

25 Peillaube, E. *Caractère et Personnalité*. Paris: Téquè, 1935.

26 Rapaport, David. The conceptual model of psychoanalysis. *Journal of Personality*, 1951, vol. 20.

27 Riggs, M. M. An investigation of the nature and generality of three new personality variables — Part I. The sentence test. *Journal of Personality,* 1952, vol. 21.

28 A. A. Roback (ed.): *Problems of Personality, Studies in Honor of Morton Prince* (1925) Kegan Paul, London.

29 Roback, A. A. *Personality in theory and practice.* Cambridge: Sci-Art, 1950.

30 —— *The psychology of character,* 3rd ed. London: Routledge, 1952.

31 Róheim, G. Psychoanalysis of primitive cultural types. *Intern. Jour. Psycho-Anal.,* 1932, vol. 12.

32 Sears, R. R. Personality. In: *Annual Review of Psychology,* 1950, vol. 1.

33 Skinner, B. F. *Science and Human Behavior.* New York: Macmillan, 1953.

34 Sullivan, H. S. *The interpersonal theory of psychology* (ed. by H. S. Berry and M. L. Gavel). New York: Norton, 1953.

35 Wellek, S. *Die Polarität im Aufbau des Charakters.* Bern: Francke, 1950.

Chapter IX

THE CHARACTER ASPECT IN RECENT PSYCHOLOGY AND PSYCHIATRY

A. A. Roback, Ph.D.
Head of Psychology Department
Emerson College

EDITORIAL NOTE

In psychological circles, character has fallen by the wayside. It has become associated almost exclusively with ethics; and at the most, it may be allotted some space in educational psychology texts. What has happened to it is the reverse of the Psalmist's happy-ending reflection; for we might say that "the cornerstone of our whole social organization has been condemned by the (psychological) masons." Here and there, however, there is a sign of a changed attitude. It is, of course, not in the animal laboratories that such indications will manifest themselves but in the clinical bivouac of life.

The writer has detached the subject of character from that of personality for the very reason that it was being regarded as the obscure and minor adjunct of the more inclusive department. In recent years, however, we have learned, from biology and physics, that often the tiny nucleus is worth far more than everything else in the unit involved.

A. A. Roback's Psychology of Character, *which originally appeared in the International Library of Kegan Paul (London) went through several editions and was translated into Spanish and German. The enlarged edition of 1952 ran into 780 pages. During the period between the first and fourth printing, interest in character had lagged. Whatever the reasons—and it would take us far afield to dwell on them, although they certainly should be analyzed—it is beginning to dawn upon some of the vanguard in psychology that (a) character is not merely a blind alley of personality (b) that it is not another name for personality traits* in toto *(c) that it is a mistake from the standpoint of scientific organization to disdain it. Logical positivism may rule it out of its court on the fallacious premise that it belongs to an axiological frame of reference. We may yet establish, nevertheless, that it is a biophysical product i. e., a distillation of certain unit characters. And if we are to dismiss the subject* ab initio, *how can we ever hope to prove the point?*

TRENDS IN THE PSYCHOLOGY OF CHARACTER

It has been customary to treat character together with personality, and gloss over the former with a single remark or two, and for this reason two separate chapters have been allotted to the two topics, which are distinct and should not be deliberately confused. The source of this confusion lies in the fact that the term "character" has been taken in the sense of a characteristic, a unit character, largely a biological concept, and so popularized by Francis Galton.

In *Psychological Abstracts,* there is no single rubric for character, not even a subrubric. It seems to be a wandering topic, an adjunct, now attaching itself to personality, which is itself a subdivision of "complex processes," and now thrown in with development psychology, or, again, falling into the class of behavior deviations, or found under personnel psychology. In brief, it is all over the place, and yet, it would have been more reasonable to gather all the character items and place them into a special class.

R. Heiss (1936) is perhaps alone of the Germans to voice a similar protest when in his *Die Lehre vom Charakter,* he complains "In designating this foundation, 'character', in the stricter sense, we must take cognizance of the fact that this concept of character was hardly treated in the literature and frequently would even be discarded as a 'value-colored' or 'ethical' concept. To be sure, common usage recognizes well the import of this sort of character, when someone is spoken of as *having* character or is without *character.* But scientific inquiry has concerned itself little with this sense . . . So that by and large, character was understood to mean the total personality" (p. 268).

Even as late as 1954, the term *characterology* was what the European session on personality at the fourteenth International Congress in Montreal went by; and the present writer, a discussant at the session, expressed his puzzlement at the nomenclature which brought American investigations under the rubric of personality and European (predominantly German) views under the head of characterology. One might think that characterology was adopted as a term because personology is a hybrid formation. The Americans seem to be quite content to let the Europeans use the word characterology, thus suggesting a gap between their own empirical approach and the more philosophical one of their colleagues in Europe.

The relation between personality and character has not always been clearly demarcated. Sometimes the one is made more inclusive, at times the other. According to some (Hans Thomae) personality embraces the external behavior aspects, while character refers more to the inner potentialities. There is no need, however, to shear the term character of its general and significant sense, nor is it meet for us to dismiss character from psychology as G. W. Allport (1937) does by saying that "character is personality evaluated and personality is character devaluated."

Were we to accept Allport's diphasic view, then a winning smile, when appreciated and designated as such, would come under the head of character, while reliability or persistence, when only noted, though not evaluated, would be pigeonholed under personality. For one thing, the evaluative phase of personality has its place also in the study of personality. It deals with such questions as the criterion of personality, but character has its own subject-matter and problems; and although it leads to the normative eventually, it does not deal with it exclusively. While Allport regards character "an unnecessary concept for psychology", it is nevertheless true that character may be treated descriptively, genetically, integrationally, etc., in a word, under the same heads as personality is discussed in the selfsame book.

DIFFERENT STUDY ANGLES

It would seem as if the ethical side of character had so overshadowed the psychological portion that the moment one mentions character (outside of the biological sphere) it is immediately associated with ethics. Roback's (1925, 1927, 1954) definition of character as "an enduring psychophysical disposition to inhibit instinctive tendencies in accordance wth regulative principles" may be regarded as a psychological rather than an ethical definition. It affirms that persons of character will do such and such, and why. The "ought" is something outside this sphere. Hence the exhortative aspect is left to the moralist, pedagogue, or preacher. Characterology, then, is the large field of character study from different angles with a view to establishing the descriptive as well as the exhortative facts of character. As a phase of personality it is a *descriptive* study, but since it projects out into the ethical sphere too, it has a *normative* side, and of course in character education it shows its *applied* facet.

It is not easy to keep personality traits separated from character. Does tact belong to the former or to the latter? The same question may be asked about ambition and a number of other traits. By and large, the answer will hinge on *the amount of effort it takes to resist an opposing tendency.* Our definition of character will be of some service in all such cases. Again, it may be asked: Why is it necessary to institute a division between character and personality, when character is a phase of personality? The reason is, of course, the significance of character in society. It is not just a phase. It is the most important phase of personality. Through its manifestation, progress is possible, and even if it should be only the mark of a small minority, there is at least some germ of it in every normal person. There is no reason why character cannot stand as an important component of personality, which embraces the conative development from unconscious strivings toward a conscious goal of social value, rated in terms of (a) constancy and (b) consistency, and therefore predictability.

The "stable character" would presuppose an integration of such traits and attitudes that acts performed by the agent could be subsumed under a general rule, if not a law. The "strong character," in popular parlance, would connote a singleness of purpose, good or bad in the social sense, whereby an objective is pursued in spite of difficulties and temptations. Finally, when the individual is always prompted to regard his acts or their consequences as affecting others (*interindividual consistency*) we have the so-called "good character."

The study of character has had its vicissitudes. At times, it was fostered even by empiricists like J. S. Mill, and certainly by idealists and religious thinkers. But the psychology of character was taken up only in the way of prolegomena or as a propaedeutic to ethics.

EMPIRICAL APPROACH

It must not be supposed that problems of character failed to occupy the minds of educator and practitioner alike. Attempts to get to the root of character came from many sides, but the work was not organized. As early as 1912, G. G. Fernald made an attempt to discover incipient delinquency by the administration of tests, but it has been shown that the discrimination of right and wrong or any moral judgment scarcely offers any reliable estimation of moral integrity. It was about a decade later that tests were devised by Voelker (1921), Cady (1921), Franzen (1922) and Raubenheimer (1925), as well as by Hartshorne and May, to actually place the subject in a life situation in order to probe his trustworthiness, aggressiveness, overstatement, etc.

FACTORIAL ANALYSIS

Meanwhile, E. Webb (1915) on the basis of factorial analysis of certain correlations, reported finding a character element corresponding to the persistency of motives. That is by no means the whole of character. It merely answers to that which is generally referred to as strength of character. The core is really social consistency i. e., a single measure for oneself and others in the matter of conduct. That this measure will be a constant is to be taken for granted, otherwise it is not a measure but an arbitrary tendency.

There was no dearth of books with the word "character" included in the title, but *The Psychology of Character,* growing out of a lengthy essay entitled "Character and Inhibition" (*Problems of Personality,* ed. by A. A. Roback) seems to be the first historical and systematic account of character as a psychological entity, as seen through various lenses (behavioristic, psychoanalytic, intuitive, etc.). A couple of years later came the landmark in this field, the gigantic Character Education Inquiry which M. A. May and H. Hartshorne conducted at Teachers College, Columbia University, over a period of five years with a staff of forty collaborating. The outcome was a series of three volumes and the upshot was that traits are specific, that habit and the situation are the only things to be considered. One may cheat in one situation and not in another. The technique of the experiments was admirable, but the fallaciousness of the conclusion was due to a superficial handling of the results, in that the motivation was not analyzed. Again it may be doubted whether children are suitable subjects in a character investigation.

Weakness of Specificity Theory

Since a whole chapter was devoted to this inquiry in *The Psychology of Character* (3d. ed., 1952), it would scarcely be worth while going over the ground again. May and Hartshorne were, at the time, influenced by the specificity doctrine of Thorndike, which colored all the work produced at Teachers College. If a trait is only a label that does not correspond to some biophysical tendency in the individual, then acts cannot be said to stem from some constant mould, but will be a function of the individual's whim in response to a given situation. Conduct is then unpredictable. At no time should we be able to say that *A* is honest, charitable, unselfish, considerate, or courageous, were we to accept the verdict of the May-Hartshorne investigation.

Even at Teachers College a dissenting voice was heard a few years later, when G. B. Watson (1932), called attention to the need of greater insight into the behavior involved and a better characterological approach before measurement can be properly assessed. Watson's critique may be amplified. Unless we have a solid basis first with premises that have been properly considered, the results of the tests are anything but conclusive. We may even doubt their validity; for to take one instance, it is not so much that there are different kinds of dishonesty, but that the individual is *motivated* in different ways (because of his make-up) in a variety of situations which have been subsumed in the popular mind under a single label. An analysis of the label will disclose the fact that it covers diverse traits.

Another critic of the specificity doctrine in the treatment of character was P. Lecky, who trenchantly exposed the weakness of the May-Hartshorne Inquiry in a small book (1945) which comes remarkably close to the views expressed earlier in *The Psychology of Character*. "If every act" he writes, "is the function of a specific situation, then since transfer is virtually negligible and since the same situation admittedly occurs but once, it follows that behavior is not predictable at all . . . and a science which can make no predictions is worthless". (p. 13)

What may be regarded, in a sense, as a sequel to the Inquiry discussed above is the extensive investigation by F. J. Havighurst and H. Taba (1949). Here it was not so much character as such which was studied directly but reputation, since the results were gained as a result of interviews with teachers and fellow students about adolescents, on the supposition that "the measures of reputation yield as adequate a picture of character as do several measures of conduct in actual test situations" (p. 309)—a belief which must first be proven. That an outgoing, genial person may take on a halo, and an introvert strike somewhat adversely is too well known to require elaboration. One of the important conclusions of the study which may precipitate discussion is that "moral character could be understood only in relation to the over-all personality of the individual. Good character means one thing in one type of personality and something quite different in another. Character is formed differently in different people."

PSYCHOANALYSIS

The psychoanalytic approach to the study of character is through the avenue of the unconscious—the repressed residues of very early experiences in life: principally the Oedipus and castration complexes and the development of the sexual drive from the pregenital (oral, anal, phallic) to the fully genital level. According to Freud "the permanent character traits are either changing perpetuations of original impulses, sublimations of them, or reaction-formations against them." Sublimation diverts an originally undesirable impulse into some socially valuable activity, while a reaction-formation just masks it, without doing either the individual or society any good. Much was said about the oral character (sadism) the anal character, (compulsion, miserliness, orderliness) and the urethral character (ambition).

When W. A. White (1921) entitled his book *Mechanisms of Character Formation,* he had those mechanisms in mind, and was not concerned with the more typical elements of character, which later began to take on more significance in the psychoanalytic system, as the topographical scheme of *id, ego,* and *superego* became one of the most solid planks in the Freudian platform. When Freud toward the close of his life veered toward the ego principle and took more interest in the superego, then, and then only, could we clearly perceive the relation between psychoanalysis and what is generally understood as character, for it is in the realistic ego and the superego that the cognitive-volitional is grounded just as the affective is rooted in the id.

With all the dissidents, Jung, Adler, Stekel, and Rank, as well as the para-Freudians in general—Horney, Fromm, Reich—character has been a major consideration, no longer to be brushed aside as an inconsequential detail for either science or therapy. Whether character is a protective armor or a burdensome hard shell which engenders neurosis, it is at least something to be reckoned with. In the Freudian system, the rigidly ethical person is set down as belonging to the anal-erotic type, and a sensitive conscience is associated with a guilt complex and a sadistic component turned inward, surely the least acceptable of the many theses constituting psychoanalysis.

THERAPY VS. CHARACTER BUILDING

Freud, as is well known, was primarily concerned with treating and curing patients. As a physician, he cared little about the morals or character of those who consulted him, except in so far as the ill effects interfered with the therapy. His business was to relieve the patient, and therefore he was far more interested in the symptoms and their formation than in traits as such. Recognizing that the neuroses originated in the conflict between sexuality and the ego, between the *amo* and the *veto,* he and his immediate coadjutors delved in that direction, especially when they found the neurosis more accessible.

Later, it was noticed that the ego instincts or drives had been neglected, and more attention was now given to those than in the past, until emphasis began to shift to the ego, and with it to character, which seemed to stand out like a thick wall that must yet be negotiated before some new excavation could be done. It was only during the last dozen years of his life that Freud reckoned with this newly discovered framework; and as a matter of fact, thanks to the new insight, psychoanalysis started on a new course. It was no longer a matter of ferreting out repressed complexes but looking into the resistances which held these repressions as in a vice. And here Freud came to grips with the problem of character. From then on more of the psychoanalytic literature is devoted to the subject, while some of his disciples who have diverged recently from the orthodox party line have made character, as we shall see in another section, the crux of their study. Indeed, it was the inability to see eye to eye with Freud on fundamental questions of character interpretation and morality which precipitated the rift.

To what extent Freud himself was influenced in this direction may be gleaned from his writings shortly before his death in which he states: "Every analyst of experience will be able to think of a number of cases in which he has taken permanent leave of the patient *rebus bene gestis*. There is a far greater discrepancy between theory and practice in cases of so-called character-analysis. Here it is not easy to predict a natural end to the process . . . the business of analysis is to secure the best possible psychological conditions for the functioning of the ego . . ." (*Internat. Jour. Psycho-Anal.* 1937, vol. 18, p. 403.)

It is evident then that he thought the ego, including the superego, far more inscrutable than the id, and felt that this region was destined for future investigation.

What Freud has overlooked in his likening conscience to the sense of taboo guilt is the regulative principle, which gives character its stamp of validation. The taboo is an internalization of a tribal custom, but the regulative principle, like liberty, requires universalization. It is not thrust upon us from without. These principles are the very opposite of the taboo. Men of character often lose life or limb in fighting the group imposition. Certainly Freud seems to have had no faith in human values; as for respect for moral origins, his libidinal doctrine is its very nemesis. If our ethical conduct depends wholly on whether our libido has been arrested at the oral, anal, or urethral level or has been developed to the genital point, where sexual intercourse is performed satisfactorily, there can be no standards possible of assessment; and character can be the result only of fortuitous, even if determined, events in the past. Characteristics, in the biological sense, would be a better name for it. Freud has imbibed at the font of the enlightenment philosophy, and a nondescript and indifferent relativity has been the outcome.

INDIVIDUAL PSYCHOLOGY

Adler divides character traits into two classes: the aggressive and non-aggressive. Among the first are included vanity and ambition, jealousy, envy, avarice, and hate, while the non-aggressive type comprises seclusiveness, anxiety, faint-heartedness, and uncouth behavior.

Adler does not believe in the inheritance of character traits. They are the consequence of the style of life. Children seize upon those qualities in their elders which bring them closer to their goal; and if laziness is seen as a means of gaining this objective, then they will become lazy as a matter of course. Of course that sounds wide of the mark, but Adler was ready to bolster a theory. Laziness does mean an easy life to some, but certainly not to all, or even the majority, and laziness is not something acquired by emulation. Adler made more of character than Freud, but unfortunately it was at the mercy of a hypothesis which played havoc with the facts. If the goal of superiority directs the development of character, then traits are only devices or tricks adopted to reach that end, good or bad, mainly bad because the goal of superiority (as a self-end) in itself, is amoral.

A Psychoanalytic Voluntarist

Otto Rank, who is known particularly for his attempt to make the birth trauma the basis of all neurosis, diverged from Freud's system to the extent that he prescribed for his patient a self-disciplinary course which is aptly labelled "Will-Therapy." As for para-Freudians like E. Fromm, his stand on value problems and moral judgment may be gathered from this statement. "Neurosis itself is in the last analysis a symptom of moral failure" (1947, p. VIII).

Para-Freudians Stress Character

Similarly, Karen Horney declared (1939) that "an absence of value judgments belongs among those ideals we should try rather to overcome than to cultivate," and "Our knowledge of cause and effect in psychic ailments should not blind us to the fact that they do involve moral problems . . . The moral problems are an integral part of the illness."

Although Freud and Adler and Rank are no longer contemporary, their psychology has influenced so many present-day writers that their views would need to be reviewed in bare outline in this connection, especially as the character angle of depth psychology is usually omitted in textbooks.

CHARACTER CONSISTS OF GETTING RID OF IT (!)

Reich's use of the term, character, is somewhat deceptive; for to him it would consist of breaking the rigid and hard shell and the resistances which it generates. Character, in this sense, is tantamount to the full genital development, which means getting rid of the armor and becoming flexible and free like the jelly fish—a rather novel conception of character. Yet Reich moves in the framework of character and is preoccupied with it, though he may pervert its goal.

In recent years, psychiatry and clinical psychology have been paying more attention to the matter of character, although in many instances, personality and character traits have not been differentiated. We hear much of the compulsive or obsessional or hysterical character. Now it may well be that there are certain character traits which are correlated with the compulsive or the hysteric, but as such these types do not fit into the categories of character, simply because they lack the volitional and evaluative gradations which all character treatment implies.

CHANGE IN CLINICAL TREND

There is some evidence that the pendulum is swinging in this self-regulative and autonomous direction and away from the *ego—a-passive-theatre* view, current in Freud's generation. Only 25 years ago, such a position would be derided in most clinical circles as smacking of the pastoral; but without injecting religion into clinical situations or even bringing ethics into therapy, the rôle of the volitional, the characterial ego, is beginning to make itself felt. Although primarily a researcher in learning, O. H. Mowrer (1952) has shown reluctance to accept either Pavlovian, Thorndikian, or Freudian explain-alls of neurosis and its paradox, feeling, as he does, that there is something of a moral deficit involved, and is inclined to look for the source of the trouble in the cognitive-volitional make-up, instead of the wholly affective, as orthodox psychoanalysis was wont to insist on. The neurotic has learned how not to learn; and this learning deficit is, in the last analysis, a moral deficit. Perhaps Mowrer goes too far in the opposite direction. If he were not moral, the conflict would not have arisen; and that is the difference between the neurotic and the delinquent. It might be safer and fairer to say that the neurotic is atoning for temptations — undergoing a heavy penance.

Mowrer comes close to the para-Freudians who inject a characterial note into the psychoanalytic rhapsody when he speaks of "voluntary and consciously directed action" instead of habit as an antidote to neurosis (1953, p. 175). He is not even averse to introducing such archaic phrases as "freedom of choice" and "moral responsibility" in his argument, which runs along the lines of self-determinism. Neurosis to him is punishment in order to guide the individual in the future (p. 181).

Apropos of this issue, it may not be irrelevant to mention that in his doctoral dissertation, *The Interference of Will Impulses,* the present writer, discussing the applications of the experimental results, argued that "whether we yield or not, we are following the lines of least resistance. . . . The hero is actuated by his idea just as the coward is determined by his. What really distinguishes their modes of behavior is the value judgment which attaches to their respective ideas." A decade later, in his *Psychology of Character,* the codicil is added that "there is a difference also in the genesis of the act. The praiseworthy act has been released by an idea which it has taken effort, perhaps struggle, to build up."

More and more clinical studies are appearing in which character figures not merely in the sense of just any personality trait, but in the volitional frame. Out of a number of illustrations, for which there is no space here, let me but refer to a typical one by A. F. Valenstein, J. J. Michaels, and Marg. Evje (1953) in which the authors found one group of neurotic veterans (A) who had fullfilled their military obligations without any psychiatric involvements, yet breaking down at the close of the war, while the other group (B) became mentally disabled during service, but did not seek psychiatric aid as soon after discharge as group A. In group A, the men were of a tougher fibre, appeared to have a stronger ego. "Of all the variables, the A group conspicuously gave evidence of perseverance at work, good service performance, and self-discipline. . . . They tended to exploit symptoms to a lesser extent, and this may reflect a heightened sense of duty that probably prevailed." The conclusion brings out that such individuals were able to perform without disability while in service only to break down after demobilization, due to their compulsive type of character. "The self-esteem of these individuals is dependent on the quality of their performance. . . . They critically evaluate their achievements in terms of personal success or failure, masculine adequacy or inadequacy, and they drive themselves relentlessly to success". In the strong ego, endurance of tension, inhibitiveness, and high purposiveness will be the most salient qualities, and these go with the mildly compulsive. Excessive compulsiveness will lead to rigidity and obsessive neurosis.

CHARACTEROLOGY IN APPLIED FIELDS

In Switzerland, Franziska Baumgarten has busied herself with studies of a characterological nature. While still in Poland, she had engaged in exploring deceitfulness among children. In 1936, there appeared her survey of gratitude among children, analyzing four types, and offering a number of interesting observations e. g., that gratitude is correlated with specific kinds of intelligence (not the practical kind, however). The question arises whether what the children promise they would do to repay kindness is to be taken seriously i. e., can be said to tally with what they actually would perform.

Baumgarten's researches are not primarily pedagogical. She is interested more in applied psychology; personnel matters, vocational psychology, etc. Her objective is thus practical, yet her results based on non-projective tests and questionnaires, as in her vocational investigations (1941), contain much that is useful for the theoretical study of character. It is true that it is often difficult to separate personality traits from character qualities, but it would seem that she stresses the latter more often.

A SOCIOLOGICAL VIEW

In the chapter on personality, it has already been remarked that sociology is becoming greatly interested in psychological topics, and offers its own definitions and formulations in a sphere which, although somewhat related to it, is nevertheless scarcely within its bailiwick. To the sociologist, there is no individual, but an interpersonal, institutional, or social set of relations. The person, to the sociologist, is simply a bundle of rôles.

Let us take a recent text, that by Hans Gerth and C. Wright Mills on *Character and Social Structure* (1953) and see how *character* fares there. According to these authors, man may be viewed under four aspects, each envisaged by a different concept. There is (a) the *organism,* a biological term relating to structural mechanisms (b) the *psychic structure,* which takes in feeling, sensation, and impulses, as well as perception and purpose. Then, there is (c) the *person,* i. e., the social actor, who plays his part; and it is for us to discover the motives which lead him to assume this or that rôle, and finally there is (d) the *character structure,* which is "the most inclusive term for the individual as a whole entity. It refers to the relatively stabilized integration of the organism's psychic structure linked with the social rôles of the person. On the one hand, a character structure is anchored in the organism and its specialized organs through the psychic structure: on the other hand, it is formed by the particular combination of social rôles which the person has incorporated from out of the total roles available to him in his society. The uniqueness of a certain individual, or of a type of individual, can only be grasped by proper attention to the organization of these component elements of the character structure". (p. 22)

It is evident that the term "character" as employed here does not comport with the concept in vogue, that it is merely an over-all label for a conglomeration of traits, motives, mechanisms, interrelations. Character here is not differentiated from personality, and we are not sure whether person and personality are synonyms in this context, for the latter term does not appear in the book. Hence, we have nothing specific to put our finger on. Definitions are useful when we can see illustrations before us.

CHARACTER EDUCATION

It is somewhat odd that while the subject of character has been in the ascendant among professionals, there has been nothing like a concerted effort to come to grips with the practical problems of character, which have become rather acute, especially in the present generation. Not so long ago, character education was one of the fundamentals uniting the interests of the teacher, the church, the home, the court; and even moral philosophy and the psychology of personality had certain stakes here. Not only articles in the hundreds but a large number of books dealing with character building saw the light in the decade between 1925 and 1935. Within the last fifteen years or so, there has been a decided drop in emphasis and output in quarters which fairly bristled with interest. What has happened to cause this decline? Certainly it cannot be said that the issues are no longer actual. Juvenile delinquency has been more rampant than ever, so much so that it is a threat to the school as well as to the community. There is no need of speculating on the causes. The situation alone counts for our purpose; and that is too well established.

ETHICAL RELATIVITY

One reason for the disorganization among workers from different fields is probably that character education has come to connote a species of sermonizing and nothing more. Years ago, inspirational books like those of Smiles had a great appeal. Of late, the intellectual public has become if not *blasé,* then at least more sophisticated; and those with any scientific pretensions are chary of touching anything which does not have a technical prospect, so that the results could be brought under some scientific aegis. What has become of all the character-education and character-inquiry institutes? If they work hand in hand with religious organizations, then they are not likely to be recognized in scientific circles; and the psychologists, criminologists, and social psychiatrists have set themselves different tasks, in which adjustment and statistics are the *urim* and *thummim* on the breastplates of the modern foundation-priests, for whom the term "character" is almost taboo, savoring of the popular approach of the old-time pedagogue and clergyman. And foundations control the experimental Rialto.

What has led to this is not only the advance of scientific standards and demands, but also the expansion of ethical relativity, and the whittling away of values as mere cultural excrescences, largely as a result of Freudian psychology, as we have already seen and, what is at present even a greater influence, sociology and cultural anthropology. When Herbert Spencer, some 75 years ago, began to promulgate his views on ethical relativism in a series of works, he was but a lone eagle or lone wolf, depending on our own attitude. Sociology was scarcely born then, and cultural anthropology had only been conceived. In the present age of physical relativity, it is only to be expected that ethics and character would be slanted in the same direction. If we all have a sense of guilt, and if there are unconscious motives propelling us toward misdeeds, if all charitable acts are the result of reaction-formations or the camouflage of sadism, then, of course, it would be futile to talk about character, in any volitional sense. Again, if right and wrong behavior is only a function of the particular locality and set of mores, then one can be held responsible only from a legal but not an ethical standpoint. Character, then, is no longer fraught with meaning, and at best is only a name for a consolidation of social relationships.

PRESENT-DAY PSYCHOLOGY

Whether or how long this relativistic dominance is to last cannot be foretold. It is quite possible that a compromise will be made, and the volitional aspect of character will once more be studied—and not only in Catholic institutions. The relativistic extremists may yet become aware of the fact that society cannot thrive on a principle which makes short shrift of all principles; and that we must study the matter of character more deeply if only to keep the world from toppling despite its technically solid foundation, for with every technical improvement, the threat to peaceful living seems to become greater, and the ampler the facilities, the more pronounced the tendency toward conflict. By disregarding the import of character we are widening the breach between knowing and living. By examining the concept anew in the light of fresh data from other fields, in addition to sociology and Freudian tenets, we stand to gain both theoretically and practically.

BIBLIOGRAPHY

Allport, G. W. *The Nature of Personality; Selected papers.* Boston: Addison-Wesley, 1950.

Baumgarten, F. *Die Dankbarkeit bei Kindern und Jungendlichen.* (Beiträge zur Charakter- und Persönlichkeitsforschung). Bern: Francke, 1936.

Baumgarten-Trämer, F. *Der Charakter und die Charakterbildung.* Bern: 1936.

——*Die Charakterprüfung der Berufsanwärter.* (Beiträge zur Charakter- und Persönlichkeitsforschung) Zurich: Rascher, 1941.

Cady, V. M. The Psychology and Pathology of Personality. *Journal of Delinquency,* 1922, vol. 7.

Fernald, G. G. The Defective Delinquent: Differentiating Tests. *American Journal of Insanity,* 1912, vol. 68.

Gerth, H. and Mills, C. W. *Character and Social Structure.* New York: Harcourt Brace, 1953.

Havighurst, F. J. and H. Taba. *Adolescent Character and Personality.* New York: Teachers College, 1949.

Heiss, R. *Die Lehre vom Charakter.* Berlin-Leipzig: Gruyter, 1936.

Klages, L. *Persönlichkeit, Einführung in die Charakterkunde,* 1927.

Lecky, P. *Self-Consistency; A Theory of Personality.* New York: Island Press, 1945.

Lersch, Ph. *Der Aufbau des Charakters.* Leipzig: 1938.

LeSenne, R. *Traité de caractérologie.* Paris, 1945.

Mounier, E. *Traité du caractère.* Paris: Ed. du Seuil, 1946.

Mowrer, O. H. Learning Theory and the Neurotic Paradox. In: *Learning Theory and Personality Dynamics*. New York: Ronald, 1952.
—— Motivation in Neurosis: In: *Current Theory and Research in Motivation. A Symposium* (ed. by J. S. Brown). Lincoln, Nebr.: Univ. of Nebraska Press, 1953.
Rohracher, H. *Kleine Einführung in die Charakterkunde*, 6th ed., 1952.
Roback, A. A. Character and Inhibition. In: *Problems of Personality* (ed. by Roback). London: Kegan Paul, 1925.
—— *A Bibliography of Character and Personality*. Cambridge: Sci-Art, 1927.
—— Character, in *Encyclopaedia of the Social Sciences*, 1930, 1935.
—— *The Psychology of Character*, 3rd enl. ed. London: Kegan Paul, 1952.
—— *History of American Psychology*. New York: Library Publishers, 1952.
Thomae, H. *Persönlichkeit, eine dynamische Interpretation*. Bonn: Bouvier, 1951.
Valenstein, A. F., Michaels, J. J. and Evje, Marg. Aspects of Character in the Neurotic Veteran. *Journal Nervous and Mental Disease*, 1953, vol. 117.
Verdun, M. *Le Caractère et ses correlations*, 2 vols. Paris, 1950-51.
Watson, G. B. Tests of Personality and Character. *Rev. of Educ. Research*, 1932, vol. 2.
Webb, E. Character and Intelligence. *British Journal of Psychol. Monog. Suppl.*, vol. 1, part 3, 1925.

PART II
Branches

CHAPTER X

CHILD PSYCHOLOGY

JOHN E. ANDERSON, Ph.D., LL.D.

Professor of Psychology and Director, Institute of Child Welfare
University of Minnesota

EDITORIAL NOTE

No introduction is necessary to child psychology. It has always been the most important subdivision of genetic psychology. Some universities have especially encouraged research in that particular branch, and even separate institutes have been founded to train workers with children and conduct investigations on child development. Yale, Teachers College at Columbia, the University of Iowa, the University of California and the University of Minnesota have been especially active in that direction. Although there are not many textbooks on child psychology, those that have appeared within the last decade or so are of a high order. One must also point with satisfaction to the authoritative volume edited by Leonard Carmichael (2d edition, 1954) which is almost encyclopedic in scope.

The contributor invited to write the chapter in our own volume is Dr. John E. Anderson, Ph.D., (Harvard) and LL.D. (Wyoming) who founded the Institute of Child Welfare at the University of Minnesota in 1925 and was its Director until 1954 when he gave up administrative responsibilities to accept a research professorship in the Institute. He has been President of the American Psychological Association (1942-1943); President of the Society for Research in Child Development (1941-1944); Vice-President of the American Association for the Advancement of Science (for Psychology Section, 1934), and Editor of the Psychological Bulletin *(1942-1946). He has served on the National Research Council, the Social Science Research Council, and on various educational commissions.*

Dr. Anderson was Chairman of the Infant and Preschool Section of the White House Conference on Child Health and Protection (1929-1930), a member of the White House Conference on Children in a Democracy (1939-1940), and a member of the Mid-Century White House Conference on Children and Youth (1950).

In addition to many scientific and popular articles, he is the author of the Psychology of Development and Personal Adjustment, (1949); Happy Childhood, (1933) *and is joint author of the* Young Child and His Parents (2d. Ed. 1930); *of* Child Care and Training (7th ed. 1947).

CHILD PSYCHOLOGY

A human being moves through the life cycle from birth to death. The first third of his life is spent in growth and in developing behavior to enable him to meet the demands of adult life. What he is and what he does depends partly upon what is unfolded and partly upon what is demanded of him by the stimulation all about him. He is a system with high input and high outgo operating in a time dimension. As he moves forward in time, every aspect of his being becomes organized in some fashion. Patterns of cognition, thought, emotion and action appear.

It is the business of the psychologist to study this patterning in all its aspects. But patterning may be analyzed in terms of the momentary stimulation and immediate action or in terms of trends over a long period. The actions of the moment and the pattern of an entire life are the ends of a continuum that can be divided and studied in many different ways. For the developmental psychologist, the primary interest lies in long time trends; he sees the infant become the child; the child, the adolescent; the adolescent, the man; and the man, the senescent.

It is my purpose to consider some of the more general aspects of this develomental course upon which so much research has been done in recent years. So rich is the field and so brief my space that I can only select within narrow limits. I have chosen to emphasize principles that contribute to general understanding rather than details and urge the reader to turn to the scientific literature for the documentation of what is here sketched in compact form. Any such selection is obviously determined by the writer's own bias and by the demands of his own theoretical system. He can, however, hope that the model bears some resemblance to the realities of the behavior he seeks to represent in symbolic form.

The child is an energy system. For our purposes, we can best think of a human being as an energy system which is constantly taking in from the environment and constantly expending energy upon it. On the physico-chemical side food comes in and energy is expended in activity. On the neuro-psychological side, stimulation comes in through sense organs and is transformed into impulses which cause muscles to move. The circuits between sense organs and muscles are the devices through which the energy derived from the transformation of food is directed. Energy exchange is a vital characteristic—through it, living is manifest. With death interchange ceases and problems disappear.

Regarding the child as an energy system has important practical consequences. Many naively think of docility, obedience, quietness, lack of energy, as indicators of good adjustment. Actually, the reverse is the case. Many of the "good" children of the good old days were probably badly nourished. Studies made in France, Spain, and Germany show that children when they first meet marked food deprivation become very active. But soon by lying around much of the time they reduce their effective relation to the environment. For an energy system, education and training become matters, not of eliminating energy, but of guiding it into desirable and socially acceptable channels.

The child exists in time. The energy system, which is the human being, exists in time. As infant, child, adolescent, adult, senescent, the person is adjusting in time and is becoming. Every parent watches the dependent, stationary infant become the independent and free moving adult. Every teacher sees relatively inept and inadequate children who come in the Fall, go out nine months later with increased skill and competence. In observing this process, we view not the day or the week, but the month and the year. The present is related to the past and to the future.

Development is first of all a continuous transformation in time in which changes are slight over short periods, but marked over long ones. Because these changes cumulate, variability among and within individuals increases because more factors enter to determine behavior as time passes.

When the growth of each part of the body, each structure, organ, organ system, or psychological function is studied, each is found to grow at a different rate and to reach a terminal point at a different time. Hence, general measures of growth are aggregates of many smaller growths, each of which can be studied in and for itself.

In infancy and early childhood the growth process is so vigorous and all-powerful that the development of virtually every structure and function is positively correlated with every other. As the over-all rate slows down more differentiated types of growth appear, intercorrelations drop, and the individual moves into the adult phase, in which there is substantial though not complete independence of function.

In addition to the basic growth process with its powerful urge toward maturity, the organism possesses great ability to recover from deprivations and insults of all types. This capacity for self-repair and recovery is greater in the early stages and decreases as structures and functions age. When children who have been in deprived environments are placed in good environments of high stimulating quality, forward progress is rapid and recovery great.

All children grow in some degree, whatever happens to and about them. Even in an environment of great deprivation some growth occurs. But in a good environment, a child can realize the full possibilities of his growth, while a poor or deprived environment holds development to a minimum. Between these minimum and maximum possibilities lies the area in which those who deal with children, work.

This range of possibility can be called a growth potential.

Its range is determined by nature. What happens within that range is determined by nurture. The egg cells of mice and elephants resemble each other in size and appearance, yet one has a growth potential for six inches of body length and slight weight, while the other has a potential for eight to ten feet of body length and tremendous weight. The child's various capacities vary in potential; the limits for height are narrower than those for weight; those for intelligence are narrower than those for emotional and social behavior. As scientists and practitioners we explore the range between these limits for each structure and function and for the whole combined in order to discover the most favorable conditions for maximum development.

For scientific and practical purposes, development is divided into a number of categories about which we orient our thinking. Commonly we speak of the following areas: physical growth, motor skills, language, intelligence, problem solving, emotional behavior, social behavior, interests and activities, and adjustment. In each area investigators picture the growth process in detail by showing the changes that occur with time.

Between birth and maturity in each of these areas, marked increases in the child's level of functioning occur. In general, increase is most rapid in the early years and slower as maturity is approached. There is more difference between a two and a three-year-old for most aspects of development than between a fifteen and a sixteen-year-old. In considering this principle one must recognize also that within any group of children, substantial differences among individuals are found not only in the general rate of development but also within the particular areas. Although there is some correlation between position in the different areas, the differences are large enough to warrant their study as relative independent aspects. Within any major developmental area and for the person as a whole evidence indicates consistency in the pattern of development from one child to another, even though there may be marked differences in rate. Growth and development are orderly processes in this sense.

The picture of development, is one of a very complex organism made up of many parts and functions, moving in an orderly way from birth to maturity. The whole aggregate can be viewed as the personality of the child and concern can go, not only to the problem of how adaptation takes place within each area, but also to the manner in which the child as a whole meets the problems presented to him by his own internal development and by the demands of the environment in which he lives. Viewed in this way there are several nodal or key points in the cycle from conception to maturity that are particularly important. One is birth, when the environment of the child is radically changed as he moves from the relatively constant environment of the womb to the varied environment of the outside world with its demand for adjustment to new stresses.

A second comes at the end of infancy, when the infant, because of the development of locomotion, becomes a free-moving, active person seeking stimulation and because of the development of language, becomes able to communicate with his fellows and to respond to symbolic as well as direct stimulation from them. Within a relatively short time as the combined result of locomotion and communication the entire orientation of the person to the environment is changed.

A third occurs around six or seven years when the child develops the capacity to dissociate qualities from the objects in which they are embedded and moves into a world of generalization, abstraction and freer manipulation of symbols. Within a few years the intellectual mobility gained transforms most of the child's relations to his environment.

A fourth occurs with puberty, when, due to physical and glandular changes, the adolescent becomes interested in the opposite sex and organizes his social relations in a different manner. What is sometimes overlooked, is that there is a parallel, but not necessarily related, development in mental level which makes him more responsive to future goals and still more concerned with the symbolic and abstract. Again a substantial reorientation occurs.

It should be noted, in thinking about these nodal points, that proportionately the reorganization is less drastic as we move along the developmental course, because at each succeeding point in time, more and more of what is to be the final whole is *in* the system that is developing.

Great differences exist in the manner in which the developmental pattern within an area or for the whole person are modified by stimulation and the learning which results from stimulation. At all ages the person possesses some capacity to modify or change his behavior. Obviously there are some advantages to early learning under desirable auspices since early learning facilitates subsequent progress and establishes the priorities upon which skills of higher level can be developed. But some current theories emphasize early learning as more important than learning at any other time and suggest that the patterns acquired in infancy and early childhood can never be changed. These ignore both the capacity of the organism for self repair in a changed and good environment and the fact that given some opportunity to adjust, the developing organism meets life situations as they come and moves forward into new situations. However there are some unusual conditions under which fixations occur that give early learning great dominance. But for most growing persons apart from the great amount of overlearning which accompanies early learning and the priorities established, we need not assume that behavior in a growing organism becomes rigid early and is essentially unmodifiable in the later course of development.

All later experience is related to earlier experience in the sense that selective factors growing out of that experience continue to operate as the person moves forward in time. Every person is a creature of the past who brings a unique character to the present. But he is also a forgetting animal, as he lives in a continuously stimulating environment which crowds out earlier experiences and weakens his hold upon the past. Thus, new stimulation may blot out much of what has gone before and change him. In the stimulation received, much of what has gone before is reinforced and much of what has been learned earlier suffers extinction. Viewing the tremendous input and outgo of the living human being, the irregular time intervals between experiences of a similar type and the somewhat erratic attachment of reward and punishment to the responses made, it is little wonder that life in the "natural" situation acquires a degree of complexity that cannot be duplicated in the laboratory. Survey of the amount of stimulation and the number of sources from which it comes reveals an amazing input into a system which is already active and in which incoming stimulation must compete for its place. Hence, simple conceptions of behavior in terms of momentary stimulus-response mechanisms fail to picture the developmental process. To know the child we must know, not only the immediate stimulation, but also something about his past experience and something about the values and goals which result from that experience.

As with other living animals, the human being moves in the time dimension from an infancy in which he is almost completely dependent, to an adult life, in which he is an independent and free-moving organism. Viewing the psychological aspects of development broadly, we can ask what this movement does for him.

First, it greatly increases the number and variety of stimuli to which he can respond. Next, he moves from the few and limited skills of the infant to the almost limitless and varied skills found in adult life. Third, progress is from concern with the immediate present to memory of the past and anticipation of the future both of which come more and more to affect all conduct. Fourth, his psychological and social space enlarges so that he reacts to what is remote in space and time as well as to what is close at hand. Fifth, the level of his behavior is raised as his capacity to meet and solve problems of greater and greater difficulty increases. Sixth, as he gains competence he moves from limited control of himself and of the environment to increased control of himself and of others and thereby to greater freedom as he becomes less and less situation-bound.

The child has resources. What does the child bring to his life situation? From a long biological history carrying resources that have come to him from his ancestors, he moves into an environment that will use his potentials in various ways. Not all of what he is or has, is apparent at birth—for many years he will unfold. In the prenatal period and in infancy the course of his behavior is very largely internally controlled. For example, he cannot be taught to walk ahead of his normal time. Under the most favorable conditions, walking may be advanced about two weeks; under the most unfavorable conditions, it may be delayed about two weeks. But as he grows older his behavior is more and more determined by the stimulation present in the environment and his capacity to learn. Swimming may be acquired over a wide range of ages or not acquired at all. There are then developmental features which can be modified only slightly depending on opportunities or facilities; others that can be modified in some degree and still others that can be greatly modified.

The resources which the individual child brings with him are many, varied and in some degree uncorrelated. As behavior becomes organized his particular traits and characteristics become bound together into patterns and potentials that enable him to meet a wide variety of situations. To some degree, as patterns appear there is less dependence upon any particular item that was part of his original make-up and more dependence upon the structure of which the item has become a part. Thus in a very real sense the life process takes the raw material of heredity and out of it organizes and builds new personalities.

The child moves into a preformed culture. The child, with his resources that become manifest at various points in development, grows up in a particular context or a culture which is already formed before he comes into it. It is a world in which in general he must adapt to its demands. In England, his strength, speed, and motor coordinations will be used in playing cricket; in the United States in playing baseball. Born in France, he learns French; born in England, he comes to speak English. In this preformed world the child acquires the knowledge, skills and attitudes that surround him. Nevertheless, the level at which he functions within the skills, knowledges and attitudes to which he is exposed depends upon his resources and the opportunities given him to develop them.

In recent years great advances in understanding human behavior have come from the analysis of the contexts in which the child develops. Materials and equipment obviously vary with cultural level and socio-economic status. But attitudes toward child training and behavior also vary. Homes into which children are born already have theories about the handling of children which are in part determined by the family's social status. Most children come into homes which are dominated by middle-class concepts of obedience, docility and conformity. But some children from infancy onward are trained to be aggressive and not to respond to ordinary social patterns, while others are exempt from many of the social controls that we accept as natural when we think back to our own training. It is of some interest that the children from the extremes in terms of social status, i.e., from upper-upper and from the lower-lower social groups are more likely to have difficulties in adjustment.

Any description of these relations usually comes as a revelation since most of us naïvely assume that all children are trained much as we were trained. But great numbers of children are reared under radically different concepts of right and wrong, and of what is valuable and what is not valuable. For example, in one study boys from a two-block area in New York City were found to talk about what they were going to do when they got to Sing Sing. In these two blocks some 60 per cent of the adult males had spent some time in the New York State prisons and talked casually about their experiences in the presence of their sons. What was abnormal as a goal for the ordinary boy came to be accepted as normal by these boys who took over the value systems of their fathers. Similarly with respect to facilities. One child comes from a home in which there is a good children's encyclopedia, a newspaper, a half-dozen different magazines and a library of five hundred books. Another

271

child in the same grade comes from a home in which there is no newspaper, no telephone, no magazines, and, perhaps, only one or two books.

The implements through which much of the culture comes to the child center in the home and parents. Parents are both selectors and interpreters; they not only choose the play equipment, the pictures on the wall, and the magazines taken in the home, but also by precept and example transmit values and attitudes to the child. Later on the school, the child's associates, and the modern communication devices such as the radio, the movies, and television add their part to the child's background.

The peer culture is very important for the child. The child also participates in another cultural stream known as the peer culture. Many persons think of stimulation as coming mainly from adults to children. But actually, much behavior is determined by the pressures of associates. The nine-year-old boy educates the seven-year-old boy; the thirteen-year-old girl, the eleven-year-old girl, and so on. Studies of children's games such as hop-scotch, bounce-the-ball, and marbles, show a line of cultural transmission virtually unmodified by adult interference or training over many years. Often games start from a common base; small variations which are handed on from one child to another in time within an area create regional differences about a common base. So important is this transmission that the control of children's organizations is taken over quickly by authoritarian societies in order to use the demands made and the examples set for nine-year-olds by eleven-year-olds and for eleven-year-olds by thirteen-year-olds to support the regime in power.

With development, selection is inevitable. At birth the child has an indefinite number of possibilities in the sense that he may go in any one of many different directions depending on what the environment affords. But his time is limited; he lives only twenty-four hours a day, of which one-half is spent in sleeping and eating. Since he is so organized that he cannot do everything at once, choice is necessary. For example, he cannot play the piano while throwing a baseball or study while he is playing tag.

Many of his choices are made by other persons. Parents provide facilities and equipment and by their attitudes favor or condemn various activities. The school as an agent of society decides what the child shall study. Boys with good bodies and good motor co-ordinations who go into athletic pursuits develop a different type of social life than do boys with poor coordinations who blunder in the use of their bodies. Selection whether done by the child or for him begins early and sets essential features of the life pattern as its effects cumulate in later behavior.

A good example of the selection made for children is found in the persons or committees that decide on the school curriculum. In choosing material for different age and grade levels they have to decide whether thirty minutes a day in the fourth grade at age nine should be spent on arithmetic or social studies. Serious errors in their choices will not, however, be discovered until demands for skill arise many years later. In World War II much money was spent teaching simple arithmetical processes to adults who had to work with various types of instruments, gauges and mechanical devices. Because the war needs for arithmetic were pressing, society could not wait for another group of children to mature. Decisions made 10 to 15 years earlier that reduced the time available for numbers and increased the time for other school subjects were determining factors.

Progressively greater and greater specialization seems to be an inevitable part of growth in any environment. In our culture, the person with the widest range of interests and activities is the eight-and nine-year-old boy. By 22 years the range of his interests and activities has been more than cut in half. Actually he is more effective and more deeply concerned with fewer activities. Often it is said that growth involves purchasing of efficiency at the cost of versatility.

As he develops, the child meets and masters one situation after another. Viewed in its broadest aspects, development involves meeting and mastering one problem after another as time passes. At each age level, the growing person faces problems characteristic of that level. As he gains competence, he moves through and beyond that level. For example, in the earliest period of life, up to two and a half years, there is much concern with gaining control over eliminative processes. By two and a half years almost all children are competent. From one to three years, eating habits are mastered and from two to six years many of the skills involved in dressing. From six to ten years the child in school is acquiring skill in reading. In adolescence, social dancing is mastered.

To describe this progress in detail, great amounts of space would be needed for the hundreds and even thousands of skills the ordinary person in our culture acquires and which we take for granted. But certain general principles can be brought out.

First, some of the problems presented to the growing child arise out of his growth and are largely the result of internal factors. For example, he finds himself with his new ability to walk and as a result must build many new skills in the wider world of space. Another example is furnished by the changes in his body at the beginning of adolescence which call for many new adjustments.

Second, the world about him makes many demands upon him. Not only do parents and teachers expect children to acquire certain competencies at particular ages but they also insist that they do so. The boys and girls about him who have acquired competencies in particular areas put pressure upon him, society tells him to go to school at six and expects him to learn to read whether he likes it or not. Thus both directly and indirectly the developing human being is faced with demands for doing in a time order.

Third, in each area in which he must become competent, the child begins ineffectively with many errors and poor performance. With time, much practice and motivation, some degree of mastery is attained, at the least enough to get along, at the most exceptional skill. Almost without end, given some instruction or example, some motivation, some opportunity to practice, and some regard for good performance and some unpleasantness for poor performance, reasonable competence will come. Generation after generation of human beings learn to handle knives, forks, and spoons, to dress themselves, to ride tricycles and bicycles, to read and write and so, on and on, through a host of activities. In a very real sense development is a forward progression through one skill after another, one situation after another.

With competence, the particular demand loses its character as a problem. The growing person moves on to other areas and levels and finds that his skill frees him for attack on other and in general problems of a higher order. The child of four, learning to lace his shoes, takes thirty minutes. Months later he laces his shoes in a minute or a minute and a half. Our present interest is not so much in the minute and a half as in the twenty-eight and a half-minutes saved which becomes available for meeting other demands and for engaging in other activities. The adolescent boy takes thirty minutes for shaving the first time. But, after shaving a thousand and more times, a man takes two or three minutes.

Suppose we cut across the growing person at any particular time. One skill is just coming in, another is half developed and in another mastery has been attained. In some areas the person is competent; in others, a novice. At any moment he has a repertoire which we can view as assets and liabilities. This repertoire will be composed of skills at various levels; of patterns of knowledge at various degrees of completeness; of attitudes and value systems; and of emergency and learning mechanisms which enable him to build new ways of meeting situations and stress. From such horizontal assessments educational, advisory, and guidance services can be established for aiding the child in his on-going course.

The child who is out-of-step lives in a different psychological world. If the growing person moves along with other children of his age or developmental status and is not far behind them, little difficulty arises. He is taken somewhat as a matter of course by parents, teachers, and associates. If he moves somewhat faster, but not too fast, he is likely to receive some recognition or acclaim which will operate to facilitate his progress.

For example, consider the boy who wets the bed, as compared

with one who has gained control of elimination. The bed-wetter's mother, father, doctor, nurse, teacher, brothers and sisters know that he is a bed-wetter. Hence, all act differently with him in some situations than they do with a boy who has developed normal controls. For the boys with control i.e. competence, there is casualness and acceptance; for the boy without control, there is concern, exhortation, punishment and ridicule. The child who is out of line in the developmental sequences whether they arise from internal needs or external demands thus meets very different pressures than does one who moves along the normal sequences. Similarly with reading at seven, or social dancing at fifteen. The boy who fails to develop skill in reading mechanics and comprehension by ten has many difficulties which may make him quite a different person at fourteen in terms of his relations to others, than is the boy who takes life's demands in stride. Social life and personal expectation differ for the boy or girl who dances well at sixteen as compared with those of a boy or girl who is not a good dancer.

It is important to recognize the principle that the difficulties which arise for the child out-of-step appear not only in the particular skill itself but also in its relations to other activities and to other persons. Good descriptions of behavior abnormalities in growing persons can be written in terms of disturbances of developmental sequences and the overlay of social pressures which result and make for more difficulty. We must understand those who are so unfortunate as to be out-of-step and seek methods to return them to effective relations. But for all children a basic job is giving children more than an even chance of meeting the situations presented by life in its unfolding. If, in addition, we can give them some possibility for creative living, we will have made a positive contribution to them and to society.

The child develops in a world of relations with others. No person lives to himself. Instead, like a goldfish, he is in a world in which what he does is observed by others. But unlike the goldfish, what he does changes the behavior of others. In turn, his behavior is modified by what others do. Thus arises the series of interrelated, circular, and feed-back reactions which cumulate over time and result in striking trends and deviations in behavior that are inexplicable except in terms of multiple causes operating in time.

On the one hand through the development of his own skills, knowledge and attitudes under the pressures exerted upon him by others and the facilities available to him, he comes to fill roles or perform certain functions in society. Upon these roles both he and other persons come to rely. Society is an enormously specialized organization made up of many interacting individuals with many interlocking relations. The boy comes to have a vocation, to be a father, to serve in the military, etc. etc. Each of these different roles has well defined responsibilities in terms of social demands. In these reciprocal relations with others, personal expectancies which determine his future behavior arise. At the same time those associated with him at various levels develop expectancies with regard to this performance. His personality is organized more and more in terms of these patterns of expectancy and value which carry forward into situation after situation. In general the resulting continuing structure comes to elicit consistent responses from others. Thus continuity and order come into life.

The result of development is then a highly organized and structured person with a variety of skills and attitudes upon which other persons react in consistent fashion. Each person is unique in that he has followed a particular developmental course which broken down becomes the impact of different experiences upon a different combination of original traits. But because human beings in original constitution are basically more alike than different and because the stimulation within any culture has substantial similarity, human beings can be classified in various ways. Principles for predicting development and behavior within describable limits of error can be established. The resulting scientific generalizations have substantial practical value. Two major but interrelated descriptions of facilitating environments emerge and bring us to the conclusion of this paper.

Competence is facilitated in an environment that encourages wide concern early and deep concern later. Already we have pointed out that the eight- and nine-year-old has the broadest range of activities and that with development the range will narrow. Since many of his traits and capacities are essentially uncorrelated, the early environment should permit varied stimulation that will make it possible for him to explore both himself and his possibilities. Such broad and varied experience will ensure that the inevitable specialization which accompanies growth will not be too narrow and will utilize those parts of his makeup that will bring him good skill and some recognition. He can thus achieve a satisfactory way of life and a realistic view of himself.

Later opportunities should be concerned with depth. Evidence indicates that good adjustment is related in some manner to the depth of a person's concern. In clinics, the difficulties that arise with children who are reasonably successful in particular activities are few in comparison with those among children who have failed to develop channels for emergency expenditure. So far as adjustment is concerned, it seems to make little difference whether the success comes in athletics, school subjects, extracurricular pursuits or social activities. What is important is that there be some one or more areas of activity, which can function as a polarizing or organizing agent. Far too frequently the outcome of growth is a thwarted, blocked, ineffective, inadequate, and unhappy kind of person. In a good environment the growing person is given an opportunity to become vitally concerned with an activity that is important to him and about which he can organize his life.

Personality development is facilitated as confidence in the environment is transformed to confidence in self. Early life is concerned with establishing a stable environment with respect to stimulation and emotion that will permit the child to establish consistent reactions and build up the patterns or habits which will enable him to meet difficulties. For instance, the mother who tells her three-year-old child at night that she will spank him if he does not go to sleep, and the next day on the streetcar tells him that she will spank him if he does not keep awake, sets up a situation that makes learning very difficult, because punishment is not clearly attached to one alternative. By security we mean consistency that permits habits to evolve. But we also include a beneficial and friendly atmosphere rather than a noxious and negative atmosphere. Environments for younger children could well be examined in terms of consistency and stability of stimulation and the emotional atmosphere in order to discover the situations and experiences that promote good behavior oganization. In the evacuation of young children in Britain in the early stages of World War II, much distress and emotional tension appeared. But if in their new environment there was a familiar piece of play equipment their difficulties decreased and in some instances disappeared. Objects or activities which were familiar and to which children had built stable reactions, functioned as devices for reducing emotional tension and increasing security.

In adolescence, the confidence of the child in his environment should be transformed. He moves into a world in which, as a self-reliant and independent person he becomes responsible for his own actions. To survive he must be able to meet difficulties and to bounce back from them. Adolescence is the period of emancipation from the home, when new found impulses drive the person to establish a home of his own and to support himself by a vocation. How can the security feelings developed in early childhood be transformed into an interest in meeting problems, in solving situations, in carrying on as a responsible person? Obviously in view of the nature of development, a beginning in the encouragement of self reliance must be made early and some experience provided in solving problems and meeting situations. But after puberty these opportunities must be expanded.

In a real sense development is a process in which we introduce into earlier periods smaller and more limited situations and problems which the child can meet in terms of the level he has attained in order that he may grow strong and capable enough to meet similar situations of a larger and more dangerous type later on without failing or becoming emotionally disturbed. Skill and emotional factors are interrelated—development is not a matter of sharply defined distinctive categories but a unitary process—there is but one person moving from infancy to adult life.

CHAPTER XI

ADOLESCENCE

KARL C. GARRISON, Ph.D.
Professor of Education, University of Georgia

EDITORIAL NOTE

Although adolescence has been treated as a division of child psychology, there is no question about its being the most important part of child psychology or even genetic psychology as a whole, as it is at that age that the consequences begin to show. *We may* speculate *on what is happening in the child's unconscious, but the adolescent is, in comparison, transparent, even if it is a transitional stage which he passes through. It was Stanley Hall who saw the significance of this phase of life, when he brought out, just 50 years ago, his two volumes on adolescence. The textbooks which have appeared since have been less encyclopedic and more devoted to surveys of special investigations. Long-term studies, subsidized by foundations, have produced a mass of results, which however, have yet to be adequately evaluated. The influence of war conditions on growing youth, the alarming manifestations of juvenile delinquency, on a large scale, the efforts of unstable home conditions and social tension— these and other factors have been studied from various observation points. As this is being written, there appears an odd report of a UNESCO expert on child psychology stating that he is skeptical of the alleged ill effects of the movies or pornographic literature on the child, and that we are ignorant of the influences, good or bad.*

In Dr. Karl C. Garrison, who taught at a number of institutions in various parts of the country before his appointment as Professor of Education at the University of Georgia, in 1948, we have a specialist on the subject, whose textbook, Psychology of Adolescence, *has already enjoyed four editions. His* Psychology of Exceptional Children *has come out in the second edition. His most recent work is entitled* Growth and Development *(1952). In addition he is co-author of several well-known books in the general area of educational psychology, and a contributor to educational and psychological periodicals.*

THE ADOLESCENT

The scientific study of adolescents may be said to have begun early this century with the appearance of two volumes, entitled "Adolescence," by G. Stanley Hall. The adolescent years are described by Hall as a period of "storm and stress." He made use of adolescent diaries in arriving at a better understanding of the characteristics and aspirations of adolescents. Following the voluminous writings of G. Stanley Hall a great deal of literature on adolescence appeared, in many cases exceeding scientific data bearing on the various problems and topics presented.

The past two or three decades witnessed a widespread interest in this period of life. From primitive times down to the twentieth century it was generally customary for an individual to pass from childhood into adulthood in a relatively short period of time. The lengthened school program, the industrial revolution which led to child labor legislation, and the increased leisure among growing boys and girls have combined to bring the problems of adolescents to the forefront.

Studying adolescents. While the use of diaries did not bring forth a large body of scientific knowledge about the nature of adolescents, it did help to create an interest in this age-group and motivated students of adolescent psychology to explore various techniques for studying adolescents. Following World War I, important centers for child study were established at Columbia University, University of Iowa, University of California (Berkeley), University of Minnesota, Michigan State College, and elsewhere. These studies brought forth an enormous body of information about the physical, mental, emotional, and social development of children and adolescents. Both cross-sectional and longitudinal studies were conducted, with an increased attention gradually being given to longitudinal studies. In addition, many studies have been made with different groups of adolescents as subjects in which specific problems related to the effects of various forces and conditions on the personal and social development of adolescents have been studied.

An examination of these studies reveals that an increasing number have dealt with the effects of peer culture, social-class structure, social climate of the home and school, and group dynamics on the personal and social development of adolescents. This growing trend may be observed in two textbooks which have appeared during the past two decades.[1] These are Garrison, *Psychology of Adolescence* (1934), and Cole, *Psychology of Adolescence* (1936). There are recent textbooks by Cruze, (1953), Horrocks (1951), Hurlock (1949), Josselyn (1952), Kuhlen (1952), Malm and Jamison (1952), and Schneiders (1951) which have brought together the results from research and furnished a comprehensive picture of adolescent growth and personality characteristics. Certain outstanding trends may be observed in the textbooks during this period. Among these may be listed the following:

1. An increased recognition of the importance of peer relationships.
2. A recognition of the effects of class on the personal and social development of the child and adolescent.
3. An inclusion of recent findings bearing on the physiological changes during adolescence.
4. A better understanding of the developmental tasks of the presentday adolescent.
5. An application of recent findings in education and sociology to the guidance of adolescents.
6. Increased attention to individual and group dynamics.

Physiological changes. Adolescence marks the beginning of sexual maturity. The typical American girl matures sexually sometime between the ages of 10 and 15 years, with the average age around 12.5 years. This is significantly earlier than her European cousin matures and earlier than her mother and grandmother.[2] The age range for sexual maturation of the American boy is from one and one-half to two years later than that for the girl, with the average around 13.5 or 14 years. The period required for complete sexual maturity for girls following the first menstruation covers about two years; while that for boys is slightly longer.

Since sexual maturity comes at such widely different ages, there are marked differences in the degree of sexual maturity attained by a group of teen age boys or girls.[3] This presents difficult problems of adjustment, especially for those who deviate considerably in their sexual development from the average.[4] The girl whose sexual maturity occurs early finds herself in a difficult position. She is not only advanced beyond that of the girls of her age, but is considerably out of line with boys of her age-group. The boy who matures early is not in quite as great a difficulty, although he is out of line with other boys of his age level. His changing voice and increased interest in girls are likely to bring laughter and ridicule from his less mature classmates. Likewise, the boy or girl who is late in reaching sexual maturity will not display the interest in social activities involving both sexes displayed by other members of the group. The boy, in particular, who is already slower in developing than girls, will now be several years behind the girls of his age-group in his sexual development. This condition furnishes a source of frustration for some adolescents.

Investigations of the skeletal development of the same children over a number of years have furnished standards which allow for significant differentiation of sexual maturity, within similar age groups. The skeletal age is usually measured by the formation of new areas of ossification and the changing outline of the bones. The ossifications of the bones are rather far advanced at the beginning of adolescence. At the age of 13 about 70 per cent of the area of a girl's wrists shows ossification, and there is a considerable slowing down in rate of development at this period. Individual growth curves show that there is a very close correspondence between skeletal development and sexual development.[5] This correspondence may be noted as early as the seventh year. The skeletal development of the child furnishes a good basis for determining his general physical development and for predicting his mature size.

There is, however, a lack of uniformity in the growth of different parts of the body. Adolescence is accompanied by an increase in lung capacity and an increase in the size of the heart. Tests of strength of arms, strength of back, endurance, and rate of tapping will show that there is a pronounced acceleration with the advent of puberty. Closely connected with increased muscular development are the obvious changes of voice in early adolescence. These are much more evident in the case of boys than girls and constitute one of the external signs of the advent of puberty. The voice of young men at maturity will vary widely in pitch and other qualities. Also, pronounced differences will be found among adolescents of the same developmental level. The voice of the female is not subject to such an outright transformation. In maturity the female voice may be little lower, if at all, than it was in childhood.

During the adolescent years marked changes take place in the structure of the skin and in the activity of the skin glands. The endocrine glands play an important role in the physiological changes that take place during adolescence.[6] This may be observed in connection with the skin glands, sweat glands, formation of hair, and other secondary sexual characteristics. In our society, many problems, interwoven with customs and conventions, emerge as these physiological changes appear.

Impact of technology. This half-century has been one of transition from an agrarian-urban culture to an urban-industrial culture.[7] In the early American family the child was taught to do chores and make an important contribution to the family's economic enterprise. Thus, by the time the boy or girl reached the adolescent years, he was no longer an economic burden on the family. To adapt to this condition, the early schools operated only in the mid-winter months, when there was little work to be done in the fields. Under such a system much emphasis was given to family obligations. The adolescent was ready for marriage at an early age. He usually remained in the community and assumed responsibility for the security and protection of his parents when they reached old age.

Although the American family has its roots in an agrarian culture, it has changed a great deal as a result of technology. The adolescent of today is concerned with growth in independence of the family unit, and no longer has his obligations to his family emphasized at all points. Furthermore, the home has become more democratic in nature. The ideal of parent-child coöperation is stressed. The welfare of the individual child is given first consideration. The parent is required to send the child to school well up into the adolescent years. Health and other welfare provisions are provided for children and adolescents in cases where the home is unable to provide these. Thus, the presentday adolescent has health and educational advantages which were not provided for most adolescents a half-century or more ago. He is brought up with the feelings that the future is his own, and that a social security program will largely relieve him of the obligations of taking care of his aged parents.

The presentday adolescent is more concerned with modern problems and living personalities than was the adolescent fifty years ago. This is borne out by a study reported by Averill in which it was noted that 78 per cent of adolescents fifty years ago chose as their ideals historical characters, whereas today only 33 per cent choose such characters as their ideals.[8] Also today's adolescents fail to identify themselves ideally with characters from literature, which intrigued one out of eight adolescents fifty years ago. The present day adolescent finds his ideals in flesh-and-blood figures—individuals identified with sports, radio, movies, television, business, and other contemporary figures. Although adolescence may be regarded as an age of idealism, the presentday adolescent is more practical in nature than were the adolescents of previous generations. This has been revealed in their wishes and aspirations about their future.

The adolescent and his peers. For most children early and late childhood are characterized by neighborhood group and gang activities. With the onset of pubescence, belonging to a social group acquires increased significance. It is through desirable peer relations that adolescents are able to solve many of their problems.[9] If they are able to obtain approval, recognition, and status in their group they have solved one of the major problems of social adjustment. The young adolescent must conform to the standards, and subscribe to the values of the group if he expects to be accepted by the group. Thus, the young adolescent is likely to conform slavishly to the behavior pattern of the group. Older adolescents have already achieved status, and are instrumental in forcing younger adolescents to submerge their interests and standards to that of the group.

The attainment of a satisfactory role among peers is a developmental task faced by the growing child. This task is enlarged with the onset of adolescence, for now the individual is faced with the problem of attaining satisfactory relations with members of the opposite sex. He must learn the complementary roles found in a heterosexual society. Boys and girls who fail to achieve satisfactory roles find growing up, and particularly social development, a most unpleasant task. The desire for social approval is perhaps keener during the teen years than at any other time of life. Also, the factors that contribute to social acceptability changes with age. This was shown in a study by Kuhlen and Lee of the factors that contributed to social acceptability of sixth, ninth, and twelfth grade boys and girls.[10] The trait *friendly* appeared at all grade levels. A major change noted for both boys and girls is the reduction in importance of good looks and the increase in the importance of more sociable traits.

Social pressures become complicated for the adolescent. The words "permanents," nail polish, scuffed shoes, lipstick, and the like, become important to the girl as she progresses into adolescence. Biological needs will withstand much treatment and even some torture, if necessary to gain status and acceptance. Girls will go without sweets and other carbohydrates in order to reduce weight. They will avoid sleep in order to conform, and if it is currently popular will avoid exercise when possible. The boy, on the other hand, is confronted with the problem of developing the masculine physique and playing the male role. He will undergo strenuous exercise, and challenge the dictates of his parents when these are important for peer approval. The failure to attain a satisfactory role presents a critical problem to the adolescent.[11] Studies have revealed several important findings relative to the adolescents' relation to their peers.

1. The relative importance of peer approval increases as the individual grows into adolescence.
2. Pre-adolescents and adolescents like to imitate their peers or those slightly older than they are.
3. Early adolescence is accompanied by the formation of cliques. These cliques play an important part in satisfying certain felt needs of adolescents.
4. Social class plays an important role in determining the membership of cliques and social acceptance during adolescence.
5. Good peer relations during pre-adolescence is perhaps the best assurance available for good peer relations during adolescence and post-adolescence.

Adolescent personality. Studies of adolescent personality during the 30's were primarily concerned with the frequency of different types of behavior exhibited, with little concern about how these behavior responses fitted into the personality of the adolescent as a functioning individual. A careful study of the background of these responses will show that similar overt responses may appear as a result of different needs and conditions and thus present different implications. One adolescent may display withdrawal because of a feeling of inadequacy, while another one withdraws from the group as a display of negativism or a protest against certain actions of the group. This functional concept of personality has been very well presented in a volume by a number of specialists in this area.[12] Recent studies of personality formation have emphasized the notion that physical and psychological factors are interrelated in all behavior. Thus, marked changes in personality can be expected to occur during adolescence.

The advent of adolescence is marked by important internal changes involving the maturation of the sex glands. In addition there is a broadening of acquaintances. Increased knowledge and understanding furnish a basis for insight into problems which affect the individual self. These forces and conditions operate to produce what may be termed the adolescent personality; however their ultimate effect will be determined to a large degree by the home influences, group expectancies, and peer relations during early childhood and the pre-adolescent years. Research findings offer considerable evidence that the early years are extremely important in personality development.[13] Overall patterns of personality of the adolescent seem to be largely predetermined by his early social relationships—the retiring child becoming a retiring adolescent and the aggressive child becoming an aggressive adolescent.

The adolescent has often been referred to as the problem boy or girl. A more accurate and apt description of the adolescent is that of an individual faced with many problems. Havighurst has pointed out that there are certain developmental tasks which the adolescent must achieve in order to lead a satisfactory life and to advance through the various stages of normal growth toward maturity.[14] The adolescent is striving toward independence from family control. In his strivings he often displays ambivalent behavior. He is also striving to be accepted by his peers, and becomes a nearslave to social conformity to his peer group.

With the ripening of the sex glands there is a keen desire for the adolescent to win the approval of members of the opposite sex. This leads to an increased interest in personal grooming— an interest often almost completely lacking among boys during the pre-adolescent years. Studies by Centers revealed that adolescents manifest class consciousness that follows the adult pattern of evaluating class structure and occupations.[15] However, adolescents showed more upward displacement of their own class status than did adult groups. This accounts for many frustrations and conflicts among adolescents. Many of the problems of the adolescent, particularly those from the middle-class group, arise out of family or group expectancies. The middle-class ideology has traditionally supported the postponement of pleasure and the prolongation of education.[16] This has led to more role-conflicts among middle-class than among lower-class adolescents. The conflicts most prevalent among adolescents from the lower social class relate to material things such as lack of the use of an automobile, inadequate clothes, and the like.

Exceptional children and adolescents. There are four distinct categories of children which need special attention at school, if they are to have adequate opportunities for the development of their abilities. These pupils represent about one-eighth of our school population. The approximate per cent in each of the four categories has been estimated as follows:[17]

Mentally gifted	2 per cent
Mentally retarded	2 per cent
Physical defects or disease or disorder	6 per cent
Emotionally disturbed or socially maladjusted	2.5 per cent

The gifted child has been generally described as one possessing a very high IQ as determined from standard intelligence tests. The typical gifted pupil of the Terman study read more books than did most children, but was clearly no bookworm.[18] He displayed normal interests in sports, made collections of beetles, Indian arrowheads, and match covers, and showed a superior personality development. Gifted eleven-year-old pupils from the Hunter College Elementary School for young gifted children showed a general superiority in abilities in art judgement, music memory, science, and mathematical abilities when measured by standard tests.[19] Pronounced individual variability was noted among the gifted children in their abilities and interests.

The mentally retarded child is significantly inferior in learning complex and abstract materials. This inferiority appears when he first enters school, but becomes more observable as he progresses into more complex kinds of learning. The mentally retarded adolescent will be unable to compete successfully with others of his age in the traditional school subjects. His deficiency will be most marked in activities requiring reading and listening comprehension, following complex directions, gaining insight into problem situations, and generalizing from rules and principles encountered at school. The mentally retarded adolescent is often frustrated because of the failures encountered at school.[20] This may account in part for the excessive number of mentally retarded usually found among the delinquents.

Any physical condition which limits the adolescent's ability to participate in the activities of the group is a handicap to him in his personality development. Concerning this Maberly has pointed out:

> Where no special steps are taken to assist the handicapped to accept or to overcome their difficulties, there follows a distortion of normal development whereby the child fails to make personal relationships and is very liable to display anti-social behavior. He sets out to satisfy his own needs at the expense of those towards whom he feels neither affection nor loyalty.[21]

Cerebral palsy dominates the picture of the handicapped. There are in excess of 200,000 children and adolescents who are affected by cerebral palsy, or about seven to a population of 110,000. A mental diagnosis of 500 palsied cases revealed that less than 40 per cent were average or above.[22] Sensory handicaps were more frequent among these children than in an unselected group; while speech defects, due to motor difficulties connected with cerebral palsy, occurred in 54.6 per cent of the 500 cases.

Heart disease is recognized as the greatest of all threats to the health of American children. The most common form of heart disease among children is that associated with rheumatic fever. There are now over 1,000,000 cases in the United States. And, although this is a disease of all ages, it preponderantly involves children from the age of five to fifteen. One of the most dangerous characteristics of the disease is its tendency to become chronic with frequent, increasingly serious relapses. Malnutrition, tuberculosis, and even cancer (in the form of leukemia) frequently appear as debilitating conditions during childhood and adolescence. The extent to which physical defects and debilitating conditions act as a handicap will depend upon such factors as: (1) the severity of the handicap; (2) the duration of the handicap; (3) changing characteristics of the handicap; (4) the attitude of peers toward the handicap; (5) the attitude of adults toward the handicap; and (6) the nature of the educational and social program for the handicapped.

The present-day child is regarded as a dynamic individual growing and developing in accordance with the various forces and conditions of his environment. He is from an early age beset with maladjustments resulting from thwarting of basic needs or conflicts between certain needs. When these frustrations or conflicts are not resolved in a satisfactory manner, they lead to symptoms of neuroses. Many of the difficulties experienced by adolescents and post-adolescents are simply a continuation of these persistent unsolved problems of childhood—in many cases accentuated by changed social conditions and physiological maturation. Another group of problems which appear during adolescence are those related to the developing sex drive. The appearance of an increased sex drive may seriously affect the harmony established between the socializing forces and the dynamic *self*. The ideals and concepts established during the earlier years may not be wholly in harmony with the drives and aspirations of the adolescent years. Thus conflicts appear in the form of feelings of guilt, depressed states, anxieties, and the like.[23]

The symptoms of personal and social maladjustments will vary from individual to individual. Case studies show that they are closely related to conflicts and frustrations in life. Due to the complex nature of personality patterns, it is very difficult to classify forms of maladjustments into clear-cut categories. Two general types of maladjustments may be observed: aggression and withdrawal. Unsocialized aggressive tendencies may be observed in such acts as bullying, fighting, defiance of authority, and the like. Socialized aggressive behavior may be socially acceptable or not. Unacceptable socialized behavior may be found in group stealing, gang mischief, and the like. Withdrawal behavior tendencies are revealed in shyness, seclusiveness, daydreaming, jealousy, and the like.

Both the patterns of unsocialized aggressive behavior and that of withdrawal behavior appear to involve deep-seated emotonal disturbances resulting from intense frustrations and conflicts. Unsocialized aggressive types are seldom found among girls, since they are under greater pressure from their parents and peers to conform to well-established behavior patterns. Shyness and timidity are outstanding characteristics of a number of pre-adolescents and adolescents.[24] These maladjusted forms of behavior represent an effort toward adjustment just as do other forms of behavior.

FOOTNOTES

[1] A brief review of the literature is presented by Brickman, W. A. The psychology of adolescence. *School and Society,* 1946, vol. 64, pp. 225-231.

[2] Shuttleworth, F. K. The adolescent period. *Monogram of the Society for Research in Child Development,* 1938, vol. 3, No. 3.

[3] Ramsey, G. V. The sexual development of boys. *American Journal of Psychology,* 1943, vol. 56, pp. 217-233.

[4] Stolz, H. R. and Stolz, L. M. Adolescent problems related to somatic variations. *Forty-third Yearbook of the National Society for the Study of Education,* 1944, Part I, pp. 80-99.

[5] Simmons, K. and Greulich, W. W. Menarcheal age and the height, weight, and skeletal age of girls 7 to 17 years. *Journal of Pediatrics,* 1943, vol. 22, p. 548.

[6] Greulich, W. W., Dorfman, R. I., Catchpole, H. R., Solomon, C. J. and Culotta, C. S. Somatic and endocrine studies of puberal and adolescent boys. *Monographs of the Society for Research in Child Development,* 1947, vol. 7, No. 3.

[7] Edwards, N. The adolescent in technological society. *Forty-third Yearbook of the National Society for the Study of Education,* 1944, Part I, Chap. X.

[8] Averill, Lawrence A. The impact of a changing culture upon pubescent ideals. *School and Society,* 1950, vol. 72, pp. 49-53.

[9] Tyron, Caroline M. The adolescent peer culture. *Forty-third Yearbook of the National Society for the Study of Education,* 1944, Part I, Chap. XII.

[10] Kuhlen, Raymond J. and Lee, Beatrice J. Personality characteristics and social acceptability in adolescence. *Journal of Educational Psychology,* 1943, vol. 34, pp. 321-340.

[11] See *Examiner Manual for the SRA Youth Inventory, Form A,* 1949.

[12] Blake, Robert R. and Ramsey, Glenn V. *Perception: An Approach to Personality.* New York: The Ronald Press, 1951.

[13] See Banham, Katharine M. The development of affectionate behavior in infancy. *Journal of Genetic Psychology*, 1950, vol. 76, pp. 283-289.

[14] Havighurst, Robert J. What adolescence is like. *National Parent Teacher*, 1950, vol. 45, pp. 26-28.

[15] Centers, R. Social class identification of American youth. *Journal of Personality*, 1950, vol. 18, pp. 290-302.

[16] See Ort, Robert S. A study of role conflicts as related to class level. *Journal of Abnormal and Social Psychology*, 1952, vol. 47, pp. 526-530.

[17] *Health in Our Schools*. Twentieth Yearbook of the American Association of School Administrators, 1951, p. 214.

[18] Terman, Lewis M., *et al. Mental and Physical Traits of a Thousand Gifted Children: Genetic Studies of Genius*. Stanford University Press, 1925.

[19] Wilson, Frank T. Some special ability test scores of gifted children. *Journal of Genetic Psychology*, 1953, vol. 82, pp. 54-68.

[20] See Kimball, B. Case studies in educational failure during adolescence. *American Journal of Orthopsychiatry*, 1953, vol. 23, p. 406.

[21] Maberly, A. Delinquency in handicapped children. *The British Journal of Delinquency*, 1950, vol. 1, p. 128.

[22] McIntire, J. T. On the education of the cerebral palsied. *Journal of Educational Research*, 1947, vol. 40, pp. 561-568.

[23] See Mohr, George J. Psychiatric problems of adolescence. *Journal of the American Medical Association*, 1948, vol. 137, pp. 1589-1592.

[24] Lowenstein, P. and Svendsen, M. Experimental modification of the behavior of a selected group of shy and withdrawn children. *American Journal of Orthopsychiatry*, 1938, vol. 8, pp. 639-653.

SELECTED REFERENCES

Cole, Luella. *Psychology of Adolescence,* 4th edition. New York: Farrar and Rinehart, Inc., 1954.

Cruze, Wendell. *Adolescent Psychology and Development*. New York: The Ronald Press, 1953.

Garrison, Karl C. *Psychology of Adolescence,* 4th edition. New York: Prentice-Hall, Inc., 1951.

Havighurst, R. J. and Taba, H. *Adolescent Character and Personality*. New York: John Wiley and Sons, Inc., 1949.

Horrocks, John E. *Psychology of Adolescence; Behavior and Development*. Boston: Houghton Mifflin Co., 1951.

Hurlock, Elizabeth B. *Adolescent Development*. New York: McGraw-Hill Book Co., 1949.

Jones, Harold E., *et al. Adolescence*. Forty-third Yearbook of the National Society for the Study of Education, Part I. Chicago: School of Education, University of Chicago, 1944.

Josselyn, Irene M. *The Adolescent and His World*. New York: Family Service Association of America, 1952.

Kuhlen, Raymond G. *The Psychology of Adolescent Development*. New York: Harper and Bros., 1952.

Malm, Marguerite and Jamison, Olis G. *Adolescence*. New York: McGraw-Hill Book Co., 1952.

Schneiders, Alexander A. *The Psychology of Adolescence: A factual study of the conduct and personality of youth.* Milwaukee: Bruce Publishing Co., 1951.

Shuttleworth, Frank K. *The Adolescent Period: A photographic atlas.* Monograph of the Society for Research in Child Development, No. 2, vol. 14, 1949.

Symonds, Percival M. *Adolescent Fantasy.* New York: Columbia University Press, 1949.

CHAPTER XII

EDUCATIONAL PSYCHOLOGY

GORDON C. HANSON, Ph.D.
Professor of Educational Psychology,
University of Wichita, Kansas

EDITORIAL NOTE

The first branch of psychology to have definitely flourished in America was educational psychology. It was also the first division of applied psychology to have developed toward the end of the pre-scientific period. One might have easily anticipated this from the very fact that teaching is actually an everyday performance over a considerable period of the day; and of course it had already had its psychological moorings in Europe, largely through the efforts of Herbart.

Educational psychology is a difficult subject to survey briefly. It consists of so many segments. Originally it connoted the application of psychological facts to the problem of teaching the young. We may all remember how critical William James was in his Talks to Teachers *about those who insisted on a detailed knowledge of psychological facts, especially the nervous system, as a chief qualification. Münsterberg, too, was never tired of exposing the pedantry of such a view.*

At the present time, educational psychology leans heavily upon dynamic theories (depth psychology) sociological and anthropological data, and goes into the problems of adjustment of the pupil as well as into matters of curriculum planning, administrative work, and other areas which at one time would have been considered as tangential or irrelevant.

Textbooks on educational psychology differ widely as to content, because the selection of material will often depend upon the type of individual the author is and his past and present interests. Educational psychology in itself is highly specialized and divided into smaller sectors. Thus secondary schools, institutions for defectives, classes for exceptional children, and many other subjects must be treated separately.

Dr. Gordon C. Hanson is professor of Educational Psychology at the University of Wichita, Kansas, and a frequent contributor to the periodical literature.

PRESENT-DAY PSYCHOLOGY

INTRODUCTION

Educational psychology is one of the applied fields of psychology; in fact, its subject-matter probably has been explored more extensively than that of any other area in the wide range of psychological investigation. Since psychology deals with human behavior and most, if not all, behavior involves learning, the principles of educational psychology are basic to an understanding of any field in psychology. Living effectively in any kind of social setting will involve some kind of learning. The man selling insurance or the mechanic in the garage has to learn to adjust to new situations continuously; hence principles of learning apply.

Educational psychology is as old as man. As a formal science it it comparatively recent in its development. Actually it grew up after the First World War. We are prone to think of it in terms of the professional education for teachers since every teacher education program has its "Introduction to Educational Psychology." As we all recognize, fundamental to teaching is the study of human behavior or personality—its growth, development, and guidance under the socializing process of formal and informal schooling. Adequate social behavior is possible only because persons can and do learn. Human learning is the core of educational psychology.

In order to understand the learning process we have to understand the innumerable factors that influence the development of the human personality, internal and external. The knowledge gained from biology, sociology, social psychology, clinical psychology, anthropology, physiology, neurology, genetics, endocrinology, *et al*, is useful in achieving an understanding of personal development. Whether educational psychology should be looked upon as a social science or as a biological science is a moot question. The fact remains that the human biological organism develops in a social setting. We cannot study the child adequately in any other way than in terms of his biological potentiality as that develops in a specific environment.

Most of the early scientific psychologists were interested in learning as such and their experiments were directed toward some specific area of learning, such as animal, maze, industrial, or classroom. Both Thorndike and Dewey did considerable work in animal learning. As psychology came into its own as a science, men like William James, G. Stanley Hall, Cattell, Baldwin, Titchener, Münsterberg, McDougall, Woodworth, and many others contributed to the thousands of experiments which have given educational psychology its basis as an applied field.[1] In the twentieth century the pioneers in applied psychology as related to education in the broadest sense were Terman, Thorndike, and Judd. Every educational psychologist is familiar with Thorndike's three volume *Educational Psychology* and Judd's *Psychology of High School Subjects*.

As previously indicated, what is studied in educational psychology is pertinent to a study in any field of human endeavor. No complex behavior excludes learning. What a person knows or does is influenced by his previous experiences and his ability to adapt them to a present situation. Whether a man is in business, industry, or farming he still has to learn to function effectively as a social creature and, so long as he has a dynamic culture, he has to learn to adjust constantly to the new demands made upon him. What we know and continue to discover as pertinent to learning in school is equally pertinent to effective work elsewhere in society. While we live we should endeavor to learn to live efficiently so as to achieve more with less expenditure of effort and time. In education therefore we are primarily concerned with efficiency in learning, first as it is applicable to school situations and then as it is applied in all situations in life. In this chapter we shall confine our thinking to what psychology is contributing to the development of efficiency in the learning process through the school's program.

OBJECTIVES OF EDUCATIONAL PSYCHOLOGY

Educational psychology's position in the preparation of teachers can be seen only in terms of the objectives for the American school system. Any group of objectives, based on our philosophy of equal educational opportunity for every child in America, would involve goals for the development of adequate behavior consistent with our social thinking. Included would be:

1. Civic-social responsibility
2. Occupational efficiency
3. Recreational and esthetic appreciation
4. Recognition of individual differences
5. General or liberal educational training
6. Physiological efficiency or good health
7. Moral and esthetic character
8. Exploration and guidance in growth

The "Seven Cardinal Principles" as described by the Committee for the Reorganization of Secondary Education in 1918 state the aims as health, command of fundamental processes, worthy home membership, vocational training, citizenship, worthy use of leisure time, and ethical character.[2] Seen in perspective, the teacher's job is first to understand the child's problem and then to know enough about the learning process to help him achieve the aims of American education. Our objectives for the field of educational psychology, stated in terms of American education and the teacher, are:

To acquaint the teacher with research techniques in the field of education.

To help the teacher understand learning, both as a process and as a product.

To aid the teacher in understanding child behavior as related to the modification of that behavior.

To help the teacher understand the social adjustment process in all its interrelationships.

To help the teacher to better understand society's rôle in the educative process.

To help the teacher understand and use evaluative materials and criteria effectively.

To help the teacher to understand and to use visual aids in learning more efficiently.

To help the teacher to gain an understanding of individual differences.

To help teachers to evaluate different philosophies of education in terms of their contributions to child development.

To develop the teacher's understanding of guidance activities with respect to the total educational program of the school.

To develop the teacher's understanding of fundamental principles of counseling and related activities to the extent required to insure an initial level of competence appropriate to counseling in schools.

To inspire confidence in the student to the point where he can effect an individual solution to personal, educational, and vocational problems.

To develop the teacher's understanding of the relationship between learning and the discipline of the social science field.

To guide prospective counselors in evaluating personal characteristics which bear upon the child's future success or failure as an American citizen.

To the extent that educational psychology is able to help teachers realize in the classroom and through the co-curricular activities the objectives of American education can it be justified as necessary in the education of teachers.

In looking through school catalogues it is evident that educational psychology looms large in the training of teachers. Interest in the field is increasing. Every college of education wants to know what body of knowledge will help teachers to be more effective on the job and thereby help to develop better learning habits in children. Ideally, what teachers should know about successful achievement parents also should know. Roughly the area of study could be broken up into two large fields—studying the learner and studying the learning process. In studying the learner we want to know the nature of, or fundamental principles involved in the growing process, how physical growth and motor development takes place, the nature of mental development, how to understand emotions and gain emotional control, how to achieve a desirable social adjustment. The learning process would include the theories of learning, motivation of learning, acquiring tools for learning, thinking and problem solving, guidance and the evaluation of learning.

Theory of Learning

Learning today is influenced by the entire scope of psychological development, by the type of experimentation and surveys conducted, and by the interpretation of results. Several theories have played a significant role in the development of educational psychology, namely, the Connectionist, the Conditioned Response or Behaviorist, the Purposivist, the Gestalt or Field Psychology and the Freudian.[3] Each has contributed a great deal to our understanding of the learning process in the child. However, few educational psychologists today tend to think of a "School" of Psychology as the one right school of thought. New developments modify all interpretations.

Thorndike is usually regarded as one of the early exponents of the Connectionist School. Learning to him in his early experience consisted of bond formation, i.e., the formation and strengthening of the connections between situations (S's) and responses (R's). Thorndike himself says, "That a connection S_1—R_1 exists in a certain organism means . . . simply that there is a probability greater than infinitesimal that if S_1 occurs, R_1 will occur."[4] "Satisfiers" and "Annoyers" are basic to the learning process in this theory. Their presence or absence induces appropriate responses to be re-enforced or inappropriate responses to be eliminated. When a situation "satisfies" the learner, "he does nothing to avoid it" but rather behaves in such a way that he can maintain it or renew it. On the other hand, when a situation "annoys" the learner, he "does nothing to preserve it," often "doing things for putting an end to it."[5]

"Satisfiers" and "Annoyers" were thought to have an important part in learning, the one stamping in connections and the other stamping out. Later, as a result of his research work, Thorndike maintained that the after-effects of "satisfiers" are positive and predictable while those of "annoyers" are not. The implication to learning in the classroom seems to be that learning should be so structured that the child gets a feeling of accomplishment—a positive type of motivation. Sandiford expresses the idea well when he says "learning seems to be best explained as a function of reward."[6]

CONDITIONING OR STIMULUS-RESPONSE ASSOCIATION

The idea of a person's responding to a stimulus is not new nor even a modern idea. Pavlov's classic experiment with the dog, the salivation to the sound of a bell, furnishes the modern early experimental background. In the event of conditioning the connection is often an anticipatory one. The importance of this anticipatory adjustment is educationally quite significant—ready at hand, involuntary or habitual foundation for all subsequent voluntary behavior. To a large extent it defines the character of the active desires which set the goals toward which the organism strives in its trial and error learning. Thus the mind set, the organic pattern, and the readiness are determined. How to establish and control the anticipatory adjustments through effective stimuli are the prime concerns of persons interested in conditioned response. Success depends upon:

1. State of the organism at the time.

2. The response to "satisfier" or "annoyer" stimulus must occur after the response to the cue stimulus, and before the latter has altogether subsided.

3. The second stimulus must be stronger than the first.

4. The second stimulus must follow the first with relative consistency until the conditioned response is established.[7]

GESTALT PSYCHOLOGY

In Gestalt psychology learning is considered as an organizing process much more so than in connectionism and behaviorism.[8] When there is recognized similarity between the new problem and the learner's previous experience the learner can reshuffle congruent previous experiences and see them in the new context or pattern. It is a process of fitting the new into the old and reorganizing the perceptual processes so as to get significantly new experiences. At the time of the perception the learner has achieved insights into his problem, that is, he has seen at least an essential relationship. The process involves two interchanging or even simultaneous operating activities, generalization and differentiation.

Several basic implications for teaching emerge, namely:

1. Presentation of the whole problem in relation to the parts.
2. Pacing especially in recognition of where the pupil is in his stage of readiness.
3. Cognitive and emotional readiness to learn on basis of previous learning experience.
4. Teacher's assurance of sufficient help so as to give the pupils an understanding of the problem in proper perspective.
5. Emphasis on seeing relationships so as to get better permanent learning.

PURPOSIVIST

The purposivist group[9] in psychology place a great deal of emphasis on the goals or purposes for behaving. Intelligent behavior, in particular, would include a great deal of recognition or emphasis on a plausible reason for behaving in a particular way under a specific circumstance. Naturally, the more clear-cut the purpose for doing something, the greater is the motivation for the behaver. "All behavior is motivated" as P. T. Young states in the first sentence of his text, "The Motivation of Behavior."[10] As is readily seen purposive psychology includes the whole field of motivation. The purposivists try to study the "Whys" of behavior. By providing the proper motives for good behavior they hope to get socially desirable responses.

FREUDIANISM

Freud has contributed to the field of educational psychology through his emphasis on present behavior as being indelibly influenced by past behavior, the "conscious" and the "unconscious". Freud's followers have deemphasized "sex" and interpreted behavior more in terms of total development, especially in terms of human relationships and the endless interrelationships throughout life. Despite the fact that Freud himself perhaps over-emphasized sex, he has influenced educational thinking tremendously in that he focused attention on the total development of the child from conception on, thus men and women in the educational field have begun to see in proper perspective the place of previous experience in the child's learning process.[11]

MOTIVATION IN LEARNING

Learning involves change or adjustment. In order to learn a child needs some kind of motivation. Teachers are naturally interested in how to motivate the child most effectively so as to increase the quantity and quality of learning. Teaching method implies an attempt at better motivation. Numerous books have been written on the improvement of learning in recent years.[12] Psychological experimentation is quite extensive in this area of learning. One thing stands out in our experimentation: no single factor ever operates to influence learning. Rather, innumerable factors interact in the learning process so that to understand motivation we have to understand the child's background and how it interacts with present stimuli.[13] Some of the more common factors influencing a child's learning are:

1. Present physiological condition.
2. Pleasant or unpleasant sensory reactions.
3. Fatigue and exhaustion.

4. Degree of success or failure in learning.
5. Being put in position where status is jeopardized.
6. Discouragement by people deemed important.
7. Being ostracized or ignored by people who are significant to learner.
8. Praise or blame in terms of when, how, where, by whom.
9. Uncontrollable fears previously acquired.
10. Undesirable home conditions and experiences.
11. Negative or positive cultural influences.
12. Degree of genuine self-confidence, self-assurance, self-reliance.
13. Failure to reach level of aspiration.
14. Purpose for learning and clearness in seeing purpose.

Anything that impinges itself on personality can affect a child's learning, pro or con. No list of influences could ever be complete since what motivates one child may or may not motivate another. Briefly stated, the child learns because he is biologically equipped under stimulation for learning. Under proper motivation in the home, the community, the school, the various organizations and play groups to which the child is exposed, he tends to be motivated to learn a socially approved body of knowledge. In recent years social psychology has demonstrated the terrific impact of society on the behavior of the child, positive or negative, in terms of social goals.

Acquiring Tools for Learning

Much attention is now being given to learning of the motor skills and to the learning of skills for effective living. Motor skill is tied closely to social skills. How to improve motor skill has been studied extensively in such child developmental laboratories as those at Yale, Columbia, Iowa, Minnesota, California, and Catholic University. Studies have been made of height and weight and body proportions and their effect on behavior, varying patterns of growth, differences between boys and girls in the maturing processes, differences within the sexes, adjustments that have to be made to bodily changes, especially in adolescence, the effect of these changes on heterosexual interests, the effect of motor development on the personality of the child.

As a result of numerous child studies, we are more aware of the need for learning the language arts in adequate personality development in time and place. Today we think of the language arts as including speaking, reading, spelling, and writing. We recognize, for example, that the child usually learns to speak before he can read, write, or spell. In our culture he is handicapped to the extent that he is deficient in oral or written communication for effective living. We spend a great deal of time emphasizing the art of speaking, developing a vocabulary, and learning to read as an adjunct to speech—"language written down." We emphasize that at first the child learns to read and then gradually shifts more to reading to learn. Spelling and writing become significant tools in the process of learning how to use language effectively. Efficiency in all the language arts is required for success in learning in school as emphasized in our reading programs.[14] Personal adjustment in our day demands varying degrees of speech and reading facility.

Another tool that in our culture looms large is that of numbers or mathematics in its broadest aspect. In our type of society effective living is becoming more dependent on the whole mathematical field. For good adjustment in school and in the out of school situation, the effective handling of numbers is increasingly more significant. Since education today is looked upon as a life-long process, in many vocations learning more about "math" is a constant process in the art of making a living. It becomes closely related to success and failure, in school or on the job. Many a child in school is looked upon as a failure by his classmates because he is deficient in arithmetic. As in any other field, his failure here may seriously affect his all-round learning as well as impair his personality development. Since teachers are aware of the totality of personality development, they are getting more concerned with trying to improve all learning, including mathematics. They realize the hazard of labeling the child. Educational psychologists are trying to find out how to teach mathematics more effectively and thus develop an interest in the subject. How to get children to like mathematics is a persistent problem in every school. Much study on this phase of education needs to be done.

NATURAL AND SOCIAL SCIENCE FIELD

For adjustment in a complex society we are aware that children need to learn the fundamental facts of the natural science field. How to develop selective learning in this area is a vital problem. The average child can in no significant measure learn everything—no one could—so one of our larger problems is training him to select his material in such a way that he has the necessary knowledge for effective thinking in specific situations. Certain facts in physics, chemistry, and geology he will have to know to live on a somewhat intelligent plane. How to learn them and be able to apply them is a crucial educational problem.

Closely related to the natural and biological fields is the social science area. Understanding how people live in a physical world is of prime importance and is basic to all psychology. Without adequate human relations no physical world would or could serve people effectively, therefore educational psychologists are concerned with establishing the proper relationship between man and his world. What a child needs to know about sociology, psychology, economics, political science and education is pertinent to his social development. As in the natural science field we are concerned with selecting the most pertinent facts and principles in terms of the child's need and then discovering ways in which this knowledge can be learned in a meaningful way for the individual child. Needless to say, we have not yet discovered the secret for teaching effective human relations and citizenship.

In the whole field of learning in school it is evident that the teacher has the task of training children in:

1. What is important to learn.
2. How to learn important things efficiently.

More and more we are looking at the problem of learning from the viewpoint of the efficiency engineer—greater output in less time at less cost in terms of energy expenditure on the part of both pupil or teacher. The teaching problem involves knowing enough about the learning background of each child and then being able to select the right material which will fit into the learning pattern of the child. Each field has its own problems for each, in time and place, has its cultural prestige and significance.

GUIDANCE OR COUNSELLING

As long as man has existed there has been some form of informal guidance of children. Only recently have we found it necessary, as a result of the changing structure in society, to organize definite guidance programs for children. In the early schools of the United States the teacher in the classroom did any counselling that was deemed necessary in the rural society of the time. Most of it, however, was done by the parents. In the twentieth century the job became too complex, largely as a result of mass education and the ever increasing complexity of society with its steadily increasing body of knowledge. No one will question the fact that today the child has many more decisions to make as to his future growth and vocational choice than was true yesterday. What he must do to achieve success is too involved a process to be understood with his limited knowledge. In mass education individual attention to the child's needs is extremely difficult especially in the junior and senior high school periods. Today more attention is focused necessarily on counselling by trained counsellors who have studied specifically in the fields of child development, personality problems, gathering case histories, tests and measurements, vocations, interviewing, and allied subjects. This field is a specialty of educational psychology and, from the school's viewpoint, of tremendous significance.

The trend in the training of teachers today is to stress more work in guidance in such subjects as child development, mental hygiene, adolescent psychology, principles of guidance, exceptional children, and occupational information.[15] In the secondary field this training is a particularly important phase of teaching. For the average child the most significant counsellor is the classroom teacher—only the severe cases go to the professional worker. The adolescent today has not only the problem of learning to live satisfactorily with people but he has to make a vocational choice and prepare himself to be adequate in his vocation. Along the way, he needs the mature help of a teacher who knows reasonably well what he needs and is willing to help him achieve his goal. With the aid of understanding teachers who know how to help the child, many problem children can become well-adjusted and live a satisfying worthwhile life. Educational psychology must furnish the training and assure sufficient knowledge for the average teacher's needs. Every teacher training institution today does some work in guidance.

THE LEARNER: PHYSICAL GROWTH

To understand the learner the educational psychologist has to borrow from the biologist's and the child psychologist's storehouse of information. It is a biological organism that learns to behave, therefore too much emphasis cannot be given to biological development. Notice that the Committee on the Reorganization of Secondary Education put *health* as the number one Cardinal Principle of Education. We cannot know too much about the physiological growth of the child, his strengths and his weaknesses, for they influence his social reactions. As mentioned earlier in this chapter, child psychologists are intensely interested in how children grow and differ in their growth because these differences help motivate much of the child's social behavior. For a time we likely overstressed hereditary factors, then we went to the other extreme and overemphasized the influence of environment. At the present time we likely have hit the middle road where we recognize that heredity without environment is an impossibility or vice versa.

Every teacher should recognize the significance of: first, the cephalocaudal trend in development in relation to its effect on learning; second, mass or general activity as it gives way to more specific, localized, precise, orderly activity; third, continuous development even though differences in rate and time are peculiar to the person; fourth, sequence as being about the same in all people; fifth, capacity on basis of growth to predict development; sixth, each phase of growth with certain characteristics peculiar to that stage of development—many so-called forms of problem behavior are normal when they occur; seventh, every person's normally passing through each stage of development in a definite sequence.[16]

MENTAL DEVELOPMENT

Since mental development is merely a part of total development, it is necessary to think of psychological development in terms of the best possible child care and stimulation. The child's mental growth comes as a result of widened temporal dimensions. The younger the child, the more his responses, his interests, his activities are concerned with the process of occurring. As he ages he is increasingly able to react in terms of recollections from the past and anticipation of the future. As he is stimulated to learn he increases his ability to use symbols and thus profit more from past experience. The teacher is well aware that a child is fortunate who has a broad developmental experience because more and more, he is able to go from concrete experience to the abstract. The higher his intelligence the greater his ability to use the abstract and to concentrate for longer periods of time in problem solving.

Mental development begins at conception though it gets an added spurt as soon as the child gets into the external environment. Intelligence, as every teacher knows, is well along in development in the preschool days but the great spurt comes when the child learns to read and gets into an organized school program for learning. Though heredity no doubt is a basic factor in intelligence it is not operating in a vacuum. To the extent that the school furnishes a stimulating environment is the school able to develop the child intellectually. It is rather significant that totality of behavior is involved and that the child learns to be intelligent. Knowledge is involved in mental growth. For a short time there was a tendency to discredit the learning of facts and to emphasize "personality development." Even psychologists sometimes lose perspective! We now recognize that the home and school have a vital role in developing the child intellectually. Intelligent behavior can come only when there is sufficient knowledge to know how to behave adequately. Mental development is shown in the adjustment process. The school has a definite part to play in trying to adjust the child to life and in this process the most important factor is mental development—the thinking process. The school must help with furnishing the tools for thinking as well as developing skills in using those tools.

Basically the school must try to develop the child's ability to use his sensory processes effectively—train him to hear, to see, to smell, to touch, etc. The school has a definite function in giving experience in observation of likeness and difference in sensory discrimination. Though the concrete experiences will always be present in schoolwork the tendency should be toward moving into the abstract realm of thinking where the mastery of language looms large. In mental development we should stress the accumulation of information or knowledge, the use of words and relative meanings, the comprehension in language usage, the ability to understand and follow directions, the ability to see relationships, opposites and similarities, analogies, spatial relations, inferences. In reality, since mental development involves the development of intelligence or intelligent behavior, the educational psychologist is concerned with trying to develop a child to behave "intelligently" in time and place. This involves knowledge and skill.

SOCIAL AND EMOTIONAL DEVELOPMENT

Educational psychology is concerned particularly with the emotional and social development of the child. To a large extent the child's learning is influenced by the kind of emotional reactions he exhibits in social situations. The school is obliged to deal with all phases of his development. Perhaps the most important aspect long range is emotional control, since the emotional states influence the whole development of the child, including his adjustment to the school situation. Emotional reactions are learned, therefore can be controlled. If the schools can furnish the necessary satisfying experiences we can help develop self-controlled people. Much of our difficulty hinges on the kind of competitive social situations to which the child is exposed in school. Where comparisons are made adversely and the child is ranked in terms of his performance we have difficulty with adjustment. Other person's ideas in regard to the performance play an important part in the child's reaction. What the child learns, quantitatively and qualitatively, will depend largely on how he in turn reacts emotionally to living. This is included in the field of mental hygiene. Prescott deals admirably with this topic in his book "Emotions and the Educative Process."[17] Educationists, as well as parents, are concerned about such emotional states as anger, hostility, vindictiveness, fear, aggression, regression, withdrawing. To the extent that the school can aid parents in taking care of the child's adjustment problems on an emotional plane can the school serve the child's educational needs. In the training of teachers we are particularly concerned with giving them an adequate background for understanding the child's emotional and social needs. Courses in mental hygiene, child development, adjustment, and guidance are designed for this purpose.

A teacher must recognize that most emotional difficulties are intimately connected with the socializing process—the feeling states of being important, wanted, noticed, useful, loved, respected. The school has the job of organizing the school program so as to develop adequately in every child feelings of or for:

1. Social sympathy
2. Expanding friendships
3. Popularity based on affection
4. Group loyalties

5. Socially acceptable responses to competition
6. Maturing social consciousness with aging
7. Social significance of followership and leadership
8. Discipline in work situations so that success is possible

A teacher should know that a successful social performance in school is influenced by the total personality development. Included are such factors as:

1. Physique—evaluated in terms of development in time and place.
2. Prevailing social attitudes.
3. Personal likes and dislikes.
4. Mastery of certain facts.
5. Moral values deemed significant in community, home, or school.
6. Knowledge of social facts and skills deemed significant.
7. Educational values regarded important to society and to person.
8. Language facility in social situations.
9. Property qualifications.
10. Approved home evironment.
11. Church affiliations.
12. Social level of family.
13. Kind of habit system.

Educational psychology, in view of the aims of American education, is placing increasingly more emphasis on teaching what may help in better personal adjustment. We emphasize continually better understanding of the moral and social values deemed important for acceptance in our culture, better cooperation in living together in social units, more wholesome values achieved through social-centred effort, better work habits for the purpose of gaining more satisfaction through achievement thus better acceptance by the group, more conscientious efforts to serve society, better self-discipline and emotional control in trying situations, and a more discriminating sense of worth of the individual in society. All this involves promoting a better mental health program. As all mental hygienists realize, this is a program that involves the effort of all society.[18]

The educational psychologist, borrowing from the experience of clinical psychology and psychiatry, is concerned also with the abnormal cases in the classroom. Degrees of maladjustment are found in every child under certain circumstances. We are attempting to train teachers to recognize some of the symptoms in order to better understand the child, also to recognize that deviant behavior has a cause for its existence and that to get socially approved behavior involves sympathetic understanding and guidance by the teacher. An efficient teacher can achieve success with his guidance in most classroom cases. Some problems however, are so involved that experts are needed in getting at the root of the trouble. At all times teachers must recognize that no two children have the same backgrounds nor are they going to react the same to any social situation, in school or outside the school.

A point of view that is gaining headway rapidly is that everyone who comes in contact with the child is in part responsible for his psychological welfare. We are recognizing slowly that we are "our brother's keeper." Several recent texts in mental hygiene have emphasized this point of view in trying to answer the question, "Who is responsible for the mental hygiene program?"[19]

EVALUATION IN EDUCATION

Without knowing the results of one's effort little or no progress can be made in developing a more effective program. The more objective the evaluation, the greater value it is to the school and to the teacher. In our early education only subjective judgments were used. Now, however, we are in the early stages of getting objective measurements. In every teacher education school there is a standardized course usually entitled, "Tests and Measurements." This course usually deals with the function of objective tests, the various types of test items, the methods of standardization, their strengths and weaknesses, their validity and reliability. Objective testing is in reality a product of the twentieth century. It is true that Dr. J. M. Rice in 1894 prepared an objective spelling test and that Thorndike in 1909 came out with his Handwriting Scale, but it was after the Binet Scale was adapted for American use that objective measurement began to be widely used. Perhaps the best evaluation today is done in achievement.

In current testing we try to get objective measurements in intelligence, in personality, in aptitude, in achievement, in attitudes, in special skills, in reaction time, and numerous other phases of child development. We emphasize wide sampling, objectivity, and norms. In fact, educators are accused of worshipping norms. It is true that some of the standardized tests are useful; however, some of them are of little or no value.

Our main objective for testing, whether it be subjective or objective, is to evaluate development in the pupil and to evaluate our own teaching. In the school situation learning and teaching are interdependent. Good learning usually accompanies good teaching. We are gradually going beyond the stage where we pass judgment on the pupil as a result of a test score to the stage where we ask the question, "Why?" It is through evaluation, used discriminatingly, that we have the possibility of passing sound judgments on the curriculum of the school, the teaching methods, the training of teachers, the effective teaching personality, the equipment and physical environment for learning, as well as the personal achievement of the student. Taken from this broad point of view, evaluation is an indispensable tool in the learning process and in the modern school system. Throughout this symposium testing is referred to many times as it is one of the psychologist's important tools.

Most of our objective measurement in the grades has been in terms of school achievement. In most progressive schools we are giving achievement tests at least once a year. But we have scarcely touched the other phases of personality development. We have been prone to judge the efficiency of a school on the basis of a few facts found from a statistical analysis of achievement. Scholastic achievement is only one phase of the total program. However, it is a start at least in evaluation. That educational psychology is aware of total personality evaluation is shown in the number of departments we have working in this area in our larger universities. As an example we can cite the work of the Committee on Human Development of the University of Chicago and such illuminating studies as "Elmtown's Youth" and "Adolescent Character and Personality."[20]

In the better secondary schools we have added personality and vocational aptitude testing. Many schools today use such tests as the Strong "Vocational Interest Blank" or the California "Occupational Interest Inventory". Most schools use some form of intelligence testing. Specialized tests for vocational use are being developed. Since we look upon the secondary school as a terminal school for the majority of high school students, we are trying to prepare them for living in terms of their vocational choice. This makes vocational counselling loom large in any high school program. Even though thousands of tests are available, no one is able to make any absolute predictions. We are forced to do the best we can with our limited knowledge of the individual's background as derived from fragmentary case histories, the limited information we can get from interviews, the obvious limitations of tests, the scholastic achievement records, and any other bits of information we can gather that may be of use. Perhaps the greatest lack is found in the teacher himself with his lack of knowledge and the skills to use the knowledge he has and the bias inherent in his own training. Not until we get cumulative information concerning the child's total development can we presume to speak with dogmatic certainty.

BIBLIOGRAPHY

[1] Roback, A. A. *History of American Psychology.* New York: Library Publishers, 1952.

[2] Bulletin, 1918, No. 35, *Cardinal Principles of Secondary Education,* U. S. Bureau of Education.

[3] Hilgard, Ernest R. *Theories of Learning.* New York: Appleton-Century-Crofts, 1948.

4 Thorndike, E. L. Fundamentals of Learning. New York: Teachers College, Columbia U., 1932, p. 19. Quoted in: Forty-first Yearbook, National Society for Study of Education, Part II, p. 146.

5 Sandiford, P. Connectionism, Origin and Features. Forty-first Yearbook, Nat. Soc. Study Ed., Part II, p. 114.

6 Postman, L. The History and Present Status of the Law of Effect. Psychological Bulletin, vol. 44, No. 6, Nov. 1947, pp. 489-563.

7 Hull, Clark L. Conditioning Outline of a Systematic Theory of Learning. Forty-first Yearbook, National Society for the Study of Education, Part II, pp. 68-72.

8 Kohler, W. Gestalt Psychology. New York: Liveright Pub. Corp., 1947. Hartmann, George W. The Field Theory of Learning and its Educational Consequences. Forty-first Yearbook, Nat. Soc. Study Educ., Part II, p. 191.

Lancelot, W. H. Permanent Learning. New York: John Wiley & Sons, Inc., 1944.

9 Tolman, E. C. Purposive Behavior in Animals and Man. New York: Century, 1932.

10 Young, Paul T. Motivation of Behavior. New York: John Wiley & Sons, Inc., 1936, p. 1.

11 Roback, A. A. History of American Psychology. New York: Library Publishers, 1952, Part 3.

12 Burton, William H. The Guidance of Learning Activities. New York: D. Appleton-Century Co., 1944.

Kingsley, Howard L. The Nature and Conditions of Learning, New York: Prentice-Hall, Inc., 1946.

Lancelot, W. H. Permanent Learning. New York : John Wiley & Sons, Inc., 1944.

13 The Forty-ninth Yearbook of the National Society for the Study of Education, edited by Nelson B. Henry, III. The University of Chicago Press, 1950, Pt. 1.

14 Gates, A. I. The Improvement of Reading. New York: The Macmillan Co., 1949, Ch. 1.

15 Jones, Arthur J. Principles of Guidance. New York: McGraw-Hill Book Co., Inc., 1951.

Tyler, Leona E. The Work of the Counselor. New York: Appleton-Century-Crofts. See Appendix C.

16 Garrison, Karl C. Growth and Development. New York: Longmans, Green & Co., 1952, Pt. 1, 2.

17 Prescott, D. A. Emotions and the Educative Process. The American Council on Education, Washington, D. C., 1918.

18 Fenton, N. Mental Hygiene in School Practice. Stanford: Stanford University Press, 1949, Part 5.

19 Bernard, Harold W. Mental Hygiene for Classroom Teachers. New York: McGraw-Hill Book Co., 1952.

Katz, Barney and Lehner, George F. Mental Hygiene in Modern Living. New York: The Ronald Press Co., 1953.

20 Hollingshead, August B. Elmtown's Youth. New York: John Wiley & Sons, Inc., 1949.

Havighurst, Robert J. and Taba, H. Adolescent Character and Personality. New York: John Wiley & Sons, Inc., 1949.

CHAPTER XIII

PSYCHOMETRY

J. P. GUILFORD, Ph.D., LL.D.
Professor of Psychology, University of Southern California

EDITORIAL NOTE

Psychological testing is a comparatively recent accretion of psychology. Aside from the earlier groping attempts of Galton in England, Toulouse in France, and J. M. Cattell in the United States, this branch really burgeons up with Alfred Binet and H. Simon in France. But it was in the United States that it began to spread with increasing rapidity. Lewis M. Terman may be looked upon as the successor of Binet, but who has contributed far more than the founder, cut off in the prime of life, as he was about to systematize his findings. Terman has not only given us the first rigid standards and norms of the Binet tests but has trained a whole generation of mental testers. To speak of the great service of testing in all sorts of institutions and in the organization of national defence and mobilization would be dispensing well-known information.

Dr. J. P. Guilford, who at present is Professor of Psychology at the University of Southern California, has been one of the foremost workers in this branch of psychology, having served as director of several research units in connection with the army air force training centers, and attaining the rank of Colonel in the army. He also was decorated with the Legion of Merit. Among the many offices he has held are: President of the American Psychological Association (1949-1950), *President of the Psychometric Society and of the California Color Society. He has been a prolific writer—author of over* 100 *scientific papers and a number of manuals and textbooks such as* Laboratory Studies in Psychology (*New York,* 1934), Psychometric Methods (*New York,* 1936 *and* 1954), General Psychology (*New York,* 1939 *and* 1952), Fundamental Statistics in Psychology and Education (*New York,* 1942 *and* 1950). *He also edited* Fields of Psychology(2d ed. 1950).

Psychological Tests

The impact of psychological science and technology upon the general public in the U. S. A. is felt in many ways. It can probably be said without much fear of contradiction that of all the direct influences of psychology, that attributable to psychological tests is by far the most prevalent and decisive. At the time of World War I and after, it was often reported as a remakable fact that nearly two million American, adult males had been given the Army Psychological Examination, Alpha or Beta. The impetus toward mass testing carried over into civilian life, in institutions of higher learning as well as in industry. World War II brought with it much improved and extended programs of psychological testing in the various branches of the armed services. More than eleven million service personnel were examined with one or more tests. In the Army Air Force, approximately 600,000 men who were applying for classification for training as flying personnel took a battery of twenty tests which required as much as ten hours of their time. These represented about half of the number who had taken previously a three-hour qualifying examination. The impetus to testing in civilian life following World War II seems somewhat in proportion to the increase in testing efforts during that War.

It is the purpose of this chapter to present a survey of the field of psychological tests as that field appears to one observer today. The chief concern will be with the psychological test as an instrument of measurement. It will therefore be necessary to consider briefly theories pertaining to tests and test scores. Although practice in testing has always outrun theory, the gap has been narrowed somewhat in recent years, with the consequence that tests have been considerably improved and they are sometimes used in a much more enlightened manner than formerly. There is still much to be gained in the latter direction. We shall also consider how theory is affecting practices in psychological testing. We shall be concerned with testing of various kinds, in the measurement of interests, attitudes, and temperament traits as well as aptitudes. We shall not be concerned with the various uses of tests, except incidentally, or with certain kinds of tests—projective tests and achievement tests. We shall begin with test theory.

PSYCHOLOGICAL-TEST THEORY

Modern psychologists have generally seemed to be afraid of theory. Perhaps it has been because so many of their colleagues have tended to confuse theory with fact. Some of the bolder and more discriminating among them, however, have taken advantage of the contribution that theory has to offer, at the same time recognizing its proper place. There are theoretical aspects latent in whatever a scientist does, of course, but latent theory is likely to be nebulous, shifting, and rather impotent.

In the development of psychological tests, there were, on the psychological side, some general ideas of the nature of human abilities. The pioneers, Galton, Binet, and Cattell, could not have proceeded as they did without having in mind certain conceptions of human intellect and the kind of mental tasks it would take to discriminate between those with more or less of that important human quality. On the side of measurement, however, although Galton was also a pioneer in the development of statistical ideas and applications, on the background of present theory of psychological measurement the founding fathers appear rather naive. Nor did their followers overcome this deficit very rapidly, for it is only within the past quarter century that suitable psychological-measurement theory has been developed. In many ways, as we shall see, the development of measurement theory has also facilitated to a marked degree the development of psychological theory.

THEORY OF RELIABILITY

About 50 years ago, Spearman made the first important step in theory of measurement by means of tests when he developed the concept of reliability. The key idea was to regard each obtained test score as the sum of two components, a *true* component and an *error* component. The true component is the individual's actual status with respect to the psychological quality measured, on the scale of measurement. The error component is an increment (or decrement) determined by many things, other than the person's status, operating at the moment. In a perfectly reliable test there are no errors of measurement. The larger and more variable the error components, the less reliable the test. Incidentally, Spearman's announcement of the idea of reliability did very much to instill new life into the lagging test movement. The low correlations that were then being found between different tests of intellect and between test scores and grades of university students had been rather discouraging. The low correlations could be accounted for in part on the basis of unreliability of the test scores.

Besides putting new life into the test movement, Spearman's theory of reliability led to some immediately useful statistics and eventually to the more important body of theory under the heading of factor analysis. Spearman defined reliability as the proportion of true variance in a set of test scores and suggested methods of estimating this proportion in terms of a coefficient of correlation between scores derived from the same test (or an alternate form of it) when applied to a sample of individuals. He also demonstrated that the longer the test (when lengthening is effected by adding more of the same kind of items), the proportion of true variance increases more rapidly than the proportion of error variance. A long test is therefore more reliable than a short one of the same kind and the reliability of the long test can be estimated from the known reliability of the short one by means of the famous Spearman-Brown formula (developed independently by Wm. Brown).

Another statistical outcome of Spearman's work was the formula for correcting an intercorrelation between two different tests for attenuation. Attenuation is a lowering of the amount of correlation by the presence of errors of measurement in the scores. A coefficient of correlation corrected for attenuation gives an estimate of the correlation between two measures, with the influence of errors of measurement eliminated. This procedure gives a more accurate picture of the validity of a test, where validity is indicated by a coefficient of correlation between test scores and criterion measures.

FACTOR THEORY

From his formula for correction of a coefficient for attenuation, Spearman derived what he thought was proof that among tests of cognitive abilities the intercorrelations are due entirely to a single, general, common factor G. Others, notably L. L. Thurstone (1947), have demonstrated that more generally the intercorrelations among different tests may best be accounted for by the assumption of more than one common factor. Thus, factor theory, building upon Spearman's original ideas, has become generalized to what is called *multiple-factor theory*. The most prevalent conception today is that there are a number of common factors and that usually more than one such factor in a test is needed to account for the intercorrelations with that test. Within any circumscribed area of tests—cognitive, perceptual, temperament, or interest—we may find that one of the factors is common to all the tests in that area and hence may be regarded as a g factor, but this is not essential. Thurstone believes that Spearman's G is best indicated experimentally as a "second-order" factor, which is a factor among factors. Of the "first-order" factors that are found directly from intercorrelations, none is usually found to be general. British psychologists (Burt, 1941) very commonly follow Spearman, however, by extracting a general factor in any area in which they are working. This is usually possible, if one insists upon it. American psychologists do not insist upon a g factor and usually do not find one.

Multiple-factor theory takes an important step beyond the theory of reliability with which Spearman started. It accepts the idea of summing true and error components in test scores. It breaks down the true component of a test score, however, into contributions from different factors, some of which are common factors (found in more than one test) and one of which is specific to this particular test. The specific component contributes to true variance and hence to reliability, but it does not contribute to intercorrelations of this test with other tests. Hence, only the common-factor components contribute to test validity. A test can be valid, then, to the extent that the variable with which it is correlated possesses the same components, regardless of its reliability. Thus, some tests of low reliability can have greater validity than other tests of high reliability.

According to factor theory, the common-factor components, like the true and error components, combine in an additive fashion to produce a total score. Any person's obtained score is a sum of his factor scores (assuming that he has a true status in each factor), each weighted appropriately, plus his weighted status in the specific component, plus the error component. Many critics balk at accepting the idea of summation of components. They do not believe that, even granting that human abilities and other traits exist as separate unities, the contributions of factors actually combine by addition to produce results. This objection indicates a misunderstanding of the role of a mathematical theory. A mathematical theory is used to provide a model for description and understanding of phenomena. The applicability of the model can be tested by predicting results, then testing by empirical operations to see whether those results follow as they should. In general, such predictions from factor theory have held up very well (Guilford, 1948). We can then say that events of the kind observed in psychological testing take place *as if* a summative operation were going on. Thus we do not ask whether the factorial picture is the *true* one, but rather whether it gives us the power to predict and control psychological events. Certainly no other theory has worked as well. This does not mean, of course, that we shall never have a better one.

ITEM-SUMMATION THEORY

Another theoretical approach that was designed particularly for the test that is composed of items is a summation theory of a different kind. It assumes that a total test score is a sum of item scores. In a typical test, each item is scored on a scale of two points, zero and one. Since the total score is a summation of such component scores, it is possible to derive means, standard deviations, and an estimate of reliability for the total scores from a knowledge of item statistics—item means, standard deviations, and intercorrelations. Among the advantages of this general theoretical approach are the many useful deductions that can be drawn concerning the optimal combination of items for a test that is designed to accomplish certain objectives. Thus, by the proper selection of items one can control the shape of the frequency distribution of total scores, the mean, standard deviation, and reliability. Another important outcome is in the form of computing formulas, among which are the well-known Kuder-Richardson formulas for estimating reliability.

HOMOGENEITY OF TESTS

A rather different type of theory is concerned primarily with the number of consistent and meaningful discriminations among individuals that a test provides. Among theorizers who have espoused this type of theory are Jane Loevinger (1947) and Louis Guttman. They define a perfectly homogeneous test as one such that each person passes every item up to a certain level of difficulty and fails every item of greater difficulty. Thus, from each person's total score one would be able to say which items he passed and which ones he failed. There is no particular utility in making such a prediction, but a highly homogeneous test has certain desirable properties. It is a very reliable test, and according to Guttman we can conclude that it measures only one common factor. When we have a one-factor test the scores have univocal meaning. A test that measures two or more common factors yields psychologically ambiguous scores. If a certain person makes a moderate score we do not know whether he is about average in all the factors measured by the test or whether he is high in some and low in others. One-factor tests are rare, however, and it is possible that even highly homogeneous tests in the Loevinger-Guttman sense may measure more than one factor. For many purposes tests with more than one factor serve very well; for other purposes, to be pointed out later, univocal or one-factor tests are very important.

SOME EXAMPLES OF TESTS IN COMMON USE

We shall pass in review some of the common types of tests in current use and note some of their general features.[1] Tests may be categorized in several ways. In terms of personality modalities (type of traits), we have tests of aptitudes, interests, attitudes, and temperament traits. In terms of basic test theory, some tests aim to measure single common factors and some do not. Some (such as intelligence tests) yield a single, omnibus score, while others (such as interest and temperament inventories) provide multiple scores, one for each trait.

APTITUDE TESTS

Roughly speaking, aptitude tests measure readiness to learn. For example, one can say that Binet's original scale was designed to measure aptitude for learning school subjects. For many years the practice of aptitude measurement sought to label each individual with a single score for intelligence or mental ability. Spearman's championship of a single intellectual factor may have helped to foster the practice. Even today we have many tests whose goal is a single numerical index for each individual. Among the individually administered intelligence tests in common use today are the *Stanford Revision* of the *Binet* test (Terman and Merrill, 1937), the *Wechsler-Bellevue Intelligence Scale,* and the *Wechsler Intelligence Scale for Children.* Among the group intelligence tests in common use are the *Otis Mental Ability Test* and its derivative, the *Wonderlic Personnel Test.*

In connection with vocational guidance and vocational selection of personnel it has been realized that an intelligence test should be supplemented with special tests of clerical aptitude and of mechanical aptitude. The much more analytical approach provided by the measurement of factors in aptitude—the primary mental abilities, as Thurstone calls them—has not gained much vogue as yet. It is coming to be realized, however, that for the classification of personnel into different kinds of assignments and for vocational-guidance purposes factor tests are very much needed. In the classification of personnel it is not only a question of how much ability each person has but is he better in ability X than he is in ability Y, and better in ability Y than he is in ability Z? The Thurstone *Primary Mental Ability Tests* were the first of their kind, each test emphasizing a different common factor—verbal comprehension, numerical facility, spatial orientation, word fluency, and so on. The U. S. Employment Service in recent years has committed itself to testing along factorial lines. Other published batteries of factor tests are the *Guilford-Zimmerman Aptitude Survey* and the *Factored Aptitude Series* by Joseph E. King.

The number of aptitude factors there may prove to be is as yet only a guess. French (1951) includes more than 40 factors in the aptitude list. The number is likely to exceed 50 by a substantial margin when all are discovered and identified.

Interest Tests

In the field of interests, the prevailing type of instrument for measurement is of the questionnaire or inventory type. Verbal questions are asked concerning likes and dislikes, and preferences. Two general principles have been followed in developing interest inventories. The popular *Strong Vocational Interest Blank* (one for men and one for women) was developed by an almost entirely empirical approach. By asking several hundred questions of samples of people who had been working in their professions for a number of years, Strong determined what answers were more characteristic of each group. For example, in setting up a scoring key for interest in the profession of medicine, if his medical group gave a certain answer much more often than the average person in all other groups combined, Strong gave that answer a positive weight. The more any examinee's answers to the keyed items resemble those of medical men in general the greater his score for interest in medicine, and so on for each vocation in turn. There must be a scoring key for every vocation for which interest is to be measured. Many such scores are highly intercorrelated, in which case differential measurement is poor.

The other general approach to interest measurement is somewhat more rational. It assumes that there are basic human interests and that they are the same wherever you find them. The prediction of interest in any particular vocation is then a matter of using weighted composite scores derived from the basic interest scores, or, more commonly, profile patterns of scores. A popular instrument based on this principle is the *Kuder Preference Record,* which now provides scores in ten general areas. The selection of areas was determined by seeking the goal of low intercorrelations of scores. All scores are given meaningful designations, such as persuasive, musical, artistic, mechanical, scientific, and so on. The only attempt to assess basic interests incorporating what is generally known concerning the factors in the domain of interests is represented by the *Guilford-Shneidman-Zimmerman Interest Survey.*

ATTITUDE SCALES

The measurement of attitudes was initiated by L. L. Thurstone some 25 years ago. His technique is still unique among those employed in the development of attitude scales. An attitude scale in the Thurstone manner is composed of statements of opinions varying in degree of favorableness or unfavorableness toward an institution, a social group, or an issue. Thurstone derives a numerical value on a scale of 11 points for each opinion as judged by a number of qualified observers. Having a set of scaled opinions on a subject, he asks each person whose attitude is to be measured to say which statements express his own feelings. His position on the scale is then determined by the values of the opinions that he endorses.

Rensis Likert, after experimenting with other procedures,

came to the conclusion that items of opinion may best be selected in the same way that test items in general are selected, that is, by way of item-analysis procedures. An item is selected for inclusion and a response is weighted according as the item correlates with a previously accepted criterion of the attitude continuum in question. Louis Guttman has developed a procedure known as "scale analysis" which aims at a collection of items with very high level of homogeneity, in line with homogeneity theory mentioned above.

TEMPERAMENT INVENTORIES

The prevailing type of temperament test in use at the present time is the personality inventory, usually composed of questions about personal habits, feelings, beliefs, opinions, and likes and dislikes. It is not always assumed that the examinee's answers are truthful nor is it regarded essential that they be truthful. It *is* important that his answers indicate how he stands in some trait, as determined by correlational evidence. The interpretation of traits thus measured does place heavy reliance, however, on self descriptions. Some inventories provide secondary scores intended to indicate something about probable veracity and capability for self report.

The nature of an inventory cannot be well understood without considering its general history. The inventory got its start when R. S. Woodworth designed a screening instrument for military use during World War I. The obvious approach was to ask all the promising questions concerning common symptoms that would possibly be reported in psychiatric interviews. A large number of symptomatic responses given by one person was taken to indicate potential pathology. The Woodworth inventory was followed by Donald Laird's *Personal Inventory C 2,* Floyd L. Allport and Gordon W. Allport's *A-S Reaction Study,* and the *Personality Schedule* by L. L. Thurstone and Thelma G. Thurstone. The Laird Inventory was designed to give a score for the trait of introversion-extroversion; the Allport inventory **a** score for the trait of ascendance-submission; and the Thurstone inventory a score for general maladjustment or neurotic tendency. R. G. Bernreuter initiated a new trend in personality inventories by incorporating the scoring for all these traits, plus his own proposed trait of self sufficiency, from the same list of 125 items. This definitely makes for economy, but because the same items are scored for so many traits, some very high intercorrelations of scores result.

An empirical approach, similar to that used by Strong, has been followed in the development of two well-known inventories, the *Humm-Wadsworth Temperament Scale* and the *Minnesota Multiphasic Personality Inventory,* known as the *MMPI.* In the development of the former, Doncaster G. Humm and Guy W. Wadsworth added rationality by following the personality theory proposed by the psychiatrist A. J. Rosanoff. According to this theory, six fundamental traits of normal personality are exhibited in extreme degree by six pathological groups. Responses to some 300 items are scored according as each pathological group—for example, manic, hysteroid, epileptoid, and so on—differs from a non-pathological group in answering the same questions. The *MMPI* was developed similarly by S. R. Hathaway and J. C. McKinley, without adherence to the Rosanoff theory and with some differences in the pathological groups selected. Both instruments were designed to differentiate between each of several pathological groups and presumably normal individuals. Their use *within* normal groups rests on the assumption that differences in their scores mean the same kinds of discriminations as those between normal and pathological groups.

The first attempt to introduce factors of temperament as the variables to be scored in personality inventories were made by the writer. A factor analysis of items, all of which had been accepted as capable of distinguishing between extroverts and introverts, showed at least three varieties of introversion-extroversion as well as other primary traits that seem unrelated to that popular hypothetical dimension. The outcome has been in the form of three inventories—*Inventory of Factors STDCR, Inven-*

tory of Factors GAMIN, and the *Personnel Inventory.* Roswell H. Johnson, R. B. Cattell, and L. L. Thurstone have also published inventories designed to measure primary traits of temperament.

The dissatisfactions with inventories as a method of measurement have continued as their use has become very widespread. The situation is one of crying need for the assessment of temperamental qualities of personnel in the absence of anything promising to take their place. It should be remembered that inventories were originally designed to replace the personal interview, which is much more costly and which is not usually designed to yield scores. It would be best to look upon the personality inventory as a written, systematic, group interview. The source of information is from the interviewee himself, as it is in an interview. The answers come through the observations and the reflections of the person assessed. The proof of what his responses and his scores mean is in terms of intercorrelations of this information with other information. The meanings of scores as revealed by this approach, including factor analysis, seem to be promising of somewhat objective and valuable information. The extent to which the information is distorted by the many possible sources of bias has never been accurately determined for the inventory in usual practice.

PERFORMANCE TESTS OF TEMPERAMENT

An alternative to the inventory, for measuring interests and attitudes as well as for measuring temperament, is in the form of performance tests, objectively scored if possible. Since the pioneer attempts of June E. Downey in the *Downey Will-Temperament Test,* there have been practically no published performance tests of non-aptitude traits. Much research in this area is going on at the present time. Most tests of this character prove to be disappointing when intercorrelation studies are made of them. Most of them fail to show much strength in any common factor. Notable exceptions to these statements are to be found in the results reported by H. J. Eysenck (1949, 1952),

who appears to have had unusual success in the direction of
genuinely objective temperament tests.

BIBLIOGRAPHY

Burt, C. *Factors of the Mind*. London: University of London Press, 1941.
Cattell, R. B. *Description and Measurement of Personality*. Yonkers-on-Hudson: World Book Company, 1946.
—— *Factor Analysis*. New York: Harper and Sons, 1952.
Cronbach, L. J. *Essentials of Psychological Testing*. New York: Harper and Brothers, 1949.
Eysenck, H. J. *Dimensions of Personality*. London: Kegan Paul, 1947.
—— *The Scientific Study of Personality*. New York: Macmillan, 1952.
Ferguson, L. W. *Personality Measurement*. New York: McGraw-Hill, 1952.
French, J. W. Description of aptitude and achievement tests in terms of rotated factors. *Psychom. Monog.*, No. 5.
Gibson, J. J. (Ed.) *Motion Picture Testing and Research*, Washington, D. C.: Government Printing Office, 1947.
Goodenough, F. L. *Mental Testing*. New York: Rinehart, 1949.
Greene, E. B. *Measurement of Human Behavior*, 2nd Ed. New York: Odyssey Press, 1952.
Guilford, J. P. Factor analysis in a test-development program. *Psychol. Rev.*, 1948, *55*, 79-94.
—— *Psychometric Methods*, 2nd Ed. New York: McGraw-Hill, 1954.
Guilford, J. P. and Lacey, J. I. (Eds.) *Printed Classification Tests*. Washington, D. C.: Government Printing Office, 1947.
Gulliksen, H. *Theory of Mental Tests*. New York: Wiley and Sons, 1950.
Lindquist, E. F. (Ed.) *Educational Measurement*. Washington, D. C.: American Council on Education, 1951.
Loevinger, J. A systematic approach to the construction and evaluation of tests of ability. *Psychol. Monog.*, 1947, *61*, No. 285.
Melton, A. W. (Ed.) *Apparatus Tests*. Washington, D. C.: Government Printing Office, 1947.
Super, D. E. *Appraising Vocational Fitness*. New York: Harper and Brothers, 1949.
Terman, L. M. and Merrill, M. A. *Measuring Intelligence*. Boston: Houghton Mifflin, 1937.
Thurstone, L. L. *Multiple Factor Analysis*. Chicago: University of Chicago Press, 1947.
Vernon, P. E. *The Structure of Human Abilities*. London: Methuen, 1950.

FOOTNOTE

[1] The tests mentioned here represent the best examples of their types. It is impossible to mention even all the well-known tests in the space available here.

Chapter XIV

ANIMAL AND COMPARATIVE PSYCHOLOGY

Sherman Ross, Ph.D. and Wendell I. Smith, Ph.D.

The University of Maryland and Bucknell University

EDITORIAL NOTE

To the man in the street it often comes as a surprise that so many of the American laboratories are given over largely to the study of animal behavior. Even the educated find it somewhat puzzling that the rat, pigeon, or guinea pig, should take up so much of the psychologist's time. Every one, however, with a psychological background understands the reasons for this preoccupation. There are, naturally, those investigators who find it "lots of fun" to experiment on infra-humans, but even there, one might hazard the opinion that there is more business than pleasure involved.

It goes without saying almost that the pooling of the results in child psychology and animal psychology bring us to rock bottom facts. The ontogenetic and the phylogenetic accounts of learning, e. g., provide a social foundation for that vast department. Animal experimentalists are respected by the profession as a whole because of their technique, their patience, and scientific procedure. Their results are seldom questioned, unless the methods are clearly at fault, but their theoretical conclusions and extrapolations are not always on a par with their empirical observations. For one thing, we are not certain whether the animal psychologist is not judging, say, the rat's behavior from his own human motivational vantage point. Then, again, it is doubtful whether what happens in the cage or the maze can fully apply to homo sapiens.

Dr. Wendell Smith, Associate Professor of Psychology at Bucknell University, and Dr. Sherman Ross, Associate Professor of Experimental Psychology at the University of Maryland, have had wide experience as researchers, and have contributed extensively to the periodical literature.

The Current Status of Comparative Psychology

Any attempt of estimate the contemporary status of comparative psychology of necessity must consider this discipline in the light of the history of the science of psychology. This shall be our first task.

An excellent historical review of the development of comparative psychology was published over 25 years ago by C. J. Warden.[1] This scholarly evaluation deals with five epochs representing important stages of development of comparative psychology. These are: (1) ancient animal lore, (2) the Greek influence, (3) early and middle ages, (4) Sixteenth Century to Darwin, and (5) the modern experimental movement. Warden says: . . . "few modern disciplines possess a richer heritage of opinion and discussion than comparative psychology, few have been more consistently exploited in ages past by men of . . . diverse interests, temperament and training. The philosopher and the theologian, as well as the naturalist, both trained and untrained, have attempted to solve the riddle of the living organism and its behavior."[2] In recent times in the solution of this riddle we can center our interest about the importance of Darwin as a great pioneer and forerunner of modern comparative psychology. We should like to introduce our points in a different way.

The recent history of American psychology can perhaps be characterized as responding to two major forces. The first is a force from outside and the second is a force from inside of psychology.

Psychology has become socially important. In the office, the factory, the armed forces, the clinic, the schools, etc., we find psychologists working. World War I and II and the intervening economic depression provided the needs and the opportunities which have resulted in a phenomenal growth of the profession of psychology. In this great growth of the social importance of psychology, comparative psychology as a discipline has probably suffered.

The other force in which we are interested is the apparent great need for large scale theory construction present among psychologists. Koch[3] has treated this point mainly in relation to learning theory. For the present context, however, his point that a crisis exists on the current theoretical scene is applicable. This crisis resulted from the demand for accelerated theoretical progress stemming from the marked increase in both the social recognition and the social responsibilities of applied psychology during the post-war period. We must in evaluating theoretical psychology start with accepting the premise that "psychology is in a pre-theoretical stage, and that the central problem, . . . is . . . to assay realistically how psychology can be made to move towards adequate theory."[4]

A general emphasis on "objectivity" has strongly influenced research workers studying the behavior of animal subjects. Initially this important trend came about as a reaction against loose anecdotal reporting and speculation on the behavior of animals. In all probability an objective, quantitative manner of thinking and working has become so well developed, as to provide a rigid frame of reference through which animals were observed and studied. The counter-reaction, a sort of subjective rebirth in the hands of skilled and sophisticated psychologists has proven fruitful.

An observer from another planet studying our history and culture might make an observation that about 100 years ago must have been an important time for psychologists. Darwin's work appeared in 1859. Freud was born in 1856. So far as current students can discover, a French physician, Philipeaux,[5] used rats for his experiments on adrenals as early as 1856. In addition to other important forces operating on psychologists, one should like to suggest that possibly these three forces:

Darwin, Freud, and rats have something in common for our present discussion.

As we indicated it is not our purpose here to trace the development of comparative psychology or of the study of animals. This task has been well done by others.[6, 7] We shall take as our first task to review the current state of affairs regarding comparative psychology. Our second task shall be to attempt to understand how this state came about. As a final task we shall indicate what we believe lies ahead for comparative psychology.

THE CURRENT SCENE

In 1920, A. A. Roback[8] wrote: "Comparative psychology, like its mother science, has had a long past and a short history. In fact it is doubtful whether it has had any history. There is no department or field in psychology which has been changing color, all the time since its inception, as much as comparative psychology."[9] That the color of comparative psychology has changed in the more than three decades since Roback wrote the lines above is attested to in Russell's inaugural lecture in 1951 at the University of London. Russell[10] remarked:

"For some reason the interest of psychologists in phylogenetic studies seriously waned, until, I have been told, not a single department of psychology in the country maintained an animal research laboratory. Much of the work in this branch of comparative psychology was taken over by scientists in other disciplines and there it remains even today, although there is now a revival of interest in work of this kind."

The situation in this country is slightly different. Possibly we can paraphrase Russell in the following lines to make our point. For some reason the interest of psychologists in phylogenetic studies has seriously waned, until, we have been told, there is not a single department of psychology in the country, which does *not* maintain a rat colony.

No one has presented the situation in a sharper, clearer, more instructional or more entertaining manner than has Beach[11] in his presidential address delivered before the Division of Experimental Psychology of the American Psychological Association in 1949. In this paper Beach has traced the initial development and subsequent decline of comparative psychology in the United States. He is most careful to indicate that the study of the Norway rat has been the prime favorite of psychologists working with animals. He has reviewed the contents of the *Journal of Comparative and Physiological Psychology* and its earlier forms, the *Journal of Comparative Psychology,* and the *Journal of Animal Behavior.* His conclusions are clearly supported. As supplied by these journals, contributors to these journals over some 30 years have done more and more experiments on fewer and fewer species. An earlier analysis by Schneirla[12] published in 1946 showed similar trends.

Let us start by what may appear to be a bold statement about the nature of psychological investigation. Let us temporarily believe that of all the species on the earth that the human is the most important to us as scientists and as citizens. Let us further believe that efforts to investigate, describe, understand, predict, control, etc., the behavior of this species is a task of such magnitude that many diverse scientists are hard at work and making some progress. We would like temporarily to have you hold the idea that psychologists believe both of these statements and that their efforts are centered about human beings. Further, we want to support and encourage such an attitude for several good reasons. We want, however, to examine these methods and techniques by which we can achieve better understanding of human behavior.

The centering of psychology about human behavior may seem to some of our colleagues to be rash, since they can point to many significant research workers whose main work has been with rats. This comment leads us into our major initial concern.

WHY DO PSYCHOLOGISTS STUDY ANIMALS OTHER THAN HUMANS?

Let us initially state a series of reasons which are relatively obvious and clear as to why infra-human organisms are studied by psychologists. First, there may be reasons of convenience: ease of securing subjects, control of subjects, shorter breeding cycles, etc. Second, there may be procedural reasons: operative studies which cannot be done on human subjects. Third, the investigator might be interested in the specific organism for some reason.

Waters[13] has identified two motives at work in the study of comparative psychology. The first is a better understanding of the animal, and the second, the discovery of principles which will lead to a better understanding of human behavior. Some workers have suggested that the major function of comparative study of animals is akin to the use of animal subjects in pharmacological research.[14] Let us consider the first of these motives.

In the recent past a major contribution to the literature of animal behavior was made by N. L. Munn.[15] This volume was dedicated to an analysis of the literature on rat behavior. In the period from 1933 to when Munn's book was in preparation, there was a fourfold increase in the literature on the rat. This increase in the number of studies represented new fields of investigation, such as behavior disorders, social behavior, emotional behavior and systematic psychology. Munn says: "Indeed it can be said that material on the rat now covers every important area of psychological research."[16] He adds that even the clinical field is included, since rats are used in determining the effects of conflict and shock therapy and in evaluating the basic psychoanalytic concepts. Learning theory is today "rat oriented", and the section in this book is now about 30,000 words compared to an earlier treatment of 5,000 words.

In the editor's introduction to this major work, Leonard Carmichael presents some ideas which are significant to our purposes. He says: "The study of basic psychological processes in man is always complicated by the human being's use of language and by the influence that social learning has on almost every human capacity. It is not an exaggeration to suggest, therefore, that in the study of the behavior of the typical mammal such as the rat, the scientific psychologist is able to approach certain of his problems in the same spirit that the modern physicist approaches a basic consideration of his field in the study of subatomic phenomena."[17]

It is precisely the commonly held assumptions so well phrased by both Munn and Carmichael which we wish to consider.

Munn in the *Handbook* describes animal psychology as a branch of psychological science which concerns itself with the behavior of animals, in contrast with the behavior of plants and of human beings. He finds it possible to distinguish four overlapping branches of animal psychology: (1) *the psychology of special animals,* such as the dog, cat or horse; (2) *comparative psychology,* referring to comparisons of one animal form with another; (3) *phylogenetic psychology,* tracing the evolution of psychological processes from lower to higher organisms; and (4) the *research tool,* providing an instrument through which fundamental problems of general psychology may be investigated. Munn stresses that the chief interest on the part of psychologists is with the rat as a research tool. We most certainly can agree with him in his general statement that studies with the rat have supplemented what we know about human psychology and that new problems and new methods have been suggested by such studies.

However, one can readily argue whether or not the rat is a *typical* mammal. There are some 66,000 living species in the phylum *Chordata,* and about 15,000 in the class *Mammalia.* The variations among these species in structure and function are extremely wide. Can we, should we, choose the rat as typical?[18]

In an extremely valuable paper appearing in 1951, Christie[19] has called to task a major series of research studies of the rat. His words and meaning are clear: ". . . animal experimenters are not studying the principles of behavior, but the behavior of cage-reared rats."[20] He argues further that the exclusive use of cage-reared rats might unduly limit the body of behavioral data, thus restricting the theoretical inferences made from the analyses of the data.

Still another weakness of basing a psychology of the typical mammal on the data which have been obtained thus far lies in the general failure to consider the importance of and control of genetic sources of variance in rat subjects.[21]

If *comparative* psychology is defined broadly as the study of the differences and similarities in behavior among the types of living organisms, then a rat psychology is insufficient. What is implied in this definition is a discipline of serious contrasts ". . . with emphasis upon the significance of differences as well as similarities in capacities and adustment patterns."[22]

In a sense there does seem to be a clear trend discernible on the current scene. Psychologists have not developed a discipline of comparative psychology.

Let us attempt to review briefly some of the ideas we have developed. Psychologists, operating in an environment where the science is of increasing social importance, driven by a premature need to build large scale theories of behavior, have found a useful research tool—the domesticated albino rat. The interest of psychologists in this tool has been largely to derive general laws of behavior. Several important features of the tool have not been attended to with appropriate intensity, i.e. the sampling represented, the peculiar individual history of laboratory reared subjects, the role of hereditary contributions, etc.

Psychologists have not been vitally interested in the evolutionary problem. In general they have not been interested in the rat *qua rat*. The research tool idea has been the dominant one in the climate of the emphasis on rigid objective measurement which has characterized American experimental psychology.

It is interesting to consider that the basic problems of our science still remain to be explored. Fashions in verbal labellings have changed. We now have more elaborate statistical and electronic techniques. We are pushing, perhaps prematurely, to theory building. We are man-centered. We are called upon to answer needs and demands of the world about us. But the basic problems are still with us. Our learning theorists do not worry too much about the "unlearned" in behavior. The problem of ontogenetic development even in the tool (rats) we use has hardly been assessed. We have gone ahead ". . . to merge super-ficially similar kinds of performance in very different animal types under the same phenomenal headings." Our attacks on the problems of intelligence, perception and social behavior are all roundly criticized by Schneirla.[23] In regard to social behav-ior of animals, a recent review by Smith and Ross[24] of some 250 studies reported between 1939 and 1950 shows the pressing need for a comparative psychological study of social phenom-ena. A sounder theoretical orientation, a wider range of sub-jects, and improved research techniques were called for.

A clear state of affairs, we believe, is discernible on the con-temporary scene. Rats have become a prime test tool for many psychologists in the search for general laws of behavior. As ex-pected there have been reactions, important ones, against this state of affairs. The reactions have had a general direction, and this direction is *not* towards the development of a comparative science.

We should like to present as a sample of the reaction against the situation described above, some of the challenging thinking of a distinguished contemporary social psychologist, S. E. Asch, on the "Biological Concept of Man".[25]

In evaluating the effects of Darwin's contribution, Asch sup-ports the idea that psychology "directed its effort to demonstra-ting that men are not as different psychologically from lower organisms as had been generally supposed. . . . In the hands of later psychologists the main consequence of the doctrine of evo-lution was not to enrich the realm of biological phenomena to include the unusual properties of men—their particular capaci-ties for social life, their potentialities for science and art—but to reduce the latter to the model of action in lower organisms. The strange consequence of Darwin's thought was although it placed men in nature, it also stripped them of the qualities most dis-tinctive of humanity—their social relation, speech and art. . . . The result was a dehumanization of the concept of man, which dominates much of current thought and from which psychology has by no means recovered. A considerable effort was directed to forming a psychology based predominantly as the study of lower organisms, the principles of which were generalized to the human level. This shift was marked by a radical omission or devaluation of specifically human characteristics. . . ."[26]

The whole problem of the specific *unique* characteristics of our species, to which Asch refers, is an important problem. It has been dealt with many times by oversimplified assumptions of equivalence as we have indicated. We contend, nevertheless, that only from the point of view of comparative study can a solution to the problem be approximated.[27]

A recent article by Josephine Semmes presents another interesting observation for our analysis.[28] It might be considered paradoxical that the study of integrative mechanisms of behavior has become almost the exclusive province of the animal psychologist. Semmes says: "Complex processes, such as learning, problem solving, and concept formation, are studied primarily in infra-human animals, which, whatever their virtue, are not noteworthy for these abilities. This displacement of the human subject by the rat or monkey appears to rest on two related articles of faith: First, that the taxonomy of cognition is mature enough to allow study of the interrelation of established variables in simpler and better controlled situations that the use of animals permit. Second, that the laws and mechanisms which are uncovered in one species will apply equally well to others, and that a complete 'phylogeny of behavior' merely awaits appropriate adjustment of the constants on some fundamental equation."[29] Semmes outlines a significant program of research on agnosia in human clinical patients. She warns: ". . . Even if we had the answer for the monkey, we still would not necessarily have it for man. A truly comparative attitude should prevent us from hasty generalizations from one species to another even within the primate series."[30]

It would be inappropriate and inaccurate to leave the reader at this point with the impression that little or nothing of value is being accomplished currently. One would suppose that the current scene is best represented in the various professional journals and publications purportedly devoted to studies in animal behavior and the comparative method. The *Annual Review of Psychology*[31] (appearing since 1950) has devoted one brief chapter in each volume to a presentation of a critical review of the literature on comparative and physiological psychology. In the 1953 issue, for example, some 16 pages of a total of 458 are devoted to comparative psychology. Some of our colleagues would question the wisdom of calling much of even this small amount of material *comparative*. Lorenz[32] in an extensive discussion of the application of the comparative method to the study of instincts, writes:

". . . it is all the more misleading if psychologists . . . apply the same term (the comparative method) in a very loose sense to all behaviour studies concerned with different forms of life. I must confess that I strongly resent it . . . when an American journal masquerades under the title of 'comparative' psychology, although, to the best of my knowledge, no really comparative paper ever has been published in it."

Even if we assume that some psychologists are publishing their research findings in vehicles which "masquerade" as being intended for comparative psychology, it is still of some interest to determine just what topics are being investigated.

From the *Annual Review* for the four-year period during which they have been published, it appears that roughly one-third of the studies reported on animal behavior have been concerned with investigating, predominantly by observational techniques supplemented by experimental situations, in natural and semi-natural habitats (e. g. zoölogical parks), such phenomena as (1) methods of orientation to aspects of the environment, (2) forms and characteristics of social behavior (3) learning (4) sexual behavior (5) experience during infancy and (6) extensive descriptions of selected behavior patterns which are considered to be predominantly innate in character. The formal laboratory studies have been concerned with much the same range of topics, and, in addition, intelligence and sensory and perceptual processes. Since these annual reviews of the literature are based upon the full range of scientific publication, it is clear that the area is not completely static.

In the study of social behavior and the processes of learning in particular, American psychologists have been attempting comparative studies. On the current scene, one of the most interesting developments is the appearance of research programs at zoölogical parks and behavior stations and farms. This work frequently has involved the combined uses of experimental techniques in field studies. At the Roscoe B. Jackson Memorial Laboratory, Bar Harbor, Maine, for example, a program of research on genetics and the social behavior of mammals, particularly the dog, has been underway for seven years during which time a number of significant studies have been completed. Through the administrative device of utilizing a small permanent research staff to provide continuity for the program it has been possible for many workers to produce worthwhile data as visiting investigators during the summer.[33] Similar attempts have been made at Jackson Hole, Wyoming, and at the New York Zoölogical Park (Bronx Zoo). There are obvious potential values in program research of this nature. First, the behavior station becomes a base for the development of large animal colonies with known genetic and experiential histories. Second, such a research center becomes a clearing house for developing, discussing, and testing new concepts. This is made possible by cross-fertilization from workers in other fields such as genetics, physiology, biochemistry, ecology and zoölogy. Third, the interdisciplinary value of bringing together workers with widely differing training and skills should result in the development of broad theoretical frames of reference within which the data can be organized and interpreted. That these values are not illusory is evident from the quality of production from such centers as the Laboratory of Primate Biology and the American Museum of Natural History with which such distinguished psychologists as R. M. Yerkes, H. W. Nissen, D. O. Hebb, T. C. Schneirla and F. A. Beach (to indicate but a few) have been associated.

A serious difficulty faced in large scale research planning has been the procurement of research workers who are interested in and qualified to deal with comparative psychological problems. Since current graduate training and public demand are most often biased in the direction of human applied psychology, relatively few adequately trained, broadly oriented psychologists are being produced from our graduate programs in psychology. Consequently, it is not surprising that the bulk of comparative and phylogenetic studies appearing in the literature emanates from disciplines other than psychology. This has been particularly true of recent European investigations. As a corrollary to this development, studies of animal behavior are likely to appear in the professional publications of the disciplines with which these investigators identify. It is equally obvious that psychologists are not the only scientists who are interested in the study of animal behavior. We only want to make the point that the continuing threads of comparative psychological thought are being supplied largely by workers who do not identify themselves with psychology.[34]

Perhaps this is nowhere better illustrated than in European studies of animal behavior, particularly those concerned with analyses of innate behavior patterns. K. Z. Lorenz for more than fifteen years has been engaged in studies of innate behavior as revealed in a "laboratory free" environment, i. e. under field conditions or in a semi-natural habitat such as may be provided for animals kept as pets. By combining experimental techniques (often highly original) with field observations, Lorenz and others have collected sufficient data to provide some support for a theory of behavior based chiefly on the concepts of releasing stimuli and releasing mechanisms. These concepts have become popular among a number of investigators, and in England and on the continent a sizable literature on the subject has developed. Even though a number of studies have appeared in English, and both Lorenz and Tinbergen[35] have supplied fairly comprehensive and detailed discourses on the theory,[36] only the beginnings of the effect of the Lorenz-Tinbergen school have been felt to this time among American psychologists.

Since most of the research by adherents of the Lorenz-Tinbergen school has been on birds, fish, and insects, it is too early to say whether or not the theory has the generality required for a true comparative science. At the very least, the theory has been exceedingly stimulating to a large group of European investigators. From another point of view an important impetus has been given to the problems of early development by the recent volume of Hebb.[37]

Future Trends

It is hard to discern at this time the future of comparative psychology. If we have painted a dismal picture of the current scene, it may be a true one. Certainly we can foresee the greater development of the applications of psychology to industrial, business, military, personal and social problems. We can surely expect further theoretical development in our science. We can expect also that many of the needs we have indicated will be answered in part. In large part, however, so far as comparative psychology is concerned, we suspect that our colleagues in the biological sciences will have a great influence. In the strong leadership of Lorenz, Tinbergen, Thorpe, Hediger and others in England and on the continent we have a strong group of interested biological workers studying behavior. Their impact is being felt in contemporary psychology. In this country, the influence of Allee and his students (among others) exert a strong influence in the study of behavior by biological scientists.

Whether or not the area of the study of the behavior of animals which in our field has produced such pre-eminent men as Yerkes, Thorndike, Watson, Lashley, Köhler, Hull, Tolman—to mention only a few—will continue to be a major ground for work remains to be seen. We have not developed a discipline of comparative psychology. Perhaps we shall not. Perhaps we should not. It is our conviction that the comparative method in the study of behavior will persist and develop. If this development is not in the field of psychology it will develop in other fields. We have as psychologists become man-centered in our thinking, phenomenon centered in our theory and technique centered in our studies. The fundamental problems of our science remain.

On a more concrete level, it is our conviction that in the United States, at least, we shall witness an increase in interdisciplinary research on problems of animal and human behavior. Furthermore, it is expected that, with the impetus from an increasing interest in animal behavior on the part of professional workers in the agricultural sciences, the large state universities and colleges will also contribute heavily to research.

As the demand for applied psychologists is satisfied, it seems possible that a greater number of the promising young scientists will turn to basic research including the use of the comparative method.

Finally, the use of certain animals as tools for research (e. g. rats, fish, birds, etc.) will eventually lead to a relatively complete inventory of the behavior patterns of these and other species making comparisons of homologous behavior patterns possible.[38]

No one has more sharply discerned the issues nor better stated a significant program of comparative psychology than has T. C. Schneirla in his recent paper on conceptual trends in comparative psychology. He has carefully and critically treated several basic concepts and their status. We hold with him that "The answer to challenges of the relevance of animal-behavior evidence for human psychology is not that, in the absence of such evidence, irresponsible conclusions will be drawn and applied in any case, both in lay and in scientific circles. More significant is the greater breadth of view which can be obtained through comparative methods in studying the wide range of psychological problems."[39]

The growth of the specialized analytical program of research on the rat which we have pointed out as a significant characteristic of the contemporary scene is, of course, fruitful. We hope, however, that newer workers in psychology will accept the broader challenge and carry out the program indicated.

FOOTNOTES

1 Warden, C. J. The historical development of comparative psychology. *Psychol. Rev.*, 1927, *34*, 57-85 and 135-168.

2 Warden, 57.

3 Koch, S. Theoretical psychology, 1950: An overview, *Psychol Rev.*, 1951, *58*, 295-301.

4 Koch, 298.

5 Philipeaux, J. M. Note sur l'extirpation des capsules surrenales chez les rats albinos (*mus rattus*). *C. R. Acad. Sci.*, 1856, *43*, 904. Cited from: Richter, C. P. Domestication of the Norway rat and its implication for the study of genetics in man. *Amer. J. Hum. Genet.*, 1953, *4*, 273-285.

6 *Op. cit.*

7 Warden, C. J. and Warner, L. H. The development of modern comparative psychology. *Quart. Rev. Biol.*, 1928, *3*, 486-522.

8 Roback, A. A. The scope and genesis of comparative psychology. *J. Phil. Psychol., Scient. Meth.*, 1920, *17*, 654-662.

9 Roback, 654.

10 Russell, R. W. *The comparative study of behaviour.* London: H. K. Lewis, 1952, 16.

11 Beach, F. A. The Snark was a Boojum. *Amer. Psychol.*, 1950, *5*, 115-124.

12 Schneirla, T. C. Contemporary animal psychology. In: *Twentieth century psychology*, P. L. Harriman (Ed.) New York: Philosophical Library, 1946.

13 Waters, R. H. Historical background of comparative psychology. In: *Comparative psychology*, 3rd ed., C. P. Stone (Ed.) New York: Prentice-Hall, 1951, 28.

14 Hilgard, E. R. *Theories of learning.* New York: Wiley, 1948.

15 Munn, N. L. *Handbook of psychological research on the rat.* New York: Houghton-Mifflin, 1950.

16 Munn, viii.

17 Munn, vii.

18 McCutcheon, F. H. The viewpoint and progress of comparative physiology. *Scient. Monthly*, 1952, *74*, 297-302.

19 Christie, R. Experimental naïveté and experiential naïveté. *Psychol. Bull.*, 1951, *48*, 338.

20 Christie, 338.

21 Scott, J. P. Genetics as a tool in experimental psychological research. *Amer. Psychol.*, 1949, *4*, 526-530.

22 Schneirla, T. C. A consideration of some conceptual trends in comparative psychology. *Psychol. Bull.*, 1952, *49*, 559-597.

23 *Ibid.*

24 Smith, W. I. and Ross, S. The social behavior of vertebrates: A review of the literature (1939-1950). *Psychol. Bull.*, 1952, *49*, 598-627.

25 Asch, S. E. *Social psychology.* New York: Prentice Hall, 1952, 9-11.

26 Asch, 11.

27 An enchanting satirical, although not necessarily sound, treatment of

the problem of the unique human capacities may be found in a recent novel by Vercors, *You shall know them*. Boston: Little, Brown, 1953.

[28] Semmes, J. Agnosia in animal and man. *Psychol. Rev., 60*, 140-147.

[29] Semmes, 140.

[30] Semmes, 144.

[31] *Annual Review of Psychology*, vols. I-IV. Stanford, California: Annual Reviews, Inc.

[32] Lorenz, K. Z. The comparative method in studying innate behaviour patterns. In: *Physiological Mechanisms in Animal Behaviour*. New York: Academic Press, 1950, 239-240.

[33] Ross, S. and Scott, J. P. Opportunities for psychological research at the Roscoe B. Jackson Memorial Laboratory, Bar Harbor, Maine. *J. gen. Psychol.*, 1953, *48*, 87-89.

[34] This may not be the best arrangement.

[35] Lorenz, K. C. *King Solomon's Ring*. London: Methuen & Co., 1952. (See also 32).

Tinbergen, N. An objective study of the innate behavior of animals. *Bibliotheca Biotheretica*, 1942, *1*, 40-98. *The study of instinct*. London: Oxford Univ. Press, 1950.

[36] In brief, Lorenz believes that it is necessary to differentiate between the instinct *per se* and *instinctive behavior*. The instinct is an innate movement form, a stereotyped behavior pattern, which will be 'released' or evoked by appropriate stimulating conditions. Instinctive behavior is used to refer to the complete behavior pattern evoked of which the instinct is the core composed of endogenous activities. The releasing mechanism according to Tinbergen "must be a special neuro-sensory mechanism that releases the reaction and is responsible for its selective susceptibility to such a very special combination of sign stimuli." (p. 41-42). This relationship between sign (releasing) stimuli and the innate releasing mechanism is vaguely anaiogous to a lock and key relationship. In practice, it has been found that fairly specific stimuli arouse and result in a highly stereotyped reaction energized by accumulated specific energy in the organism. The possibility of modification of the instinctive behavior is admitted by Lorenz under the term "imprinting" which may occur during a very brief period following birth. Tinbergen has broadened the concept to include a learning process similar to the typical conditioned response form.

[37] The work and thinking of D. O. Hebb (*The organization of behaviour: a neuro-psychological theory*, New York: Wiley, 1949) regarding ontogenetic development may prove to be more exciting to American psychologists. Hebb's notions are being tested actively at McGill and elsewhere.

[38] We have recently reported such an attempt in regard to hoarding behavior in the mouse (Wendell Smith and Sherman Ross, The hoarding behavior of the mouse, *J. genet. Psychol.*, 1953, *82*, 279-297, 299-307, 309-316). A recent review of sensory capacities of infra-human mammals (Philip Ash, The sensory capacities of infra-human mammals: Vision, audition, gustation, *Psychol. Bull.*, 1951, *48*, 289-326) clearly indicates that only a few of the many available species have been studied. Of these species investigated (mainly one or two), small sample sizes are generally employed, in experiments involving non-comparable methods. The extent of our ignorance of the basic sensory capacity characteristics of animals is unfortunately, relatively great.

[39] Schneirla, *op. cit.*, 590.

CHAPTER XV

ABNORMAL PSYCHOLOGY

PHILIP L. HARRIMAN, Ph.D.
Chairman, Dept. of Psychology, Bucknell University

EDITORIAL NOTE

Abnormal psychology is not talked of so much now as in the teens of the century, when courses and textbooks on the subject were relatively plentiful. Has there been less abnormality since? That can hardly be the answer; for we know that nervous disorders have increased, or at least, they cry for help more than in the past. What has happened is that psychoanalysis has liquidated the distinction between normal and abnormal, and, then too, clinical psychology has established its empire, in many cases absorbing the practical phase of abnormal psychology. In the early period, abnormal psychology was oriented according to normal psychology. The one seemed to be on the debit side and the other on the credit side of the ledger. All this has been changed. We really do not know what is the norm except on the strength of a theory (adjustment, rationality, adequate libidinal development, integration) and there is no pari-passu relationship between the normal and the abnormal, i. e., the problems of the latter are different.

Is clinical psychology the same as abnormal psychology? While they sometimes overlap, yet, in the strict sense, the two cannot be equated. The clinical psychologist is primarily a practitioner; the abnormal psychologist is a theoretician, usually giving courses in an institution and engaging in research. That the two often change parts or combine duties does not invalidate the dichotomy. Abnormal psychology has now been assigned a minor rôle in a larger organization, whereas before it constituted the whole division.

Dr. Harriman has studied at Colgate, Harvard, and New York University, where he received his Ph.D. A man of wide interests, he is at home in the classics and has taught English before devoting himself entirely to psychology. He is at present Chairman of the Psychology Department at Bucknell University.

The Field of Abnormal Psychology

Because of its origins in a wide diversity of inquiries, both non-scientific and scientific, abnormal psychology covers an infinite variety of topics. Superstitious beliefs and practices, well-intentioned and objective investigations of occult phenomena, mental disorders, various psychological events that occur but rarely in normal individuals, behavior under conditions of extreme stress or great excitement, superiorities and deficits in intelligence—these are a few of the topics that have been subsumed by the term *abnormal psychology*. In fact, almost any topic not readily included in a treatise on the normal behavior and experience of normal persons has been relegated to discussions that bear this rubric. Even those topics which excite interest, such as dreams, sleep, hypnosis, or the psychological effects of drugs and intoxicants, are frequently omitted from textbooks in general psychology, only to find a place in this field. Certainly, "it is a broad, elusive, and ill-defined subject." Even a cursory examination of some of the older textbooks reveals the incoherence and indefiniteness of this field of psychology as it was delimited fifty or more years ago.

Two important references have been chosen for the purposes of this brief introduction. They serve to emphasize the fact that abnormal psychology is a very broad field of psychology and that it includes about anything which might not be coherently integrated into a systematic presentation of facts, principles, and theories of any other field. The first reference is a quotation from Jastrow, one of the American pioneers in teaching the subject. He wrote that abnormal psychology is one of the divisions of psychology which embraces—

> ". . . the study of the various forms of illusions and hallucinations; of the phenomena of trance, hypnotism, auto-

matism, and allied states; of the psychic effects of drugs or intoxicants and of diseased bodily conditions; of the impairment of the faculties in old age; of the unusual mental manifestations of individuals or classes under the dominance of social or extreme emotions (fright, panic, psychic epidemics); of real or alleged manifestations purporting to transcend the ordinary laws and limitations of human intelligence (possession, telepathic phenomena), as well as the more specific types of lack of development, or loss or impairment of faculty, constituting the various forms of mental disorder or insanity."[1]

The terminology, of course, includes some words that are quaint as read by the contemporary student of psychology. The point to note, however, is that the definition connotes the wide diversity of topics which at one time were subsumed under this division.

The second reference deals with a textbook, once of great importance in the field of abnormal psychology, written by Coriat.[2] He dedicated the book to his eminent friend Dr. Morton Prince, whom he calls the great pioneer in the field. Drawing heavily from the theories of Prince and, in particular, from Continental psychologists, he gave primary emphasis to subconscious influences and to dissociation as causative factors in abnormal behavior. When, in 1921, he published a revision of his well-known book, he included the brilliant contributions of Freud, but he found no need to alter any of his basic positions. To Coriat, the term *abnormal psychology* had a rather precise connotation. He looked upon it as a comparatively late development of scientific medicine, a development which drew attention to the psychological causation of certain types of illness. Many topics which could not logically find a place in other medical treatises, he implied, might gain a hearing if presented in texts on abnormal psychology. Though he did narrow the field considerably more than did Jastrow, he found it broad enough to include discussions of such topics as sleep and dreams, "the mysteries of our psychic life;"[3] colored hearing or synesthesia; psychotherapeutic and preventive techniques in mental disorders; and the complexities of memory functions.

It would be quite difficult, therefore, to initiate this account of abnormal psychology by giving a brief definition of the subject. In fact, there are many definitions of it. As a result, the modern psychologist breaks the subject down into a number of separate and distinct fields, the most important of which is psychopathology. At least, most contemporary books and journal articles written by contemporary experts in this field deal with facts, theories, diagnostic techniques, and therapeutic procedures relating to patients with mental disorders. Those psychologists who are interested in "impairment of the faculties in old age" are coming to be known as gerontologists. Students of "manifestations purporting to transcend the ordinary laws and limitations of *human intelligence*" deal with what is now called parapsychology. Similarly with other topics included in Jastrow's oft-cited definition of abnormal psychology, they have either faded out of interest or they have grown into highly specialized fields.

At the outset, it is obvious, this chapter deals with a division of psychology that may no longer exist. For a while the American Psychological Association, Division 12, indicated by an asterisk those psychologists who wished to be included in the directory as having a special interest in abnormal psychology. Only twenty or so indicated such a choice in 1947. Now they, too, have been merged into the ranks of clinical psychologists. The *Journal of Abnormal and Social Psychology,* founded by Morton Prince, now contains articles that deal with practically none of the topics dealt with in the early issues of this publication. The change is not to be deplored. On the contrary, it indicates the achievement of a degree of maturity in psychology. Those facts and theories which are of importance in contemporary psychology have been clarified, worked over by experimentalists, tested and expanded in clinical practice, and incorporated into the growing science. Many other topics have been relegated to a sort of psychological museum, there to remain as subjects of considerable interest to the historian. Still others, such as "specific types of lack of development," have come to form special fields of scientific inquiry, in this example, the field of diagnosis and treatment of mentally defective individuals. The growth has been healthy and vigorous. A backward look is worth a bit of time. Only by looking backwards can one see what abnormal psychology was at one time. Then there may be occasion to regret some of the specialization of the present day, even to lament the demise of interests once the preoccupation of students of abnormal psychology.

II

OCCULTISM AND PSYCHICAL RESEARCH

The roots of abnormal psychology, and particularly those phases of the subject which relate to mental disorders, lie deep in the occult. In the *Sacred Disease,* Hippocrates sought to dispel the superstition that paranormal influences cause epilepsy. Nevertheless, unscientific beliefs about this disorder, and many others as well, have continued into modern times.[4] Again and again old beliefs reappear, though in new guise; and the fallacious opinion that personality aberrations or mental diseases are caused by mysterious influences survives in many places even today. Heinroth, a professor of medicine at the University of Leipzig, wrote in a sober treatise for medical students in 1818:

> Where God is, there is strength, light, love, and life. An evil spirit abides, therefore, in the mentally deranged; they are the truly possessed.

Not only are various influences not to be explained scientifically at work in producing mental illness, but also they are said to cause strange events. Tables are said to move without the mediation of any known force; persons separated by great distances are said to be able to communicate with one another in ways not to be accounted for by natural science. Many of these beliefs may be traced back into remote antiquity, and they have survived into the present, though under modern guises.[5]

At least three eminent psychologists have been interested in these phenomena. Gustav T. Fechner was a firm believer in the prevalence of occult forces in the world. Under the pseudonym of Dr. Mises he wrote voluminously about them. William McDougall was a believer. He, too, made excursions into what may be termed "borderland science." The enthusiasm of William James for these studies is well known.[6] Many persons in England, France, Germany, and the United States once took a keen interest in occultism. Some of them were well educated, gifted in writing, and prominent in the intellectual community. The field is characterized by fraud, deception, and trickery on the part of those who claim to have supernatural powers. It is likewise marked by a lack of critical sense by those who are attracted to believe in these matters. Now, however, there does seem to be some revival of interest in what is termed parapsychology. Carefully designed experiments have brought to light data which are either rejected as nonsense or interpreted to indicate the need for further research. Abnormal psychology was, in part, sired by those who, like James, sought for insights into psychological functions through a study of those who were apart from the everyday life of everyday individuals.

III

Inquiries into the Nature of Religious Experiences

One of the most original series of psychological research was initiated in America half a century ago. This movement took the form of an empirical inquiry into the nature of religious experience. Starting out from the belief that abnormal personalities display in exaggerated form those traits which are present in the normal, the pioneer research dealt with emotional conversion experiences. The first major report was made by Starbuck, who interpreted a large number of personal records contributed by those who had experienced religious conversions.[7]

The dramatic nature of many of these accounts drew much

popular attention to this field. Though Starbuck emphasized a naturalistic interpretation of the phenomena associated with conversion, many eminent persons, lay and clerical, believed in the supernatural aspects of religious experiences in all their varieties and manifestations. James, invited to give a series of lectures at Edinburgh, chose to speak upon these matters.[8] He explored the "inner world" of saints and mystics. He by-passed the religious experiences of normal persons, and gave emphasis to the abnormal phenomena associated with unusual, abnormal, extraordinary individuals. Transcendental hypotheses must be set up, he implies, if we are to investigate religious persons empirically. Within a few years enthusiasm for this line of psychological inquiry died down. Nevertheless, one effect has remained to influence the development of abnormal psychology. The field deals with matters which necessitate new hypotheses not customarily found in general psychology; which, supposedly, throw into exaggerated view trends present in the normal; and which, obviously, have a morbid connotation.

IV

Origins of Abnormal Psychology in Legal Practices

In 1843, a man suffering from what would now be called delusions of persecution attempted to assassinate Prime Minister Peel. He killed Sir Robert's secretary, was taken into custody, and tried for murder. The jury brought in a verdict of "not guilty by reason of insanity." Subsequently, the House of Lords attempted to formulate a policy for the guidance of courts of law when this type of case occurred. Even today eminent lawyers debate these points with typical redundancy and verbosity. Whether crime is committed wilfully or whether it indicates mental ill health is still a question. At least, the old idea of retributive justice for all offenders has been weakened by the growth of understanding of psychology. Modern enlightenment has forced the legal authorities to take cognizance of many psychological facts, theories, and principles relating to abnormal psychology. More than a hundred years ago Esquirol identified a pattern of behavior which he called "monomania". This term designates activity which may lead an individual to commit an offense, not because of wilful intent, but because of obsessive, uncontrollable delusions. Terms like "constitutional psychopath inferior" and "psychopathic personality," unsatisfactory though they are to a scientific psychologist, do imply a recognition of abnormal determinants in some offenders against the mores and the legal codes. Because of their histories, psychology and psychiatry still tend to place heavy emphasis upon single individuals, considered apart from the social influences which affect personality development and behavior. Until very recent times, the growth of abnormal psychology from the field of legalisms, as well as from all other "parents," took place in singular independence of the cultural influences which certainly affect behavior.[9] The individual was considered, more or less, as living *in vacuo*.

Court procedures have affected the course of development in the field of abnormal psychology to some extent. Sensational newspaper publicity in some trials has familiarized the public with a variety of terms drawn from the expositions of facts and theories in psychopathology. Humanitarians have sought to educate the public in objective, scientifically tenable concepts about abnormal persons who commit offenses and who must be institutionalized as a result. The development of psychology as a science, however, has been far more influential in correcting outmoded legal practices than has the growth of enlightenment in law been in affecting the field of psychology. Persons who suffer from mental illness or from mental deficiency are likely to have a difficult time even today in adjusting to community life. Those who deviate to an extreme degree are still likely to be held accountable if they run counter to the law.[10] The need for a recognition of social determinants in abnormal behavior is still in need of a hearing, particularly in courts of law.[11] The community is frequently beset by problems relating to young delinquents, school children who cannot proceed at the normal rate from grade to grade, "problem individuals," eccentric and misfits, and mental defectives. These individuals often occasion troublesome difficulties when they appear before a court of law. Psychological work involved in diagnoses of their problems was one of the major influences towards a development in abnormal psychology. Now psychology has advanced far beyond diagnosis and "labeling" of deviant personalities. Nevertheless, great impetus to modern developments came from studies of "problem individuals" brought before law enforcement agencies many years ago.

V

LITERATURE AND THE FIELD OF ABNORMAL PSYCHOLOGY

Using the term *literature* in a very broad sense, one can discover many examples to indicate an interest in strange happenings, remarkable characters, aberrant psychological functions, and irrational determinants of behavior in familiar works of literature. The Old Testament, for instance, abounds in references to dreams. Browning, the themes relating to nature having been more or less exhausted, turned to psychological functions for the themes of many of his poems. He depicted the intricacies of human motivations, he gave insights into personality, and he analyzed the wealth of emotions. Since normal persons are likely to be thought dull, stodgy, and uninteresting, the novelists depicted individuals who had unusual motives, incentives, frustrations, feelings and emotions, fantasies, compensations, and innumerable other experiences. *Silas Marner,* to choose but a single example at random, presents a complete, logical analysis of the behavior of a man. Long before psychologists had fully recognized the importance of irrational motives and nonintellectual determinants in mental functions, these were being exploited by dramatists. In fact, some of the newer hypotheses in psychopathology have their roots far down in the field of literature. Though the scientific jargon of the modern student is recent, the underlying concepts are very old. Freud pointed out this fact very clearly in many of his publications. Now that abnormal psychology has more nearly come of age, its concepts have proved useful in the enrichment of literary studies.

The traditional patterns in literary criticism laid down by such persons as Georg Brandes and Matthew Arnold have yielded to challenging new points of view. These concepts are derived principally from the theories of Sigmund Freud. Not only have they vitalized the study of literature, ancient and modern, but also they have opened up many new ideas for creative literature. The concept of 'stream-of-consciousness' was known centuries ago, and Thomas Hobbes described it fully in the Leviathan (1651). The possibilities of using it in fiction, however, were not successfully employed until James Joyce's *Ulysses* (1921). Other concepts in abnormal psychology have furnished themes for widely known works of literature. Superstitions about hypnotism (in this instance properly called by the older term, *mesmerism*) furnish the plot for Du Maurier's *Trilby*. Knowledge of the concept of psychopathic personality is revealed by Erskine Caldwell in many short novels and stories. Plots dealing with a wide variety of symptoms seem to have a special appeal for the reading public today. As in the case of law, psychology contributes more to modern literature than it receives from it. Nevertheless, there is a growing belief that superior writers are able to obtain insights which would be of considerable value to psychologists informed about them. Consequently, there is the beginning of an interest in literature on the part of those who study abnormal psychology.[12] Evidence of this interest, feeble though it may be now, is shown in a number of analyses of famous literary works in the *Psychoanalytic Review* and in a newsletter published by the Modern Language Association since 1951.

VI

Abnormal Psychology and Psychiatry

The roots of abnormal psychology extend deeply into the division of medical art and science that is now called psychiatry. Facts and theories about diagnosis and treatment of mentally disturbed patients have assumed such a dominant position in the contemporary field of abnormal psychology that most of the older topics have faded into significance. As a result, a term more appropriate to designate this branch of psychology might be *psychopathology*. The history of the gradual emergence of scientific concepts in psychopathology is an interesting account.[13] There appear to be three distinct, though overlapping, periods in the development of scientific views about mental disorders. First, there were the ancient notions that all illness, especially when psychological functions are deranged, indicates disfavor with the gods. Next came a period of total neglect. The mentally disturbed were assigned to the category of non-human species. Subsequently, there was the gradual rise of humanitarian concepts regarding the psychologically disordered. One of the most eminent physicians to take intelligent care of disordered patients was Philippe Pinel (1745-1826). Against opposition he was able to have the chains removed from demented patients. He said:

> The mentally sick are far from being guilty people. They are ill. Their unhappy state deserves all the consideration which suffering men and women ought to receive. The physician should attempt with simple and appropriate methods to restore them to sanity.

Pinel was vigorously against such extreme and neglectful forms of treatment as that of weakening patients by letting blood, using drugs indiscriminatingly, or giving them violent shocks by suddenly immersing them in ice-cold water. He sought to arouse his colleagues to exercise the same type of therapeutic procedure in treating the mentally ill as they had been taught to employ in dealing with the physically sick.

The emergence of enlightened, humanitarian attitudes about mental disorders brought about an intensive study of various types of mental aberrations. The procedure, following the accepted practices in all scientific inquiries, was that of isolating various symptoms, defining them precisely, and delineating the circumstances under which each of them might be diagnosed. Knowledge was systematized and integrated. Based in part upon clinical observations and in part upon ingenious speculative principles, this knowledge about mental disorders soon began to emphasize classification of the various syndromes. Emil Kraepelin (1855-1926) is generally recognized as the greatest of modern nosologists in psychiatry. He brought together the various descriptive terms and concepts and organized a systematic psychiatry. His influence upon psychopathology remains as a potent determinant of the course of development which this branch of knowledge has followed.

Chiefly, the Kraepelinian point of view has furnished incentives for more adequate concepts whereby to understand and treat the mentally disturbed. Many of the leaders in this field were stimulated by Kraepelin to undertake critical analyses of his nosology. Some of them became critical of the basic assumptions upon which his entire system rests. They found it to be static. They believed that his philosophy of science was based upon the concepts of traditional atomistic physics rather than upon concepts in biology. This fact, they believed, misled him in his efforts to ground psychopathology upon a firm basis. Concepts appropriate for scientific studies of inert, isolated bits of matter, it was objected, are not applicable to the study of living organisms. Thus, there arose a variant of the old controversy between anatomists and physiologists, physicists and biologists, those who advocate reductive analyses vs. those who take a holistic view.

The quarrel has profoundly affected the course of development in contemporary psychopathology. As an immediate, intrusive outcome, there are challenging points of view put forth by various leaders in the field. Accord seems to have been reached upon but two major points. First, there is a general tendency to reject the Kraepelinian emphasis upon classificatory schemata as the end-all in psychiatry. Quite to the contrary, there is a growing interest in the psychodynamics of each individual patient. Though, for convenience in institutional procedures, it is necessary to pigeonhole the disorders, in actual practice the individual patient is the center of reference. This trend has been carried to such an extreme that a sort of patient-society dichotomy has been implied. First, there are indications that medical practitioners are commencing to realize that social scientists may have much to contribute to a better understanding of the dynamics of the patient. Secondly, there seems to be a growing readiness to welcome bold hypotheses and concepts as yet not validated by experimental research. This interesting situation has led to the formation of many divergent schools of thought in the general area of psychopathology. Not only have various conceptual systems been formulated, but also a wide variety of diagnostic and therapeutic procedures have been utilized far in advance of their empirical validation. A pragmatic spirit appears to be prevalent at this stage. Apparently, it is a time when clinical evidence and intuitive judgments are likely to be welcomed, even though a rationale is still lacking to support them.

Behind any illness there is a patient. Whether the illness be categorized in the traditional dichotomy as mental or physical, a human being is involved. Sociological and psychological aspects of the patient's life are now regarded as being of utmost significance in diagnosis, treatment, and rehabilitation of the individual who is ill. These statements are likely to be construed as obvious truisms. Actually, however, the recognition of all the implications in them marks a milestone in the history of psychopathology. Even today there is an inadequate understanding of the sociological involvements in this field, though some evidence indicates that progressive developments are likely to occur within a few years.

Regarding the psychological factors behind the pattern of symptoms exhibited by the patient, tremendous advances have been made. Though it would be an oversimplification to attribute this progress to a single person, Sigmund Freud (1856-1939) is generally considered to be the greatest modern innovator in the field. His importance for contemporary psychopathology can scarcely be over-emphasized. Terms and concepts which he introduced in his voluminous publications have become integral parts of the corpus of modern knowledge, not only of psychopathology, but also of many cognate areas. Stimulating discussions have arisen over the validity, the applicability, and the ethical import of his views. He won ardent proponents, and he incurred the wrath of able critics. Few other men in the history of ideas have ever succeeded in arousing so many divergent and controversial thoughts in Western culture. The intellectually curious still wonder whether Freud is the greatest psychologist since Aristotle or whether his views are nothing but an evanescent reflection of interests characteristic of a decadent age.

Freud's contributions may be briefly considered under three headings. First, he developed a mode of therapeutic procedure for use with the mentally ill. In 1893, Freud, then working with an older physician named Josef Breuer, reported successful treatment of a young patient who suffered from various hysterical symptoms. This he did by hypnotizing the patient, and then encouraging her to verbalize all her mental conflicts. "Mental catharsis" was achieved thereby. The patient really knew about the origin of all her symptoms, but she was consciously unaware of it. The underlying, causative factors were in her unconscious.[14] Gradually, Freud systematized a method whereby his patients could achieve release of unconscious emotional tensions through a technique of free association. Thus, the cause, the various hysterical symptoms arising therefrom and the cure once the causes had been verbalized, evolved as a method for treating neurotic patients.

Secondly, Freud and his disciples developed a new point of view in psychopathology as a logical extension of this method. Throughout his long and active life, Freud constantly revised his theories. Hence, it becomes difficult to state within this brief chapter the major characteristics of his point of view. Of course, it is important to note that he emphasized the unconscious determination of many psychological functions involved in neurotic behavior. He observed that many of his patients exhibited an obsessive interest in sex. He also noted that they met the issues of life in immature ways. Woodworth, therefore, has summed up Freud's point of view by saying that it emphasizes "repressed infantile sexuality" as the causative agent in neurotic disorders.[15] Neuroses always involve repressions; the determinants are unconscious; the causes lie deep in the early life of the patient; and the sex drive is inevitably at the root of the problem. Though these statements are nothing but sophomoric generalizations, they do epitomize the popular understanding of Freud's point of view.

Thirdly, Freud is regarded, at least by his most devoted followers, as the greatest of philosophers. His theories, in consequence, are extended to cover matters far beyond the narrow confines of the psychiatrist-patient relationship and beyond the formulation of a theory of psychopathology. They are considered to furnish a basis for understanding the metaphysical questions of the meaning of existence. They are considered to be applicable to psychotherapy; to an understanding of history, interpersonal relationships, creative activities, economics, and politics; and also to religious aspirations.

Traditional emphasis upon descriptive analyses of mental symptoms has gone. Classification of individuals upon a basis of arbitrary typology has yielded to attempts to understand the unique dynamic factors behind the aberrations. This trend has stimulated a great deal of theorizing about the nature of personality. There has been a great shift in abnormal psychology. On the one hand, there seems to be an enthusiasm for novel theories which have pragmatic value. If they contribute to a better understanding of the patient, they are utilized. Pending validation by the procedures of science, they win tentative acceptance because of their immediate, practical value. In general, these challenging theories have a degree of unity, though in superficial aspects they may be as far apart as the poles. They emphasize the motivational-affective dispositions of the individual; and, by corollary, they play down the rational, intellective functions.

On the other hand, these theories of personality have stimulated a considerable amount of experimentation with new types of appraisals of the quality of adjustment. A hasty marriage has been effected between *Gestalt-theorie* and Freudian theory in order to provide a frame of reference for the interpretation of data accumulated through the use of novel tests. The rapid growth of these new conceptualizations has been stimulated by the wide use of so-called projective techniques. The best-known of these techniques is the Rorschach series of inkblots. The subject perceives a series of ten blots, which, of course, are chance forms, but are likely to be interpreted in meaningful ways. Presumably, unresolved conflictual tensions and unconscious needs influence the interpretations of the blots, and thereby the investigator may find a "royal road" to the unconscious dynamics of the individual who is tested by this technique. Not only are specific indices as to various personality traits likely to be revealed, but also there may be a revelation of the total configuration, or *Gestalt,* which, by definition, is the personality. Success in Rorschach appraisals has led to enthusiasm for devising numbers of ingenious techniques for "global" studies of personality.[16]

Thus, both research and theorizing in the field of psychopathology have had far-reaching effects upon contemporary psychology. The impetus to this work has arisen from a practical need to bring to bear upon unhappy, disturbed persons all those resources of psychology which might be helpful for them. Psychopathology, which is the legitimate offspring of abnormal psychology, is now in a dominant position in the general field of psychology. Its influence has extended to nearly every other subdivision within psychology. A new profession is now in the making. This is the profession of clinical psychology. The practitioner is said to be adept in the traditional administration and interpretation of psychological tests and measures, to be skilled in the use of projective techniques, to be qualified in diagnosis of mental illnesses, and to be able to contribute much to the therapeutic work needful with those patients who have psychological difficulties. Owing to the fact that the whole field of abnormal psychology is marked by rather loose concepts, dogmatic formulations justified historically but not empirically, and challenging, though divergent, theories, it is natural that conflicts should arise. Those who are certificated to practice the medical arts and sciences are inclined to resent what seems to be an invasion of their territory. Clergymen, the traditional advisers and helpers for those in trouble, object to encroachment upon their function. Educators also may be disturbed by what seems to them to be an indefensible extension of the teaching arts. They may not be able to see how a maladjusted person could be "straightened out" through generalized procedures rather than through specific, contentful learning experiences. Such a heated controversy has been generated that no little personal animus has been involved. The existence of such attitudes within any province of science indicates that it is still in its infancy; prospects for achieving maturity may be bright but adulthood is still far away. At the present time, psychopathology exhibits every sign of vigorous, healthy growth, though, to be sure there are obvious "growing pains."

VII

CONCLUSION

The field of abnormal psychology, as its pioneers defined the subject, is now a matter of interest only to the historian of psychology. Many of the topics which were at one time of considerable importance have either been relegated to special fields or have been dropped out of treatises on abnormal phenomena. Now the dominant enthusiasms of "abnormal psychologists" relate almost exclusively to psychopathology. The "social climate" fosters the rapid growth of new theories of personality dynamics, new techniques for personality appraisals, and new methods in psychotherapy. More than half the members of the American Psychological Association are now interested in these matters, whereas a few decades ago the principal interests were in "traditional, brass-instrument experimentation" and in teaching psychology to college students. Certainly, Morton Prince would not recognize the field of abnormal psychology were he able to scrutinize it today. Perhaps he would find that there is no such field within the province of psychology. He would be amazed, however, to observe how potently the subject designated as psychopathology has influenced the course of contemporary psychology. His amazement would be tinged with gratification, one may assume, for he was most enthusiastic about the possibilities for a "dynamic" psychology. It was Freud, however, not Prince, who should be considered as the "father" of contemporary psychopathology. As for what was once termed abnormal psychology, that field has evaporated, faded away, been occupied by new tenants. No matter what the metaphor, the plain fact is that it no longer exists.

FOOTNOTES

1 Definition of abnormal psychology in the *Dictionary of Philosophy and Psychology*. New York: Macmillan, 1901.

2 Coriat, Isador H. *Abnormal Psychology*. New York: Moffat, Yard, 1910.

3 *Op. cit.*, 2nd ed., p. 138.

4 For an important survey of persistent superstitions about mental illnesses, see A. D. White, *History of the Warfare of Science with Theology*, Chaps. XIII-XVI. New York: D. Appleton, 1896.

5 See J. G. Frazer, *The Golden Bough*. New York: Macmillan, 1922. See also Joseph Jastrow, *Fact and Fable in Psychology*. Boston: Houghton, Mifflin, 1900.

6 For an informative account, see R. B. Perry, *Thought and Character of William James*, Chapter LXI. Boston: Little, Brown, 1935.

7 Starbuck, E. D. *Psychology of Religion*. London: Walter Scott, 1899.

8 James, W. *Varieties of Religious Experience*. New York: Longmans, Green, 1902.

9 For an important discussion of sociological influences upon personality, see S. K. Weinberg, *Society and Personality Disorders*. New York: Prentice-Hall, 1952.

10 See M. S. Guttmacher and Henry Weihofen, *Psychiatry and the Law*. New York: Norton, 1952.

11 Bloch, H. A. *Disorganization: Personal and Social*, Part II. New York: Norton, 1952.

12 See Caroline Shrodes, Justine Van Gundy, and R. W. Husband, *Psychology Through Literature*. New York: Oxford, 1943.

13 For a readable discussion, see Gregory Zilboorg and G. W. Henry, *A History of Medical Psychology*. New York: Norton, 1941.

[14] The details of this case are reported in Sigmund Freud and Josef Breuer, *Studien über Hysterie.* Vienna, 1895.

[15] Woodworth, R. S. *Contemporary Schools of Psychology,* p. 141. New York: Ronald, 1931.

[16] See, for example, J. E. Bell, *Projective Techniques.* New York: Longmans, Green, 1948.

SELECTED REFERENCES

Coriat, Isador H. *Abnormal Psychology.* New York: Moffat, Yard, 1910.

Freud, S. *Basic Writings of Sigmund Freud.* New York: Modern Library, 1938.

Lindner, Robert M. *Prescription for Rebellion.* New York: Rinehart, 1952.

McDougall, W. *Outline of Abnormal Psychology.* New York: Scribner's, 1926.

Tomkins, S. *Contemporary Psychopathology.* Cambridge: Harvard Press, 1943.

Zilboorg, G. and Henry, G. W. *History of Medical Psychology.* New York: Norton, 1941.

Chapter XVI

SOCIAL PSYCHOLOGY

Eugene L. Gaier, Ph.D.
Assistant Professor of Psychology, Louisiana State University

EDITORIAL NOTE

Sociologists have been eager of late to appropriate this field to themselves. There are many experimentalists, particularly in animal psychology and the special senses, who are ready to cede that territory. In some institutions social psychology has been merged with sociology, or is incorporated into a new set-up called "Social Relations" or "Human Relations". However, psychology cannot afford to give up this large area. It is no longer, of course, what McDougall thought it to be nearly fifty years ago, and it has developed differently from the way the founders (H. Steinthal, M. Lazarus and W. Wundt) have shaped it. It has become linked with almost every department in psychology (perception, personality, learning). Its expansion has been enormous, psychoanalytic trends, anthropology, and sociology giving it its special impetus.

Dr. Eugene L. Gaier has written a balanced chapter, and while not including all the variegated elements that go to make up this field, he has covered most of the ground. Receiving his degrees in three different universities (the doctorate at The University of Chicago) he has been at the Training Research Laboratory of the University of Illinois, as Research Associate in Psychology and is now an Assistant Professor at Louisiana State University. He is the author of a monograph on Selected Personality Variables *and a number of articles.*

SOCIAL PSYCHOLOGY

In the process of casting off the bonds which confined it to studies in the tradition of McDougall, social psychology has become increasingly concerned with the development of the individual in the broader context of the family and community with their complexity of cultural influences. Whereas social psychology was formerly addressed to the individual, his specific attitudes and his isolated reactions, it has now come to view the organism not as an isolated unit, but as part of a community interacting in a social structure. Research in most areas, especially that of prejudice, has moved from the study of the college sophomore in the classroom in the direction of clinical studies and field investigations. The varieties of problems precipitated by World War II have been largely responsible for this changing focus in theoretical approach, methodological daring and research interests in social psychology.

The most comprehensive statement of the trends and developments of research of social phenomena during World War II is contained in the four volumes of *Studies in Social Psychology in World War II*.[25, 45, 46, 47] Replete with methodological and technical advancements, these four volumes represent a new high in contribution to fact and theory in social psychology.

Volume I, *Adjustment during Army Life,* is concerned with the personal adjustment as it is affected by Army experience, morale factors, job satisfaction, and attitudes toward Negro soldiers. Volume II, *Combat and its Aftermath,* deals with combat motivations and fears, psychoneurotic symptoms, and combat attitude and behavior. Volume III, *Experiments on Mass Communication,* is directed at experimentation in mass communications with an evaluation of the film programs introduced for improving knowledge and attitudes towards the objectives of war. Volume IV, *Measurement and Prediction,* discusses the problem of prediction and contains summary statements of the research design, analysis procedures and scaling techniques employed by the Research Board sponsoring these four volumes.

The need for integration of the findings of different disciplines in the study of social-psychological problems has been increasingly felt and recognized. Attempts at coordination have, however, been few in number and sterile in result. Due perhaps to the traditional opposition of the individual and society—an opposition established by the dualistic social philosophy of the nineteenth century—recognition of the mutual reinforcement of the individual and his society has been slow to develop. With recent emphasis on the interdependence of the individual and his culture there is emerging a more dynamic and integrated approach to the study of individual and group behavior. The value synthesis becomes apparent when one considers the handicap psychology faces in its efforts to understand the development of the human mind without reference to the cultural patterns internalized in the process of its development. A deemphasis of such variables as human intellect and personality imposes similar limitations upon social anthropology in its atttempts to understand cultural patterns.

One of the outcomes of this broader outlook has been an increasing overlap of the subject matter of social psychology with other fields of psychology and with other disciplines. Interdisciplinary inquiries, with attempts at integration, have grown to embrace such broad areas that it is difficult for one to obtain discussion of the current trends and issues in contemporary social psychology within a psychological frame of reference. Attitudes and public opinion, group processes, leadership and morale, mass communication media, international relations and tensions, social class structure, action research and group dynamics,— these areas have been made the rightful subjects for investigations by psychologists, sociologists, cultural anthropologists, educators, psychiatrists, and economists. This growing utilization of inter-disciplinary methods and concepts has enriched social psychology, for it encompasses developments within each discipline, as well as the advantages of integrative theorizing.

These developments have thrown social-psychological research into a state of flux and influx—flux of what is to be considered the rightful subject matter of social-psychology study and the influx of a multiplicity of approaches, concepts, methodologies, and theoretical models for interpreting the old and investigating the new. It has become increasingly apparent that no one discipline is capable of handling all the intricacies involved in studying personality structure and functioning, socialization, and group dynamics. And no one technique is adequate to obtain the necessary data.

The purpose of the present chapter is to discuss current research and technical developments in social psychology with particular reference to major trends and issues. This chapter is not intended as a review of the literature, since the latter is provided each year by the *Annual Review of Psychology.* [9, 28, 36, 43] In view of the vast number of publications that could be classified as social-psychological, it is necessary to be highly selective. Thus, only a small fraction of the multitude of investigations that could be cited will be mentioned, and these primarily for the purpose of illustration. In this discussion, attention will be devoted first to considerations emerging from the study of the individual in a social context. Subsequently, specific problems indigenous to the field will be examined.

CULTURE AND PERSONALITY

The social structure of a society is not the result of chance. Rather, the distinctive qualities of a society are the products of a continuous development which can be calibrated to the principles of learning theory. Some deterministic psychologies, nevertheless, have tended to ignore the crucial role played by the cultural norms and institutions in the development of individual personality. Since the process of transmission of attitudes, ideas and behavior is primarily social rather than genetic, the individual tends to become the type of person his society attempts to make him. The fact that different cultures have produced distinctive types of personality, and the apparent correlation between the cultural configuration to which a child is exposed and the type of adult he becomes is evidence substantiating this generalization.

One of the major attempts at rapprochement of various disciplines has been the psychiatric study of the basic personality structure by Kardiner. [27] He has interpreted in dynamic terms the data supplied by Linton, Dubois, and West on the Comanche, the Alorese, and the mid-Western American. Kardiner reports that varying personal dispositions tend to arise from exposure to sharply contrasting institutions and social practices. By examining the relationships between personality and culture in three contrasting societies, Kardiner traces how the basic personality structure, shared by most members of a society, is related to prevailing child care practices, how such a personality comes to be receptive to some and not to other types of culture patterns, and how cumulative changes in certain social practices in turn affect the personality structure. Gorer[21] also finds "evidence" for a typical national character. He develops the theory that this character is an outgrowth of a rejection of the father and acceptance of the mother figure of authority.

Typical of the investigations of personality variations among subcultures and social classes have been the work of Centers,[13] Davis,[14, 15] Warner[48, 49] and Hollingshead.[24] In contrast to the quantitative approach of Centers, Hollingshead is less interested in the determination of class consciousness than in presenting an interpretation of the social pattern among adolescents in one community. He found that each of the five different social classes in Elmtown has value systems and modes of behavior which distinguish it from other classes. In a similar vein, Davis and Havighurst[16] have stressed the psychological techniques involved in differential class training in child-rearing practices, property rights, and control of aggression. Warner,[50] with his qualitative methods for determining social class, has treated the conflicts of social class patterns with educational and social ideals. His work is corroborated by Hollingshead[24] who found that the treatment accorded adolescents in school by their teachers varied according to the social class to which the adolescent belonged.

Three conceptualizations of the relationship between social status and personality appearing in the literature may be distinguished. The basic notion arises out of evaluations of individuals and families made by members of a community, with especial reference to participation and reputation in the various social units.[49] Such observations are made explicitly when individuals talk of themselves and their families in relation to other persons and their families, and they are reinforced in interviews where people not only refer to their own status position but place others in terms of social participation and reputation. A second aspect arises out of the tendency to categorize people one does not know as person or families by using "objective" criteria.[50] These are often phrased in terms of economic factors. Many of these criteria have a basis in fact, for they are symbols of differences and are used by members of a community to place people prior to more intimate interaction and subsequent acceptance or rejection.

The third conceptualization of status arises when reference is made to the individual's or family's point of view. These family-value attitudes not only tend to organize and control behavior but lead to perceptions that initiate particular kinds of affect accompanying thought and behavior. These value-attitudes are acquired drives, learned in the family and other social agencies through imitation and identification. They are reinforced by social rewards and punishments, are organized in a hierarchy, and are present at varying levels of consciousness.

A basic problem in measuring social status has been the development of an index for predicting social class participation and family reputation, as evaluated by the community. The work of Warner and his associates[50] has been directed towards developing an index based on socio-economic factors for predicting social class participation and reputation. The core of this problem has been to develop an Index of Status Characteristics which correlates highly with the class participation and reputation of individuals and families.

Centers[13] developed a theory as to the origin of social class consciousness based on his interviews with a cross-sectional sample of the nation. He has proposed an "interest group theory" which holds that the individual's status and role with respect to economic processes of a society impose certain attitudes, values and interests relating to his role and status in the political and economic sphere. Thus, the individual is identified with those who share his value, and in Centers' definition, his social class. When asked how they decided on whether a person was in their class, his interviewees named as most important how the person "feels and thinks about certain things". The emphasis upon shared beliefs, plus the communality of emphasis on proprietorship in the middle class, and "working for a living" in the working class, is the crux of Centers' approach.

Great interest has been shown in the problem of the influence of the social or cultural environment on test performance. The most widespread approach has been to determine what the lower-class and ethnic cultures in our society are like. A sizable number of anthropological and sociological field studies have been made of the various social and ethnic groups in America. Davis, working at The University of Chicago, has made use of these findings in his attempt to construct intelligence tests applicable to all classes of American children. While it may appear to be manifestly impossible to have a cultural fair test, since symbol systems must be used, Eells, Davis and Havighurst[18] have asserted that it is possible to base a test on a range of experience which has been empirically determined to be sufficiently common to the majority of children in our society. Their approach has emphasized the need to employ test items which are equally familiar and motivating to children from the range of socioeconomic and ethnic groups who will eventually take these tests.

PERCEPTION

Considerable evidence has indicated that in a learning or social situation, stimuli are selectively perceived in a manner consistent with the individual's motivation at the time. This motivation is a function of his particular needs, his momentary set, and his goals, as well as the structure of the stimulus. Investigations in the area of perception have demonstrated that the striving for meaning and organization in unstructured and/or ambiguous situations reflects both the present need system and the expectancies of the individual.

In the investigation of the fundamental dynamic relations between the individual and the environment, it is essential to keep in mind the actual total situation in its concrete individuality. Behavior reflects the relationship between aspects of the personality and of the environment. And the experiences of the individual are an interaction between the internal and objective conditions.

The problem of perception becomes important in social psychology because human behavior is dependent on how the organism perceives his world. Basically, two major issues are involved here. Cantril[12] has made the distinction between ordinary and social perception. In perceiving a desk, one may expect nothing from this piece of furniture, yet how it affects our purposes determines what we see. This is non-social perception. In perceiving another man, however, we expect something from him, and he from us. Thus, in social perception there is an interaction between perceiver and perceived, which must account not only for our purposes but for his purposes too. According to Cantril, such purposes and expectancies are of primary importance in perception. If our judgments of behavior are to have any predictive value, we must take past learning into account and connect this with the purposes and expectancies of the person.

Bruner and Postman[10, 11, 37] differ from Cantril in that for them all perception is *social perception*. Perception is conceived as a compromise between what a person wants to see and what he is given to see. The perceiver performs four functions; he *selects* from the multitude of stimuli presented to him, since it is impossible for him to perceive *everything* in the field. Secondly, he organizes what is selected and then *accentuates* certain percepts at the expense of others. Lastly, what is seen repeatedly in any given perceptual situation is a function of the *fixation* of past perceptual responses in that situation. These authors conclude that ". . . the four functions of the perceiver —selection, organization, accentuation and fixation—reflect his prevailing state at the time of perceiving. That prevailing state is compounded of the organism's needs, his values, his hopes, his past experiences, his culture—in short, all those items of his past history which have gone into making him what he is."[10]

These researchers have divided their perceptual studies into two parts: the one concerned with "attributive perception" such as the studies of size, movement, and brightness, and the other dealing with the speed and course of the recognition processes under varying motivational states. They have attempted to explain these phenomena by two intervening mechanisms. One they have called *accentuation* referring to a central process leading to systematic tendencies in attributive judgment, and serves to increase the saliency of those things which are personally relevant. The other intervening mechanism may be termed *availability*. This points to the fact that perceptual mechanisms operate to select and maintain those aspects of the environment congruent with the prevailing state of the individual. Thus, perception has as its goal the construction of a meaningful and stable environment; and this environment must be congruent with reality on the one hand and the needs and dispositions of the individual on the other. In other words, sense perception is conceived as a first line of defense against would be catastrophic situations and as a sensitizer to adaptive opportunities.

To demonstrate how values organize perceptions, subjects were given the Vernon-Allport scale.[38] Adjectives describing each of the six values (e. g., aesthetic, religious, political, etc.) were then tachistoscopically presented at subthreshold levels. A relationship was found between threshold of recognition and values of subjects; that is, an "economic" man tended to perceive more quickly the words associated with economic value. In accounting for this process of selection, a principle of resonance was postulated: we see more readily that which resonates with our values. To account for the subject's thresholds on which they scored low, a principle of defense was expostulated: We actively defend ourselves against that which is inimical to us.

The evidence presented, together with the theoretical stand taken by Bruner and Postman, have been premised on the assumption that perception, as indeed all cognitive processes, must be regarded as activity subserving the adjustive needs of the individual. Their research has been concerned with the manner in which needs, internalized values, and various forms of stress effect both the relative saliency of objects and symbols in the perceptual field and also the readiness with which these objects and symbols are perceived.

1. Personally relevant objects in the perceptual field undergo accentuation, as measured in experiments by an increase in apparent size. Certain reality demands, such as the need to use the object as an instrument, work against such accentuation.

2. As measured by the determination of recognition thresholds in a tachistoscopic situation, perceptual selectivity is believed to favor the recognition of values, or objects associated with the prevailing interests of the subjects.

3. When encountering threatening stimuli, the individual shifts from defensive avoidance of the stimuli and becomes vigilant and perceptually selective towards the threat. In Bruner's words, "... both at the fantasy level and in perceptual organization, increased need leads not only or necessarily to gratification responses, but may lead to instrumentally oriented activity."[9]

4. "Perceptual behavior may be usefully conceptualized in terms of learned response dispositions whose acquisition and performance are governed by general principles of associative learning such as frequency, recency and effect. . . . Motivational selectivity in perceptual discriminations is often mediated by and is a consequence of, the operation of these general principles of learning. There is little evidence for direct sensitizing effects of motivational conditions on perception."[10]

In view of the available evidence, it appears that the most important variables in perceptual research continue to be: (a) the intensity of the individual's needs; (b) the restraining or threatening nature of the situation; (c) the relation of the experimental situation or stimuli to the individual's needs; (d) the nature of the subject's personality; and (e) the problem of initial set and selectivity. It should be emphasized, however, that the variables affecting perceptual selection and distortion are still not adequately identified, measured, or validated.

Earlier, Jaensch postulated a *unity of style* within each individual he believed could be detected by means of a few perceptual tests. His somewhat politically-controversial results have suggested that there may be "perceptual styles" in different types of reasoning. Food deprivation was shown to have a significant effect on word association, on the interpretation of neutral pictures, and the completion of drawings (Sanford).[41] Support for this finding was also reported by Levine, Chein and Murphy[32] who presented ambiguous drawings behind a ground glass screen to hungry and satiated subjects. Hungry subjects perceived the pictures more frequently as food objects than did the satiated subjects.

Social pressures and group norms have also been reported to have an appreciable effect on individual perception of the autokinetic phenomena. Sherif[42] demonstrated that the frame of reference of the individual determined the scale by which the stimuli were judged. Personal values were demonstrated to be the determinants of what the individual selects from his environment by Postman and Bruner. It should be noted, however, that Bruner and Postman do not study the particular individual in perception. Group data has been studied to sustain their hypotheses about a theory of personality, but deviations from these hypotheses are not explained.

Closely allied to the research on the influence of need in perception is the conceptualization and explanation of suggestibility. Many investigations on suggestion have involved the assumption that a type of response to stimulation exists that is different in nature from other kinds of responses and these have been termed suggestibility. Individuals were found to differ in their capacity to elicit these special responses and was taken as evidence as reflecting fundamental personality traits called suggestibility. At present, two major views dominate the conceptualization on suggestion. Asch, Block and Hertzman[5] contend that suggestion or prestige suggestion alters the entire cognitive context in which a judgment is made, and change in context is responsible for the changed reasoning process. Krech and Crutchfield,[30] on the other hand, define the structure in terms of motivation, learning and perception. They assert that there is no particular response to a stimulus that may be termed suggestion; it is merely a tension-reducing cognitive reorganization. The suggestibility of the individual is a function of the person's immediate psychological field, and individual needs, emotions and beliefs are stressed rather than the experimenters' "tricks of the trade." Instead of looking for different degrees of suggestibility among different subjects, attention must now be turned to the difference in the immediate psychological field of the individual.

PREJUDICE AND INTER-GROUP TENSION

Research and theory on prejudice and minority group intolerance is currently oscillating between two major orientations: emphasis on individual frustration and causation versus stress on social learning. In the first type of explanation, frustration gives rise to insecurities and hostilities which are subsequently directed toward ethnic or minority groups. The sources of these frustrations are to be found in the environment operating upon the individual during his early preschool and school years, and increasingly in the larger social structure as he matures. The individual's prejudices are not necessarily determined by the frustration experiences in the family and early peer relations; they may simply predispose him to seek an outlet for the hostility and aggression brought about by personal thwarting.

The other side of the coin is pictured in terms of cultural learning through indoctrination and habituation. Prejudice develops out of adult values and the status quo to which the individual is exposed, as well as out of social situations generating insecurities. In order to play his role as a member of a particular group, the individual must accept the values of the group as his own. As a consequence of these pressures, he may find himself on the group for the determination of what is right and what is wrong. From this approach, prejudice may also be an outgrowth of a competitive struggle between certain material and psychological returns. In this context, it is important to note that aggression toward minorities may not derive from the frustration per se, but from the economic and prestige advantages to be gained from such aggression.

These two interpretations of the nature of prejudice are not contradictory. Rather, they are varying levels of explanation which reflect the multiple levels of approach towards prejudice postulated by Allport.[3] Defining prejudice as the "negative attitudes toward human beings that are held because of their membership in a certain group," Allport has distinguished six levels where he believes the causes of prejudice must be investigated: (a) the stimulus object; (b) the phenomenological; (c) personality dynamics and structure; (d) the situational; (e) the socio-cultural; and (f) the historical. Since prejudice is a product of multiple causation, Allport asserts that analysis at each level will contribute to the understanding of prejudice.

Perhaps the most significant shift in the thinking on prejudice has been the departure from the consideration of prejudice as a phenomenon independent of inter-group relationships and attitudes. Much impetus for this changing research emphasis can be attributed to the very provocative and extensive studies of the Berkeley group on the authoritarian personality. In this series of studies, the deeper personality dimensions involved in prejudices have been explored.

The study of the authoritarian personality by Adorno and his associates[2] represents a large scale investigation of prejudiced and non-prejudiced subjects that has set the stage for many studies of the personality correlates of prejudice. In an attempt to determine what kinds of people were authoritarian or undemocratic, a close degree of association was found between a number of basic personality patterns and ideological systems. The forces of this interest lie in the so-called authoritarian personality syndrome defined by conventionality, rigidity, an exaggerated adherence to conventional values as cleanliness and order, repressive denial power orientation, fear of imaginary dangers, exploitative tendencies and black-white thinking. The extent of the presence of this syndrome appears to depend, in part, on the nature of the parent-child relationship. There was also a degree of inconsistency characteristic of the reaction of these people towards members of other groups. This took the form of responding favorably to a given group in one situation and unfavorably in another, or accepting one kind of relationship with such a group while rejecting an apparently much less personal type of contact.

While the evidence reported in *The Authoritarian Personality* on the relationship between authoritarianism and ethnocentrism has provided new insights for investigating prejudice, several questions must be answered before these relationships can be accepted as casual. Adorno and his colleagues reported that most, but not all, of their *authoritarian* subjects were ethnocentric. Conversely, most but not all of their non-authoritarian subjects expressed little or no prejudice. How can these deviations be interpreted? Can the behavior of these deviants be attributed to early child-rearing practices, family impact, peer group association, socio-economic background, and/or sub-cultural membership or reference groups? Is the *authoritarian personality* indigenous to our culture or to a unique group within our society? Or can the results obtained by the Berkeley group be interpreted as a post-war phenomenon?

The designation of specific groups towards which hostility is directed appears to be largely a function of the social pressures operating on the individual. Both Davis[15] and Bettleheim and Janowitz[7] have reported evidence pointing to the importance of the social class status system as a source as an agency for focusing existing hostilities upon certain racial and cultural minorities. These studies are representative of the investigations of the social, economic, and cultural correlates of prejudice. In their study of the relationship between social mobility and anti-Semitism of war veterans living in a large city, Bettleheim and Janowitz found that objective downward social mobility, as measured by changes in pre- and post-war employment positions, was significantly related to prejudice. Apprehension about future employment was found to be associated with ethnic intolerance. They concluded that intolerance was less a function of the

objective situation than the personal evaluation of that situation
or the subjectively felt deprivation.

Ackerman and Jahoda[1] employed case history materials
from 40 anti-Semitic subjects in psychotherapy, thus enriching
with qualitative materials the current psychoanalytic interpretations of prejudice. Their subjects who professed religious affiliations were more prejudiced than those who did not, and those
with higher conservatism scores were more prejudiced than those
with more liberal dispositions. Similarly, those who accepted parental attitudes were more prejudiced than those who did not accept them. These two kinds of evidence have been reconciled by
Ackerman and Jahoda by relating them to the ego-integrative
forces which stem from the person constantly seeking to associate and order his experiences into a consistent pattern, and to the
divisive forces of a complex society in which the requirements
for status in one aspect of life are antithetical to those of others.
Bettleheim and Janowitz also recognize that personality structure
cannot alone entirely explain why their subjects were more prejudiced toward one group than another. One might argue, in view
of this evidence, that the defensive needs of the individual, the
social structure of the community and the ethnic realities of the
moment must all be taken into account.

Frenkel-Brunswik[20] presented evidence for the existence of
a basic variable, "tolerance versus intolerance of ambiguity,"
in both the emotional and cognitive orientation of the individual.
Support has been given to this conceptual scheme by some preliminary results yielding motivational and cognitive correlates of
ethnic prejudice in a large sample of school children. Existence
of this general attitude towards ambiguity in objects and object-
relations was found in the prejudiced children's description of
their parents, their reactions to parental figures on the TAT, and
in their adherence to social values and norms. Conflicting tendencies were dichotomized in interpersonal relationship, as well
as in the social fields. Thus, those found incapable of tolerating
conflicting emotions or value-judgments were generally incapable
of viewing objective stimuli in several different ways. One ex-

periment revealed higher perseveration scores for prejudiced children when they had to identify each card in a series of pictures which changed slowly from a dog to a cat. This work suggests that tolerance of ambiguity may be equated with the ability to think in probabilities rather than escape into an all-or-none type of conception. This might also involve a tolerance for several hypotheses about a given problem or the ability to shift fairly rapidly from one hypothesis to another.

This latter hypothesis was an outgrowth of the work of Frenkel-Brunswik and was tested by Rokeach.[40] In the use of problem-solving methods to discriminate between prejudiced and non-prejudiced subjects, he found that prejudiced subjects perseverated significantly more often in a complex method of solving problems for which an initial set had been established. Non-prejudiced subjects more often perceived the shorter and more direct solution that could also be employed to solve the tasks. On the basis of these findings, Rokeach hypothesized a general rigidity factor which manifests itself as prejudice on the personality level, and the inability to restructure the field or to change set on the perceptual and problem-solving level.

In conclusion, attention should be called to the specific methods and techniques utilized in the research studies cited. The intensive interview approach was used by Ackerman and Jahoda, Adorno, and Bettleheim and Janowitz. The study of prejudice has also been approached via group therapy sessions, the Rorschach, TAT, sociometry, and the responses of groups in concrete life situations. Of great interest for research on the dimensions of prejudice is the unidimensionality of attitude scales reported by Kramer[29] and the indications of the intensity with which an attitude is held.

GROUP PROCESSES

One of the productive developments of the study of the individual as a group member and a cultural product has been the interest in the group as a unit for study and analysis. Dissatisfied with the sweeping hypotheses about social organization and behavior developed by Freud, LeBon and Jung, Moreno and Lewin and their students have called for systematic experimental research under controlled laboratory conditions of the ways in which individuals actually function in real life situations as members of small groups. This work, primarily by members of the Survey Research Center of the University of Michigan, has been initiated and pursued in the expectancy that experiments on small manageable units will yield reliable laws which can be applied to the understanding and prediction of all group behavior. Many investigations have emphasized the patterns of behavior characterizing small group organizations. Attention has also been directed to the problem of leadership as it related to communication, the degrees of cohesiveness and group productivity, and the intra-group interaction processes of what has come to be called group dynamics. The study of the effects of psychological climate on group morale and group personality, have proven very relevant for public administration and organization of industry.

Research into the nature of the structure and dynamics of small groups has broadened the scope of social psychology to include new methodologies as well as to embrace a new vocabulary from other disciplines. Concepts such as group productivity, syntality, cohesiveness, action research, viscidity, role, and status and the like have all been outgrowths of the work done on group processes. As summarized, by Lippett,[34] the five major objectives of this research on group structure and functioning are:

". . . (a) to apply experimental methods to the behavior of small groups and to the behavior of individuals in the group setting; (b) to attempt an integration of work in the fields of industrial psychology, social psychology, sociology and social anthropology; (c) to isolate the comparative properties characteristic of small groups of different kinds operating under different conditions on different tasks and to attempt translation of these properties into field theory; (d) to develop measurement applicable to small group behavior; and (e) to apply findings to such socially useful activity as supervisor training, leadership training, group therapy, etc. . . ."

The extent to which these objectives have been realized, or are likely to be realized in the future, must be evaluated against the background of the diverse and somewhat ambitious approaches introduced in this area since its inception in the early thirties. Benne and Levit[6] have distinguished nine approaches employed in research on the nature of groups from the period of 1930 to the present. These include (a) the sociometric approach by Moreno,[35] (b) the study of work organization as a feature of group life typified by the Ohio State Leadership Studies; (c) the psychoanalytically oriented investigations of the motivational and emotional aspects of group life (Redl,[39] Bion);[8] (d) the study of the interaction of group members within specific situations; (e) the influence of a group on the behavior and attitudes of individual members (Sherif,[42] Asch);[4] (f) group decision-making and the processes leading from goal setting to the formulation of the solution (Lewin);[33] (g) the communication in small groups; (h) the study of groups in their "natural" habitat typified by Whyte's[51] study of street-corner society; and (i) study of leadership-membership function (Stogdill).[44]

The experimental investigation of behavior in its natural context while simultaneously evaluating the effectiveness of the introduction of change programs has been called action research of group behavior. Implicit in this approach is not only the investigation of conflicts and prejudices based on the responses of interviewees in the situation (e.g., housing projects, Air Force combat crews, factory workers), but the encouragement and introduction of variables for the changing of group behavior. Action research is applied which attempts to arrive at conclusions and recommendations for change and growth with the people studied participating in a research role.[26] Several intensive studies have been carried out on the effects of residence in segregated bi-racial housing projects in an attempt to study the effects on the reduction of prejudice (Deutsch and Collins,[17] Festinger).[19]

The Ohio State Leadership Studies have been undertaken on the assumption that the variables of organization can be isolated and defined so as to permit systematic investigation through experimentation. Working within this framework, Stogdill[44] has asserted that the existence of organization is dependent on the cooperation and performance of individuals who play different roles. He defends the measures of authority and leadership as aspects of measures of organization, even though the measurements have been made in terms of the numbers and relationships among the members. For Stogdill, leadership exists only in so far as individuals, as members of a group, are differentiated as to the influence they exert upon the organization. As a result, the leadership influence of any one member will be determined to a large degree by the total leadership structure of the organization. Leadership is thus defined in terms of the influence among group members.

The approach to the study of leadership appears to be derived from two opposed theoretical views: the leader is conceived as a symbol of authority or as an embodiment of superior personal traits, versus the "heroes-are-made-not-born" approach in which leadership appears to be regarded as a manifestation of social-psychological interaction. Evidence for this last view was presented by Sherif.[42] He found that in a group, the extreme opinions seem to lose out and settle around a group norm. Thus, a good leader has the sensitivity to modal group opinion. Arbitrary change of policy on the part of the group leader would not result in an accommodating change on the part of the group. Accordingly, group pressures appear to determine both leadership and conformity.

PUBLIC OPINION POLLING AND COMMUNICATIONS

The long needed re-examination of public opinion research was touched off by the criticisms levied against the pollsters in the face of the erroneous prediction of the 1948 election results. The hithertofore held assumption concerning polling was found inadequate: that the thoughts and habits of people can be pinned down, defined, and catalogued if a sample of people is asked enough questions and these answers are statistically arranged and interpreted.

The greatest amount of interest in post-November 1948 research has been in the direction of the study of the factors in the interview situation leading to bias in the results obtained, the development and application of improved mathematical models for the measurement of opinion, and the development of indirect methods and projective techniques in an effort to give depth to attitude study and free it from the limits set by the insight and cooperation of the interviewee. Attention has also been directed to the problem of interviewer bias, the problem of interviewees who are reluctant to be interviewed, as well as the problems of coding open-ended questions, and the process of recording of the respondent's replies.

Making a prediction of voting behavior from responses obtained in interviews involves a number of steps. And at each step, this procedure includes technical difficulties of a formidable sort. Errors made in any of the steps, viz., sampling design and instructions, questionnaire design, selection of interviewers, deciding how to allocate the "no opinion" group, or the "not at home" group, making adjustment for trends and sudden shifts in opinions, interpretation of the results—may serve to contaminate the results obtained at later stages of the analysis. Nevertheless, the task of interviewing is still entrusted to the lowest paid, least trained, and most impermanent members of the staff. The interviewer is often apt to cut corners to satisfy the category requirements in the interest of speed and convenience.

In assessing interview bias, Hart[25] points to three characteristics of the interview situation demanding further analysis: First, that it is a social artifact varying with a host of factors. For example, the public opinion poll has the appearance of consensus of opinion, yet little or no opportunity is usually allowed the respondent for re-stating the question with little possibility for a "meeting of minds." Secondly, interviewees vary widely in their ability to interpret the situation and the questions asked. Each respondent is a bundle of conflicting loyalties, responsive to a dozen pressures—his family, his friends, his past, his party, and sometimes to the political issues at stake. If these are not in harmony, his opinions may be contradictory, depending on whether a particular question hits him at the moment in his role as a Texan, Democrat, veteran, Lion, amateur cook, or art patron. Thirdly, interviewers are known to vary widely in their capacity to influence responses. Hart reported a positive correlation between respondent and interviewer opinion which is more marked in small population areas where the interviewer may serve the role of conformity agent. Discrepancies in race, religion, and class between interviewer and respondent may hamper rapport and distort the results in the direction of conformity. In addition, interview bias results most when the interviewer has either strong biases on an issue or none at all, since part of the bias is exercised in the selection of his respondent. Ambiguous answers also tend to elicit projection on the part of the interviewers classifying the interviewees, and trained people introduce as much bias as untrained interviewers.

Harris and Connelley[22] have suggested the following five recommendations for reducing interview errors: (a) use of the Guttman scale to reduce error or at least make the error determinable since such scales are less dependent on single questions; (b) increased interview training and participation, with higher salaries to obtain more highly trained individuals; (c) separation of the drudgery of enumeration from the task of interviewing, to be carried out by a separate staff in double enumeration; (d) use of more permanent interviewing staffs; and (e) omission of costly and time-consuming call backs and remote calls which add but a minimum to sampling precision.

Viewed in perspective, the nature and methodology of the measurement of attitudes and public opinion have taken on new meaning and significance, as well as a great sense of responsi-

PRESENT-DAY PSYCHOLOGY

bility. Four major trends have emerged from the work carried out in this area:

1. The widespread popularity of public-opinion survey results have encouraged people to think concretely and face up to issues that might otherwise have remained in a somewhat nebulous state in their own minds. This has applied not only to those questioned and interviewed, but to the newspaper audience who wonder what they themselves would have replied in response to the questions. At the same time, these results have affected beliefs and attitudes by gaining their attention through headlines and sheer repetition.

2. Public opinion polls have been instrumental in exposing to public appraisal such rarely publicized issues as birth control, sexual attitudes and practices, venereal disease, cancer, mental health and the like. People who formerly would not dream of making public pronouncements on such matters have little hesitation in addressing their opinions to poll interviewers.

3. The polls have spotlighted areas of ignorance and inconsistency—housing, prejudice, educational practices, medical care.

4. The polls have been able to counteract the work of various pressure groups by skillful analyses and interpretations of their results.

The study of mass media has continued under the aegis of the formulation set down by Lasswell: Who says what, to whom, in what context and to what effect. Lazarsfeld[31] has conceptualized this definition of the purposes of communications research in the following five dimensions:

1. Control analysis: Who determines the content of mass media?

2. Content analysis: What is contained in the media and how is it described?

3. Audiences as such: What are the characteristics of the media audience and how can these characteristics be measured?

4. Effect studies: What is the effect of the communication on the audience and how can it be measured?

5. Functional analysis: What are the relationships of media to each other, as well as to the other aspects of the social system?

The criteria for the classification of various media have been divided into three types: *primary* characteristics such as age, sex, economic level, education; *psychological* characteristics based on personality test scores or attitudes on a variety of issues; and *communication* habits, the reading or listening habits of the audiences.

The most comprehensive studies conducted in mass communications were reported by Hovland, Lumsdaine and Sheffield[25] in Volume III of the Studies in Social Psychology in World War II. In its implications, this volume is a very important contribution to mass media of research both in its improvements of old research tools as well as its daring in the development of new ideas and concepts.

Outlook

Some of the major issues and trends in the present status of social psychology have been treated in the present chapter. Some attention should now be given to the desirable directions that social psychology might well take in order to function more effectively both in the laboratory and the marketplace. First, let us consider the content of social psychology. In the past, much of the content has been only remotely related to the actual community behavior of the individual. For social psychology to make a difference in the actual contribution, content should be selected and emphasized which has maximum applicability. The content should not only be drawn from the various areas of psychology (viz., child, adolescent, learning, clinical, abnormal, and mental hygiene) but should also include relevant materials from the fields of cultural anthropology, medicine, psychiatry, biology, and sociology.

A second question for discussion is whether a course in social psychology should be designed to influence changes in behavior or merely to increase the students' store of knowledge in this subject area. The scientist's ethical position would be somewhat more tenable if the *influencing* were left to the action researcher and the clinician. Nevertheless, courses in social psychology often fail to influence the behavior of the students because the principles and theories are learned apart from their application.

Basic to the research in social psychology is the problem of methodology. Only recently have the necessary statistical and conceptual tools been introduced. The present techniques of analysis are a response to the demands of research rather than an obvious, logical outgrowth of developments in theory. The present concern with statistical techniques, coupled with a closer cooperation of the clinician and the applied psychologist, have contributed to the recent rise in the interest of the relationship of attitudes with underlying personality structure. But perhaps the outstanding factor in preparing the climate for this approach has been the rapid obsolescence of the "unit" conceptualization of the individual.

The direction of future work in social psychology must be affected by the cooperation that has been achieved among the various disciplines. Stimulated by the preliminary results of inter-disciplinary inquiries with its more encompassing interpretations and methods, social psychologists have been offered the richest subject matter for systematic investigations to date. Many of the problems available for investigation lend themselves to intensive study with available methodologies, while others call for newer techniques, and structure greater preparedness to study situations of stress and flux.

REFERENCES

1 Ackerman, N. W. and Jahoda, M. *Anti-semitism and emotional disorder.* New York: Harper and Brothers, 1950.

2 Adorno, T. W. *et al. The authoritarian personality.* New York: Harper and Brothers, 1950.

3 Allport, G. W. Prejudices; A problem in psychological and social causation. *J. Soc. Issues,* 1950, 4, 1-26. (Supplement)

4 Asch, S. Effects of group pressure upon the modification of and distribution of judgments. In: *Groups, Leadership, and Men,* edited by Guetzkow, H. Pittsburgh: Carnegie Press, 1951.

5 Asch, S. E., Block, H., and Hertzman, M. Studies in the principles of judgments and attitudes: I. Two basic principles of judgment. *J. Psychol.,* 1938, *5,* 215-251.

6 Benne, K. D., and Levit, G. The nature of groups and helping groups improve their operation. *Rev. of Educ. Res.,* 1953, *23,* 289-308.

7 Bettleheim, B., and Janowitz, M. *Dynamics of prejudice.* New York: Harper and Brothers, 1950.

8 Bion, W. R. Experiences in groups, I-VI. *Human Relations,* 1948, *1,* 314-20, 487-96.

9 Bruner, J. S. Social psychological and group processes. In *Annual Review of Psychology.* Stanford: Annual Reviews, Inc., 1950, vol. I, 119-150.

10 Bruner, J. S., and Postman, L. An approach to social perception. In *Current trends in social psychology.* 71-118. Pittsburgh: Univer. of Pittsburgh Press, 1948.

11 —— Symbolic value as an organizing factor in perception. *J. soc. Psychol.,* 1948, *27,* 203-208.

12 Cantril, H. The nature of social perception. *Trans. N. Y. Acad. Sci.,* 1948, Series II, *10,* 142-153.

13 Centers, R. *The psychology of social classes.* Princeton: Princeton Univer. Press, 1949.

14 Davis, A. American status systems and the socialization of the child. *Amer. soc. Res.,* 1941, *6,* 345-54.

15 Davis, A. Socialization and adolescent personality. *Yearbook nat. soc. Stud. Educ.,* 1944, *43,* 198-216.

16 Davis, A., and Havighurst, R. J. Social class and color differences in child-rearing. *Amer. Sociol. Rev.,* 1946, *11,* 698-710.

17 Deutsch, M., and Collins, Mary E. *Interracial housing: A psychological evaluation of a social experiment.* Minneapolis: Univer. of Minnesota Press, 1951.

18 Eells, K., Davis, A., Havighurst, R. J., Herrick, V. E., and Tyler, R. *Intelligence and cultural differences.* Chicago: Univer. of Chicago Press, 1951.

19 Festinger, L. S., Schacter, S., and Back, K. *Social pressures in informal groups.* New York: Harper and Brothers, 1950.

20 Frenkel-Brunswik, E. Intolerance of ambiguity as an emotional and perceptual personality variable. *J. Personal.,* 1949, *18,* 108-143.

21 Gorer, G. *The American people.* New York: W. W. Norton and Co., 1948.

22 Harris, Natalie, and Connelley, G. M. A symposium on interviewing problems. *Inter. J. opin. att. Res.,* 1948, *2,* 69-84.

23 Hart, C. Problems of measuring public opinion. In Schramm, W. *Communications in modern society.* Urbana: Univer. of Illinois Press, 1948, pp. 156-166.

24 Hollingshead, A. B. *Elmtown's youth: The impact of social classes on adolescents.* New York: Wiley, 1949.

25 Hovland, C. I. *et al. Experiments on mass communication. Studies in social psychology in World War I,* vol. 4. Princeton: Princeton Univer. Press, 1949.

26 Jahoda, Marie, Deutsch, M., and Cook, S. W. *Research method in social relations*. Part one: Basic Processes. Part two: Selected techniques. New York: Dryden, 1951.

27 Kardiner, A. *The psychological frontiers of society*. New York: Columbia Univ. Press, 1947.

28 Katz, D. Social psychology and group processes. In: *Annual Review of Psychology*. Stanford: Annual Reviews, Inc., 1951, vol. 2, 137-172.

29 Kramer, B. M. Dimensions of prejudice. *J. Psychol.*, 1949, *27*, 389-451.

30 Krech, D., and Crutchfield, R. S. *Theory and problems of social psychology*. New York: McGraw Hill, 1948.

31 Lazarsfeld, P. Communication research and the social psychologist. In Dennis, W. (Ed.), *Current trends in social psychology*. Pittsburgh: Univer. of Pittsburgh Press, 1948, 218-273.

32 Levine, R., Chein, E., and Murphy, G. The relation of the intensity of a need to the amount of perceptual distortion (a preliminary report). *J. Psychol.*, 1942, *13*, 283-293.

33 Lewin, K. Group decision and social change. In *Readings in social psychology*. New York: Holt, 1952.

34 Lippett, R. A program of experimentation on group functioning and group productivity. In Dennis, W. (Ed.), *Current trends in social psychology*. Pittsburgh: Univer. of Pittsburgh Press, 1948, 218-273.

35 Moreno, J. L. *Who shall survive?* Washington, D. C.: Nervous and Mental Diseases Publishing Co., 1934.

36 Newcomb, T. M. Social and group processes. In *Annual Review of Psychology*. Stanford: Annual Reviews, Inc., 1953, vol. 4, 183-214.

37 Postman, L. The experimental analyses of motivational factors in perception. In *Current theory and research in motivation: A symposium*. Lincoln: Univ. of Nebraska Press, 1953, 59-108.

38 Postman, L., Bruner, J. S., and McGinnies, E. M. Personal values as selective factors in perception. *J. abnorm. soc. Psychol.*, 1948, *43*, 142-154.

39 Redl, F. Group emotion and leadership. *Psychiatry*, 1942, *5*, 573-596.

40 Rokeach, M. Generalized mental rigidity as a factor in ethnocentrism. *J. abnorm. soc. Psychol.*, 1948, *43*, 259-278.

41 Sanford, R. N. The effects of abstinence from food upon imaginal processes: A further experiment. *J. Psychol.*, 1937, *3*, 145-159.

42 Sherif, M. *An outline of social psychology*. New York: Harper and Brothers, 1948.

43 Smith, M. B. Social psychology and group processes. In *Annual Review of Psychology*. Stanford: Annual Reviews, Inc., 1952, vol. 3, 175-202.

44 Stogdill, R. M. Leadership, membership, and organization. *Psychol. Bull.*, 1950, *47*, 1-14.

45 Stouffer, S. A. *et al. The American soldier: Adjustment during army life. Studies in social psychology in World War II*, vol. I. Princeton: Princeton Univer. Press, 1949.

46 —— *The American soldier: Combat and its aftermath. Studies in social psychology in World War II*, vol. II. Princeton: Princeton Univer. Press, 1949.

PRESENT-DAY PSYCHOLOGY

47 —— *Measurement and prediction. Studies in social psychology in World War II*, vol. IV. Princeton: Princeton University Press, 1950.

48 Warner, W. L. *Democracy in Jonesville: A study of equality and inequality*. New York: Harper and Brothers, 1949.

49 Warner, W. L., and Lunt, P. S. *The social life of a modern community*. Yankee City Series, vol. I. New Haven: Yale University Press, 1941.

50 Warner, W. L., Meeker, M., and Eells, K. *Social class in America*. Chicago: Science Research Associates, 1949.

51 Whyte, W. F. *Street corner society*. Chicago: Univer. of Chicago Press, 1943.

402

Chapter XVII

APPLIED PSYCHOLOGY

Harold E. Burtt, Ph.D.
Chairman, Dept. of Psychology, Ohio State University

EDITORIAL NOTE

It is difficult to believe that there was a time within one's memory that applied psychology did not exist, and that there were such ace psychologists as Titchener, who would have no truck with it. In less than fifty years, applied psychology virtually non-existent before the day of Münsterberg, has come to dominate the whole science, particularly when we consider the clinical sphere as applied. It is not at all strange; for mathematics, physics, and chemistry have had a similar history in that respect; and that should have been expected, in view of the fact that man is interested in furthering his practical aims and satisfying his needs. With the great technological advances even during the past couple of decades, new fields have opened up for the applied psychologist. Since there is nothing which touches man but has a psychological aspect, it follows that all endeavors and activities, whether economic, medical, legal, artistic, industrial or even religious, can be psychologically approached.

It is well that applied psychology is not stressed in institutions of learning. The attraction is too great for students who are thinking in terms of material reward rather than developing a scientific spirit and that is probably the reason why Titchener, a scientist of the highest integrity, could not become reconciled to it as an academic study.

Dr. Harold E. Burtt may be regarded as the successor of his famous Harvard teacher, Hugo Münsterberg, in that special domain. Heading the psychological department at Ohio State University, he is also serving as consultant for some industrial corporations. In addition to a number of articles, he has brought out several successful and solid textbooks on applied psychology, one of these dealing with legal psychology.

Trends in Applied Psychology

Initial interest in applied psychology developed around the turn of the century. Some psychologists shifted their attention from general laws to individual differences and the practical implications of those differences. Cattell did some preliminary work with mental tests of college students and Binet developed his intelligence scale for school children. The American Psychological Association took some cognizance of the trend with its Woodworth and Wells Committee on Tests. By 1910 there was enough material for Whipple's test manual.

The whole movement received considerable impetus from Hugo Münsterberg who had a broader grasp of the problems than did others at the time. He wrote books touching on educational, medical, legal, and business phases of psychology and finally pulled a lot of this material together in his comprehensive *Psychotechnik*. Much of this material was rather crude by present standards. Statistics had had comparatively little impact on the psychological profession. Tests were validated primarily by comparing average scores made by groups that were high and low in the criterion and a correlation coefficient was something that was discussed in hushed tones.

Münsterberg was one of the few all-around applied psychologists. At that time it was possible to be familiar with practically everything that had been done in the field. Nowadays there is great specialization and anyone attempting to write even a cursory survey of the field is aware of his incompetence in some aspects.

The first World War gave applied psychology considerable impetus. The greatest activity was in the field of personnel testing with much of it focussed on the Army Alpha Intelligence Test. There was, however, some interest in training methods, in the discovery of emotional difficulties and in public attitudes. After the armistice some of those who had been concerned with psychological problems in the armed forces carried that interest back to civilian life and applied psychology was on its way.

Academic courses on the subject were developed. Some consulting work was done by individuals or by groups and organizations specifically devoted to professional psychology such as the Psychological Corporation were formed.

The present survey will consider applied psychology as contributing to four major fields,—education, medicine, law, and business. While there are numerous outlying fields which might be construed as applications of psychology the foregoing are the four conventional psychotechnologies. Some of the highlights of the last twenty-five or thirty years will be noted.

THE EDUCATIONAL PROCESS

Instruction aids. Trends in educational psychology will be discussed under three aspects: (1) the educational process, (2) techniques of measurement, and (3) the raw material of education, that is individual differences and their development. With reference to the first of these we may note the development of devices and aids for instruction. Objective examinations constitute one instance. These are more reliable than the essay type of exam made up by the individual teacher—reliable in the sense that different people grading the same paper would give pretty much the same score. Another type of instructional device is aimed at self-instruction. With pupils differing as they do in native capacity there is economy if some of them can proceed on their own. Typical is a manual for self study in arithmetic including practice exercises and tests which the pupil may give himself to determine whether he needs more practice of a given sort. Then there are little machines on which a student may punch keys according to the alternative answers on a question sheet. If he punches the correct key, that is gets the right answer, the machine steps along and he knows he is correct, but if his answer is wrong the machine jams and he has to try another alternative. In this way he determines progressively whether he knows the answer to the various questions in the exercise. A third class of devices comprises so-called teaching aids, notably moving pictures and radio. Instructional films of a wide variety have been developed and, on occasion, an educational broadcasting station provides material which is picked up by receivers in the school room. This may be supplemented with printed material previously distributed. This medium is even used to teach the teachers in the sense that the radio or TV station may broadcast a panel of experts discussing educational problems, some of which may have been submitted by individual teachers in the listening area.

Acceleration. A second trend with reference to the educational process is acceleration.[1] Hitherto, academic progress has been pretty much in step with chronological age. There is even some folklore about the unfortunate consequences of getting out of step, such as social maldevelopment. We now realize that the rate of progress does not necessarily need to be the same for everyone. A little accelerating has been done in individual cases through the years as when an occasional pupil skips a grade. But apparently these variations in the rate of progress could be made more general and perhaps the program might even be altered so that almost everybody could accelerate a little. An investigation of the possibility of integrating the high school and the college curricula was carried out by several preparatory schools and the colleges to which most of their graduates went. They planned the last two years of secondary school and the first two years of college as a unit, removing duplications and filling gaps. It was found, for instance, that a third of the pupils repeated in college a beginning course in the science that they had in prep school. This particular investigation came up with a proposal for a seven year program to replace the usual eight years, that is four years in high school and four in college.[2]

Another acceleration project dealt with the possibility of earlier admission to college. With many young men having to enter military service at about the age of eighteen it seemed desirable to get them as far along in their education as possible by that time. Several colleges experimented with admitting high school students who had not completed their course and were not over sixteen and a half years of age. Individuals were selected who seemed ready academically and had sufficiently mature personality. The progress of these students was satisfactory according to the first year's results. They were compared with matched groups of similar aptitude but who had graduated from high school and entered college at the "normal age". In one sample for which results are available the experimental group outdistanced the rest of the freshman class and in most cases outperformed their matched or control group. They also seemed well adjusted to college life.[3]

Guidance. A third trend regarding the educational process is an increased emphasis on guidance. The modern teacher does more than just teach certain subjects. One type of guidance concerns how to study. Investigation has indicated that study skills are picked up pretty much at random and some of them are quite ineffective. Even capable students sometimes have very inefficient study habits. Manuals are available for systematic approach to one's method of studying and in some institutions actual academic courses on study skills are available. Material of this sort is often covered in orientation lectures given to college freshmen.[4]

Another type of guidance is vocational. Some efforts of this sort go back fifty years but with the recent development of psychometric procedures and the validation of vocational tests and some of the job analysis work done by the War Manpower Commission and the various state employment services, vocational guidance can now be implemented much more satisfactorily. The exploration of aptitudes, interests, and opportunities is central in this program. Teachers to an increasing degree are called upon for this type of service.

Guidance on the part of school personnel sometimes extends to mental adjustment problems. We realize now that poor progress in school may be due to personal factors of a clinical nature. To some extent the teacher helps in the exploration of these factors and may do therapy in a small way. Some of the methods will be discussed in the next section on clinical psychology.

This enlargement of the teacher's role to include various phases of guidance has led to the emergence of the school psychologist. Many states now make provision for certifying personnel appropriately trained to carry out such functions. In a typical instance a person who is qualified for the ordinary teacher's certificate takes an additional year of work with emphasis on clinical psychology and is then certified as a school psychologist. A major function of such a person is the guidance activity just mentioned although a school psychologist also does a lot of psychometric work such as school surveys.

Social emphasis. A fourth educational trend is an increasing emphasis on social development. The school as originally constituted was concerned mainly with transmitting certain information and developing certain skills. While this policy equipped the pupil for some subsequent life activities it overlooked the fact that he would spend his life in a social environment and part of his success would depend on adjustment to such an environment. Hence it became apparent that we needed to train the pupil for living in modern society. A present-day remedy is to give the student more social experiences in the class room, in other words socialize the instruction. The pupils work in groups on joint projects, conversation is permitted, and there is much social give and take in the process. There are experimental indications that when the whole school room atmosphere is somewhat democratic instructional progress is more satisfactory.[5] Teachers-in-training now get considerable emphasis on socialized methods and actually participate in such projects in the courses they take themselves with a view to bringing home to them the techniques they may use subsequently in their own classes. A wholesome by-product of this process is a certain amount of training for leadership. When youngsters work on educational projects there are many opportunities for someone to serve as chairman of a committee or otherwise play a leadership role.

MEASUREMENT TECHNIQUES

Educational psychology has made extensive use of mental

measurement techniques. The initial emphasis was on measuring intelligence. Some of this stemmed from observed differences in the rate of progress of school children and the possibility that intellectual differences might account for this. With the development of group intelligence tests following the pattern of World War I Army Alpha such measurements in schools have become almost routine. However, it was realized presently that this was only part of the story and that other aspects of the individual were equally important. Interests constituted the next category coming in for extensive measurement. The interest inventory of the type developed by Strong has played an increasing role. It has been used by school people in connection with vocational guidance where it develops that the student's stated interest in vocations may not be very basic. Another psychometric development involves personality. School adjustment, vocational success, and general life adjustment often depend on aspects of personality. Some of these may be modifiable. At any rate it is desirable to have information about the personality of the pupil. Some such tests are of the inventory type while others employ projective methods. These will be discussed in connection with clinical methods (*infra*). Measurement of attitudes, likewise, has received considerable emphasis. A major concern has been the evaluation of public opinion. But if the school is interested in developing or changing attitudes it needs to know what they are to start with. Attitude scales have been developed for this purpose and much research has gone into perfecting fine points of technique.

INDIVIDUAL DIFFERENCES

Educational psychology is interested in the raw material with which it deals. The central problem here is the individual differences between pupils. Binet brought the problem into focus when he developed his intelligence test. Goddard and Terman did some of the early work along these lines in this country. The developments in psychometrics just discussed have helped. A trend worthy of special mention is the increasing interest in persons at the upper end of the intelligence scale. Earlier work dealt with the more obvious lower end of the scale and the educational problems arising from mental defect. Terman, however, took a look at the upper end of the scale, located a sample of youngsters with high intelligence quotients and followed them up for many years. They were generally successful in life and in few instances suffered any handicap resulting from their intellectual superiority. Now various agencies are attempting to discover outstanding intellectual talent and insure that it gets adequate educational opportunity.

Another aspect of the raw material of education is the extension of developmental psychology to cover the entire life span. Initial interest was primarily in people of school or college age. Now we are looking into the later years. This involves problems such as the adjustment of different ages when three generations of the same family are living together. An aspect which extends beyond educational psychology is the field of gerontology which has developed in the last decade or so. One problem is the employability of people in their later years. Another is their adjustment to retirement and preparations for it as it approaches.[6]

DIAGNOSIS

Turning now to the second major technology, the application of psychology to medical problems, we may note some trends in the diagnostic aspect of clinical psychology. The recent emphasis on psychotherapy will be mentioned presently but until the late thirties the main contribution of psychology was diagnosis. The typical clinical team included medical personnel and a psychologist, with the latter contributing only to the diagnostic aspect.

The interview is the old stand-by in clinical diagnosis and probably always will be, but the development of clinical tests is of some interest. The test most frequently used at the outset was the Binet test which gave the clinician some opportunity to observe the client in action as well as yielding an intelligence quotient. Some maladjustment, to be sure, stemmed from low intelligence.

Personality inventories were developed in an effort to supplement the clinician's judgment as to personality deviations. These inventories reached their peak in the thirties. The Minnesota Multiphasic Inventory is one of the best known and the Guilford-Martin is a more recent instance. Inventories of this sort have some validity provided the client marks the answers truthfully. There is always the danger with such instruments of malingering on the part of a subject who might wish to fake some deviation so he would not be imprisoned or drafted or who might wish to misrepresent himself as more stable and better adjusted or more extrovert than he actually was. This problem is not as great with such instruments used in the clinical situation as it is in the industrial situation. In the former case the client is more apt to be seeking help and thus cooperate in facilitating his diagnosis. The case of delinquents is a notable exception. It is possible, however, to introduce items or scoring patterns in order to detect a person who is deliberately misrepresenting. There are certain types of response which he is more inclined to make than is a person who is answering the items truthfully. The K scale developed for the Minnesota Multiphasic is an instance.

Projective methods. Interest in the personality inventory has been supplanted more recently by enthusiasm over projective techniques. The Rorshach ink blot test has received more attention than any of the other projective devices. There is considerable variation among clinical psychologists in their attitude toward this particular test. Some regard it as the last word and practically make a cult out of it while others consider it merely another good instrument in the hands of a competent clinical psychologist. In academic circles the trend seems to be to include it as part of the curriculum for a well trained clinical psychologist but not to train persons exclusively as technicians who would merely administer the test for a psychiatrist and score it in standard fashion without using their own clinical insight. Other projective tests have centered around pictures, for instance the Thematic Apperception Test which asks the client to tell stories about a series of pictures. Then there are the Blacky cartoons involving a dog and his relatives. Supposedly the client will project with less resistance when the picture involves animals rather than humans.

PSYCHOTHERAPY

In the late thirties clinical psychologists began to move into the field of therapy. To be sure there had been a little of this hitherto, but the psychologists had been regarded primarily as diagnosticians. In fact it was not until the second world war that they began to operate very extensively in the therapeutic field. This trend was precipitated by the large number of mental cases resulting from the war and the inability of medical personnel to cope with anything like the therapeutic case load.

Interview. The conventional clinical interview often serves somewhat of a therapeutic function. While it is initially directed toward diagnosis it often shades over into therapy and the line is difficult to draw. The client, for example, may in the course of the diagnostic interview get some things out of his system, thus obtaining some therapeutic release. Or, the interview may culminate in some direct advice which becomes obvious to the clinician.[7]

A trend in interviewing which has aroused considerable interest is the client-centered or non-directive type of interview. It was found that some clients could not accept advice very readily and it proved advisable to arrange it so that the client apparently worked out his own solution. Some of the conventional interviewers did this anyway without making a deliberate effort. But one school of interviewing made this non-directive aspect a little more specific.[8] The atmosphere was permissive, the client did most of the talking, and gradually achieved insight himself. The counselor was careful not to pass judgment such as indicating that something was "too bad". This method has received considerable criticism, perhaps because some enthusiasts followed it a bit blindly disregarding the desirability of using other techniques in certain individual cases. It is certainly advisable for a therapist to be familiar with different methods. Many practitioners feel that with a broad background the clinician should determine which method or which combination of methods would be most effective with a particular case.

Psychoanalysis is a field that cannot be overlooked in any review of psychotherapeutic methods. Freud and his followers, especially the psychiatrists, have been using some of these principles for many years. As some of these people, particularly since the war, have entered academic circles there has been more interest in psychoanalysis on the part of the clinical psychologists. The original method followed a free-association technique looking for complexes which often were centered around some instinctive core. Then these complexes were released or brought to the surface (catharsis). As the psychologists worked into this picture they gave somewhat less emphasis to instinct and even Freud, himself, later admitted that catharsis was not the whole story. Some psychologists find the techniques of interest because they make possible a much more extended observation of a client and he exhibits himself much more fully than he would in a laboratory situation. This may contribute somewhat to theory as well as helping the client.

A group of psychologists have pursued this technique still farther and attempted to apply learning theory to psychoanalysis.[9] At least they are able to apply it by analogy. Their notion is that neurotic habits and symptoms are learned and so are repressions. The emphasis is on drive, cue, response, and reinforcement. Transference has always been important in psychoanalysis. The client develops an emotionalized attitude similar to that toward his relatives. In other words, the therapist is made to resemble a relative and the emotion is transferred. In this way it is possible to determine how the client feels toward other people. Some of the recent psychoanalysts make transference a special case of generalized responses. The emotional tendencies generalize more strongly to the therapist because the avoidance tendencies are less strong. Then the therapist helps the client label them and thus gets them into the patient's reasoning and planning activities. This apparently is the current trend in psychoanalytic therapy but interestingly enough this point of view is also making some contributions to psychological theory.

Play therapy is another recent development. It is something like catharsis. The child "plays out" situations rather than "talking out". This is an especially good release for hostile and aggressive tendencies. It also makes for a good relation between the therapist and the client because the therapist tends to let the client be himself. If other types of therapy are then used, this good relationship carries over. The technique is limited for the most part to children. They are given indestructible and expendable materials which they can throw around or mess up without having too much feeling of actually doing wrong. Puppets serve quite effectively in this way. Very often these may represent members of the family or persons with whom the child has some conflict. The play may help him put his conflict into words and perhaps the therapist can then help him attain further insight into his problem.[10]

Group therapy. Clinical diagnosis and therapy are time consuming. Sometimes repeated interviews of an hour or so are necessary. It was quite natural, then, that after our experience with group tests versus individual tests we should explore the possibility of group therapy as compared with individual therapy. In practice such therapy may vary from what is essentially a lecture by the therapist to very spontaneous group discussion with the therapist inconspicuously keeping them on the subject or occasionally interpreting something. It received considerable impetus from military use. Military personnel who seemed to have adjustment problems were brought together in small groups and usually started off with a gripe session. However, with a little guidance the discussion went on from that point and got into individual problems in a helpful way. While the original motive was one of time saving, it develops that the group technique has some intrinsic advantages. For instance, a reserved patient finds that his anxieties are less unique than he had imagined and so he expresses them. Sometimes the group can suggest alternative solutions that might not occur to the individual himself. The older patients tend to reassure the newer ones. Excellent rapport frequently develops in the group. With the therapist playing an inconspicuous role there is little tendency for dependency upon him to develop as it sometimes does in an individual interview. This type of thing has been going on informally for a long time as when camp counselors chat with small groups and sometimes turn up adjustment problems. However, in the last decade or so there has been more formal recognition of group therapy.[11]

Psychodrama may be considered one of the techniques of group therapy which merits a bit of additional emphasis. The participants act out roles according to their needs and some skill is necessary in assigning roles. An individual who is suffering from too submissive an attitude may be given a domineering role and may develop some desirable habits in the process of playing that role.

Research. Clinical psychologists are engaged in numerous research projects designed to improve their techniques. In recent years they have shown increased research sophistication. For instance, in the study of personality traits there has been considerable use of factor analysis methods. Or, again, projective methods are not only merely taken for granted but are evaluated experimentally. Clinical psychologists these later years have a good statistical background and are competent in experimental design.

TYPE OF CLIENTS

The foregoing developments in diagnosis and therapy constitute the main trends in clinical psychology. However, a few less technical points may be mentioned. One is a change in the type of clients. In the old days it was almost exclusively children. Those who had trouble in school or difficulty in getting along with their parents were brought to the clinic. Included also were delinquent youngsters referred by courts or other agencies. Nowadays, especially in the post-war years, clinical psychologists have dealt more and more with adults. Much of this stemmed from mental cases arising in the war. With the increased veteran case load the psychologist was called upon and it became apparent that his techniques were applicable at the adult level. Many clinical psychologists now are operating in institutions which are primarily for adults such as veterans' facilities.

MAGNITUDE

Clinical psychology used to be one of the minor professional fields. In the first war, for instance, there was little beyond the development of a neurotic inventory for diagnostic purposes. In the second war, as mentioned above, numerous military cases required diagnosis and therapy. In 1946 the Veterans Administration wanted more clinical psychologists for its hospitals than there were competent clinical psychologists in the country. This need has not slackened. The V. A. now estimates that by 1960 it will need for its existing and authorized hospitals 825 clinical psychologists whereas it now has only 276. For its regional offices it will need 360 as against a present 124.[12] It has been subsidizing the training of clinical psychologists in recent years and the U. S. Public Health Service is doing likewise. The latter agency is interested also in the mental health of non-military cases. The magnitude of interest in clinical psychology may be further evidenced from the fact that the clinical division is the largest one in the American Psychological Association.

INTERPROFESSIONAL PROBLEMS

For the clinical psychologist the relations with other professions are perhaps a bit more critical than is the case with other professional psychologists. The obvious problem is getting along with medicine. There was a time when the medical profession looked askance at the clinical psychologists altogether. As indicated above the increased case load has changed this to some extent. In some institutions the clinical psychologist is getting along very well with the medical personnel and they are cooperating in joint programs. Private practice by clinical psychologists appears to arouse more opposition, at least in certain places. A few states do have certification for practicing psychologists and in other states efforts to secure legislation have been blocked. At present the clinical psychologist is doing more therapeutic work in institutions than in private practice. His future status is still problematical.

TESTIMONY

We now come to the third psychotechnology,—the application of psychology to legal and criminal problems. One application is to testimony or evidence because of the possibility that errors in testimony may result from causes which are essentially psychological in nature. Witnesses who previously observed something may have made some initial mistake in perception. Their attention at the time of observation may have been inadequate. They may have forgotten details in the period between the observation and the testimony and they may even make errors because the questions asked involve an undue amount of suggestion.

This is an aspect of legal psychology where there has been little progress. Münsterberg outlined some of the problems in 1912. There have been two books written by lawyers called "Legal Psychology" and one by the writer of the present review (1931). That is about all. To be sure there are many findings in the psychological literature that might contribute to this field of testimony. Experiments have demonstrated how some questions are loaded with suggestion and how children or young people are more suggestible than older persons. But this sort of thing has not worked into the legal structure specifically. If a psychologist reads case reports in the law library, he will find many rulings which obviously involve psychological principles without actually saying so. Rarely does he find a psychologist giving expert testimony about the reliability of evidence. Again, relatively few law schools have any psychology in their curriculum although in a few places courses on legal psychology are available to pre-law students. However, at the present time the American Bar Association has a committee which is exploring the desirability of some psychological instruction in law schools.

CRIME DETECTION

Association reaction. In the preceding section we were concerned with the witness who is presumably trying to tell the truth. There is the other type of witness or suspect who is trying to conceal the facts. There has always been considerable interest in determining from the suspect himself whether or not he was guilty. Inasmuch as lying and deception involve emotional components there have been efforts to tap some objective indication of these components. The earliest effort along this line was the association reaction technique in which stimulus words are given, the subject responds with the first associated word and the reaction time is recorded. Analysis of the reaction times for critical and control words and also the quality of responses sometimes yields results of interest. The procedure has been pretty much routine through the years with little in the way of new developments. Some of the early investigations brought out the importance of different parts of speech such as nouns and modifiers as introducing a constant error in the reaction time and there have been studies of the comparative merits of visual and auditory stimuli.

One development, however, should be noted, namely the manual response technique first suggested by Luria.[12a] The subject presses a key with his finger at the same time he speaks his response word. This key, however, operates pneumatically and the finger is clamped to it so that a continuous record of the position of the finger is secured on the polygraph tape. If the voice keys likewise record on the polygraph it is possible to note how well the subject synchronizes his two responses and to observe any qualitative variations in the manual pattern. The interpretation is for the most part qualitative although there have been efforts to measure such things as latent period. Luria, himself, used the technique in some criminal cases. It has not been employed to any extent in actual police practice inasmuch as they seldom use the association test anyway.

The conventional association reaction method has been used by psychologists here and there somewhat informally. Perhaps one unscrambles a local case on the campus but it is not written up in the literature. The writer knows of a number of persons who have done this sort of thing. However, the association reaction technique is not undergoing any major developments and is not used to any great extent in actual practice.

Blood pressure and breathing. The most widely used variables in the field of psychological crime detection are blood pressure and breathing with more emphasis on the former. Serious interest in blood pressure as a diagnostic device began in about 1914 with the work of Marston in Münsterberg's laboratory. Periodic readings were taken every minute or two in ordinary medical fashion while the subject was being questioned. While encouraging results were obtained, it became apparent that there was need for a continuous record because of what might happen emotionally in between readings. Such a record became possible by means of a device which put a moderate degree of pressure in a cuff on the arm and then stepped this pressure down to atmospheric pressure so it would operate an ordinary recording tambour. The adjustment of the apparatus was tricky and recording tracings on a long kymograph tape with lamp black and shellac was a nuisance. However, Larson in the police laboratory at Berkeley, California, did use this apparatus for some of the pioneer work in interpreting blood pressure tracings to indicate deception.[13]

A big development came with the advent of metal bellows for pneumatic recording to replace the old rubber tambours and with barographic pens to trace with ink on a moving paper tape. It was possible to make a bellows sufficiently sensitive to light changes in pressure in the cuff on the arm so that it could operate another metal bellows at atmospheric pressure which did the recording. With this improvement in recording devices more people began to use them. Among these were Keeler who originally understudied Larson and Darrow who approached the problem from a practical and a theoretical standpoint. The crime detection laboratory at Northwestern University incorporated these techniques in its program and presently various law enforcement agencies employed people who had received training at such laboratories. Instrument makers sensed a market and developed standard units.

While the instruments were being perfected the methods of interrogation became somewhat standardized.[14] We always use control questions on which it is known that the suspect will tell the truth as well as critical questions about the crime. Categorical questions or at least those in which talking is minimized are standard practice. The interpretation of the polygraph tracing also follows a somewhat uniform pattern. On each question the blood pressure rises slightly and then drops again after a few seconds but with deception the rise is apt to be a little higher and a little longer. An examining technique which is sometimes applicable is the peak-of-tension test. The suspect is confronted with a series of articles, one of which resembles the one that he may have stolen and the examiner goes down the line asking him about each one. If he is guilty and sees the crucial one coming, he is apt to build up tension gradually until he passes the crucial item.

With reference to breathing there have been no outstanding developments although the breathing is almost always recorded simultaneously with the blood pressure. There have been research indications that the inspiration-expiration ratio might be diagnostic. However, it is necessary to secure breathing records for several breaths before and after each answer and then make very detailed measurements of the tracings. Few practical workers have bothered with this. The usual interpretation of the tracing is merely qualitative although sometimes one will note something as specific as an immediate repression of breathing on a crucial question when lying or an increased depth of breathing with a latent period of fifteen or twenty seconds after the question. The breathing and blood pressure tracings are the ones most frequently used by agencies employing these psychological techniques in a large way.

Electrodermal. There has been moderate interest in the electro-dermal response as a method of crime detection. At least it occurs with emotional stimuli. Originally it was difficult to get an actual tracing on a polygraph, but recording galvanometers are now available. In class-room demonstrations it has been common practice to connect a subject through an appropriate circuit to a meter which would deflect as the skin conductance changed. It was simple enough to demonstrate such deflection when the subject was startled or embarrassed. This led to the development of devices for actual crime detection in which deflection of a meter was used rather than a continuous graphic record of conductance. There is some attempt to determine the normal deflection on the control questions and then interpret greater deflection on critical questions as indicating deception. Some of those who are handling such units commercially report successful use. The writer knows of at least one person using a graphic record who is enthusiastic about it. On the other hand, there has been some unfavorable criticism of the electro-dermal relative to the blood pressure-breathing technique. Darrow has tried them simultaneously and concluded that the blood pressure was more sensitive to emotions of ideational origin such as those involved in deception, whereas the electro-dermal was more responsive to emotions of sensory origin such as startle. At the Northwestern laboratory where both had been tried carefully the judgment was distinctly in favor of the blood pressure. The controversy has not been resolved at the moment and may even be clouded a bit by the interests of instrument makers. At any rate, in actual practice the blood pressure-breathing technique is much more frequent.[15]

These polygraph techniques are quite widely used. Some 200,000 persons have been examined in the last 20 years. Approximately 100 police departments use such examinations. Several departments of the Federal Government do likewise. Plants of the Atomic Energy Commission where security is highly essential examine their critical employees periodically with the polygraph. Military units employ these methods in the interrogation of prisoners. The methods are used in the employment offices of financial agencies in order to predict how good a financial risk an applicant may be.

Misuse. Along with the increased use of polygraph methods there comes the danger of incompetent operators. Some of the instrument makers, to be sure, do provide a modicum of training in the use of their instrument. Also some public agencies operate a "school" for training operators. In addition to incompetence there is sometimes an unfortunate orientation of the examiner toward the securing of a confession rather than an objective scientific determination of the facts. It is impossible to tell how wide-spread this tendency may be. Much depends upon the background of the examiner. If he came up through a scientific laboratory of some sort the chances are that his attitude will be more nearly what it should be. Suppose someone is employed as a chemist in a crime laboratory but also doubles in operating the polygraph. With his scientific background he can probably be counted on to take a wholesome scientific attitude toward the polygraph.

Polygraph as evidence. There has been some interest in the use of the polygraph in the field of evidence. A defendant is examined by a polygraph expert who concludes that the defendant is innocent. Defense counsel then attempts to introduce the expert to testify accordingly. For the most part courts are still following a 1923 precedent which is unfavorable to the admission of such expert testimony. One trend, however, is of some interest. In Wisconsin in a case of murder resulting from a hold-up, counsel for both sides agreed in advance to have the defendants examined at an appropriate laboratory and agreed to waive any question of admissibility of the evidence. The expert came to a quite definite conclusion as to who drove the car and who did the shooting and testified accordingly. This evidence went to the jury along with the other evidence. Under these circumstances the admission of the expert's testimony would be much more defensible from a scientific standpoint. The expert is not retained by either party and in those marginal decisions which sometimes occur he would not be influenced by knowledge of who was paying the fee. Even the most impartial expert sometimes finds it difficult to make these marginal decisions under the usual circumstances. An interesting procedure has been adopted by a few states whereby if a case necessitates expert testimony prosecution and defense each pay half the cost of the expert and the latter is selected by the court. This arrangement could well cover the polygraph expert. However, it is probable that the greatest usefulness of this technique will always be as an "investigation aid". For instance, if a crime has been committed and several suspects are under consideration, it is possible by these methods to delimit the problem quite expeditiously and determine which is the most likely suspect. Then efforts can be concentrated on that person for the time being, at least, rather than devoting unnecessary time to all suspects. These techniques have vindicated themselves in this investigation aid function time and again.[16]

DELINQUENCY

The modern attitude toward delinquents stresses individual differences,—why he slipped and what we should do to him. Naturally psychology has a stake in this. Through the years there have been many studies of samples of delinquents with intelligence tests, personality measurements, and clinical examinations. Other scientists have explored such factors as home conditions and economic status. Originally there were two sharply defined points of view. One school attributed delinquency primarily to feeblemindedness or mental disorder which, in turn, were hereditary. The other school explained everything in terms of environment. The present trend is to recognize that nobody has all the answers and that even if those who stress heredity and those who stress environment do their utmost to reduce delinquency their joint efforts will still be inadequate. Current practice is to find out what actually is involved in the individual delinquent case and then let the chips fall where they may. This leads to a variety of preventive efforts. Social agencies are taking steps to provide better living conditions, recreational facilities, and security in general. The psychologists promote mental hygiene and personality adjustment. Courts now refer many cases to appropriate agencies for psychological study and recommendation. Psychologists are employed in counseling capacity in institutions for the delinquent. Some of this takes the form of vocational guidance looking toward their subsequent vocational adjustment when they leave the Big House. Sometimes it is directed toward attitudes and emotional outlets.

A further aspect of individualization in criminology is adjusting the punishment to the individual delinquent. The parole system implements this aspect. A basic problem is predicting actual success on parole. Statistical studies have been made of different variables that are related to keeping out of trouble. Regression equations are being developed in which the different variables are weighted to predict parole success with a practical degree of validity.

TRADEMARKS

Trademark or trade name infringement often involves psychological considerations. The basic mechanism is confusion in recognition. A customer goes into a store looking for Sozodont tooth paste and comes out with Kalodont. The original manufacturer may take legal steps to prevent the competitor from using the confusingly similar trade name. Basically the question is the extent to which the "unwary purchaser" looking for a brand will erroneously recognize another as the one he had in mind. If the psychologist is consulted, he conducts an experiment on recognition in which subjects are given a series of names containing, for instance, the name of the plaintiff followed by a second series of names which contain that of the defendant. The subjects go through the second list indicating which names were in the first list. The percent who make mistakes on the alleged infringing name may be noted and compared with some over-all figure which reflects the general difficulty of the experimental conditions and the frequency of mistakes that are to be expected just by chance. Initial studies along this line were reported many years ago. Various psychologists have handled similar projects in subsequent years. Little has been reported in the literature but the writer knows of a number of recent cases of expert testimony based on such experiments.

APTITUDE TESTING

The earliest activities of industrial psychologists dealt with the measurement of aptitudes in order to predict vocational criteria. Münsterberg's study of motormen was the classical instance. These efforts received considerable impetus in the first war with the Alpha and Beta group intelligence tests, and special tests for aviators and gun pointers. This field of aptitudes occupied most of the attention of industrial psychologists in this country during the inter-bellum years. In Europe, to be sure, there was some consideration of industrial efficiency, fatigue, monotony, and ventilation. Such problems over here were handled for the most part by engineers.

Probability of success. A few technical developments in this field of aptitudes may be mentioned. The first step was better procedures for validating tests. Instead of determining average test scores for two extreme criterion groups the entire distribution was used and correlation coefficients between test scores and criterion computed. Partial correlation came into use for weighting the predictors in a regression equation and thus improving over-all validity. Then various methods were devised to make more convenient the interpretation of an applicant's test score in terms of probability of success in the job. A typical table makes possible interpretation like the following. If a "good" punchpress operator is defined as one who is in the top thirty percent of the present employees in that job and we have a validity of .60 for a test and decide to select, say, the top fifty percent of the applicants, then what proportion of these applicants will be "good" in the sense defined above?

Factor analysis is a recent development that has made some contribution to aptitude testing. By intercorrelating the tests and making appropriate analysis it is possible to get some notion as to what underlying factors the tests actually are measuring. Then in revising the tests or developing others for the same purpose it is possible to aim them more directly at these basic factors. This should result in a somewhat shorter battery of tests and thus save time and cost in the employment procedure. The goal is tests which are factorially pure. This approach is especially important if we are hoping to use the same group of tests to predict various criteria, with different weightings of course. If our concern is merely a battery of tests for a single job and we have no intentions beyond that one job, then an ordinary regression equation may suffice.

New tests. Many new tests have been developed. In some military projects it has been possible to develop quite complicated instruments with which the subject works continuously at a series of problems. Some of these tests have been more satisfactory than those developed in the typical industry where research time and equipment construction cost must be limited. Another noteworthy development is in personality tests. We have long been aware of our inability to measure such things as tact, enthusiasm, or getting along with people. While some personality tests of the inventory type have been fairly satisfactory in clinical situations they have not worked out well for industry. If an applicant is called upon to evaluate himself, he will attempt to do it in such a way as to get the job rather than to state how he actually feels about things. A solution for this difficulty that has shown considerable promise is the forced-choice test. Here the person has to choose from alternatives the one which best describes him. The alternatives have previously been selected experimentally so that they will have about equal preference value for a subject but will have discrimination value against some personality criterion. The subject cannot determine which alternative would be most apt to get him the job and so marks the test more or less truthfully. The expert who knows the "key", however, can derive the personality score.

Some attention has been devoted to predictors other than tests. The Life Insurance Agency Management Association, for example, has sponsored extensive research upon items of personal information (biographical) which might correlate with a selling criterion. These items are weighted in a regression equation much like tests. Considerable reliance is sometimes placed on a rating scale for evaluating the applicant's personality. But instances have been encountered in which the rater actually wished to bias the results, that is to "control" his ratings. An instance would be an officer who wished to keep a subordinate in his unit or wished to get rid of him. To counteract this difficulty the forced-choice technique has been adapted to rating scales and the rater is called upon to state which of the two alternatives best describes the individual although they are of such a nature that the rater cannot tell which is the more favorable.

BASIS OF JUDGMENT

The criterion has always been a fundamental consideration in personnel psychology because tests are selected and modified in order to predict it. One recent development has been to use more than one criterion for a given job. In clothing manufacture it proved desirable to have one criterion based on speed and one on accuracy because some of their products were turned out rapidly and of moderate quality while others were high quality jobs.

Then there has been some development of new types of criteria. The nominating technique was developed originally in military groups. Air force pilots are asked to select from among their fellow pilots the one whom they would most like to have flying wing-on. Similarly, minor executives select the man they would rather have working at the next desk. Another technique is the critical incidents method. This involves describing incidents which were especially important or significant in the occupation. Air force personnel, for example, are asked to describe incidents which nearly involved a crash. Or workmen describe what they consider mistakes on the part of their supervisors. This is a bit like the procedure sometimes used in rating scales where the rater is required to justify his ratings by reporting some instance in support of it. This critical incidents technique is also used in job analysis; likewise in machine design in order to improve instruments by noting critical errors that have been made in reading them.

Differential prediction. A final development in the field of aptitude testing has not been fully perfected as yet but is worth mentioning. It is termed differential prediction. The usual procedure has been to consider one applicant at a time and, if there is more than one job available for him, predict his chances of success in the different jobs and employ him for the one where he has the highest probability of success. However, the problem really is more complicated especially if we have a number of applicants with different probabilities of success in the different jobs. Moreover, some jobs may be more important than others for the entire enterprise. For job *A* it may be very urgent to get a person who has a very high probability of success whereas in job *B* a person with only mediocre probability of success might be reasonably satisfactory from the overall standpoint. The ideal thing would be to employ these applicants in the various jobs in such a way as to promote the maximum overall efficiency of the entire organization. This becomes quite complicated statistically and at the present time we are merely in process of working out appropriate methods.[17]

Engineering Psychology

The last decade has shown an interesting development in the field of engineering psychology, otherwise called applied experimental psychology.[18] Here the orientation is not so much to fit the man to the machine but rather to fit the machine to the man. It gets into such considerations as design of machinery or equipment. Originally there was some interest in this field as one minor phase of the psychology of industrial efficiency but now it has developed into a very considerable field in its own right. It is possible to approach problems of machine design by determining what portion of the error in the operation may be in the machine, what part in the man, and what part in the interactions between the two.

Display systems. A major type of study in this field deals with display of information. With visual information an instance would be the legibility of signs as dependent on the width of strokes in the letters. Instrument scales constitute another field where considerable study has been made. The kind of marks on a dial make a big difference in the accuracy with which the dial may be read. Or, again, the relation between the two hands on an altimeter and what each one registers may be quite significant. There are problems concerning the relation between the direction in which a knob turns and the direction in which an indicator moves. Actually most of us have certain stereotyped notions about this and anything which violates our stereotype tends to lower efficiency. In the field of auditory display we have such problems as signal-to-noise ratio. In the tactual field there have been studies of the shapes of knobs which can readily be discriminated by touch without looking at them.

Control systems. Coordinate with problems of display are those which involve designing control systems. If the operator is turning some kind of a dial in order to track a moving target, his accuracy depends on the amount of friction in the control. There are similar problems in gear ratios, such as the optimal relation between the extent of movement of the control and the corresponding movement of the display. Workers in this field are beginning to write equations for motor behavior somewhat analogous to equations for servo systems involving input, output, and feedback. The pursuit of these analogies is leading to some interesting theoretical considerations likewise.

TRAINING

There is quite a bit of interest in training on the part of industrial psychologists. In fact, there is enough material coming out now to warrant the publication of Industrial Training Abstracts. Some of the articles deal with the training of special groups such as apprentices, sales people, and especially foremen (*infra*). There has been some investigation of the possibility of predicting trainability as contrasted with predicting actual production on the job. There are studies of the effect of knowledge of progress on the training program and the comparative merits of short range and long range goals for the learner. Special techniques in training have been explored. These include conference methods and role playing for certain types of trainees such as sales people. Teaching aids similar to those used in schools are being taken over by the industrial training people.

SOCIAL EMPHASIS

Measurement of morale. A conspicuous trend in industrial psychology is the increased emphasis on the social aspect. In the old days it was largely a matter of efficiency as influenced by work methods and motivation. Now we are aware that a contented employee is more apt to be an efficient one quite apart from any other desirable results. Industry itself is aware of this fact and frequently there is a vice president whose entire job is industrial relations. One of the first considerations in this connection is the measurement of morale. Attitude scales have been taken over from other social fields where the techniques were originally developed. Executed anonymously, they can indicate the general morale level of a group of workers. Interviews also are used for this purpose although good rapport and the workers' confidence are necessary if worth-while information is to be secured. The interview may also explore specific sources of discontent as well as getting at overall morale level. Another measurement technique that has been used in a limited way is to get the employees to write essays in connection with a contest in which they describe their jobs, favorably or otherwise. Naturally in the hope of winning a prize most of them try to say nice things about the job but it is possible to analyze the results in terms of conspicuous omissions.

Some general contributions of the psychologist to industrial relations may be mentioned. One such is countering the over-emphasis on financial incentives. There are many other sources of satisfaction or dissatisfaction,—recognition of accomplishment, opportunities for self-expression, friendly inter-personal relations with peers or with supervisors, annoyances in the working conditions. It is becoming obvious, too, that work satisfaction is related to overall life satisfaction. The industrial psychologist finds himself dealing with a whole man and not with one who becomes a different personality when he punches the time-clock in the morning.

Supervision. First line supervision is a critical spot in industrial morale. This point came out dramatically in the now classical Hawthorne studies of the Western Electric where drastic changes in working conditions and procedure could be introduced with no unfavorable effects on production when the group was under a very fine type of supervisor.[19] Awareness of the importance of supervision has led to much more careful attention to foreman training programs. Such programs frequently include material on how to teach and how to handle people and get along with them. In the second war there was a good deal of this type of training given to supervisors in the war industries. There were concise programs such as JIT (job instructor training) and JRT (job relations training). Even the engineering science management war training (ESMWT) program included some of this material. It has reached the point now where some organizations which have a lot of plants scattered around the country maintain a central school for the training of supervisors. An essential part of the curriculum is human relations and the program includes case studies and role playing.

Leadership. Another phase of this social emphasis is recent research on leadership. We used to be interested primarily in the traits of the leader but now we are more concerned with his actual behavior. We find out what he does, how much time he spends in each kind of activity and the people with whom he spends his time. We determine the extent of his responsibility and authority or how far he delegates authority.[20] We are finding out what constitutes an effective group and we are encouraging groups to do some self-evaluation. This research will eventually lead to a higher type of leadership on the part of industrial supervisors among others. In fact some current research is using such supervisors as experimental subjects.

MARKETING

Business psychology gives some consideration to problems of marketing. Early interest dealt with the effectiveness of different kinds of copy or the factors which tended to catch attention such as size or color. A notable recent trend is the increased emphasis on techniques of measurement. Some of this measurement is done for research purposes and some for actual operation of the advertising program. Psychology has contributed considerably to this field although not all the work is done by psychologists. Some professional psychologists are employed full time by advertising agencies and one of the recent books on advertising psychology is written by two such persons.[21]

These efforts at measuring the impact of advertising take several directions. One type deals with opinion rating. This is largely a matter of getting people to look at advertising copy and indicate the extent to which it might induce them to purchase something. This sometimes takes the form of a consumer jury, that is, a group of people who are called upon periodically, and paid a small fee for their trouble, to pass judgment on forthcoming advertisements or specific appeals.

A second type of measurement involves what might be called concurrent methods. The best known of these is the telephone co-incidental method. Thousands of people are called every day and inquiry made as to the radio program to which they are listening at the time. This procedure is carried one step further in the mechanical devices which may be installed in a radio or television receiver and which will record on a moving tape for a period of a week or more just when the set was on and the frequency to which it was tuned. Another concurrent method is the diary of purchases which people may be induced to keep. They may be given a free basket of groceries every so often for filling out the schedule which includes everything they have bought.

A third method is a recall test in which the person is merely asked what advertisements or what radio programs he recalls having seen recently or he may be asked to what programs he listened yesterday or who is the sponsor of a specified program. A fourth possibility is recognition tests. The most frequent instance of this is the technique in which an interviewer goes through a magazine quickly with a respondent and the latter indicates which pages he remembers having seen. Passing mention might also be made of tabulating inquiries in response to advertisements and of actual sales records although these do not have any particularly unique psychological slant.

Ethics

With psychology now taking the form of a profession as well as a science and with many psychologists helping people in various practical problems it is natural that ethical considerations should arise just as in many of the other professions. There have been noteworthy efforts of the American Psychological Association or of local groups of psychologists to attempt to insure that those rendering psychological services are qualified to do so and conform to ethical principles. There is no nation-wide legislation along this line but in some states the psychologists have succeeded in getting legislation for licensing or otherwise certifying psychologists who practice there. In such instances it is possible to set adequate standards in the way of training and to keep the pseudo-scientists out. Only a few states have such arrangements, however, at the present time.

Meanwhile the American Psychological Association is policing its own membership. It has established the American Board of Examiners in Professional Psychology which, on request, considers a person's record and gives him various examinations and then if he qualifies issues him a Diploma. As the public becomes educated to the significance of this diploma practitioners lacking it will probably have difficulty in securing clients.

The Association has also formulated a code of ethics which it hopes the membership will observe.[22] This deals with such things as client-relationships, the client's welfare, confidential relations with clients, fees, referrals, and discretion in the way the psychologist informs the public of available services. There is also mention of ethical standards in research, in reporting, in popular writing and in relationships with colleagues. There will always be some pseudo-scientists and occasionally a psychologist who ought to know better goes unduly "commercial" but nearly all of us who are using psychology professionally are keeping our activities on a commendable ethical plane.

FOOTNOTES

[1] Pressey, S. L., *Educational Acceleration*. Bureau of Educational Research Monograph, No. 31, Ohio State University, 1949.

[2] *Bridging the Gap Between School and College*. Fund for the Advancement of Education. New York, 1953, pp. 127.

[3] Fund for the Advancement of Education. *Ibid.*

[4] Robinson, F. P. *Effective Study*. New York, Harper's, 1946, pp. 262.

[5] Lewin, K., Lippit, R., and Escalona, S. K. *Studies in Topological and Vector Psychology*. University of Iowa Studies in Child Welfare, 1940, 16, No. 3.

[6] For a general reference on this section see, Pressey, S. L. and Robinson, F. P. *Psychology and the New Education*. New York, Harper's, 1944, pp. 654.

[7] For a general review of psychotherapy see: Snyder, W. U. Present Status of Psychotherapeutic Counseling. *Psychol. Bull.*, 1947, *44*, 297-369.

[8] Rogers, C. R. *Counseling and Psychotherapy; Newer Concepts in Practice*. Boston, Houghton-Mifflin, 1942, pp. 450.

[9] Dollard, John and Miller, Neal E. *Personality and Psychotherapy*. New York, McGraw-Hill, 1950, pp. 488.

[10] Axline, V. M. *Play Therapy*. Boston, Houghton-Mifflin, 1947, pp. 451.

[11] Anon. *Group Psychotherapy*: a Symposium. New York, Beacon House, 1945.

[12] *American Psychologist*, 1953, *8*, 263.

[12a] Burtt, H. E. Motor Concomitants of the Association Reaction. *Journal of Experimental Psychology*, 1936, *19*, 51-63.

[13] Larson, J. A. *Lying and its Detection*. University of Chicago Press, 1932, pp. 453.

[14] Inbau, F. E. *Lie Detection and Criminal Interrogation*. Baltimore, Williams and Wilkins, 1942, pp. 142.

[15] For discussions pro and con see: Trovillo, P. V. A History of Lie Detection. *Journal of Criminal Law*, 1939, *29*, 848-881 and *30*, 104-119. MacNitt, R. D. In Defense of the Electro-Dermal Response and Cardiac Amplitude as Measures of Deception. *Journal of Criminal Law*, 1942, *33*, 266-275.

[16] For a review of present status see: The Polygraphic Truth Test. A Symposium. *Tennessee Law Review*, 1953, *22*, 1-64.

[17] Thorndike, E. L. The Problem of Classification of Personnel. *Psychometrika*, 1950, *15*, 215-235.

[18] Fitts, P. M. Engineering Psychology and Equipment Design. In Stevens, S. S. *Handbook of Experimental Psychology.* New York, Wiley, 1951, pp. 1287-1340.

[19] Roethlisberger, F. J. and Dickson, W. J. *Management and the Worker.* Harvard University Press, 1939, pp. 615.

[20] Shartle, C. L. Leadership and Executive Performance. *Personnel,* March, 1949, pp. 11.

[21] Lucas, D. B. and Britt, S. H. *Advertising Psychology and Research.* New York, McGraw-Hill, 1950, pp. 765.

[22] American Psychological Association. *Ethical Standards of Psychologists.* 1953, pp. 171.

BIBLIOGRAPHY

Berrien, F. K. *Practical Psychology*, New York, Macmillan, 1952, pp. 640.
Bingham, W. V. *Aptitudes and Aptitude Testing,* New York, Harper's, 1937, pp. 390.
Burtt, H. E. *Applied Psychology,* New York, Prentice-Hall, 1948, pp. 821, abridged edition 1952, pp. 465.
Burtt, H. E. *Legal Psychology, New York,* Prentice-Hall, 1931, pp. 467.
Chapanis, A., Garner, W. R. and Morgan, C. T. *Applied Experimental Psychology,* New York, Wiley, 1949, pp. 434.
Harrell, T. W. *Industrial Psychology,* New York, Rinehart, 1949, pp. 462.
Hepner, H. W. *Psychology Applied to Life and Work,* New York, Prentice-Hall, 1941, pp. 770.
Inbau, F. E. *Lie Detection and Criminal Interrogation,* Baltimore, Williams and Wilkins, 1942, pp. 142.
Louttit, C. M. *Clinical Psychology of Children's Behavior Problems,* New York, Harper's, 1947, pp. 661.
Lucas, D. B. and Britt, S. H. *Advertising Psychology and Research,* New York, McGraw-Hill, 1950, pp. 765.
Pressey, S. L. and Robinson, F. P. *Psychology and the New Education,* New York, Harper's, 1944, pp. 654.
Roethlisberger, F. J. and Dickson, W. J. *Management and the Worker,* Cambridge, Mass., Harvard University Press, 1939, pp. 615.

Chapter XVIII

MILITARY PSYCHOLOGY*

Charles W. Hill, Ph.D.
Colonel, Department of the Army, U.S.A.

* This manuscript was reviewed by the following military psychologists whose helpful comments and criticisms are greatly appreciated by the author: Dr. M. P. Crawford, Human Resources Research Office, George Washington University; Dr. L. E. Baker, Office of the Assistant Chief of Staff, G-1, Department of the Army; Dr. Glen Finch, Human Factors Division, Directorate of Research and Development, Department of the Air Force; Dr. H. E. Page and Dr. D. D. Smith, Office of Naval Research, Department of the Navy. This does not relieve the author of any responsibility for all statements contained herein, nor does it mean that these persons or their agencies endorse the contents of this chapter. The author is also indebted to Captains J. B. Bennet, Jr. and L. S. Brice, Office of the Assistant Chief of Staff, G-1, Department of the Army, for their untiring efforts in the collection of the bibliographical material.

EDITORIAL NOTE

This is probably the first time that a chapter on military psychology is included in a general psychological volume of this sort. The editor has no particular taste for this regrettably growing branch, and wonders what the American pioneers of scientific psychology would have thought about dignifying such a growth, e.g., James with his "Moral Substitute for War", Titchener with his aversion for even a harmless applied psychology. Nevertheless, since we are living under conditions which are war-seared and war-fringed, and since preparations and counter-preparations are being made on a large and even terrifying scale, and as many psychologists have been engaged in national defence, it is only reasonable to indicate how the science has affected and has been affected by the two world wars, and how it is being employed at the moment in the various arms of the war machine.

Colonel Charles W. Hill who has received his Ph.D. in experimental psychology at Vanderbilt University, after obtaining his bachelor's degree from the U. S. Military Academy, is certainly well qualified to present the over-all picture. He served in the Coast Artillery Corps in the United States, in the Philippines prior to 1940; and with anti-aircraft artillery in the South Pacific, during World War II. From 1951 to 1954, he was on duty in the Pentagon as Chief of the Human Relations and Research Branch, Office of the Assistant Chief of Staff, G-1, Department of the Army. He is currently serving as G-1, V Corps in Germany.

It is evident that Colonel Hill's account is both comprehensive and possibly the most informative we have yet had from a psychological angle. It may be said that this branch did not exist before the first World War, and once initiated, it has made more rapid strides than any other—a sad commentary on our times.

PRESENT-DAY PSYCHOLOGY

INTRODUCTION

Military psychology, as a category of scientific activity, contains all the traditional academic sub-fields of the science of psychology which contribute to the solution of military problems. It is an applied category, somewhat analogous to industrial or educational psychology, but broader than any other such applied field in its inclusion of learning, perception, motivation, etc. A noted psychologist, with many years of experience in the military situation, has recently stated that "it would be difficult to find a topic in general psychology which, in some clear relation or other, does not have a bearing on military psychology".[19] Many of the problems which concern the military psychologist are shared in common with one or more of the other applied fields, while many more are unique to the military situation.

The military services are primarily interested in obtaining the most efficient performance from the maximum number of individuals made available to them. The objectives of military psychology may therefore be stated generally as follows: (1) to provide screening instruments and techniques that will discriminate between those who can be utilized in some military capacity and those who cannot; (2) to provide classification instruments and techniques that will sort out those selected into the general job areas most suitable to each one's abilities and capabilities; (3) to develop training methods and devices that will expedite the learning process as the capabilities are transformed into military abilities; (4) to develop management methods and techniques that will assist the commander in providing the necessary leadership, in maintaining high motivation and morale, and in welding assemblages of individuals into unified, cohesive groups; and (5) to insure that all weapons, equipment, and supplies are designed with the capabilities and limitations of the average operator and maintenance man in mind. A more detailed account of these "military objective" categories may be found in the address referred to in the introductory paragraph.[19]

Each of the three military services has a different set of problems within the five areas listed above, although there will usually be a common nucleus which will be shared by all. The Army, Navy, and Air Force, therefore, have each developed an organization for psychological research peculiar to its own requirements. Coordination among the services is maintained by the Office of the Secretary of Defense by means of continuous exchange of information and the direction of joint projects.

Once problems have been identified and requirements for research officially stated, the research project itself may be conducted by an in-service agency or by contract with a civilian university or private research organization. This distinction is usually based upon the degree to which the military situation must be involved in the study. Projects which may be taken off into the laboratory, as it were, are appropriately assigned to civilian contractors; while those which involve "troops in the field" are more efficiently conducted by the in-service researchers. This is not a complete dichotomy, however. There are a number of factors which may operate to make some military-situation studies quite feasible for certain contractors; and conversely, military research agencies may often be found conducting their own laboratory-type projects with ample justification.

The methodology, results, and conclusions of completed research projects are published by each military research agency in its own series of reports. These reports are distributed to all interested agencies both within and without the Department of Defense. They are also placed on file in a central office known as the Armed Services Technical Information Agency, or ASTIA. In addition, the individual research scientists, who participated in a particular project, may write a paper based upon that study and submit it to one of the professional journals. Such a paper is a personal product of the psychologists concerned and is handled by the journal editor in the usual manner.

Much of the research sponsored by the military services, especially those studies which have produced important results, has been published in the professional journals as described above. This is probably more true of the laboratory-type than of the field-type research. It is believed that these journal articles will be covered in the other chapters under their appropriate academic categories. This chapter, therefore, will focus its attention upon those studies with a real military flavor, that were conducted in the military situation employing military subjects. Such a restriction is further justified by the practical necessity for covering the vast amount of research sponsored by the three services within the allotted space of this chapter.

A further curtailment of the field of military psychology is imposed upon this chapter by considerations of security. It is obvious that a certain amount of military research, even in the science of psychology, is of a classified nature and cannot be reported here.

SELECTION

This section will be devoted to recent efforts of the military psychologist to provide the military operator with tests and techniques that will indicate which men can be made into good soldiers, sailors, and airmen, and which will become a liability. In this endeavor the current tendency is toward the principle of "screening out" or the rejection of only those for whom there is little or no hope of success. This is in contrast to a "skimming the cream" policy, which has been influential in the past, under which all doubtful cases would be treated on the "safe" side of rejection. This new philosophy of making the most out of the maximum number may be found quite clearly expressed in the report on a recent symposium concerned with the selection of military manpower.[10] It should not be assumed, however, that all the criteria presently being used for selection purposes are in complete agreement with this new trend.

The two principal criteria for selection into the armed services are general intelligence and physical fitness. The measurement of general intelligence was pioneered in the military situation with the development of the old Army Alpha in World War I. Since that time, continuous work has been devoted to this type of instrument thereby producing a succession of new and improved forms. All of these variants have been objective, paper-and-pencil tests attempting to get beneath the superficial layers of achievement and culture.[39]

Recent efforts have been directed toward (1) the improvement of individual items (2) the sharpening of sensitivity around the cutting-score, (3) the extension of adequate discrimination throughout the range, and (4) the broadening of the culture-content of the items. Two new alternative forms of the AFQT* (3 and 4) have been produced which embody verbal analogies, arithmetic reasoning, mechanical and spatial relations. With the introduction of these tests into the operational situation, renewed activity will begin with a view toward having two more forms ready by 1955 or 1956.

The Armed Forces have a motivational problem to contend with that does not occur in other screening situations. When participation is not entirely voluntary, there will always be a certain number of "applicants" who will not respond whole-heartedly to the call of duty and country. Low scores obtained by such individuals will be measures of performance only, with greater than normal discrepancies between these scores and the capabilities they represent. Special scoring keys have been developed for the AFQTs which will detect such discrepancies when they exist.[7] These keys are based upon empirical differences in test item responses of two groups, one of low mental ability which was highly motivated to pass, and the other of normal ability which was deliberately attempting to fail. Exploratory work is proceeding with various kinds of items that will permit the negatively motivated to express themselves in a different manner from those of low intelligence. These items, if successful, would be used in special tests in conjunction with the AFQTs.

Another line of research endeavor in the armed services is directed toward the problem of selecting individuals who have not been exposed to the normal cultural environment of the U. S. Non-verbal or semantic tests are being developed in order to avoid the achievement aspects of practically all other tests of

* Armed Forces Qualifications Test.

general intelligence.[47] These new tests employ pictures and symbols, and the testees are measured upon their ability to manage and interpret this abstract material.

In line with the philosophy of utilizing the maximum number and kinds of personnel, a considerable amount of research is directed toward the so-called marginal personnel. The principal questions in this area have to do with what costs are incurred when standards of acceptance are lowered along the several dimensions of usefulness, such as mental ability, emotional stability, physical fitness, etc. The analysis of World War II records has been used extensively to find answers to these questions. In general, such analyses have found that marginal personnel did just about as well as their "normal" brethren in terms of promotions, awards, disciplinary actions, hospitalizations, etc. A study of illiterates showed them to be below average on all such criteria, but the differences were small.[21] This study also produced several techniques for predicting those illiterates who would be most likely to succeed in training and in later performance on the job. The Verbal-Arithmetic subtest of the AFQT and a special Non-language Qualification Test have both been found to be quite useful in determining which illiterates can perform successfully in the military situation with or without special literacy training.[6] The other side of the coin has also been presented through research which has attempted to include the various "cost" variables that operate to the disadvantage of utilizing marginal personnel. One such series of studies has shown that there is a definite increase in lost time and administrative expense as acceptance standards are lowered along the various scales listed above.[24]

The military psychologist working in this selection area is the test and measurement psychologist or psychometrician. This kind of research is the oldest and most accepted of all psychological research in the armed services. The meaningfulness of discriminations along the dimension of general intelligence is disputed by few in military circles. In fact, it could be argued that this acceptance has gone too far, to the detriment of other factors. The practical success of these discriminations, however, has largely been responsible for the entrée of psychologists into other military operational areas where indifferent toleration is gradually giving way to problem-solved satisfaction.

CLASSIFICATION

The next major problem encountered by the military psychologist is that of getting the various individuals, who are selected for the armed forces, most appropriately located in terms of their abilities and potentialities. The principal dimensions currently employed in this task are aptitudes and physical profiles. The general philosophy of the military operator in regard to classification is that all personnel should be "fighters" first and foremost, and that technical specialization is of secondary importance. This concept has been gradually changing with the realization that there may be an inverse relationship between technical and fighting abilities in some instances. In view of the multiplicity and diversity of military jobs, however, it is doubtful that fungibility will ever cease to be an important requirement.

A number of aptitude tests have been developed involving such factors as reading, arithmetic, pattern analysis, mechanics, electrical information, clerical speed, and radio and automotive information. These tests have been organized into batteries with aptitude areas, composed of two or three tests each, which give differential predictions among the various military occupations and job families.[14, 38] Validation studies are continuously in progress designed to establish the relationships between the various test areas and technical school success.[58] Job performance validities have varied from just under .30 (fire control and food inspection) up to just over .50 (radio repair, cartography, and preventive medicine).[18]

The recent conflict in Korea provided the opportunity to check the aptitude areas against success in combat. For the foot soldier, the results were not too encouraging.[48] The aptitude area which is currently used for assigning men to the

Infantry produced *r*s of only .16 to .21. This area involves arithmetic reasoning and pattern analysis. Slightly better results (*r*s = .18 and .24) were obtained from a combination of the best three tests (arithmetic reasoning, mechanical aptitude, and radio code) which do not presently constitute an aptitude area.

Looking forward to the time when psychological classification will be desired along additional dimensions, the military psychologists are engaged in numerous studies designed to establish the predictive ability of other human factors. A considerable amount of exploratory work has been accomplished in the noncognitive fields of interests, personality, motivation, and personal history data.

An early approach to the tapping of interests was in terms of activities preferences. Triads of military activities were developed with the testee required to select the one he liked most and the one he liked least. Further work has produced several thousand items of various kinds relating to a few selected military occupations. In addition to interests, these items attempt to assess attitudes, personality traits, and biographical information which is believed to be significant.[33] Validity studies of instruments derived from these items are currently in progress. Little relationship was found with ground combat performance in Korea.[30]

Another approach has been directed at personality traits and motivational states by employing projective testing techniques. One recent project has produced a series of thematic-apperception type picture stories which will be validated against performance in several occupational areas. Another study has utilized a great many diversified techniques in the assessment of personnel for special type of work situation.[35] In addition to the usual intelligence and aptitude tests, this project integrated interest and personality appraisal by means of (1) personal interviews, (2) biographical information blanks, (3) interest tests, (4) sociometric techniques, and (5) projective methodology. This study is still in progress.

The military psychologist involved in the problems of classification is again the psychometrician. He is attempting to improve the classification of military personnel by continuous polishing of the aptitude tests which have been accepted for operational use, and by the development of new predictive instruments which will get at such non-cognitive factors as interests, attitudes, and personality traits. Once these new tests have proved themselves in terms of reliability, validity, and standardization, there is no reason to doubt that the military operator will accept and utilize them completely just as he has their forerunners, the intelligence and aptitude tests.

PROFICIENCY MEASUREMENT

It is believed appropriate at this time to devote a special section to the subject of proficiency measurement. This category of research is carried on as a necessary part of projects in all the major operational areas. In order to develop instruments, methodologies, and techniques that will increase the efficiency of military personnel, there must be quantitative standards of this efficiency. In other words, appropriate criteria must be identified and quantified to pave the way for prediction and validation, change and evaluation.

Paper-and-pencil tests have been found to be the easiest to construct and the simplest to administer. Unfortunately, they prove to be adequate criteria only in connection with individual performance in some technical fields. They appear to fall short in the measurement of group performance and individual performance where psychomotor skills predominate over mental abilities. Attempts are being made systematically to investigate the relative value of several kinds of paper-and-pencil tests together with some selected performance tests. A study which used sound-motion pictures as the stimuli found such a test to be highly reliable but not much better than the current paper-and-pencil test.[12]

The most obvious answer to the need for better performance measures is the job-sample test. The content of such a test is provided gratis, and its face validity is perfect. It merely remains to be firmly structured and standardized. A number of such tests have been developed in the services for simple, routine jobs such as machinists, electricians, and enginemen.[55] When the job is complex and integrated with other jobs, however, there is still a critical need for a true performance test.

One of the most active and most promising areas of criterion research today is that of group performance measures. The combat squad, the bomber crew, and the naval ship crew—all require measures which will cover the numerous factors that influence the productivity of such a group. The performance test must also include a representative sample of all the essential on-the-job activities, and should be reliably assessed by as small a number of judges as possible. Such a test has recently been developed for the Infantry rifle squad in which the four basic combat tasks are included together with job knowledge and certain attitudes and interpersonal relationships within the squad.[22] NCO's normally available can be used as umpires and the scoring system is as objective as possible.

A battery of performance tests was developed recently for analyzing the difficulties which combat air crews experience in working together and for training these crews to function more effectively as teams.[52] Three kinds of tests were utilized: (1) problem solving, (2) group-interaction picture stories, and (3) an adaptation of Bavelas' group squares test. Sufficient discriminations were achieved to indicate that this battery could predict field performance.

Last but far from least in importance, we come to a type of proficiency measurement that is widely used and has many ramifications in other areas as well. The methodology of ratings has been the subject of much intensive research over a period of many years. Rating scales, in addition to serving as stop-gap criteria in all areas of personnel research, have also been employed extensively in an administrative role. Recent studies have produced considerable evidence bearing upon the adequacy of various rating techniques, the effects of certain rater characteristics upon their ratings, and the importance of certain rating conditions.[2] An average of several ratings was found to be more accurate than any single rating. Ratings by identified raters were as valid as were ratings by anonymous raters. Certain characteristics of raters, such as general ability and efficiency, can have as important an influence on ratings as the subject characteristics of the ratees themselves.

In the area of proficiency measurement it can be seen that the current trend is toward the development of standardized performance tests, especially those which will handle small groups operating in their normal military function. At the same time, work continues to improve the "tried and true" paper-and-pencil tests, the job-sample tests, and especially the techniques of rating, which have been and will continue for some time to be the workhorses of the criterion problem.

TRAINING

Once the determination has been made as to what occupation the new military man is most likely to be successful in, the next step is the obvious one of teaching or training for that particular job. The chief concern of the military is to get a well qualified combat man or specialist into his pay-off job as soon as possible after recruitment or induction. The time spent in military service by all too many of the young and able is much too short for the numerous demands and the high costs involved.

Basic or orientation training presents many interesting problems. First, there is the question as to just how much of what subjects the military man should receive during this initial training period in order that he be basically grounded and ready to proceed in any direction within his particular service. Current research is attempting to relate the course content of the various preliminary training periods forward to on-the-job performance and backward to selection and classification procedures.[9] A second question is concerned with the optimum length of this training period, and this independent variable has been manipulated to a certain extent with inconclusive results.[50]

After basic training, the military man must be taught the

specific skills of whatever job he has been pointed toward. The most unique and, in a sense, the most important of these jobs are those directly related to combat. Current research is attempting to devise new techniques for training on (a) the various military weapons, such as the M-1 rifle, automatic weapons, and artillery pieces;[20] (b) fire control apparatus such as radar, director, and bombsite;[3] and (c) the driving of vehicles such as trucks, tanks, small boats, and air-craft. Controlled comparisons are being made between traditional methods and experimental methods involving distributed practice, knowledge of results, appropriate incentives, and the early teaching of the whole procedure. Special emphasis is devoted to the fundamental motor skills which underlie all of the above areas.[27, 42]

The skilled individuals must then learn how to function smoothly together as a team. Small unit training is finally receiving its fair share of attention with the recent advances in measurement as discussed in the preceding section. Standardized procedures with structured courses and check lists for judges have been developed for the Infantry squad. Similar approaches are being taken with the aircrew, the gun section, and the combat information center.

Behind the combat man stands the technical specialist, a man of ever-increasing importance in this new atomic-electronic age. Although the production of such specialists is not peculiar to the military, the services do have unique problems in view of the limited time such personnel are available to them, the small remuneration they can offer, and the rough living conditions that must be tolerated. An intensive effort is being made to shorten the time required to train electronics maintenance men by means of (a) revision of job specifications to eliminate nonessentials, (b) establishment of meaningful standards for assignment to such instruction, and (c) more effective presentation of the difficult content.[54] The technical schools within all the services are receiving a critical examination these days. Groups of educators and psychologists have carefully looked into several schools and made valuable recommendations concerning the administration of students, the organization of the curricula, and areas amenable to more detailed research.

The one and only aspect of human resources research that perhaps could be said to be overemphasized is that concerned with training aids and devices. Aids such as charts and small models have long been recognized as valuable assistants to the platform instructor. With the development of the flight trainer in World War II, a new era of complex simulators, models, and synthetic trainers of all descriptions was ushered in. The face validity of these gadgets is overwhelming to the layman, and the trend toward their proliferation is still unchecked. Some few attempts have been made to evaluate completed devices and to develop principles which may be applied to their design, but the task is an enormous one and there is still much that remains to be done.

A training procedure that has received a lot of research attention within the services is the use of movies and film strips. The great advantage of being able to give standardized instruction to any number of large groups has resulted in increased use of this medium. Like training devices, however, the effectiveness of films should not be taken for granted. Unlike training devices, motion pictures and film strips have been subjected to a considerable amount of analytical research. One recent study has shown that learning increases consistently with multiple examples of the process to be learned.[34] Another study provided evidence in support of the superiority of guided-practice over unguided-practice in the teaching of a fairly simple task.[29] An extensive series of integrated studies has recently culminated in a comprehensive report covering the most preferable procedures to be taken in the selection, playing, production, utilization, evaluation, and revision of training films.[11] From time to time a few selected films are taken from the regular operating list and evaluated by research techniques. The results of these projects are fed back into the film research program.

With the coming of age of television, the same system of investigation that had been developed for motion pictures was applied to this new medium. After a number of aspects had been examined, a comprehensive survey was undertaken to ascertain just what facts were known that could be applied to military training and what kinds of specific research was needed to complete the picture.[17] From this baseline a research project has been initiated which will compare the actual learning resulting from the use of television in basic training with the learning accomplished without television.

Research in the training area is conducted by "learning" psychologists. They have a considerable number of established facts and low-order laws "on the shelf." Thus, much of their research can be by way of determining the transferability or generality of this stock when applied to the military situation. Military operators have long accepted the value of research designed to produce training aids or devices, but they have not been critical enough to require the evaluation that is essential. Films and television have also been welcomed by the military and, fortunately, more research has been devoted to the "proof of the pudding" with these new media. Research directly aimed at the basic methods and techniques of training have not fared as well as the "gadget" oriented approach. The need for research assistance is not apparent to the military instructor; in fact, it would seem to impugn his abilities in this field. When significant specific facts are obtained, however, they are welcomed by the military operator and put to good use. The areas receiving major emphasis at present are (a) basic training, (b) small unit training, and (c) technical school instruction.

Personnel Management

Not only during the training period, but also throughout the entire operational career of the serviceman there is a continuous need to maintain his motivation and morale at reasonably high levels. It scarcely needs repeating that the most careful selection and the most thorough training are both greatly reduced in effectiveness if the individuals concerned are low in "spirits" and negative in their attitudes. The military commander must be continually concerned with the attitudes and feelings of his men, their tendencies and sets, and the influences of fatigue, fear, and other stresses upon their behavior.

The initial period of adjustment to military life and the military situation is a particularly sensitive one. The average American boy has lived through a childhood and teen-age that was radically different from the community living and regimentation of the barracks. It would be of great value for the military commander to know the most appropriate techniques that would introduce the average boy to this new regimen with a minimum loss of effectiveness through negative attitudes, neurotic tendencies, AWOLism, homesickness, lonesomeness, etc. One recent study has found that adjustment is enhanced by a sharp break with home life and a minimum of contact with family and old friends during the critical period.[13] The evidence also indicated that supports in the form of friendly attitudes on the part of immediate superiors and associates were of great help. Another study is currently under way investigating the peculiar problems of adjustment to shipboard life in relation to the objectives of recruit training immediately prior to the first embarkation. The results of this study can be utilized in the revision of training procedures as well as in the modification of management methods aboard ship.

The unique nature of so many military jobs together with rough living conditions and increased probability of injury or death makes the motivational factors of great importance in the attempts of the military commander to get the maximum performance from his men. In addition, there is bound to be more resistance to incentives of all kinds when the jobs bear little relation to civilian pasts or expected futures and when the assignment process is involuntary. Although much can be accomplished by fear and punishment, there is an ever-growing realization that the highest and most sustained performance can only be achieved through the positive techniques of rewards and incentives, as the good leaders have always known. A study recently conducted in the submarine service has shown that over half of the disqualifications for this type of duty are the result of inappropriate motivation.[32] Several predictors were suggested such as attitude toward authority, ability to verbalize, and the possession of definite goals.

The measurement of motivation and morale is a most difficult undertaking. The military services have traditionally used such indices as AWOL rate, church attendance, VD* rate, re-enlistment rate, courts martial, etc. in assessing unit morale.

The attitude survey is still the principal methodological tool for collecting data in this whole intangible area although there have been considerable advances in the direction of increased intensity of probing. A series of short studies has demonstrated that attitude questionnaires can be scored so as to provide a reliable measure of attitudes toward military service, and that such attitudes are positively related to both school and on-the-job performance.[53]

Several new approaches to the use of attitude surveying have recently been developed. One of these has employed the questionnaire to get at basic social values.[23] Some of the findings indicate that (a) differences in motivation may be reflected in attitudes toward authority, (b) certain social attitudes are related to peer-nominations for leadership, and (c) the failures in a training situation are more closely related in social attitudes to the successful men than are those who voluntarily withdraw from the situation.

In view of the shortcomings that exist in the measurement of morale, very little has been done toward the development and scientific evaluation of new management techniques. One recent project worth mentioning, however, attempted to determine the value of encouraging complaints as a factor in increasing morale.[8] It was found that such a practice made a significant difference in morale scores when compared to a group whose complaints were suppressed.

There is a steadily increasing awareness within the three services of the need for some attention to be paid to the non-

* Venereal Disease.

cognitive aspects of individuals when small groups are composed. The increased ability to measure group performance discussed above has highlighted the fact that reliable predictions of performance cannot be made when intelligence, aptitudes, and skills only are considered. Some early approaches involved the measurement of certain attitudes or personality factors which were believed to be significant and attempts to relate these to group productivity. In some cases various sociometric techniques were employed. More recently, perhaps in response to weaknesses revealed in the early studies, the emphasis has shifted to the development of models which could satisfactorily handle the complex of variables involved. One project has attempted to cope with the task of specifying an optimal assembly of identical small units in the standard situation where there would be restricted numbers of each job available. [43] This task would be in addition to the primary one of predicting group performance from combinations of individual measures. Another related project has produced a model which incorporates four diverse requisites that are considered essential: (a) the specific environmental constraints and stimuli which govern the behavior of the group, (b) the temporal relationships of the group behaviors, (c) intra-group communications as the key processes, and (d) the close interrelations of social behaviors and job-related behaviors. [44]

The final aspect of personnel management to be discussed is that pertaining to psychological stress. This is a most important area in the military situation and unfortunately, one that has very little research evidence to be contributed. Although the usual stresses of the civilian world, such as failure, noise, rejection, shock, etc. are also of interest to the military, of much greater concern are the unique conditions of combat. Only a modest start has been made toward obtaining the many answers which are needed as to what "kinds" of men will make good fighters and what kind will break and run, what kinds of supports are required on the battlefield, what factors should be used in selection and which may be amenable to training, and what indoctrination procedures may be helpful in minimizing the effects of stress. One project involving threat and failure stress upon perceptual-motor performance has shown that both kinds of stress will produce decrements in performance initially with later recovery as well as greater variability within subjects.[15] Current research is investigating the value of selected orientation and training procedures in the introduction of personnel to stressful military occupations, and the personality factors which are primarily responsible for enabling the individual to perform adequately in the face of death and bodily injury.

The problems of personnel management are being attacked by the social psychologist with the attitude survey as his primary tool. The area is a most difficult one, a fact which is exemplified by its retardation within the total science of psychology, yet a most important one from the viewpoint of the military commander. The weaknesses of opinion surveying are realized and efforts are being made to improve this technique by means of more intensive interviewing as well as to develop other methodologies. In spite of the concern of the military for these problems, the related research is not well supported. The intangible nature of the variables together with the general feeling that "you can't change human nature" makes it difficult for the potential contributions of research to be understood.

LEADERSHIP

The key to successful personnel management may be said to be the quality of leadership which applies the techniques in question. The importance of leadership is such that it is believed warranted to devote a special section to the research in this area. In general, the military psychologist is concerned with four inter-related problems of leadership: (1) the selection of leaders, (2) the determination of leadership factors, (3) the training of leaders, and (4) the evaluation of leaders.

There seems to be little doubt that the dimensions of intelligence and aptitudes will contribute very little to the prediction of leadership. Certain minimum levels are necessary, but once these levels are achieved the problem becomes one of personality variables and social interaction. A recent multi-disciplinary study has produced new evidence that interest and intelligence tests add nothing to leadership prediction.[45] Instead this study has shown that the more intangible variables seem to have the most promise. Attitude and value questionnaires, personality inventories, projective tests, and peer ratings all proved of sufficient value to warrant continued use and refinement. Another series of studies has produced conclusions which are compatible although not identical with those just mentioned.[37] Self-description items proved to have considerable validity. Objectively-scored projective techniques were believed to offer great promise with further refinements, although they were not as useful as the self-description blanks. The rating scale portions of evaluation instruments indicated useful validity.

Rating scales have proved to be particularly effective in another series of studies wherein success as a junior officer with troops was predicted from a combination of "aptitude for service" ratings by seniors and peers upon military cadets.[31] Combat performance ratings showed substantial agreement $(r = .52)$, while general non-combat efficiency produced similar relationships.

Through the use of questionnaires and factor analysis procedures a recent study has attempted to discover the relative importance of the major factors involved in noncommissioned officer leadership.[36] The most important factor proved to be a general over-all impression of good leadership combined with intelligence and job competence. Two other factors pertained to disciplinary strictness and moral character. It is interesting to note that the latter two factors did not seem to interact with the general opinion of leadership.

A comprehensive, ten-year study of leadership is participated in by one of the services and a number of reports containing fresh and interesting evidence upon the multiple aspects of leadership have been produced to date.[49] Only a few of these facts can be presented here. One phase is concerned with "status expectations" as aspects of organizational relations. Here it was found that status expectations were reciprocated more frequently when they conformed to the formal organizational structure. Status reciprocity apparently gives permanence and predictability to the structure of interactions among members. Another phase was designed to test the hypothesis that behavior patterns will be different for the various positions occupied by leaders. The results of factor analysis indicated a marked tendency for similar specialties to appear with high loadings on the same factor. The final phase to be reported here had to do with the problem of criteria and their relation to several variables describing what leaders do and how they do it. An important variable was found to be the leader's own description of the extent to which he delegates responsibility.

The battlefields of Korea have been used quite extensively for the purpose of gathering incidents of both good and bad leadership behavior. In one study, the "critical incident" technique was employed to provide the basis for constructing a number of structured situational tests.[16] These tests are being used in the evaluation of leadership training. They have been found to be satisfactory in regard to objectivity, reliability, and agreement with other measures of success. Another project succeeded in obtaining reports of actual situations demonstrating effective and ineffective leadership in the combat zone.[46] These incidents have been classified as human relations, communications, personal conduct, organization and planning of duties, administration and supervision of duties, and execution of duties. They will be used as case studies in school instruction and as raw data for further analytical research.

There still remain many more questions than answers within the general area of leadership. It is an area of great importance to the military, although the consensus of commanders would not recognize the existence of any special problems. This factor is further complicated by the multiplicity of leadership phenomena in the military situation. The military psychologist recognizes the existence of three factors in the leadership situation: the leader, the followers, and the specific situation involved. He also accepts the fact that certain potentials may be inherited that will facilitate leadership, but that much progress can be achieved through training. The noncognitive variables seem to offer the most promise for the analysis and prediction of leadership. The identification of these variables and their subsequent measurement must be greatly improved. Ratings, especially peer ratings, have proved to be the most valuable in both the prediction and evaluation of leadership behavior to date, but continued effort is necessary in order to devise more objective and reliable techniques.

THE DESIGN OF WEAPONS, EQUIPMENT, AND SUPPLIES

The final area of major importance to the military psychologist is that of the design of materiel with the capabilities and limitations of the human operator and maintenance man in mind. The traditional practice of worrying about the human aspects of "hardware" development after the equipment has been produced is still the general rule, but there seems to be a growing realization that this procedure is extremely wasteful both in time and money. The design engineer, as well as the military operator, is coming more and more to accept both the human engineer and the psychophysiologist, whose basic work on the human senses, perceptions, and motor coordination supports this important area.

One recent study involved a survey of all research findings pertaining to the most efficient utilization of existing equipment and personnel in radar-scope detection.[1] This review also produced some recommendations for the improvement of operational practices and directions for future research. It was emphasized that scope operation involves two kinds of activity, detection and tracking, which probably have quite different psychological requirements. Another review study has summarized the results of recent research on the design of knobs and levers for making settings on scales and scopes.[25] A series of studies has indicated that the human operator is still the best mechanism for detecting and tracking a radar target in the presence of noise.

In the auditory area, a project was recently initiated to investigate the relation between certain auditory selection tests and proficiency in sonar performance.[51] A completed study in the same area inquired into the time required for the ear to regain its ability to hear after exposure to a loud noise.[40] Results showed the ear to recover rapidly; recovery is complete within about one-third of a second when the stimulating tone is roughly the intensity of average speech.

Continuous research is being carried out on a multitude of visual problems. The sensitivity of stereoscopic rangefinding to binocular depth illusions has been demonstrated in the laboratory. A number of integrated projects have been directed toward the solution of problems involving both vision and audition in combination. These studies have already provided data on the input rate of information which the human individual is capable of accepting.

Motor coordination has been subjected to a number of detailed investigations. These studies have been concerned with the military aspects of such factors as (a) transfer of training,[26, 5] (b) distribution of practice,[41] and (c) knowledge of results.[4]

A comprehensive survey of the status of, and requirements for, human engineering services in one of the armed forces was recently conducted.[56] It was found that only 7 per cent of all man-machine systems which needed human engineering were receiving it. Furthermore, there was a gap, due chiefly to poor communication, between the production of research results and their application to equipment design.

The application of the products of psychophysiological research to "hardware" design has been furthered by the recent development of human engineering handbooks which attempt to present such facts in a clear, concise, and logical fashion. The first handbook of this kind presented its data primarily for the benefit of human engineers.[28] Experience with this early hand-book indicated that, because of the shortage of human engineers and a certain amount of resistance on the part of design engineers, it would be better to construct the handbook so that it would be meaningful directly to the design engineer. At least one new manual has been produced based on this new concept.[57] At the present time, all three services are working jointly to produce a comprehensive handbook which will set forth the general principles underlying the design of all military equipment.

Through the use of the handbooks mentioned above and directly from the results of psychophysiological research, the armed forces have introduced human engineering principles into the design of innumerable pieces of equipment, weapons, and supplies. Certain areas, of course, have progressed more rapidly than others. Individual clothing, rations, and field equipment have long been developed with the human consumer in mind, while individual weapons still have not been so influenced to any significant degree. The design of crew-served weapons have received some attention, but this has been spotty and there still remains much to be done. The major focus of recent attention has probably been the design of crew compartments, such as submarines, bomber aircraft, tank turrets, and various critical areas on surface ships. Studies of this nature have resulted in the rearrangement of equipment, reductions in personnel required, redesign and relocation of displays and controls, and the substitution of man for machine or vice versa at various points in each particular system.

The military psychologist working in this general area of human engineering is the general-experimental psychologist with an orientation toward physiology. In addition to conducting basic experiment in audition, vision, perception, and motor coordination, he is forced into the application of fundamental data to the actual design of material by the lack of "psychophysiological engineers" and by the cold reception still accorded his work by the regular design engineer. The importance of human engineering is recognized by the majority of military operators, however, although the shortcomings of the design engineer are not so clearly discerned and the need for supporting psychophysiology is rarely perceived.

The further development and increased use of human engineering handbooks should be of great value in the "selling" of this type of service to the design engineer as well as to the military operator. The easily-demonstrated benefits from past and current improvements in the design of crew-served weapons, fire control centers, and restricted crew compartments will also insure that the military consumer is satisfied with this important research activity and willing to support more in the future.

CONCLUSION

This chapter has attempted to describe the psychological research activities carried on within the three military services during the past several years. In so defining military psychology, it should be noted that this differs somewhat from Geldard's conception, which includes all psychological research contributing to the solution of military problems.[19] The value and close integration of these "outside" contributions is recognized, but their arbitrary exclusion is believed justified in a review of this kind. Civilian research has been covered, however, in those cases where it was sponsored by the Department of Defense as an integral part of the human resources research program.

As a comprehensive review of the current state of military psychology, this chapter leaves much to be desired. Admittedly, there has been no attempt to make it definitive. A severe restriction has been imposed throughout by the requirements of national security. This restriction has operated with special force upon the areas of training and human engineering. Further, it was deemed wise to concentrate upon projects which were conducted within the military situation under the assumption that the more "civilian" research would receive adequate publication attention elsewhere. Finally, the determinations as to inclusion or exclusion within this chapter were inevitably influenced by the relative saliency of the various projects within the writer's perceptual field and other miscellaneous personal biases. It is believed, however, that some general idea as to current activities within the Armed Forces can be gathered from the foregoing account. Psychological research appears to be firmly established in the military services today. The contributions of the psychometricians to the solution of the many complex problems involved in the selection and classification of personnel have been recognized and appreciated. To date these discriminations have been made in terms of aptitudes and intelligence only, but it should not be long before the non-cognitive dimensions are employed as well. Slowly but surely, the potential "pay-off" of psychological research directed toward training and human engineering problems is being perceived by the military operator. The problems themselves have always been **clearly seen, and now the possibilities of scientific assistance** are being recognized, not because of abstract articles and "sales talks" directed at high levels, but by virtue of actual results produced by the research worker in the field. Recent advances in the development of small-unit performance tests have been of great assistance in this endeavor.

Research directed toward the improvement of management techniques is not looked upon very favorably by the military operator today. For one thing, the problems themselves are not clearly perceived, if at all, by the military operator. It is an area where the techniques are considered to be pretty much an art, and the current state of psychological methodology does little to disturb this viewpoint. There is an immediate and urgent need for (1) the isolation and definition of standard dimensions, (2) the quantification of such variables as may be discovered, and (3) the development of reliable and valid objective measures. A great deal of workable knowledge has been acquired by the military through years of experience concerning leadership and the control of men. The science of psychology will have to produce some facts and procedures that are clearly more effective before its rightful place in this area will be recognized.

PRESENT-DAY PSYCHOLOGY

The opening sentences of the introduction of this chapter indicated that military psychology referred to an applied category. This is certainly true as far as the problems or requirements are concerned, and it is also true in regard to the interest, emphasis, and focus of the military operator. The applied label ceases to apply only when the total research effort is subjected to detailed description. Then it can be seen that research at all levels is sponsored by the military services as required to solve any particular problem. When answers are needed at each succeeding lower level, the literature is carefully searched and current workers in the field are contacted wherever they may be. If the evidence has not yet been obtained, then supporting research and even basic research becomes an essential part of military psychology, and is so recognized and supported by military psychologist and operator alike.

BIBLIOGRAPHY

[1] Bakan, P., Kappauf, W. E., and Payne, M. C. Review of Psychological Research Bearing on Radar-Scope Interpretation in ADC Operations. *Technical Report 53-26, Human Resources Research Center, Air Research and Development Command*, USAF, August 1953.

[2] Bayroff, A. G. and Haggerty, Helen R. A Study of Officer Rating Methodology XI. Summary of Major Findings. *PRB Report 910, Personnel Research Branch, The Adjutant General's Office*, Department of the Army, December 1952.

[3] Beverley, R. F., and Kausler, D. H. Effect of Practice on Circular Error and Its Components in Visual Bombing. *Research Bulletin 52-10, Human Resources Research Center, Air Training Command*, USAF, February 1952.

[4] Bilodeau, E. A. Speed of Acquiring a Simple Motor Response as a Function of Systematic Transformations of Knowledge of Results. *Research Bulletin 52-33, Human Resources Research Center, Air Training Command*, USAF, November 1952.

[5] Bilodeau, E. A. Transfer of Training between Tasks Differing in Degree of Physical Restriction of Imprecise Responses. *Research Bulletin 52-40, Human Resources Research Center, Air Training Command*, USAF, **December 1952.**

[6] Bolanovich, D. J., Jones, W., Frankfeldt, E., and Lovelace, N. R. Development of Instruments for Selecting Men for Military Service under Reduced Mental and Literacy Standards for Induction. *PRS Report 927, Personnel Research Section, The Adjutant General's Office*, Department of the Army, 25 February 1952.

7 Bolanovich, D. J., Jones, W., and Lovelace, N. R. Development of a Scoring Key for Identifying Failures Due to Negative Motivation on the Armed Forces Qualification Test. *PRS Report 960, Personnel Research Section, The Adjutant General's Office,* Department of the Army, 19 June 1952.

8 Briggs, L. J., and Roe, R. M. Morale as a Function of Opportunity to Register Complaints. *Technical Report 53-4, Human Resources Research Center, Air Training Command,* USAF, March 1953.

9 Brown, C. G. Final Report on Research on Problems of Navy Recruit Training. Report prepared for *Bureau of Naval Personnel,* Navy Dept. February 1953.

10 Carmichael, L. and Mead, L. C. (Eds.) *The Selection of Military Manpower.* Washington: National Academy of Sciences — National Research Council, 1951, pp. iii, 269.

11 Carpenter, C. R. Logistics of Sound Motion Pictures for Military Training. *Human Engineering Report SDC 269-7-31, Navy Special Devices Center,* Navy Dept., September 1952.

12 Carpenter, C. R. et al. The Development of a Sound Motion Picture Proficiency Test. *PRB Report 991, Personnel Research Branch, The Adjutant General's Office,* Department of the Army, 31 January 1953.

13 Christie, R., Walkley, A. T., and Maisel, R. An Exploratory Study of Factors Affecting Transition to Army Life, as summarized in *PRB Bulletin 53-3, Personnel Research Branch, The Adjutant General's Office,* Department of the Army, August 1953.

14 Cowles, J. T. Development of an Alternate Form of the Airman Classification Battery AC-1. *Research Bulletin 52-5, Human Resources Research Center, Air Training Command,* USAF, February 1952.

15 Deese, J. and Lazarus, R. S. The Effects of Psychological Stress upon Perceptual-Motor Performance. *Research Bulletin 52-19, Human Resources Research Center, Air Training Command,* USAF, June 1952.

16 Flanagan, J. C., Sivy, J., Lange, C. J., and Jacobs, O. Development of an Objective Form of the Leaders Reaction Test. *PRS Report No. 930, Personnel Research Section, The Adjutant General's Office,* Department of the Army, 30 April 1952.

17 Fritz, M. F., Humphrey, J. E., Greenlee, J. A., and Madison, R. L. Survey of Television Utilization in Army Training. *Human Engineering Report SDC 530-01-1, Navy Special Devices Center,* Navy Dept., 31 December 1952.

18 Fuchs, E. F., Woods, I. A., and Harper B. P. Prediction of Job Success in Eight Career Ladders. *PRB Report 997, Personnel Research Branch, The Adjutant General's Office,* Department of the Army, February 1953.

19 Geldard, F. A. *Military Psychology: Science or Technology?* The American Journal of Psychology, July, 1953, Vol. 66, No. 3, pp. 335-348.

20 Goldstein, M., and Rittenhouse, C. H. The Effects of Practice with Triggering Omitted on Performance of the Total Pedestal Sight Gunnery Task. *Technical Report 53-9, Human Resources Research Center, Air Research and Development Command,* USAF, May 1953.

21 Hagen, E. P., and Thorndike, R. L. A Study of the WW II Navy Careers of Illiterates Sent Through Literacy Training. *Research Report, Bureau of Naval Personnel,* Navy Dept., April 1953.

22 Havron, M. D., Fay, R. J., and McGrath, J. E. The Effectiveness of Small Military Units. *PRS Report 980, Personnel Research Section, The Adjutant General's Office,* Department of the Army, 30 September 1952.

23 Hollander, E. P. Problems and Techniques in the Evaluation of Motivation Among Naval Aviation Cadets. *A Special Report, U. S. Naval School of Aviation Medicine,* Navy Dept., 9 March 1953.

24 Hunt, W. A. *Neuropsychiatric Selection as a Contribution to Military Efficiency.* Prepared under contract with Office of Naval Research, Navy Dept., 1952.

25 Jenkins, W. L. Design Factors in Knobs and Levers for Making Settings on Scales and Scopes. *Technical Report 53-2, Wright Air Development Center, Air Research and Development Command,* USAF, February 1953.

26 Jones, E. I., and Bilodeau, E. A. Differential Transfer of Training between Motor Tasks of Different Difficulty. *Research Bulletin 52-35, Human Resources Research Center, Air Training Command,* USAF, December 1952.

27 —— Retention and Relearning of a Complex Perceptual-Motor Skill after Ten Months of No Practice. *Research Bulletin 53-17, Human Resources Research Center, Air Research and Development Command,* USAF, June 1953.

28 Kennedy, J. L., et al (Handbook Staff). Handbook of Human Engineering Data for Design Engineers. *Technical Report No. SDC 199-1-1, Special Devices Center, Office of Naval Research,* Navy Dept., 1 December 1949.

29 Kimble, G. A., and Wulff, J. J. The Effect of "Response Guidance" on the Value of Audience Participation in Training Film Instruction. *HFORL Report No. 34, Human Factors Operations Research Laboratories,* Air Research and Development Command, USAF, April 1953.

30 King, S. H., Klieger, W. A., Campbell, J. T., Johnson, C. D., and Yaukey, D. W. Validation of Personnel Measures against Combat Performance of Enlisted Men in Korea VI. Self-Description Items. *PRS Report 965, Personnel Research Section, The Adjutant General's Office,* Department of the Army, 14 July 1952.

31 King, S. H., Campbell, J. T., Johnson, C. D., Klieger, W. A., and Yaukey, D. W. Studies of the Performance of Officers in Combat I. Relationship of West Point Measures to Later Combat Effectiveness. *PRS Report 969, Personnel Research Section, The Adjutant General's Office,* Department of the Army, 22 August 1952.

32 Kinsey, J. L., and Weybrew, B. B. Etiological Factors in the Disqualification of Submarine Personnel. *U. S. Naval Medical Research Laboratory Report No. 226, Bureau of Medicine and Surgery,* Navy Dept., 22 June 1953.

33 Klieger, W. A., Lubin, A., and Roy, H. L. Self-Description Instruments for Classifying Enlisted Men. *PRB Report 990, Personnel Research Branch, The Adjutant General's Office,* Department of the Army, June 1953.

34 Lumsdaine, A. A. et al. The Value of Using Multiple Examples in Training Film Instruction. *HRRL Report No. 25, Human Resources Research Laboratories, Headquarters Command,* USAF, May 1952.

35 Medical Research Laboratory Memo Report 52-11. The Assessment of Submarine Candidates: Studies in Progress. *Medical Research Laboratory, U. S. Naval Submarine Base,* Navy Dept., 16 October 1952.

36 Moore, J. V. A Factor Analysis of Subordinate Evaluations of Noncommissioned Officer Supervisors. *Research Bulletin 53-6, Human Resources Research Center, Air Research and Development Command,* USAF, April 1953.

37 Parrish, J. A., and Lieffler, June C. Research in the Army's Enlisted Leaders' Course Program. *PRS Report 986, Personnel Research Section, The Adjutant General's Office,* Department of the Army, 4 December 1952.

38 PRS Report 808, Development of Aptitude Areas for Classification of Enlisted Personnel in the Army. *Personnel Research Section, The Adjutant General's Office,* Department of the Army, 18 October 1949.

39 PRS Report No. 976, Development of Armed Forces Qualification Test and Predecessor Army Screening Tests, 1946-1950. *Personnel Research Section, The Adjutant General's Office,* Department of the Army, 5 November 1952.

40 Rawnsley, Anita, and Harris, J. D. Studies in Short Duration Auditory Fatigue IV. Recovery Time. *Report No. 187 Medical Research Laboratory, Bureau of Medicine and Surgery,* Navy Dept., 30 January 1952.

41 Reynolds, B., and Bilodeau, Ina, McD. Acquisition and Retention of Three Psychomotor Tests as a Function of Distribution of Practice during Acquisition. *Research Bulletin 52-27, Human Resources Research Center, Air Training Command,* USAF, August 1952.

42 Reynolds, B. The Effect of Learning on the Predictability of Psychomotor Performance. *Research Bulletin 52-32, Human Resources Research Center, Air Research and Development Command,* USAF, November 1952.

43 Roby, T. B. Problems of Rational Group Assembly Exemplified in the Medium Bomber Crew. *Research Bulletin 53-18, Human Resources Research Center, Air Research and Development Command,* USAF, July 1953.

44 Róby, T. B., and Forgays, D. G. A Problem-Solving Model for Analysis of Communication in B-39 Crews. *Research Bulletin 53-30, Human Resources Research Center, Air Research and Development Command,* USAF, August 1953.

45 Rohrer, J. H., Bagby, J. W. Jr., Wilkins, W. L. *The Potential Combat Officer.* A Technical Report prepared by Tulane University for the Bureau of Medicine and Surgery, Navy Dept., 1952.

46 Ruch, F. L. Incidents of Leadership in Combat. *Research Memorandum No. 3, Human Resources Research Institute, Air University,* USAF, January 1953.

47 Rulon, P. J. and Schweiker, R. F. Validation of a Non-Verbal Test of Military Trainability. *PRB Report 1076, Personnel Research Branch, The Adjutant General's Office,* Department of the Army, June 1953.

48 Sharp, L. H., Campbell, J. T., Johnson, C. D., and Yaukey, D. W. Validation of Personnel Measures Against Combat Performance of Enlisted Men in Korea. II. Army Classification Battery and Related Variables. *PRS Report 940, Personnel Research Section, The Adjutant General's Office,* Department of the Army, 9 April 1952.

49 Shartle, C. L., Stogdill, R. M., *et al.* Studies in Naval Leadership, conducted by The Ohio State University Research Foundation under contract with the Office of Naval Research, Navy Dept., 1953.

50 Smith, R. G. Jr. A Comparison between Eight-Week and Twelve-Week Basic Training Programs. *Technical Report 53-5, Human Resources Research Center, Air Training Command,* USAF, March 1953.

51 Stuntz, S. E. Current Program of Research in Selection of Submarine Sonar Operators. *Report No. 201, Medical Research Laboratory, Bureau of Medicine and Surgery,* Navy Dept., 21 December 1952.

PRESENT-DAY PSYCHOLOGY

52 Torrance, E. P. Crew Performance in a Test Situation as a Predictor of Field and Combat Performance. *HFORL Report No. 33, Air Research and Development Command,* USAF, March 1953.

53 Tupes, E. C., and Yarnold, J. K. Military Attitude as a Predictor of Air Force Success; Preliminary Studies of the Attitude Survey. *Research Bulletin 52-23, Human Resources Research Center, Air Training Command,* USAF, July 1952.

54 Wickens, D. D., Stone, G. R., and Highland, R. W. A Study of the Retention of Electronics Fundamentals during Basic Radar Mechanic Training. *Research Bulletin 52-36, Human Resources Research Center, Air Research and Development Command,* USAF, December 1952.

55 Wilson, C. L. and Mackie, R. R. Research on the Development of Shipboard Performance Measures. (In Five Parts) *Personnel and Training Branch, Office of Naval Research,* Navy Dept., 25 November 1952.

56 Wohl, J. G., Nagay, J. A., and Taylor, F. V. *Human Engineering in the U.S. Navy.* A study by the working group in human engineering, Office of Naval Research, Navy Dept., February 1953.

57 Woodson, W. E. *Human Engineering Guide for Equipment Designers.* U.S. Navy Electronics Laboratory, Navy Dept., 15 February 1951.

58 Zachert, Virginia, and Ivens, F. C. Fourteen Air Force Technical School Validity Studies for the Airman Classification Battery AC-1B Based on Samples Including Negroes and WAF. *Research Notes PERS 52-4, Human Resources Research Center, Air Training Command,* USAF, January 1952.

CHAPTER XIX

INTRODUCTION TO EXPERIMENTAL PARAPSYCHOLOGY

J. B. RHINE, Ph.D.

Director, Parapsychology Laboratory
Duke University

EDITORIAL NOTE

No doubt there will be psychologists who will wonder why parapsychology should be treated as a branch in a volume of this sort. Only recently, a well-known physiological psychologist discussing theoretical models intimated that no matter what the evidence in laboratory experiments, he would take no stock in parapsychology because it made no sense to him, i. e., it does not fit into the system of science such as we know it.

It is not for us, however, to reject out of hand a body of data gathered in a number of institutions, simply because the conclusions might militate against orthodox psychology. Let us be skeptical, by all means, but let us not ignore. The psychologist must deal with every phase of human activity; and if psychical research is a human endeavor which has attracted at least some outstanding minds, then it is within our larger purview. We feel, at any rate, that students of psychology should have at least an idea as to what it is all about; so that they can take a stand toward it. The great sin of official psychology seems to be ignoring minority activities and convictions. If parapsychology turns out to be little more than folklore or superstition, it still does not warrant our making short shrift of it before it has had its day in court. Let us first be enlightened; then we can discuss intelligently.

It is gratifying that the chapter on parapsychology has been written by the leading exponent of this doctrine. Dr. Joseph B. Rhine has come to this field not through theology but by way of science, for he was a plant physiologist and instructor in botany before embarking on his new career. He received his Ph.D. at the University of Chicago, where he had obtained the B. S. and M. S. degrees. Since 1940, he has been Professor of Psychology and Director of the Parapsychology Laboratory at Duke University. His book on Extra-Sensory Perception *appeared in 1934,* and was followed by other volumes like New Frontiers of the Mind, The Reach of the Mind and New World of the Mind. He is also co-author of Extra-Sensory Perception After 60 Years, and Co-Editor of the Journal of Parapsychology.

PARAPSYCHOLOGY

Parapsychology is admittedly the most controversial branch of psychology today. The reasons for this may be apparent from the definition: Parapsychology is the branch of psychology that deals with occurrences that defy physical explanation.

As in all branches of psychology, there are in parapsychology two general types of manifestation, subjective experiences and objective effects. Most parapsychological (or *psi*) phenomena consist of experiences and, like all experiences, they have to be communicated to become available for scientific-study. The most familiar *psi* experience is *extrasensory perception,* a cognitive response to external events or objects without the aid of sense organs. Extrasensory perception or ESP may apprehend either an objective event, as in *clairvoyance,* or the mental state of another person, as in *telepathy;* and the definition includes the awareness of events that are displaced in space and even in time.

The other type of *psi* manifestation is complementary to ESP. It is to the overt behavior of the individual what ESP is to sensory perception. It might be termed an "extramotor response." Any direct mental effect upon the physical environment not involving the motor functions belongs under *psychokinesis* or PK, the direct action of mind on matter. It is presumably a reaction upon the object by means of the same underlying psychophysical interaction that must necessarily be involved in the extrasensory perception of the object. In *psi* phenomena as a whole, then, are represented a subject-object interaction not involving the sensorimotor system by which subject-object relations are most commonly and familiarly maintained.

General psychology in America, however, has in its philosophy become almost an adjunct of physical science, and it has closely followed physical theory in its search for explanatory principles. Accordingly, *any* findings at all in the field of parapsychology as defined would have to be revolutionary. The establishment of any *psi* phenomenon by sound experimental method challenges the underlying philosophy that has dominated psychological thought. While it is true that many individuals in psychology and psychiatry have on other grounds challenged this physicalistic philosophy of man, it still remains beyond dispute that *general psychology has today no other fundamental explanatory principles at its disposal than those of physics*. It does not know where else in the natural order of things to attach its fundamental theory of personality other than to physics. The only alternative is supernaturalism which the sciences, of course, reject. Among the conventional natural sciences the universe has come to be accepted as physical.

Parapsychology, therefore, is not only a challenge to the concept of the organism as a wholly physical system, it is a refutation to any and all of the philosophies of nature that restrict their fundamental principles to physical theory. In a word, it offers to psychology as a natural science evidence of a nonphysical order in nature—a psychological one.

*   *   *

In parapsychology, as in all the sciences, unexplained happenings in nature—spontaneous phenomena—preceded and eventually led up to the necessary experimental tests. The shift from casual observation to experiment began with the mesmerists and hypnotists of the nineteenth century and led to the formation in the last quarter of the nineteenth century of psychical research societies in various countries of Europe and in America. While at first psychologists played only a minor part in these pioneer developments, by the first quarter of the twentieth century experiments were in a few instances introduced to the university laboratory of psychology, notably at Harvard and Stanford in this country and at Groningen in The Netherlands.

Troland at Harvard made a short-lived effort at telepathy experiments, and Coover[1] at Stanford concealed his really encouraging finding under an unreasonable demand for significance from which it took decades to recover. In the early twenties, however, Professor Heymans at Groningen sponsored telepathy experiments in which Brugmans[2] played the most active part, and at Harvard Professor McDougall sponsored the work of Murphy and that of Estabrooks[3] on a similar line. The more persistent and systematic experimental work in parapsychology at Duke University began in 1930 under the sponsorship of Professor McDougall.

Following publication of the first Duke report on extrasensory perception in 1934,[4] similar experiments began in a number of other American and European colleges, mostly in laboratories of psychology. A number of graduate degrees were granted for theses on parapsychological researches; a "studentship" (or scholarship) in psychical research was established at Trinity College in Cambridge University, and in 1953 the University of Utrecht established a professorship in parapsychology. Parapsychology has been a subject of interest on an international scale with active work on every continent and in most countries where free research is done.

In selecting the review material to follow, large areas of the research field are necessarily slighted, but an outlet for the student may be found to this larger field in the list of references at the end of the chapter.

*   *   *

In the appraisal of the research in a new field such as parapsychology the quality of the methods used should properly become the center of attention. And the more disturbing to prevailing theories the new results appear to be, the better the research procedures have to be and the more confirmation is needed for acceptance.

The most outstanding feature about the methods in *psi* research is the excessive range of precautions taken. There is, in the experiments that are designed to be more crucial, an order of safeguarding that will not be found anywhere else in all the natural sciences. No experiments in psychology have been carried out with anything like the extensive precautionary measures that were used for example, in the Pratt-Woodruff and in the Soal and Goldney experiments in extrasensory perception, which will be discussed below.

Another characteristic of parapsychology is the seemingly endless repetition of the experiments year after year and decade after decade, reestablishing the occurrence of some form of *psi* capacity over and over again, as if the earlier work had not been done.

This excessive precaution and repetition would suggest that there is something wrong with the framework in which these research findings are being regarded. Obviously it is more than a question of experimental method itself; it is, rather, a matter of philosophical attitude. And it is clear that the establishment of a *psi* principle would clash inescapably with the physicalistic view of man that prevails today in psychology. Naturally, the *psi* researches meet with head-on (if not head-down) resistance from those who are prepared to reject new facts if they do not fit old theories. And that, according to the 1952 Warner survey of psychologists' opinions[5] of ESP and its comparison with an earlier survey, applies to a large percentage of the profession in America. A large number of these psychologists are even so frank as to say that they do not need to consider the evidence; they know on *a priori* grounds that *psi* phenomena are impossible.

But for those who will consider results on their merits, there are, as in every field, two broad general categories of method, each necessary to its own stage of a scientific investigation. There are, first, exploratory methods or techniques and, second, there are techniques for verifying or establishing a conclusive finding. About the first exploratory techniques there is no need for a full account here. They include the analytical study of spontaneous case reports that seem to involve *psi;* they also include cases collected by the professional man who deals with firsthand human experiences, the psychiatrist, the minister, the clinical psychologist, the anthropologist. These men may find spontaneous or semi-spontaneous occurrences that appear to have *psi* elements and an exploratory study may lead to a valuable research idea. Or, again, the exploratory techniques may be more or less experimental and involve preliminary testing of individuals who have had *psi* experiences or who may be suspected of having had them.

The more crucial verification experiment differs from the exploratory study in requiring the exclusion of all the known alternatives to the hypothesis being tested. Not only must the alternatives, such as chance, sensory cues, recording errors, and the like, be excluded, but, other forms of possible *psi* function than the one being tested must be eliminated also, at least if the aim of the experiment is a definite conclusion as to which kind of *psi* phenomenon is involved.

In simple outline the test methods that have become standardized for work in this field can be briefly described and the details left to the handbooks on methods now available.[6a][6b] For the elemental testing of ESP of the clairvoyant type it is necessary only to have, for example, a pack of cards in randomized order and maintain them in a position that rules out all possible sensory contact on the part of the subject who is asked to identify them. If the cards are completely screened from sensory contact and the order is unknown, it then remains to be seen whether the subject can identify enough cards in the pack (or in the series) to exclude the theory of chance coincidence. To make recording safe from error, the card record should be made in ignorance of the call record.

There is little fundamental difference between the ESP tests of the telepathic type and the one just described except that the precautions needed are more complicated. In most of the older telepathy tests one person, called the sender or agent, was asked to look at an object, let us say a card chosen from a random pack, and the receiver or percipient subject, located out of sensory range, attempted to identify it. When in the early Duke work it was recognized that this test fully allowed for the possibility of clairvoyant ESP as well as telepathy, the test was improved by having the sender not have a card or other object present but use a code or a system for the subjective selection of the symbol of which he would think at the appointed time. The receiver would then have to rely on the sender's thought as the target. However, the discovery still later of the capacity for ESP of future events opened up the alternative possibility that the subject in a telepathy test could, instead of getting the sender's thought, be precognizing the record sheet when the sender's record was later decoded and the actual symbols put down. It was then recognized that a code would have to be used that would *never be revealed* in a way that would make precognitive clairvoyance of the record a possibility. In order to meet the requirement of having an independent recheck made of all experimental records, however, a technique was needed where-by the code could be indirectly communicated to an assistant. This difficulty was eventually surmounted, but by so detailed a procedure that the original reports[7a] [7h] will have to be consulted for its description.

The concept of precognition, or the ESP of a future event, seemed at first simple enough as a test problem. All that appeared to be needed was the procedure of having the subject attempt to predict what the card order would be when the pack was duly shuffled. However, a series of fresh counter-hypotheses arose out of the very researches themselves, which led eventually to the need for a very complex procedure. The changes were aimed at excluding every possibility that the final target order had been made to conform to the already recorded predictions. The randomizing procedure now in use is quite an elaborate ritual.

The method of testing the mind-over-matter hypothesis, psychokinesis, proved to be simpler than those needed for telepathy and precognition. The common procedure of dice-throwing provided a basic technique for PK testing; the subject was instructed to attempt to influence the fall of the dice by direct action of the will. Various precautions were taken to prevent the use of skill in the dice-throwing, such as the use of special cups and mechanical dice-throwers. The effect of possible dice-bias was eliminated or neutralized, for example, by the requirement that the dice be thrown an equal number of times with the different faces of the die as target. Then, with experienced experimenters following certain established routines of reading the dice and recording, sufficiently good conditions for *exploratory* purposes were provided. For the final stage of *verification,* however, the investigators relied primarily on the analysis of the records for certain internal differences explainable only by PK; later on, photographic recording of the dice was added to the procedure of complete mechanization of the dice throwing.

In both the ESP and PK branches of *psi* inquiry it was necessary to estimate the statistical significance of the run scores or score totals in order to deal with the question of chance. With the experiment set up in such a way that the probability of success for each trial was known, it was possible to apply the convenient binomial method of computing the theoretical standard deviation for a given series of trials. Then, by dividing the score deviation from mean chance expectation by this standard deviation, a critical ratio (cr) was obtained. The probability of so large a cr occurring by chance is given in the Normal Probability Integral Tables. Various other methods of evaluation have, of course, been used. In general, *the application of statistics to the* psi *data has been continuously under the watchful eye of competent statistical authorities,* and an extensive literature is now available covering the basic procedures of evaluation. Not only has the weight of authority been behind the use of statistics in the *psi* work, but a vast amount of empirical testing of the usage has been carried out, using *psi*-test data in various cross-checks, tests of distribution and the like.[8a] [8b]

It is, however, on the psychological methods that the greatest emphasis is needed today. It has long been recognized that a *psi* test consists of a great deal more than the mechanical procedure and the statistical techniques. *Psi* does not operate independently of the mental conditions of the subject. Moreover, it is elusive and has to be coaxed and cultured. Careful selection of subjects is needed in the first place, and careful coaching thereafter may be required to inspire the kind of motivation and general reaction conducive to the exercise of the *psi* capacity. The ability is completely unconscious and is commonly inhibited by a stream of conscious activity.

But if the subject has a normal interest, especially a simple curiosity to find out how high he can score in the test, and if the surroundings are not distracting or unpleasant he is likely to be able to score above mean chance expectation for a few short runs. If he is embarrassed or critical or is very doubtful about his ability, he is even more likely to score on the negative side of the mean; that is, his *psi* ability may still be active but in effect its aim may be diverted, causing him to miss the target at which he is aiming, perhaps mistakenly hitting a neighboring card in the sequence or systematically confusing one symbol for another. Also, if the subject is allowed to continue with the test for too long a time, his scoring rate is likely to drop. That is especially likely to occur if he is asked to continue through a long session without being told his scores. Boredom, monotony, and a logical attitude are destructive, but mild novelty and playfully challenging situations are likely to help him to do his best.

*   *   *

In appraising the results of the parapsychology experiments in general, the first question to consider is that of whether or not a case has been made for the occurrence of any *psi* phenomenon. Because of the prevailing philosophy of science which equates nature with physics, it is plain that this first question is the most difficult one for the average scientist to take up. Once the materialistic philosophy is successfully refuted, however, (an accomplishment that requires only one established exception) it should be possible to come down to ordinary scientific standards in parapsychology. It should then be much easier to answer the many further questions that remain, questions of what kinds of phenomena there are, under what conditions they function, what general psychological and biological characteristics *psi* may have, and, in general, what the whole natural history and rationale of *psi* capacity will reveal.

The decisive research on which the beginning work at the Duke Laboratory was pegged is known as the Pearce-Pratt series.[9] It has the advantage of standing unchallenged by even the most unreasonable of the critics during the most heated stage of the controversy over parapsychology. While the full details must be left for the inquirer to find in the original reports, the essential outline is as follows: A standard deck of twenty-five ESP cards (containing the following symbols: star, circle, square, waves, cross) was shuffled by the experimenter and turned face down on the table. The cards were removed one from the back of the pack without the faces being seen and, after being kept for a minute in the center of the table as a point of "exposure," were put in another pile, still face down, at another corner of the table. One hundred yards away in another building the percipient, who had synchronized his watch with that of the experimenter, attempted to identify the cards as they were "exposed." As a check on the good faith of the two, each made his "record" in duplicate and sealed one copy in an envelope for independent delivery to me. At the end of the designated series of twelve runs through the pack, or three hundred trials, it was found that the score average was 9.9 hits per 25 where mean chance expectation is 5.00. The odds that so high a scoring rate would not occur by chance alone is of the order of millions of millions to one. Sensory contact was completely ruled out and there was no basis for rational inference. A study of the card order revealed no evidence of unusual recurrent patterns. The performance had to be due either to extrasensory perception or to fraud. And because it was anticipated that there might be those who would prefer the fraud alternative, a second half-series was planned in which I sat in with the experimenter as a second observer so that I could observe the adequacy of the precautions.

The average score thus secured was almost the same, 9.3 instead of 9.9.

The scoring obtained in the Pearce-Pratt series just described is actually above the level reached by the same subject when the cards are within a yard of his body (8.0). No process is known in physics today that could operate to convey an impression of these cards to the subject 100 yards away and produce results that were not affected by a distance comparison of 100 to 1. The wave frequencies required, the barriers to be traversed, and the other physical characteristics of the test situation combined to render a physical theory untenable. Once this point became clear, we predicted that *time* should logically have no more relationship to success in ESP tests than *distance*. (The underlying premise is that it is physical change that affords the basis for the experience both of space and of time and that the one is not separable from the other.) Later experimentation confirmed the prediction.[10a] [10b]

Anyone familiar with the history of science would not expect a finding so revolutionary as the Pearce-Pratt series of ESP tests to have been accepted by the orthodox. There was, in fact, a heated controversy precipitated, especially by the attacks of a number of critical psychologists in America, where it should be remembered the behaviorist movement, the extreme form of physicalism in psychology was having its greatest vogue. As would be expected, these attacks did not spring from the less mechanistic schools of psychology; not for example, from the followers of any form of purposive or personalistic psychology, nor from any of the depth psychology groups, and not from the Gestalt school. The published criticism was confined entirely to American and Russian psychologists.

One of the most heavily safeguarded experiments ever carried out in the field of psychology is that known as the Pratt-Woodruff series of ESP tests performed in the Duke Laboratory in 1939. The series was partly a response to a critical article prepared by seven leading experimental psychologists in the U. S. A. who published a paper[11] stating the requirements that would satisfy them in an ESP experiment. Combining their suggestions with the experience of workers in the field of parapsychology, Pratt and Woodruff designed a test based on the screened-touch-matching technique.[12] Under these tightly controlled conditions a highly significant positive result was obtained. The subjects were volunteer students and staff members and were unselected. The details of procedure and precaution are much too elaborate even for outlining here.

Somewhat later in London, Soal and Goldney, carried out a comparably well-controlled series of ESP tests with a single gifted individual as subject.[13] This subject, Mr. B. S., had been tested earlier, had scored but little above the chance level, and had already been dropped when the attention of Soal, the experimenter, was drawn to a displacement effect—a tendency to deflect hits from the direct target to the adjacent ones in the sequence. Soal found that B. S.'s records showed highly significant displacement, and (with Goldney) he began new experiments with him. The results of the lengthy series of tests and the high rate of scoring that prevailed throughout, leave no room for argument about the exclusion of the chance hypothesis. Here, too, the precautions taken for the testing were so much more extensive and thorough than those usually found in the field of experimental psychology as to render any rejection of the results on the ground of methodology unworthy of consideration.

As far as possible over the years, criticisms of the *psi* investigations were met with new modifications in the experiments. Sometimes these had to be incidental; for example, the demand for a repetition by an experimenter with a negative attitude was satisfied incidentally by Soal's work, for Soal had entered into it with a manifestly critical attitude toward the Duke experiments.[14] Likewise, the more apparatus-minded critics insisted that the recording and checking be done by machine in spite of the fact that the safety and objectivity in such experiments as those mentioned above could not be surpassed by mechanical aid. By now, however, a sufficient number of experiments have been carried out with the use of machines to answer this demand.

Among these are the experiments of Tyrrell[15] and of Kahn on ESP[16] and those of McConnell, Snowden and Powell[17] on PK.

The *rational* picture of the *psi* findings, however, is as impressive as are the specific experimental results themselves. First of all, the *psi* experiments only confirm what has been suggested over and over again as a result of the study of large collections of spontaneous psychic experiences. The *psi* hypothesis is not something conceived *de novo* from the abstract; the kind of ability designated as *psi* has been assumed by all the religions of the past as the basis of prophecy, prayer, revelation, seership, communion, omniscience, and the like. The same suggestion of the occurrence of *psi* arises, too, in medicine; for example, in association with hypnosis and with psychoanalysis. From the MacRobert survey[18] of psychiatric opinion of the ESP research it is evident that literally hundreds among that profession have had first-hand encounters with what appear to be *psi* effects. This does not mean, of course, that there is anything pathological about *psi;* rather the evidence indicates there is not.

But quite apart from all these supporting associations, the types of *psi* phenomena are, within themselves, far more rationally interrelated than is realized by any but the most careful student of the field. Consider, for example, how reasonable it is to find that there is in psychokinesis a counterpart to the subject-object relationship represented in clairvoyant ESP. Again, how logically consistent ESP turns out to be in its defiance not merely of a consistent relationship with either space *or* time alone but with *both*. These consistencies can be pursued much farther and wider than these bare statements imply. The whole scope of *psi* findings to date includes many things that would have had to be logically predicted had they been approached in that way, such as the apparent independence of the *psi* function of barriers between subject and object, the absence thus far of any evidence of relationship with mass or size of object (e.g. dice) in the PK experiments, or of size or angle or position or other physical characteristics of the targets in ESP tests. But the topmost logical consideration is the comparatively equal success obtained in telepathy and clairvoyance tests. It seems most logical to conceive of *psi* as transcending these target differences, since it has shown independence of relation to the other far-ranging differences of condition and of target for which the tests have been devised to subject it. If size, distance, position, and location of target mean nothing, why then should objectivity or subjectivity of target? The point is, the explanation of the *psi* function is consistently outside the categories of nature with which we have become familiar through the senses and the study of physics. It is not a confused or uncertain matter. The picture of lawfulness it presents will surely appeal to the reason of any scientist whose philosophy permits him to reason freely about new findings.

Within the realm of psychological relationships, too, there is a wealth of rational considerations that have emerged from the *psi* studies of recent years. Particularly outstanding is the clarity brought into the interpretation of experimental results by the recognition of the irrecoverably unconscious character of the *psi* function. It is now clear that *psi* is the most completely unconscious capacity that has been brought to the attention of the psychologist. It is not to be confused with the recoverably unconscious functions familiar to depth psychology. The subject in a *psi* test is *completely* unaware of the operation of the ability. Recognition of this fact makes immediately understandable the subject's inability to improve on his performance in *psi* tests, to distinguish between success and failure, and to report reliably as to when his *psi* capacity is likely to be successful. Awareness of this characteristic of the deep unconsciousness of *psi* goes far to explain the uncertainty that attaches to *psi* performance in test demonstrations of it. It is not surprising, therefore, to find that a subject may fall into a practice of using *psi* to miss the target consistently even while consciously aiming to hit it. It is understandable, too, that, without the subject realizing what is taking place, his ability to demonstrate his *psi* capacity may decline in the course of the run or other unit of the test series. All of the peculiarities of performance that have been shown by the analyses of test data are better understood since the unconsciousness of the *psi* function has been recognized.

Some further understanding of the place of *psi* in the personality as a whole has been contributed by the studies of the relation between performance in *psi* tests and certain measures of personality variables. The primary finding is that thus far, throughout all the vast amount of work done on the topic, no personality type stands out as a *psi*-personality type. No single trait or combination of traits have been discovered yet as the key to the selection of outstanding performers in *psi* tests. Instead, the many valuable studies made by Stuart, Schmeidler, Humphrey, and others, have generally indicated that the personality state and traits associated with high or low scoring relate to the subject's adaptability to the test situation. There is no reason yet to think that any fundamental tie-up with the *psi* capacity of the individual himself has been revealed.

As a matter of fact, the newer studies in the field of biology suggest that these *psi* capacities are not even confined to man. Exploratory studies indicate they are to be found at least in the horse, the dog, and the cat. That is as far as the inquiry has gone. If *psi* is found throughout the animal world, it will be easier to conceive of it as an early evolutionary acquisition, prior to the development of the complex cerebrum, perhaps even presensory. Its unconscious level of operation, its presence in animals, its utilization of an energetic influence not apprehended by the sense organs and not subject to the familiar time-space-mass relationships, all together point clearly to a distinct order of reality of which personality is a partial derivative. There is, then, a place in nature for human experience that is nonphysical, yet lawful, in its own way. Yet this nonphysical order of nature is by its very interaction with physical energies indicating an interrelationship with the physical world within some larger concept, one that is still beyond realization. There is thus possible a relatively dualistic, as well as a relatively monistic, structure to the person; but no ground for an extreme or unqualified characterization either way. Above all in importance, the discovery of *psi* must result eventually in the liberation of psychology from its present stifling bondage to physicalism, a bondage that has long been barring it from its own legitimate domain, the world of distinctively mental realities.

FOOTNOTES

[1] Coover, John E. *Experiments in Psychical Research,* Stanford University Press, 1917.

[2] Brugmans, H. J. F. W. Some experiments in telepathy performed in the Psychological Institute of the University of Groningen. *Compte-Rendu du Premier Congrès International des Recherches Psychiques,* 1921.

[3] Estabrooks, G. H. A contribution to experimental telepathy. Bull. 5, *Boston Soc. Psych. Res.,* 1927, 1-30.

[4] Rhine, J. B. *Extrasensory Perception.* Boston: Bruce Humphries, 1934.

[5] Warner, L. A second survey of psychological opinion on ESP. *J. Parapsychol.,* 1952, *16,* 284-95.

[6a] Humphrey, E. M. *Handbook of Tests in Parapsychology.* Durham: Parapsychology Laboratory, 1948.

[6b] West, D. J. *Tests for Extrasensory Perception.* London: Society for Psychical Research, 1953.

[7a] McMahan, E. A. An experiment in pure telepathy. *J. Parapsychol.,* 1946, *10,* 224-42.

[7b] Soal, S. G. The experimental situation in psychical research. *J. Parapsychol.,* 1949, *13,* 79-100. (see pp. 92-97).

[8a] Huntington, E. V. Is it chance or ESP? *Am. Scholar,* 1938, 7, 201-10.

[8b] Rhine, J. B. *et al. Extrasensory Perception after Sixty Years.* New York: Henry Holt, 1940, pp. 22-48.

[9] Rhine, J. B., and Pratt, J. G. A review of the Pearce-Pratt distance series of ESP tests. *J. Parapsychol.,* 1954, *3,* 165-177.

[10a] Rhine, J. B. Evidence of precognition in the covariation of salience ratios. *J. Parapsychol.,* 1942, *6,* 111-43.

[10b] Humphrey, E. M., and Rhine, J. B. A confirmatory study of salience in precognition tests. *J. Parapsychol.,* 1942, *6,* 190-219.

[11] Dunlap, K., and others. Adequate experimental testing of "extrasensory perception" based on card sorting. *J. Parapsychol.,* 1939, *3,* 29-37.

[12] Pratt, J. G., and Woodruff, J. L. Size of stimulus symbols in extrasensory perception. *J. Parapsychol.,* 1939, *3,* 121-58.

[13] Soal, S. G., and Goldney, K. M. Experiments in precognitive telepathy. *Proc. Soc. Psych. Res.,* 1943, *47,* 21-150.

[14] Soal, S. G. Fresh light on card-guessing — some new effects. *Proc. Soc. Psych. Res.,* 1940, *46,* 152-98.

[15] Tyrrell, G. N. M. The Tyrrell apparatus for testing extrasensory perception. *J. Parapsychol.,* 1938, *2,* 107-18.

[16] Kahn, S. D. Studies in extrasensory perception. *Proc. Amer. Soc. Psych. Res.,* 1952, *25,* 1-48.

[17] McConnell, R. A., Snowden, R. J., and Powell, K. F. MS awaiting publication.

[18] MacRobert, R. G. Current attitudes of American neuropsychiatrists toward parapsychology: a survey. *J. Parapsychol.,* 1948, *12,* 257-72.

ADDITIONAL REFERENCES

Fisk, G. W., and Mitchell, A. M. J. ESP experiments with clock cards: a new technique with differential scoring. *J. Soc. Psych. Res.*, 1953, *37*, 1-14.

Forwald, H. A further study of the PK placement effect. *J. Parapsychol.*, 1952, *16*, 59-67.

Humphrey, E. M. Success in ESP as related to form of response drawings: I. Clairvoyance experiments. *J. Parapsychol.*, 1946, *10*, 78-106.

—— Success in ESP as related to form of response drawings: II. GESP experiments. *J. Parapsychol.*, 1946, *10*, 181-96.

James, W. "Final impressions of a psychical researcher." *Memories and Studies.* New York and London: Longmans, Green and Co., 1911.

McDougall, W. Editorial introduction. *J. Parapsychol.*, 1937, *1*, 1-9.

Osis, K. A test of the occurrence of a psi effect between man and the cat. *J Parapsychol.*, 1952, *16*, 233-56.

Rhine, J. B. *The New World of the Mind.* New York: William Sloane Associates, 1953.

—— Telepathy and clairvoyance reconsidered. *J. Parapsychol.*, 1945, *9*, 176-93.

—— The problem of psi-missing. *J. Parapsychol.*, 1952, *16*, 90-129.

—— The psychokinetic effect: a review. *J. Parapsychol.*, 1946, *10*, 5-20.

—— *The Reach of the Mind.* New York: William Sloane Associates, 1947.

Rhine, J. B., and Humphrey, E. M. The PK effect: special evidence from hit patterns. I. Quarter distributions of the page. *J. Parapsychol.*, 1944, *8*, 18-60.

Rhine, L. E. Subjective forms of spontaneous psi experiences. *J. Parapsychol.*, 1953, *17*, 77-114.

Soal, S. G., and Bateman, F. *Modern Experiments in Telepathy.* New Haven: Yale Press, 1954.

Schmeidler, G. R. Some relations between Picture-Frustration ratings and ESP scores. *J. Personal.*, 1950, *18*, 331-43.

Schmeidler, G. R., and Murphy, G. The influence of belief and disbelief in ESP upon individual scoring levels. *J. exper. Psychol.*, 1946, *36*, 271-76.

Soal, S. G. and Bateman, F. *Modern Experiments in Telepathy.* London: Faber and Faber, 1953. Also, New Haven: Yale University Press.

Soal, S. G., and Pratt, J. G. ESP performance and target sequence. *J. Parapsychol.*, 1951, *15*, 192-215.

Stuart, C. E. An analysis to determine a test predictive of extra-chance scoring in card-calling tests. *J. Parapsychol.*, 1941, *5*, 99-137.

Thouless, R. H. Thought transference and related phenomena. *J. Parapsychol.*, 1952, *16*, 23-40. (Reprinted from the *Proceedings of the Royal Institution.*)

Thouless, R. H., and Wiesner, B. P. The psi processes in normal and "paranormal" psychology. *J. Parapsychol.*, 1948, *12*, 192-212.

CHAPTER XX

CONTEMPORARY HISTORIES OF PSYCHOLOGY

RALPH WALDO ERICKSON, Ph.D.

Chairman, Department of Psychology
Mississippi State College for Women

EDITORIAL NOTE

This is probably the first time that a review of histories of psychology appears in a general survey of psychology, which is a sign of the times. In a French volume by Foulquié and Deledalle, entitled La Psychologie Contemporaine (1950), *we find the statement that "the Americans lack a truly complete history of psychology." The senior author, in a review of Roback's* History of American Psychology, *in* L'Ecole *had occasion to modify his observation, saying "Mais notre remarque n'est plus vraie depuis l'ouvrage de M. Roback. . . ."*

The impression was gained abroad that Americans were not concerned with the history of science. In a sense it is true, because nearly all of the historians of mathematics, physics, biology, chemistry, psychology, and medicine as well as science in general, in the United States, are not of Anglo-Saxon origin, and very few are natives of America.

Nevertheless, there is at present a growing interest in the subject of history. Dr. Erickson has examined critically a goodly number of psychological books which may be considered historical, including American, German, British, and French works.

Dr. Ralph Waldo Erickson took his Ph.D. degree at the University of Minnesota. In 1929, he began teaching mathemathics and physics in Minnesota colleges, later shifting to psychology. During the war, he was personnel consultant and clinical psychologist in the Army. After the war, he was head of the testing service at Carleton College for some time and has been head of the Department of Psychology at Mississippi State College for Women, since 1947.

HISTORY OF PSYCHOLOGY

In the preface to his *History of American Psychology,* Roback has made the observation that Americans and Canadians have shown great interest in the history of psychology, judging from the number of histories that have been written. Similarly, Boring cited half a dozen histories that have come out between the two editions of his *A History of Experimental Psychology.* Yet most of these histories are apt to be devoted to special fields, such as schools of psychology, American psychology, medical psychology, physiological psychology, experimental psychology, or biographical subjects. Psychology has grown so extensively that it is very difficult to write a history that covers all the main branches.

MURPHY

While some of these histories are quite brief (such as those of Baldwin and Pillsbury) [1] that of Gardner Murphy [2] is an ambitious attempt to trace the developments of most of the important fields of psychology. Although he admits neglecting some fields such as those of sensory processes, mental testing, applied psychology, abnormal psychology, comparative psychology, and learning theory, still they are not ignored completely. A whole chapter, for example, is devoted to the measurement of intelligence, and abnormal psychology obtains consideration in discussions of physiological psychology and personality.

Murphy divides his history into four sections: one on the antecedents of modern psychology, the second on the rise of the research spirit, the third on psychological schools, and the last on representative research areas. The earlier of the two editions also had an interesting appendix on German psychology by Klüver. The section on antecedents begins with the time of Homer and is followed by short accounts of the leading philosophers and psychologists up to the middle of the nineteenth century.

The section on the rise of the research spirit begins with a short account of science in general during the early nineteenth century followed by an account of the work of Weber, Fechner, Johannes Müller, and Beneke. There are then two chapters on British psychology with an unusually good account of the impact of evolution on psychology and the social sciences. Coming back to the continent, there are chapters on psychiatry (primarily French), German physiological psychology, and on Wundt and his students. These are followed by chapters on topics like memory, neurology (cortical localization and the neurone theory, with a separate section on Sherrington), and learning. Finally, there are three chapters on William James, Structuralism and Functionalism, and the Würzburg School, which probably should have been placed in the next section.

Besides the three chapters just mentioned, the next section includes short objective accounts of behaviorism, associationism, gestalt psychology, field theory, and the psychoanalysts. One might disagree on placing Hull, Skinner, and Tolman with the associationists instead of under behaviorism, and more space probably should have been devoted to them. The last section does not attempt to cover all research areas, dealing only with intelligence, physiological psychology, child psychology, social psychology, and personality. On the whole, however, in less than five hundred pages, Murphy's history probably covers more ground than any we now have.

BORING

As a student of Titchener, it is natural that Boring should devote his history to that of experimental psychology and dedicate the first volume to him.[3] His work, however, is not entirely restricted to the experimental in the Titchenerian sense, as it also goes into physiological psychology, animal psychology, educational psychology, schools of psychology, and even philosophy. The two editions of the first volume are much alike, but the introductory approach is quite different. In the first, there is a brief account of science and philosophy up to the nineteenth century in an introduction of thirty pages. In the second edition, with the exception of the physiologists, most of this is omitted, and replaced by a discussion of the naturalistic versus the personalistic views of history. While Boring appears to be influenced by Tolstoi's arguments in favor of the naturalistic, still his history is largely personalistic, almost biographical in character. Otherwise the two editions are much the same up to the contemporary period.

After the introduction there are two sections on the origins of experimental psychology in science (physiological psychology, in first edition) and in philosophy. The first section centers around Bell, Magendie, Johannes Müller, Gall and Spurzheim, the physiology of the brain, Weber, hypnotism, and reaction time. The section on philosophy begins with a page on Aristotle and continues with accounts of the modern classical philosophers from Descartes to Kant (with the omission of Spinoza). The next section on the founding of experimental psychology has a chapter each on Fechner, Helmholtz and Wundt. There follow three sections on the establishment of modern psychology in Germany, Great Britain, and America. (The first edition groups them together, with Brentano, Stumpf, and G. E. Müller placed in the preceding section). In the German section, the complexities of the content-versus-act psychologies are considered with the result that Titchener gets lost between the Würzburg school and the Act school, while Külpe gets spread both before and after Titchener in connection with these same schools. Short accounts are given of British psychologists, such as Ward, Sully, and McDougall, but most of the chapter on Great Britain goes to Darwin and Galton. The two chapters on American psychology begin with James and his contemporaries, whom he considers as pioneers. The second chapter is on functional psychology as a school at Chicago and at Columbia, with added sections on the development of educational psychology, and mental tests.

The last section of Boring's history is devoted to later trends in modern psychology but is actually a continuation of the preceding chapter on schools of psychology with a chapter on brain function, placed after the chapters on Gestalt psychology and behaviorism and before that on dynamic psychology. Under dynamic psychology, Boring includes several schools, such as those of Freud and McDougall, as well as Lewin and other Gestalt psychologists, Tolman (who is also classified as a behaviorist), Murray, and Woodsworth (also dealt with in the chapter on functionalism). The section on behaviorism in the first edition is expanded in the second into a chapter on behavioristics, in which Jennings is included with Loeb, Thorndike with Hunter, the positivists (Comte as well as Carnap) with J. Mck. Cattell, the psychoanalysts and the Würzburg school with behaviorism. Even stranger is the attempt to combine the metaphysical system of logical empiricism with a method of definition (operationsm). On the whole, Boring has moved into the behavioristic camp sufficiently to hold that "the behaviorist can eat the cake of consciousness and have it too."[4] No attempts are made to answer the criticisms of Roback and Heidbreder (who are mentioned in the notes), while those of the present writer are completely ignored.[5]

In the sequel to his history, Boring restricts his account to sensation and perception, expanding much of what was treated in a more general way in the first volume. The account is much more scientific, with philosophical background largely eliminated. The result is a work packed with interesting detail and revealing the training of Titchener.

ROBACK

While neither Murphy nor Boring has much to say about American psychology before the time of William James, nearly a third of Roback's history is devoted to this period.[6] The account goes back to colonial days when psychology was buried quite deeply in philosophy or religious dogma. The influence of the Scottish school of philosophy and of German idealism is clearly pictured, as well as that of science and medicine. While psychology was dominated to a large extent by theologians, Benjamin Rush, a physician, had built up a psychophysical parallelism at the beginning of the nineteenth century. At about the time of the Civil War, his son, James Rush developed a system which leads Roback to call him the first behaviorist, although he apparently had no influence on the later movement of that name. In this pre-James era, it is also pointed out that John Dewey began his career under the influence of idealism, and that his early textbook of psychology was idealistic.

In the second section of his history, entitled "Psychology Comes of Age", Roback gives extended treatment to William James, G. Stanley Hall, Ladd, Cattell, Baldwin, Titchener, and Münsterberg. More than usual appreciation is given here to Hall and Münsterberg, and Cattell is definitely taken out of the behaviorist camp. With regard to Münsterberg, Roback regards him: "In his day, the most famous psychologist in the world, with the possible exception of Wundt".[7] While it would be difficult to convince most psychologists of this, still a strong case is presented to prove that Boring has underestimated him in his history. Roback is certainly correct in pointing out that Münsterberg's fame has suffered from his being both a German and a Jew. For the terrific anti-German propaganda before and during the first world war (even more vicious than during the second world war) affected academic circles as well as the general public. Add to this the strong anti-Jewish feeling smoldering below the surface (as it did in Germany before Hitler), and it was inevitable that Münsterberg would suffer.

Part three of Roback's psychology is devoted to the schools of psychology. As the structuralism of Titchener is considered in the preceding section, the discussion begins with a consideration of functionalism, passes to behaviorism, then to the dynamic psychologies, operationism, factorial analysis, semantics, and the neo-scholastics. The chapter on functionalism contains an interesting letter of Angell's showing that his opposition to behaviorism was greater than generally known. In the chapter on behaviorism, the fundamentals of the movement are traced to Max Meyer rather than John Watson, with roots extending back to James Rush. Watson is reduced to not much more than a promoter: with most of the attacked concepts now coming back into the general picture. Psychology once more has to consider problems of consciousness, instinct, and purpose.

Dynamic psychology is covered in several chapters embracing such diverse investigators as Morton Prince, Freud, McDougall, Woodworth, Köhler, Lewin, Tolman, G. W. Allport, Murray, and Troland. It would appear that the term is getting too broad to be useful in distinguishing schools, as practically all psychology is dynamic, being based on the needs of the organism. In this connection, Roback shows that the greatness of McDougall was not properly appreciated in this country (although he was in England). Similarly, the chapter on Gestalt psychology gives a higher estimate of this movement than Boring is willing to grant. When one considers the dominant position of behaviorism with its attempt to keep out everything non-behavioristic as being unscientific, the impact of the Gestalt movement has been terrific. Intellectual horizons became widened and even philosophy became respectable. Instead of becoming a minor branch of physiology, psychology became a science in its own right, without loss of consciousness.

ETHNIC PRODUCT OR CULTURE?

In his discussion of the Gestalt movement, Roback has brought up a question which is usually ignored because of emotional reactions. In pointing out that most of the early leaders of the movement were Jews, he suggests that an ethnic rather than a religious interpretation should be made. This could be either a gene linking or family tradition. Such a position requires considerable courage, as it exposes him to the charge that his position is essentially that of Houston Chamberlain, E. R. Jaensch, and Hitler. Where there is little or no scientific evidence, it is as easy to build up unfavorable stereotypes as favorable ones. In fact, Jaensch is the only one who has presented any experimental evidence, and that would doubtless be regarded as biased. For what kind of gene linking or family tradition would predispose toward Gestalt on the part of Jews? Would it not be much easier to use the cultural factors? Probably the best solution is in the dominance of the German universities throughout the whole of Central and Eastern Europe. It is quite likely that all the leaders were familiar with the works of the precursors of the movement. In addition, there was often physical contact, as well as through German psychological journals present in the universities of the Scandinavian and Baltic countries. Wertheimer, Köhler, and Koffka were working together on the experiment leading to the 1912 article that precipitated the movement, while Lewin was a student of Köhler's at Berlin. It would be difficult to imagine that Rubin and others had not been influenced by Wertheimer's article, just as the sale of Köhler's, Koffka's, and Lewin's books in this country indicate a great interest in the movement as a movement regardless of the religious or ethnic position of the authors.

It would seem desirable, however, to indicate in a history, facts of interest to the reader, and Roback is quite correct in considering items of religion and nationality of importance. But there seems to be no necessary connection between Gestalt and either the Jewish religion or a Jewish ethnic group.

DIVERSITY IN AMERICAN PSYCHOLOGY

With regard to the last chapters, Roback points out, in contrast to Boring, that operationism can be used in a mentalistic psychology as well as in a behavioristic one, and that there are limits to its use, even in physics. In the section on factor analysis, there is a discussion of the British versus the American position of factor interpretation with Roback tending to be somewhat skeptical of the whole movement. The section on semantics, on the other hand, indicates that Korzybski should be taken more seriously than he usually is, if for no other reason than the interest in semantics that he has aroused. The last school is the neo-scholastic which is usually passed by as a remnant of the Middle Ages. Roback presents some of the contemporary leaders both in this country and in French Canada, but the final impression is that the Catholic Church has not moved very far from Thomas Aquinas. The last chapter gives a brief summary of some of the branches of present-day psychology.

To sum up the three leading present-day histories of psychology in this country: Murphy has given us the best balanced although brief account; Boring an excellent picture of the experimental side, but somewhat biased towards behaviorism on the theoretical side; while Roback, leaning in the opposite direction with a slight emphasis on Gestalt psychology, gives an excellent picture of American psychology.

BRITISH HISTORIANS

BRETT

Passing next north of the border, we find the monumental three volume treatise of G. S. Brett of Canada.[8] From the contemporary point of view, the work is out of date as the last volume was published in 1921, limiting the account to that date as well as suffering from a shift in interest in historical topics. To remedy these defects, a one-volume edition has recently been edited by R. S. Peters, of England, who has omitted sections of the original and added an introduction, a final chapter, and introductory comments before each chapter.[9] The omissions are at times whole sections, at other times only a paragraph or less, or footnotes only. On the whole, most of the original material is retained, although the order of presentation is often changed. All of the first chapter on primitive thought is omitted, but most of the account of the Greeks through Aristotle is retained. The three chapters on Plato and the five on Aristotle are practically intact. The individuals of the next few centuries with the exception of the material on the Stoics and Epicureans is largely removed. While most of those left out, with the possible exception of Cicero and Plutarch, are now regarded as minor individuals, it is rather odd that the chapter on Oriental psychology should be eliminated. The increasing interest in India, Egypt, and Persia makes this omission a distinct loss.

While many of the early Christian accounts are retained, Brett's discussion of Tertullian, Gregory of Nyssa, and Nemesius is taken out, leaving a rather large blank between Origen and St. Augustine. Most of the medieval period has only short omissions, with the next large omission being the chapter on the expansion of psychology in the 17th century, primarily devoted to education and literary writers. Peters believes that literary men and ethical teachers do not belong in psychology as their theories can not be tested in the laboratory or consulting room.[10]

In the 18th century, most of the minor philosophers between Leibniz and Kant are omitted, as are in the 19th century, the German Idealists. In the chapter "From Fechner to Wundt", one is surprised to find both Stumpf and G. E. Müller missing. Of the last two chapters on the progress and scope of modern psychology, only the section on William James is retained.

As an appendex to Brett, Peters has added a chapter on 20th-century trends. Short accounts are given of most of the schools with his chief attention centered on Freud because of his "overwhelming importance and influence."[11] A short section on child psychology and intelligence tests leads up to factor analysis with emphasis on Spearman (Thurstone is almost completely ignored). The chapter ends with a short survey of physiological and social psychology and with the question of whether psychological laws are possible.

On the whole, one wonders whether the new Brett is an improvement on the old. By using smaller print the three original volumes are condensed into one, but Peters has probably added more words of his own than he has removed of Brett's, so that it is still a very large work. It would be a tremendous task to condense such a work, but the removal of parts is always a delicate task. The result is still somewhat too dependent on philosophy, with too little discussion of 19th-century empirical and experimental psychology, and too little on the antecedents of the modern schools. One might also object to some of the rearrangement, in which Peters adopts a classification of topics that changes Brett's more chronological order. For example, Brett had a section devoted to an age of transition which included the Scottish School, Mill, Herbart, and Beneke, among others. This was followed by a section on modern psychology which included Wundt. Peters, on the other hand, places Wundt in a chapter on the observationist tradition along with Locke, Berkeley, Hume, and Mill. The result is that Wundt is placed before Kant, Herbart, and Beneke.

SPEARMAN

Coming next to another distinguished Englishman, we have Spearman's *Psychology Down The Ages*.[12] It is not a history in the usual sense of beginning at a definite time and considering successive contributions in a chronological manner. Instead, the author has taken various topics like intelligence, thought, or emotion, from various points of view such as a philosophical one, as faculties, as subject to law. Each of these in turn is illustrated by references to historical figures without any historical context. As a result, the same person may be referred to many times throughout the work; while several people widely separated in time may be referred to within a short space. For example, Flugel, Lotze, Titchener, and Nemesius are mentioned in that order on the same page.[13] To completely appreciate the work requires considerable previous historical background.

Spearman divides his work into two parts, a structural and a functional. The structural is divided into three sections: the subject matter of psychology, the problem of faculties as powers, and the interrelationships of the parts of the psyche. The functional part is divided into two sections: laws of psychology and correlational results. Spearman gives a rather pessimistic view of the structural part: philosophy has been of little help and has been a source of trouble (yet he makes more references to Aristotle than to anyone else, with Plato a close second), too little has been obtained from physiology, while associationism, Gestalt psychology, and faculty psychology are all failures. With regard to Gestalt psychology, he goes so far as to regard it as a confusion of objective and subjective configurations, which is not even original. By oversimplification he traces the movement back to Aristotle by way of Aquinas, Brentano, Meinong, Ehrenfels, and Krueger. It is also interesting that Spearman considers Krueger as the head and founder rather than Wertheimer. The latter is given credit for the law of *Prägnanz,* while the *phi*-phenomenon experiment of 1912 is considered as of little significance.

The functional view is regarded by Spearman as more hopeful with the possibility of laws throughout psychology, but especially with the possibility of correlational studies leading to his position of general, group, and special factors. This section is essentially a defence of his position against the attacks of American critics. While he doesn't go so far as Peters in ignoring Thurstone, still one is left with the impression that the rivalry of Thurstone and Hotelling—Kelley should cancel them out, leaving Spearman's position intact. Possibly Spearman resents the reduction of his system to a part of Thurstone's (the special case of unit rank).

Flugel

Another British author who has written an excellent history in spite of its brevity is J. C. Flugel.[14] Beginning with the year 1833, brief accounts are given to most of the leading figures from Herbart to the modern schools. His treatment of both American and Continental psychologists, specially the German, compares quite well with that of the British. French psychology, however, is almost completely ignored. Spearman is probably over emphasized, especially as the American workers in this field are treated quite casually. With regard to Münsterberg, Flugel differs quite radically with Roback. Although admitting that he had exerted considerable influence, Flugel holds that "Münsterberg never developed into an important psychologist."[15] Flugel also differs from Spearman with regard to the Gestalt school. After admitting the possibility of Spearman's criticism that this school has overemphasized the unitariness of configurations, he believes that it has nevertheless played an important rôle in perception, and has proved a valuable counterweight to behaviorism.[16]

German Historians

Coming next to Germany, the triple tragedy of the Treaty of Versailles and of being the loser in two world wars, with the consequent impoverishment of the country, has led to a considerable curtailment in publications, including histories of psychology. Accordingly, the best-known works in this field were those of Dessoir and Klemm, published before the first world war.[17] Between the wars, however, there appeared the work of Müller-Freienfels, which is of primary importance.[18]

Müller-Freienfels

The work begins with a short historical introduction up to about 1880, and then considers the various psychological movements in detail. This presentation may seem unusual to the American reader for it is presented from the European point of view, which places emphasis on topics which are usually ignored by Americans or shifted to philosophy. That is not to say that Müller-Freienfels is out of sympathy with American psychology or lacks knowledge of it, for at one time he had been a student of William James.

Like Spearman, Müller-Freienfels finds it necessary to consider the modern development of psychology in parallel movements. There are only six of these, however, and each shows the historical relationships in an unusually clear manner. The first section deals with the analysis of consciousness; not only into its elements (with corresponding syntheses), but also in connection with the totality of consciousness. In this way he is able to consider the interactions of the sensationist school influenced by English and French philosophers from Locke to Mill and Taine; the primarily German school, headed by Wundt and his followers, influenced by philosophers from Leibniz and Kant; finally the primarily Austrian school, beginning with Brentano and eventually culminating in the Gestalt movement.

The second section deals with physiological psychology, and includes not only a consideration of the problems of localization, but also problems such as Kretschmer's types of physique, and biological problems such as Driesch's vitalism. The third section shifts emphasis to the motor side with James, Functionalism, Behaviorism, the Russian reflexologists, McDougall, Woodworth, Ribot, Bergson, Piéron, Klages, and Müller-Freienfels himself as representative. While James is too large to be placed in such a narrow category, Müller-Freienfels presents considerable evidence for his interpretation. Of interest here is also the placing of Münsterberg as one of the leaders of the functionalist school.

The fourth section deals with the dynamic factors underlying consciousness, the problems of capacities and dispositions, while the fifth includes hypnosis and the psychoanalytic schools. The sixth section takes up a broadened social psychology including folk psychology, cultural and race psychology, even including a discussion of Spengler. In conclusion, an appendix is added on parapsychology, to consider the widespread interest in this field. He is aware of the emotional attitudes of many psychologists toward the various contributions until he reaches the real difficulty involved. This difficulty is that no amount of evidence is satisfactory until the causal relationships are explained.

On the whole, this history of Müller-Freienfels is very helpful in showing relationships not only among psychologists but also in connection with other fields of science. There is no hesitation in taking material from philosophy, biology, sociology, or anthropology with the result that there is a feeling of freedom of interpretation and a broadening of one's point of view.

French Historians

In considering French psychology, most histories are apt to

be satisfied with a chapter on abnormal psychology and a few paragraphs on Ribot, Binet, Piéron, and Piaget. It is therefore a pleasure to find a work by Paul Foulquié, assisted by Gérard Deledalle, which is essentially a historical introduction to contemporary psychology.[19] Most of the work is by Foulquié, with Deledalle furnishing the chapter on American experimental psychology. The introduction gives a short philosophical account of French philosophy from Descartes to Cousin, with a page devoted to the British associationists. This is followed by a section on the new psychology in three chapters: one on the German developments from Fechner to Wundt (4 pages) and on the French developments (Ribot, Binet, and Dumas in 18 pages), one on American psychology; and the third on non-conscious psychologies. The American chapter is quite comprehensive, beginning with James and the schools, including Holt, Washburn, and Calkins, and continuing with accounts of animal psychology, social psychology, and the measurement of intelligence. The chapter on psychology without consciousness begins with Pavlov and Bekhterev, continues with the French school of Piéron and Guillaume, and ends with an account of American behaviorism (Watson, Max Meyer, Weiss, Tolman, and an unusually extensive treatment of Kantor).

The second section of Foulquié's work, dealing with the renewal of subjective tradition, includes discussions on James, Bergson, and Delacroix. While Delacroix is best known in this country for his studies on mysticism, it may seem strange to place James in the subjectivist tradition. But just as he can be placed as a forerunner to functionalism and behaviorism, and as Müller-Freienfels could place him in a motor setting, so Foulquié presents good evidence for his position. Evidently the many-faceted James is difficult to exhaust. Bergson is largely unknown to American psychologists (although well known to philosophers), but he has evidently had a considerable influence on French psychology. The second chapter, on subjectivism in Germany and France, deals with the Würzburg school, the imageless thought controversy, and the works of

Dilthey, Spranger, and Jaspers. The third chapter, on the unconscious, links together such movements as Christian Science, hypnotism (the Paris and Nancy schools), Babinski, and Coué, with the psychoanalysts. To the usual discussions of Freud, Adler, and Jung is added that of Szondi, who is usually considered in America as merely the author of another projective test.

The last section considers various syntheses of the objective and subjective. The first, on the Gestalt movement, traces this school from Ehrenfels, through Krüger, the Graz school, and the Berlin school to Köhler and Koffka. The second chapter presents two French schools, one which he labels a psychobiological movement, the other the psychology of the governor or conductor. In the first of these he includes Pradines, Burloud, and Ruyer. Perhaps Foulquié should also be placed here, as all four are greatly influenced by Bergson, emphasize the importance of the will, and stress the goals or ends which give meaning to life. The second French school is represented by Janet and Lagache who combine a humanistic with a clinical approach to psychology. Finally there is a chapter on phenomenology which is traced through Brentano, Husserl, Heidegger, and Jaspers to modern existentialism. It is rather interesting that Brentano and Husserl are placed in the existential tradition rather than with the Gestalt movement, and that Kierkegaard is given no credit at all as the originator of existentialism.

It is evident from this work that histories which ignore French psychology have serious omissions, and that the influence of philosophy is still sufficiently great to make modern European psychology unintelligible to those ignorant of it. Psychology still rests apparently on a philosophical foundation.

Space permits only the mention of works devoted to special topics. Zilboorg's account of medical psychology, for example, gives an excellent history of the demonological concept of medical disorders.[20] Oberndorf in his history of psychoanalysis relates how the medical profession succeeded in excluding lay analysis in this country in spite of Freud's desires.[21] He also frankly reveals that failures in treatment are more numerous than psychoanalysts usually admit. While on this topic, mention should also be made of the first volume of Ernest Jones' biography of Freud, which includes the Fliess period, based on letters that Freud wanted destroyed.[22]

On the history of physiological psychology, we have Fearing's work on Reflex Action, while Hilgard gives an account of learning theories.[23] The current trend series, edited by Dennis, also has historical significance, especially the volume on *Current Trends in Psychological Theory*.[24] On the schools of psychology, there are the excellent accounts of Heidbreder and Woodworth, while the Psychologies of 1925 and 1930 are now classics.[25] As source books in the history of psychology, the older work of Rand is now supplemented by the readings of Dennis.[26] In terms of autobiography, Murchison's collection now runs to four volumes.[27] Finally, shorter accounts are given in periodicals, such as that on clinical psychology by Watson, and that on Italian psychology by Misiak and Staudt.[28]*

Editorial Note

* Since Dr. Erickson corrected the proofs, the volume *Catholics in Psychology: A Historical Survey,* by H. Misiak and V. M. Staudt (N. Y.: McGraw-Hill, 1954) has appeared.

FOOTNOTES

1 Baldwin, J. M. *History of Psychology; A Sketch and an Interpretation,* Putnam, 1913. Pillsbury, Walter B. *The History of Psychology,* Norton 1929.

2 Murphy, Gardner. *Historical Introduction to Modern Psychology,* Harcourt, Brace, 1928 and 1949.

3 Boring, Edwin G. *A History of Experimental Psychology.* Appleton-Century Crofts, 1929 and 1950.

—— *Sensation and Perception in the History of Experimental Psychology.* Appleton-Century, 1942.

PRESENT-DAY PSYCHOLOGY

[4] *Op. cit.*, 2nd ed. p. 659.
[5] Roback, A. A. *Behaviorism and Psychology*. Sci-Art Publishers, 1923.
—— *Behaviorism at Twenty-five*. Sci-Art Publishers, 1937.
Heidbreder, E. *Seven Psychologies*. Century Co., 1933, pp. 234-286.
Erickson, Ralph W. An Examination of Prof. Edwin G. Boring's System of Psychology. *J. Gen. Psychol.*, 1941, pp. 63-79.
—— An Examination of the System of Prof. L. S. Lashley. *J. Gen. Psychol.*, 1950, pp. 243-260.
—— An Examination of Edward C. Tolman's System of Psychology. *J. Gen. Psychol.*, 1948, 73-90.
[6] Roback, A. A. *History of American Psychology*. Library Publishers, 1952.
[7] —— *op. cit.*, plate 17 opposite p. 272.
[8] Brett, G. S. *A History of Psychology*, 3 vols. Allen Unwin Ltd., 1912 and 1921.
[9] Peters, R. S. *Brett's History of Psychology*. Allen Unwin, 1953.
[10] Peters, *op. cit.*, p. 135.
[11] —— *op. cit.*, p. 693.
[12] Spearman, C. *Psychology Down the Ages*, 2 vols. Macmillan, 1937.
[13] —— *op. cit.*, vol. 2, p. 89.
[14] Flugel, J. C. *A Hundred Years of Psychology*. Macmillan, 1933.
[15] —— *op. cit.*, p. 213.
[16] —— *op. cit.*, p. 250.
[17] —— Dessoir, M. *Geschichte der neureen deutschen Psychologie*, 1894.
—— *Outlines of the History of Psychology*. Macmillan, 1912.
Klemm, O. *History of Psychology*. Scribners, 1914.
[18] Müller-Freienfels, R. *The Evolution of Modern Psychology*. Yale, 1935.
[19] Foulquié, P. and Deledalle, G. *La Psychologie Contemporaine*. Presses Universitaires de France, 1951.
[20] Zilboorg, G. *A History of Medical Psychology*. W. W. Norton, 1941.
[21] Oberndorf, C. P. *A History of Psychoanalysis in America*. Grune and Stratton, 1953.
[22] Jones, Ernest. *The Life and Work of Sigmund Freud*, vol. 1. Basic Books, 1953.
[23] Fearing, F. *Reflex Action*. Williams and Wilkins, 1930.
Hilgard, E. R. *Theories of Learning*. Appleton-Century-Crofts, 1948.
[24] Dennis, Wayne, et al. *Current Trends in Psychological Theory*. Univ. of Pittsburgh Press, 1951.
[25] Heidbreder, Edna. *Seven Psychologies*. The Century Co., 1933.
Woodworth, R. S. *Contemporary Schools of Psychology*. Ronald Press, 1948.
Murchison, Carl (ed.). *Psychologies of 1925*. Clark Univ. Press, 1926.
—— *Psychologies of 1930*. Clark Univ. Press, 1930.
[26] Rand, B. *The Classical Psychologists*. Houghton-Mifflin, 1912.
Dennis, Wayne (ed.) *Readings in the History of Psychology*. Appleton-Century, 1948.
[27] Murchison, Carl (ed.) *History of Psychology in Autobiography*, 4 vols. Clark Univ. Press, 1930 on.
[28] Watson, R. I. A Brief History of Clinical Psychology. *Psychology Bulletin*, 1953, *50*, pp. 321-346.
Misiak, H. and Staudt, V. Psychology in Italy. *Psychology Bulletin*, 1953, *50*, pp. 347-361.

PRESENT-DAY PSYCHOLOGY

BIBLIOGRAPHY

1 Baldwin, J. M. *History of Psychology; A Sketch and an Interpretation.* Putnam, 1913.

2 Boring, E. G. *A History of Experimental Psychology.* Century-Appleton-Crofts, 1950.

3 —— *Sensation and Perception in the History of Experimental Psychology.* Appleton-Century, 1942.

4 Brett, G. S. *A History of Psychology,* 3 vols. George Allen and Co., 1912 and 1921.

5 Dennis, Wayne (Ed.) *Current Trends in Psychological Theory.* Univ. of Pittsburgh Press, 1951.

6 —— *Readings in the History of Psychology.* Appleton-Century, 1948.

7 Dessoir, M. *Outlines of the History of Psychology.* Macmillan, 1912.

8 Erickson, R. W. An Examination of Prof. Edwin G. Boring's System of Psychology. *J. General Psychology,* 1941, *24,* pp. 63-79.

9 —— An Examination of Edward C. Tolman's System of Psychology. *J. General Psychology,* 1948, *39,* pp. 73-90.

10 —— An Examination of the System of Prof. K. S. Lashley. *J. General Psychology,* 1950, *42,* pp. 243-260.

11 Fearing, F. *Reflex Action.* Williams and Wilkins, 1930.

12 Flugel, J. C. *A Hundred Years of Psychology.* Macmillan, 1933.

13 Heidbreder, Edna. *Seven Psychologies.* The Century Co., 1933.

14 Hilgard, E. R. *Theories of Learning.* Appleton-Century-Crofts, 1948.

15 Jones, Ernest. *The Life and Work of Sigmund Freud,* vol. 1. Basic Books, 1953.

16 Klemm, O. *History of Psychology.* Scribners, 1914.

17 Misiak, Henryk, and Staudt, Virginia. Psychology in Italy. *Psychological Bulletin,* 1953, *50,* pp. 347-361.

18 Müller-Freienfels, R. *The Evolution of Modern Psychology.* Yale Univ. Press, 1935.

19 Murchison, Carl (Ed.) *History of Psychology in Autobiography.* Clark Univ. Press, 1930-1952.

20 —— *Psychologies of 1925.* Clark Univ. Press, 1926.

21 —— *Psychologies of 1930.* Clark Univ. Press, 1930.

22 Murphy, Gardner, *Historical Introduction to Modern Psychology.* Harcourt Brace, 1949.

23 Oberndorf, C. P. *A History of Psychoanalysis in America.* Grune and Stratton, 1953.

24 Peters, R. S. *Brett's History of Psychology.* George Allen and Unwin, 1953.

25 Pillsbury, Walter B. *The History of Psychology.* Norton, 1929.

26 Rand, B. *The Classical Psychologists.* Houghton Mifflin, 1912.

27 Roback, A. A. *Behaviorism and Psychology.* Sci-Art Publishers, 1923.

28 —— *Behaviorism at Twenty-five.* Sci-Art Publishers, 1937.

29 —— *A History of American Psychology.* Library Publishers, 1952.

30 Spearman, C. *Psychology Down the Ages,* 2 vols. Macmillan, 1937.

31 Watson, Robert I. A Brief History of Clinical Psychology. *Psychological Bulletin,* 1953, *50,* pp. 321-346.

32 Woodworth, R. S. *Contemporary Schools of Psychology.* Ronald Press, 1948.

33 Zilboorg, G. A. *A History of Medical Psychology.* Norton, 1941.

PART III

Dynamic and Clinical Psychology

CHAPTER XXI

SOME RECENT EXPERIMENTAL WORK IN PSYCHODIAGNOSTICS

WERNER WOLFF, Ph.D.

Chairman, Department of Psychology
Bard College

EDITORIAL NOTE

Psychodiagnostics may be defined as the interpretation of personality traits from external symptoms, such as the features, facial expression, vocal inflection, gait, gesture, handwriting, and numerous other manifestations. Its place in psychology has not been secure, because somehow fragmentary experiments by skeptical investigators have yielded negative results in certain respects, which, by way of transfer, are damaging to the subject as a whole. It is thought to appeal to popular "gold-brick" demands, and that is another reason for its cavalier treatment among American psychologists, who put almost all their faith in tests, both direct and projective, interviews, ratings, etc.

Psychodiagnostics covers a large area. It is of great use in some of the applied aspects, personnel work, e.g., but it plays a considerable part in clinical psychology too. In a sense it is an ancient art, dating from Hippocrates, but recently it has been filtered through the prism of dynamic psychology, which lends it added weight.

Dr. Werner Wolff, who has contributed the chapter on this branch, has done much research along these lines. He calls his own approach "experimental depth psychology". Shortly after obtaining his Ph.D. at the University of Berlin, he served as Visiting Professor of Psychology at the University of Barcelona. He later was research associate and lecturer at Vassar College. At present, he is Head of the Psychology Department at Bard College. Dr. Wolff has worked on a variety of projects. He is the author of several volumes, such as The Expression of Personality (*New York,* 1943), The Personality of the Pre-School Child (*New York,* 1946), Abnormal Psychology, Diagrams of the Unconscious (*New York,* 1948), The Dream: Mirror of Conscience (*New York,* 1952), Values and Personality, What is Psychology? *and a large number of articles. He is also editor of* Personality, *and secretary-general of the Inter-American Society of Psychology.*

EXPERIMENTAL DEPTH PSYCHOLOGY AND
PSYCHOSYNTHESIS

EUCLIDEAN PSYCHOLOGY

Psychology and psychiatry have been called the science of the mind, following the physical model of science with its postulates of control, analysis, and prediction. The ideal of such a model was the machine, in which all operations could be controlled, the mechanisms of which could be analyzed, and the performance of which could be predicted. Operations, mechanisms, and predictions could be duplicated after the master design. In a machine the connections of its elements are fixed and the sum of its parts, fitting ingeniously into each other, constitute the whole. The machine only operates by a correct interdetermination of its parts, and therefore its function verifies the adequateness of its structure. Science attempted a similar rational design.

The concept of rational design is based upon Euclidean geometry which developed from a design on a plane surface. According to Euclidean geometry the three angles of a triangle add up to two right angles. But this is only true if we draw the triangle on plane paper; it is not true any more if the triangle is drawn on a sphere or on an egg. Similarly, many other of Euclid's theorems do not work any more if the diagrams are used upon a material other than a plane surface. The relationships of our mathematical schemes change according to the material we employ. For physical science it was necessary to develop non-Euclidean geometries adapted to different materials, each of them with its own particular mathematical expression.

For instance, according to Einstein, our measures of length and of time vary with our motion. Two events that are simultaneous for one observer are separated for another observer who moves with different motion. The concept of fixed distances had to be given up just as the concept of fixed cause and effect relationships, and therefore of a fixed predictability. According to Planck's quantum theory, we cannot observe the course of nature without disturbing it, as he demonstrated it with the behavior of electrons; in order to see the electron we have to use light, the energy of which will disturb the electron's behavior in an unpredictable manner. For chemistry the idea of fixed entities had to be given up. Here the combination of two entities produces a new one, a new whole which is not any more the sum of its parts. For instance, from our knowledge of the properties of oxygen and of the properties of hydrogen, we cannot deduce that their composition produces water, which, according to the theory of emergence, emerges as something new.

Although psychology and psychiatry attempted to follow the model of the physical sciences, they did not accept the new orientations which were brought in by the new theories of the physical sciences. They still apply to man a scheme as if he were a plane surface. They still operate with a fixed relationship of stimulus and response without considering the dynamics and the motion of the system in which they appear. With the assumption of a rigid determinism of cause and effect it was hoped to make general predictions applicable to everybody, neglecting the dependence of cause-effect relationships on an individual setting.

With the ideal of a quantitative determination of reactions one forgot that a very high or a very low quantity may transform the quality. Searching for the causes of behavior, the investigator analyzed behavior into its elements making the assumption that any complex behavior is a sum of reflexes,

A

B

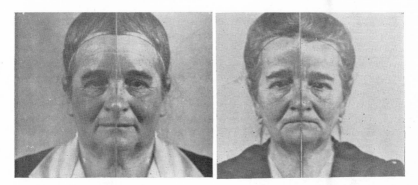

R—R   R—R

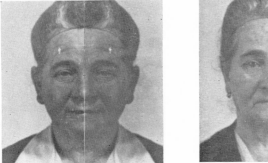

L—L   L—L

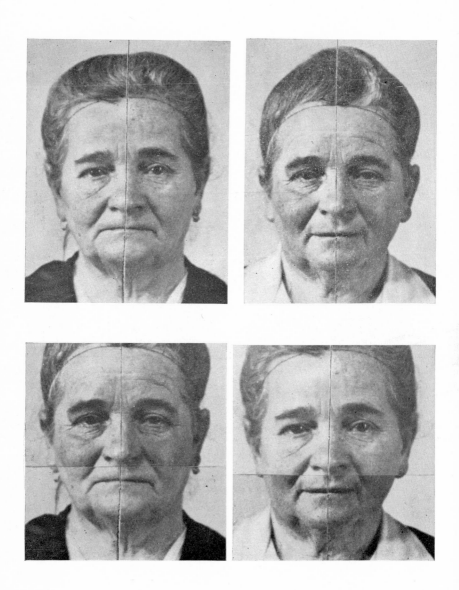

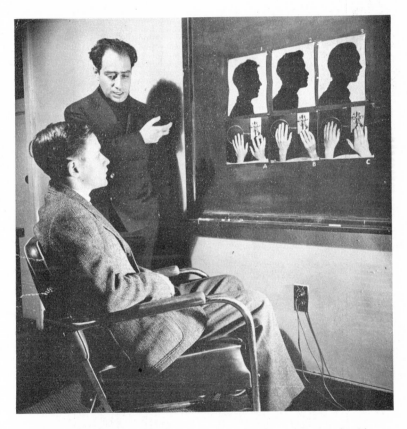

A subject tries to match hands and profiles; he does not recognize his own
profile (2) and his own hands (C). The other correct matchings are: 1—B,
3—A.

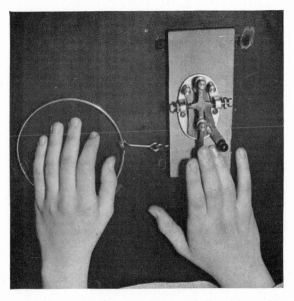

A subject's hands are photographed without his knowledge, while he is asked to extend his hands beneath a curtain and to push a key at a given signal.
Courtesy of Life Magazine

A subject's profile is photographed without his knowledge, during a supposed experiment in perception.
Courtesy of Life Magazine

conditioned responses, or of habits. According to the environmental thesis, the environment pushes the buttons of the human machine; according to the instinctual thesis, man's emotions and drives move the clockwork. The environmental thesis lent itself best to experimentation since outside stimuli could be measured and statistically evaluated. The instinctual thesis, revived by psychoanalysis, did not permit experimental proof. Under the ideal of specialization the environmental thesis and the instinctual thesis were mutually exclusive.

NON-EUCLIDEAN PSYCHOLOGY

With the conception of the unconscious, a stimulus did not necessarily produce a predictable response. A stimulus could produce a reaction that was indifferent, creative, or neurotic. The reaction could be an immediate response, a delayed response, it could produce a repression, sublimation or transformation. But since any stimulus enters an already present organization, its relationship to this organization allows us certain predictions; these predictions, however, are not general ones, but derive from the individual system to which they are applied. A psychology of interrelationships moves to the foreground. It is not the analysis of elements but their synthesis which becomes an object of investigation. Although Freud called his procedure psychoanalysis he introduced the concept of psychosynthesis. He deals with a synthesis of stimuli from the environment without and man's psychological organization within. Freudian psychotherapy recognized that our perceptions of the outer world depend on our inner processes or perceptions within, that our social maladjustments are reflections of inner personal maladjustments, that distortions of reacting to the so called objective reality are projections of inner psychic distortions. Psychotherapy was no longer directed toward the Euclidean surface-model but plumbed the depth of personality, and the relationship between cause and effect was no longer considered a fixed resultant but a dynamic product.

PRESENT-DAY PSYCHOLOGY

EXPERIMENTAL DEPTH PSYCHOLOGY

Modern psychology may be roughly divided into experimental psychology and depth psychology. Experimental psychology tries by apparatus and tests to bring all human reactions under laboratory conditions and to evaluate the results obtained by statistical methods. With the ideal of objectivity the phenomena are described rather than interpreted, and the description is made in quantitative rather than in qualitative respects. But laboratory psychologists became aware of this fact, as G. W. Allport expressed it in 1924:

> With analyzing, testing, and correlating most of these investigators became blind to the true nature of the problem before them,—the traits are there, but the personality is lacking.—We must have a supplementary and very different type of technique.*

Depth psychology, especially as practiced by psychoanalytic schools, shies away from experimental procedures. They point out that human reactions have to be interpreted rather than described, since a description deals only with the surface behavior which usually has little to do with the underlying motivation, reflecting the true psychological phenomenon, unique in each personality. The psychological phenomenon must be interpreted, and being unique, it cannot be generalized. Therefore, the interpretation must be made in qualitative rather than in quantitative respects. Excluding laboratory conditions, Freud himself admitted in 1933: "Not long ago, medical men of an American university refused to consider psychoanalysis as a science because it did not permit experimental proof."** While experimental psychology deals with surface behavior and with the effects of stimuli, depth psychology focuses upon the depth of personality, searching for the causes of stimuli.

* Allport, G. W. The Study of the Undivided Personality. *J. Abn. & Soc. Psychol.,* 1924-25, *19,* p. 132.
** Freud, S. *New Introductory Lectures on Psychoanalysis.* New York: 1933.

A third alternative appears with an approach by means of analysis or by means of synthesis. Especially Gestalt theory introduced the concept of synthesis in psychological phenomena. Perceptual phenomena cannot be understood by dividing them into their single elements: A painting, or a piece of music is perceived as a whole, and by the synthesis of elements perceived, the whole is more than the sum of its parts. With these mutually exclusive approaches which we simplified by labeling them Euclidean versus non-Euclidean, experimental psychology versus depth psychology, the approach by analysis versus synthesis, psychology could not develop a unified psychological system as the physical sciences had succeeded in doing.

Experimental depth psychology is an attempt in this direction. The new realms discovered by depth psychology can no longer be eliminated from a study of the total personality, but the scientific methods of experimental psychology have to be used if the observations of depth psychology are to be controlled, validated, and made predictable. The method of analysis has to be combined with that of synthesis, if we grant that any single psychological phenomenon depends on its relationships with other psychological phenomena and their setting. The Euclidean approach, aiming at generally applicable formulas, has to be combined with a non-Euclidean one, adapted to different materials. The over-all theoretical aim of experimental depth psychology is a synthesis of methods and of observations in the field of personality.

THE SYNTHESIS OF EXPRESSIVE BEHAVIOR

For an experimental study of personality, attempting to find general formulas, we have to use those manifestations of personality which all men have in common and which can be observed under experimental conditions: control, repetition and prediction. If personality is expressed in man's postures and in man's movements, we can use such expressions as man's face, hands, posture, voice, gait, gestures, and his handwriting for an experimental study of personality.

We have first to clear up the "if" because a counter-thesis states that man's postures and movements are not determined by personality but are based upon imitation, upon conditioning and learning, or simply chance. Expressive behavior may be an imitation of movement patterns frequently perceived; it may be learned like walking and speaking; and it may be a product of chance like the materials of writing (pen and paper).

If imitation, learning, and chance determine expressive behavior our various forms of expression can not have anything in common, since the individual has learned or imitated a certain way of speaking from one person and a certain way of walking from another, and a chance factor can not interrelate any forms of expression. On the other hand, if our various forms of expression have certain expressive qualities in common, a common seal of personality must have patterned them. To decide this question experimental depth psychology introduced the *matching technique*.[54, 55]

Photographs were taken of the face, of the profile, and of the hands; the voice was recorded, and the gait was filmed; handwriting specimens and samples of style retelling a story were procured. In matching experiments, subjects were asked to match one type of expressive behavior with another of the same person. Facial photographs of three persons were to be matched with three photographs of their hands, handwriting samples with their voices, gait with style of retelling a story, and other combinations. The chance expectancy for a correct matching of three pairs is one of three. Since the number of correct matchings obtained in these experiments was, on the average, one and a-half to two times the chance expectation, we concluded that an individual expresses the same characteristics by different means. The expressive quality seems to be determined by a *common denominator* that cannot be found in outside factors such as imitation and conditioning or chance, but has to be assumed as working from within the organism or through man's personality.

We now investigated whether the recognition of common

THE MATCHING TECHNIQUE

Musical notations to be matched with the names of three composers:

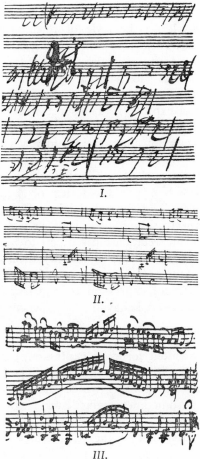

I.

II.

III.

A. Bach
B. Beethoven
C. Mozart

Try to recognize in the form and the rhythm of the notes the rhythm of the musical expressions of the composers.

Correct matchings: I-B; II-C; III-A.

characteristics in forms of expression was accompanied by common characteristics in the interpretation of their expressive qualities. Subjects gave personality characteristics from photographs of the full face, the profile, the hands, the voice, the gait, the handwriting, the style of retelling a story. Neutral observers compared the characteristics given by many subjects about the same form of expression, crystallizing a common denominator out of the various descriptions; then, in new matching experiments, the common denominator was matched with the forms of expression. The success obtained averaged 77 per cent as against 23 per cent to be expected by chance, thus establishing a common characteristic for each of the expressive forms.

The next step aimed at a correlation between the common characterization of a person's forms of expression with his everyday behavior. The characterizations of expressive forms of several persons were submitted to subjects who knew these persons from daily life relationships. In 60 to 90 per cent of the cases our subjects were able to identify their friends from the descriptions of their forms of expression. These results indicate that a form of expression reflects personality traits that correspond to the overt behavior of the person judged.[64, 65, 68]

The Synthesis of Identification and Interpretation

When we presented forms of expression, such as the photographs of faces and hands or the recordings of voices to subjects who knew the persons whose forms of expression they perceived, they sometimes immediately identified them and therefore we did not obtain a character interpretation which led to the identification of the person they had judged. If a person sees his own photograph and if he hears his own voice, we can expect him to recognize himself immediately; but if this is not the case, we may be able to receive an interpretation without identification. Such a self-interpretation in the absence of self-recognition may yield an unbiased self-analysis on the basis of expressive behavior.

For testing reactions on self-confrontation, forms of expression were recorded without a person's knowledge: a concealed microphone recorded his voice, a hidden camera took pictures of his face. While the subject stretched his hands through a curtain with the apparent purpose of measuring his speed of reaction while pushing a button, his hands were photographed from behind the screen; and his gait was filmed by a hidden movie camera. In order to exclude outer factors of recognition when the films were later shown to the subjects, they all had to wear the same kind of suit and their faces were blotted out in the film.[60]

Handwriting samples were photographed and enlarged and presented in a mirrored form. In the experiment the subject was confronted with the voice recordings of three persons speaking the same sentence, one of the voices being his own, the other two those of his friends. Would he recognize himself? A corresponding experiment was made with profile silhouettes and photographs of hands. We made the surprising observation that, in a majority of cases, a person does not recognize his own form of expression although he recognizes those of his friends. In cases of non-recognition we obtained interpretations which were not biased by identifications. The question now arose whether a self-interpretation in the absence of self-recognition is in some way different from an interpretation by other people of other people. A comparison of all judgments immediately showed that the self-judgments in a state of unawareness (these are referred to as unconscious self-judgments) were usually longer than all the other judgments. Furthermore, these unconscious self-judgments are in general significantly more favorable or unfavorable than the judgments *of* others and they are more favorable or unfavorable than judgments *by* others. By counting the words and by ranking the judgments these observations can be objectified. *Unconscious self-interpretation showed affective qualities such as overvaluation,* for instance, by reporting "a most interesting personality", or "a genius", *or an undervaluation,* for instance, by characterizing oneself as "almost a criminal", "highly neurotic", "terribly disagreeable". The split between identification and interpretation, combined with the affective degree of unconscious self-evaluation indicates the involvement of inner psychological processes during the act of self-confrontation. Our procedures had opened a way to study depth processes by experimental methods.

The absence of self-recognition as an isolated phenomenon can be explained by the assumption that our voice heard in a recording sounds different from the way we hear it through our bone resonance; that we do not recognize our profile because we rarely observe it in the mirror; and that we do not recognize our hands because we do not expect to see them detached from the body as in a photograph. However, the synthesis of the missing identification with a characteristic type of interpretation indicates that these explanations fall short. By interrelating the absence of self-recognition and the affective self-interpretation, we come to the conclusion that the absence of self-recognition is not due to outer factors, but to intra-psychological factors such as an inner resistance.

The Self-Image in the Experiment

The process of self-interpretation in the absence of self-recognition was investigated by an association experiment. We used the descriptive terms given in a self-judgment and presented them as stimuli-words upon which the subject had to give his associations. Subjects reacted to their own terms in two characteristic ways: They produced wishes or fears. For instance, a young student described his own mirrored handwriting as made by a person of Indian type who had a certain superiority and artfulness, and the fine strokes of the handwriting reminded him of fine wrought-iron gates. The associations revealed that the subject, being of a Nordic type, had the wish-image to be a dark Indian. Suffering from inferiority feelings, he strove for superiority; scientifically-minded, without an understanding of art, he mostly admired artistry. Suffering from a lack of reserve, he wished to have a fence, an artistic fence "of fine wrought-iron gates." While his statements referred to wish-images, statements of other people about themselves (although less preponderantly) also referred to fear-images, such as fearing to be neurotic or criminal, etc.[66]

Thus, the interrelationship between the absence of self-recognition and the emotional self-interpretation in terms of wishes and fears suggests that a person does not recognize himself because he has another psychological image of himself. But the lack of self-identification also may be related to processes of memory: We do not remember the image of ourselves. Psychoanalysis suggested the emotional determination of what we remember and what we forget, and our experimental technique could verify this assumption. We read to our subjects a story with which they were unacquainted, asking the subjects afterwards to retell the story as exactly as possible. The reproduction was recorded and compared word by word with the original text. The words which a subject had omitted or changed were given as stimuli-words for his associations, mixed with an equal number of words which he had correctly recalled. In 55 per cent of the cases we obtained emotionally negative associations with the omitted words, while we only obtained 16 per cent of emotionally negative associations with the recalled words. Similarly, emotional factors in memory were investigated by reading to subjects six pairs of positive and negative proverbs in a mixed order. Examples are: Positive: "a good winter brings a good summer." Negative: "a bad day never has a good night." Compared with an investigation of general optimism or pessimism of a person, we found that pessimists tend to forget positive proverbs and (although less accentuated) *vice versa*. Both experiments, confirmed by repeat procedures, indicate a tendency for material that cannot be synthesized with personality to be eliminated from recall, as it is eliminated from perception.[67]

Indirect Methods of Synthesizing
Intrapersonal Tendencies

One aim of experimental depth psychology is the development of indirect methods for diagnosing personality. In paper and pencil tests as well as in many depth approaches, the individual explored may easily become aware of what the investigator is driving at. He therefore may modify his responses in accordance with what he assumes to be expected of him. This aim, to hide the conceptual denominator of the experimental approach, had to be combined with the aim at converging approaches to personality. But we do not only have to consider that various approaches to the same goal validate our results, if corresponding reactions are obtained, but we also have to consider the fact that a personality trait is not an isolated element, effective only in one area of personality. The same personality trait may determine our decision, our memory, and our perception and our preference and our rejection. A personality trait synthesizes our various reactions, and exploring them we need a synthesis of many approaches. It thus became desirable to construct converging approaches with the same conceptual denominator which was to be hidden and which had to appeal to different reactions such as those of perception, memory and decision. Thus, the same or equivalent diagnostic material was to be presented as a test of decision or of choice, as a memory test, and as a test of perception. Although "equivalent" tests may check the reliability of responses, they do not indicate the motivation for the response. An approach to motivation was made by investigating the relationships of reactions through a matching method which would correlate the various concepts investigated.

The following test was called the *crossroad test* because it was based upon the selection of opposite directions. We chose five pairs of personality traits aimed at investigating the degree of their presence and their interrelationships. These pairs were:

A. Egoism   B. Altruism
C. Introversion   D. Extraversion
E. Impulsiveness   F. Self-control
G. Feeling   H. Rationality
I. Passivity   J. Activity

The author composed 25 stories in each of which one of the trait pairs was emphasized. The subject was asked to tell what his choice in the situation would be; since similar situations reappeared five times, a consistency of choice was assumed to be significant.

In a second approach, the same story was read to the subjects; later they were asked to recall them as exactly as possible and the forgetting was evaluated in terms of the trait pairs. In a third approach, the same concepts referring to the five trait pairs were presented in a perception test in which these words were written unspaced on a typewriter and between any two words representing concepts were put meaningless words, obtained by spelling the preceding word backward. The subject was asked to perceive the words in each row during ten seconds.

In a fourth approach the subject was to imagine four colors: red, blue, green, and yellow, and to match each of our key concepts with one of the four colors.

A comparison of all reactions allowed to diagnose consistency and degree of a trait, while the color matchings of concepts, indicating which differing concepts were grouped together under the same color, revealed their interrelationship. The test serves to illustrate the possible avenues of synthesizing intrapersonal tendencies. In its present stage, the crossroad test is only one of many methods of selecting from numerous trends those that seem to be distinctive for a subject, indicating some direction for intensive study within the framework of psychosynthesis.[64]

THE SYNTHESIS OF FORMS AND EXPRESSION

Verbal expression in self-interpretation without self-recognition was characterized by a larger number of words used. The arithmetical mean of all judgments of others was 34.4 words;

of self-judgments it was about double, namely, 66.9 words. This characteristic form corresponded to the characteristic of expression, namely, of a greater emotional impact.

Another investigation indicated that characteristics of expression were related to characteristics of form. Classifying the terms used for describing expressive qualities for the different forms of expression, and evaluating their distribution statistically, the investigator learned that the profile elicited terms that referred to the sphere of will to a higher degree than did the other forms. In the hand, the sphere of vitality; in the voice, the sphere of attitudes; in the gait—the social sphere, and in the style of retelling, the intellectual sphere were dominant.

The relationship between form and expression was also investigated by experiments with full-face photographs. Full-face photographs were taken, and prints were made from each side of the negative. The dull side gave the usual photographs and the glazed side gave mirror pictures. Bisecting each of these pictures and combining the right side and the mirrored right side, we obtained a full face consisting only of the right side of the person. The same was done with the left side. A person's reactions to his own right side or left side picture were significant. In some cases the subject did not recognize his distorted photograph, but even if he did so, his reaction to the two pictures was significantly different.

In right-handed people the right half of the face is more expressive, related to the corresponding dominance of the left cerebral hemisphere, which is also the seat of the dominant conscious activities. The left half of the face, less featured, seems to have a less conscious expression. It appeared that a person's preference for the left half of the face was related to an accentuation of unconscious processes. For instance, in mental diseases and under hypnosis, the left side was preferred. Associations about each facial part indicated that the left side elicited more wish and fear images than the right side. Each facial part was frequently related to father or mother and also in this respect the preference or rejection of one part was significant. The left part of the face is less expressive and its form seems not to change so much during the course of life as does the right side of the face.[61]

When we combined facial pictures from photographs taken at different ages of a person's life, the basic features seemed to remain consistent and the left side of the face remained always less expressive. Similar observations were made with animal faces, death masks, and mummies, indicating that certain relationships between expression and form seem to be basic properties of the individual.

A synthesis of form and expression was finally investigated with movement patterns on the basis of graphic movements in handwriting and in drawings. The question whether a synthesis of form and expression is a product of learning or inherent in the organization of personality was investigated with scribblings and drawings of preschool children who had no previous training in drawing. At different times the children were asked to draw a man. Samples in groups of three children, each with three drawings were shuffled and given to neutral observers with instructions to match the drawings of the same child. The matchings, successful in 100 per cent of the cases, indicate the presence of a characteristic style of expression before any learning of drawing takes place. Children, when asked to draw what they hear, drew certain pictures upon hearing the phonographic records of a march and of a waltz. The march produced more angular, the waltz more rounded patterns, indicating that the child is able to transform certain expressive qualities into certain forms.[62, 70]

Children's drawings of their families indicated that their attitude to their father and mother, to their siblings, and to themselves appeared with various formal characteristics of the drawings. It was significant which figure came first and which was put at the end, the distance between figures, used as stimuli to elicit the child's associations, showed that emotional attitudes are spontaneously expressed by certain forms.[71]

LAWS OF EXPRESSION AND OF FORM IN THE SIGNATURE

A writer frequently expresses compulsive thoughts in his signature. The Earl Jowitt, former Lord Chancellor of Britain, questioned in his book *The Strange Case of Alger Hiss* the methods used in the trial. The questioning attitude of the writer seems to

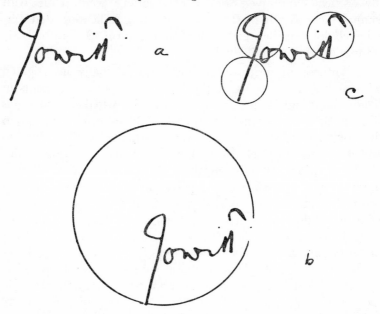

be incorporated in the question mark put above the end of his signature (a), developed from an original t-bar.

The integration of this question mark into the form principle of the signature can be demonstrated by the author's method of graphometry. The length of the first stroke, used as a radius for a circle made in the upper point of this initial stroke touches the dot of the question mark, last movement of the signature (b). The length of the last stroke, namely the "t" is exactly one fourth of the first stroke's length (c). Different laws of simple proportions were found to appear in everybody's signature, alluding to the existence of individual formulas of expression.

THE SYNTHESIS OF MOVEMENTS

The synthesis and organization of movements in expressive behavior can be investigated in handwriting, since handwriting is a recording of movements and forms upon paper. These graphically recorded movement patterns can be measured in their size and in their position and interrelation of elements. Such measurements have led the author to the discovery of unconscious formulas of movement organization. The lengths, distances, positions, and shapes of graphic elements were found to be simple proportions of one movement that appears with the start, the end or the middle of a signature. Each element of handwriting, including dots and flourishes, was disclosed as part of a configurational scheme. These unlearned, unconscious proportions in handwriting, usually appearing in simple mathematical relationships, also were present in scribblings of pre-school children, thus independent of learning. They appeared with African children, thus independent of culture; they were present in the blind, thus being independent of perceptual processes; they remained in mental illness, in epileptic seizures and during emotional shocks. They even appeared in the transfer from right-hand writing to left-hand writing in cases where the right hand was lost; thus they were independent of a person's normal equilibrium. Measurements of handwriting specimens during a person's life period, starting with his early childhood, indicate a consistency of these configurations which, however, do not remain rigidly fixed but may change in simple mathematical proportions.[73]

A relation between these formulas of configuration and synthesis in graphic movements and certain personality structures was evident in states of elation and depression, with a loss of control and under inhibition. In states of elation and loss of control, such as after an emotional shock and after epileptic seizure, movements tended to increase in simple proportions. In states of depression and under inhibition, such as in imprisonments and at the decline of life, movements tended to decrease in simple proportions; that is, the forms and relationships increased or decreased one, one and one-half, two, three or even more times as compared with their average size. It, therefore, seems that the synthesis of form and expression and the synthesis of movements depend on formulas of configuration, determined by the changing factors of personality.[63]

DREAM SYNTHESIS

The investigation of dreams by experimental methods has been limited to a study of external stimuli in their relation to the production of dream-images and to classifications of dream-images, while psychoanalytical investigations used dream images only as stimuli for associations within the therapeutic process. Experimental psychology as well as depth psychology isolated dream images from their context, aiming at a classification of symbols. Dream synthesis focuses upon the organizational scheme of dreams, upon the individual dream center, and upon the interrelationship of dream elements. Comparing dreams with day-dreams and fantasies and dream-images with the associations elicited by them, we conclude that dream thinking is distinguished from waking thinking in quantitative rather than in qualitative aspects and that its object is not only thoughts patterned by drives and emotions, but also thoughts patterned by reason and ethical considerations, both related to our social problems and to our immediate situation. The synthesizing function of the organism which we observe in its physical processes and its mental operations, which govern perception and expression and the configuration of movements, appears in dreams by neglecting the categorizing functions of time and space. The dream becomes a self-observation from the total aspect of lived time and from the total aspect of the individual's actions and reactions. This synthesis is stimulated by movements of crisis and of decision, dramatizing the dream before the forum of conscience. These observations were made through our development of an interpretative technique of dream synthesis in correspondence to the dream's function of synthesis.

This technique may be summarized as follows: Dreams are recorded word for word, then each word is presented to the dreamer as a stimulus word for his associations, in a sequence different from that of the original dream. The synthesizing element in the association chain to each dream stimulus word, that is, the key-association, is used for the translation of each dream image, by replacing it or by qualifying it.

We observed that such a dream translation gives a coherent and meaningful story which qualifies the content of the dream. Since associations to the dream-images were obtained in a sequence different from that of the original dream and still elicited thoughts which, rearranged in the sequence of the dream, gave a coherent story, it appeared that there is an intimate connection between waking associations and unconscious dream thoughts, and that both follow a configurational scheme.[79]

Psychosynthesis and the Creative Process

An approach to imagination has been much neglected by experimental psychology, while depth psychology investigated imagination, the creative process and the personality of the artist solely with a stereotyped scheme of psychoanalytic interpretation. According to the concepts of experimental depth psychology, the creative process was explored by converging approaches and in terms of the creative artists themselves. In one experimental series, student artists (painters, sculptors, poets, composers, and dancers) analyzed three specimens of their own work in terms of motivation and intention. Their work was also analyzed by a group of observers, and the areas of agreement between creator and observer were investigated. In addition to these free interpretations, a questionnaire was developed and given both groups, artists and observers. The agreement between artist and observer was greater as regards the reactions to the questionnaire than in regard to the free interpretation. But the observers agreed more among themselves than with the artist. When painters were shown their paintings in color slides, projected through a tachistoscope and in short exposure of 1-300th of a second, many artists were not able to identify their paintings, but they could describe color and movement. A set of questionnaires interrelated types of self-perception, of artistic perception and art appreciation and of artistic creation. These tests pointed at two groups of artists namely those for whom art is a self-expression and those for whom art is a form of communication. The communicating and self-expressing type indicate differences in their motivation, in their patterns and goals of the creative process.

Investigating the reactions to geometrical forms and symbols, once given as visual stimuli and another time in verbal description, we approached a psychology of the symbol in art; patterns of imagination and their consistency were studied with doodlings, with a completion of started form patterns, with the use of associations and projections upon Rorschach and the TAT cards, with the completion of stories, with reactions to paradoxical situations, with reactions to sounds, to movies, to paintings; and by comparing the degree of realistic and fantastic imagination. For the latter purpose our subjects were asked to imagine a house and describe in writing how it would look; after the description was finished, they had to imagine the most fantastic house. The time for each performance was measured, the number of words used was counted, and the imagery used was compared with that used by other approaches. Investigating the memory of stories told, we found sensory types, namely, people who emphasized in their memory visual or auditory or kinesthetic elements, who emphasized objective observation or emotional attitudes, etc. An interrelationship of all these data approaches a synthesis of expression in the creative process, while measurements of artist's drawings, similar to our studies in handwriting, approach a synthesis of form principles in the creative process.

The measurement of lines and forms in an artist's drawings reveals the center of the drawing and with it its unconscious frame of reference. By studying the consistency of these proportions and centers in various drawings, we may be able to deduce the unconscious theme of the artist, and his general artistic motivation.[82]

PSYCHOTHERAPY AND PSYCHOSYNTHESIS

Since Freud the orientation of modern psychotherapy has been an analytic one. The complex behavior of a patient is analyzed into its single reactions, with the attempt to find out single events that had conditioned his pathological reactions. But the psychotherapy applied operates like a screening system; from all events which the patient reports, those are especially selected to which the therapeutic system is attuned. The Freudian psychoanalyst focuses especially upon the patient's sexual experiences, the Adlerian upon his inferiority-superiority feelings and power drives, the Jungian upon his moral and religious tendencies, neo-Freudians upon the social and cultural implications. Through the structure of the therapeutic system the patient's single life events are strung up as a series in which past experiences, present attitudes, and goals for the future have the same location on what we might call the Euclidean psychogram. The patient, surveying this plane design of his psychic forces, recognizes his stereotype in which his entire life is brought upon one formula. Through analysis the isolated events lose their threat and the patient recognizes that he was driven by the combination of these events, by their quantitative power. Although this analytic method has been successful, many patients experience a pauperization of experience and a conceptual limitation of thinking in terms of the system with which they have been treated. From the point of view of psychosynthesis the patient has to discover the unique theme of his personality. He does not look at one single aspect of his personality screened by a specific therapy. From the concept of synthesis, the interrelationship of events becomes more important than the single events themselves. The patient should see himself as the synthesizer of his life pattern, of being the driver rather than being driven.

The patient has to become detached from himself, to be led away from a two-dimensional view to an "airplane view" of his personality. It is from this perspective that he may recognize the inadequate connections between his various attitudes towards life, enabling him to make an overall new synthesis.

From this point of view there emerges a new therapeutic technique. In the therapeutic sessions, the therapist records the complete account of the patient with as little interference as possible. In a later typewritten transcription, each concept is numbered. After several sessions of repeated concepts, conceptual groups are noted. Together with dream synthesis the patient is made aware of his neurotic patterns rather than of isolated elements, of interrelationships between his sexual, social, and moral attitudes rather than of the single attitudes themselves, and his experiences are dealt with in terms of his total existence rather than as isolated phenomena. If the patient becomes aware of the fact that he is the weaver of his life rather than its victim, if he recognizes that an early traumatic experience had caused a total switch of his attitude to life, he becomes able to change his targets and to synthesize his inner and outer reality, the conflict of which has caused the neurosis. (76, 77, 83)

Culture Synthesis

A culture is more than the summation of its collected data; it has a definite design which is dependent on the relationship of each element to the other and to adjacent cultures as well. In order to understand a culture, it is essential to establish a synthesis or a core where the various relationships converge. Since a culture is a fusion of epochs and individuals, a culture synthesis is based upon the various concepts as revealed in works of art, legends, ceremonies which are treated like the mental associations of an individual; and just as we look for synthesizing factors or common denominators in an individual's associations, so we search for common themes in cultural concepts. If a culture is represented by the works of various authors which are unified in a collective book, such as the Bible or the sacred books of the East, the thought material is largely amalgamated and integrated by tradition so that it can be treated like the mental material of one person.

The reactions of various authors to the same concept may be treated like the associations of one person to one stimulus word. The interrelationships of these associations reveal the symbolic meaning of a concept. The interrelationship of all main concepts of a culture gives us the synthesis or world-conception of the culture. The synthesis of the ethnologist should follow the synthesizing principles of the culture under investigation. The result of such a culture synthesis is quite different from that of a psychoanalysis of cultures, because the culture-synthesist does not project any frame of reference or any preconceptions upon his material as do those who analyze a culture in terms of their own culture. For instance, an attitude which in our cultural frame of reference would be termed as submissive may have the meaning of being meditative in an Eastern culture; a person's subjective ideal of being realistic may cause his negative evaluation of the emphasis on imagination in other cultures.

With reference to any particular school of thought, cultures are interpreted according to certain key-concepts. For instance, according to the psychoanalytic school of thought, cultural symbolism is largely investigated in sexual terms. For making a culture synthesis we collected all available data, dividing them into similar data, interrelated data, and contradicting data. Similar data enforce our knowledge, interrelated data expand our knowledge of a cultural pattern, and contradicting data hint at the dynamic issues. After a cultural pattern has emerged, this pattern is compared with that of other current cultures from the aspects of similarity, interrelationships, and contradictions. A culture synthesis is not only a behavioral description of cultural patterns but an attempt to formulate its postulates and its contribution to a world view.[74, 78]

One example may illustrate the difference of interpretation

of a symbol in terms of psychoanalysis and in terms of the culture concerned. The importance of the snake in the Aztec culture, in which this animal was deified as the "plumed serpent" would lead to the psychoanalytic concept of a phallic culture, and, synthesizing this concept with other manifestations of this culture, for instance, their sacrifice of the human heart, the sacrifice would be interpreted as a castration symbol. However, according to the ancient Aztec sources, such a synthesis would represent our school of thought but not the ancient Aztec one. The plumed serpent appears as a symbol of the clouds that change their form as does the serpent, its poisonous bite is a symbol of lightning, its devouring large animals is a symbol of clouds covering the sun. The serpent's contracted and outfolded state corresponds to the single cloud and to its outfolding over the sky. With this outfolding the serpent becomes a symbol of all-embracing and all-pervading force. The animal's property of shedding its skin is not only a symbol of the transformation of the tempestuous sky into the sunny one, but it is also associated with the transformation of death into life. Synthesized by this conceptual pattern, the sacrifice serves to pacify the world serpent by giving food to it, thus conjuring the transformation from death into a new life, a concept which was a collective wish-image of the Aztecs. Our example illustrates the need not only for a synthesis of cultural concepts but also for a synthesis in terms of the cultural pattern itself.[84]

Synthesis and the Diagnosis of Personality

The apparently divergent topics that experimental depth psychology deals with, as well as the different methods which their investigation demands, nevertheless are closely interrelated and converge in new approaches of diagnosing personality. Concerning personality traits we encounter the same dangers as with the cultural traits. Paper and pencil questionnaires put an individual into the strait-jacket of an isolated inquiry which might not be relevant within his total trait pattern. We might, for instance, judge a child a liar, although, within his age level, he displays only fantasy. According to investigations of experimental depth psychology, traits are insignificant if detached from their synthesizing pattern; and expressive forms reflect a personality synthesis rather than isolated aspects. For instance, if masculinity and femininity are not determinants of psychic processes, they will not be reflected upon expressive movements such as handwriting. Thus, one of the great limitations in the diagnosis of the cultural or the individual personality is the danger of formulating an inadequate question, that is, a question which either cannot be answered by the material or which leads in directions which are inappropriate with reference to the pattern.

The approaches to personality by experimental psychology through reaction experiments, paper and pencil questionnaires and by means of projective tests give only one segment of personality, isolating it from its total configuration, whether this segment deals with areas of intelligence, of introversion-extraversion, ascendance-submission, or with any typological aspect. Experimental psychology investigates the present status of a personality aspect without considering its motivations through the past or its goals in the light of the future. Although depth psychology and certain projective methods include the determining tendencies of causes and of goals they, too, focus upon selected segments of personality. If we compare psychological descriptions of case material with case material as represented in novels, we experience that the psychologist's personality sketch enumerates traits rather than integrating them. We might say that the stereoscopic depth dimension is missing, the traits are not synoptically used.[77]

If psychology is to give depth to a diagnosis of personality, it has to use synthesizing approaches. This is attempted by experimental depth psychology. Since the production of a synthesis is facilitated by giving a thesis and an antithesis, we aimed at the juxtaposition of procedures. Thus, our approaches to diagnosing personality were based upon approaches to the conscious and the unconscious level, to personality as seen by the person himself and by others and in the judgment of oneself and of others. The expression of personality was viewed through a synthesis of various expressive qualities such as voice, facial expression, gestures, gait, and handwriting. The synthesizing functions of the individual himself were studied in the configuration of his movement patterns in handwriting, of his mental patterns in his associations and through his dreams. His ways of perception and of memory were brought to a convergence with his ways of creative expression. The synthesizing function of mental processes was found to have its most extreme representation in the formation of symbols, and the genesis of symbolic thinking was followed up through a psychology of young children, of the dream of the artist, of neurotics and psychotics, and of ancient cultures.

An approach to the structure of symbol formation is designed to facilitate the discovery of symbolic expressions of the individual, the apprehension of which would give a new dimension to the diagnosis of personality. Converging methods seem to advance the ultimate aim at discovering individual formulas of personality which, through their structure, would enable us to reconstruct motivations of the individual's past and to make predictions about the individual's future course of action.

EXPRESSION SYNTHESIS

The theory of expressive movements implies that inner psychological processes press towards their outer manifestation, in which inner tensions are discharged or expressed. Clinical observations of psychoanalysis and psychosomatics support this theory of expressive behavior, indicating that all expressions of the organism are *symbols* of psychosomatic functions, which are determined by motivations and by goals, and that these individual processes modify all learned behavior. In this sense our individual expression is considered to be a direct reflection of inner processes, especially of those which are emotionally attuned. *Emotion* directly transformed into *motion* makes expression to a psychograph of its processes.[81]

Diagnostic techniques based upon a subject's movements, his handwriting, walking, speaking, have been erroneously identified with projective techniques. They are of a different order, because they deal with the *direct* expression of personality. The sound movements of the voice, the movement patterns of gait, the graphic movements, as visible in handwriting, are direct manifestations of inner processes, without the medium of foreign material and without necessarily involving the transforming function of projection. Characteristic of all projective techniques is the use of a prepared stimulus, which may be presented verbally, visually, or as an object, testing the subject's reaction to this impression, while expressive techniques usually refer to spontaneous situations.[5, 12]

While projective techniques elicit a person's desires, fears and defenses, emphasizing the repressed and suppressed aspects of personality, expressive techniques focus upon a person's actual behavior, upon the realized aspects of personality. Projective and expressive techniques both are used to explore depth processes of personality and to measure experimentally those intrapersonal dynamics which psychoanalysis observes during psychiatric treatment. But while projection involves man's unconscious ascription of his own needs and qualities to his environment, expression involves the unity of his conscious and unconscious style of response. *Expression synthesis* deals with the unique characteristics of behavior, with its patterns of configuration, and with its consistent style. Expression appears in movement, form and content. In a painting, for instance, we distinguish the expressive value of motion of brush strokes from the form of composition and from the content of representation. But the same holds true for any sphere of expression, thus pointing to the relationship between *movement* as an indication of drives, *content* as an indication of experience and *form* as an indicator of integration.

Bibliographical Survey of Studies on Expressive Movements and on Experimental Depth Psychology

Experimental depth psychology introduced a systematic research of man's expressive movements such as his voice, his face, hands, gait, style, his patterns of thinking, and his handwriting within the unity of his expressive behavior. A large number of observations from many different angles validated the main hypothesis of definite relationships between expressive movements and certain characteristics of personality. In the following we give a brief survey of some of the main studies, preceding and following the present author's investigations.

Voice and Personality. The present author's observation that man's forms of expression reveal his personality has been confirmed by various researches. According to several studies, correct judgments of personality and constitutional factors could be made from listening to the voices of speakers over the radio.[2, 20, 59, 64]

Style of Speech and Personality. Speech patterns and styles distinguish various clinical pictures of psychological disturbances and characteristics of literary and artistic style correspond to definite personality characteristics.[10, 46, 52, 64]

Facial Expression and Personality. A relationship between facial expression and personality has been observed since Aristotle. Matching experiments proved definite relationships between facial expression and certain personality traits, or personality sketches and patterns of living.[6, 7, 8, 24, 34, 53, 64, 65]

Hands and Personality. The individual expressiveness of man's hands was recognized in the 18th and 19th century. According to modern investigations the form of the hands seems to be related to constitutional personality patterns and the expressiveness of the hands seems to be related to their muscular tension.[16, 18, 28, 58, 64, 68]

Gait and Personality. Individual characteristics of rhythm and of tempo determine the individual movement patterns of gait and seem to relate gait to psychomotor types; during the war a study of these movement patterns was helpful for the assessment of men.[1, 4, 14, 19, 39, 44, 60, 64]

Handwriting and Personality. The studies of handwriting are the most extensive ones of all investigations of expressive movements. They started with the observations of the Italian physician Camillo Baldi in 1622. With investigations of pressure and of speed handwriting movements can be measured quantitatively. Also regularity, tension and blockage and form principles can be measured and standardized.[9, 31, 33, 45, 48, 63, 73]

Doodling Drawing, Painting and Personality. Principles similar to those found in handwriting have been observed with scribblings, doodlings, and with drawings or paintings, which equally transfer motions as a record of emotions and personality traits. Certain formal criteria, for instance, in children's drawings are positively correlated with certain personality traits, and the differences in the drawings of the human figure give general diagnostic indications.[5, 29, 38, 56, 62, 64, 70, 73]

Motion and Personality. The length and direction of movements appear to be in predictable relationships to moods and emotions; for instance, lines drawn during pleasant thoughts expand while they contract during unpleasant moods; the same has been observed in movements of throwing rings on to a target. Comparative studies of line drawings of mental patients indicate a definite relationship between motor characteristics and mental states.[12, 23, 35, 43, 64, 73]

Perception and Personality. Experiments of the present author and many recent studies in perception indicate that our perception of objects and of our environment depends on expressions of personality. Wishes, expectations, prejudices and pleasant-unpleasant memories influence what we perceive.[15, 21, 41, 64, 73]

Memory and Personality. Not only what we perceive but also what we retain depends on personality factors as demonstrated clinically by psychoanalysis and experimentally by the present author and other investigators of memory. Emotionally tuned experiences influence the recall of concepts, situations, or single words which had been memorized, by forgetting or changing them.[11, 64, 67]

Thought and Personality. Associations, the elements of thought, are patterned by typological and emotional factors of personality; types of thinking, such as serial (methodical) thinking and synoptic (intuitive) thinking are characteristic of personality organizations.[42, 47, 64, 76] A link between thought patterns and expressions of personality is demonstrated by the present author in relationship to the dream[79] and to the creative process.[82]

Attitude and Personality. A relationship between bodily physique, attitudinal patterns, and expressions of personality has been recognized since ancient times. Attitudinal patterns of various stages of individual development, of the normal and abnormal personality and cultural-national stereotypes go together with characteristic expressions of personality to which approaches are made by experimental depth psychology.[49, 50, 51, 64, 66, 72]

Consistency in Personality. The characterological qualities of expressive movements can be validated by tests and daily-life explorations, but the best verification can be found by studying the consistency of expression in a cross-sectional and in a longitudinal approach. The cross-sectional observation that the same or corresponding expressive value underlies man's various forms of expression is found as early as the Bible. In Proverbs, 6:13 we find: "A naughty person, a wicked man walketh with a forward mouth. He winketh with his eyes, he speaketh with his feet, he teacheth with his fingers."[3, 8, 17, 22, 64, 70, 73]

The observation of a unity of expression, for instance, reflected upon gait, posture, facial characteristics and gesture was tested by matching experiments, advanced by the present author and by others. Studies on longitudinal consistency, namely, over many years in a person's life, indicate a developmental stability in a person's basic expressions. A consistency of movements and movement organizations was discovered by the present author, with signatures from different periods of a person's life.[73, 80, 81]

The Dynamics of Personality. Psychoanalytic observations on the dynamics between conscious and unconscious processes, on tension systems in personality and on the expression of wish-images and fear-images, were a special object of experimental depth psychology which through a study of expressive movements was able to test psychoanalytic insights into the depth

540

of personality by means of experimental methods. Most of the findings were supported by repeat experiments of other researchers, such as the experiments on self-recognition, [25] on the expressive value of the voice,[2] on gait,[44] on facial parts,[34] on the matching method applied to expressive movements,[54], [55] on intra-personal consistency,[3] and on configurational tendencies in handwriting.[31]

Methods of experimental depth psychology have been applied to psychiatry,[36] to child study,[13] to art therapy,[38] to diagnosis,[5, 12, 30, 57] to social psychology,[26] and the present author has related them to his studies in cultures and values.[74, 75, 78]

Aims of Experimental Depth Psychology. Studies of experimental depth psychology radiate in various directions and focus upon different aspects of personality, because they emphasize the phenomena of organization, integration, and the unity in personality, and are occupied with four main aims:

First: To discover general laws of expression, characteristic of everybody's personality.

Second: To find methods which allow us an experimental verification of diagnosing an individual's personality.

Third: To integrate the various observations into a new system of understanding and predicting behavior.

Fourth: With all three aims together, experimental depth psychology hopes to contribute to the development of a science of personality in which general laws, individual applications, and a theoretical system form a unity that, parallel to the physical model of the universe, may establish a psychological mode of man's personality.

Each of these aims needs methodological procedures, the soundness of which must be checked by independent research at different laboratories, by cross-validation in the diagnosis of the same subject, by successful prediction and through the discovery of new principles.[85]

BIBLIOGRAPHY

1 Allport, G. W. *Personality; A Psychological Interpretation.* New York, 1937.

2 Allport, G. W. and Cantril, H. Judging Personality from the Voice. *J. Soc. Psychol.,* 1934, *5,* 37-55.

3 Allport, G. W. and Vernon, P. E. *Studies in Expressive Movement.* New York: Macmillan, 1933.

4 Anders, P. Ueber den Individuellen Eigenrhythmus beim menschlichen Gange, etc. *Pflueg. Arch. f. d. Ges. Physiol.,* 1928, *220,* 287-299.

5 Anderson, H. H. and Anderson, G. L. *An Introduction to Projective Techniques.* New York: Prentice Hall, 1951.

6 Anon. Personality. Psychology Seeks Clues in Faces, Manners, Bearing. *Life,* Jan. 18, 1943, 98-104.

7 Anon. Open Book. *Time,* July 12, 1943, 90-92.

8 Arnheim, R. Experimentell-psychologische, Untersuchungen zum Ausdrucks-problem. *Psychol. Forschg.,* 1928, *11,* 1-132.

9 Baldi, C. *Trattado Como da Una lettera Missiva si Conoscano la Natura equalita dello Scriviente.* Bologna, 1644.

10 Balken, E. and Masserman, J. The Language of Fantasy. *J. of Psychol.,* 1940, *10,* 75-86.

11 Bartlett, F. C. *Remembering.* Cambridge: Cambridge Univ. Press, 1932.

12 Bell, J. E. *Projective Techniques.* New York: Longmans, Green, 1948.

13 Bender, L. *Child Psychiatric Techniques.* Springfield: Thomas, 1952.

14 Bogen, H. and Lipman, O. Gang und Charakter. *Beih. z. angew. Psychol.,* vol. 58, 1931.

15 Bruner, J. S. and Krech, D. *Perception and Personality,* a symposium. Duke University, 1950.

16 d'Arpentigny, C. St. *La Chirognomie ou l'art de reconnaître les tendances de l'intelligence d'après les lignes de la main,* 1843.

17 Downey, J. B. *Graphology and the Psychology of Handwriting.* Baltimore: Warwick, 1919.

18 Duffy, E. Level of Muscular Tension as an Aspect of Personality. *J. Gen. Psychol.,* 1946, *35,* 161-171.

19 Enke, W. Die Psychomotorik der Konstitutionstypen. *Z. f. Angew. Psychol.,* 1930, *36,* 237-287.

20 Fay, P. J. and Middleton, W. C. Judgment of Spranger Personality Types from the Voice as Transmitted over a Public Address System. *Char. and Pers.,* 1939, *8,* 144-155.

21 Franklin, J. C. *et al.* Observation of Human Behavior in Experimental Semi-Starvation and Rehabilitation. *J. of Clin. Psychol.,* vol. 4, 1948, 28-45.

22 Gesell, A. Some Observations of the Developmental Stability. *Psycho. Monog.,* 1936, *47,* 35-46.

23 Goodenough, F. L. and Brian, C. R. Certain Factors Underlying the Acquisition of Motor Skill by Preschool Children. *J. Exper. Psychol.,* 1929, *12,* 127-155.

24 Guilford, J. P. An Experiment in Learning to Read Facial Expression. *J. Abn. and Soc. Psychol.,* 1929, *24,* 191-202.

25 a) Huntley, W. Judgments of Self Based Upon Records of Expressive ᷉havior, *Thesis.* Harvard Univ., 1938.

PRESENT-DAY PSYCHOLOGY

b) —— Judgments of Self. *J. Abn. and Soc. Psychol.,* 1940, *35,* 298-427.

26 Klineberg, O. *Social Psychology,* New York.

27 Koffka, K. *Principles of Gestalt Psychology,* New York, 1935.

28 Lavater, J. C. *Physiognomische Fragmente,* 1775-78.

29 Machover, K. *Personality Projection in Drawing of the Human Figure.* Springfield, Ill.: Thomas, 1948.

30 Muller, J. B. Character and Personality Tests. *Psychol. Bull.,* 1934, *31,* 501-524.

31 Margadant, S. V. *Practice and Psychology of Graphometry.* The Hague, Netherlands, 1952.

32 Martin, W. E. Identifying the Insecure Child; The Wolff Security Test. *J. genet. Psychol.,* 1951, *78,* 217-232.

33 McAllister, C. N. Researches on Movements Used in Handwriting. *Yale Psychological Laboratory Studies,* vol. 8, 1900.

34 McCurdy, H. G. Experimental Notes on the Asymmetry of the Human Face. *J. Abn. and Soc. Psycho.,* 1949, *44,* 553-55.

35 Mira, E. Myokinetic Psychodiagnosis: A New Technique for Exploring the Conative Trends of Personality. *Proc. Roy. Soc. Med.,* 1940, *33,* 173-94.

36 Moore, T. V. *One Hundred Years of American Psychiatry.* New York: Columbia Univ. Press, 1944.

37 Murphy, G. *Personality.* New York: Harper & Brothers, 1947.

38 Naumburg, M. *Spontaneous Art in Therapy and Diagnosis.* New York: Grune and Stratton, 1952.

39 OSS Assessment Staff. *Assessment of Men.* New York: Rinehart & Co., 1948.

40 Piaget, J. *The Child's Perception of the World.* New York: Harcourt Brace, 1929.

41 Postman, L. and Murphy, G. The Factor of Attitude in Associative Memory. *J. Exp. Psychol.,* vol. 33, 1943, 228-238.

42 Rapaport, D. *Organization and Pathology of Thought.* New York: Columbia Univ. Press, 1951.

43 Remmers, H. H. and Thompson, Jr. L. A. A Note on Motor Activity as Conditioned by Emotional States. *J. Appl. Psychol.,* 1925, *9,* 417-423.

44 Ricker, L. H. Self-recognition from Motion Picture Studies of Gait. *Thesis,* Gainsville: University of Florida, 1950.

45 Roman, K. G. Tension and Release. *Personality Symposium,* No. 2, 1950, 57-61.

46 Sanford, F. H. Speech and Personality: A Comparative Case Study. *Char. & Pers.,* 1942, *10,* 169-198.

47 Sanford, R. N. The Effects of Abstinence from Food Upon Imaginal Processes. *J. of Psychol.,* 1937, vol. 2, 129-36, and vol. 3, 145-59.

48 Saudek, R. *Experiments with Handwriting.* New York: Doran, 1926.

49 Seeleman, V. The Influence of Attitude upon the Remembering of Pictorial Material. *Arch. Psychol.,* No. 258, 1940.

50 Sherif, M. *The Psychology of Social Norms.* New York. Harper, 1936.

51 Stone, C. P. and Baker, R. G. The Attitude and Interests of Premenarchal and Postmenarchal Girls. *J. of Genet. Psychol.,* vol. 54, 1939, 27-71.

52 Taylor, H. C. Social Agreement in Personality Traits as Judged from Speech. *J. Soc. Psychol.,* 1934, *5,* 244-48.

[53] Vernon, P. E. Some Characteristics of the Good Judge of Personality. *J. Soc. Psychol.*, 1933, *4*, 42-58.

[54] —— The Matching Method Applied to Investigation of Personality. *Psychol. Bull.*, 1936, *33*, 149-177.

[55] —— The Evaluation of the Matching Method. *J. Educ. Psychol.*, 1936, *27*, 1-17.

[56] Waehner, T. S. Formal Criteria for the Analysis of Children's Drawings. *Amer. J. Orthopsychiat.*, 1942, *12*, 95-104.

[57] Watson, G. B. Character and Personality Tests. *Psycho. Bull.*, 1933, *30*, 477-487.

[58] Wolff, C. The Form and Dermatoglyphics of Hands of 115 Different High Grade Boys. *Brit. J. Med. Psychol.*, 1947, *21*, 38-49.

[59] Wolff, W.* The Experimental Study of Forms of Expression. *Character and Personality*, vol. 2, 1933, 168, 176.

[60] —— Involuntary Self-expression in Gait and other Movements; an Experimental Study. *Character and Personality*, vol. 3, 1935, 327-344.

[61] —— The Right and the Left Face. *Ciba Symposia*, vol. 3, no. 11, 1942.

[62] —— Projective Methods for Personality Analysis of Expressive Behavior in Preschool Children. *Character and Personality*, vol. 10, 1942, 309-330.

[63] —— Graphometry: A New Diagnostic Method. *Psychol. Bull.*, vol. 39, 1942, 456.

[64] —— *The Expression of Personality. Experimental Depth Psychology.* New York: Harper & Brothers, 1943.

[65] —— Experimental Psychology and Depth Psychology. *Ciba Symposia*, vol. 7, 1945, 1-14.

[66] —— Wish Image and Fear Image. *Ciba Symposia*, vol. 7, 1945, 15-26.

[67] —— Emotional Factors in Memory. *Ciba Symposia*, vol. 7, 1945.

[68] —— Example of a Study on Forms of Expression. *Ciba Symposia*, vol. 7, 1945, 32-36.

[69] —— The Mystery of the Easter Island Script. *J. Polynesian Society*, vol. 54, 1-38. Wellington, N. Z., 1945.

[70] —— *The Personality of the Preschool Child.* New York: Grune & Stratton, 1946.

[71] —— *Expressive Movement Chart, Evaluation of Emotional Trends in Preschool Children.* New York: Grune & Stratton, 1947.

[72] —— *What is Psychology?* A Basic Survey. New York: Grune & Stratton, 1947.

[73] —— *Diagrams of the Unconscious; Handwriting and Personality in Measurements, Experiment and Analysis.* New York: Grune & Stratton, 1948.

[74] —— a) *Island of Death: A New Key to Easter Island's Culture through an Ethno-psychological Study.* New York: Augustin, 1948.

b) Three Mysteries of Easter Island. *The Scientific American*, February, 1949, 50-55.

[75] —— One Plus One = ? An inquiry into methodology, perception and values. *Personality*, Symposium No. 1, 1950, 68-74.

* The Author has published many papers in German, French and Spanish scientific journals; we only refer here to contributions in the English language.

76 —— *The Threshold of the Abnormal; A Basic Survey of Psychopathology.* New York: Hermitage House, 1950.

77 —— *Values and Personality.* New York: Grune and Stratton, 1950.

78 —— *Changing Concepts of the Bible; A Psychological Analysis of its Words, Symbols and Beliefs.* New York: Hermitage House, 1951.

79 —— *The Dream: Mirror of Conscience.* New York: Grune and Stratton, 1952.

Films

80 —— *Unity of Personality.* Pennsylvania State College Film Library, 1944.

81 —— *Symbols of Expression.* Pennsylvania State College Film Library, 1952.

82 —— In Preparation: *The Psychology of the Artist.* Imagination and the Creative Process.

83 —— *Contemporary Psychotherapists Examine Themselves;* a quantitative evaluation of the opinion of 43 leaders in various schools of psychotherapy. Springfield: Thomas, 1955.

84 —— *The World of Symbols;* the psychological origin of signs, letters, ornaments and magic images.

85 —— *The Synthesis of Personality in Experiment, Psychotherapy, Thought pattern and Theory.*

Chapter XXII

PROJECTIVE TECHNIQUES IN CONTEMPORARY PSYCHOLOGY

Leopold Bellak, M.A., M.D.

EDITORIAL NOTE

One of the undreamed of developments in the mental sciences is projective testing. Although it is not a part of psychoanalysis it would scarcely have stood its ground without the stress laid on the unconscious by Freud. Projective testing, even if it has not gained the quantitative precision of intelligence testing has become a major method of probing the human psyche, largely because it provides safeguards against conscious maneuvering in answering questions of a direct nature.

The contributor in this case, Dr. Leopold Bellak, who has studied medicine at the University of Vienna, has had wide contacts and gained fresh points of view by reason of his psychoanalytic training, his psychological research at Harvard University, and his supplementary medical training at New York Medical College where he received the American doctorate in medicine. As a staff member of St. Elizabeth Hospital in Washington, in 1944-46, he had excellent opportunities to advance in psychiatry. Thereafter he studied at and was graduated from the N. Y. Psychoanalytic Institute.

In addition to numerous articles, Dr. Bellak is the author of the following books: Dementia Praecox; Manic-Depressive Psychosis and Allied Disorders; Projective Psychology (*co-ed.* L.T. Abt); Psychology of Physical Illness (*ed.*); The T.A.T. and C.A.T. in Clinical Use; The Children's Apperception Test; Supplement to the Children's Apperception Test *and the* TAT Blank. *Dr. Bellak has taught at the City College of New York, at the New York Medical College and the New School for Social Research and at N. Y. University and is a Fellow of the American Psychiatric Association, the American Psychological Association, and the American Psychoanalytic Association, as well as of other learned and professional societies.*

PRESENT-DAY PSYCHOLOGY

HISTORICALLY SPEAKING

Projective techniques owe their current prominence about as much to the personnel problems of the Second World War as intelligence testing was indebted to an impetus from the manpower demands of World War One. Highly specialized people were necessary for the complex machinery of destruction, notably in the Air Force. A tremendous investment of time and money had to be made into the training of soldiers; too often the human factor—emotional maladjustment—caused breakdowns and rejections; techniques which might be able to reduce incidence of poor investments became of utmost importance. Projective methods came to the forefront in appraising personalities in this context. The quantitative side of the story of projective methods can be illustrated, for instance, by the increase in bibliography on the Thematic Apperception Test, from 11 items in 1941, as collected by Sanford and White,[52] to a total of 663 items ten years later, as listed by Holt in the *TAT Newsletter*. The Rorschach bibliography has gone through even greater avalanching.

The atmosphere of urgency led, on the one hand, to powerful strides of development, and, on the other hand, brought about a misuse of techniques insufficiently known and applied to too wide an area. Older academic psychologists without any clinical knowledge had to become self-styled experts, and in turn trained younger psychologists with an insufficient background. The result is that the postwar years are primarily so far a time of stocktaking, attempts at validation, re-examining of notions cherished for some years, and generally a period of more cautious appraisal and increasingly more appropriate use of projective techniques.

The entire field of American Psychology has been profoundly changed by the Second World War. The American Psychological Association has increased tremendously in size of membership, and by far the largest single section is the clinical one. Psychologists especially concerned with projective techniques banded together at first in the Rorschach Society with a mimeographed "Rorschach Research Exchange"; later they formed a nationwide Society for Projective Techniques and an excellent *Journal for Projective Techniques*. Psychology had become a profession with Boards and certificates; projective techniques became the most important tool of the professional clinician.

Certainly one important avenue to understanding any phenomenon is the historical one. Therefore, it was attempted to state the current status of projective techniques to serve as a backdrop for its development. The progress of these aspects of psychology might serve as an illustration of Hegelian notions of thesis, antithesis, and synthesis. Psychology started its modern phase in the psychophysiological laboratories of Wundt as an atomistic science; it remained as such not only in Titchener's hands, but in essence also for the behaviorists who would deal with single conditioned responses, even in the clinical field (such as attempting to deal with a phobia by deconditioning the subject to a single object!). Much of psychological statistics is predicated on atomistic notions, with the concept of the parameter an ever-disturbing nemesis. Gestalt psychology was one form of negating the atomistic approach; psychoanalysis another. Projective methods were originally primarily a synthesis of laboratory psychology and psychoanalysis. Hermann Rorschach was interested in responses to form and color, and influenced by his interest in association as a psychoanalyst. Murray, creator of the second most important projective method, the Thematic Apperception Test, worked in an academic psychological setting, as a psychoanalyst; already in Murray, Gestalt notions emerge in his concept of need-press syndromes (though in his case organismic concepts were probably largely mediated by his training in organic chemistry).

ATTITUDE OF ACADEMIC PSYCHOLOGIST

But if projective techniques had become holistic clinical instruments in a development away from the laboratory, we have already started on a new series of developmental steps: the

550

academic laboratories have become interested in the perceptual problems inherent in projection, as exemplified by experiments of Bruner and Postman.[14] Psychology of personality, which had to develop away from the brass instruments, is engaged in a return play in experimental laboratories via theories of personality conceived in terms of the psychodynamics of perception as stimulated by projective tests.

Projective techniques themselves have become subject of inquiry by the experimental psychologist. On the other hand, projective techniques and dynamic psychology pertaining to them have been incorporated in an increasingly important and even more holistic aspect of behavior than clinical psychology, namely social psychology. Psychodynamics has been related to social behavior, and projective techniques are prominently being used in the work.

The term "projection" was first used in a definite psychodynamic frame of reference by Freud in 1894 in the paper: The Anxiety Neurosis.[20] It is from that paper on "The Anxiety Neurosis" and the one in 1896 "On the Defense Neuropsychosis"[21] and the case of Schreber[22] that American psychology took until very recently the meaning of projection as a defense mechanism, whereby ego-alien thoughts and feelings were ascribed to the outside world (instead of recognizing them in oneself). Freud, however, had clearly stated in "Totem and Taboo"[23] that projection—far from being an exclusively pathological process is part of every perception; as Bellak[6] attempted to formulate it: every contemporary apperception is influenced and structured by all previous memory percepts.

L. K. Frank[19] must be credited with having coined the current use of the term "projective methods", in 1939. Hermann Rorschach had done his *Formdeutungsversuche* from 1911 to 1922, without relating them to the concept of projection. A number of procedures and experimental stimuli which must be considered "projective" had been used to elicit personality variables earlier in the twentieth century, as reported by Tomkins[49] and by Bellak,[1] for instance. None of these early attempts were in definite relationship to a theory of personality or even a specific frame of reference for interpretation. I do not doubt that this could even be said for Rorschach. Though a psychoanalyst, his perceptual interests were only tenuously related to psychoanalytic theory. Murray and Morgan were the first to have a hypothesis about fantasy formation, to demonstrate it experimentally,[32] and to select stimuli methodically which would produce fantasy useful for diagnostic inferences.

Clinically Speaking

The Rorschach Method doubtlessly dominates the field of projective techniques internationally and in the United States. Hermann Rorschach[39] who worked on this technique, in essence from about 1911 to his untimely death in 1922, must have been a unique and outstandingly gifted person. Being the son of a Swiss drawing teacher must have contributed to his interest in perception and form. Being a psychoanalyst and somewhat exposed to Jung, association experiments came natural to him. The rigid experimental spirit in which he conducted his experiments commands admiration even today.

Rorschach

While at first used only in Europe, the bulk of the development of the Rorschach doubtlessly took place in the United States. The first American paper seems to have been published in 1930 by Beck.[3] To start with, there were papers consisting, in essence, of case studies as e.g., by Rickers-Ovsiankina.[36] By 1940, books which helped to disseminate knowledge (Bochner and Halpern,[13] Klopfer and Kelley[27]) were published. Then came a series of attempts to facilitate and make uniform the scoring. A number of scoring forms and location charts, etc., were devised. Then it was attempted to find methods for more economy in administration and interpretation. Individual Rorschach is a time-consuming, cumbersome technique; therefore, methods of group administration were devised. Outstanding among them is Harrower's Multiple-choice Rorschach,[24] and Munroe's development of the Inspection technique of scoring to reduce time and labor. Later, the Bühlers and Lefever[16] further attempted to streamline Rorschach work by developing what they called "The Basic Rorschach Score" as a reference for interpretation and evaluation of records. Other endeavors headed in the direction of the development of syndromes or signs for organicity (Piotrowski) [34], suicidal tendencies, schizophrenia, and all other clinical conditions. Only within the last year or two has there been more work on children's Rorschach, as by Ford,[18] and attempts to standardize their responses in age ranges.

In the postwar years, there has been an increasing vigor in the experimental exploration of Rorschach tenets and underlying hypotheses. Possibly the most intensive attention was received by the concept of color and color shock in the Rorschach. Lazarus,[28] Rockwell et al.[37] used chromatic and achromatic cards to see what, if any, difference is produced by the colors. Sipola's experiment[45] deserves particular attention. Her main conclusion was that nothing has been added magically by color except that concept formation has to take two factors into consideration—form and color. She sees this simply as a task which may be well handled by the normal, may produce blocking in the neurotic, and may lead to bizarre responses in the psychotic. Schachtel[43] contributed outstandingly to the study of the M responses. There were a great number of studies of repeat reliability and ability to differentiate various groups by means of the Rorschach. Roe[38] has investigated a number of occupational groups by means of the Rorschach; the Rorschach has been applied to the anthropological study of many different cultures.

TAT

Aside from the Rorschach, and following in this order, the Thematic Apperception Test, the Szondi Test, and Figure Drawing are probably the most widely and most often used of projective techniques. The Thematic Apperception Test deals with structured social situations, and therefore, elicits more content than the Rorschach; it lends itself, therefore, less well to a percept analytic approach and better to a psychodynamic study of the nature of fantasies, wishes, fears, and the defenses against them. Murray has advanced his own need-press syndrome system of personality for the interpretation of the TAT which, however, has hardly been taken up.[33] Tomkins,[49] Rapaport,[35] Bellak,[7] and Wyatt,[35] are among the many who have offered their own approaches. The TAT has been used in a great number of clinical studies of all sorts and is used in relation to psychotherapy. Aside from the fact that many modifications of the TAT were made to explore and suit different cultural contexts (as pioneered by Henry[25]), the TAT has fathered a large family of similar tests designed to test special function or special areas. The MAPS Test by Shneidman[44] supplies movable figures on a background to which TAT-like stories are to be told. Thompson[48] created a form of the TAT supposedly better adapted for Negroes, using Negro characters as stimuli. The Children's Apperception Test and its Supplement by Bellak and Bellak[11] uses animal pictures instead of humans for children from 3 to 10 years of age. The Tomkins-Horn Test[50] uses pictorial situations particularly adapted to industry, and there also exists a Vocational Apperception Test.[26] Rosenzweig's Frustration Tolerance Test[40] must be considered a descendant of the TAT, as well as the Symonds Make-a-Story-Picture-Test for Adolescents, and Blum's Blacky Test.[12] In a somewhat different category belongs Van Lennep's "Four Picture Story Test" which was developed by the author quite independently of the TAT in Europe, in the 1930's, but reached the public eye only in the late 40's.[51]

SZONDI AND OTHER TESTS

The Szondi Test also uses pictures, but not to have stories told about them. It consists of a series of pictures of faces which the subject is asked to rank-order according to preference. Named after its originator, the test was developed approximately in 1939 and was originally intimately integrated with Szondi's drive theory and notions of genetics.[47] Deri[17] almost single-handedly brought the test to the American scene and adapted it theoretically and practically. While the test has become quite popular clinically, its theoretical and experimental status is unclarified as yet.

Figure Drawing was originally designed by F. Goodenough as an intelligence test for children, but was adapted by K. Machover[30] as a projective test for personality diagnosis. It differs from the other three tests mentioned in that it permits motor expression of drives and of the defenses against them, this subsemantic level sometimes permitting of insights where more verbal methods fail. The procedure can be dramatically insightful, but is particularly difficult to standardize and to put on a reliable experimental basis.

Among the promising tests belongs Sargent's interesting Insight Test[42] which is of the paper and pencil variety. The patient is asked to answer certain questions concerning a situation stated and diagnostic inferences are made from that. The *Mosaic Test,* originated by Lowenfeld, has not found very wide acceptance, while on the other hand the *Bender-Gestalt Test* can only be put in the class of projective tests with some difficulty. More prominent are the various *sentence completion* tests (Levy).[29] Here also belongs the *House-Tree-Person-Test* by Buck, the *World Test* (consisting of many figures which may be manipulated by children), and dozens of other tests in part designed in the United States and in part in Europe. Graphology, too, has somehow been included among projective methods. Furthermore, practically all the individually administered intelligence tests have been made instruments of projection: the answers which the subject gives are not only evaluated in terms of intelligence levels, but also in terms of personality characteristics. Projective tests are not only the most important instruments in psychodiagnostics; they, as already mentioned, have been applied to the study of people in different cultures: they have also been used as instruments in action research and for the investigation of social problems: they are widely used in selection processes for business and industry, for the armed forces, for professional schools, and others. A number of comprehensive textbooks have been written encompassing all the projective techniques (Bell,[5] Abt and Bellak,[1] Anderson and Anderson[2]), permitting an easy overview and serving as excellent sources for reference and teaching.

THEORETICAL GROUND

The *theoretical* problems of projective techniques can be characterized by the fact that they have largely been techniques in search of a theory. Too much has been grouped under the heading of projective techniques. Some of the techniques are concerned with the study of the *content*, with what the patient says (the TAT and its descendants); other tests are primarily concerned with *structural, formal,* and *expressive aspects,* such as the Rorschach and Mira's technique,[31] and to a certain extent Figure Drawing, and Graphology. Another function investigated by some of the techniques are the *Gestalt functions* of personality as exemplified in the Bender-Gestalt Test, the Mosaic Test, and the Rorschach. The *body image* and *self-image* is another sphere of activity entered into by the Rorschach, but first of all by Figure Drawing. Finally, *methods of preference* enter in under the heading of projective techniques; the Szondi, for instance, is based upon a system of selective choices as personality indicators, while color choice in finger painting, selection of figures in Dell play, choices of material in the MAPS, and others belong in this category.

EGO VS. DRIVES

It is no wonder that methods so divergent in their nature have more easily been subsumed under a common name than under a single theory. Projective methods up to now probably were almost wholly considered under the aegis of a drive-centered psychology of personality. It is time that a step be taken in projective theory which psychoanalysis undertook two decades ago: towards a consideration of ego psychology.

The psychoanalytic concept of the ego characterizes its functions as those of perception, organization, execution, hierarchical selection, and as an intermediary between drives and the outside world. An ego psychological theory seems to be able to subsume all the many approaches included under projective techniques to date, and permit a dynamic approach not only to drive content, but also to the formal characteristics and the defenses which have become of signal interest in psychodynamics.[8]

Projective techniques have been plagued by the fact that they were originated for the clinical idiographic study of personality, while they are now expected to fulfill the tough-minded criteria of nomothetically oriented academicians. Projective methods are expected to meet the standards of reliability and validity which have been associated with intelligence tests and other more easily quantified procedures.

There is no doubt that it would be gratifying if projective methods could be properly held in rein statistically. Certain aspects of these techniques certainly can and will be tabulated in norms. Particularly formal aspects of behavior on projective tests lend themselves to comparisons of a quantitative nature, e.g., the comparison of the performance of one individual to the performance of a sample population (*interpersonal comparisons*).

INTRAPERSONAL VS. INTERPERSONAL COMPARISONS

However helpful such normative data can be, they will probably always remain only of supportive significance. Unlike other tests, the validity of projective techniques must lie in intra-test comparisons and intra-personal comparisons.[4], [9] In the intra-personal comparisons the variables compared are those of the test behavior (latent personality features) and those of the overt behavior in reality. In intra-test comparisons the repetitiveness of significant patterns throughout various parts of the test has to serve as a measure of the significance of the variables. Until this unique feature of tests concerned with the unconscious is appreciated, no real statistical peace will be achieved.

FUTURE PROSPECTS

The most ambitious question is of course: What is the next phase projective techniques will go into? Presumably, testing of limits, validation, and restatements of rules and basic assumptions will be one important development. Probably most of the war and postwar growth of projective techniques will disappear and leave only half a dozen as the hard and useful nucleus. Specialized techniques for specific areas of applicability may survive in addition.

Development of projective techniques will have to be geared to the development of clinical psychiatry and its syndromes. Probably the largest single use of projective techniques is made in attempts of the differential diagnosis of schizophrenia. The poor quality of diagnostics by projective techniques is inextricably linked with the poor existing psychiatric nosology. How can one very well expect an instrument to diagnose a condition which is practically not defined by the experts on that condition? If psychologists are supposed to be useful members on the clinical team, psychiatrists will have to contribute stable concepts of their own.

Clinical psychologists generally, and those using projective techniques particularly, will require more opportunities to familiarize themselves with *homo sapiens*. Internships in hospitals are an excellent step in that direction, but not the whole answer. It enables psychologists to become familiar with the vagaries of psychotics primarily, but hardly with the minds of neurotics and those who fall into a group of what one might call "normals". One result of the narrowness of experience of the current crop of psychological clinicians is the fact that they are familiar to a certain extent with psychotic processes but not with the range of peculiarities found in non-psychotic minds and therefore consider many productions psychotic which to the best knowledge of clinicians with broader and longer experience are not at all so.

Professional schools for clinical psychologists (instead of academic graduate schools) will probably be one answer to the necessities of training.

A central Projective Research Registry for the collecting of international data of projective techniques may go a long way toward making these obstreperous clinical tools acceptable instruments of nomothetic science. Such a Registry might also serve as a body of experts to thesis advisors and students; it might initiate research in areas where it is needed and integrate independently started projects in a way which would facilitate the comparison of data obtained by different investigators.

BIBLIOGRAPHY

[1] Abt, L. and Bellak, L. *Projective Psychology;* A clinical approach to personality. New York: Alfred Knopf & Co., 1950.

[2] Anderson, H. H. and Anderson, G. L. *An Introduction to Projective Techniques.* New York: Prentice-Hall, Inc., 1951.

[3] Beck, S. J. Personality diagnosis by means of the Rorschach Test. *Amer. J. Orthopsychiatry,* 1930.

[4] —— Introduction to the Rorschach Method: A Manual of Personality Study. *Amer. Orthopsychiat. Ass. Monog.,* Vol. 1, 1937.

[5] Bell, J. E. *Projective Techniques*: A Dynamic Approach to the Study of Personality. New York: Longmans, Green and Co., Inc., 1948.

[6] Bellak, L. The Concept of Projection: An experimental investigation and study of the concept. *Psychiatry,* 1944, *4,* 353-370.

[7] —— *Guide to the Interpretation of the TAT and Analysis Sheets.* New York: Psychological Corp., 1942.

[8] —— Ego Psychological Theory of Projective Techniques. *J. Proj. Tech.,* Vol. 18, No. 3, 154.

[9] Bellak, L., with the collaboration of Eileen Ort. Thematic Apperception Test and Other Apperceptive Methods, in *Progress in Clinical Psychology,* edited by L. Abt and D. Brower, Vol. I, Sec. 1. New York: Grune & Stratton, Inc., 1952.

[10] Bellak, L. and Abt, L. *Projective Psychology*: A clinical approach to personality. New York: Alfred Knopf & Co., 1950.

[11] Bellak, L. and Bellak, S. S. *Children's Apperception Test* (1948) and *Supplement to the Children's Apperception Test* (1952), C. P. S. Co., P. O. Box 42, Gracie Sta., New York 28, N. Y.

[12] Blum, G. *The Blacky Test.* New York: Psychological Corp., 1950.

[13] Bochner, R. and Halpern, F. *The Clinical Application of the Rorschach Test.* New York: Grune & Stratton, Inc., 1942.

PRESENT-DAY PSYCHOLOGY

14 Bruner, J. S. and Postman, L. Tension and Tension-Release as Organizing Factors in Perception. *J. Personality,* Vol. 15, 1947, pp. 389-413.

15 Buck, J. N. The H-T-P Test. *J. Clin. Psychol.,* Vol. 4, 1948, pp. 151-158.

16 Bühler, C., Bühler, K. and Lefever, D. W. *Development of Basic Rorschach Score with Manual for Directions,* No. 1, Rorschach Standardization Studies. Los Angeles, 1949.

17 Deri, S. *Introduction to the Szondi Test.* New York: Grune & Stratton, Inc., 1949.

18 Ford, M. *The Application of the Rorschach Test to Young Children.* Minneapolis: U. of Minn. Press, 1946.

19 Frank, L. K. Projective Methods for the Study of Personality. *J. Psychology,* Vol. 8, 1939, pp. 389-413.

20 Freud, S. The Anxiety Neurosis, in *Collected Papers,* International Library, Hogarth Press, Vol. 1, 1940.

21 —— *Defense Neuropsychoses,* International Psychoanalytical Library, Vol. 1. London: Hogarth Press, 1940.

22 —— Psychoanalytic Notes on an Autobiographical Account of a Case of Paranoia (Dementia Paranoides), in *Collected Papers,* Vol. III, pp. 387-470.

23 —— Totem and Taboo, in *Basic Writings of Sigmund Freud,* edited by A. A. Brill. New York: Modern Library, 1938.

24 Harrower, M. R. Modification of the Rorschach Method for Use as a Group Test. *Rorschach Research Exchange,* Vol. 5, 1941, pp. 130-144.

25 Henry, W. E. The Thematic Apperception Technique in the Study of Culture-Personality Relations. *Genet. Psych. Monog.,* Vol. 35, 1945, pp. 3-315.

26 Herzig, S. A., Ammons, R. B. and Butler, M. N. A Projective Test for Vocational Research and Guidance at the College Level. *J. Appl. Psychol.,* 1950, *34,* 97-111.

27 Klopfer, B. and Kelley, D. McG. *The Rorschach Technique.* Yonkers, N. Y.: World Book Co., 1942.

28 Lazarus, R. S. The Influence of Color on the Protocol of the Rorschach Test. *J. Abnorm. & Social Psychol.,* 1949, *4,* 506.

29 Levy, S. and Sacks, J. M. The Sentence Completion Test, in *Projective Psychology,* edited by L. E. Abt and L. Bellak. New York: Alfred Knopf, Inc., 1950.

30 Machover, K. *Personality Projection in the Drawing of the Human Figure.* Springfield: C. C. Thomas, 1948.

31 Mira, E. Myokinetic Psychodiagnosis: A New Technique for Exploring the Conative Trends of Personality. *Proceedings of the Royal Society of Medicine,* Vol. 33, 1940, pp. 9-30.

32 Morgan, C. D. and Murray, H. A. A Method for Investigating Fantasies: the Thematic Apperception Test. *Archives of Neurology and Psychiatry,* Vol. 34, 1935, pp. 289-306.

33 Murray, H. A. *Thematic Apperception Test.* Cambridge: Harvard University Press, 1943.

34 Piotrowski, Z. A. The Rorschach Method of Personality Analysis in Organic Psychoses. *Psychol. Bull.,* Vol. 33, 1936, 795.

35 Rapaport, D. *Diagnostic Psychological Testing,* Vol. I. Chicago: The Year Book Publishers, Inc., 1946.

36 Rickers-Ovsiankina, M. The Rorschach Test as Applied to Normal and Schizophrenic Subjects. *Brit. J. Med. Psychol.,* 1938, *17,* 227-257.

[37] Rockwell, F. V., Welch, L., Kubis, J. and Fisichelli, V. The Effect of Repetition with Color Removed. *Monatschr. f. Psychiat. u. Neurol.*, 1948, *116*, 321.

[38] Roe, A. Analysis of Group Rorschachs of Biologists. *Rorschach Res. Exch. & J. of Proj. Techniques*, 1949, *13*, 25.

[39] Rorschach, H. *Psychodiagnostik*. Bern: Hans Huber, 1932.

[40] Rosenzweig, S. The Picture-Association Method and Its Application in a Study of Reactions to Frustration. *J. Personality*, 1945, *14*, 3-23.

[41] —— Apperceptive Norms for the Thematic Apperception Test, I. The Problem of Norms in Projective Methods. *J. Personality*, 1949, *17*, 475-482.

[42] Sargent, H. *The Insight Test*. New York: Grune & Stratton, Inc., 1953.

[43] Schachtel, E. G. Projection and Its Relation to Character Attitudes and Creativity in the Kinesthetic Responses. *Psychiatry*, 1950, *13*, 69.

[44] Shneidman, E. S. The Make a Picture Story (MAPS) Projective Personality Test: A preliminary report. *J. Consult. Psychol.*, 1947, *11*, 315-325.

[45] Sipola, D. M. Influence of Color on Reactions to Ink Blots. *J. Personality*, 1950, *18*, 358.

[46] Symonds, P. *Picture Story Test*. New York: Columbia University, Bureau of Publications.

[47] Szondi, L. *Szondi Test, (Testband)*. Bern: Verlag Hans Huber, 1947.

[48] Thompson, G. E. *Thematic Apperception Test: Thompson Modification*. Cambridge: Harvard University Press.

[49] Tomkins, S. S. *The Thematic Apperception Test*. New York: Grune & Stratton, Inc., 1947.

[50] Tomkins, S. S. and Horn, D. *Tomkins-Horn Picture Arrangement Test*. Mimeographed.

[51] Van-Lennep, D. J. *Four Picture Test*. The Hague, Netherlands: Martinus Nijhoff, 1948.

[52] White, R. W. and Sanford, R. N. *Thematic Apperception Test*, Mimeographed. Cambridge: Harvard Psychological Clinic, 1941.

[53] Wyatt, F. The Interpretation of the Thematic Apperception Test. *Rorschach Research Exchange*, 1947, *11*, 21-25.

CHAPTER XXIII

MILESTONES IN PSYCHOANALYSIS

Leon J. Saul, M.D. and Andrew S. Watson, M.D.*

EDITORIAL NOTE

While Freud was alive, there was only one brand of psychoanalysis. Popularly Jung, Adler, Stekel, and Rank would be referred to as psychoanalysts, but eventually different labels had to be thought of, like "Analytical Psychology", "Individual Psychology", etc.

Dr. C. G. Jung was approached for a statement on the latest development of his school, which could have been supplied by one of his followers, but that did not materialize. Stekel's and Adler's position, however, have their exponents in the volume.

The choice of Dr. Leon J. Saul to represent psychoanalysis in this volume seems to have been well considered in view of the fact that he has given us a balanced account of the recent developments. While it is true that the para-Freudian angle might have received extended treatment, the reader will find more on the subject in subsequent chapters, especially the one on psychotherapy by Dr. Gutheil.

Dr. Saul received his M.A. at Columbia University and M.D. at the Harvard Medical School, where he was for a time a Teaching and Research Fellow. During World War II, he served at first as Lieut.-Commander and then Commander in the U.S. Naval Reserve. At present he is Professor of Clinical Psychiatry at the University of Pennsylvania and Psychiatric Consultant to Swarthmore College. Emotional Maturity (*Philadelphia* 1947) *and* Bases of Human Behavior (*Philadelphia,* 1951) *are the titles of his two books. He has also written about forty papers in neurophysiology, psychoanalysis, and psychosomatic medicine.*

Dr. Watson is a practicing psychiatrist in Philadelphia.

PSYCHOANALYSIS

The history and development of psychoanalysis, perhaps as much or more than any other science, reflect the genius and accomplishment of one man, Sigmund Freud. His pioneer work and the impact of his personality have greatly influenced the course of this relatively young science.

Freud aimed to understand the history, current dynamics and the economics (quantitative factors) of the patient, in terms of each other. He showed how the historical method could be used for understanding the present-day motivations and how current behavior, feelings, thoughts, memories and dreams were conditioned by early experiences and the emotional life of childhood. That such early conditioning may also shape the character of a group[20] is clearly illustrated in the development of psychoanalysis itself. In this brief sketch of the milestones of psychoanalysis, it seems appropriate to begin with the significant factors in its early history.

EARLY INFLUENCES

Just as all newborn babies are affected by certain experiences which they have in common and by specific, individual ones as well, so new fields must go through certain phases characteristic of them all, and also through others which are individual.

Anatomy became respectable only after centuries of struggle. Astronomy grew against opposition. So did bacteriology. Semmelweiss showed the way to eliminate childbed fever (which killed roughly half the women delivered in hospitals at that time) and was martyred for his work. The antagonism to Darwin's conclusions has died down but is not yet extinguished. In the early days, Freud and the psychoanalysts met strong general opposition, an experience they had in common with most important innovators.

Such opposition has its effects not only upon the men who suffer from it, but through them, upon the academic discipline as well. An atmosphere of closeness, defensiveness, and suspicion was generated in the psychoanalytic group by such opposition, as was a strongly felt need to control training and thus access to the group. These natural reactions are still strong, for many men now prominent in the field were students of psychoanalysis in its beginnings, and themselves felt the pressure of general opposition.

Although the early reception of psychoanalysis may have been much like that which greeted other infant fields, yet psychoanalysis reacted in certain characteristic ways. These characteristic reactions were "overdetermined" by specific factors. Among these factors a few seem to have been specially effective in shaping the later character of the field.

1. Psychoanalysis Originated and Developed Outside of the Universities

Since faculties are composed of human beings, it should not be surprising that discoveries can be opposed within the universities themselves. That this was the case, in the early days, for psychoanalysis, was fateful for the new field in that it added to the influences tending toward isolation. Although there were advantages in isolation, the opportunities for discussion and understanding by workers in different disciplines were missing.

2. Psychoanalysis Developed With a Certain Coldness Toward Official Medicine

Perhaps this derived in part from Freud's difficulties with the university; perhaps in part from the hostility of the medical society when he reported to them his experiences with Charcot, and views on hysteria in men as well as in women.[27] The fact that Freud attracted sympathetic and brilliant laymen encouraged the isolation, not only from medicine, but from academic psychology as well. Into the presentation of the findings of psychoanalysis there crept disparagements of other psychological work.

3. Freud Chose to Devote Himself to Creative Work in His Own Field

As Freud said, psychoanalysis was his creation. Its origins were marked by the domination of his genius, and he attracted followers who fitted with his own personality. He provided an excellent model for behavior in the face of opposition, in that he refused to engage in polemics and followed the motto, "the only answer is good work." Shunning a waste of energy in answering critics and opponents, he devoted his forces to creative studies in his own field. [27]

Further, as a deliberate choice of methodology, Freud endeavored to keep himself as uninfluenced by other thinking as possible, while making observations and formulations in this difficult field of unconscious motivation and processes. That it was a fruitful procedure was proven by his work. Fifty years later, with discipline strong enough to stand on its own, and with methods, facts and theories well established, such isolation would seem anachronistic.

4. Emotional Resistance, Mingled With Rational Criticism, Clouded Issues

The content of psychoanalytic theory aroused strong emotional resistance and this factor introduced difficulties into distinguishing between legitimate criticism and what were only rationalizations for the hostility born of fear and offended feelings. The individual analyst was tempted to say that the critic could not comprehend the facts because of his emotional resistance, and thus he could avoid answering rational criticism as well. Even when he was right, this situation added its bit to the isolation in which the infant field was growing up.

5. Psychoanalysis Attracted Many Students With Hopes for Personal Help from the Field

Naturally, a field dealing with emotional problems will attract persons interested because of underlying hopes of finding in it answers to their own difficulties. There have been good results from this. It has long been noted that doctors study with the greatest devotion those diseases from which they suffer. Knight has pointed out that many psychoanalysts in the early days had difficulty in personal relationships and found a refuge in psychoanalysis.[28] Psychoanalysis absorbed their interests and became their whole lives; and the isolation sometimes encompassed the pattern of their living.

6. EUROPEAN INFLUENCE ON INDIGENOUS DEVELOPMENT

The development of psychoanalysis has been marked by another unusual feature during its early adolescence at least so far as the United States is concerned. Most new fields unfold indigenously. A discovery made in one country, is reported in other countries and developed in these other countries by their own workers. In the earlier days of psychoanalysis, physicians went to study in Vienna with Freud and returned to introduce psychoanalysis in this country. Then, owing to conditions in Europe, a considerable number of European analysts, came to this country and began to influence the development of the field here. In the early thirties a movement began in the United States to declare its independence from the International Psychoanalytic Association under the close control of which American psychoanalysis had been. In 1936 the American Psychoanalytic Association declared its right to veto rulings of the International and the movement culminated in 1938 in resolutions which made the American association truly autonomous, although still a member of the International.

Meanwhile the influx of European analysts, especially from Vienna, continued, and later, with World War II, many American analysts served in the Armed Forces for the duration. The older of the European analysts could not serve and, during this period, came naturally into control of the local societies and of the American Association. This has resulted in a second, current effort to re-establish independence from their control, particularly in regard to official recognition of individuals, institutes, and societies, and to keep the development of this young science democratic and academically free. It is interesting to note that at the present time 82% (399) of the members of the American Psychoanalytic Association and 73% of the current candidates in training are members of the American Psychiatric Association. Many of these men are products of the finest universities and medical schools in this country, stable, of high caliber, and superior academic capacity. They will carry forward the developments of the field, increasing its depth and breadth in sound ways.

The above six factors, among others, contributed strongly to the characteristics of this growing field, certain of which are of special importance. One of these characteristics was an emotional atmosphere in which science was colored by a fervor which had something of the intensity and quality of a religious mission. Psychoanalysis, a research method, a science of the mind, and a form of treatment developed as a "movement".[4] There was a sense of having something very precious which would save the world, and which must be jealously guarded by the chosen, initiated few from a world bent on diluting or destroying it. Even the initiated were not to be trusted entirely and must be carefully watched.[37]

This emotional climate had its effect on the intellectual development of psychoanalysis. The sense of mission, and fear of dilution and loss, led to a form of teaching which has influenced almost all modern analysts. Although psychoanalysis is an exquisitely clinical field, based upon the most careful, detailed, sustained observation of the individual and his utterances, yet it has been taught in many institutes as a body of theory which the students must learn, and then, in the third year, *apply* to patients.[7] This has the effect of making the theory itself sacred and unalterable rather than making it an ever-evolving help in understanding facts. There are exceptions, and there is an ever increasing tendency to return to Freud's emphasis upon "the ever green fields" of factual observation.[5]

Freud called the theory "superstructure", even referred to

some of it as "our mythology", although at one time he sought to use parts of it as a shibboleth, a test of whether a person was a psychoanalyst. However, later he wrote, "It may thus be said that the theory of psychoanalysis is an attempt to account for two observed facts that strike one conspicuously and unexpectedly whenever an attempt is made to trace the symptoms of a neurotic back to their sources in his past life: the facts of transference and of resistance. Any line of investigation, no matter what its direction, which recognizes these two facts and takes them as the starting-point of its work may call itself psychoanalysis, though it arrives at results other than my own." [16]

Another effect of the emotional feeling of mission, superiority, and suspicion has been the development of psychoanalysis as a closed system and the retardation of its integration with other sciences. This has not been unproductive. Yet there are many problems which cannot be solved within the framework of psychoanalysis itself, either as a method or as theory. In Freud's terms, there are "causal networks"; however specialized disciplines may be, reality is a continuum. The mental and emotional life of man is not an isolated phenomenon, but is part of nature. It cannot long be studied without reference to the knowledge of other sciences about it.

Great advantages have been derived from the kind of upbringing psychoanalysis has had at the hand of its parent. The "religious" atmosphere strengthened it in the early days and has given it a sense of force and vitality and inner cohesiveness. [27] Freud's original methodology of working uninfluenced has had excellent effects in fostering concentration upon one method and what it can yield, and has increased mastery of it. The work in relative isolation established methods, facts, and theories, and helped psychoanalysis to stand upon its own feet in the world of medical science. The child has now grown to adolescence. There are fresh orientations to be achieved and in this process some growing pains seem inevitable.

PRESENT-DAY PSYCHOLOGY

INFLUENCE OF UNIQUE TRAINING

A special feature of psychoanalysis, of great influence in its evolution, is the personal analysis, generally considered the most essential part of the candidate's training. Its value has been fully established.[32] It is indispensable.

In this analysis for training, as in any therapeutic analysis, the analysand, through prolonged contact with his analyst, reporting all of his thoughts and feelings, comes to react to the analyst as though he, the analysand, were in part the child reacting to his parents or other important figures of his childhood. Hence the analysand tends to depend upon, submit to, and identify with the analyst. This is a great responsibility for the analyst and it requires of him a personality make-up of the very highest integrity and an unusual degree of maturity to enable the analysand to develop truly in his own way and to have full independence of mind for use, not only in life, but academically in psychoanalysis.

Where divisions have occurred in psychoanalytic groups, it is very rare for a student not to side academically with his analyst. And yet, a few analysts have freed the minds of their analysands so well that the analysands have risen to prominence as independent thinkers, often disagreeing with their analysts. To help the analysand mature, the analyst must not only be mature himself but must understand maturity.[39], [29], [34]

If the analyst is a man (or woman) of topnotch academic capacity and maturity, then his influence is highly favorable. If he has not achieved this, then the younger men he has analyzed are apt to continue in his image, with his prejudices. There is probably no other field in which both the student and the evolution of the field itself are so strongly influenced by the teacher and the personalities in it.

The importance attached to the personal analysis was not entirely understood by leaders in related sciences. Perhaps the fervor previously mentioned seemed attached to this part of training and so served to precipitate a hostile reaction. As the conditions which enforced the isolation of the young science began to disappear, so also did the elements of mystery surrounding the training of psychoanalysts. With easier understanding, the emphasis on personal analysis is less and less a source of difficulty to workers in other fields.

INFLUENCES OF CONTENT

Certain early findings of psychoanalysis have so influenced it during the formative period that later changes have been rendered difficult.

1. THE EARLY EMPHASIS UPON SEX

Freud was struck by the prominence of sexual material and references in the associations and dreams of his patients and began his studies with a detailed exploration of this factor in connection with the etiology of neurotic symptoms. This study resulted in a broadened meaning of the term "sex". Freud showed that genital sensations are a more dominant form of feelings which are also experienced in other areas of the body, especially the mouth and anal regions.[23] This led to the conclusion that all pleasure is basically sexual pleasure—from sucking to driving an automobile. "Sexual" was used as an equivalent of "sensual". It was seen also as the foundation of "love". In Freud's latest formulation it became part of Eros, a term Freud used to mean the force which tends to bind protoplasm together as cells, multicellular organisms and even as societies.

This expanded meaning of "sexual" had several consequences. A certain confusion was introduced because, in psychoanalytic literature, the term might mean specifically genital sexuality, any pleasure, or even the forces of life.

Further, all pleasure was considered to arise as sexual pleasure basically in connection with the mother during infancy, the father being the interloper and rival, at least for the male child. Thus every investigator could come out with only one conclusion: the oedipus complex. If a man enjoys driving an automobile, this is pleasure, hence sexual and hence originally in relation to his mother, and other drivers must be competitors, or fathers. The effects of such thinking have been both stimulating and narrowing. This by no means denies the importance of the oedipus complex, which is an expression, toward the parents, of the underlying sexual rivalry seen in mammalian and other animal forms.

2. The Late Acceptance of Hostility as a Vital Force

Another effect of the early discovery of sexuality was the exclusion of hostility as a force in its own right in the neuroses. Early in his studies, Freud, while referring repeatedly to the importance of hostility in his patients and in human affairs, nevertheless insisted that it be formulated only as a part of the sexual drives. Late in his life he expressed astonishment that he and his followers could have overlooked the importance of this motivation. He went so far as to state, briefly yet explicitly, that he believed all guilt feelings to derive from hostility and only from hostility. [18]

His final theory was dualistic; the forces of life (Eros) bringing together protoplasm, opposed by an equally powerful tendency toward death (thanatos), one expression of which, turned outward from the organism, is hostility.

It is fortunate for the development of psychoanalysis that Freud made a formulation according full importance to hostility. So powerful has been his influence that if his earlier rejection of the vital significance of hostility had stood unrevised, valuable current research might have gone unused or opposed. Even with Freud's recognition of hostility, tradition still interferes with full appreciation of its fundamental importance. There is an emotional tendency to linger in the realm of the psychoanalytically more proper, "deeper", more standard, and an inertia against seeing the fight reaction, the rage and guilt under which a patient suffers and which cry for relief. Late recognition of this by Freud, and the emphasis of current thinking and research are spelling good progress in this direction.[26]

3. THE LIBIDO THEORY

Through a remarkable feat of observation and interpretation, Freud was able to formulate his libido theory. Originally this presented a rather rigidly stratified picture of human development, in terms of the oral, anal, and phallic stages during which the foundations of the personality were laid, followed by the latency period, adolescence, and maturity. These stages were further studied and subdivisions suggested, especially by Abraham.[1]

The horizontal concept of the personality in terms of fixed stages of development led to an effort to relate each neurosis to a particular stage. The fixed stages of the libido theory reinforced the fixed entity view of neuroses, then thought of as "disease entities".* A person "had" hysteria—this was related to the oedipal phase. Another patient suffered from "compulsion neurosis"—this was related to the anal stage. One was to think of the whole patient in terms of being on one or another level of development.

While there is considerable truth in this view, Freud recognized that the relationships are more involved and much less simple than was first thought, and loosened his concept. "Our attitude to the phases of libidinal organization has in general altered somewhat. We formerly emphasized the way in which one phase gives place to the next; nowadays we direct our attention more to the facts which indicate how much of each of the earlier phases persists side by side with, and later organization, and obtains permanent representation in the economy of the libido and in the character of the individual."[21]

This loosening of the concept of fixed, horizontal stages of development led to the addition of vertical concepts as well. A view developed of the personality as motivated by certain major forces, each of which has its own developmental history, its own connections with these earlier stages and its own unique expres-

sion. For example, Freud, in many places, points out the fundamental importance of dependence. In fact, he attributes neuroses
to the long period of the child's dependence upon the mother.
However, he did not get around to making a separate formulation of dependence. Hence, dependence is usually thought of in
connection with the "oral" stage of development rather than as
a major force in its own right with other connections in addition
to the oral. So too, full and explicit appreciation of their significance has not yet been accorded to hostility and to the progressive forces toward responsibility, productivity and independence.
(31), (11)

The formulation of the early stages of development have received the greatest attention, quite naturally, because it is during
these early formative years that the child is subjected to those
influences which make for him emotional problems in his later
adult life. The analyst daily sees the emotional problems of the
adult and focuses upon their sources in these early stages.

The solution of the neurotic problem, i.e. of the persisting,
warped childish reactions, must lie in overcoming these early
fixations and in freeing the emotional development so that the
person can achieve enjoyment from mature attitudes and patterns of behavior. This is leading to increasing emphasis upon
the later development particularly to work upon the meaning
of maturity, "object interest" and "genital level". Their importance, both theoretically and therapeutically is now coming
to be increasingly recognized.

The various motivations mentioned above are now receiving
more focused attention in their relationships, not only to the
libido theory, but in all observable connections, and in relationship to other observation and theories in bordering fields, such as
biology and physiology.(10), (28), (33), (43)

SHIFTING EMPHASES

The trends in content just discussed are reflected in shifts
of emphasis in the field of psychoanalysis. Freud noted that, as

study progressed, interest shifted from *what was repressed* to the nature and operation of the *repressing forces*. Even those of his followers who adhere most rigorously to his early thinking have continued this shift.

1. INTEREST IN THE OPERATIONS OF THE EGO

Anna Freud begins her book, *The Ego and the Mechanisms of Defence,* with the statement that the study of the ego had been unpopular because many analysts considered that the scientific and therapeutic value of their work was in proportion to the "depth of the psychic strata upon which attention was focused." The transfer of interest to the *ego,* it was felt, "was a beginning of apostasy from psychoanalysis as a whole . . . With problems such as the adjustment of children or adults to the outside world, with concepts of value such as those of health and disease, virtue or vice, psychoanalysis was not properly concerned. It should confine its investigation exclusively to infantile fantasies carried on into adult life, imaginary gratification, and the punishment apprehended in retribution for these." She goes on to say that there was some indication for this in the past when psychoanalysis was built up from the study of the *id,* but that this is no longer valid when we apply it for treatment. From the beginning, analysis, as a therapeutic method, was concerned with the ego and its operation; the investigation of the id and its mode of operation was always only a means to an end. And the end was invariably the same; the correction of those abnormalities and the restoration of the ego to its integrity. She sees it as the task of analysis to acquire the fullest possible knowledge of the ego, superego, and id and their relationship to one another and to the outside world.[14]

The earlier emphasis on the fantasies of patients is sometimes hauntingly present in the feeling that an analysis filled with fecal penises dangling from breasts is deeper and more effective, even as treatment, than one that emphasizes the ways in which the ego defends itself against rejected motivations and frees itself from them in favor of mature functioning. Anna Freud's work marked a growing tendency of psychoanalysis to develop in the direction of reality, and of seeing its own findings in realistic perspective.

2. RECOGNITION OF THE ROLE OF EXTERNAL REALITY AND TOTAL PERSONALITY

The experience of the last war demonstrated that even the strongest of men will break under external pressures maintained for long enough periods. The rôle of the total personality and its relationship to the external world demanded understanding. War experiences emphasized the importance of external reality in affecting even the deepest inner psychic realities.

The kinds of patients who now come for treatment demand an appreciation of the same sort; a recognition of the total personality, not only in the production of symptoms but in the trajectory of a whole existence.[2] Freud foresaw this when, as A. A. Brill told the senior author, he said that analysis would emerge with the next generation from preoccupation with the neuroses into the broad ocean of characterology and the total personality.

Analytic work with children, based on direct observation, has submitted theory to the test of reality.[13] This approach submits the "superstructure" of theory to the continual questioning, testing, and modifying of an expanding empirical base.

War experiences, the kinds of patients who now come for treatment, and the direct studies of children have supported a growing tendency in the analytic field to face the realities of the psychic life in relationship to the external situation in which the person lives his life and for which he is partly responsible.

3. PSYCHOANALYTIC THERAPY AS EMOTIONAL REEDUCATION

The growing recognition of the rôle of external reality has led analysts to see that cures are not accomplished by the mere process of unearthing early fantasies, and that preoccupation

577

with these usually signifies regressive escape from real life and its responsibilities.*

The process of cure in psychoanalysis lies basically with the use of the transference relationship as an instrument for correcting the effects of those influences during childhood which warped the development, thereby freeing the individual for growth toward emotional maturity. "If," wrote Freud, "the patient puts the analyst in the place of his father (or mother), he is also giving him the power which his superego exercises over his ego, since his parents were, as we know, the origin of his superego, the new superego now has an opportunity for a sort of *after-education* of the neurotic; it can correct blunders for which his parental education was to blame . . . In all his attempts at improving and educating the patient, the analyst must respect the patient's individuality." And, adds Freud, "the amount of influence he may legitimately employ will be determined by the degree of inhibition of development present in the patient. Many neurotics have remained so infantile that in analysis they can only be treated as children."[17] Hence the necessity for the analyst to be mature. "After-education" has also been called the "corrective emotional experience."[8] It is readily intelligible in Pavlovian terms as "deconditioning" and "reconditioning."[12]

That analysts themselves resist these changing emphases is to be expected and may be traced to the influences on the field already discussed. Moreover, most people, even in their professional lives, continue to operate within a conceptual framework which they learned years before. In the light of this expectancy, it is gratifying to review recent growth of psychoanalytic thinking beyond the exclusive effects of early influences to increasing awareness of the relation of these early influences to the interrelationships of dependence, hostility, inferiority and prestige needs as well as the rôle reality and maturity play in the therapeutic processes.[25]

PROGRESS IN TREATMENT PROCEDURES

Psychoanalysis developed from the observation of the patient and its roots lie in therapy. Its evolution is reflected in progress in treatment techniques. Alexander and French see the main periods in the development of psychoanalytic therapy as: 1) cathartic hypnosis, 2) waking suggestions, 3) free association, 4) transference neurosis, and 5) emotional reëducation.[8]

Originally patients were selected pretty much to fit the early standard psychoanalytic method of treatment. This method consists of close observation and keeping in touch with the patient's life by having daily interviews. It was dictated by certain conditions of practice, and to a considerable extent by Freud's recognition that psychoanalysis was a new field and that research interests were primary.

In the past fifty years, however, a good deal has been learned; psychoanalysis has become known to the public; patients of a great many different kinds and a wide variety of problems come for help. They can no longer be treated primarily for research interest. Moreover, the diversity of their personalities and problems requires much greater knowledge, perspicacity, and flexibility on the part of the analyst. He must indeed understand, as Anna Freud expressed it, the total personality in relation to its functioning in the outside world. It is only to be expected that on the basis of increased knowledge, changed social and professional climate and patients of different types and kinds, that the original mechanics of treatment would develop a corresponding flexibility. However, a particular resistance arose against increasing flexibility since the daily interviews on the couch are looked upon as a trade-mark of the analyst, a sign of his identity as his specialty permeates the rest of psychiatry. But no single prescription can fit all cases. The five or six 50-minute sessions per week and the lying on the couch, if rigidly insisted upon as a fixed essential in every case, begin to appear in the light of ritual. Although this technique continues to provide the basis of analytic procedure, yet more and more it is not adhered to blindly, but is used as a means to an end.[8], [24], [31], [36], [42], [44], [45]

Witnessing the different personalities, backgrounds and expanding varieties of patients, analysts have felt more and more that no set mechanics, such as number of hours per week, could be uncritically applied in every case. What one individual, with his particular personality makeup and emotional problem might specifically require, another might not tolerate or do well with. At first, any alteration in the formal procedure, any smaller number of hours per week, was equated with superficial, non-analytic psychotherapy. But probably all experienced analysts have on occasion seen patients fewer than five times a week and have otherwise adapted the technique to the goals. Freud in 1910 wrote, "We are . . . now coming to the opinion that the analytic technique must undergo certain modifications according to the nature of the disease and the dominating instinctual trends in the patient . . ." In 1919 he stated, "We are ready to admit incompleteness of our understanding to learn new things and to alter our methods in any way that yields better results."[19], [22]

Another factor of considerable weight is experience and skill. What an analyst of twenty years experience does, if he uses his full powers, is not something which bears no relation to technique. Psychoanalysis is a science and a therapy that can be used by such analysts as a fine instrument, adaptable to the widest variety of persons, problems and situations. Thus there has come to be recognized, amidst conflicting opinions, *analytically based therapy,* which only experienced analysis can employ skilfully.

EMERGENCE FROM ISOLATION

Paralleling the inner growth of psychoanalysis, the other sciences and society have shown an increasing interest in its concepts. Pressing social and political problems have caused thinkers in other fields to consider how individual attitudes and behavior develop and to turn to psychoanalysis for suggestions. Patients, especially in the United States, make increasing demands. Changing educational philosophies have raised questions of cause and effect in the development of children. Certain analytic findings cast light on obscure problems of physiological medicine. The last war not only affected psychoanalysis, but introduced a large number of people to the field, its concepts, and techniques. Both the inner unfolding of this new science and the widening range of demands made on it are bringing about an end of its isolation.

In this country, the pendulum has swung from the early antagonism to official medicine over to the other extreme. Each time the issue has come up in the national society, the overwhelming sentiment has been for considering psychoanalysis (for therapy) as a branch of medicine.

The trend toward the integration of psychoanalysis with other sciences within the universities is reflected in its rapid acceptance into the medical schools since the last war. Medical schools having analysts as professors, or as important members of their faculties, now include, to mention only some which come to mind, such universities as Harvard, Yale, Columbia, Temple, Cincinnati, Chicago, California, Southern California, Illinois, Tulane, Maryland, North Carolina, Pittsburgh, Washington, Western Reserve, Northwestern, Jefferson, New York (University), Pennsylvania, Colorado, and State University of New York. Hospitals also, such as Michael Reese, in Chicago, Mt. Sinai, in New York, Harper Hospital in Detroit, have predominantly analytic staffs for their department of psychiatry.

Today, the young men who come for training in psychoanalysis are M. D.'s and psychiatrists. Some of them have had research interests and research experience. They have seen the concept of psychoanalysis give rise to the field of Psychosomatic Medicine.[6] They have seen it permeate the thinking of general psychiatry to the extent of shaping what is called "dynamic psychiatry,"[33] a psychiatry based upon an understanding of human motivation and its development. They have seen its influence in experimental work on animals and its effects on cultural anthropology. They see the potential emergence of psychosociology. As they master the difficult field of psychoanalysis they see that it is strong enough and secure enough to take its place in the family of sciences.

Part of the original narcissism of the early days lay in the consciousness of the great contribution that psychoanalysis had to make to other fields. For reasons already discussed, little attention was paid to what other fields could contribute to psychoanalysis. A milestone in its development has been the opening of two-way roads to the other sciences. There is an increasing recognition that the concepts of physiology, such as Cannon's fight-flight reaction and homeostasis,[43] and Pavlov's work on conditioning are vital to understanding phenomena of the human mind which are dealt with daily by the analyst.[12] Geza Róheim, so long concerned with the application of psychoanalytic insights to anthropology, has recently published a book which seeks to draw upon anthropological data to help understand dreams.[35]

Everywhere in the psychoanalytic field there is a growing acceptance of the fact that analysis cannot solve all its problems within its own framework. Depressive reactions are better understood because they are seen in animals as well as human beings. Dejong has shown that the catatonic reaction is a defensive reaction of the nervous system used by all species as far down the evolutionary scale as reptiles.[9] Men like French, Kubie, Alexander, Margolin, Erikson, Senn, Spock, Masserman, Grinker, Mirsky and very many others (who, we hope will forgive us for not making this list exhaustive) have brought to psychoanalysis their knowledge of physiology, psychology, biophysics, anthropology, sociology and other related fields and have used this knowledge to further psychoanalytic understanding. The recognition that psychoanalysis cannot solve all the problems it sees in patients by staying within its closed framework has released it to an enriching exchange with other sciences.

CURRENT RESULTS AND THE FUTURE

It is not easy to evaluate the effects of all these advances. It seems that perhaps a major result is the emergence from psychoanalysis, which has been a science and a tool of investigation, of "psychodynamics"—a new basic science in which psychoanalysis is integrated with the knowledge of the other related sciences— biology, physiology, anthropology, sociology and the like.[33] Here the old isolation, superiority, and suspicion of the child is replaced by the understanding and coöperation of maturity. This has not yet been thoroughly achieved, but there is noticeable movement in this direction.

The science of psychodynamics is now itself an infant, but the outlines of this new science are already recognizable. Resting upon psychoanalysis and upon the related sciences as well, it will provide a firm foundation for understanding psychoanalytic knowledge in terms of biology and physiology, on the one hand, and the social sciences, on the other.[38] Freud stated in many places that one day psychoanalysis would rest on a biological basis. Psychodynamics will provide a basic science for the student of human thought and behavior. It will open up a variety of new techniques of investigation and a variety of new techniques for treatment, not only of the individual but of the problems of social life. The essay style of article, so appropriate for Freud in exploring a new humanistic field, will gradually give way to the scientific style in which adequately controlled data are presented and conclusions are rigorously tested as in other sciences. Quantitative methods are already being introduced.[41]

Some analysts very understandably fear that these advances may cause the treasured core of psychoanalytic understanding of the unconscious to become diluted or dissipated. However, in the light of the history of science, the opposite is far more likely to occur. Psychoanalysis, in finding its place among the sciences, will be more secure and more sound than ever and it will attract the best of scientists and practitioners. Not in "splendid isolation" but with mature diminution of its narcissism, psychoanalysis will make its contribution to man's effort, through understanding himself, to save himself from destruction, and to achieve maturity on a wide scale, and so realize the full potentials of his nature.

On Para-Freudianism

It has been strongly urged on the part of the editor that a discussion of para-Freudians be included in this chapter. To do so is decidedly against my own judgment for several reasons. Chief among these is the fact, as it seems to me, that this reflects most unfavorably upon psychoanalysis itself. Sciences are not the exclusive work of any one man no matter how great his genius. They represent knowledge of reality gained by many workers. There are physicists, not Newtonians and para-Newtonians. There is the medical specialty of brain surgery and not Harvey Cushingites and para-Harvey Cushingites.

Disagreement is part of the very essence of science. A scientist reports his work, knowing that others will do their best to tear it apart. If it withstands these initial criticisms, then it must stand up against attempts by others to repeat it. In this way a better grasp of reality, which is what science seeks, is gradually achieved.

To distinguish different groups such as Freudians and para-Freudians is to represent psychoanalysis as, not a science, but a religious cult. It is to say that there can be no progress because Freud is the final authority. It is to say that authority rests solely in what one man wrote at one time rather than in the vast universe of reality. Thus I believe such terms as "para-Freudian" should be shunned completely for they are an insult to all concerned. They make it appear that there is a group called "Freudians" who are cultish devotees who impose a discipline and thought-control like that of religious or revolutionary fanatics, and are not interested in the truth but in people's beliefs; who do not welcome originality and science but who forbid it and seek to purge it.

This is not, as the rest of this chapter shows, what I believe psychoanalysis is. The disagreements between its members are not only part of the growing pains of a new field but are, as mentioned above, part and parcel of every live science. I have heard some of the best brains in physiology attack each other's work and ideas mercilessly in an evening meeting and then all go out for beers feeling that they had spent an exciting, congenial, scientifically profitable and most enjoyable evening.

If, in spite of these considerations, I am nevertheless pushed to discussing para-Freudians, I would do it historically. The first outstanding para-Freudian was, of course, Freud himself. He repeatedly disagreed with himself and took new positions. Anxiety, as every analyst learned, came from repressed libido, but then Freud said that anxiety really was the force which caused the repression. Freud described clearly how one phase of libidinal organization gave place to the next, but then he stated that the earlier phases could persist side by side with the later organization. Freud considered that sexuality was a basic instinct and aggression was only a quality; but then he said that aggression was a force of power and importance equal to that of the erotic drives. He even went so far as to say that it is from aggression alone that all guilt derives. When "The Ego and the Id" was published, it was, if I am correctly informed, understood by very few of the analysts, who were accustomed to thinking in the former terms of conscious and unconscious alone. Had anyone else but Freud written this book, it is likely that it would not have been accepted. Freud emphasized the oedipus complex as the "nuclear complex" of neuroses but later he saw the part played in neuroses by the "blunders" of the parents. Freud also used his own terms in different ways. For example, he used "repression" in four different ways, finally decided that he must define it, did so, but then did not stick to the definition. He even referred to psychoanalysis as "after-education" although it was usual for analysts to maintain hotly that psychoanalysis was not education, and he wrote that the term psychoanalysis is properly applied to any psychotherapy which works through the resistance and the transference. In technique also Freud was para-Freudian. Walther Schmideberg reports doing a control under Freud's supervision in which he saw the patient at her home with her sitting up facing the analyst and knitting. Moreover Freud stressed the fact that the analytic technique developed out of the study of hysteria and that it would have to be modified as it was applied to other clinical problems. These are only a few random samples.

The other great para-Freudian was Ferenczi, an outstanding experimentalist and, of course, a close friend and co-worker of Freud.

Freud's daughter, Anna, could not keep to the spirit of her father without being herself para-Freudian. She wrote bluntly that psychoanalysis cannot be confined to depth psychology. She then went on to study the ego, recognizing that this might be looked upon as "apostasy." In a recent lecture, she said that in a child guidance clinic (which she now directs) it is no longer possible to wait 100 or 200 hours before making a diagnosis. One must gain an understanding of the patient in the very first few interviews.

Compared with the radical ideas of Freud and Anna Freud, anyone who nowadays could by any stretch of the imagination be called para-Freudian is in reality a thoroughgoing conformist whose ideas represent no more than differences in emphasis. Franz Alexander has created something of a stir because he studied physical symptoms psychoanalytically. Thereby he contributed greatly to the new field of psychosomatic medicine and helped to integrate psychoanalysis with medicine. He and his group spent eight years in a conscientious study of the psychoanalytic technique, raising the question of whether the depth and permanency of treatment is *necessarily* proportional to the frequency of the interview. In science others study a man's work, then repeat it, honestly and sympathetically, and see if they reach the same conclusion. Whatever their results, they then publish them. If a systematic eight-year study of an important aspect of psychoanalysis is to be labelled as para-Freudian, then no Freudian could raise his head without shame among scientists.

While Anna Freud turned to the study of the Ego, Karen Horney was especially interested in the effects of cultural factors and of current reality. Freud, I am told, recognized her as a top analyst and asked why she did not come to see him.

That the powerful feelings of people, which psychoanalysis studies, are directed to each other is an obvious fact. Harry Stack Sullivan gave this explicit recognition by using the term "interpersonal." He was also especially interested in how people communicate with each other—an aspect of knowledge which has become a little more recognized and respectable since the introduction of cybernetics by Norbert Wiener. Sullivan was primarily concerned with the psychoses, especially schizophrenia. Frieda Fromm-Reichmann has also worked very largely with psychoses. Hence the observational material of these workers differs somewhat from those of analysts who have an exclusively office practice with neuroses. If, as Freud explicitly stated, the psychoanalytic technique must be modified more and more as one gets away from hysteria, we can certainly expect that different techniques and observations will emerge from the study of the psychoses. Workers such as these have shown what an important contribution psychoanalysis does have in the psychoses and how much is to be learned from them.

Psychoanalysis is a broad field and its workers study various aspects of it, expand its frontiers, and by so doing deepen and enrich it.

Psychoanalysis cannot be a little cult of dictatorial fanatics who grade people in accordance with the purity of their beliefs in the true faith and, announcing that they are the chosen people, mete out labels to those who think and experiment and base their knowledge on reality.

Psychoanalysis is a science. It is a young and as yet not well developed one but is maturing rapidly. It must be broad enough to include all conscientious workers. Science is questioning. Psychoanalysis must be happy to have every aspect of its field expanded, explored, experimented with. Only in this way can it grow as a science and as a medical specialty, add to human knowledge and be of increasing use in alleviating human suffering. Every sincere worker in this field is a psychoanalyst. There are young ones and old ones, good ones and bad ones, experienced ones and inexperienced ones, but they are not Freudians and para-Freudians. Science is a cathedral built by many hands. It rests upon the solid ground of reality which is its only authority.

FOOTNOTES

* The authors wish to express their gratitude to Catherine (Mrs. Andrew S.) Watson for editorial assistance in preparing this chapter.

* The concept of disease entities is no longer so fixed, even in medicine. The neuroses appear more and more as "ways of reacting"—everyone has all the mechanisms, only one or another may be more or less prominent. For example, a person with a strong schizophrenic reaction may also show some paranoid projection, some compulsive behavior and some hysterical symptoms. It is a matter of degree, intensity, and proportion.[40]

* The recovery of the "traumatic memories" is important in the ways reported by Freud in his Studies in Hysteria. But regarding infantile fantasies, Freud, in 1909, writing in a footnote to the "Case of an Obsessional Neurosis", said: ". . . The present success of the treatment was precisely what stood in the way of this (reconstruction of infantile phantasies). The patient recovered, and his ordinary life began to assert its claims: there were many tasks before him which he had already neglected far too long, and which were incompatible with continuation of treatment. I am not to be blamed, for this gap in analysis. The scientific results of psychoanalysis are at present only a by-product of treatment aims, and for that reason it is often just in these cases where therapy fails that most discoveries are made. . . ."[15]

BIBLIOGRAPHY

[1] Abraham, K. *Selected Papers of Karl Abraham.* International Psychoanalytical Library No. 13. London: Hogarth Press Ltd., 1949.

[2] Alexander, F. Neurosis and the Total Personality. *Medical Journal and Record,* August 4, 18, September 1, 1926. Reprint by A. R. Elliot Publishing Company.

[3] —— The Sociological and Biological Orientation of Psychoanalysis. *Mental Hygiene,* 1936, 20, 232-248.

[4] —— Psychoanalysis Comes of Age. *Psychoanalytic Quarterly,* 1938, 7, 299-306.

[5] —— *Fundamentals of Psychoanalysis.* New York: W. W. Norton & Co., 1948.

[6] —— *Psychosomatic Medicine: Its Principles and Applications.* New York: W. W. Norton & Co., 1950.

[7] —— *Psychoanalytic training in the past, present and the future. A historical review.* Address to the Association of Candidates of the Chicago Institute of Psychoanalysis, October 26, 1951.

[8] Alexander, F. and French, T. *Psychoanalytic Therapy: Principles and Application.* New York: The Ronald Press Company, 1946.

[9] Dejong, H. H. *Experimental Catatonia.* Baltimore: The Williams and Wilkins Co., 1945.

10 Erickson, E. *Childhood and Society.* New York: W. W. Norton & Co., 1950.

11 Fenichel, O. *Psychoanalytic Theory of Neurosis.* New York: W. W. Norton & Co., 1945.

12 French, T. M. Interrelations between Psychoanalysis and the Experimental Work of Pavlov. *American Journal of Psychiatry,* 1933, *12,* 6.

13 Freud, A. Observations on Child Development. *Psychoanalytic Study of the Child,* International Universities Press, Vol. VI, 1951, 325.

14 —— *The Ego and the Mechanisms of Defence.* New York: International Univ. Press, Inc., 1946.

15 Freud, S. A Case of Obsessional Neurosis. *Collected Papers,* Vol. 3. London: Hogarth Press, 1950, 345.

16 —— On the History of the Psycho-analytic Movement. *Collected Papers,* Vol. 1. London: Hogarth Press, 1950, 287.

17 —— *An Outline of Psychoanalysis.* New York: W. W. Norton & Co., 1949.

18 —— *Civilization and Its Discontents.* London: Hogarth Press Ltd., 1930.

19 —— Future Prospects of Psychoanalytic Therapy. *Collected Papers,* Vol. II. London: Hogarth Press Ltd., 1933.

20 —— *Moses and Monotheism.* New York: Alfred A. Knopf, 1939.

21 —— *New Introductory Lectures in Psychoanalysis.* New York: W. W. Norton & Co., 1933.

22 —— The Turnings in the Ways of Psychoanalytic Therapy. *Collected Papers,* Vol. II. London: Hogarth Press Ltd., 1933.

23 —— Three Contributions to the Theory of Sex. *The Basic Writings of Sigmund Freud.* New York: Modern Library, 1938.

24 Fromm-Reichmann, F. *Principles of Intensive Psychotherapy.* Chicago: University of Chicago Press, 1950.

25 Grotjahn, M. and Gabe, S. Psychotherapy—Outline of its History in present situation, in *Modern Abnormal Psychology,* Philosophical Library, 1953.

26 Hartman, H., Kris, E. and Loewenstein, R. M. Notes on the Theory of Aggression. *The Psychoanalytic Study of the Child,* vols. 3 and 4, 9. New York: International Universities Press, 1949.

27 Jones, E. *The Life and Works of Sigmund Freud.* New York: Basic Books, Inc., 1953.

28 Knight, R. P. The Present Status of Organized Psychoanalysis in the United States. *Journal of the American Psychoanalytic Association,* vol. 1, 1953, 197-221.

29 Levine, M. *Psychotherapy in Medical Practice.* New York: Macmillan & Co., 1948.

30 Masserman, J. Psychoanalysis and Biodynamics—an Integration. *International Journal of Psychoanalysis,* 1953, *34,* Supplement, 1-30.

31 Mittelmann, B. Analysis of Patients without Acute Symptoms. *Psychoanalytic Review,* 1945, *32,* 181-196.

32 Oberndorf, C. P. *A History of Psychoanalysis in America.* New York: Grune & Stratton Inc., 1953.

33 Rádo, S. Psychodynamics as a New Basic Science. *American Journal of Orthopsychiatry,* 1946, *33,* 405.

34 Redlich, F. C. The Concept of Normality. *American Journal of Psychotherapy,* 1952, *6,* 551-576.

35 Róheim, G. *The Gates of the Dream.* New York: International Universities Press, 1953.

36 Rosen, J. N. The Treatment of Schizophrenic Psychosis by Direct Analytic Therapy. *Psychiatric Quarterly,* 1947, *21,* 3-37, 117-119.

37 Sachs, H. *Freud, Master and Friend.* Cambridge, Mass.: Harvard University Press, 1944.

38 Saul, L. J. *Bases of Human Behavior.* Philadelphia: Lippincott Co., 1951.

39 —— *Emotional Maturity.* Philadelphia: Lippincott Co., 1947.

40 The Nature of Neurotic Reactions. *American Journal of Psychiatry,* 1950, *106,* 547-548.

41 Saul, L. J., Sheppard, E., Selby, C., Master, G. and Sachs, D. *An Attempt to Quantify Emotional Forces using Manifest Dreams:—A Preliminary Study.* Presented at meeting of American Psychoanalytic Association, New York, December, 1953.

42 Schmideberg, M. Short Analytic Therapy. *Nervous Child,* 1949, *8,* 281.

43 Selye, H. *Stress: A Treatise based on the Concepts of the General Adaptation Syndrome and the Diseases of Adaptation.* Montreal: Acta, Inc., 1950.

44 Thompson, C. *Psychoanalysis: Evolution and Development.* New York: Hermitage Press Inc., 1953.

45 Whitaker, C. A. *The Roots of Psychotherapy.* New York: Blakiston Company, 1953.

CHAPTER XXIV

MIDCENTURY PSYCHOSOMATICS

JAMES W. D. HARTMAN, Ph.D.
Veterans Administration Center, Wichita, Kansas

EDITORIAL NOTE

Psychosomatic medicine is committed to the theory that bodily ailments either have their origin in, or at least are affected by, certain mental states. The conception certainly is not new, and, as the present writer has shown in his Psychology of Character, *(3rd ed. 1952) by quotations, has been formulated with some clarity by Friedrich Schiller, whose poetry has far overshadowed his medical essays. Both in France and in Germany, the idea of the physical and mental interrelationship in disease has taken root, but it was only within the past two decades that psychosomatics had begun to develop into a substantial body of sifted opinion worthy of a place in science. While it is regarded as a branch of medicine by physicians and psychiatrists, there is no reason why it could not with equal justice be allocated to psychology. It seems to be a borderland between the two; and psychoanalysis has brought the neighbors together more closely, for Franz Alexander has been a leading spirit in this movement.*

Dr. James W. D. Hartman, of the Veterans Administration Center in Wichita, Kansas, has written a general review of the literature in compact form. His interests have been largely in clinical psychology.

PRESENT-DAY PSYCHOLOGY

INTRODUCTION

Interest in the mind-body relationship, which is referred to today as psychosomatics, has been present since the time of the early philosophers. Organized effort to utilize the products of thinking in this area is evident as early as 1806 in the form of a medico-psychological journal established by Reil and Hoffbauer in Germany (Stainbrook, 1952). In 1843 the *Annales Médico-psychologiques* was published. During the 19th century, there was built up an experimental and an empirical body of knowledge with an extraordinary body of hypotheses. During the 20th century there have developed the psychological systems and the psychotherapeutic skills as well as a tremendous amount of intensive research.

Within the last 20 years there has been a renewed and intensified interest in the area of psychosomatics, perhaps stimulated in 1935 by Dunbar's *Emotions and Bodily Changes,* which is an integration of some 2200 pertinent publications.

Since 1939, The American Psychosomatic Society, its forum for scientific discussions and its professional journal have become very important. During World War II the somatic effects of excessive anxiety were clearly demonstrated. Following World War II, the large number of professional people who rushed to study in this area included psychologists, physicians, social workers, anthropologists, and people in many other disciplines, all of whom have contributed to the vast literature in this field.

"Psychosomatics" means many things to different people. It is seen as a form of medical philosophy, as a conjoint research approach, and as an application of psychosomatic principles and methods in certain forms of somatic sickness (Hoch, 1952). Cobb (1950) proposes that it is a conceptual approach to relationships, not new physiological or psychological theories or new therapeutic approaches to illness. The term 'psychosomatics' is probably most often thought of in relation to the way emotions express themselves in disease or in deviation from normal physiological functioning. However, Murphy (1947) points out that it properly includes all psychophysiological relationships including normal physiology and psychology. Just as emotional stresses can create disturbances in physiological function, emotional satisfactions can have profound psychosomatic consequences.* On the other hand, Hoch (1952) believes its popularity rests on its claim that it is able to treat and to cure a certain group of disorders which formerly did not yield to a pure somatic approach of treatment.

If psychosomatics has any claim to being a specialty it must be in its function of reintegrating the psyche and soma in the medical specialties of psychiatry and medicine. The need for such was pointed out as early as 1899 by James Putnam in his Shattuck Lecture, when he said, "I should rate a thorough preliminary course in psychology . . . far above a knowledge of botany or zoölogy, and as following closely on chemistry and physics as a preparation for the work of a general practitioner."

METHODOLOGY

Emotion is as much an organic force as other physiological manifestations, but we cannot at present adequately measure emotions. Our greatest handicap is that we do not have a special methodology for psychosomatic investigations but only a coördinated use of already existing methods. A substantial groundwork for these had been laid at the close of the 19th century, at which time Morton Prince, Freud, and Janet had already described psychosomatic conditions from clinical observations. Through Kraepelin and Buccola, Wundt's laboratory had introduced the methods of experimental psychology into psychiatry in Germany and Italy. All this had been made possible by earlier contributions of such men as Féré and Tarhanoff with the psychogalvanic reflex, and Weber, Binet, Kiesow, Mosso

---

* Since this has gone to press I have been made aware by personal communication of the article now in press by Saslow, G., Guze, S. B., Matarazzo, J. D., "Psychosomatic Medicine and the Psychologist", in Pennington and Berg (1954). It presents an excellent critical evaluation of research approaches to psychosomatics by psychologists.

and Gent in psychophysiology. Now it is believed that social-environmental stimuli are as important as physical stimuli, but we do not yet know how environmental stimuli translate themselves into organismic responses.

The existing methods which have been used, and which have contributed much to the existing literature, are clinical, experimental, hypnotic, sociological, psychological, qualitative analysis and statistical correlations of quantitative measurements. These have been organized and discussed by Hoch (1952) and the following is based largely on his presentation of the subject.

Clinical: This method is probably the earliest and most widely used. Here it is used to refer to the method of treating a patient psychotherapeutically and appraising the results of the treatment in terms of the amelioration or elimination of the somatic pathology.

Qualitative Analysis: The psychoanalytic investigation is essentially a qualitative one trying to find what conflicts in what constellation produce the emotional disorder. Symbolisms and latent verbalizations and behavior are analyzed for qualitative values. Qualitative values often forewarn of a symptom which has not yet made its appearance.

Experimental: "Here it is tried to register alterations of organic function under the influence of spontaneous or artificially produced emotional states. (The registration of spontaneous emotional alterations is very difficult because quite often the experimental set-up itself influences the outcome.) The trouble with this method is that even in obvious emotional deviations like constant anxiety, the emotional condition is often fleeting, or changes over into another set of reactions—for instance, anxiety into rage. Furthermore, we usually register changes only in the organs we feel are pathologically affected but we do not set up recordings on organs supposedly not involved. Then usually the experiment confirms our preconceived hypothesis that only the sick organ is affected by a particular emotional state. It is possible in a given peptic ulcer case that the emotional state not only influences the stomach but the vasomotor system in other organs, too, even to the same degree. The changes in the stomach are recorded, the others are not, and a specific stimulation of the stomach is then concluded. The experimental approach is nevertheless very promising if properly linked with simultaneous psychodynamic observations. Related or conditioned reflex studies in the experimental neuroses of animals throw light on basic adaptive responses without interference of a structure of social values. Conditioning experiments in humans are very few and not worked out methodologically as well as in animals." (Hoch, 1952).

Hypnotic: This method was used more widely and perhaps more effectively some years ago. Hoch (1952) emphasizes that this method was of great help in our understanding of how much the mind can affect somatic function and he emphasizes further that suggestive forces are present in any situation including the experimental situation as well as the evaluation of the results.

A difficulty is that the quality and intensity of the suggestive forces can not be characterized precisely.

Sociological: These studies are limited in number and special methods need to be devised for psychosomatic problems.

Psychological: These studies are also limited in number. They indicate, like the projective techniques, the psychodynamic forces present in the patient and are able therefore to provide valuable information for further research or for use in evaluating the individual as a whole for diagnostic and treatment purposes. Systematic studies, such as Frankle's (1952) use of the Minnesota T-S-E Inventory and the Cornell Index, Form N-2 to investigate the relationship between emotional repression and the occurrence of psychosomatic symptoms, provide valuable material for evaluating psychological theory in the area of psychosomatic relationships.

Statistical: Dunbar (1947) noted several years ago that

"where the method of correlation of single or several random quantitative measurements are employed, confusion reigns." Hoch (1952) holds

> This is still evident. Many measurements used are not as exact as implied and often the statistical evaluation of the results is unsound. Nevertheless, some progress has been made in registering the autonomic component of emotions with the psychogalvanic reflex and skin temperature method and other measurements even though they are not fully satisfactory, being at times over- and at other times under-sensitive. It is a striking observation that single deviations from the norm are not so important as the lability of the regulation in the emotional and vegetative homeostasis.

While the inadequacies are widely recognized, statistical techniques are probably the most widely utilized.

Anthropological: Studies comparing cultures such as Suarez' (1950) study of the indigenous peoples of Africa and America, on frequency of arterial hypertension among other things, give insight into the social, cultural, and economic stresses which are forever changing and which obviously play some rôle in the changing frequencies of diseases in our own culture.

APPROACHES

The psychological aspects of psychosomatics are important not only in understanding the illness but in the treatment thereof. There have been not only widely different approaches from many different but related fields, such as general biology, comparative anatomy, physiology, psychology, psychoanalysis, anthropology, clinical medicine and many others (Saul, 1944), but also widely different approaches from within the field of psychology. Here we find techniques borrowed from related fields to help point up the psychological aspects, from the simplest and most objective kind of empirical observation and correlation of isolated factors, to the most subjective and inductive evaluations based on latent meaning of symbolic material and emphasizing "feelings" and relationships.

In the postwar years there has been a trend starting with amassing on the one hand correlational coefficients of isolated specific factors and on the other hand psychoanalytic explanations of every somatic complaint, or as stated in another way, (Hoch, 1952) emphasizing the meaning of the symptom which is purely psychological or the effect of the stimulation, i. e. the tension, which is purely physiological. Today the trend is toward attempting to link the two together. There is some feeling that the two are, in reality, one and that there are merely two approaches, subjective and objective, and that the psyche might be more adequately defined in terms of the soma; as, for example, Grace and Graham (1952) suggest that emotion should be defined in terms of the attitude and its associated physiological changes.

Psychosomatic Relationships

There are many theories on how the psyche influences the soma; Bargen (1950) discusses some of these:

It has been suggested that when psychic impulses are intense and long sustained, anatomic damage may result in some digestive organs.

As an individual makes interpretations of his life situations, various emotional states are produced. The manifestations of these reactions that are under the control of the voluntary nervous system may be suppressed, but those which involve the autonomic nervous system cannot be suppressed so that the various organs enervated by this system are stimulated. Long continued stimulation has been known to produce deleterious physical effects in various organs. Many of the deleterious impulses reach the various organs involved by way of the vagus nerves and their branches. A tenseness may be produced in skeletal muscles of various parts of the body; for instance, in the muscles of the back of the neck,

which may frequently be the origin of occipital head-
aches. In the other muscle groups, stiffness and various
aches and pains may arise. Similar impulses conveyed
by the vagus nerves to the stomach may result in gastric hypermotility and hypersecretion.

These are only a few of the well recognized involuntary nervous reactions and emotional responses which
have been thought to alter individual life situations.

Man is characterized by his capacity to think and to
reason with symbols and not alone by his gross behavior. Most of man's everyday relationships with his
fellow men are on a symbolic level. Things have meaning and value and are capable of evoking responses
which are only understood as their symbolic meaning is
known. 'One man's meat is often another man's poison'
solely because of the unique symbolic meaning which
has been given to the 'meat'. Food preferences and dislikes often are rooted in personal symbolism to the point
at which palatability is not solely a matter of the nutri-
tious value of the food. The external appearance of a
person, or even what he says, is not always the reflection
of what he thinks and feels.

There is a vast amount of literature, mostly controversial, but
a small amount of which seems to be reasonably validated data
on the physiological effects of emotion. The findings presented
in this chapter have generally withstood rigid validation studies
and/or critical appraisal by reviewers.

In 1944, Saul contributed a representative account of the psychodynamic approach to the physiological effects of emotional
tension. Since that time psychoanalytic interpretations have
been applied to about every conceivable psychosomatic problem, as is evidenced by Masserman's experience in his presentation to a group of internists on the general topic of psychosomatic medicine, in 1953, wherein he attempted to present a
satire on the practice of attributing all physiological disturbances to psychic factors. He found that his satire based on the

psychodynamics of the ingrown toe nail was heralded by many psychosomaticists as a brilliant formulation which should be of utmost value in treating ingrown toe nails. This is a significant "sign of our times" in the area of psychosomatics inasmuch as this is accompanied by a growth in realization by the authorities in the field, that while the individual formulations for many specific disorders are stimulating and logical they do little in the final analysis to differentiate one disorder from another on the basis of psychological factors. Hence the reader will be asked, for the most part to refer to Saul (1944), Alexander (1941, 1950) and the vast psychoanalytic and psychosomatic literature for the psychodynamic formulations. At the present time the generalized psychological factor of emotion is still elusive to attempts to control it experimentally and label it in its different forms, such as anger, fear, love, hate, etc. so as to study their differential effects. There has been success in establishing through systematic study, the presence or absence of "emotional" stress and some of its effects. These studies, for the most part, form the basis of the material presented here. It is representative and not all-inclusive in scope.

THE DIGESTIVE SYSTEM

Two authors, Altschule (1953) and Bargen (1950), have reviewed the literature pertaining to the relationships of emotion to the functions and organs of the digestive system. The following is drawn, in main, from these two reviews.

Saliva, in the presence of strong emotions such as fear or anger, changes in the direction of being more alkaline (Starr, 1922, 1923). The emotion causing hyperventilation resulting in a lowered blood carbon dioxide could be the sequence. Salivary production is increased in chronic schizophrenics (Eysenck, 1944).

Esophagus: Emptying time can be prolonged by the influence of emotion. Cardiospasm can occur as a result of emotional reaction (Wolf and Almy, 1949). Sensitivity to pain created by esophageal distention is increased by emotional stress (Chapman and Jones, 1944).

Stomach: It is generally accepted that startle, a variety of strong feelings and emotions, and fatigue result in a cessation of peristalsis, decreases in tone and delay in emptying. It is also generally accepted that in the absence of sudden strong emotions, which cause cessation of secretion, the volume and acidity of gastric secretions undergo greatly varying changes as a result of mild emotion, except in patients with ulcer, where it is found consistently to increase (Wolff, 1949).

Gaskill (1950) found, in his study of patients with peptic ulcers, two common factors, i. e., a conflict in the attempt to repress their strong passive-dependent wishes and a significant degree of hostility. These were integrated into several different personality types.

In neurosis, especially under conditions of stress, gastric motor activity can be increased (Mittelmann and Wolff, 1942) but in schizophrenics it is normal or decreased (Northcote, 1932).

Liver: Bargen (1950) reports an increase may occur in the secretion of hippuric acid during anxiety states, while Pesky, *et al.* (1952) report that the hippuric acid test is not influenced by stresses, including psychoanalytic ones. Faints are followed by a marked decrease in hepatic circulation. The arterial pressure becomes normal long before the hepatic circulation (Bern, *et al.*, 1951). During emotional stress the liver of the diabetic patient may switch to ketone metabolism (Bargen, 1950).

Altschule's (1953) review finds no evidence that hepatic functions are influenced by neurosis. He finds hepatic functions in manic-depressives, involutional, and schizophrenic psychoses are generally reported to be normal. Some deviations in functioning are reported but not consistently, and there is no evidence that emotion *per se* causes impairment of hepatic or biliary function.

Small Intestine: Bargen (1950) notes that nothing which influences the intestinal function seems to be primarily or secondarily associated with emotional stress or nervous tension.

Large Intestine: Emotional upset is usually accompanied by increased colonic motor activity which may result in a spasm, but some specific feelings may produce atony. Flushing or pallor of the mucosa is also found, with flushing being the more common. Different emotions give different effects in the same person; but the same emotion does not give an identical effect in different persons.

Recurrent diarrhea alternating with constipation and chronic spastic constipation, often associated with dyspareunia, are both syndromes commonly found in psychoneurotic patients.

The course of such colonic disturbances as irritable colon, spastic colon and mucous colitis is influenced predominantly by emotion according to Altschule (1953) who feels that evidence also supports the idea that there is a parallel in severity between colonic function and disorders of personality. He does not accept evidence that specific psychological factors are causal factors in these colonic disorders.

Emotional upset is important in the exacerbation of ulcerative colitis, causing, in patients with this disease, colonic spasm, oversecretion, hyperemia, and sometimes hemorrhage. In patients with ulcerative colitis, emotion produces the normal wave-pattern associated with constipation (Kern, *et al.*, 1951). While it is recognized that the disease of ulcerative colitis may cause emotional disorders, it is not accepted that emotional disorders are the causal influence in ulcerative colitis (Altschule, 1953; Bargen, 1950).

Theories concerning the place emotion fills in gastro-intestinal disorders or the exact nature of the psychosomatic relationship have not been validated. Altschule (1953) states the following:

A tentative conclusion concerning the rôle of emotion in gastro-intestinal disorders is that neurosis is the primary etiologic agent in some or most instances of hysterical dysphagia, irritable colon, spastic colon, and possibly mucous colitis, although unusual sensitivity of the reacting organs cannot be disregarded as a possibility. On the other hand, it is probable that primary etiologies are unknown in peptic ulcer and ulcerative colitis. Nevertheless, emotional factors have an important determining influence on the course of any chronic disease of the gastro-intestinal tract. This is largely because persistent emotion causes spasm, presumably through activation of the parasympathetic nervous mechanisms; spasm is already present or is easily produced in many gastro-intestinal diseases, and many of the discomforts experienced in these conditions are caused by it.

There is much yet to be determined:

An important phenomenon, not adequately studied by psychiatrists, [or by psychologists or any other researchers] is the frequent development of emotional disorders in patients with chronic gastro-intestinal diseases. Among factors to be considered in this area are: the discomforts, such as pain or diarrhea, associated with eating, and the consequent interference with an important source of physical and emotional satisfaction; the effects of special diets in interfering with enjoyment of food and with social life; the effects of recurrent pain present for long periods, particularly in young persons; the markedly debilitating effects of malnutrition, dehydration, anemia, and fever; interference with social life associated with vomiting or diarrhea; the effects of economic deprivation owing to the cost of medical care over long periods and to interference with the patient's ability to work at his usual level of efficiency; the peculiarly depressing effect of diarrhea that lasts for more than a few days; and effects on the patient of changes in family life and attitudes brought about by his disease. (Altschule, 1953).

THE CIRCULATORY SYSTEM

A most comprehensive analysis of the literature in this area has been done only recently by Altschule (1953). Most of the information presented here is based on his review.

Hematologic Changes: The leukocyte count and total number of blood lymphocytes rise during and/or shortly after emotional stress. (Garrey and Butler, 1929; Goldberg and Lepskaia, 1926, 1927). Several hours later, there is a delayed fall below the initial level of the total number of blood lymphocytes (Goldberg and Lepskaia, 1926, 1927; Goldwyn, 1928; Hoagland, 1947; Hoagland, *et al.*, 1946), and a fall in blood eosinophil count (Frost, *et al.*, 1951; Humphreys, *et al.*, 1950; Renold, 1951; Truelove, 1951). Clotting time is accelerated following emotional upset. (Macht, 1952; Schneider and Zangari, 1951).

The probable development of hematological changes in patients with mental disorders is summarized as being not significantly different from changes found in normals unless the patients with mental disorders have other conditions complicating the problem. It is probable that most of the abnormal deviations reported result from factors other than the mental disturbance, such as failure of the investigator to appreciate the full "normal range" of hemoglobin concentration, or such as dehydration, or tuberculosis and other infections common in crowded unsanitary institutions. (Altschule, 1953).

Metabolic Changes: Emotion is followed, after an interval, by a rise in blood sugar level. After a half or three-quarters of an hour from the onset of the stress, the maximum level is reached and then falls below the starting point. (Schou, 1937). Whether glycosuria is found or not depends on the level reached in the blood and on the renal threshold for sugar. Relationships between specific personalities and variations in blood sugar concentration have been suggested and studied without convincing success. (Hammett, 1920). Emotional effects on blood sugar and the output of glucose by the liver, which is increased during emotion, cause the same changes as an injection of epinephrine. (Bearn *et al.*, 1951).

Faints produce an appreciable increase in blood lactate level (Bearn, *et al.*, 1951) which can be explained as a result of an epinephrine discharge and a development of stagnant anoxia.

A summary of the findings regarding the probable effects of

metabolic factors in neurotics and psychotics indicates they usually show a normal fasting blood sugar level, but abnormal deviations of carbohydrate metabolism are reported variously and non-uniformly. It is generally believed that they have difficulty accepting carbohydrate which is important because the function of the brain depends entirely on the utilization of carbohydrate and one amino acid. Alcohol, which is one carbohydrate that can be utilized by patients with mental disorders, may serve as a better source of energy than glucose and hence is a possible factor in alcoholism. Neurotic obese patients show no specific metabolic pattern. (Altschule, 1953).

Cardiac Output and Work: Emotional reactions such as apprehension, startle, anxiety, tension may increase cardiac output by as much as two-thirds or more. (Goldberg, *et al.*, 1951; Wescott, *et al.*, 1951; Duncan, *et al.*, 1951). There is evidence for and against a relationship between type of emotion and circulatory change. (Duncan, *et al.*, 1951; Hickam, *et al.*, 1948; Stevenson, *et al.*, 1949; Wolff and Wolff, 1946).

Anxiety has the same effect on the cardiac output of patients with heart disease but without failure, as of normal subjects. (Stevenson, *et al.*, 1949). It increases the pulse rate, but has little or no effect on the cardiac output of patients with congestive failure. (Hickam, *et al.*, 1948).

Cardiac Rate: Studies show that emotion usually produces an accelerated heart rate often briefly preceded by an abnormally slow rate (Altschule, 1953).

Altschule also summarizes the literature on patients with neurosis or neuro-circulatory asthenia and manic depressive patients as showing that their pulse rate is normal or increased, whereas in the schizophrenic patient it may be high, low, or normal.

Startle produces a sudden rise in pulse rate, usually followed by a quick fall below the initial level, another rise and diminishing fluctuations with succeeding startles. (Blatz, 1925). Startle anticipation produces similar but less marked changes. (Blatz, 1925; Skraggs, 1926).

Simple startle produces excessive increases in pulse rate in neurotic or neuro-circulatory asthenic patients. (Meakins and Wilson, 1918). Patients with a recent onset of neurosis, neuro-circulatory asthenia, or schizophrenia show an excessive rate increase from standing; this is not found in patients with a chronic disease, and, in general, psychotic patients' pulse rate changes are normal or similar to those in neurosis. (Altschule, 1953).

Intense concentration sometimes produces increased cardiac rate. (Gillespie, 1924). This is true more often when the concentration is on solving geometrical rather than philosophical problems. (Gley, 1881).

Telling lies increases cardiac rate while psychotic patients telling of their hallucinations show no change. (Adler and Larson, 1927). Word associations cause variations in pulse rate. (Darrow, 1929). However, it is still questionable whether the direction of fluctuation depends on the emotion related to the association as indicated by the contention that unpleasant associations retard the rate and pleasant ones increase it (Darrow, 1929).

Circulation Time: Emotional tension usually accelerates circulation time. The data generally indicate that in neuro-circulatory asthenia, manic-depressive, involutional, and schizophrenic psychoses it is normal or somewhat accelerated. (Butler, 1941; Cohen *et al.,* 1948; Cotton, *et al.,* 1916; Friedman, 1945; Spillane, 1940). However, there is some disagreement on this. (Freeman, 1934, 1938; Gottlieb, 1936). In hysterical hyperventilation, circulation time is normal. (Sattler, *et al.,* 1951).

Venous Pressure: During emotional upset, measurements of pressure in the right auricle show no deviation from the normal, (Hickam, *et al.,* 1948; Stead, *et al.,* 1945) although it has been commonly recognized that slight rises in peripheral venous pressure do accompany emotional upsets and the rise falls to normal as the patients relax. (Altschule, 1953). Venous pressure is normal for patients with neuro-circulatory asthenia at rest, (Cohn, *et al.,* 1948; Friedman, 1945) standing at rest, (Friedman,

1945) after exercise, (Friedman, 1945) in hysterical hyperventilation, (Sattler, 1951) and in the manic-depressive, involutional and schizophrenic psychotics who are relaxed. (Altschule, *et al.*, 1947; Altschule and Tillotson, 1948; Krinsky and Gottlieb, 1936; Martinengo, 1933; Silverskiöld and Amark, 1943). However, non-relaxed psychotics may show slight elevations.

Arterial Pressure: Emotional stress results in an elevation of arterial blood pressure, (Greenfield, 1951; Palmer, 1950; Schneider and Zangari, 1951; Stevenson, *et al.*, 1949) resulting from a systolic but not a diastolic pressure rise. Attempts to establish a relationship between arterial pressure changes and the quality or intensity of the feeling or emotion present have produced both negating and confirmatory results. (Altschule, 1953).

Cohen *et al.* (1948), Friedman (1945) and Wolff and Wolff (1946), generally agree with many earlier authors that neurotic or neuro-circulatory asthenic patients' arterial pressures are usually normal or slightly elevated with the systolic pressure rising more than the diastolic, which rises slightly if at all.

Greenblatt, *et al.*, (1951) found low blood pressure to be related to anorexia nervosa, and Altschule (1953) reports various earlier authors who relate it to propensity for fainting, faints, chronic fatigue, and neurasthenia.

Patients with hysterical convulsions show a rise in arterial pressure. (Bing, 1906). Arterial pressure rises in neurotic subjects under conditions of emotional stress the same as (Jost, 1941; Palmer, 1937) or somewhat more (Malmo and Shagass, 1952) than in normal subjects. Normal and neuro-circulatory asthenia subjects experiencing distress following exercise show the same rise in arterial pressure; however, it takes more exercise for normals (Cotton, *et al.*, 1916). Neurotics experiencing anxiety while performing exercise may show excessive rises in arterial pressure (Wolff and Wolff, 1946).

Altschule (1953) summarizes the vast literature relating to the psychoses. Manic patients show only occasionally elevated arterial pressure. Depressed patients often show an elevation. Involutional psychotic patients usually show hypertension and schizophrenic patients show arterial pressures in, below, and above the normal range. Word associations sometimes produce a rise in arterial pressure in psychotic patients (Solomon, *et al.*, 1939). Emotional stress may produce no change in arterial pressure in depressive patients (Harrowes, 1933) but excessive changes in schizophrenics (Malmo and Shagass, 1952). Arterial pressure rises in schizophrenics when they're telling lies but not when they're telling of hallucinations (Adler and Larson, 1927). Standing, by early but not chronic schizophrenics, produces an abnormally large rise in diastolic arterial pressure (Pfister and Schweiz, 1937; Pfister, 1938). Many chronic schizophrenics show a tendency toward a lowering of arterial pressure.

Pheripheral Blood Flow: Emotion is related to cutaneous vasoconstriction in the hands and feet (Horwitz, *et al.*, 1951; Ray, *et al.*, 1946) and when emotion or concentration produces acral cutaneous vasoconstriction, the skin temperature over the face rises. Anxiety in normal persons produces a vasoconstriction that is mostly limited to the skin (Greenfield, 1951).

Cortical impulses are important in vasomotor phenomena (Chapman, *et al.*, 1949, 1950; Pool and Ransahoff, 1949). The frequency of stimulation applied to the cortex determines whether peripheral constriction or dilatation occurs (Grant, 1951). Strong pleasurable emotions may give rise to the same peripheral vascular phenomena as unpleasant emotions (Binet and Courtier, 1897); (Angell and Thompson, 1899); (Mittelmann and Wolff, 1939). Emotional vasoconstriction occurs due to startle (Binet and Courtier, 1895) and anticipation (Hallion and Comte, 1894) but disappears during sleep (Day and Klingman, 1939). Conditioned vasomotor responses (Jones and Scarisbrick, 1946) may be more easily developed in subjects with unstable peripheral vascular systems (Gottschalk, 1946).

Neurotic patients show a decrease in blood flow to the hands (Abramson, et al., 1941; Jung and Carmichael, 1930) and abnormally high acral vasoconstriction during emotion, anti-cipation of discomfort (Hallion and Comte, 1894, 1895), attention (Theron, 1948), or mental effort (Breiger, 1913). Patients with anxiety states (Van der Merwe, 1940), hysteria, or neuro-circulatory asthenia (Soley and Shock, 1930) show abnormally high vasoconstrictor activity. The usual vasoconstriction is caused in an hysterical patient by touching an apparently anesthetic area (Hallion and Comte, 1894, 1895). The emotionally unstable person's excessive vasoconstriction disappears during sleep (Day and Klingman, 1939). Conditioning of peripheral vasomotor mechanisms is shown more readily in patients with hysterical personalities (Marinesco and Kreindler, 1934) or with unstable vasomotor systems (Gottschalk, 1946) than in normal persons. In schizophrenia (Abramson, *et al.*, 1941; Altschule and Sulzbach, 1949; Baruk, *et al.*, 1950; Henschel, *et al.*, 1951; Jung and Carmichael, 1930; Severin, 1916) and often in manic-depressive psychoses, the acral blood flow is usually diminished, forearm flow is less affected, and the carotid pulse waves are usually normal (Mendel, 1876). A further decrease in acral flow is shown in patients with schizophrenia or manic-depressive psychoses in stressful situations (Wiersma, 1913) but not during mental stimuli or concentration (Breiger, 1913; Cuppers, 1913; Ziegler and Cash, 1938). Excessive, delayed, emotional constriction may be shown by catatonic patients (Jürgens, 1940).

Cardiac Rhythm: Normal subjects under emotional stress do not commonly show arhythmias other than sinus tachycardia or bradycardia. Neurotics show arhythmias more commonly than normal persons. Psychotics show abnormally long or markedly short P-R intervals more frequently than normal persons (Altschule, 1953).

Hypertension: Emotional factors have a strong influence on the disease of hypertension (Hambling, 1951, 1952; Jost, 1952, Reiser, 1951; Altschule, 1953). There is evidence that indigenous peoples of Africa who are to a great extent free from the tension of daily existence and who are not preoccupied with the modern tensions found in America, are relatively free of signs of arterial hypertension (Suarez, 1950). In addition, the personality and emotional settings for the outbreak of symptoms of essential hypertension have been described for patients studied (Hambling, 1951). But in general evidence that emotional factors are causal agents is viewed with skepticism (Murphy, 1950; Binger, 1951; Altschule, 1953).

Attempts to relate hypertensive disease to specific personality structures have been unsuccessful (Reiser, *et al.*, 1951; Storment, 1951; Weiss, *et al.*, 1950).

The problem of hostility as an influencing factor in hypertension is consistently reported (Alexander and French, 1948; Hambling, 1951, 1952; Dunbar, 1948; Fain, 1950; Weiss, 1950; Lowy, 1951). Lowy (1951) discusses the psychological behavior of the patient with benign hypertension:

> Psychological analysis of these patients suggests that they have difficulties in facing authority in the broader sense, including religion, patriotism, loyalty. They are afraid of criticism and of being inadequate. Deep down they are rebellious and find potential or actual criticism rather unjustified. As they lack self-assertiveness, it appeals to them more to please than to voice their objections and to justify themselves frankly. Many of them are so afraid of anticipated failures that they choose 'an occupation below their actual capacity' (Dunbar). This fact becomes a further source of resentment against their lot which, neurotically, they attribute to the hostile world around them. Outwardly they tend to behave correctly, and many of them are manifest perfectionists, for the sake of approval by their fellow men as well as for their own satisfaction.

Anxiety, in hypertensive subjects, produces an increased elevation of arterial pressure (Jost, *et al.*, 1952; Palmer, 1937) and cardiac work, but the cardiovascular physiology of anxiety is different from that of essential hypertension (Altschule, 1953).

Altschule also points up an important finding for understanding the psychosomatic relationship in essential hypertension:

> Excellent work in animals and more recently in man has extended knowledge bearing on nervous pathways that carry vasoconstrictor impulses from the brain. The existence of vasoconstrictor centers in the hypothalamus has long been known; it has recently been shown that stimulation of the frontal cortex, especially that of its posterior orbital surface, elevates blood pressure (Chapman, *et al.*, 1949, 1950; Pool and Ransahoff, 1949). The location of this area in the general region in which is situated cortical representation of visceral changes and of somatic movements associated with expression of emotion is highly significant.

Neuro-circulatory Asthenia: This condition has been variously diagnosed "irritable heart," "effort syndrome," "anxiety neurosis," "neurasthenia" and "neuro-circulatory asthenia." (Weiss, 1952). At the present time psychiatrists use the terms "anxiety neurosis" and "neurasthenia" for ailments which other medical specialists diagnose as neuro-circulatory asthenia—both of them referring to the syndrome referred to by the British as "effort syndrome" and diagnosed during the Civil War as "irritable heart." (Weiss, 1952).

Weiss (1949, 1952) summarizes the characteristics of the patient diagnosed as a neuro-circulatory asthenic:

> (1) . . . the symptoms are those of psychoneurosis; (2) The family history shows a high incidence of psychopathology; (3) longitudinal study of the life history indicates neurotic personality structure; (4) cross-sectional study of the life-history at the time of onset of symptoms shows emotionally disturbing events that are specific for that particular personality structure; (5) discussing this material brings out meaningful behavior on the part of the patient; and (6) dealing with this material has psychotherapeutic value.

Both the nature of the symptoms and the physiological changes that are induced by exercise in patients with neuro-circulatory asthenia are similar to those found in various types of neurosis. Physiological changes in patients with neuro-circulatory asthenia are greater on the average, although overlapping between groups is great. During exercise a metabolic disorder occurs which can account for the inability to perform (Altschule, 1953).

Miles and Cobb (1951) point out a need to differentiate between neuro-circulatory asthenia and anxiety neurosis on the basis of an identifiable physiogenesis for neuro-circulatory asthenia.

Weiss (1952) contends the term neuro-circulatory asthenia is inadequate and harmful, calling "attention to a part when the disorder is one of the whole" and leads to complacency regarding the psychological factors—and it would seem that the proper psychiatric designation with added qualifying terms would be more satisfactory.

Headache: Emotional stress may create carotid arterial dilatation which is a precursor of attacks of migraine and probably other types of headache. Hence, this is one mechanism by which emotional stress may cause headache (Altschule, 1953).

Note: The exact nature of the relationship between emotion and the circulatory system in all its aspects is far from being understood but some things of importance about the relationship are recognized. Altschule (1953) makes the following statement:

> Physiologic effects of emotion on the circulation in health and disease are many and varied. Their importance lies in the facts that they exacerbate cardiovascular diseases, that their manifestations may resemble those of coronary sclerosis or myocardial insufficiency and hence lead to erroneous diagnosis, and that their occurrence may call attention to the presence of emotional disorders not previously recognized.

No comment has been made on the effect of disease itself in causing emotional upset that in turn unfavorably affects the initial condition; this is true when the condition is organic heart disease or cardiovascular neurosis. Except for the fact that the cardiovascular changes in startle reactions are similar in nature if not in degree in various persons, no consistency is encountered in the occurrence or character of cardiovascular phenomena that may appear in relation to environment factors influencing the psyche. The emotional significance of a given factor to the individual determines the occurrence and, in a measure, the severity of the response to it. . . . However, except in a small number of instances in which the nature of the cardiovascular response to emotional stress is evidently determined by neurotic identifications or by previous conditioning, there is no indication of the mechanisms that cause the appearance of each of the various types of cardiovascular change.

Circulatory manifestations of emotion in psychotic patients are not likely to be troublesome, except in presence of serious heart disease, but in non-psychotic persons they are of great clinical importance. (Altschule, 1953).

Cutaneous Functions

Sweating of the palms, soles, the front of the face and the axillas is caused mainly by emotion. Sweating of the palms and soles does not result from warming. (Kuno, 1930, Shelley *et al.*, 1950). Sweating of all these areas may occur as a result of mental concentration. Although the mechanism of emotional sweating is not yet understood, it is known that palmar sweating is markedly influenced by the cerebral cortex. (Altschule, 1953). Insensible perspiration is also increased by emotion. (Schou, 1937). Cold, moist, cyanotic hands are commonly recognized signs of emotional disorders. This sweating is stimulated by the sympathetic nervous system which also induces vasoconstriction resulting in a lowered cutaneous temperature (Altschule, 1953).

Fever may be a result of vasoconstriction. Neuro-circulatory asthenia has been related to an elevation of rectal temperature. (Friedman, 1944). Prolonged psychogenic fevers are possible (Carmichael and Luider, 1934; Deutsch, 1926) but, generally, they are brief. Cutaneous vasomotor changes may result in fever in psychosis but this does not occur often because of a reduced heat production found especially in chronic schizophrenia (Altschule, 1953).

Neurotic patients commonly experience itching and develop or exacerbate cutaneous lesions (Rothman, 1941). Emotional changes are associated with the production or exacerbation of various cutaneous lesions (Altschule, 1953). Local neuro-dermatitis is an external manifestation of chronic emotional tension (Huber, 1949).

A neuro-dermatitis scale (Allerhand, *et al.*, 1950) has proven useful in identifying functional cases from a total sample. They describe the neuro-dermatitic patient as a person who is some-what tense and restless and unable to relax easily, who has strong needs for recognition and success, who prides himself on his own strength and vitality, who tends to be impatient and irritable and to see the demands of others as infringements and impositions. Interspersed with these tendencies there appears the sentimentality stressed in earlier studies, admitted touchi-ness, and intermittent feelings of disappointment with other people and with the world in general.

THE PROBLEM OF OBESITY

Many physiological and hereditary factors have been investi-gated in relation to obesity but no intrinsic metabolic, endocrin-ological or central nervous system abnormality has been found in the usual case. The conclusion presently held most widely is that obesity is due to an excessive inflow of energy exceeding the outflow, such disproportion being caused primarily by overeating. Hereditary, constitutional, hypothalamic or other factors may play a part but hyperphagia is the only consistent and necessary symptom (Brobeck, *et al.*, 1942, 1943; Rytand, 1943; Friedgood, 1950) and it may be influenced by many factors.

Bram (1950) offers a physiological explanation for the good humor of the obese individual. "There is a constant fight for blood between the belly and the brain." The full stomach demanding more blood at the expense of the brain, lends a sense of composure, of relaxation, and of happy indolence and repose to the emotional centers. Seeking this outlet habitually despite increasing weight, the tensive individual becomes the calm, jolly, roly-poly "fatty". Yet he worries over his obesity.

Blazer in his studies with obese women (1951) offers a psychological explanation:

> The core of the problem is that the compulsive eater unconsciously has given up the struggle to preserve a non-derogatory attitude toward herself, so that she is only able to have a shallow, defensive rapport with others. In the same way her work life is routine, her creativeness is half-hearted and self-depreciatory. But since all human beings, to survive, must have some kind of security if they are not to be flooded with anxiety, she retreats to an earlier stage historically, in her emotional development; to the unweaned level where the nipple and emotional security were one and the same thing.

Usually these patients' sex life is inadequate and they may use accessory defenses resembling those occurring in the submissive, over-aggressive, or withdrawn schizoid.

The average case of obesity presents a typical psychosomatic problem. The glandular or endogenous form of obesity is unusual. (Bram, 1950; Bayles, 1950). Hamburger (1951) reports that some form of disturbed intrafamilial relationships in the patient's home during the formative years is a consistent finding. Broken homes, openly rejecting parents, and overprotective, "smothering" mothers are examples. (Bruche, 1943, 1948;

Lurie, 1941; Selling, 1946; and Levy, 1936) have all pointed up the "smothering" mother of the obese patient.

The prognosis for obesity depends on the prognosis for the underlying emotional conflict of which hyperphagia is thought to be a symptom; whether it be an acute or chronic external stress or frustration, a psychological disease such as for example hysteria, substitute gratification for cravings of love, affection and security, or a physiological factor.

Whether fat people overeat and become obese rather than developing other symptoms such as depression, alcoholism, drug addictions, peptic ulcer, etc., because of unknown physiological, hereditary, or psychosocial emotional factors is an undetermined question which merits serious research attention.

Psychosomatic Mechanisms

Much theorizing has been done regarding psychosomatic mechanisms in the production of illness. Effort has been made attempting to relate single psychological factors with about every physiological factor known. By and large the results have shown that this approach to understanding psychosomatic problems is inadequate and it is fairly generally accepted in the literature today that multiplicity rather than specificity of causal factors is the only successful avenue to understanding this type of illness. Stevenson and Mathews (1953), Heath (1952), Grinker and Robbins (1954), Lipshutz (1952), Rosen (1952), MacKenna and Macalpine (1951).

In regard to specificity of cause Grinker and Robbins (1954) say: ". . . 'two-variable' correlations which are operational procedures in all current psychosomatic formulations dichotomize and fracture the field and unjustifiably are based on the assumption that the two variables are significant for each other in lineal, cause and effect relationship. For this there is no adequate theoretical evidence and, practically, these concepts do not explain psychosomatic function or dysfunction except by disregarding important empirical data." Grinker and Robbins (1954) favor a "field" theory of psychosomatics, an application to specific behavior of a formulation which seems similar to the integration of personality theories formulated by Rosenzweig (1944). Stevenson and Mathews (1953) have organized the available fact and theory on psychosomatics and much of the following is based on their presentation.

The theoretical formulations regarding organ selection seem to fall in the following general areas: organ weakness or inferiority; a purposeful function; symbolic purposiveness; and specificity of personality structure or emotional constellation. Each theory is said "to be founded on nuclear factual material but each is individually incapable of comprehending all psychosomatic phenomena" (Stevenson & Mathews, 1953).

Organ weakness or inferiority may have environmental or hereditary causes and may involve whole portions of the nervous system or a single organ. The facts are that a predisposition to disease of certain organs runs in certain families; the strength of the genetic factor varies with different diseases; and morphological and physiological characteristics differ in victims with different diseases. It is probable that constitutional factors exert an etiological influence at all different levels of the organism— physiological and structural. Victims of a given disease do not all show the stigmata delineated by the quoted studies in constitutional medicine for that disease.

A purposeful function involves such feelings as anger, giving postural and physiological preparation to attack; fright, giving postural and physiological preparation to run (The physiological changes in both of these are similar, but not identical, for all people. The differences are caused by other factors); depression, giving an emotional and physical withdrawal from stress; restrained aggression, giving behavioral withdrawal but physiological preparation for anticipated attack (when action becomes imminent, physiological changes occur in preparation for imminent action). Abdominal visceral depression may indicate the individual has given up and is no longer struggling or is engaging in full mobilization of his defensive forces depending upon the corresponding cardio-respiratory and muscular changes. The depressive, restrained aggressive, and anxiety states are at least three affective states to which visceral changes can be related. Complications arise because these affective states rarely occur alone.

In symbolic purposiveness localized symptoms may be symbolically expressive of the psychic content or motivation. Hysteria gives the most pronounced examples of the influence of belief and symbolic expression on the production of symptoms. Other symptoms arise in relation to what seem to be obvious symbolic expressions. On the other hand symbolic bases have been conjectured for psychosomatic symptoms much more often than it has been possible to validate them. This leads to irritating confusion in the interested reader who learns from one report that diarrhea is a part of a riddance pattern and in another report that it is an overcompensation for oral aggression by the urge to give.

Theories on specificity of personality structure or emotional constellation are shown in research to have great overlapping, lack of consistency, and much contradiction. Individuals with multiple psychosomatic symptoms create confusion in the application of symptom type personality hypotheses i.e. ulcer personalities, etc. Profit in studying the different personalities of patients with different disorders results when the illness involves the total behavior of the person or there is a disease of the total organism; e.g. accident proneness, obesity, alcoholism, etc. Similarities between personalities of all persons with psychosomatic disease are more striking than are the differences in personality between persons with different psychosomatic disease. Cobb (1950) says of his earlier description of the personality of patients with mucous colitis: "Today I would say that this is a good description of many patients with mucous colitis, but that it could be almost as accurately applied to patients with bronchial asthma or peptic ulcer." The common personality feature of patients with psychosomatic illness is that of excessive dependency which results from frustration and hostility with related factors of guilt, anxiety, and physiological tension. There are mature, neurotic, psychotic, character disorders and physiological "outlets," for tensions produced during life stresses and it is a rare person, even among the most seriously ill, who uses only one of these "outlets" at all times.

Important factors in the production of psychosomatic phenomena are those which:

1.   Produce unresolved tension. This involves a stressful life situation, and a personality which permits the stress to produce unresolved tension within the individual.

2.   Govern the channeling of tension generated with the Central Nervous System. Involved here are the threshold of excitation of different structures of the Central Nervous System; the prevailing attitude and affective state with which the individual encounters the stressful situation; the symbolization or organ language; and the facilitation and conditioning.

3.   Govern the response of stimulated organs; e.g., end organ inferiority, end organ disease, acquired, end organ stimulation, duration, and other physical factors acting concomitantly.

4.   Govern the production of symptoms or complaints during stress such as concomitant physical stresses and focusing of attention by the subject on his body. Following this presentation of the above information, Stevenson and Mathews point up what seems to be the present-day trend of thinking in the approach to understanding and dealing with psychosomatic problems. "The various factors listed above have different importance in different persons and even different importance in the same person at different times. The actual occurrence of physiological changes and of symptoms is related to the sum of all the factors operating at one time. When this sum reaches a certain number we or the patient speak of an illness, but the liability to the illness and some disorder or disease have been present long before this. We should not speak of psychosomatic disorders as 'psychogenic' or as 'constitutional' or refer to them by any other such categorical words. Rather they should be thought of as the end result of a series of events with many steps along the way. This

series of events may appear to be initiated by some easily visible
life stress such as marriage, death, or a demotion. But the way
in which a person reacts to this stress both in his outward behavior and in the physical changes of his body is a highly individual matter which can be understood only by the appreciation of many factors. Somewhere between the objective stress
and the physiological disturbances the symbolizing functions of
the forebrain become involved, sometimes with the influence on
the molding of physiological changes and sometimes without
such influence. But in any case each symbolization is only one
of the many factors to be considered. If the physician's efforts
to understand psychosomatic disorders are dominated by a need
to attach a causative rôle to symbolism in every case, he must
often be misled and confused. The preoccupation with the symbolic purposiveness of symptoms has led, in our opinion, to a
neglect of other factors. At the physical level, more importance
should be attached to those physical factors—whether of constitutional origin or acquired later—which govern the channeling of nervous impulses in a given direction and which influence
the reaction of the end-organ to such nervous impulses. At the
psychological level more importance should be attached to those
factors leading to the accumulation of tension which cannot be
discharged in constructive mastery of problems and which is
channeled into the various viscera."

Lhamon and Saul (1950) comment on the significance of the
psychosomatic symptom in relation to maturity of the personality: "Probably psychosomatic symptoms occur in all sorts of
personalities. Not only does the psychosomatic symptom not necessarily signify an infantile personality, but it often signifies just
the opposite. The psychosomatic symptom is often a partial
vegetative regression which prevents psychological regression; in
this sense individuals with psychosomatic symptoms may be the
opposite of infantile. Thus an important executive in a corporation was severely disappointed when a desirable promotion was
given a competing friend; although he maintained a friendly
helpful behavior, his rage became apparent in a contemporary

dream from which he awakened with a bout of painful colitis. In this case a localized and partial somatic regression prevented breakdown of a mature reaction. Contrariwise, an academically and politically successful college student had to be restrained from physical assault at being disappointed over honor society elections. In such a psychological regression, the behavior is clearly less adult than with our executive.

"An individual is not an homogeneous entity. It is necessary to study the individual impulses in detail as well as their interactions and their final common paths in a person's official reactions, as well as their specific relations to the symptoms. In this way we can hope to narrow the gap between the physiological and psychological data and to emphasize those forces which actually affect the physiological functioning of an organ."

In every field where medical information is being applied or studied in relation to the human being, psychosomatic relationships are being or can be recognized. The areas covered somewhat intensively in this chapter are samples of what has been or is ready to be done in many areas where the soma is influenced by the psyche and vice-versa. Many of these areas such as urogenital functions, respiration diseases, allergies, dysmenorrhea, plastic surgery, orthodontics, orthopedics, anterior-pituitary, posterior-pituitary and sensory functions, etc. already have vast numbers of studies accomplished. A class of illnesses which has become popular for analysis recently results from the doctor-patient relationship and is termed iatrogenic.

Interest in any one area leads to impractical amounts of frustrating reading; for despite the vast literature, few basic questions have been answered. The psychosomatic method for experimental study has still not been developed to help answer such questions. Creative research in any of these areas is of immeasurable benefit to a large segment of the people receiving medical treatment today, and it is hoped that such research will eventually produce useful information concerning psychosomatic mechanisms.

BIBLIOGRAPHY

Abramson, D. L., Schkloven, N., and Katzenstein, K. H., *Arch. Neurol. & Psychiat.* 45:973, 1941.
Adler, H. M., and Larson, J. A., *J. Abnorm. & Soc. Psychol.*, 22:364, 1927.
Alexander, F., In Portis, S. A., *Diseases of the Dig. Syst.* Philadelphia: Lea & Febiger, 1941.
Alexander, F., *Psychosom. Med.* New York: W. W. Norton & Co., 1950.
Alexander, F. and French, T. M., *Studies in Psychosom. Med.* New York: Ronald, 1948.
Allerhand, Melvin E., Gough, Harrison G., and Grais, Melvin L., *Psychosom. Med.*, 12:387, 1950.
Altschule, M. D., and Sulzbach, W. M., *Arch. Neurol. & Psychiat.*, 61:44, 1949.
Altschule, M. D., Sulzbach, W. M., and Tillotson, K. J., *Neurol. & Psychiat.*, 58:717, 1947.
Altschule, M. D., and Tillotson, K. J., *Neurol. & Psychiat.*, 59:469, 1948.
Altschule, M. D., *Bodily Physiol. in Mental and Emotional Disorders.* New York: Grune & Stratton, 1953.
Angell, J. R., and Thompson, H. B., *Psychol. Rev.*, 6:33, 1899.
Bargen, J. Arnold, *Gastroenterology*, 15 (4) : 581-591, 1950.
Baruk, H., Melzer, R., and Joubert, M. P. *Ann. Med. Psychol.*, 108 (2): 243, 1950.
Bayles, Spencer, *Amer. J. Med. Sci.*, 219:104-107, 1950.
Bearn, A. G., Billing, B., and Sherlock, S., *J. Physiol.*, 115:430, 1951.
Bern, A. G., Billing, B., Edholm, O. G., and Sherlock, S., *J. Physiol.*, 115: 442, 1951.
Binet, A., and Courtier, J., *L'Année Psychol.*, 2:87, 1895.
Binet, A., and Courtier, J., *L'Année Psychol.*, 3:65, 1897.
Bing, R., *Klin. Wochenschr.*, 43:1180, 1906.
Binger, Carl, *Psychosom. Med.*, 13:273-276, 1951.
Blatz, W. E., *J. Exp. Psychol.*, 8:109, 1925.
Blazer, Alfred, *Int. Rec. Med.*, 164:24-30, 1951.
Bram, Israel, *Arch. Pediat.*, 67:543-552, 1950.
Breiger, E., *Zeitsch. f. d. ges. Neurol. u. Psychiat.*, 17:413, 1913.
Brobeck, John R., *Yale J. Biol. and Med.*, 15:893, 1942-43.
Bruche, H., *Psychosom. Med.*, 2:141, 1940.
Bruche, H., *Amer. J. Dis. Child.*, 59 (2) : 739, 1940.
Bruche, H., *Amer. J. Dis. Child.*, 60 (2) : 1082, 1940.
Bruche, H., *J. Pediat.*, 19:365, 1941.
Bruche, H., *Am. J. Orthopsychiat.*, 11:467, 1941.
Bruche, H., *Am. J. Psychiat.*, 99:752, 1943.
Bruche, H., *Bull. New York Acad. Med.*, 24:71, 1948.
Butler, A. G., *Med. J. Australia*, 1:667, 1941.
Carmichael, H. T., and Luider, F. E., *Am. J. Med. Sci.*, 188:68, 1934.
Chapman, W. P., and Jones, C. M., *J. Clin. Invest.*, 23:81, 1944.
Chapman, W. P., Livingston, K. E., and Popper, J. L., *J. Neurophysiol.*, 13:65, 1950.
Chapman, W. P., Livingston, R. B., and Livingston, K. E., *Arch. Neurol. & Psychiat.*, 62:701, 1949.

PRESENT-DAY PSYCHOLOGY

Cobb, S., *Emotions in Clinical Medicine*. New York: W. W. Norton & Co., 1950.

Cohen, M. E., White, P. D., and Johnson, R. E., *Arch. Inst. Med.*, 81:260, 1948.

Cotton, T. F., Rapport, D. L., and Lewis, T., *Heart*, 6:269, 1916.

Cotton, T. F., Slade, J. G., and Lewis, T., *Heart*, 6:227, 1916.

Cuppers, E., *Zeitsch. f. d. ges. Neurol. u. Psychiat.*, 16:223, 1913.

Darrow, C. W., *J. Exp. Psychol.*, 12:267, 1929.

Darrow, C. W., *Psychol. Bull.*, 26:185, 1929.

Day, R., and Klingman, W. O., *J. Clin. Invest.*, 18:271, 1939.

Deutsch, F., *Med. Klin.*, 22:1213, 1926.

Dunbar, H. F., *Emotions and Bodily Changes*. New York: Columbia Univ. Press, 1935.

Dunbar, H. F., *Mind and Body*, 263 pp. Random, 1947.

Dunbar, H. F., *Synopsis of Psychosom. Diag. & Treatment*. St. Louis: Mosby, 1948.

Duncan, C. H., Stevenson, I. P., and Wolff, H. G., *Psychosom. Med.*, 13:36, 1951.

Eysenck, H. J., and Yap, P. M., *J. Ment. Sci.*, 90:595, 1944.

Fain, Michel, *Rev. franç. Psychoanal.*, 14:367-383, 1950.

Frankle, A. H., *Psychosom. Med.*, 14:252, 1952.

Freeman, H., *Psychiat. Quart.*, 8:290, 1934.

Freeman, H., *Arch. Neurol. and Psychiat.*, 39:488, 1938.

Friedgood, H. B., (chap. 10) William's *Textbook of Endocrinology*. Philadelphia: W. B. Saunders, 1950.

Friedman, M., *War Med.*, 6:221, 1944.

Friedman, M., *Am. Heart J.*, 30:325, 1945.

Friedman, M., *Am. Heart J.*, 30:478, 1945.

Friedman, M., *Am. Heart J.*, 30:557, 1945.

Frost, J. W., Dryer, R. L., and Kohlstaedt, K. G., *J. Lab. and Clin. Med.*, 38:523, 1951.

Garrey, W. E., and Butler, V., *Am. J. Physiol.*, 90:355, 1929.

Gaskill, H. S., in Bockus, H. L., *Postgrad. Gastroenterology*. Philadelphia: W. B. Saunders Co., 1950.

Gillespie, R. D., *J. Physiol.*, 58:425, 1924.

Gley, E., *Arch. de Physiol.*, 13:742, 1881.

Goldberg, H., Eliasberg, E. I., and Katz, L. N., *Circulation*, 5:38, 1951.

Goldberg, A., and Lepskaia, M. W., *J. Physiol. et path. gen.*, 24:715, 1926.

Goldberg, A., and Lepskaia, M. W., *Zeitsch. d. ges. exp. Med.*, 56:181, 1927.

Goldwyn, J., *Arch. Neurol. and Psychiat.*, 19:110, 1928.

Gottlieb, J. S., *Arch. Neurol. and Psychiat.*, 35:1256, 1936.

Gottschalk, L. A., *Psychosom. Med.*, 8:16, 1946.

Grace, W. J., and Graham, D. T., *Psychosom. Med.*, 14:243, 1952.

Grant, R., *Ann. Rev. Physiol*, 13:75, 1951.

Greenblatt, R. B., Barfield, W. E., and Clark, S. L., *J. Med. Soc. Georgia*, 7:299, 1951.

Greenfield, A. D. M., *Lancet*, 1:1302, 1951.

Grinker, R. R., and Robbins, F. P., *Psychosom. Casebook*. New York: The Blakiston Co., Inc., 1954.

Hallion, L., and Comte, C., *Arch. de Physiol.*, 26:381, 1894.

Hallion, L., and Comte, C., *Arch. de Physiol.*, 27:90, 1895.

Hambling, John, *Brit. J. Med. Psychol.*, 24:242-253, 1951.

Hambling, John, *Brit. J. Med. Psychol.*, 25:39-47, 1952.
Hamburger, Walter W., *Med. Clin. N. Amer.*, 35:483-499, 1951.
Hammett, F. S., *Am. J. Physiol.*, 53:307, 1920.
Harrowes, W. McC., *Trans. Med. Chir. Soc. Edin.*, 113:10, 1933.
Heath, R. G., *Med. Clin. of N. A.*, 36 (2) : 305, 1952.
Henschel, A., Brozek, J., and Keys, A., *J. Appl. Physiol.*, 4:341, 1951.
Hickam, J. B., Cargill, W. H., and Golden, A., *J. Clin. Invest.*, 27:290, 1948.
Hoagland, H., *J. Aviat. Med.*, 18:450, 1947.
Hoagland, J., Elmadjian, F., and Pincus, G., *J. Clin. Endocrinol.*, 6:301, 1946.
Hoch, Paul H., *Psychoanal. Rev.*, 39:213-221, 1952.
Horwitz, O., Peirce, G., and Montgomery, H., *Circulation*, 4:111, 1951.
Huber, W. R., *Arch. Derm. Syph.*, 59:293-302. Chicago, 1949.
Humphreys, R. J., and Raab, W., *Proc. Soc. Exp. Biol. and Med.*, 74:320, 1950.
Hunt, J. Mc V., *Personality and the Behavior Disorders.* New York: Ronald Press Co., 1944.
Jones, M., and Scarisbrick, R., *Psychosom. Med.*, 8:188, 1946.
Jost, H., *Child Development*, 12:9, 1941.
Jost, Hudson, Ruilmann, C. J., Hill, T. S., and Gulo, Martha Jo., *J. Nerv. Ment. Dis.*, 115:35-48, 1952.
Jost, Hudson, Ruilmann, C. J., Hill, T. S., and Gulo, Martha Jo., *J. Nerv. Ment. Dis.*, 115:152-162, 1952.
Jung, R., and Carmichael, E. A., *Arch. f. Psychiat.*, 107:300, 1930.
Jurgens, B., *Arch f. Psychiat.*, 111:88, 1940.
Kern, F., Jr., Almy, T. P., Abbot, F. K., and Begdonoff, M. D., *Gastroenterol.*, 19:492, 1951.
Krinsky, C. M., and Gottlieb, J. S., *Arch. Neurol. and Psychiat.*, 35:304, 1936.
Kuno, Y., *Lancet*, 1:912, 1930.
Levy, D. M., *Arch. Neurol. and Psychiat.*, 36:991, 1936.
Lhamon, William T., and Saul, Leon J., *Psychosom. Med.*, 12:113-115, 1950.
Lipshutz, Daniel M., *Amer. J. Psychother.*, 6:683-693, 1952.
Lowy, S., *Amer. J. Psychother.*, 5:362-366, 1951.
Lurie, Olga R., *Amer. J. Orthopsych.*, 11:452, 1941.
Macht, D. I., *J. Amer. Med. Assoc.*, 148:265, 1952.
MacKenna, R. M. B., and MacAlpine, Ida, *Lancet*, 1:65-68, 1951.
Malmo, R. B., and Shagass, C., *Psychosom. Med.*, 14:82, 1952.
Marinesco, G., and Kreindler, A., *J. de Psychol. Norm. et Pathol.*, 31:722, 1934.
Martinengo, V., *Schizophrenie*, 2:157, 1933.
Masserman, Jules H., *Amer. J. of Psychiat.*, 110:324, 1953.
Meakins, J. C., and Wilson, R. M., *Heart J.*, 7:17, 1918.
Mendel, E., *Virch. Arch. f. Path. Anat. u. Physiol. u. f. Klin. Med.*, 66:251, 1876.
Miles, Henry H. W., and Cobb, Stanley, *New England J. Med.*, 245:711-719, 1951.
Mittelmann, B., and Wolff, H. G., *Psychosom. Med.*, 1:271, 1939.
Mittelmann, B., and Wolff, H. G., *Psychosom. Med.*, 4:5, 1942.
Murphy, B. W., *N. Z. Med. J.*, 49:284-289, 1950.

PRESENT-DAY PSYCHOLOGY

Murphy, Gardner, "Personality; A biosocial approach to origins and structure." Harper Bros. Publishers, 1947.
Northcote, M. L. M., *J. Ment. Sci.,* 78:263, 1932.
Palmer, R. S., *New Eng. Jour. Med.,* 216:689, 1937.
Palmer, R. S., *J. Amer. Med. Assoc.,* 144:295, 1950.
Persky, H., Gamm, S. R., and Grinker, R., *Psychosom. Med.,* 14:34, 1952.
Pfister, H. O., Schweiz, *Arch. f. Neurol. u. Psychiat.,* (supp.): 77, 1937.
Pfister, H. O., *Amer. J. Psychiat.,* 94 (Supp.) : 109, 1938.
Pool, J. L., and Ransahoff, J., *J. Neurophysiol.,* 12:385, 1949.
Ray, G. B., Ray, L. H., and Johnson, J. R., *Amer. J. Psychiat.,* 147:630, 1946.
Reiser, Morton F., Rosenbaum, Milton and Ferris, Eugene, B., *Psychosom. Med.,* 13:147-159, 1951.
Renold, A. E., Quigley, T. B., Kennard, H. E., and Thorn, G. W., *New Eng. J. Med.,* 244:754, 1951.
Rosen, Samuel Richard, and Appel, Jesse, *Psychoanal. Rev.,* 39:322, 1952.
Rosenzweig, Saul, *Psych. Bull.,* 51:248-256, 1944.
Rothman, S., *Physiol. Rev.,* 21:357, 1941.
Rytand, D. A., *Proc. Soc. Exper. Biol. and Med.,* 54:340, 1943.
Sattler, T. H., Marguardt, G. H., and Cummins, G. M., Jr., *Amer. Med. Assoc.,* 146:1125, 1951.
Saul, L. J., chap. 8 in J. McV. Hunt's *Personality and the Behavior Disorders.* Ronald Press, 1944.
Schneider, R. A., and Zangari, V. M., *Psychosom. Med.,* 13:289, 1951.
Schou, H. I., *Acta Psychiat. et Neurolog.,* (Supp.) 14: 1937.
Selling, L. S., *Am. J. Orthopsych.,* 16:163, 1946.
Severin, G., *Monatsschr. f. Psychiat. u. Neurol.,* 40:265, 1916.
Shelley, W. B., Hovath, P. N., and Pillsbury, D. M., *Medicine,* 29:195, 1950.
Silfverskiöld, B. P., and Amark, C., *Acta Med. Scandinav.,* 113:191, 1943.
Skraggs, E. B., *J. Comp. Psychol.,* 6:303, 1926.
Soley, M. H., and Shock, N. W., *Am. J. Med. Sci.,* 196:840, 1930.
Solomon, A. P., Darrow, C. W., and Blaurock, M., *Psychosom. Med.,* 1:118, 1939.
Spillane, J. D., *Brit. Med. J.,* 2:739, 1940.
Stainbrook, Edward, *Psychosom. Med.,* 14:211-227, 1952.
Starr, H. E., *Am. J. Psychol.,* 38:394, 1923.
Starr, H. E., *J. Biol. Chem.,* 54:55, 1922.
Stead, E. A., Jr., Warren, J. V., Merrill, A. J., and Brannon, E. S., *J. Clin. Invest.,* 24:326, 1945.
Stevenson, I. P., Duncan, C. H., and Wolff, H. G., *J. Clin. Invest.,* 28:1535, 1949.
Stevenson, I. P., and Mathews, Robert A., *The Jr. of Nervous & Mental Disease,* Vol. 118, No. 4, Oct. 1953, pp. 289-306.
Stevenson, I. P., and Wolff, Harold G., *Psychosom. Med.,* 11:223, 227, 1949.
Storment, Charlyne T., *Psychosom. Med.,* 13:304-313, 1951.
Suarez, Ramon M., *Bol. Assoc. Med. P. Rico,* 42:519-532, 1950.
Theron, P. A., *Psychosom. Med.,* 10:335, 1948.
Truelove, S. C., *Clin. Sci.,* 10:229, 1951.
Van Der Merwe, A. B., *Psychosom. Med.,* 10:347, 1940.
Weirsma, E. D., *Ztschr. f. d. ges. Neurol. u. Psychiat.,* 19:147, 1913.
Weiss, E., *Principles of Psychodynamics,* 268 pp., Grune, Stratton, 1950.

Weiss, Edward, *Psychosom. Med.,* 14:150-153, 1952.

Weiss, E., and English, O. S., *Psychosom. Med.,* 2nd Ed., pp. 59. Philadelphia: W. B. Sanders & Co., 1949.

Westcott, R. N., Fowler, N. O., Scott, R. C., Hauenstein, V. D., and Mcguire, J., *J. Clin. Invest.,* 30:957, 1951.

Wolf, S. J., *Ann. Int. Med.,* 31:637, 1949.

Wolf, S. J., and Almy, T. P., *Gastroenterol.,* 13:401, 1949.

Wolff, G. A., and Wolff, H. G., *Psychosom. Med.,* 8:293, 1946.

Ziegler, L. H., and Cash, P. T., *Amer. J. Psychiat.,* 95:677, 1938.

Chapter XXV

CLINICAL PSYCHOLOGY

W. G. Eliasberg, M.D., Ph.D.

EDITORIAL NOTE

Clinical psychology is at present the most important province of our science. No branch of psychology has had a parallel success, which, in one sense, argues failure on the part of the average human. It cannot be said, as often it has been in connection with organic medicine, that we have always been victims but didn't know it. Clinical Psychology has become a full-fledged professional department, and its practitioners constitute by far the largest and probably the most affluent division of the American Psychological Association, over 1,000 members.

Clinical psychology cannot be encompassed in a single chapter. It would rather take a series of volumes to deal with it. Dr. Wladimir G. Eliasberg has introduced the subject by raising several central issues. Some of the subsequent chapters are also on various phases of clinical psychology.

Dr. W. G. Eliasberg holds both a Ph.D. from the University of Munich and an M.D. from the University of Heidelberg. He was an intern in Prof. Kraepelin's Hospital and lectured at the University of Munich, at Rutgers University, Newark College. He was the founder and secretary general of the "Allgemeine aerztliche Gesellschaft fuer Psychotherapie," and editor of the "Allgemeine aerztliche Zeitschrift fuer Psychotherapie," Psychiatric consultant to the Bulova Watch Co., honorary member (1935) of the Prague Association for Psychotechnics, honorary member (1952) of Allgemeine aerztliche Gesellschaft fuer Psychotherapie. He is a frequent contributor to the periodical literature, having published hundreds of scientific papers in scores of journals, on a variety of topics. Child psychology, industrial and business psychology, sociology, criminology and forensic medicine have occupied much of his attention, but his wide scope of titles places him in the category of those whose interests expand as they grow older. In addition to articles, he has brought out monographs and books, among them A Textbook of Propaganda, *a book on the problem child, and has collaborated on various encyclopedias and other collective volumes. He is associate editor of the* Journal of Group Psychotherapy.

Introduction

The present problems of clinical psychology can be understood only in their development; therefore, a chapter on Clinical Psychology must start with a historical survey from which the following basic problems emerge:

clinical psychology
(a) as a science
(b) as a profession.

The latter part comprises the personal problems of the clinical psychologists in their relationships with psychiatrists, the public and employers (employment problems). This chapter, then, will deal mainly with those tasks, scientific and organizational, which may confront clinical psychology in the near future. Current discussion and non-controversial routine will be taken up only as a background; these have been surveyed recently by Robt. W. White[33] and Robt. I. Watson,[32] (*cf. also Handbook of Applied Psychology*). To write on clinical psychology, one should be familiar with psychology, of course, but also with psychiatry. A personal remark is in order, the writer, being a psychiatrist (M.D.) and a psychologist (Ph.D.), has taught social and applied psychology as well as psychiatry. He has no axe to grind.

Historical Remarks

There appeared in Germany from 1783 to 1793 a periodical called *Magazin zur Efahrungsseelenkunde,*[25] with Carl Philipp Moritz as editor, Moses Mendelssohn, Kant's critic, Salomon Maimon, Kant's former student, the physician, Marcus Hertz, and many others as contributors.* An officer in the Prussian Army of Frederick the Great reported on a soldier who murdered, actuated by a need for punishment. This was more than a hundred years before Freud. There were introspective reports on aphasia, on dreams, on psychotherapy, in short this periodical developed what today is called clinical or clinical-dynamic psychology, psychopathology and psychiatry (*cf.* W. G. Eliasberg: "Pre-History of Aphasia"[10] and "He Murdered to Get Hanged").[11]

After the *Magazin* had ceased publication, in 1793, psychology reverted to scholastic, *a priori,* logically and philosophically oriented systems. The textbook writers of that time put the emphasis on dichotomies rather than on experiences, let alone experiments. The next step ahead came from the physiologists, men like Donders, Helmholtz and others, who found in their sporadic glances over the fence enough that was interesting; psychology is beholden to them for many important findings, mostly in the field of general experimental psychology.

Helmholtz[19] has an interesting story to tell. When he was called to Königsberg to the chair of physiology, an aged and learned professor, who was concerned with the "reorganization" of the University, entreated him to divide physiology, to hold forth on the philosophical part, leaving the lower experimental part to a young instructor (Hermann Helmholtz, *Vorträge und Reden,* Vol. II, p. 179, Braunschweig, Vieweg 1896).

Notwithstanding the hopeful beginnings of experimental interests early in the 19th century (E. H. Weber), the situation in psychology remained as described vividly in Helmholtz' words, to the last third of that same century, the time when Wundt's laboratory opened. Meanwhile, psychiatrists, working in hospitals independently of psychology, were applying crude intelligence tests for the purpose of sifting normality, so-called, from various degrees of dementia. The concept of normality was an intellectual one. It seemed sufficient to apply the lawyers' idea that a man is normal, if he knows what he is doing. It was the age of legal responsibility, competence and economic egoism, all three based on the assumption that normal behavior is guaranteed, if the necessary insight is present. Finally, the psychologists who in the beginning were trained in medicine as well as in the psychological laboratories of Lotze, Fechner and Wundt, took over.

The turning point came when William Stern published his work on individual differences in 1900, later incorporated in his larger book on Differential Psychology in its Methodical Foundations in 1911.[30] In William Stern's publications, the development of clinical psychology is well reflected. Very early in his career, he embraced the various aspects of differential and applied psychology. He turned to the developmental stage of childhood, both monographically (Testimony of the Child Witness; The Language of the Child; The Development of Language; The I. Q.) and in the general psychological survey of early childhood.

Other applications followed: objective industrial psychology, psychology of aptitudes, pedagogical psychology, to name but a few. The influence of the applications on the mother-science cannot be overrated. At first, they turned toward mother like little children, but then as they grew, they themselves had more to offer for the development of the older organism of experimental general knowledge. It is the applications that force science to become concrete, to adjust its basic concepts as well as methods, and finally leave the ivory tower of the laboratory to fight it out in the market place. This has happened between the mother-science of general experimental laboratory psychology and the various fields of application that are gathered together today under the name of Clinical Psychology.

It is this unsystematic, jagged cutting line, as it were, for which clinical psychology has been blamed. Considering the achievements, both in the various fields of application and in promoting progress in general psychology, these objections are not too important. In the concept of application, some casualness must be admitted.

Clinical Psychology as a Science

In the historical introduction, it was shown how clinical psychology developed from the need to understand, and to cope with individuality. As we said, this was done naively without too many theoretical qualms. The psychological case attracted attention, and one tried to understand it with what was available in terms and concepts of general psychology. It was assumed that, on principle at least, in the pathological case, the same laws of nature obtained as in the normal case. Also, abnormal cases were, after all, frequent enough to command interest. One could understand from the pathological case that the normal one was assumed implicitly. Conversely, there was in the beginning no attempt to apply pathopsychological insights to the normal case. These various assumptions were lifted into full consciousness only when differential psychology was envisaged as a new scientific field. What had been considered a troublesome source of error later became the source of new scientific discoveries. Thus, differential psychology or individual psychology was recognized as a science of equal birthright with general psychology.

The next problem that differential psychology had to deal with was the range of variations in both the fields of normality and pathology. It was recognized gradually that there were no sharp lines between normality and pathology, childhood and adulthood, animal and human mental life, primitive and civilized attitudes of the mind. Instead of the discrete Aristotelian forms, Galilean continuity swayed that province of natural science, psychology, and it became necessary, therefore, to look into (a) correlations (b) causalities. True, it was not possible to erect fences, but it was possible to describe, and what is more important, to predict, qualitatively and quantitatively, from one fact the presence of another not yet observed. The human mind will not acquiesce, however, in mere empiricism; it seeks to understand correlations causally. If we identify a certain character in a personality, we want to know how this character originated, how one trait will influence, further, or supersede another trait. We want to know whether there are causal relationships between body-build and mind, between bumps of the skull, particular development of the brain and special development of certain identifiable psychological traits. Physiognomics, phrenology, palmistry and other disciplines belong to this group of crude causalism, but the principle as such of somatopsychic causality or at least correlation is not given up, although at present clinical psychologists are less interested in it. The final problem of differential psychology is synthesis of the individuality from the traits. In this respect differential and clinical psychology have the same task as chemistry. The chemist has gained full knowledge and mastery only, when after complete analysis, he has been able to synthesize from the elements the original compound.

In clinical psychology such syntheses are done by means of the dynamic viewpoint. Examples may be found in good Rorschach records, in the graphodiagnostic methods as used by Ludwig Klages, Richard Pauli *et al.*

Dynamic Approach

In fact, any interpretation of any test needs dynamic viewpoints. As has been shown by the writer first in 1923, and later in various papers, no test allows of direct measurement of the difficulty of the performance. One is always in need of information on how the performance was implemented, e.g., whether it was achieved with the utmost effort or reeled off easily and as a matter of routine. There is no graph that yields insights directly into objective difficulty. Only a dynamic interpretation will solve this problem. Similar experiences were gained by the author when he retrained aphasics. Neither the statistics of errors nor the time needed, neither the frequency of an achievement for a given individual nor inter-individual comparison, neither comparison between ontogenesis and phylogenesis (animals, primitives) can supersede the need for knowledge of dynamic factors.

Thus a development which is clearly visible in our present use of projective tests might have started much earlier in the routine of testing and especially intelligence testing. Many disappointments in the prediction of success in industry, business, and the professions, based on aptitude testing alone, could have been avoided. In the future, testing for military or civilian purpose will be guided by knowledge of the dynamics of personalities and groups.

It is, however, high time we became wary of building new ivory towers. Dynamic psychology can not stop at the dynamics of the individual or the group. A practical dynamic theory of the motivations has to consider average motivations in the particular locality and at the particular time. We have to consult with the sociologist and the historian as well as the psychopathologist and psychiatrist. The future of dynamic psychology will lead to the market place, not the *chi*-square (*cf. Social Science Research Council, Bulletins* 49 and 53). On the inside of the cover of *The American Psychologist,* the professional journal of the American Psychological Association, there are listed the twenty divisions of which the American Psychological Association, at present, consists. There we find general psychology, experimental psychology, measurement, personality, clinical and abnormal psychology, childhood and adolescence, counseling and guidance, and so on. One can not help wondering how with such overlapping, duplication of work can be avoided. One can not help wondering, too, where, with so many sections and cross-sections, psychology as such could find its cubicle. The genesis of clinical psychology is reminiscent of the origin of the Englishman as described by Daniel Defoe,

> *Thus from a mixture of all kinds began*
> *That heterogeneous thing, an Englishman.*

However, the Englishman exists, and there is also the comforting fact that people exist who call themselves clinical psychologists, because they are doing clinical psychology; or *vice versa,* as Robert M. Allen[1] recently wittily remarked, clinical psychology is what anyone who wants to call himself a clinical psychologist does. Said another skeptic with reference to psychotherapy: "We have left therapy as an undefined technique which is applied to unspecified problems with non-predictable outcome. For this technique we recommend rigorous training."

Whatever truth is contained in this quotation might apply to clinical psychology as well. We are reaping at present the harvest, bountiful or otherwise, of what we have sown in the short American spring of psychology. In our horror of mentalism, we have fallen prey to depart-mentalism. Ernst G. Beier[6] of Syracuse University, reports a conversation which he had in 1952 with European psychologists. They could hardly see the forest of American psychology for the trees of the departments. Be this as it may, we are not so much in need of definitions of clinical psychology and clinical psychologists as we are of developing the reliability and the validity of our predictions. This can be achieved only by widening and broadening contacts, by overcoming departmentalization, not only in psychology but among the various faculties and heads of departments. Much ingenuity in experimentation and administration will be necessary to approach this goal. In the searching beams of scientific investigation, well intentioned truisms will be recognized for what they are, thriving weeds that have to be removed.

A particular problem for research is what may be called Contract-Psychology, i.e., the farming out by the government of limited "departmentalized" projects to universities and colleges. John T. Wilson of the National Scientific Foundation quotes from Dr. C. E. Mees, the director of research at Eastman Kodak Company,

> The best person to decide what research is to be done is the person doing the research. The next best is the head of the department. After that you leave the field of best persons and meet increasingly worse groups. The first of these is the research director who is probably wrong more than half the time. Then comes a committee, which is wrong most of the time. Finally there is the Committee of Company Vice Presidents, which is wrong all of the time.[34]

This applies with inconsequential change of a few nouns to our own problems.

CLINICAL PSYCHOLOGY AS A PROFESSION

Professional problems of clinical psychology have turned up on almost every one of the preceding pages. We call the aspect with which we are going to deal professional because it entails the various social relationships in the practice of clinical psychology. Such relationships will concern the clinical psychologist and the persons with whom, for whom, on whom, against whom, he works, to wit: the clinical psychologist and his client, his client's relatives, his employer, other employees, competitors within his own group, other professional groups.

In considering these problems, two schools have raised their voice. The one believes that the whole problem is already solved by a kind of *a priori* approach. Before clinical psychology put in an appearance there existed "ethical common laws" and an "academic-scientific tradition of American culture" which adequately proscribe misbehavior. This school more or less vehemently opposes a code because laws are on principle only for those who in their heart are set to break them, the people who are looking for the loopholes, while those who would observe them, as mature persons, know in their heart what the common rules of decency are. To spell out such rules could have bad consequences. The preceding is a short resumé from Calvin S. Hall's "Crooks, Codes and Cant" (*Am. Psychol.* V7, #8, 1952, p. 431).

There is on the other hand, the work of the American Psychological Association Committee on Ethical Standards of Psychology, published in volumes 5, 6 and 7, of the *American Psychologist* (1950-51-52). This is a series of articles in which ethical standards in clinical and consultant relationships are considered in full detail. In each section a problem is posed, illustrated by incidents and summed up in a number of principles relating to the ethical conduct of the clinical psychologist. The incidents are especially valuable material. It must be said, however, that there is no organic connection between the reality of the incident and the guiding principle of conduct. If we find a high percentage of the actual population on a subway train indulging in pickpocketing, we cannot derive from this the principle that the said activity must be admitted as ethical in the said location.

Another example: If an examination of the sexual behavior of the American human male or female seems to indicate a high incidence of certain practices, that does not give sanction to such practices. It can not be admitted that ethical guidance is possible without an intimate knowledge of those actions and attitudes which, the professional oaths to the contrary notwithstanding, are considered in good standing, though ethically neutral or doubtful. What is permitted and what is mandatory? What is optional but not desirable? What is intimated but not said explicitly? What are basic interests as to financial rewards, prestige, etc.? All these make up professional ethics, and neither is the sum total identical with general ethics nor are the various parts always in ethical harmony with each other.

We shall not be successful if we try to reduce group ethical problems to individual ethical problems. The group has its own life, egotism, rules and ethics. And the basic law is that action of the group as such, and of all members individually, must not endanger the existence of the group, must, on the contrary, further the purposes of the group. What is indifferent from this angle may be unethical from the individual angle, but can be tolerated by the group. On the other hand very delicate individual conflicts, much as they may be proof of refined individual conscience, may be intolerable because of endangerment to the group. The group may in reaction expel such a member.

In this way we have found an immanent principle of group and professional ethics which will have to be applied to each of the particular problems. This principle relieves us of a state of affairs where mere subjectivity sits in judgment. The writer has shown how this principle can be put into action in such problems as morality or immorality in art, in short, in every field where it is the common denominator between general ethics and ethics of a special group that matters.

Space will not allow description of the method. Neither can we analyze all the "incidents" listed by the American Psychological Association Committee. Let us limit ourselves to one problem which in part was also taken up by Robert W. White,[33] in a tactful way. The problem we have in mind is that of therapy to be rendered by the clinical psychologist; we want to remind our readers again of our own neutrality as regards the medical-psychiatric and psychological professions. In therapy, the following social psychological relationships are involved: The client (relatives); the therapist and his competency, economic interests and reputation; the state, if state license is necessary; the professional organization, if a board of examiners grants certification; within the psychological profession: experimental psychologists; specialists in testing; specialists in personality—and social psychology; within other professions: social workers, psychiatric social workers, last but not least physicians, particularly psychiatrists. The relationships with medical psychiatrists and medical psychoanalysts is hotly debated at present. Integration can not consist of the exchange of personal amenities. Nor can there be a unity of subject-matter or viewpoints. If it were a question of mutual malice only, between psychiatrists and psychologists, we might have achieved by now that objective harmony. There would be no room for a multiplicity of viewpoints. That does not mean that there is no such malice; there is very much of it, and much social tension of the in-and-out group. But on the whole these are trivialities not worth discussing.

UNIFICATION OF AIMS

Integration can not be tantamount to giving up the differences in viewpoints; we can not hope some day to discover a heretofore hidden unity of the subject-matter. Integration and unity are not ready-made. They can not be had simply for the asking and can not be excavated, as it were. Unification is a task, the solution of which may be approached asymptotically; nor can we simply string up the different viewpoints like beads. History of science shows that differences that seemed insurmountable in bygone centuries may appear small and insignificant in our present century. Why? Because the viewpoints themselves may form new alloys, e.g., physical chemistry, or in our field, psychological psychiatry. On the other hand, viewpoints and problems may drift apart as theology and philosophy and the sciences have done.

Unity is a task, not an idea. Each period has the right to demand certain unities and to give up others. In this way experimental psychology has forced its way into the court room because Carl Marbe, professor of psychology in Würzburg, was able to enlighten the court, by means of reaction experiments, in 1911. No medical man had been able to introduce such experiments.

In thinking over the relationship to his patient, the clinical psychologist will often find it necessary to first consult with a medical man and a psychiatrist. Only the latter can tell whether the apparent psychological conflict is the first stage of a more serious mental or physical illness. The same patient's interest will counsel his being seen at frequent intervals during treatment by the physician. Physical or mental illness may develop at any time just as it develops outside of psychotherapy. Psychosomatic disorders, once diagnosed, may change their character. The patient may still believe that his colitis is "nothing but" the expression of his conflict and yet there might have developed appendicitis, which may need immediate surgical attention.

We would like to cite as witness, Max L. Hutt,[21] who gave a short survey of progress in clinical psychology in 1948. He particularly reviewed the experiences gathered in the grand style experiment of the last war. Two trends were noted, first, that of team work of the clinical psychologists with the psychiatrists and the psychiatric social workers. The other trend was toward evaluation of the tests in the context of the whole personality.

Analyses of the leading relationships and interests similar to the just mentioned relationship of the psychologists to psychiatrists and psychiatric social workers, must be carried out for other professional problems and "incidents". The critics of the code are both right and wrong. They are wrong because the law of decency is not a sufficient guide, and a collection of incidents in itself is but misleading. They are right in their feeling that a basic principle is necessary as a guide through the thickets of the incidents. Every interest, if morally acceptable and lawful, has a right to protection which can be guaranteed only through social psychological analyses; in this way we will learn in the individual case what helps and what harms the relation in question.

The assumption in clinical psychology and all its applications is that there is a consistency in the behavior of individuals and groups which is believed to be rooted "in motivational propensities, variously described as traits, attitudes, defense mechanisms, ego requirements, etc." (Leo Postman) [26]

Is this consistency and the dynamics stemming from it necessarily unconscious? This important problem was recently taken up by Gordon W. Allport in a survey of the latest developments of Motivation Theory. [3] Allport is satisfied that unless a motive is (neurotically) repressed, it is unlikely to express itself in the projective methods, possibly with the exception of the (free) association test. Allport cites experiments carried out with 36 conscientious objectors during the last war. J. Brozek, H. Guetzkow, R. Levine, *et al.*, [10] and R. N. Sanford. [29] The food motive became more and more conscious, it was not all repressed. It is in keeping with this that we find that well-integrated subjects reveal their motivations less in the projective tests and more in interviews. As we cannot know in advance with which type of subjects we are dealing, we should always employ projective together with non-projective methods. "Psychodynamics is not necessarily hidden dynamics."

It should not be so difficult, however, to find examples to the contrary. Here is one. (W. G. Eliasberg: *Freud, Veblen and Marketing*).[15] Around 1928 a manufacturer sent his market analyst out on a consumer survey to study the acceptability of a new product. The man returned with devastating results. The idea had been rejected by almost 100% of the interviewees. And they gave good reasons too: "Such practice would degrade them to the taste of the lowliest"; "No self-respecting consumer would ever stoop to that". The manufacturer disregarded the survey and went ahead anyway; the product was not a flop. Far from it. Came the time when every woman used red nail polish. What had happened? The interviewed ladies gave the answers as dictated by their superegos, but later acted in accordance with the needs of their unconscious. They may not have been aware of this at the time of the questioning or they repressed it. Perhaps they did not want to recognize their true reaction. Be this as it may, there is no use assuming that the non-neurotic, well-integrated person will always be free of hidden dynamics. Allport's formula does not cover ordinary cases of hidden non-neurotic dynamics. To what other problems does this apply? Obviously hidden dynamics is a stumbling stone that public-opinion polling has not yet been able to avoid. Conscious or unconscious resistances to self-revelation, also to revealing oneself to others, may be so strong that only through uncovering psychiatric and projective methods may we reach the depths. Such resistances, as was pointed out, are not necessarily neurotic, neither are they indicative of a weak ego-structure, or as a number of people would be inclined to assume, a strong ego-structure.

Allport's sagacity has discovered a strong trend in our present-day practice and in our literature of clinical psychology. Outside the clan there is often little mention of "tension reduction, brain drives, externalised drives, derived drives, satiation of drives but there is direct understanding of where the shoe pinches." (Harry F. Harlow,[17] Judson S. Brown,[8] Leo Postman[26]). For a survey of concrete motivations in industry, see W. G. Eliasberg's

PRESENT-DAY PSYCHOLOGY

"Challenge"; [10a] For a Survey of American literature re: Concrete Motivations, see Morris Viteles. [31]

FOOTNOTE

* Cf. on the *Magazin,* George S. Brett, *A History of Psychology,* vol. 2. London, 1921, p. 320.

BIBLIOGRAPHY

[1] Allen, R. M. What is Clinical Psychology? *American Psychologist,* vol. 7, No. 10, Oct. 1952.

[2] Allport, G. W. The Use of Personal Documents in Psychological Science. *Soc. Science Res. Council Bull.,* 1942, *49.* (With bibliography of 198 numbers).

[3] —— The Trend in Motivational Theory. *Amer. Journal of Orthopsychiatry,* vol. XXIII, No. 1, Jan. 1953.

[4] *American Psychologist, The,* vols. 5, 6 and 7, 1950, 1951, 1952.

[5] Angell, R. See Gottschalk, Louis.

[6] Beier, E. G. A Problem in International Communication. *American Psychologist,* vol. 7, No. 10, Oct. 1952.

[7] Brett, G. S. *A History of Psychology,* 3 vols. London, 1914-1921.

[8] Brown, J. S. *Current Theory and Research in Motivation.* Lincoln: University of Nebraska Press, 1953.

[9] Brozek, J., Guetzkow, H., Baldwin, M. V. and Cranston, R. A. Quantitative Study of Perception and Association in Experimental Semi-Starvation. *J. Personality,* 1951, *19,* 245-264.

[10] Eliasberg, W. G. A Contribution to the Pre-History of Aphasia. *J. of the History of Medicine and Allied Sciences,* 1950, I, 96-101.

[10a] Eliasberg, W. G. *The Challenge of Social Neuroses. J. of Nerv. and Mental Disease.* Vol. 94, No. 6, Dec. 1941.

[11] —— He Murdered To Get Hanged. *Psychoanalytic Review,* vol. 39, No. 2, April, 1952.

[12] —— Methods in Graphologic Diagnostics. *Psychiat. Quarterly,* July, 1952.

[13] —— Psychiatric and Psychologic Opinions in Court. *J. of Crim. Law and Criminology,* vol. 39, No. 2, July-Aug. 1948.

[14] —— Die Schwierigkert intellektueller Vorgänge; ihre Psychologie, Psychopathologie und ihre Bedeutung für die Intelligenz und Demenzforschung. *Schweizer Archiv für Neurologie und Psychiatrie,* vol. XXII, Heft 1 u 2. 1923.

[15] —— *Freud, Veblen, and Marketing.* Printers Ink Publ. Co., 1954.

[16] Gottschalk, L. The Use of Personal Documents in History, Anthropology and Sociology. *Soc. Science Res. Council Bull.,* 1945, *53.*

[17] Harlow, H. F. *Current Theory and Research in Motivation.* Lincoln: University of Nebraska Press, 1953.

[18] *Handbook of Applied Psychology.* D. H. Fryer and E. R. Henry, editors. New York: Rinehart, 1950, 2 vols.

[19] von Helmholtz, H. *Vorträge und Reden,* vol. 2. Braunschweig, Vieweg, 1896.

[20] Hunt, W. A. The Future of Diagnostic Testing in Clinical Psychology. *J. Clin. Psychol.*, 1946, *2*, 311-317.

[21] Hutt, M. L. What Did the Clinical Psychologist Learn from the War? *Annals of the New York Academy of Science,* vol. 49, Art. 6, pp. 907ff. New York, Oct. 8, 1948.

[22] Kluckhohn, C. *See* Gottschalk, Louis.

[23] Levine, R. I., Chein and Murphy, G. The Relation of the Intensity of a Need to the Amount of Perceptual Distortion: A Preliminary Report. *J. Psychol.*, 1942, *13*, 283-293.

[24] *Magazin für Erfahrungsseelenkunde* (Carl Philip Moritz, Ed.) Berlin: August Mylius, 1783-1793.

[25] Pauli, R. M. Arbeitsversuch als charakterologisches Prüfungsverfahren. *Ztschr. f. angewandte Psychol. u. Charakterkunde, 65,* 1 and 2.

[26] Postman, L. *The Experimental Analysis of Motivational Factors in Perception; Current Theory and Research in Motivation.* Lincoln, Nebr.: Univ. of Nebraska Press, 1953, p. 59 ff.

[27] Roback, A. A. *History of American Psychology.* New York: Library Publishers, 1952.

[28] Rosenzweig, S. Imbalance in Clinical Psychology. *American Psychologist,* vol. 5, No. 12, Dec. 1950.

[29] Sanford, R. N. The Effect of Abstinence from Food Upon Imaginal Processes. *J. Psychol.*, 1936, *2*, 129-136.

[30] Stern, W. *Die differentielle Psychologie.* Leipzig: Barth, 1911.

[31] Viteles, M. S. *Motivation and Morale in Industry.* New York: W. W. Norton, 1953.

[32] Watson, R. I. A. Brief History of Clinical Psychology. *Psychological Bulletin,* vol. 50, No. 5, Sept. 1953 (with bibliography of 121 publications).

[33] White, R. W. *The Abnormal Personality.* Ronald Press, 1948.

[34] Wilson, J. T. Government Support of Research and Its Influence on Psychology. *The American Psychologist,* vol. 7, No. 12, 1952, p. 714 ff.

CHAPTER XXVI

RECENT DEVELOPMENTS IN PSYCHOTHERAPY

EMIL A. GUTHEIL, M.D.

EDITORIAL NOTE

Long before psychoanalysis was incubated, psychotherapy served to allay mental suffering. Kant tells of treating his own spells of mental distress more or less successfully, and many lesser men and women have done the same without benefit of either psychiatrist or psychoanalyst. This is not the same as saying that all people can help themselves, or even that those individuals who have been their own physicians could not have benefited more by consulting trained men of great experience. Pierre Janet, in his Principles of Psychotherapy *was even inclined to condone quackery, so long as the patient found relief.*

Psychotherapy did not decline, curiously enough, as a result of the rise of psychoanalysis. In Germany, Hitler's professional minions sought to eradicate it because, according to them, it was wholly in the hands of Jewish physicians. C. G. Jung, in a letter to the editor of this symposium, claimed to have eased the situation for the latter by reorganizing the profession. It would seem that psychotherapy has become strengthened as a result of its new headquarters in the United States; and it has been able to add, so to speak, a new story, viz., group psychotherapy.

Dr. Gutheil who contributes the present chapter has been invited not only as a specialist in this field, but because we feel that Stekel's views should find a place in this volume.

Dr. Emil A. Gutheil, a native of Poland, received his M.D. degree at the University of Vienna where he was associated with Dr. Wilhelm Stekel as his personal assistant for about ten years and was co-founder of the Active-Analytic Clinic in Vienna, Austria. In the '30's, he joined the staff of the Mt. Sinai Hospital, and in 1947 became the Director of Education at the Postgraduate Center for Psychotherapy. One of the leading authorities on psychotherapy in the country, he has edited the American Journal of Psychotherapy *since 1947. His most recent work is the* Handbook of Dream Analysis.

I. THEORY

Freud's theories have brought about a decisive turn in the development of psychotherapy. Their impact on psychiatry as well as on contemporary thought is tremendous. Psychoanalysis not only introduced useful dynamic concepts into psychiatric thinking, but also supplied it with a vocabulary to describe mental reactions for which it was lacking adequate expressions. We can, therefore, rightfully speak of a pre-Freudian and a post-Freudian psychiatry (Wittels).

Freud's main contribution to psychiatry is that it replaced the descriptive approach to mental illness by an interpretative one, and that it focused the psychiatrist's attention on the unconscious motivation in the patient's behavior. As a consequence, psychotherapy could concentrate on the causes of the pathological condition rather than on its manifestations. What up to that time had to be treated with purely symptomatic, supportive measures could now be attacked at its source.

The Freudian doctrine developed against the continuous resistance of academic psychiatry. Ever since the efforts of its adherents have brought about a gradual penetration of analytic formulations into clinical psychiatry, a new era in psychiatry was inaugurated, that of "psychoanalytic psychiatry." It is based on insight into the dynamic processes which take place in mental disease.

WHEN PSYCHOTHERAPY AND PSYCHOANALYSIS MET

Psychotherapy in general has gained considerably from the dynamic approach. Its progress can be registered in three main directions:

I. The area of psychological exploration and the scope of application of psychotherapy have been widened. II. The human personality has been more thoroughly explored by the use of newer methods based in part on projective techniques and on deeper insight. III. The techniques of psychotherapy have been improved as a result of the lessons learned from the widening of therapeutic experience.

The progress mentioned involves research, teaching and training in psychotherapy. We can also note to what extent psychoanalysis has penetrated general medicine. This progress achieved its greater momentum after analytically trained psychiatrists began to leave the esoteric confines of their analytic societies and began to discuss clinical problems with their clinical colleagues, on the neutral grounds of clinics and hospitals.

The exposure to critique on such occasions has, in many instances, contributed to the clarification of clinical concepts within psychoanalysis. On the other hand, analysts were able to deal more successfully with biased and prejudiced opinions which used to bedevil the relations between analysts and the rest of the medical profession.

As a result of the rapprochement between psychoanalysis and medicine, there has developed a more distinct trend among analysts to coördinate purely speculative operations with the accepted clinical procedures, an increased need for psychobiologic anchoring of purely psychologic formulations, and for a scientific validation of theory and practice—i.e., for research.

Orthodoxy finds it more and more difficult to maintain itself in the fresh breezes of the free clinical investigation. This is the price psychoanalysis is paying for its general acceptance by medicine. Today, militant defensiveness is seen only in young and less experienced members of the psychoanalytic group. To quote Alexander, "the heroic phase of psychoanalysis is over."

Of course, among the "old-timers" of psychoanalysis, some complaint is still raised that psychoanalysis is being "diluted" by many of its adherents, that some of its supporters fail to conform to the original inviolate views of Freud; but their voice is fading and will probably be silenced by the inescapable course of medical history.

However, we can say that, on the whole, a liberalization of psychoanalysis is taking place all along the line. The idea gains in acceptance that psychotherapy is not the application of a uniform formula, but a process, in the course of which new principles may be discovered and old ones abolished—or confirmed. Only the *ethical principle* guiding the approach can be considered stable.

Freud's theoretical formulations have not only undergone various reforms, but have also experienced further additions and elaborations. Several attempts were made by analysts to coördinate recent advances in medicine with the original psychoanalytic concepts (Hartmann, Loewenstein and Kris).[1]

The "Libido Theory" which has been under attack by early dissidents (Adler, Stekel) has recently again been challenged by Horney and Rado.[2]

Some of the modern psychotherapeutic writers have lately come to emphasize the importance of the *psychopathology of the ego* and its defenses. Freud came relatively late to the investigation of the most conscious part of the human personality. This new research is proving particularly fruitful for the understanding of the latent and manifest forms of psychoses. It opens a wide field for clinical investigation and therapy.

SOME WAR NEUROSES BAFFLED PSYCHOANALYSTS

One factor which contributed considerably to the interest in the normal and pathological functions of the ego was the recent war experience with the "effort syndrome" and "battle fatigue," with their clinical pictures which did not fit into the existing Freudian concepts of neurosis. Concepts such as those of "a weak ego," "ego boundaries," "ego boundary cathexis," and others, were recently introduced into the psychiatric vocabulary, thanks to the contributions by Federn, Bychowski, Rado and Kardiner; these concepts help to clarify some of the intricate mechanisms which take place in neuroses, psychoses, and that partly unknown territory of "latent" psychoses. Hoch's introduction of the concept of a "pseudoneurotic schizophrenia," with its "pan-neurosis" and "pan-anxiety" represents a powerful stimulus for future research in the psychopathology of the ego.

To test the basic tenets of psychotherapy, coördinated research must be carried out. Such research is long overdue. Ever since psychotherapy began to demand its place among scientific procedures, psychotherapists have felt a growing need for investigating the inner laws governing the psychotherapeutic processes.

However, these problems have never been easy to solve. Although in all branches of medicine experiments play an important part, and observing, describing, deriving of common laws, and the working out of hypotheses, represent the main tools of research, in psychotherapy those types of research which rely on experimentation have a limited application. Experiments with patients for the sake of research are rarely done, while on the other hand, data obtained by laboratory animals (Mowrer, Masserman, *et al.*) are of use to man only to a very small extent.

Sound-recordings of psychotherapeutic sessions are widely used in research; but they offer insights into the patient's verbal behavior only, which, in psychotherapy, represents only a part of the patient's total behavior. A more extensive system by which the researcher, in addition to the sound-recording, can participate in the observation of the therapeutic development more directly (by using a one-way mirror or the like), has been proposed, but here also considerations of privacy, discretion, and other factors interfere with the practical application of the plan.

Some value for research can be derived from a comparison of data on the patient's clinical signs recorded at the beginning and at the termination of psychotherapy, a comparison of the "before" and the "after." However, since the condition of "mental health" is not a measurable factor, we lack a yardstick for such an evaluation.

PREREQUISITES OF EVALUATION

In order to evaluate a method and its efficiency, it is important to *formulate useful definitions* of the procedure, its goals and techniques. Because of its nature, the attempt at defining psychotherapy meets with marked difficulty.

Some writers (Alexander, French, *et al.*) define psychotherapy as a learning process. The therapist attempts to remove the existing defenses—erected by the patient for adaptive purposes—so that learning can proceed; the patient then may rectify his mistakes, and achieve a better adaptive level.

While there is a great need for a standardization of psychotherapeutic procedures to render the method more "scientific," thus more suitable for a scientific appraisal, the intricacies of the interpersonal relations connected with the application of psychotherapy, in most cases, place the method outside the pale of a science. Our statistical evaluations, regarding results of therapy, therefore, are all tainted by unavoidable inaccuracies.

The Berlin Institute for Psychoanalysis—the first Institute of this kind—formulated the definition of the term "cure" as follows: An essential personality change, resulting from a fundamental redistribution of instinctual energy, formerly exploited by the neurosis. The patient was considered "improved" if he had undergone essential changes of the above type, with evidence of neurosis still persisting.

The growing use of projective techniques as controls of the psychotherapeutic processes has led to the introduction of new concepts in therapy, e.g., the concept of "levels" in mental adjustment.

TOLERANCE OF FRUSTRATION

The research is also concentrating on the patient's personality and its gains achieved through psychotherapy. These gains are said to be expressed in the patient's tolerance toward frustration, his reactions to stress and other more objective data. The patient's emotional psychosomatic and psychogalvanic responses (Hoch, Wechsler, and others) offer helpful objective material for this evaluation.

In general, the measure of stress is the measure of psychobiologic responses. The researcher finds that emotionally unstable individuals are more easily frustrated than the well adjusted individual; that they can be affected more easily by, react stronger to, and recover more slowly from frustration.

Our findings in psychotherapy, even those based on clinical observations have definite sources of error. As stated above, our complex processes of applying psychotherapy are, as such, not conducive to research. Cures obtained by them are doubtful and deceptive criteria; for all methods—from Christian Science to orthodox psychoanalysis—claim "cures." Those familiar with the operation of Christian Scientists also know that there exists a factor in "cures" which can be termed "imaginary health," that sick individuals—with all their emotional and physical disabilities—in the mass-hysterical atmosphere of a Christian Science "testimonial" meeting may be induced to believe they are enjoying perfect health.

Thus we are forced to place more concrete demarcation lines around the *areas of improvement* we wish to evaluate. We can speak of (1) an "increased ego strength" deriving from a better integration of its parts; or (2) a better balance (homeostasis) between ego, superego and id, (3) we can gauge the individual's adjustment quota as regards his occupation, his interpersonal relations or his tolerance to discomforts (frustration and hostility); (4) we can compare the estimates of adjustment made at the start and the end of therapy and infer the rate of progress from the result of this comparison; (5) we can follow Freud who correlated progress with insight ("where id was, there shall ego be"), and evaluate the amount of id that was replaced by the ego.

CRITERIA OF SUCCESS

From all these points, it is clear that the evaluation is dependent—among other things—on the *value system* applied; and, for all we know, the patient may have a value system of his own. Therapy must, therefore, be appraised in terms of its importance for the individual's growth, and his specific goals. Neither the concept of "happiness," nor that of "virtue," nor even of social adjustment, can serve us in this respect; when Stekel speaks of "recovery to spite the therapist," or Bergler mentions "therapeutic success based on the patient's unconscious fear of further analysis," we can easily see that, as regards success, all the statistics and personal testimonials show a wide margin of vagueness.

The statistics of cures are tainted by many secondary factors, such as, selection of cases, definition of mental illness, type of psychotherapy applied (orthodox psychoanalysis, non-orthodox psychoanalysis, other methods), and, last but not least, by the definition of "cure."

As things stand today, we are operating with a large amount of approximations attempting to describe progress in psychotherapy which—as time goes on—will probably be replaced by a more reliable terminology.

Certainly, the question as to whether the improvement is permanent or temporary also deserves special consideration. Some of the patients we "cure" show relapses. Is the therapy at fault? Is therapy terminable at all (Freud)? What about spontaneous recoveries? Here we find a field for fruitful research.

The branching off of psychotherapy from the basic psychological conceptions is a good sign. It is a mark of growth. Gradually an "integrative" form of psychotherapy (Cameron) is developing which uses free associations, is non-directive, operates in a non-moralistic setting, and accepts the need for a biological (psycho-physiological) orientation. This development is predicated on the premise that in science we all learn from one another, enrich the total of acquired knowledge with our own clinical findings and formulations, and thus grow beyond our teachers and preceptors.

This development toward a "multi-dimensional approach" takes into account the fact that, according to the current scientific orientation, disease (or any other event) cannot be considered as provoked by this or that single cause. It is, as a rule, caused by a chain of conditions, of unequal value as provoking or contributing agents.

Modern psychotherapy, therefore, in evaluating its findings, strives toward a more effective linking of surface and depth, past and present, childhood and adulthood. Surface, present, adulthood, thus regain their dynamic importance for therapy, after having been relegated to a position of relative insignificance by the "retrospective" Freudian approach. The defenses and resistances of the ego, its reactions to aggression and frustration, the social and individual potentialities of the patient have again become objects of study. This study, however, is enriched by the analytic exploration of the dynamic forces of the depth. In many cases the new approach has necessitated changes of technique.

THE DIFFICULTY OF AGREEMENT

It is interesting and significant for the evaluation of the method that, despite all efforts of the official psychoanalytic bodies, and deliberations lasting for more than 4 years, the American Psychoanalytic Association was unable to "find a definition for psychoanalysis" that is acceptable to even a large group of members of the said Association. (*Bull. of the Am. Psa. Ass'n.,* vol. VIII, No. 1, March 1952, p. 49.) Moreover, a "strong resistance exists among the members to an investigation of the therapeutic results, even those based on their own definitions" (Oberndorf).

It was also found to be impossible to establish any true demarcation line between standard psychoanalysis (whatever its definition), analytic psychotherapy, psychotherapy, or brief psychoanalysis, for in practice all types were found to merge into one another. The vagueness of terminology and definitions in psychotherapy thus proves to represent one of the many obstacles to the scientific evaluation of the method.

A great deal of uncertainty also exists regarding the "meaning" of neurosis and the goals of psychotherapy. What are the criteria of a comparison? What is the ideal of health to be striven for? If "adaptive success" is considered a determining factor, the thing to which man is expected to adapt, is in itself vague and variable. We can say that man is well adapted if he shares the ideals of his community. But what is community? In this respect man is a part of the whole, its cause and effect, its master and its dependent. We also have as yet no unit at our disposal to measure the degree of adaptation, the degree of subjective happiness which accrues from a successful adaptation—if, indeed, "subjective happiness" is an acceptable factor in this set of values.

A scientific inquiry into the psychological fabric of the individual and his reactions to psychotherapy must be conducted backward and forward, as it were; it must include, to a great extent, his background, his physical and social environment, and also his long-range goals and strivings.

Recently, a number of leading psychologists and psychotherapists made an attempt to investigate some of the more important theoretical and practical implications of psychotherapy (Mowrer, *et al.*) by breaking down the relevant problems of the psychotherapeutic process into a number of part investigations. These workers studied psychotherapy as an interpersonal process and as a learning process; they attempted to measure quantitatively psychosomatic tension occurring in the patient during therapy; tried to record the emotional discharges in the patient (transference, resistance) and in the therapist (countertransference).

Despite all these serious attempts, however, much of what takes place in the therapeutic setting still remains a mystery. We should like to know more about the causes of our failures in therapy; understand better how successes achieved in one psychotherapeutic course compare with successes achieved after several courses of treatment; what types of patients need more than one course of therapy; what types ultimately land in institutions, regardless of any therapy; whether we have to study the entire life-history of the patient to understand his maladjustment; what part the application of a specific method of psychotherapy plays in success or failure; and many other urgent questions. Some workers have published the interesting claim that regarding ultimate results of individual psychotherapy, most of the common "schools" of psychotherapy offer the same figures (Heine). We have also heard (Glover, Oberndorf, *et al.*) that regarding the techniques used, a large margin of disagreement exists even among followers of the same school.[3]

CONTRIBUTION OF PSYCHOSOMATIC MEDICINE

In the study of problems connected with *psychosomatic medicine,* three definite stages are discernible. The first can be called the "pioneer stage," the second the "stage of expansion," and the third the "stage of consolidation." We are at present in the third phase of this development.

Among the concepts which entered into the early research in psychosomatic medicine were those of "organ inferiority" (Adler), "conditioned reflexes" (Pavlov), "physical types" (Kretschmer), "somatic destiny" (Sheldon), "genotype and phenotype" (Bauer), and others. Later the concepts of "homeostasis" (Cannon) and of "emotional thermodynamics" (Dunbar) were added, and—relatively recently—the "vector theory" (Alexander) and the "field theory" (Grinker).

All research is concerned with the mutual relations between *psyche* and *soma.* How do they affect one another both in health and disease? To what extent can physical disorders be considered psychogenic?

With the development of dynamic psychiatry, an attempt was made to penetrate psychoanalytically into mechanisms of psychosomatic interactions. This led to the formulation of theories which offered a basis for a psychosomatic therapy.

In the subsequent era, particularly after the second World War, the existing psychosomatic theories obtained wide diffusion among all branches of medicine. Shortly before the war, a representative "American Psychosomatic Society" was formed, which was concerned with the advancement of research and dissemination of related information among the medical profession. The official organ of the Society is *Psychosomatic Medicine,* a quarterly.

The search into the intricate correlations between mind and body is at present progressing steadily. However, while the scientific investigation is going on, results of some preliminary and as yet inconclusive experimental studies have obtained wide acceptance. A number of stereotyped interpretations have found their way into the literature, interpretations which seem to offer both a useful theoretical frame of reference and a prospect for an effective therapeutic approach.

It is because of this overpopularization of psychosomatic clichés, that we should become more keenly aware of the fact that a marked discrepancy still exists between theory and practice of psychosomatic medicine. Although the use of psychotherapy is advocated for all branches of medicine, the therapeutic utilization of the psychosomatic findings seems to lie almost exclusively in the hands of psychiatrists.

At a recent meeting of the American College of Physicians in Atlantic City, in which about 4,000 physicians participated, William Menninger suggested that every patient of every physician should receive from five to ten minutes of psychotherapy along with the routine medications. Brosin recommended that, to manage their cases more effectively, doctors should use "purchased supervision" from psychiatrists. Some questions arose regarding the technical procedures to be applied in referring a patient to the psychiatrist.

Little is being said about the type of dynamic psychotherapy the non-psychiatrist can use, and how he can acquire the knack and skill necessary for its application. This is probably the reason why the interest of medical men in psychosomatic medicine which, at first, was very strong, has recently cooled off considerably.

Medical practitioners are beginning to feel that the methodical application of standard types of psychotherapy in non-psychiatric practice is too complicated and time-consuming to be of real value to them, and that all they can hope to do for their patients is—to refer them to psychiatrists. They see in the theoretical dissertation on psychosomatic medicine little more than an instruction on the best ways of transferring their medical patients to the psychiatrists. Admittedly, this cannot be considered a tempting object for the practitioner's interest in psychosomatic medicine.

The time seems to be ripe for reflexion. Recently, efforts have been at work to reach a theoretical formulation which would embody a synthesis between organic and functional medicine. Especially the contributions of the so-called "Chicago Group" (Alexander, French, Grinker, Saul and others), have helped to clear some of the existing confusion and have permitted us to see the total problem from a better perspective. To some extent they make use of ideas which have migrated into medicine from other modern sciences and philosophies. They accentuate the integrative forces originating in genetic, physiological, psychological, anthropological and social forces. They include concepts of "interaction of causes and effects" within certain developmental spheres ("fields")—in preference to the concept of a (linear) "cause and effect" development in the individual. In this categorial system, "psychosomatic" medicine, "mind-body unity" and the like, become synonymous with medicine in general. It is a challenging concept, to say the least, which takes into consideration a number of varied determinants in their varying degrees of integration, including the state of "health" as well as that of "sickness," and of the many conditions that exist in between.

Time will show how useful these new ideas are in practice. However, even the boldest and farthest-reaching interpretations of psychosomatic mechanisms will not compensate for one basic deficiency which keeps on preventing the full utilization of these achievements in medical practice; the complicated standard therapeutic technique, which can be used only by psychiatrists. There is no doubt that medicine at large has greatly profited from the psychosomatic findings of psychiatrists. However, this writer is convinced that as long as psychiatry has not adopted an effective method of dynamic short-term psychotherapy which can be used successfully in non-psychiatric medical practice, psychosomatic medicine will remain, as it is at present, primarily an internal affair of the psychotherapists, with medical practitioners acting as interested onlookers.[4]

II. PRACTICE

A. THERAPY

The aims of modern psychotherapy are: normalization of the patient's behavior to a degree that enables him (1) to gain or regain a better adaptation to his environment, and (2) establish better relations with his fellow men. These aims are the synthesis of most current psychotherapeutic trends.

In recent years the area of exploration and application of psychotherapy has widened, the human personality has been more thoroughly investigated; and techniques, indications, and methodology have been improved.

At first, a small number of hysterical conditions were treated by psychoanalysis. At present, the scope of the method has widened to include psychosomatic conditions, some forms of insanity, many nervous conditions of children and some types of delinquency. However, alongside of this expansion, our insight has also extended to conditions to which the standard form of psychotherapy is not applicable, or where it is even contraindicated. This insight has been fostered by further research into the problems of psychoses, psychopathic personalities, and social maladjustments.

New psychotherapeutic approaches had to be sought and the existing ones modified. Almost from the beginning of the so-called Freudian era in psychotherapy, we find a growth of various "schools" of psychotherapy which are either offshoots of the original school, or its ramifications, or have developed independently. They concern themselves with an elaboration of the existing theories and the exploration of new vistas. This is a satisfactory sign of growth, for rigidity leads to stagnation and sterility, and every progress is marked by dissension and rebellion. Looking over the post-Freudian development of psychotherapy, we notice that "schools" are centers of crystallization of ideas, some new, some old; most, however, are related in one way or other to the basic stock of Freud's genius. They represent areas of emphasis of individual aspects of psycho-analytic theory and practice, yet each school has a definite contribution to make, each adding its own specific values.

All are striving toward a better understanding of the human personality and the mental processes in health and disease. Future psychotherapy will probably draw on all these contributions, although some of them, on closer scrutiny, prove to be, in part, restatements of concepts formulated decades ago, concepts which now appear in new contexts and are endowed with new meaning. The increased interest in the psychology of the ego, for instance, has given new emphasis to the findings of Alfred Adler on aggression and the importance of social factors in the adjustment of the individual within his environment.

VALUE OF DISSIDENTS

Freud's three early dissenters, *Jung, Adler* and *Stekel,* have fertilized several current trends in psychotherapy. Jung's anthropological views, Adler's emphasis on the socialization of the individual, and Stekel's reforms of the psychotherapeutic technique (emphasis on the "current conflict situation," or "activity" in psychotherapy, etc.) are also among the trends of present-day psychotherapy, as represented by Sullivan, Horney, Kardiner, Alexander and others. Also *Wilhelm Reich's* work on character analysis has recently obtained renewed significance.

Even the early analytic literature shows quests for reforms which involve theoretical and practical aspects of therapy. Whenever the scope of analytic therapy was widened, it was done at the expense of some of the standard rules. We can safely say that, except for some limited circles where "pure Freudian psychoanalysis" is practiced in an orthodox manner, the present practice of psychoanalysis has (fortunately) absorbed a large number of reforms, involving both theory and practice, to become essentially a "psychoanalytic psychotherapy." That is the result of inevitable, constant assimilation of progressive views fostered by improved clinical methods, renunciation of purely speculative findings and a more realistic approach to the needs of the patient.

As stated above, attempts toward abbreviation and activation of the method have been going on for a long time. *Ferenczi's* break with Freud in the early twenties was motivated by it, and so was *Rank's* dissension. Ferenczi advocated a more active form of psychoanalysis, emphasizing also, more than the original method, the display of empathy toward the patient. Rank attempted to correlate the original neuroses with what he called the "trauma of birth." Subsequently, he developed an independent active method of analytic psychotherapy which he called "Will Therapy" (recently also called "Dynamic Relationship Therapy") by which he attempted to induce the patient to use the analytic insight for deliberate (creative) psychological reorientation (Therapy=Art). During his stay in the United States he secured a definite following, especially among social workers.

Stekel's "active form of psychoanalysis" and *Alexander's* "brief psychoanalysis" represent unmistakenly rejections of the standard technique. The publications of many clinical workers add validity to such reforms. The need for them goes parallel with a reduction of the scope of indications for the standard method, mentioned above. One feels confused and bewildered when, in reading the clinical reports, one finds more and more clinical entities characterized as unsuitable for the standard form of psychoanalysis. One feels like asking, What is there that remains suitable for it?

Alexander in his work *Psychoanalytic Therapy* (1946), states: "Like most psychoanalysts, we have been puzzled by the unpredictability of therapeutic results, by the baffling discrepancy between length and intensity of a treatment and the degree of therapeutic success. That there is no simple correlation between therapeutic results and the length and intensity of treatment has been recognized, tacitly or explicitly, by most experienced psychoanalysts, and is an old source of dissatisfaction among them."

NEW TECHNIQUES NEEDED

Alexander also mentions that among the old-school psychoanalysts there is "an almost superstitious belief that quick therapeutic results cannot be genuine." Because of the "adverse propaganda" directed by some groups against any deviation from the hallowed procedure, many analysts consider the reformers as unscientific, ineffectual, wild, or outright dishonest.

Those who advocate short-term therapeutic procedures have long recognized (1) that the length of psychotherapy is not equivalent to depth, i.e., a deep penetration is possible even when less time has been consumed; (2) that the therapeutic results and the ratio of new relapses in short and prolonged procedures are the same; and (3) that an unsuccessful analytic therapy cannot become successful through the introduction of additional sessions. They are convinced that, instead, new techniques must be evolved that would fit the needs of the individual cases. Foremost of all, we must develop psychoanalytic techniques which can be applied under clinic conditions so that they can be really useful to the needs of the community. However, the techniques must not trespass against accepted scientific standards or jeopardize the therapeutic success in favor of adherence to the credo of a school.

Stekel's method of "Active Psychoanalysis" has brought about a reform of the technique in all its dimensions. It introduces the factor of activity and directiveness, the most dreaded bugbears of the orthodox procedure. It puts the analyst back into the forefront of the therapeutic process from which he has been relegated by Freud, to serve only as a screen for the patient's ruminations and a target for the patient's aggressions.

"ACTIVITY" IN DEPTH THERAPY

Stekel's therapist is not a "silent Sam," but a kindly, interested team-partner who helps the patient—on the basis of the material produced and the experiences obtained within the analytic situation—to find the best possible solution for the emotional conflicts which beset him.

Both Stekel and Alexander exert their "activity" not by hurling interpretations onto an unprepared patient, but by modulating the frequency of interviews, by "manipulating" transference to suit the particular treatment phase, by employing or omitting the couch judiciously, by interpreting details of the analytic situation, and of the patient's basic attitudes (at a time warranted by the rate of the flow of material), and by a number of other supportive measures, such as re-education, guidance, etc.

Stekel has also reformed the technique of dream interpretation so as to make it a powerful tool in collecting analytically usable material and in stimulating the patient's cooperation in therapy.[6]

In further elaboration of his theories, *Gutheil* published two works on dreams[7] in which the attempt is made to demonstrate (1) to what extent dreams can be interpreted without the patient's aid and (2) how this technique can be used to foster the diagnostic, prognostic, and therapeutic aims of the analyst. The first part of the reformed technique was designed especially to enable the analyst to deal with prepared and prefabricated "free" associations and other forms of resistance deriving from the patient's knowledge of analytic concepts.

We must not forget that during the 50 years that passed since Freud saw his first analytic patients, the *patient material* has changed considerably. This change is due, in part, to the success of the public education rendered by psychiatry and psychoanalysis to a wide circle of the public. Some of our patients today know more about psychodynamics than psychiatrists did in Freud's days. The increased insight has led not only to a slanting of the so-called "free associations" but also to far-reaching regroupings of the pathogenic complexes in the patients' minds. We are facing today many more instances of secondary repressions, amnesia, shift of defenses and of levels of cognizance than ever before. (Autoimmunization against analytic therapy?) Much of this psychopathology is due to the absorption by the patient of psychoanalytic insight and utilization of it as new psychic defenses.

This condition justifies the use of new theoretical formulations and new interpretative and therapeutic approaches, such as an intensive application of dream analysis.

Both Stekel and Gutheil protested against Freud's contention that analysts stopped publishing dream analyses and behaved "as though they had nothing more to say about the dream."[8] Gutheil pointed out that Freud could have meant only the orthodox analysts, and that the cause may have been the cumbersome and time-consuming technique they were using.

Robert Fliess recently published a critical book on dreams[9] in which he points out that in the orthodox circles the interest in dreams has been revived lately. He does not offer an explanation as to what factors may have rekindled this interest. In an aloof and somewhat arrogant manner, he mentions that some work in this respect has also been done by non-orthodox analysts, but their names remain "unquotable," and they are thus not even deemed deserving of an adverse criticism. He maintains, however, that Freud's own work on dreams was so exhaustive that only few additions could be made.

Stekel's one-time warning that not all cases we treat require, for recovery, an analytic exploration reaching back into the mother's womb, and that the "current conflict" must not be overlooked, has been gradually accepted by many experienced analysts—tacitly, or otherwise. Oberndorf states that the experienced American analysts have come to the conclusion that "only in a relatively few instances can the method be applied as (Freud) recommended it." He emphasizes that the infantile material should be submitted to the patient's catharsis only in those cases where the patient can profit from it in his current conflict situation.

This is true particularly of cases where the patient's ego is found to be weak or deficient, and the therapist is concerned lest a deep psychoanalytic penetration reduce the patient's ego defenses and thus trigger off a latent psychosis. Indeed, recent analytic contributions to the pathology of the ego have created in the minds of some psychotherapists an exaggerated fear lest the dynamic process as such cause a dormant psychosis to become manifest. Practitioners in psychotherapy are warned by their more experienced colleagues not to interpret too much in such cases, not to go "too deep" into the historical material, not to remove this or that obsessive idea—because otherwise "the ego may collapse and the psychosis break out."

LATENT PSYCHOSES

If a patient diagnosed as a case of "latent psychosis" shows a striking pathological reaction in response to therapy, this does not necessarily mean that the analyst is releasing the psychosis, or that the patient's defenses are crumbling. The patient may be "acting out" some of his complexes, and we must simply learn to deal with such behavior. The patient's psychodrama may show a wealth of meaning which can be used constructively for therapy.

The second thing we must learn is that a neurosis does not "become" a psychosis as a result of poor therapy. It does so more frequently as a result of poor diagnosis. If we fail to recognize in a patient a manifest psychosis and expose him to the standard type of psychoanalysis, the patient may, sooner or later, "experience a nervous breakdown" or commit suicide.

A psychosis does not represent an especially virulent form of neurosis. The difference between the two is qualitative rather than quantitative. Psychotic reactions occur only as symptoms of an underlying psychosis which may, otherwise, remain obscure. Conditions of severe and protracted stress, prolonged use of certain drugs or biological substances (for instance ACTH) and similar derangements of the psychobiological homeostasis, may also release a dormant psychosis. To recognize a latent psychosis, therefore, is a foremost diagnostic task.

Meanwhile recent explorations have widened the field of the

so-called "latent" and "pseudoneurotic" psychoses (Federn, Hoch, Polatin). Many such cases have remained unrecognized and were treated for many years by the classical method of psychoanalysis. It is here that the problem of releasing dormant psychoses arises. For according to the views expressed by experienced and unbiased psychoanalysts, of all psychotherapeutic approaches, the standard five-times-a-week psychoanalysis is most prone to release dormant psychoses. Other forms of psychotherapy, even those which are analytically oriented, operate in a much milder emotional climate; they do not, as a rule, produce violent transferences, overdependencies, or prolonged involvements in the infantile fantasy world. Psychotherapists who work in clinics or who are using abbreviated and active forms of psychoanalysis have no reason to be overly concerned with the problem of releasing psychoses. Unless they commit gross therapeutic blunders, their operations will be free from noxious influences.

Some psychotherapists are convinced that psychoanalysis in its original form is capable not only of releasing dormant *psychotic* reactions, but that it is also capable of releasing unwarranted *neurotic* reactions. The persistent passivity and frustration to which the patient is exposed during the many years of his therapy, as well as the artificially induced retrospection, emotional regression and dependency on the analyst, kept alive by the force of transference, generate in the patient not only conditions favorable for a breakthrough of a latent psychosis, but also release in the neurotic so much more aggression than is needed for catharsis, that new neurotic symptoms can easily be provoked. New conversions, tics, and obsessions are often induced, new anxieties are stimulated, which, under circumstances, may flood the defensive barriers of the ego. This *factitial neurosis,* superimposed as it is upon the original neurosis, must, of course, be dealt with by the therapist, a task which requires additional investment of time and effort.

Among the American psychotherapeutic schools which trace their origin to or have derived their theoretical matrix from

Freud, are also those of Harry Stack Sullivan, Karen Horney and Carl Rogers.

Harry Stack Sullivan studies the interpersonal relations (compare Adler's *"Gemeinschaftsgefühl"*) through his investigation of the relation of the patient to the therapist (transference) and of the therapist to the patient (countertransference). Sullivan tries to evaluate the patient's relation to his environment. He proceeds from the supposition (Stekel) that the transference situation reproduces not only an early family constellation (child-parent) but also the patient's most important relation toward the outside world.

Sullivan views the patient's relation toward people against the backdrop of the analytic situation. He concerns himself with the patient's character structure first and his symptoms second. He expects that an analytic reorganization of the character structure will reduce the patient's propensity toward neurotic reactions. Through his own permissive attitude he shows the patient that not all people are threatening and frustrating. He thus gives the patient an opportunity to feel protected and to abandon gradually his symptoms which no longer have to play their defensive, protective and compensatorily gratifying rôle.

Among the dissidents from the original Freudian school, we also find *Karen Horney*. She emphasizes the socio-cultural factors both in the formation of personality and in the etiology of neuroses. She disagrees with Freud on so many basic issues that one may rightly ask whether her method can still be called psychoanalysis. For instance, she denies that the development of personality is based on the individual's psychosexual development; she does not believe in the universal validity of the Oedipus complex; that neurotic conflicts necessarily result from patterns established in childhood; that libido is a core of personality. She assumes that human behavior is primarily a product of cultural influences.

The (biologically oriented) *Freud* studied —	The (sociologically oriented) *Horney* studied —
the instinctual factors —	the cultural factors;
the "inside" influences —	the "outside" influences;
the constitution —	the constellation;
the heredity —	the environment;
the infantile traumata —	the current conflicts;
the sexual urges —	the non-sexual (social) manifestations of love (being accepted);
the sexually conceived "pleasure principle" —	the socially conceived "pleasure principle" including any form of gratification;
the conflict between ego, id and superego.	the conflict between individual and environment.

While Freud considered libido as the basic principle guiding human behavior, Horney conceived of security and satisfaction as the two guiding principles of human behavior. According to her, human personality is a product of environmental forces. She, therefore, assumed that society, as a responsible agent of security, can breed or prevent neurosis. She hopefully expected that a change or improvement of society was capable of rendering the individual's life happier and healthier.

Carl Rogers has introduced what he calls a "client-centered," non-directive psychotherapy. It proceeds from the supposition that in the client (patient) there are forces for growth and "self-actualization" which motivate him toward therapy. The client, therefore, can be trusted to find a satisfactory solution for his problems, provided he can do that within the warm and permissive therapeutic atmosphere. He can explore even those of his attitudes which are shut off from his conscious awareness, and do so without experiencing too much anxiety. Having thus recognized his potentialities, he may feel induced to make better use of them. Rogers divides the therapeutic process into the following phases: [10]

(1) The individual comes for help. (2) The therapeutic situation is defined. (3) The therapist encourages free expression regarding conflicts. (4) He accepts and clarifies (for the client) the nature of his negative feelings (resistances). (5) Positive feelings are then discussed and factors evaluated that "make for **growth." (6) Insight follows the understanding and acceptance** of the "self." (7) Clarification of decisions and possible courses of action. (8) Initiation of minute but significant positive actions. (9) Further insight and encouragement through individual gains following action. (10) Increasingly integrated positive actions. (11) Decrease of need for help and feeling the therapeutic relation should end.

Among those followers of Freudian theory who introduced new techniques to improve therapeutic results, we may also mention *John Rosen*. In his *Direct Analysis*[11] Rosen describes his independence of the analytic technique. He uses the unconscious material elicited from observation and from the patient's verbal communications, to bombard the patient with it as a means of enforced insight. A basically similar approach, though much less "direct," was used by Séchehaye in her now famous case presentation.[12]

A group which represents a useful combination of psychological and physiological principles is the school of *Adolf Meyer*. Meyer, who was influenced by Freud and Pavlov, introduced into American psychiatry modern methods of compiling and utilizing the patient's case history, which includes hereditary and environmental, constitutional, social and economic, conscious and unconscious factors. He calls his approach "psychobiological." His "common-sense psychiatry," which attempts to evaluate accurately the patient's personality, (or as he calls it "the whole individual in action") aims at helping the patient to understand his self with all its psychic and somatic endowments, in order to change the "mutable," and adapt to the "immutable" internal and external factors.

PSYCHOTHERAPY AND EXISTENTIALISM

The new *European trends* are predicated upon the idea that psychotherapy needs a far-reaching philosophical foundation. According to Jaspers, "every psychotherapist is inescapably also a philosopher."

The new philosophically conditioned trend in psychotherapy goes back to Plato, Descartes, Kant, Hegel and Schelling. Although the views of these philosophers were by no means uniform and often even in contradiction with one another, they have in various ways, particularly in regard to the *theory of human existence,* contributed to the philosophical background of the main current psychotherapeutic concepts in Europe.

Kierkegaard maintained that truth lies in subjectivity and that true existence is achieved by the intensity of one's individual emotions. The "existent" individual is something unique; it is one who is in closest relation with himself and has infinite interest in his own destiny, one who has a task before him, the task of "becoming" something through maintained effort. Surrounded with uncertainty and yet able or forced to make decisions he craves fulfillment; the object of his thought and desire is the infinite. (Kirkegaard is intensely Christian, for him the infinite is Christ.)

Heidegger is strongly influenced by Kierkegaard. He maintains that Man is born into this world, a world limited by death, a world which in its temporality and solitude he experiences with anxiety. The task of living ("being-in" the world) is to find an individual formula, based on faith, for his "possibility" and following it through by a "resolute decision." (One of such "resolute decisions" must have been Heidegger's acceptance of the Nazi doctrine during the days of its temporary triumph.)

The philosophical followers of *Kierkegaard,* are *Jaspers* and *Heidegger.* The medical ones are *Binswanger, Szondi* and *Frankl.*

GROUP THERAPY

Among the advances of psychotherapy, we may mention also

the steady growth of the *group-psychotherapy movement*. This movement, too, shows a lively trend toward ramification and subdivision. Sociological, religious and psychoanalytic principles serve as rallying points of the groups. All of them have as theoretical basis the idea that a group in therapy represents a miniature world, that the individual within the group is likely to display the same reactions as he does in the world at large, and that any favorable changes effected within the therapeutic group are likely to alter the individual's position within his social environment.

The theory of group therapy incorporates the concept of the universal nature of suffering and postulates that within the group this suffering will emerge and can be dealt with as though under laboratory conditions. Hostilities, dependencies, rivalries, morbid ambitions, and all the maladjustments which exist within the human relations, can be spotlighted and ameliorated under the coöperative effort of the members of the group and its leader.

A special type of group psychotherapy represents the psychodrama originated by *J. L. Moreno*. Moreno distinguishes between three types of psychotherapy. Accepting the Shakespearean idea of the "world is a stage," he introduces a new terminology borrowed from that of the theatre. He speaks of the "monologue type of psychotherapy" to which belong therapies operating with autosuggestion, such as those practiced by Coué or by the Yogi. Most of the modern psychotherapies are of the "dialogue type" and consist of a communication between the therapist and the patient. In his psychodrama Moreno attempts to combine the monologue, the dialogue, the catharsis and the group-therapeutic principles, the latter as a part of the patient's participation in the spontaneous stage performances.

While Moreno's method is predominantly cathartic, other methods emphasize psychoanalytic and socio-reëducational points. *Schilder, Wender* and *Alexander Wolf* are in the first group, while *Moreno, Slavson* and their followers represent the second group.

In the last few years the idea of an analytically oriented group psychotherapy has obtained wide diffusion. Hospitals, social institutions, and rehabilitation groups were thus given an opportunity to benefit from the modern psychotherapeutic findings on a more extensive scale.

In further development of the concept of group psychotherapy, we have witnessed the introduction of *social adjustment groups,* such as they are advocated by *Maxwell Jones* in England. This method goes beyond group therapy. His therapy encompasses not only the patient, but all his contacts within the hospital community. Doctors and nurses, the entire administrative apparatus is involved in the rehabilitation of desocialized patients. Jones speaks of a "therapeutic community" which systematically prepares the patient for his return to normal life. Jones believes that the results obtained in this experimental setting at Belmont Hospital could not have been obtained either by individual or by the usual group psychotherapy. (*Therapeutic Community,* Basic Books, 1953.)

Adjunctive Therapy

Lately, the *hypnotic approach* has also been revived and given an adjunctive rôle within the therapeutic situation. In its present form it is not considered an independent therapeutic method but a specific intensified form of a transference relationship. (Wolberg: *Hypno-analysis;* Schilder: *Psychotherapy;* Brennan and Knight: *Bulletin Menninger Clinic,* 12:49, 1948).

Semantics

Some of the standard-school analysts make a strict differentiation between the results obtainable by psychoanalysis and those that can be secured by other forms of psychotherapy. In my opinion, this division into *psychoanalysis and psychotherapy* is arbitrary. Many analysts seem to believe (1) that a nonorthodox (though dynamically oriented) psychotherapy is, by its nature, limited to the therapy of specific problems; (2) that in a non-orthodox psychotherapy less investigation is devoted to the interpretation of the unconscious, and more to the preconscious material. (Rich. Frank: *Progress of Neurology and Psychiatry,* Grune and Stratton, New York, 1950). I have criticized this arbitrary division· as a fallacy. ("Psa. and Brief Psychotherapy," *Jl. Clin. Psychopathology,* VI, 2, 1944).

Knight (*Bulletin of N.Y. Academy of Medicine,* 28, 1949) says: "In the last analysis there is only one psychotherapy with many techniques." Kenneth Appel ("Psychiatric Therapy") writes: "There is something basically effective in the process of therapy in general which is independent of the methods employed." Shoben ("Psychotherapy as a Problem in Learning Theory," *Psychol. Bulletin,* 46, 1949) maintains that all forms of psychotherapy claim significant amounts of cure; all aim at diminishing the patient's basic anxieties; all use communications, and the doctor-patient relation as important factors in bringing about changes.

It is to be hoped that the psychotherapy of the future will arrive at a *consolidation* and *simplification* of its *terminology* which, at present, appears to divide where a *defacto* unanimity exists. It is hard, nowadays, for the student of psychiatry to find his bearings among the many psychological definitions. Is the "self" identical with the "ego"? Is the "latent" schizophrenia the same as the "pseudoneurotic" one? Are the "idealized image" and the "superego" equivalent? Are Sullivan's "interpersonal relations" the same as Adler's "community feelings" or Horney's "moving toward" another person? Is Horney's "need for acceptance" identical with Adler's "need to be important?"

A *Manual* that could lead the student out of the terminological jungle of present-day psychotherapeutic concepts would be a blessing for all concerned.

B. Training

Today we expect the psychotherapist (1) to be able to diagnose the psychological conditions underlying the patient's presenting symptom, (2) to evaluate the patient's ego strength and (3) to make a decision regarding choice of therapy, i.e., to plan the initial "strategy" of the psychotherapeutic approach. The therapist must (4) be fully familiar with the psychodynamics of the therapeutic process and also be able to reconstruct the dynamic processes that have led to the patient's emotional maladjustment. Finally, (5) the therapist is expected to have a sufficiently stable personality to warrant an unbiased and relatively symptom-free conduct of therapy.

To prepare the psychotherapist for this task, various training programs have been devised. The training requirements in the orthodox circles represent a source of controversy. The current training analysis lasts (a minimum of) 200 hours at 4 to 5 sessions a week. (Many hundreds of sessions are no rare exception). The candidate's personal qualifications, such as his therapeutic dexterity or diagnostic acumen have little influence on this rigid set-up of training.

These requirements with their associated economic repercussions, have contributed a great deal to the schisms and disagreements among the individual member societies of the orthodox group.

One of them, the so-called "Rado group," (Rado, Kardiner, Daniels, David Levy and others) formed in 1946 an "Association for Psychoanalytic Medicine" and functions as a "Psychoanalytic Clinic for Training and Research" independently of the N.Y. Psychoanalytic Society. It is affiliated with Columbia University, which offers the group candidates a residency training in "psychoanalytic medicine."

Oberndorf (*A History of American Psychoanalysis,* Grune and Stratton, 1953) deplores the fact that the training program has been "somewhat conventionalized." He feels that it "leads to stereotyped thinking and codified, even mechanized, interpretation, which satisfies the analyst's formulas but may not necessarily contribute to the patient's mastering of his difficulties . . ." Oberndorf is also of the opinion that the prolonged contact with the therapist may impress upon the candidate ideas of his analyst which he may feel obliged to propagate—at the expense of his own constructive contributions. I pointed this out in my article on "Brief Psychotherapy and Psychoanalysis" some years ago, when I predicted that the advantages of standardization of a method are far outweighed by the drawback of "inbreeding." Transferences and countertransferences, kept alive for many years of intensive personal contacts, are bound to influence the individual's capacity for independent thinking, and for a healthy self-criticism. However, Oberndorf thinks that the "undeviating adherence to Freud's original concept and scope of psychoanalysis is weakening among experienced psychoanalysts."

Alongside of this hopeful development, we note that today more and more psychiatric residents are being trained in psychoanalysis, that this training is considered essential for their specialty, that the psychiatric departments encourage this, that medical schools teach psychoanalytic concepts, that the U.S.P.H. grants fellowships in psychoanalytic training and supports institutions for this type of training.

C. PROPHYLAXIS

The results of these developments are of great value to the prevention of mental disease, and open new avenues in the social and educational fields.

In the social fields, the modern analytic findings have contributed to a better understanding of the problems of security, of interpersonal relations, the pathological strivings for power, neurotic inferiority and guilt reactions and similar maladjustments. As a result, the relations between teacher and student, teacher and parent, parent and child were improved.

All forms of psychotherapy today are directed toward prophylaxis of mental disease and economy in therapeutic procedures. Military psychiatry, and state hospitals are making extensive use of the progressive forms of psychotherapy.

A tremendous job has been accomplished by the Mental Health movement, as far as public education is concerned.

PRESENT-DAY PSYCHOLOGY

While in the not-too-distant past it was possible to hear: "You are going to a psychiatrist? You ought to have your head examined;" the need for psychotherapy and its acceptance as a legitimate approach is today fully recognized. Medical, social, and educational agencies today realize that every analyzed and cured neurotic is an investment in health for the future generations.

FOOTNOTES

[1] The Theory of Aggression. *The Psa. Study of the Child,* International Universities Press, 1949.

[2] Rado. (1) Mind, Unconscious Mind and Brain, *Psychosomatic Medicine,* II, 1948 and (2) Psychosexual Development in Health and Disease, Grune & Stratton, 1949.

Horney. *New Ways in Psychoanalysis,* W. W. Norton & Co., 1939.

Knight. A Critique of the Present Status of the Psychotherapies, *Bull. of N. Y. Academy of Medicine,* 1949.

[3] From the Editorial, *Am. Jl. of Psychotherapy,* vol. VII, *3,* 1953.

[4] From the Editorial of the *Am. Jl. of Psychotherapy,* vol. VII, *2,* 1953.

[5] Ferenczi and Rank. *Entwicklungsziele der Psychoanalyse.* Vienna: Int. Psa. Verl., 1924.

[6] *Fortschritte und Technik der Traumdeutung.* Vienna: Verl. für Medizin, 1935.

The Interpretation of Dreams. New York: Liveright, 1943.

[7] *Language of the Dream.* New York: Macmillan & Co., 1939.

The Handbook of Dream Analysis. New York: Liveright Pub. Corp., 1951.

[8] Freud, S. *New Introductory Lectures on Psychoanalysis.* New York: Norton, 1933.

[9] Fliess, R. *The Revival of Interest in the Dream.* New York: Int. Universities Press, 1953.

[10] *Counseling and Psychotherapy.* Boston: Houghton Mifflin & Co., 1942.

[11] Grune & Stratton, Inc., New York, 1953.

[12] Séchehaye. *La réalisation symbolique.* Bern: Hans Huber, 1947.

BIBLIOGRAPHY

Adler, A. *Der nervöse Charakter.* Munich: Bergman, 1922.
——*The Practice and Theory of Individual Psychology.* London: Kegan Paul, Trench, Trubner & Co., 1924.
Alexander and French. *Psychoanalytic Theory,* Ronald Press, 1946.
——*Studies in Psychosomatic Medicine,* Ronald Press, 1948.
Binswanger, L. *Grundformen und Erkenntnis menschl. Dasein.* Zürich: Niehans, 1942.
Brody, E. *et al. Psychotherapy with Schizophrenics,* International Universities Press, 1950.

Brower and Abt. *Progress in Clinical Psychology,* I, *1.* Grune & Stratton, 1952.

Bychowski, G. *Psychotherapy of Psychosis,* Grune & Stratton, 1952.

Cameron, D. E. *Objective and Experimental Psychiatry,* 1935.

——*General Psychotherapy,* Grune & Stratton, 1950.

Cannon, W. B. *Bodily Changes in Pain, Hunger, Fear and Rage.* Appleton, 1915.

De Grazia, S. *Errors of Psychotherapy,* Doubleday & Co., 1952.

Dunbar, F. *Emotion and Bodily Changes,* Columbia University Press, 1943.

Federn, P. *Ego Psychology and Psychoses,* Basic Books, 1953.

Ferenczi, S. and Rank, O. *Entwicklungsziele der Psychoanalyse.* Int. Psa. Verlag., 1924.

Fliess, R. *The Revival of Interest in the Dream,* International Universities Press, 1953.

Frank, R. *Progress of Neurology and Psychiatry,* Grune & Stratton, Inc., 1950.

Frankl, V. *Aerztliche Seelsorge.* Vienna: Deuticke, 1946.

Freud, A. *Ego and Mechanisms of Defense,* International Universities Press, 1946.

Freud, S. *New Introductory Lectures on Psychoanalysis,* W. W. Norton & Co., 1933.

Fromm-Reichmann, F. *Principles of Intense Psychotherapy.* The University of Chicago Press, 1950.

Glover, E. *Investigation of the Technique of Psychoanalysis,* Williams & Wilkins, 1950.

Grinker, R. R. *Psychosomatic Research,* W. W. Norton & Co., 1953.

Gutheil, E. A. *Language of the Dream,* Macmillan & Co., 1939.

——*The Handbook of Dream Analysis,* Liveright Pub. Corp., 1951.

——Psychoanalysis and Brief Psychotherapy. *Journal of Clinical Psychopathology,* 1944.

Hartmann, L. and Kris. The Theory of Aggression. *The Psa. Study of the Child,* International Universities Press, 1949.

Heidegger, M. *Sein u. Zeit.* Niemeyer, Halle, 1929.

Heine, R. W. A Comparison of Patients' Reports on Psychotherapeutic Experience. *American Journal of Psychotherapy,* VII, *1,* 1953.

Hoch, P. and Polatin, P. Pseudoneurotic Forms of Schizophrenia. *The Psychiatric Quarterly,* April 1949.

Hoch, P. and Zubin, J. *Anxiety,* Grune & Stratton, 1950.

Horney, K. *New Ways in Psychoanalysis,* W. W. Norton & Co., 1939.

Jacobi, J. *The Psychology of Jung,* Yale University Press, 1943.

Jaspers, K. *Allgemeine Psychopathologie,* 1913.

Jones, M. *Therapeutic Community,* Basic Books, 1953.

Jung, C. G. *Psychology of the Unconscious,* Kegan Paul, Trench, Trubner & Co., 1927.

——*Collected Papers on Analytic Psychology.* London: Baillière, Tindall & Co., 1920.

——*Psychological Types—Psychology of Individuation,* Harcourt Brace & Co., 1923.

Kardiner, A. *The Traumatic Neuroses of War,* Hoeber, 1941.

Karpf, F. S. *The Psychology and Psychotherapy of Otto Rank,* Philosophical Library, 1953.

Knight, R. P. A Critique of the Present Status of the Psychotherapies. *Bull. N. Y. Academy of Medicine,* 1949.

Kretschmer, E. *Körperbau und Charakter.* Berlin: Springer, 1936.
Moreno, J. L. Who Shall Survive? *Nerv. & Mental Dis. Publ.,* 1934.
Mowrer, O. H. *Psychotherapy,* Ronald Press, 1953.
Oberndorf, C. P. *A History of American Psychoanalysis,* Grune & Stratton, 1953.
Pavlov, I. P. *Condit. Reflexes and Psychiatry.* New York: Intern. Publishers, 1941.
——*Collected Papers,* vol. III, No. 2, 1951 (Russian).
Rado, S. Mind, Unconscious Mind and Brain. *Psychosomatic Medicine,* II, 1948.
Rank, O. *Will Therapy and Truth Reality,* Alfred Knopf, 1945.
Reid, J. R. and Feinsinger, J. S. The Role of Definitions in Psychiatry. *American Journal of Psychiatry,* 1952, *109,* 413.
Reich, W. *Character Analysis,* Orgone Instit. Press, 1945.
Rogers, C. *Counseling and Psychotherapy,* Houghton, Mifflin, 1942.
Rosen, J. *Direct Analysis,* Grune & Stratton, 1953.
Schilder, P. *Psychotherapy,* W. W. Norton & Co., 1938.
Séchehaye, M. A. *Symbolic Realization,* Int. Universities Press, 1951.
Slavson, S. R. *Child Psychotherapy,* Columbia Univ. Press, 1952.
——Ed. *The Practice of Group Psychotherapy,* Int. Universities Press, 1947.
Shoben, L. J. Psychotherapy and a Problem in Learning Theory. *Psychol. Bulletin, 46,* 1949.
Stekel, W. *Technique of Analytical Psychotherapy,* Liveright Pub. Corp., 1950.
——*The Interpretation of Dreams,* Liveright Pub. Corp., 1943.
Szondi, L. *Schicksalsanalyse,* Schwabe, 1948.
——*Triebpathologie.* Bern: Huber, 1952.
Sullivan, H. S. *The Interpersonal Theory of Psychiatry,* W. W. Norton & Co., 1953.
Wittels, F. *Sigmund Freud.* Vienna: E. P. Tal & Co., 1924.
Wolff, W. and Precker, J. *Success in Psychotherapy,* Grune & Stratton, 1952.

CHAPTER XXVII

PSYCHODRAMA AND SOCIATRY

J. L. MORENO, M.D.

Moreno Sanitarium

Beacon, N.Y.

EDITORIAL NOTE

Whether it is due to the energetic efforts of its originator or to the effectiveness of the method itself, or both, psychodrama has made something of a stir in certain clinical quarters. Dr. Moreno wants it understood that it is not the same as the Aristotelian concept of catharsis, *and is especially anxious to emphasize his detachment from psychoanalysis. His method is theoretically linked to the relationship of an individual to others, which makes him an attracting or repellent unit in a group. The view comes under the head of sociometry to which a periodical has been devoted.*

Dr. J. L. Moreno, a native of Rumania, has had a varied career as a superintendent of a state hospital near Vienna, as a health officer, in Austria, as a practitioner, as an inventor, and as an originator of the psychodrama form of therapy. He was the founder of two magazines, "Sociometry, A Journal of Interpersonal Relations and Experimental Design" (1937-), and "Group Psychotherapy" (1947-), as well as of the Impromptu Theatre and Therapeutic Theatre, and has made sociometric studies at Sing Sing Prison. Since 1936, he has been the Director of the Moreno Sanitarium. An able and dynamic organizer, he has been instrumental in the launching of several large projects, his most recent venture being the organization of the International Committee of Group Psychotherapy. He has also written and edited several substantial volumes, his latest being Who Shall Survive? *and has contributed a number of magazine essays.*

PRESENT-DAY PSYCHOLOGY

Two thousand years ago mankind underwent, as we do today, a crisis of the first magnitude. To the broad masses catharsis came from Christianity, due to the universality of its methods and the practicality of its instruments, love and confession, charity and hope, instead of from the philosophical schools of Egypt and Greece. In our time, the social and mental sciences aim at a similar accomplishment as religion once attained. Mankind's masses suffer from social and mental unrest. Catharsis will probably come again from instruments which combine universality of method with great practicality. One of the most promising methods, developed in the last twenty-five years and fulfilling these demands, is the psychodramatic method.

Drama is a Greek word which means action, or a thing done. Psychodrama can be defined, therefore, as the science which explores the "truth" by dramatic methods.

METHODS USED

The psychodramatic method uses mainly five instruments— the stage, the subject or patient, the director, the staff of therapeutic aides or auxiliary egos, and the audience. The first instrument is the stage. Why a stage? It provides the patient with a living space which is multidimensional and flexible to the maximum. The living space of reality is often narrow and restraining; he may easily lose his equilibrium. On the stage he may find it again due to its methodology of freedom—freedom from unbearable stress and freedom for experience and expression. The stage space is an extension of life beyond the reality tests of life itself. Reality and fantasy are not in conflict, but both are functions within a wider sphere—the psychodramatic world of objects, persons, and events. In its logic the ghost of Hamlet's father is just as real and permitted to exist as Hamlet himself. Delusions and hallucinations are given flesh—embodiment on the stage—and an equality of status with normal sensory per-

681

ceptions. The architectural design of the stage is made in accord with therapeutic requirements. Its circular forms and levels of the stage, levels of aspiration, pointing out the vertical dimension, stimulate relief from tensions and permit mobility and flexibility of action. The locus of a psychodrama, if necessary, may be designated everywhere, wherever the patients are, the field of battle, the classroom, or the private home. But the ultimate resolution of deep mental conflicts requires an objective setting, the therapeutic theater just as in religion, where although the devout may pray to his God in his own chamber, it is in the church where the community of believers attain the most complete confirmation of their faith.

Involvement vs. Isolation

The second instrument is the subject or patient. He is asked to be himself on the stage, to portray his own private world. He is told to be himself, not an actor, as the actor is compelled to sacrifice his own private self to the rôle imposed upon him by a playwright. Once he warms up to the task, it is comparatively easy for the patient to give an account of his daily life in action, as no one is as much of an authority on himself as the subject. He has to act freely, as things rise up in his mind; that is why he has to be given freedom of expression, spontaneity. Next in importance of spontaneity comes the process of enactment. The verbal level is transcended and included in the level of action. There are several forms of enactment, (a) pretending to be in a rôle, (b) re-enactment or acting out a past scene, (c) living out a problem presently pressing, (d) creating life on the stage, or (e) testing oneself for the future. Further comes the principle of involvement. We have been brought up with the idea that, in test as well as in treatment situations, a minimum of involvement with other persons and objects is a most desirable thing for the patient. An illustration of this is the "Rorschach." The Rorschach situation is reduced to ink blots. In the Rorschach the subjects change but the situation is always the same. It is thought to be its greatest virtue that it is pure and therefore offers an "objective" test. The psycho-analytic interview in its orthodox form too tried to be pure and objective by reducing the involvement with the analyst to a minimum. In the psychodramatic situation a maximum of involvement with other subjects and things is not only possible but expected. Reality is not only not feared but courted. Indeed, in the psychodramatic situation all degrees of involvement take place, from a minimum to a maximum. In addition comes the principle of realization. The patient is enabled not only to meet parts of himself but the other persons who partake in his mental conflicts. These persons may be real or illusory. The reality test which is a mere word in other therapies is thus actually made true on the stage. The warming-up process of the subject to psychodramatic portrayal is stimulated by num-erous techniques, only a few of which are mentioned here: self presentation, soliloquy, projection, interpolation of resistance, reversal of rôles, double ego, mirror techniques, auxiliary world, realization and psycho-chemical techniques. The aim of these sundry techniques is not to turn the patients into actors, but rather to stir them up to be on the stage what they *are*, more deeply and explicitly than they appear to be in life reality.

The third instrument is the director. He has three functions: that of producer, therapist, and analyst. As producer he has to be on the alert to turn every clue which the subject offers into dramatic action, to make the line of production one with the life-line of the subject, and never to let the production lose rap-port with the audience. For the therapist, attacking and shock-ing the subject is at times just as permissible as laughing and joking with him; at times he may become indirect and passive so that for all practical purposes the session seems to be run by the patient. As analyst, he may complement his own inter-pretation by responses coming from informants in the audience, husband, parents, children, friends, or neighbors.

The fourth instrument is a staff of auxiliary egos. These auxiliary egos or therapeutic actors have a double significance. They are extensions of the director, exploratory and therapeutic, but they are also extensions of the patient, portraying the actual or imagined personae of their life drama. The functions of the auxiliary ego are threefold: the function of the actor, portraying rôles required by the patient's world; the function of the therapeutic agent, guiding the subject; and the function of the social investigator.

The fifth instrument is the audience. The audience itself has a double purpose. It may serve to help the patient or, being itself helped by the subject on the stage the audience becomes the patient. In helping the patient it is a sounding board of public opinion. Its responses and comments are as extemporaneous as those of the patient; they may vary from laughter to violent protest. The more isolated the patient is, for instance, because his drama on the stage is shaped by delusions and hallucinations, the more important becomes, to him, the presence of an audience which is willing to accept and understand him. When the audience is helped by the subject, thus becoming the patient itself, the situation is reversed. The audience sees itself, that is, one of its collective syndromes portrayed on the stage.

The stage portion of a psychodramatic session has opened the way to action research and action therapy, rôle test and rôle training, situation tests, and situational interviews whereas the audience portion has become the common ground of the better known forms of group psychotherapy, as lecture methods, dramatic methods and film methods. Scientific foundations of group psychotherapy require as a prerequisite a basic science of human relations, widely known as sociometry. It is from "sociatry," a pathological counterpart of such a science that knowledge can be derived as to abnormal organization of groups, the diagnosis and prognosis, prophylaxis, and control of deviate group behavior.

Now that we have described the five basic instruments required to run a psychodramatic session we may ask ourselves: to what effect? We will limit ourselves here to the description of a single phenomenon, mental *catharsis* (stemming from the Greek, the word means purging, purification).

PRESENT-DAY PSYCHOLOGY

Psychoanalytic Attitude

Breuer and Freud were ignorant of the psychotherapeutic implications of the drama milieu to which Aristotle referred. It remained for psychodrama to rediscover and treat the idea of catharsis in its relation to psychotherapy. We picked up the trend of thought where Aristotle had left off. We too, began with the drama but reversed the procedure. It was not the end phase but the initial phase of the drama towards which we directed attention. *Mental* catharsis was, when we entered the scene with our investigations, to be found only in dramatic literature, in faded memories of Aristotle's old definition; and the term itself was practically out of circulation. The psychoanalysts, after a flare-up in the early 1890's, had pushed it aside. As practically every human activity can be the source of some degree of catharsis, the problem is to determine in what catharsis consists, in which way it differs, for instance, from happiness, contentment, ecstasy, need satisfaction, and so forth, and whether one source is superior in the production of catharsis to another source; indeed, whether there is an element common to all sources which operates in the production of catharsis. Therefore my aim has been to define catharsis in such a way that all forms of influence which have a demonstrable cathartic effect can be shown as positive steps within a single total process of operation. I found the common principle producing catharsis to be: spontaneity.

Extraordinary Inclusiveness

Because of the universality of the act and its primordial nature it engulfs all other forms of expression. They flow naturally out of it or can be encouraged to emerge: verbal associations, musical associations, visual associations, color associations, rhythmic and dance associations, and every other stimulus which might arouse or inhibit the emergence of one or another factor, for instance, the use of psycho-chemical starters, like sedatives, barbiturates, sodium amytal, sodium pentotal; or

685

shock methods like insulin, metrazol or electricity; or endocrin-
ological medications, such as thyroid, are fully within the
scheme of total catharsis; they may condition and prepare the
organism for psychodramatic integration. The need for the
drama can be temporarily choked, for instance, by sleep or
shock therapies. But the fundamental need for the realization
of certain fantastic imageries can not be "shocked away". Unless
the subject is reduced to a brain invalid by surgery or prolonged shock treatments, the temporarily scared patient is bound
to relapse and reproduce the same type of mental syndrome
he had before treatment began. It is into the stream of action
catharsis that all the rivulets of partial catharsis flow.

The treatment of audiences has become an important alternative to individual treatment. The relationship of the audience
to itself in a psychodramatic session, being treated by its own
spokesman on the stage, gives us a clue as to the reasons of the
cathartic effect of psychodrama. According to historians of the
Greek drama, the audience was there first, the chorus, musing
about a common syndrome. There were "keynoters" among
them but they remained within the chorus. Aeschylus is credited
with having put the first actor upon a social space outside of
the chorus, the stage, not speaking to them, but portraying the
woes of their own here. Euripides is credited with having put
the second actor on the stage, thus making possible the dialogue
and interaction of rôles. We may be credited with having put the
psyche itself on the stage. The psyche which originally came
from the group—after a process of reconversion on the stage—
personified by an actor—returns to the group—in the form of
the psychodrama. That which was most startling, new, and
spectacular to see and to feel on the stage appears to the participants after thorough exposure at a process which is familiar
to them and intimately known—as their own selves. The psychodrama confirms their own identity as in a mirror.

CHAPTER XXVIII

THE PRESENT STATUS OF KNOWLEDGE
OF ABNORMAL PSYCHOLOGY
OF THE CHILD

ERNEST HARMS, Ph.D.

Editor, The Nervous Child

EDITORIAL NOTE

Since the child can no longer be treated as a young adult and requires specific methods of investigation, it was deemed advisable to devote a separate chapter to this subject. Just as in organic medicine, the pediatrician takes his place beside other practitioners, so in nervous disorders, the child psychologist or psychiatrist brings to bear his special training and experience to meet the requirements of the case.

Dr. Ernest Harms who received his Ph.D. in Wuerzburg and on arriving in America, became Director of the Child Guidance Clinic at St. Vincent Hospital and later at the Beth David Hospital, has made a number of contributions to this field. He has worked both with subnormal and exceptional children, and has specialized in child guidance and administration. He has been editor of The Nervous Child *and is the author of* A Handbook of Child Guidance, *and* Essentials of Abnormal Child Psychology *(New York, 1953).*

Abnormal child psychology in its present state can be compared to an adolescent boy who is always outgrowing his clothes before they are worn out, whose voice has the unsympathetic gruff sound of mutation, who is full of wonderful abstract ideas and idols which he is unable to realize and who is at all times at odds with everyone in his environment and also with himself. There is no doubt that abnormal child psychology and child psychiatry have rapidly outgrown the status accorded to it a quarter of a century ago when it was called an infant science. It has not yet reached the status of a mature science but is in a confused stage comparable to a period of adolescence.

PRESENT-DAY PSYCHOLOGY

THE HISTORICAL BACKGROUND

The earlier scientific writers on the problems of childhood, the pedagogical classics, had at the beginning of the last century only a prophylactic approach to the abnormalities of juvenile mental life. There was no scientific sensitivity for the psychopathological factors of childhood until adult psychiatry had reached a point where specific mental diseases were not only recognized but where there was a new interest and insight into the genetic background of mental illness. This, however, did not lead to a real science of the mental abnormalities of childhood. It is actually only eight years since child psychiatry has been acknowledged as an autonomous specialty of general psychiatry by the official American Psychiatric Association. The assertion that the main impetus for the recent development of abnormal child psychology grew out of a desire to help the mentally impaired child and was an outgrowth of the mental hygiene movement is an incorrect or at least oversimplified statement which has been made frequently.[50] It would seem that its intention is to contribute to a myth of personal glorification. Before those mental hygienists started their publicity campaign, the real substantial and basic establishment of an abnormal psychology of childhood was developed by pediatricians. The first major writing in the field of juvenile psychopathology was to my knowledge H. Ebbinghaus' "Die psychischen Störungen des Kindesalters" (1887)[29] which appeared in Gerhardt's *Handbuch der Kinderkrankheiten*. The first sizeable American textbook in child psychiatry, Leo Kanner's voluminous book titled *Child Psychiatry*, appeared in 1935[50] and was primarily a pediatric undertaking.

If we survey the list of major publications on abnormal child psychiatry between the ones named, which covered almost half a century, we shall find that the most significant contribution came from pediatricians, and not psychiatrists. To name only one, Hector Cameron,[21] the English pediatrician who wrote the famous book *The Nervous Child* (1919), has done more

689

than anyone else to establish the notion of abnormal child psychology in the English-speaking world. In addition, it must be remembered that those who have contributed most to the general understanding of the psychological development of childhood have had a pediatric training. Karl Bühler,[16] Edouard Claparède,[25] Henri Wallon,[87] and last but not least Arnold Gesell,[35] are pediatric physicians whose scientific zest led them to research in the psychology of childhood.

A Wrong Course

One would expect that because of this general pediatric background the founders of abnormal child psychology would have theoretically accepted the pediatric approach and pediatric symptomatology as their scientific basis. In other words, they might have phenomenologically described those mental and psychological and pathological symptoms or physical pediatric ones and they might have developed from this basis a pathology and therapy. Oddly enough hardly any of them proceeded along this line. The early child psychiatrists turned to adult psychiatry to find pathological concepts for the symptoms they observed and applied them to their observations in the juvenile field. Instead of creating concepts of their own which would really fit and give an adequate somatic picture of pediatric illnesses, they used the concepts of general psychiatry which had been developed in relation to the adult and which in many cases did not fit the children.

It was not until the beginning of the second decade of this century, which has often been labeled the "century of the child," that it was realized that the understanding of the mental development of the child at various ages needed original concepts which were primarily developed in relation to this new science and not concepts of adult psychology which might be considered as acceptable hand-me-downs. One of the more important contributions which psychoanalysis has made to the scientific world has been the awareness that it created a need for an independent consideration of the psychology and psychopathology of childhood as separate from the scientific study of the mature human psyche.

WHAT PSYCHOANALYSIS BROUGHT TO LIGHT

Some psychoanalysts have maintained that the Freudian school can take credit for the creation of the whole field of child psychiatry. This, of course, is not true. There are two basic aspects in which psychoanalysis has greatly helped the development of an autonomic child psychiatry and abnormal child psychology. One is the insight common to all the psychoanalytic founders from the beginning, namely, that the sources of many serious adult neuroses originated in the childhood development of the individual.[33, 49, 91] This created the most important basis of juvenile psychopathology, namely, reversing the approach so that one did not look at juvenile pathological traits from an adult observation platform but, on the contrary, saw in them the nucleus of later pathology. By this approach the science was freed to allow an independent search for the reality of the mental life of the child and the genetic observation of its development. This was greatly assisted by the second basic contribution of psychoanalysis to child psychiatry. That is the actual phenomenological method of psychological observation which the psychoanalytic method represents, wherever it is applied factually and not as a routine based on any dogmatic concept. Particularly important have been people like Melanie Klein, an original pupil of Freud (if one disregards her abstract and abstruse theoretical conclusions) who has greatly helped to free the view for observation of the child's psychic life. Others have contributed greatly to the development of diagnostic as well as therapeutic methods by influencing existing methods of adult psychiatry or normal child psychology and turning them in the correct direction. However, there have been some bad influences, too, stemming from the Freudian school, particularly where their dogmatic thinking and mechanical application of Freudian concepts have developed into a sterile pattern of child psychoanalysis or where they have overemphasized almost meaningless abstract

691

concepts like that of infantile sexuality.[54, 65] Some extremists have, particularly when they have come into positions of influence, exercised an almost devastating effect. One can illustrate this by pointing to Frederick Allen,[3] a pupil of the analytic extremist, Otto Rank, for whom any creative and cultural expression beyond the animalistic functions was labeled masturbative. There is, however, no doubt that the positive contribution by the Freudian school to abnormal child psychology surpassed many times its negative ones.

*　　*　　*

In an attempt to systematically perceive in this short survey the present status of abnormal child psychology, it may be best to separate the consideration of the pathological and the diagnostic from the therapeutic part of the field and afterwards to record separately still other aspects, like child guidance, medical education, and prophylaxis.

PATHOLOGY

As one may expect, the status of the actual psychopathology of childhood determines the status of the entire field of abnormal child psychology as well as that of its special sections. Attempts to outline the whole field of childhood psychology have been made frequently.[5, 43, 44] However, one cannot help but feel that most of them carry the mark of intellectual construction, and almost all of them must be evaluated as preliminary products, since we have not as yet achieved that status of knowledge which lends itself to an outline of a final system of the major psychopathology of childhood. This may be illustrated by the fact that Kanner,[50] in the only major text on child psychiatry in the English language, has in his applications, resorted to an almost entirely different system of pathology in the two editions of his work. As thoughtful a worker as G. H. J. Pearson, in his struggle to find a satisfactory systematic view, offered two quite different ones in the same year.[59, 60] Of the two basic approaches to pathology, the deviative and the phenomenological-descriptive, both have been applied with either one or the other dominating, or both used simultaneously. The deviative approach, which presents pathology as deviations of concepts of normal psychology, has been limited in its successful application because of the great variety of normal theoretical concepts. The phenomenological approach, describing the patient's behavior, has been more widely applied. Its difficulties have been, in adult as well as in juvenile psychiatry, the interpretation of the phenomena. We know from famous cases that the same systems have been used for establishing as many as half a dozen different somatic pictures. In the field of childhood psychopathology, the problem is further complicated by the fact that descriptive means are limited and frequently overshadowed by adult concepts.*

Actually the short history of juvenile psychopathology is sadly limited by this circumstance. Everyone remembers the rôle that psychopathology, designated as hysteria, played at the time when Freud began his career. It was the major psychopathology in professional as well as in the popular thinking until it became dislodged by broader scientific considerations and especially by the various popular psychoanalytic concepts. Leo Kanner has presented in his book[50] the fact that there was an early phase of juvenile psychopathology where almost everything was designed as childhood hysteria. This was changed by the development of a similar unilateral psychopathology which lumped the majority of juvenile mental ailments under the new label of childhood schizophrenia.[7, 14] This unilateral approach has remained dominant for almost 15 years and has not as yet been overcome.[40, 73]

WHAT MUST BE ABANDONED

The author has made it one of his major tasks to combat and to help overcome this one-sidedness and inadequacy and to attempt to at least outline a frame for an acceptable psychopathology of childhood.[40] To this end we must give up the excessive use of concepts like childhood schizophrenia, which

Kanner, for example, tried to dissolve by separating the specific pattern of autistic concept disturbances. We must abandon completely such meaningless concepts as behavior disorder. This has become a convenient term for lumping together every other disorder which could not be designated as schizophrenia. It is necessary to reëstablish concepts like that of hysteria, where it is justified and to even take over from adult pathology the concept of depressive illness. There are quite a number of individual syndromes which have been developed lately by eager workers and which ought to be woven into the total picture, and which have a primarily phenomenological approach. However, when we proceed to the consideration of functional behavior in the individual as well as in terms of the genetic line, the deviative aspects must be applied. No system of childhood psychopathology is complete without including a consideration of deviations in thinking, emotions, and will in the child as well as deviations in the growth and development of these functions and any others which play a noticeable rôle in the mental life and development of the child.

In surveying the field of juvenile psychopathology on such a comprehensive level, we must state here something about those fields in which psychopathology plays a secondary rôle. We must mention first the wide area of what is considered mental deficiency, which is not identical with mental aberration.[20] Sarason's excellent recent book[75] has indeed stated the correct approach for any discussion at this level. Next to be considered are such nerve or general pathologies of childhood which have a considerable abnormal development.[32] An example of this is epilepsy and other seizure involvements. The great advancement we have made in the study of cerebral palsy has made it evident that there is no coincidental major psychopathology but that there is without doubt a certain psychopathology existing, with special learning disabilities. We also must not forget the psychological entanglements which accompany certain major physical ones like blindness, deafness, or arthritis as well as special learning disabilities like word-blindness or the inability to memorize[31]. And finally we must add the whole list of psychosomatic ailments and allergies which often make a more intensive psychopathological imprint upon the total nature of the child than does the less severe type of cerebral palsy.

In many respects we might say that in recent years there have been better contributions to the understanding of the secondary psychopathologies than there have been in the major syndromes.

THE DIAGNOSTIC PICTURE

Diagnostics, the technique of determining the various kinds of pathologies, should be treated separately since it involves some very special and specific aspects which make it an important part of psychopathology. We learned in our historical survey that juvenile psychopathology was primarily developed by pediatricians who did not apply their own general diagnostic methods, but had turned to adult psychiatry and applied its techniques. Children were diagnosed and evaluated as miniature adults. The psychoanalysts were the first in the psychiatric field to break with this misconception. However, long before them Wilhelm Preyer, the educator, had recognized that the psyche of the child was very different from that of the adult, and that it must be understood independently.

During the first decades of this century educators, and particularly psychologists, worked to develop concepts which would clearly separate the specific character of the normal juvenile psyche from that of the adult mind. They even emphasized a strict differentiation of psychological character in specific stages of development like infantile, pre-school, pre-adolescent and adolescent. I would like to recall that among these educational and developmental psychologists, the most prominent had a pediatric background. The most essential part of this juvenile development psychology was emphasis on the fact that a child had a specific kind of expression and interaction. We learn that a child lives in a mythological and fairy-tale world, that his world of expression is play and that his play is as serious and as important as an adult's professional life.[47, 83] We also learn that the child is unable to express major experiences in purely intellectual terms or by any other medium of adult communication, but that full expression can be found in the language of play.[26] When this fact was fully comprehended by the psychoanalytic phenomenologists, they developed a method of diagnosis within this specific frame of childhood expression. The use of toys and various play activities for diagnosis has become one of the basic patterns of pathogenic investigation.[55] Hardly any child is examined by an American diagnostician without the use of a diagnostic tool such as drawing or painting.[37, 51] Because of our desire to standardize any kind of scientific and technical procedure, the test in the field of psychological diagnosis of abnormal potentialities and abnormal characteristics has been developed into a tool which is without comparison in any other scientific field.[93] There are several thousands of tests available for children alone covering almost every conceivable phase of psychic attitude, learning and social aptitude, and character structure.[18, 38]

ON CHILDREN'S PROJECTIVE TESTS

Unfortunately, there have been too many tests produced to permit going into their general and specific applicability. Far more thought has been given to the possibility of extensive use of these tests than to the careful consideration of their limitations. Tests may be excellently prepared from a technical viewpoint but may not fit because of the impossibility of using adult forms for children. The Bellevue-Wechsler test demonstrates such limitation.[89] Others are at fault in regard to their underlying concepts, their validity, and their applicability. The famous Goodenough drawing test[36] fails in this respect because it assumes that children develop intelligence as they develop a scientific conception of the world drawn from adults' views on science. Children do not develop according to a deductive learning system. The child sees the head of a human figure first because it contains the majority of the senses with which he perceives the world. It is the most important part of the body and, therefore, all young children draw the head bigger than the body and not according to our scientific measurements. Lauretta Bender[7] fails also because of misinterpretation. She gives a child's drawing of sailboats the interpretation of sexual intercourse. In reality it is a product of a destitute child interned in a psychiatric ward which has small windows facing a river with just such boats as the only view of the outside world. David Rapaport[68] deserves great credit for having scrutinized the entire test problem in an unsurpassed critical survey and for having advanced the idea of coördinating testing in forms of batteries which attempt to eliminate overemphasis and misinterpretation through coördinated tests and by attempting to cover by means of testing sets the major features of normal and abnormal psychic expression.

Grace H. Kent's survey of the general aspect of testing[51] mental abnormalities in children is one of the best critical evaluations, although it is not one of the most recent. As a meritorious attempt at clarifying one of the most difficult and confusing tests, the Rorschach, in terms of its applicability, the work of Charlotte Bühler must be mentioned.[17] One of the best surveys of the general problem of the present state of diagnosis is that of the British psychiatrist, Muriel B. Hall.[38] Although she writes for English workers, her excellent knowledge of the American situation makes her book valid for a wider field.

Because diagnostic procedures are the same in the normal and abnormal fields, we must deny any justification of the limitation demanded by some workers that diagnosis should always aim only at clearly-known and well-defined pathological syndromes. Since most of our pathological syndromes are still vague and unclear, it is quite possible that diagnostic procedures, if properly conducted, may not only help clarify the syndrome but add considerably to our general knowledge of pathology.

THERAPY

The need for separating juvenile from adult forms of technique was recognized earlier in psychotherapy than it was in diagnosis. Diagnosis is, for the most part, observation, without the intensive participation of the patient. This was at least the earlier conception of it. Therapy is, however, in any case a more intensive activity, involving the patient. In therapy one needed to adjust to the activity pattern of the child and to come into the range of infantile and juvenile behavior in activity forms.

The first real systematic presentation of a childhood psychotherapy was presented by Erich Benjamin[9] who was an amazingly sensitive observer of juvenile mental life. He is also responsible for such original syndrome descriptions as that of *"die Trotzperiode"*, and we may consider him the first practitioner of independent child psychiatry. The Swiss Moritz Tramer has added much to these beginnings with his thinking about the various details of therapeutic work with young people. Both Benjamin and Tramer perceived their psychotherapy from an undogmatic, partly pragmatic, partly phenomenological viewpoint which set aside adult psychiatric as well as physiological pediatric concepts and used a broader general medico-psychological basis. In this development of a broader psychotherapy, they have been joined here in America by a number of pediatricians who have realized the failure of child psychiatry to offer satisfactory practical tools and to go deeply into psychology to create a practical psychopathology and psychotherapy which could be a suitable counterpart to pediatrics. With the exception of the ingenious Bret Beverly, who died prematurely, and the factual popularizer, Benjamin Spock, the best work in this line has been done by Harry and Ruth M. Bakwin who in their book *Psychological Care in Infancy and Childhood*[6] offer the most extensive coverage of the total field of abnormal child psychology.

The greatest part of the work in respect to child psychotherapy has been done by workers belonging to the more dogmatic schools of psychotherapy. The first place, of course, is taken by the Freudian school of analysis.[33] Very little actually has been done in the development and improvement of the original child analytic technique as postulated by Melanie Klein. A fantastic amount of writing has been done by academic followers, concerned almost entirely with secondary applications of Freud's least acceptable concepts of childhood, like that of infantile sexuality, which he conceived abstractly and which he never completely proved. Most of this literature of child analysis will be completely forgotten in a decade or so; but they have had a dangerous impact.[65] There are many others, however, whose names are less well known who have contributed much more and who have made unique important advances, as, for example, Lydia Dawes, with her psychoanalysis of a child afflicted with major hysteria.[27]

Apart from his great influence upon American educational thinking, Alfred Adler[1], through his Individual Psychology, has made a considerable contribution to the development of child psychotherapy, particularly in the area of social adjustment. Unfortunately the majority of Adler's followers apply his ideas only a little less dogmatically than do the Freudian proselytes. However, in general, the positive influence is considerably greater. Some of Adler's students, like Erwin Wexberg, have contributed important books to the American child-psychotherapeutic literature. Two other pupils of Adler have in an impressive handbook for teachers excellently presented the practical applications of his concepts.[79]

The influence of C. G. Jung upon child psychotherapy is rather minimal.[49] However, a number of the foremost American progressive educators, like Caroline Pratt[63] have been animated by Jung's ideas. One of the most sensitive books in the American child-psychotherapeutic literature comes from a strict pupil of Jung, Frances C. Wickes.[91]

There have been therapeutic concepts which have developed from other psychological theories. It may appear strange that the school which is strongest in America, Behaviorism, has come forward with the fewest contributions. This results, of course, from its strongly physiological background, which leads more in the direction of neurology and bio-psychiatry rather than psychotherapy.[66, 67, 70, 88] However, even this group has presented us with some specific concepts of psychotherapy as represented by Carl Rogers[71, 72] and his Chicago school of non-directive psychotherapy which, after a too radical earlier form, developed into a client-centered psychotherapy. The way in which the relationship of the therapist and patient has been presented in this approach has been criticized by Frederick C. Thorne,[85] whose therapeutic thinking is sounder and more mature and who has warned against any one-sidedness in this relationship and has denied the possibility of non-directive therapy. Thorne's brilliant argument has not yet been satisfactorily utilized in psychotherapy with children.

The most intensive attempts of developing psychotherapy with children have been, as may be expected, in terms of specified techniques among which play therapy is at present the most developed.[58] Play therapy flourishes today in various forms based on the philosophy or psychology of the worker. Very intensive attempts along this line have been made by the above mentioned Rogers Group. The method advanced by its major representative, Virginia M. Axline,[4] is not very convincing if one looks for results beyond a methodological routine. The question will always remain one that centers on what one wishes to achieve by the technique. Accordingly, one can classify the various techniques. The most primitive may be one which gives the child release from suppressed pathogenic elements. We find this aspect widely discussed and made the object of various play techniques. In finger-painting, the smear room, and in special toy sets, the child gets a chance to release and relieve, for example, pathogenic sibling rivalry by not allowing the brother into the block house or by throwing him out of an imaginary window.

There are attempts under way to find definite therapeutic measures in regard to the specific psychopathology of what today, for instance, is designated as schizophrenia or tics; but up to now no one has presented in written form a description of the treatment plan of any one of these somatic patterns. On the other hand, there are attempts under way to try to apply practically everything that lies within the scope of childhood activities for therapeutic purposes. We know of attempts to use music as well as play, drawing, painting, sculpture, dancing, dramatics, and even, most successfully, puppetry for therapeutic purposes. We have, for instance, also learned that a good game of ball on the athletic field can help much more than all the talks or schoolmasterly attempts to improve the intellectual and emotional coördination of an emotionally disturbed adolescent. We are also in the beginning of what must be called a full-fledged systematic presentation of the choice of therapeutic methods. The preliminary presentation made by Benjamin and somewhat enlarged by Tramer is still the most far-reaching achieved.

As may be expected, there has been a greater advance made in therapeutic developments in the field of special disabilities with respect to actual, systematic child psychotherapy. In such fields where the psychotherapeutic task is only a part of or plays a secondary rôle in a general pathology and is coördinated with wider educational and medical efforts, much clearer insight into the task and more definite techniques have been achieved. We are thinking here of the work with the blind, the deaf, or the mute, as well as the cerebral-palsy, polio, and cardiac child. Of course, speech disorders as well as reading and other learning disabilities belong in this field. Under the advance of psychotherapeutic insight in general, we have learned how much psychology and psychotherapy are needed to help these children. Berthold Lowenfeld, Clarence V. Huggins, Morton Seidenfeld, Harry V. Bice, and Martin Palmer are but a few of the psychologists who can claim more success along these therapeutic lines than has been achieved otherwise.

SOCIAL PSYCHOPATHOLOGY AND SOCIAL PSYCHOTHERAPY

As has been often emphasized, the human offspring is that creature which requires the most extensive social care. Disturbances, or lack of this care, become a considerable factor in the pathogenesis of every human being, and this is especially true in mental troubles. With the advance of psychiatry and especially child psychiatry, we have become more fully aware of the impact of the social aspect of human life. We know now that almost half of all pathogenic factors have to be sought in the environment and not in the innate constitutional make-up of the child.[12] It was the psychoanalyst who first pointed out the rôle of childhood and its social setting in later mental illness. We have learned that even for an infant loneliness can become a very detrimental factor.[6] The absence of or the neglect by one or both parents, the neurotic character of the parents, any imbalance between them as well as patterns of overprotection and over-discipline are also significant factors.[15] Other important factors which may contribute to the pathogenesis of mental illness are the total home setting, the relationship to siblings, the relationship to relatives, and the influence of other persons such as servants. In addition to such study of the family,[81] the street, the school and the wider community ought to be studied as sources of social psychopathology. In our urban setting, we have ample evidence of the tragic influence of some of these broader social factors. Some attempts have been made recently to present such a psychopathology of childhood as a total picture and this detailed study has helped considerably in establishing a correct focus for the understanding of individual cases.[15]

Of no less importance is the realization of the social aspects of psychotherapy. We have now come to accept the fact that in order to cure a neurotic child, the environment must either be a therapeutic one or one from which previous unsalutary social conditions have been removed. Accordingly we cannot cure a child without correcting the pathogenic attitudes of the parents, or without the removal of those factors in the environment which have been proven influential. We also know that the parents are still the best social therapeutic and educational recourse for a disturbed child, and we only consider his removal into substitute settings such as an institution when the home situation proves incurable.

Family therapy, therefore, becomes a major part of the psychotherapy of the child, and it will continue to be even more important as our general knowledge increases. The specific techniques which belong to social psychotherapy have in recent years become the center of much concern in the whole field of childhood and adult psychotherapy. The technique is known as *Group Therapy*.[51, 80] Unfortunately the whole concept of group therapy is quite confused and greatly misunderstood due to the lack of clarity of its major representatives. During the last war when large numbers of military personnel were administered psychotherapy, it became popular to take a number of them together for collective treatment. This was called group therapy, but in reality it should only have been called mass therapy. "Group" is a sociological term, and if it is to be used in its true semantic meaning, it means a number of people organically connected with definite personal relationships. The family is the primary living group and also the most characteristic, since the differentiated relationship between all the members is only too evident and strongly expressed. We had previously designated as family therapy the therapeutic work with children and parents together. This is the most specific group therapy developed for the juvenile psychotherapeutic field.

There are other forms of group therapy possible and applied. For example, when a number of strongly asocial children are put together in a play group for the purpose of social-adjustment therapy, this becomes a group which can justifiably be designated as a form of group therapy. I cannot help but emphasize here my views against the abstract and indiscriminate use of such techniques. In some cases it may be best that a child not be placed among a group of equally maladjusted children but rather placed in a group of normal ones. This again could justifiably be called a form of group therapy.

Juvenile Delinquency

There is no doubt that a major portion of the consideration of juvenile delinquency belongs to the field of psychopathology and psychotherapy. I do not wish to imply that I join those who explain and solve everything by psychology.[2] There is no doubt that law enforcement and remedial education have their part in the problem of juvenile delinquency. If we follow the history of these "crimes" of juveniles against the social environment, we find that the opinion, the popular as well as the scientific, has always been colored by the current attitudes towards sensational fads. Even our scientists have not been free from these fads. We have seen a biogenetic and hereditary, and also a purely sociological treatment of delinquency. We still see the Gluecks continue with study methods which were valid 30 years ago but which must be considered ineffectual today. On the other hand, we are at present going through a social work phase whereby the consideration of delinquency entails an unsocial snobbish attitude in the method of treating problems of differing sensitivity, which in itself seems both irresponsible and criminal.[41, 42]

We have, however, advanced in sound directions along various lines. Clifford Shaw's sociological contributions will always remain valid in the study of delinquency.[78] The work which Cyril Burt did 25 years ago demanding the study of the individual psychological conditioning was an important step forward.[19] It is not a contemporary fad but a true advance in the understanding of a delinquent when we study in detail the social background as a major factor in the conditioning and the development of a social and individual type of pathology. This does not mean that we believe every case of delinquency requires psychotherapy;[46] nevertheless, we feel that only a fraction of the psychotherapy which should be used with delinquents today is being used.[22, 62] We can only hope that the present social work faddism, as presented most tragically in a book by Alfred A. Kahn on the Juvenile Court of New York City

(1953), will be followed by an increase in the use of psychotherapy even within the judicial system. A decrease in the application of psychopathology and psychotherapy in the treatment of juvenile delinquents would be a step backward rather than forward.[13]

CHILD GUIDANCE

Although, at the present time, psychopathology and psychotherapy are regarded as subordinate, Child Guidance, if properly considered, must embrace juvenile psychopathology and psychotherapy.[39] There have been many versions and definitions of the meaning of child guidance, some of which are concerned only with a less sensitive conception of a juvenile counseling service with a routinized testing pattern.[69] I believe that if properly defined, child guidance should be developed into a field coördinate with psychotherapy.[77] It should answer many of the questions which life forces a child's mind to ponder. It should take over where the scientifically planned school education ends and where the stress of a difficult home life fails the growing mind.

American workers in this field have claimed that this child guidance approach is their discovery and have attributed its beginnings to either William Healy[42] or to the remarkable Douglas Thom.[84] Unfortunately, we must point out that child guidance was inaugurated by Alfred Adler, in Vienna, almost a decade before Healy began his child guidance service in Chicago. We could also point to similar institutions in Germany and also to the work done by the Italian psychiatrist, Sante de Sanctis, with some children about the same time.

The child guidance services created by Alfred Adler were actually the first ones organized and when they are compared with the various forms now developed they still seem modern and efficient.

Child guidance is concerned with those problems in the life of any child which it feels unable to solve. It also deals with children who make such mistakes in general behavior that they

PRESENT-DAY PSYCHOLOGY

require correction and guidance. To use the term in the meaning that Freud has given it, child guidance deals with everyday
psychopathology in the child's life.[84] Of course, the conditions
are not always severe enough to require the immediate assistance of the psychotherapist. This means that it is not necessary
for every child guidance institution to be headed by a psychiatrist. The scope of child guidance should be therapeutic
with remedial education as a secondary concern.

I myself have seriously advocated the development of child
guidance as the major technique for the assistance of youth.[39]
I have particularly emphasized the necessity of avoiding its becoming a welfare consisting of medical discipline with a routinized pattern and endless reports. If child guidance is developed properly, as a sound adjustment to the handling of
youth's problems, it can then be easily handled on the lowest
level by any teacher, clergyman, or social worker.[10] Only
those difficulties which persist and become actual personality
impairments require the services of a clinical psychologist and
only in the most serious cases should a psychiatrist be called
upon. The present trend toward having every larger school unit
equipped with a guidance specialist is a very timely development
which tends toward the improvement of the general plans for
the mental health of our children.

PREVENTIVE MENTAL HEALTH

The realization that a considerable amount of the psychopathology of our times could be avoided by certain social measures and by the correction of individual behavior has brought
into being the mental hygiene movement.[64] Those who have
advocated such changes since the Johns Hopkins psychiatrist,
Adolf Meyer and Clifford Beers began this movement have
talked a great deal without actually achieving decisive results.
Most of the good that has resulted from this movement concerned itself with the treatment of those already mentally impaired and with their fate in the mental institutions. Those who
have really advanced it have been largely the sociologists and

psychologists who have striven to give concrete views on personal and collective attitudes.[30] Few really good books on mental hygiene have been published. Among the best of these books are those which have been in existence 30 years or more and which were written by one of America's great psychiatrists, William Alison White.[92] During recent years, the mental hygiene approach has been taken up by European workers who have correctly felt that there were more psychological problems involved than mental ones. And they have therefore changed the name to psychic hygiene.[61] Work done along these lines in Switzerland points to concrete progress whereas in this country a considerable deterioration in the work in this area can be felt.

FOOTNOTE

* The best systematic survey of childhood psychopathology which I have found based on phenomenological aspects was developed by one of the earliest writers in the field, L. Scholz. His book, *Anomale Kinder,* is almost completely unknown and never quoted. Scholz, undoubtedly a pupil of Wilhelm Preyer, was an alienist in Eastern Germany. His book was published in 1912 in Berlin by S. Karger.[76]

REFERENCES

This list of suggested readings presented below is unusual inasmuch as it not only deals with the famous literature which has often been quoted, but it also presents a reading list of really worthwhile books which may be comparatively unknown. I have added the earliest books on the psychopathology of childhood to give specialists a chance to become familiar with the beginning stages of their science. A number of books listed here are noted for the first time.

1 Adler, A. *The Education of Children,* New York, 1930.

2 Aichhorn, A. *Wayward Youth,* New York, 1926.

3 Allen, F. H. *Psychotherapy with Children,* New York, 1942.

4 Axline, V. M. *Play Therapy,* Boston, 1947.

5 Baker, M. J. *Introduction to Exceptional Children.* Rev. Ed. New York, 1953.

6 Bakwin, R. M. and H. *Psychological Care During Infancy and Childhood,* New York, 1942.

7 Bender, L. *Child Psychiatric Techniques,* Springfield, Ill., 1952.

8 Benjamin, E. *Grundlagen und Entwicklungsgeschichte der kindlichen Neurose,* Leipzig, 1930.

9 —— *Lehrbuch der Psychopathologie des Kindesalters,* Zürich, 1938.

10 Bentley, J. E. *Problem Children,* New York, 1936.

[11] Born, W. *Beiträge zur Lehre von den Neurosen des Kindesalters,* Jena, 1892.

[12] Bossard, J. H. *The Sociology of Child Development,* New York, 1948.

[13] Bovet, L. *Psychiatric Aspects of Juvenile Delinquency,* Geneva, 1951.

[14] Bradley, C. *Schizophrenia in Childhood,* New York, 1941.

[15] Brown, F. J. *The Sociology of Childhood,* New York, 1948.

[16] Bühler, K. *Die geistige Entwickelung des Kindes,* Leipzig, 1918.

[17] Bühler, C. *Testing Children's Development from Birth to School Age,* New York, 1935.

[18] Burt, C. *Mental and Scholastic Tests,* London, 1921.

[19] —— *The Young Delinquent,* New York, 1925.

[20] —— *The Backward Child,* 3rd Ed., London, 1950.

[21] Cameron, H. C. *The Nervous Child,* London, 1919.

[22] Carr, L. J. *Delinquency Control,* Rev. Ed., New York, 1950.

[23] Cimball, W. *Die Neurosen des Kindes und Jugendalters,* Berlin, 1935.

[24] Claparède, E. *Experimental Pedagogy and Psychology of the Child,* Neuchatel, 1911.

[25] —— *Le Dévelopment Mental,* Neuchatel, 1946.

[26] Conn, J. H. The Child Reveals Himself Through Play. *Mental Hyg.,* vol. 23, 1939.

[27] Dawes, L. Analysis of a Case of Grand Hysteria. *The Nervous Child,* vol. 10, 1902.

[28] De Sanctis, S. *Neuropsychiatria Infantile,* Rome, 1925.

[29] Ebbinghaus, H. *Die psychischen Störungen des Kindesalters,* Tübingen, 1887.

[30] Fenton, N. *Mental Hygiene in School Practice,* Stanford, 1943.

[31] Fernald, G. M. *Remedial Techniques in Basic School Subjects,* New York, 1943.

[32] Ford, F. R. *Diseases of the Nervous System in Infancy, Childhood and Adolescence,* Springfield, Ill., 1944.

[33] Freud, S. *The Basic Writings,* New York, 1938.

[34] Fuchs, A. *Schwachsinnige Kinder,* Gueterslohe, 1899.

[35] Gesell, A. and Amatruda, C. S. *Developmental Diagnosis,* New York, 1929.

[36] Goodenough, F. *The Measurement of Intelligence by Drawing,* Yonkers, 1926.

[37] —— *Mental Testing,* New York, 1949.

[38] Hall, M. B. *Psychiatric Examination of School Children,* London, 1947.

[39] Harms, E. *Handbook of Child Guidance,* New York, 1947.

[40] —— *Essentials of Abnormal Child Psychology,* New York, 1953.

[41] Healy, W. *The Individual Delinquent,* Boston, 1915.

[42] Healy, W. and Bronner, A. F. *New Light on Delinquency and Its Treatment,* New Haven, 1936.

[43] Heck, A. O. *Education of Exceptional Children,* New York, 1940.

[44] Hollingworth, L. S. *The Psychology of Subnormal Children,* New York, 1924.

[45] Homburger, A. *Vorlesungen über die Psychopathologie des Kindesalters,* Berlin, 1926.

[46] Hoyes, J. A. *The Treatment of the Young Delinquent,* London, 1952.

[47] Hurloch, E. B. *Child Development,* New York, 1950.

[48] Ireland, W. W. *Mental Affections of Children,* London, 1898.

49 Jung, C. G. Konflicte der kindlichen Seele. In: *Jahrbuch für Psychoanalyse,* vol. 2, 1910.

50 Kanner, L. *Child Psychiatry,* Springfield, Ill., 1937.

51 Kent, G. H. *Mental Tests in Clinics for Children,* New York, 1950.

51a Klapman, J. W. *Group Therapy,* New York, 1946.

52 Klein, M. *The Psychoanalysis of Children,* London, 1932.

53 Levy, J. and Munroe, R. *The Happy Family,* New York, 1938.

54 Lewis, N. D. C. and Pacella, B. *Modern Trends in Child Psychiatry,* New York, 1945.

55 Lowenfeld, M. *Play in Childhood,* London, 1935.

56 Manheimer, M. *Les troubles mentaux de l'Enfance,* Paris, 1899.

57 Moreau, P. de T. *La Folie chez les Enfants,* Paris, 1888.

58 Moustakes, C. E. *Children in Play Therapy,* New York, 1953.

59 Pearson, G. H. J. *Emotional Disorders in Children,* New York, 1949.

60 —— The Psychiatry of Childhood. *Oxford Medicine,* vol. VII.

61 Pfister, A. M. *Die Psychohygiene,* Bern, 1949.

62 Powers, E. and Witmer, H. L. *An Experiment in the Prevention of Delinquency,* New York, 1951.

63 Pratt, C. *I Learn from Children,* New York, 1948.

64 Preston, G. *The Substance of Mental Health,* New York, 1943.

65 *The Psychoanalytic Study of the Child,* Annual, New York, 1945.

66 Rachford, B. K. *Some Physiological Factors of the Neuroses of Childhood,* Cincinnati, 1895.

67 —— *Neurotic Disorders in Childhood,* New York, 1905.

68 Rapaport, D. *Diagnostic Psychological Testing,* Chicago, 1946.

69 Reed, A. Y. *Guidance and Personnel Service in Education,* Ithaca, 1944.

70 Robin, G. C. A. *Les troubles nerveux et psychiques de l'Enfant,* Paris, 1935.

71 Rogers, C. R. *The Clinical Treatment of the Problem Child,* Boston, 1939.

72 —— *Client-Centred Therapy,* Boston, 1951.

73 Sachs, B. and Hausmann, L. *Nervous and Mental Disorders from Birth through Adolescence,* New York, 1926.

74 Strohmayer, W. *Vorlesungen über die Psychopathologie des Kindesalters,* Tübingen, 1910.

75 Sarason, S. B. *Psychological Problems in Mental Deficiency,* 2nd Ed., New York, 1953.

76 Scholz, L. *Anomale Kinder,* Berlin, 1912.

77 Schroeder, P. *Child Guidance Procedures,* New York, 1937.

78 Shaw, C. *Juvenile Delinquency and Urban Areas,* Chicago, 1942.

79 Shoobs, N. E. and Goldberg, G. *Corrective Treatment for Unadjusted Children,* New York, 1942.

80 Slavson, S. R. *An Introduction to Group Therapy,* New York, 1943.

81 Smart, M. and Smart, R. *An Introduction to Family Relationships,* Philadelphia, 1953.

82 Stockert, F. G. von. *Einführung in die Psychopathologie des Kindesalters,* Berlin, 1939.

83 Strang, R. *An Introduction to Child Study,* New York, 1951.

84 Thom, D. A. *Everyday Problems of the Everyday Child,* New York, 1930.

85 Thorne, F. C. *Principles of Personality Counseling,* Brandon, Vt., 1950.

[86] Tramer, M. *Lehrbuch der allgemeinen Kinderpsychiatrie,* 3rd Ed., Basel, 1949.

[87] Wallon, H. *Les origines du Caractère chez l'Enfant,* Paris, 1949.

[88] Warner, F. *The Nervous System of the Child,* New York, 1900.

[89] Wechsler, D. *Range of Human Capacities,* 2nd Ed., Baltimore, 1952.

[90] Wexberg, E. *Your Nervous Child,* New York, 1927.

[91] Wickes, F. *The Inner World of Childhood,* New York, 1935.

[92] White, W. A. *The Mental Hygiene of Childhood,* Boston, 1923.

[93] Witmer, H. L. *Psychiatric Interviews with Children,* New York, 1946.

[94] Ziehen, T. *Die Geisteskrankheiten des Kindesalters,* Berlin, 1917.

Chapter XXIX

INDIVIDUAL PSYCHOLOGY

Rudolf Dreikurs, M.D.
Professor of Psychiatry, Chicago Medical School

EDITORIAL NOTE

Individual Psychology is not the most felicitous term in connection with Alfred Adler's system. We know how it originated, viz., it was Adler's aim to treat man as a whole rather than as a conglomeration of complexes, all determined by certain early experiences, and without a central governor to resolve or dispel them. Adler's star had been on the wane about the time of his death, and one would have thought that by the midcentury, his name would have figured only in a history of medical psychology or psychoanalysis; but his global and ego-centered approach must have somehow clicked with later developments in clinical psychology and even psychoanalysis, so that it was found necessary to include a chapter on that sector of depth psychology, and Dr. Dreikurs was invited to state the essence of Individual Psychology in its more recent development.

Dr. R. Dreikurs received his medical training at the University of Vienna, where he was for a time Director of a Child Guidance Clinic and a Clinic for Alcoholics. On his arrival in the United States during the Nazi regime, he entered the Michael Reese Hospital as intern in psychiatry. In 1942, he was appointed Professor of Psychiatry at the Chicago Medical School. He has served on a number of university faculties and is Medical Director of Community Child Guidance Centers in Chicago. He is Lecturer in Psychology, Roosevelt University.

Dr. Dreikurs has written extensively on Child Guidance, psychotherapy and human relationships. His great interest in and wide knowledge of Adlerian psychology have rendered him especially qualified to write the present chapter.

PRESENT-DAY PSYCHOLOGY

INDIVIDUAL PSYCHOLOGY

A short description and analysis of the theory and practice of Individual Psychology as developed by Alfred Adler can merely provide a glimpse of its all-inclusive character. Its basic principles may appear simple; but their application is complex, since the very essence of Adler's "Comparative Individual Psychology" is the emphasis on individual differences.

I. BASIC PRINCIPLES

1. *The Meaning of the Name*: The term Individual Psychology does not imply a contrast to social or group psychology. On the contrary, Adlerian Psychology could be classified as a social psychology. The word "Individual" is derived from the Latin word "Individuum" which literally means "undivided," "indivisible" (*in* [not] + *dividuus* [divisible]). This meaning was more obvious in the German use of the term "Individual." Individual Psychology emphasizes not only the uniqueness of each individual, but the totality of the personality, which cannot be broken up into parts. Today, the concept of a total personality is widely accepted; but a prevalent mechanistic-deterministic orientation often prevents comprehension of such totality. Adler's system provides the general frame of reference by which a holistic concept of the personality becomes feasible and applicable, through the socio-teleological approach, characteristic of Individual Psychology. It implies a recognition of man's social nature, and the purposive character of all his actions.

2. *Man's Social Nature*: Man is a social being, a *zoön politikon*, (Aristotle). During many thousands of years of social living man became thoroughly conditioned to the social atmosphere. All human qualities characterize a person's interaction with his fellow men; all human problems are of a social nature. The deepest human desire is to belong; without others, life is meaningless. Only within the group can man fulfill himself. By developing societies, man extricated himself from the law of

the jungle, developing social laws to regulate his existence. He conquered nature to a large extent, putting natural forces into his service, be they outside of him or within himself. Biological forces no longer dominate him, but are used by him.

The fundamental human desire to belong has been called by Adler *"Social Interest."* (It is an inadequate and often misleading translation of the German term *Gemeinschaftsgefühl,* a feeling of communion). This Social Interest is the basis for man's ability and willingness to coöperate with others, to participate in and contribute to the functions of the group of which he is a part. The ability to communicate, not necessarily verbally, is innate in man, as the result of his social inheritance. However, Social Interest has to be developed and maintained for full social integration. All maladjustments are the result of an inadequate Social Interest, of a restricted feeling of belonging.

3. *Inferiority Feelings and Their Compensations*: The vital feeling of belonging is hampered by a feeling of inferiority. As soon as an individual assumes himself to be inferior to the other members of the group, he is no longer sure of his place in it. For this reason, anti-social or asocial attitudes, social and emotional deficiencies and maladjustments can be traced to an exaggerated feeling of inferiority. It does not eliminate the desire to belong, but distorts the direction of integrative efforts. It replaces the natural desire to contribute and to participate with an attempt to compensate for an actual or assumed status of inferiority by elevating oneself. As long as the individual sees some opportunity to do so in a useful way, the compensation will be sought through socially useful means; but if the individual is discouraged, he will switch from the useful to the *useless side of life* and employ methods of self-elevation useless or damaging to others. Compensatory achievements never remove the original inferiority feelings. Therefore, a real compensation never takes place. The efforts to compensate continue and lead to over-compensation, either through useful or useless means.

The striving for significance expresses itself often as a will to power. In his early writings, Adler considered such a drive as essential and universal. He changed his position in his last works, stating that each individual moves toward the "overcoming" of obstacles, not necessarily toward power; the "striving for power" or better—for personal power—is only a mistaken form of compensation for an inferiority feeling.

The human race is beset with inferiority feelings. Man is biologically ill equipped, and formed societies and developed mental abilities to compensate for his *biological inferiority,* in order to survive. With his intellectual growth, he recognized his smallness in the universe, his inevitable death and destruction. This awareness of man's *cosmic inferiority feeling* led to compensatory achievements in religion, philosophy, and art. These two types of inferiority feelings affected mankind as a whole. A third type affects the individual alone; it is the impression of a *social inferiority.* The child experiences it in the world of the adults, and each individual is exposed to it in our civilization which discontinued the cohesiveness and homogeneity of primitive society. Adler originally considered the inferiority of organs as the primary stimulus for compensatory and over-compensatory psychic activity; later he recognized the social inferiority as the incentive for compensatory efforts.

The discouragement, intensified by continuous mistaken compensatory efforts "on the useless side of life," may lead to an *inferiority complex* so that all efforts are abandoned. While the individual may not be aware of his inferiority feelings, he is fully aware of his inferiority complex which is generally used as an excuse for non-participation and withdrawal, or for special services and consideration. Similarly, *a superiority complex* is a manifestation of accentuated, but overcompensated, inferiority feelings.

4. *Purposiveness*: All human activities are purposive, regardless of whether the individual is aware of his aims or not. All actions, thoughts, and emotions have a purpose, indicating movements of the total individual. Since human life takes place in the social atmosphere, the goals of each individual are primarily of a social nature. They express his efforts to find his place

715

within the group. All character traits can, therefore, be considered as patterns of movement, not "caused", but arranged and trained. During the formative years in early childhood, the individual establishes firm convictions about his place in the groups, about the methods and approaches which he can use best, about the meaning of social living as he understands it. The goals which he sets himself as a child become fixed and are maintained throughout life; they are understandable in the childhood situation but *fictitious* when pursued in adulthood. They are the basis for his *Style of Life* which is the fundamental scheme of his unique personality structure. Nobody knows his own style of life; it was developed without awareness, due to the necessary subjectivity in the empirical search for a workable orientation. Movements in any given life situation are expressions of the basic life style, by which the situation is interpreted. Therefore, the movements and goals of the individual express his total personality; all past experiences and future aspirations converge into the one present movement. It is the total personality which is moving, neither the mind nor the body alone, or any part of either. A holistic concept presupposes a teleological approach to analysis and interpretation: it also presupposes a creative ability and self-determination of man.

5. *The Private Logic*: A child does not "know" why he does something wrong. Only if the purpose of his disturbing behavior is properly "explained" to him does he understand and respond with a *recognition reflex* (Dreikurs). It probably is impossible for man to ever be sure of his motivation. The pressure of his conscience, the acceptance of a "common sense" which he shares with the other members of his group, and finally the need to be subjective in order to move forcefully prevent full awareness of intentions when they deviate from the demands of conscience, common sense, and logical objectivity. The fictitious goals of the life style are at variance with the demands of reality, of the group. The subjective premises on which the individual operates are maintained through a *biased apperception;* it prevents him from recognizing facts which

would contradict his basic convictions and concepts. While full awareness of one's motivation will never be possible, some awareness always exists. Nothing that goes on within the individual is either clearly known or completely unknown to him. There are only various degrees of awareness, and the individual himself decides what he wants to admit to himself, again often without being aware of this very decision. He is not the victim of unconscious forces but uses his ability to conceal from himself what he does not need or want to know.

6. *Psychopathology*: The foregoing psychological principles were perceived in the study and exploration of emotionally disturbed and socially maladjusted persons. The findings, in turn, permit a clearer understanding of psychopathological phenomena. The variety of syndromes, as well as the unlimited multitude of individual personalities, do not exclude the existence of some well-defined and relatively simple principles behind the perplexing variations. (The law of gravitation explains all the movements on earth and in space by the relationship of two simple qualities, mass and distance). At the root of all psychopathological conditions is a restriction of the social interest through an intensification of inferiority feelings, concomitant with a switch from the useful to the useless side of life. This basic formula underlies each case of maladjustment, be it emotional, or social. The symptoms vary, the methods differ, but the direction is the same—away from social participation, at least in the area of disturbed functions and symptoms.

The three categories of psychopathological disorders, neuroses, psychoses and character disorders, have in common a conflict between common sense, the shared logic of accepted standards and values, and the individual's *private logic;* but the nature of this conflict is characteristically different for each disease entity. To be sure, a similar conflict exists in the so-called "normal" person: nobody always acts as he knows he should. Everybody follows his own private logic and deviates to a certain extent from the pattern of behavior which is expected of him, by others and by himself. To this extent we are all not socially adjusted. But the disturbance of our function does not imply a sizable dysfunction or neglect of function; otherwise, we would be adjudged as sick, or consider ourselves sick. Consequently, the distinction between normal and abnormal is not always simple. (Adler described a *neurotic character*—in English faultily translated into neurotic constitution—which fits the vast majority of our contemporaries).

We may say, therefore, that the "normal" individual resolves his conflict between his conscience, his common sense, and his private logic through rationalizations which are accepted by him and by the people around him. A neurosis develops as soon as *disturbances* of feeling, thinking, or bodily functions are used as rationalizations. A "symptom" emerges to "excuse" an obvious deficiency of participation and function, a non-compliance with social demands. The "sick" person disregards the demands of his conscience and common sense because he feels "unable" to comply with them. The symptom is an expression of "weakness", it is an inferiority complex.

The resolution of the conflict between common sense and private logic is quite different in a psychosis. It occurs whenever the gap becomes so great that reconciliation—even through rationalization or alibis—appears impossible, a condition probably facilitated by some organic breakdown of the cerebral functions. Common sense is then distorted and brought in line with the private logic; the psychotic creates through his delusions a reality in line with his convictions and concepts. (The mechanism involved is not pathological *per se;* we all use it in our dreams). Since the conflict is eliminated, the patient has no realization of being sick. He just creates a world of his own.

Lack of "insight" in the abnormality of his condition is also characteristic of the psychopathic personality. Only, the conflict is resolved there not by the dominance of a private logic, as in the psychotic, but by the underdevelopment of a conscience. Such a person does not share the values and convictions with the surrounding society; he may share them with a group of others like him, where he then may feel as belonging and behave accordingly. Criminals fall in this group; they are socially sick, as the neurotic is emotionally sick, and the psychotic mentally sick. Many other social adjustments can be traced to the same deficiency in values and conventions, typical of character disorders.

7. *The Theory of Neurosis*: While this short review does not permit a more detailed discussion of the psychoses and character disorders, the problem of neurosis requires further elaboration. The onset always takes place in a "crisis" situation. The element of crisis is not provided merely by the difficulty or tragedy of a particular predicament; it is the *impasse* created by a situation where the life-style does not permit functioning. Then the individual feels compelled or justified to "arrange"— although without awareness—methods of withdrawal. He tries to "safeguard" his self-esteem, his worth as a member of the group. (The term "safeguard" means what Adler called *"Sicherungen"*; it was mistakenly translated as "security." The neurotic is not looking for security, but for safeguards, a method of face-saving).

Neurotic symptoms are actually *produced* by the patient. He cannot know what he is doing, since the method of producing symptoms and maintaining them consists of deliberate efforts to *suppress* them. (There is no insomnia, unless a person "decides" that he simply *has* to sleep. For this reason, anti-suggestion, a method of inducing the patient to deliberately "produce" it, can stop any symptom, at least temporarily.) The tensions and fears behind any neurosis originate in the patient's concern with his life problems and his feeling of inability to solve them. The selection of the symptom is facilitated by certain personality patterns, by childhood training, imitation, incidental physical ailments. Organ inferiorities enable organs to "speak up" in what Adler termed their *organ dialect*. Whatever dysfunction proves effective in a patient's effort to excuse his "failure" may become a "symptom." Every neurosis has a purpose, and its function has to be understood within the total field in which the patient operates.

719

II. Personality Development

These basic psychological principles permit new insights into certain aspects of personality development.

1. *Heredity versus Environment*: The old controversy between the relative significance of hereditary or environmental factors is now resolved in a new way. It is neither heredity nor environment which shapes a child's development as such; it is the child himself who determines the significance of each. He experiences his hereditary endowment as an "inner environment", through facilities or handicaps. The child's ability to turn deficiencies into assets was demonstrated by Adler in his study of organ inferiorities, which marks the beginning of Individual Psychology. The child can react to obstacles within his own body or provided by his environment in two diametrically opposed ways. He can be discouraged and give up a function which becomes difficult, or he may try to overcome the difficulty by overcompensating for it, with a resultant special efficiency. The child does not merely react; he *acts*. It is this recognition of man's fundamental creative ability which distinguishes Individual Psychology from all mechanistic-deterministic approaches.

2. *The Family Constellation*: Whatever hereditary endowment the child has at his disposal is used by him in his efforts to find his place in his first group, which is his family. He interacts with each other member of the family almost at birth, and influences them at least as much as he is influenced by them. In many cases, the child with his rapidly developing notions of how to attain significance induces parents and older siblings to the kind of treatment he expects of them. All this takes place while no one involved is aware of what is going on.

The family constellation gives a picture of the group structure in which the child operates. The description of the family constellation can be called a sociogram (Moreno) of the early childhood group, showing the lines of alliance and competition, established with the active participation of the child. The most important person for the child's development is not father and mother, in many cases, but the sibling with whom he is in strongest competition. Competition is not identical with rivalry; the two may coincide, but need not. Competition is expressed in the differences of character, interests and temperament. The wider two siblings differ, the greater was the competition between them. Where one succeeded, the other one gave up his efforts—and vice versa. The strongest lines of competition are usually established between the first and second child in a family; consequently, these two are generally quite different. Who wins out and who loses depends on the children themselves, although the parents are the powers behind the scenes, encouraging the one and discouraging the other, and thereby establishing success and failure.

The sequence of birth provides each sibling with a special vantage in the family. He finds different opportunities depending on his position as an oldest, second, middle, youngest or only child. The only child may depend on others for his place, the oldest feels dethroned and tries to stay ahead, the second may try to keep up or overrun the first, the middle child may feel squeezed out since he does not have the rights of the older nor the privileges of the youngest sibling; the youngest may try to overrun all, or put them all into his service. However, birth order like all objective factors provides only probabilities; everything depends on the child's interpretation of his position. In each case, the child may successfully compensate for disadvantages he assumes to possess, and push the others down by elevating himself; or he may give up in defeat, either totally or in certain areas of functioning. The sequence of birth plus the information about the personality of each child and of the parents permits a clear understanding not only of the arena in which the child operated during his formative years, but also of the ways and means he employed to find a place in the family. These lines of movement became his character traits forming the basis for his personality.

3. *The Guiding Lines*: The child's methods and approaches

are the result of his groping; his personality traits are developed by trial and error, through the interaction with the other members of the family. He chooses certain guiding lines for the complexities of life in order to distinguish between right and wrong and mark off above and below. The parents primarily establish the value system for each family, and thereby provide moral and social perspectives for the children, which they may accept, reject, or feel indifferent about. Some guiding lines involve the function of either sex. Certain character traits appear as masculine or feminine, which may vary with each family. Masculinity may appear as a desirable form of superiority. However, such a masculine ideal may be resented by boys and girls. Boys may feel unable to live up to it; their "masculine protest" may be shared by girls who are impressed with women as being an "inferior" sex, and are unwilling to accept such a rôle. Other guiding lines for gaining status may be moral, physical, or intellectual superiority.

4. *The Life Style*: To find his orientation in all the maze of interactions and experiences, each child develops definite concepts about himself and the world around him. A guiding principle is generally firmly established within the first four to six years of life. Since a biased apperception makes the person impervious to experiences which contradict his convictions, the life style is maintained throughout, and can neither be recognized nor changed through the person's own efforts. If need be, this can be done in psychotherapy.

5. *The Three Phases of Childhood*: The preschool child tries to find his place within the family, the school child within the community, and the adolescent within society at large. The child's behavior in each phase depends on his self-confidence, and his feelings of belonging. Characteristic difficulties in both regards are prevalent and are responsible for aggressions and academic and social deficiencies.

6. *The Three Tasks of Life*: All problems which an adult has to face are within three fields presented by work, friendship, and the relationship with the opposite sex, through love and

marriage. Fulfillment of these three tasks presupposes social interest, courage, and the ability to give and take.

Fundamental rules for coöperation are provided by an "ironclad logic of social living." It presupposes a relationship of equals, since inequality, granting superiority to one and imposing inferiority upon another, constitutes an unstable equilibrium leading inevitably to conflict and friction. Full social functioning, which can be called social adjustment, does not merely imply compliance with social demands and conventions. Society is dynamic, in evolution, moving toward more adequate solutions to man's needs. Each individual has to participate on two social levels, meeting the demands of the group, and moving the group toward improvement. Adjustment means a precarious balance between present needs and the demands of evolution. All problems should be seen *sub specie aeternitatis,* i.e., from the viewpoint of eternity.

III. The Technique

The theoretical postulations of Individual Psychology provide the basis for specific techniques developed by Adler and his co-workers. The established technical procedures may be used differently by each practitioner; but the fundamental aspects remain the same.

1. *Psychotherapy*: Psychotherapy is primarily a learning process. The patient does not know himself, his motivations, his basic misconceptions and mistaken approaches. He knows perhaps what he is doing wrong, but not why. The Adlerian technique can be called a mirror technique. The patient is confronted with his private logic. He is not told what to do, but given to understand why he is not using good judgment or finding solutions to his problems.

Any psychotherapy based on depth psychology contains primarily four—although overlapping—phases. The first is the establishment and maintenance of a proper therapeutic relationship; the second is understanding the patient's basic dynamics (analysis); the third is helping the patient to understand himself, (insight); and the fourth is replacing his wrong premises (re-orientation). To all four phases Individual Psychology offers specific technical approaches.

The proper therapeutic relationship is one of mutual confidence. Emotional dependency of the patient is recognized and explained as an effort to relinquish responsibility and put the therapist into his service. Hostility, on the other hand, is not necessarily resistance to therapy, and may be not at all directed against the therapist primarily.

The analysis of the dynamics is gleaned from the statements of the patient, answers to selected questions, and from his overt behavior. The exploration of the background is first directed toward the present situation, which consists of the patient's complaints and his functioning on the three levels of work, friendship and sex. The question of what would be different if he were well links the subjective complaint with the objective life situation, and gives an indication of the purpose of the neurosis, i.e., against whom and what his symptoms are directed. If purpose of a symptom cannot be established, the psychogenesis of the symptoms is doubtful and organic pathology may be suspected. In this sense, the technique permits an accurate and reliable differential diagnosis between functional, psychogenic, and organic disturbances.

After an exploration of the present situation, the life style of the patient is ascertained. This is accomplished through an examination of the family constellation; it involves the field in which the patient developed his particular perspectives. Then, *the early recollections* are solicited. They indicate how the patient looks at life. He remembers from all the thousands of experiences which he had as a child only those which are in line with his basic concept of life. From these two sets of inquiries, family constellation and early recollections, the therapist can gain a picture of the patient's personality scheme[1] of his life. His basic mistakes then become obvious. They explain the present predicament.

The patient's overt behavior during the interview also shows his attitudes toward life. This is even more obvious in group psychotherapy. Additional exploration of various conflict situations in the past and in the present reveals the basic schema (pattern) on which the patient operates. All observations and findings are interpreted to the patient in an effort to help him understand himself.

Dreams are used in the same way. In them he demonstrates his private logic, by arranging conflict situations and meeting them in his own way. Dreams are considered as the factory of emotions. Through them the patient stimulates emotional attitudes in himself which are necessary for his way of movement at the time. Emotional reactions and thought processes are revealed to him as part of his movements, preparing and fortifying his actions.

The process of reorientation is the most time-consuming part of therapy, although it may sometimes occur rather fast. It is partly an intellectual process. The patient, becoming aware of his private logic, has a chance to reconsider his convictions. The difference beween "intellectual" and "emotional" understanding is that of a professed understanding as contrasted with real beliefs. He may see a point, but he does not "believe" it for himself. Additional therapeutic procedures facilitate the reorientation. The most important is *encouragement,* since discouragement is such an important element in maladjustment, and mistaken concepts are often the expression of a doubt in one's own strength and value. Interpretations make it difficult for the patient to maintain good intentions which he does not possess. The therapist "spits in his soup"—so to speak.

The process of reëducation involves a change in the value system of the patient. His social orientation is generally based on culturally induced values which are not conducive to coöperation, to inner security and inner freedom. Such mistaken values are: the need for self-elevation, overconcern with status and loss of prestige, the perfectionistic fear of making mistakes, of getting as much as possible for as little as possible. Psychotherapy cannot avoid a discussion and analysis of values in their psychological significance, either promoting emotional stability and social adaptation or endangering it. The ultimate goal of psychotherapy is the development of social interest to the fullest possible extent through the elimination of inferiority feelings. Since the basic fears of the patient are acquired in childhood and reflected in his particular life style, successful psychotherapy implies a modification of the life style through elimination of some of the most disturbing and mistaken basic convictions.

2. *Counseling*: There is no clear distinction established between psychotherapy and counseling. Since Individual Psychology is in a position to offer distinct techniques for counseling procedures, it is interested in a clarification and establishment of standards in counseling. Psychotherapy as "therapy" is primarily concerned with the treatment of illness; counseling, on the other hand, implies corrective guidance to normal people who have problems. Counseling is directed primarily to find solutions for immediate and well-defined areas of difficulties, be it vocational guidance, marital consultation, or child guidance, for parents or teachers.

The socio-teleological approach permits a rather quick and clear insight into the nature of existing problems and difficulties. All participants in a conflict are examined in their movements, resulting in the specific form of interaction, called a conflict. The counselor is, therefore, dealing with the total conflict situation, including all parts involved in it. He is not primarily concerned with what goes on *within* each party, but *between* them. Consequently, the counseling includes husband and wife, if it is marital, parents *and* child in child guidance; and if there are several children, all of them. The difficulties of the "problem child" cannot be separated from the behavior of his apparently better adjusted siblings; they are all part of the same problem.

Counseling consists primarily in giving information, be it in regard to technical details of what can be done in a given situation, or in regard to the psychological information on the private logic, the real intentions of movements of each participant. But the Adlerian orientation offers more for counseling. It is concerned with the premises for coöperation and with the factors which disturb it. For example, in this light the widespread assumption that marriage is a 50-50 proposition appears to be a fallacy; under this premise each partner is afraid of getting only 49% while 51% or more may be demanded from him. Or, the mother who apparently is concerned with the welfare of the child, when she tries to make him eat, is recognized in her efforts to impose her will on the child. The logic of social living forms the basis for an evaluation of each person's actions and movements in regard to furthering or impeding coöperation.

3. *Education*: Educational procedures can be properly evaluated by their effects. If they increase the child's social interest and courage, they are beneficial; if they diminish his self-confidence and self-esteem, they are detrimental. In this light many time-honored methods like reward and punishment appear not only as futile, but as outright damaging. They may have been adequate and effective in an autocratic society, but have lost their educational value in our present democratic amosphere. New methods are required—and are available—to stimulate growth and social adjustment. The keynote is encouragement. Learning and coöperation cannot be demanded, only evoked through interest and enthusiasm. Scolding, humiliation, and punishment evoke only rebellion but not conformity.

On the other hand, the democratic order can be preserved without suppression and hostility. Natural consequences of a disturbed order are employed instead of the previous pressure of an authority. A democratic relationship is based on mutual respect. The respect for the child can be neglected either by exposing him to humiliating and disparaging experiences, or by overprotection and spoiling. Spoiling expresses an underestimation of the child's abilities and deprives him of the necessary experience of his own strength. It also permits the child to dominate his parents and to put them into his service. Firmness and kindness express the necessary relationship of equals, based on mutual respect. This permits freedom *and* order; the child can express himself without imposing on others and ignoring *their* rights.

A new aspect has been introduced in education through the now available techniques to understand children in their motivation. The teleological approach permits a recognition of the child's goal in every one of his disturbing actions, be it his demand for attention and service, his effort to defeat power of the adults by establishing his own over them, be it his attempt to hurt in revenge or to display his utter inability in order to avoid further defeat. The "why" becomes more important in the education of children than the "what;" it permits specific remedial methods.

IV. Historical Review

The school of Individual Psychology is now some fifty years old. Adler joined Freud's discussion group in 1902. During that time he explored the influence of physical handicaps on the mind. His findings, marking the beginning of Individual Psychology, were in increasing conflict with that of Freud, and Adler left Freud's circle in 1911. In 1919, he founded several Child Guidance Centers in Vienna; in 1922 the *Internationale Zeitschrift für Individual Psychologie* began its publication which was interrupted between 1938 and 1949, and finally discontinued in 1952.[2]

In this country, Adler's psychology is often considered as a mere historical phase in the evolution of dynamic psychology. The student of psychology generally links Adler's name with the concept of the "inferiority complex" and the "will to power." If he is more informed, he may know of the "masculine protest." This limited knowledge of the significance and the all-inclusive character of Individual Psychology is the result of numerous factors. One is provided by the dominant position which one school of dynamic psychology has gained in the United States. Then there is the poor translation of Adler's books into English. Furthermore, Adler went through various, primarily three, phases of psychological formulations. The first was an organic orientation at the time when he was associated with Freud. Then came the assumption of an inherent inferiority feeling with its inevitable compensatory striving for power. Finally, he fully recognized the social significance of man and the formulations as presented in this review. Unfortunately, most books of the last and characteristic phase of Adler were written for popular consumption and, therefore, often neglected by professionals who formed their opinion of Adler's contribution only through reading the poorly translated early works.

We are witnessing a revival of Adlerian Psychology. Adler's basic tenets are re-affirmed through new discoveries by research and findings in various fields of science. Growing Adlerian groups have established training and service centers demonstrating the efficiency of their methods.

When Adler first formulated his concepts, he was often considered as unscientific. Today it is evident how much ahead of of his time Adler was, scientifically. His objections to mechanistic-deterministic concepts are shared today not only by philosophers but by physicists. The teleological approach is the basis for a new orientation in epistemology. The causal principle which assumes that a passive organism is affected by an overpowering force is increasingly discarded; the reaction of the organism to the outside force is recognized as determining the outcome of an interaction. Feedback and servo-mechanisms support Adler's concept of self-determination. The holistic concept is almost universally recognized today, although many have not yet reached Adler's formulations of how it can be practically applied. The Neo-Freudians are rediscovering Adler piecemeal. A recent survey revealed that in the opinion of orthodox psychoanalysts the so-called Neo-Freudians would be more correctly designated as Neo-Adlerians (Ansbacher). The social orientation, the purposiveness of behavior, the creative ability of man in his inner freedom, characteristic of Individual Psychology, are increasingly recognized.

Individual Psychology is very much alive, indeed. Active groups of Adlerians are organized in New York, Chicago and Los Angeles, maintaining training institutes and counseling centers, in New York the Alfred Adler Consultation Center and in Chicago the Community Child Guidance Centers. The American Society of Adlerian Psychology publishes the *American Journal of Individual Psychology*. Strong and active groups are at work in Amsterdam, London, Paris, Vienna and Zürich. The constitutional meeting of the International Association of Individual Psychology took place in Zürich, in 1954.

The purpose of organized groups of Adlerians is twofold: to maintain the knowledge and information gained through Adler and his co-workers so that it does not disappear from the accumulated body of knowledge; to make this knowledge available to the professional workers in psychiatry, psychology, education, and social science; to stimulate further research, using the existing knowledge as a springboard for further and better insight, rather than permitting research in the field to be bogged down by efforts to rediscover what already has been found.

FOOTNOTES

[1] Adler's German term *Schablone* was erroneously translated as "pattern."

[2] Alfred Adler was born in Vienna in 1870, and got his medical degree at the University of Vienna. Since 1926 he resided in New York and held professorships at Columbia University and at Long Island College of Medicine. He died during a lecture tour in Aberdeen, Scotland, in 1937.

BIBLIOGRAPHY ON INDIVIDUAL PSYCHOLOGY.*

Adler, A. Study of Organic Inferiority and Its Psychical Compensation. *Nerv. & Ment. Dis. Monogr.* Series No. 24, New York, 1917.
——*The Practice and Theory of Individual Psychology*. London: Kegan Paul, 1929.
——*The Neurotic Constitution*. New York: Dodd, Mead & Co., 1926.

——*Understanding Human Nature*. New York: Greenberg Publ., 1928.

——*What Life Should Mean to You*. New York: Little Brown & Co., 1931.

——*The Science of Living*. New York: Greenberg Publ., 1929.

——*The Pattern of Life*. London: Kegan Paul, 1931.

——*The Problems of Neurosis*. New York: Cosmopolitan Book Co., 1930.

——*The Education of Children*. New York: Greenberg Publ., 1930.

——*Social Interest, A Challenge to Mankind*. London: Faber & Faber, 1938.

Adler, Alexandra. *Guiding Human Misfits*. New York: Philosophical Library, 1948.

Bottome, P. *Alfred Adler; Apostle of Freedom*. New York: Putnam, 1946.

Dreikurs, R. *Fundamentals of Adlerian Psychology*. New York: Greenberg Publ., 1950.

——*The Challenge of Marriage*. New York: Duell, Sloan & Pearce, 1946.

——*The Challenge of Parenthood*. New York: Duell, Sloan & Pearce, 1948.

——*Character Education and Spiritual Values in an Anxious Age,* Beacon Press, 1953.

Ganz, M. *The Psychology of Alfred Adler and the Development of the Child*. New York: The Humanities Press, 1953.

Mairet, P. *The ABC of Adler's Psychology*. London: Kegan Paul, 1928.

Orgler, H. *Alfred Adler the Man and his Work*. London: C. W. Daniel, 1939.

Reiss, S. *Mental Readjustment*. London: George Allen & Unwin, 1949.

Way, L. *Adler's Place in Psychology*. London: Allen & Unwin, 1950.

Wexberg, E. *Individual Psychology*. New York: Cosmopolitan Book Co., 1929.

——*The Psychology of Sex*. New York: Farrar & Rinehart, 1931.

——*Individual Psychology Treatment*. London: C. W. Daniel, 1929.

——*Our Children in a Changing World*. New York: Macmillan Co., 1938.

Wolfe, W. B. *Nervous Breakdown: Its Cause and Cure*. New York: Farrar & Rinehart, 1933.

——*How To Be Happy Though Human*. New York: Farrar & Rinehart, 1931.

——*A Woman's Best Years*. New York: Emerson Books, 1935.

* *This list includes only books published in English.*

Chapter XXX

INTERPERSONALISM AND SOMEIKONICS

James Clark Moloney, M.D.

EDITORIAL NOTE

When Dr. James C. Moloney submitted his paper entitled "Clinical Notes on the Body Image," the editor was placed in a quandary. It was certainly a most interesting recess of the mind to explore, and yet it was not general enough for inclusion in a broad survey.

The editor then suggested that a historical introduction be added and that the title be changed. "The concept of the body image is intriguing, and if it is developed as a branch of psychoanalysis, it might give rise to a new area and require a name like someikonics, *in which case the chapter might be labeled 'Interpersonalism and Someikonics.' My main wish is to keep to some uniformity in the chapters, which are all taking up a large field. Now it would be best for your cause to* develop *your topic into a field which could be cultivated by others."*

Dr. Moloney was good enough to fall in with the suggestion and has even accepted the new coinage, as a designation for the growing collection of data dealing with the body-image and its rôle in the development of neurosis. Whether Paul Schilder, who was largely responsible for the conception of the body-image would have liked the term 'someikonics' is beyond our ken, but he certainly would have been glad that his explorations have yielded fruit.

Dr. James Clark Moloney, a psychoanalytic practitioner, has written a number of fascinating articles in American Imago *and other journals, and is the author of* The Battle for Mental Health *(New York, 1952) and* Understanding the Japanese Mind *(New York, 1954)—a volume of ethnic psychology based on personal experiences and presenting the highlights of Japanese psychoanalytic endeavor.*

WHAT IS INTERPERSONALISM?

Interpersonalism is inseparably linked with the name of the late Harry Stack Sullivan.[1] Mabel Cohn provides us with the most succinct and the clearest descriptive elucidation of interpersonalism and/or of Sullivanian psychiatry. The two are almost synonymous. Her operational restatement of Sullivan's system appears as an "Introduction" to *The Interpersonal Theory of Psychiatry*.[2]

In answer to "What is interpersonal relations?" Mabel Cohn says:

> . . . this core [communication] can be described as the psychiatry of interpersonal relations, or as the study of communication between persons, or as the operational approach to psychiatry in which the psychiatrist plays the rôle of participant observer. It rests on the propositions that: (1) a large part of mental disorder results from and is perpetuated by inadequate communication, the communicative processes being interfered with by anxiety; and (2) each person in any two-person relationship is involved as a portion of an interpersonal field, rather than as a separate entity, in processes which affect and are affected by the field.

She further elucidates Sullivan:

> The dynamic patterns of interaction must be known both specifically and also generally, in terms of types or categories of pattern. Sullivan has contributed to progress in this direction in two main ways. *First*[3] he has attempted to conceptualize in a systematic way the nature of experience. . . . In Sullivan's conceptualization, experience occurs in three modes, which he has called prototaxic, parataxic, and syntaxic. . . . Prototaxic refers to experience occurring before symbols are used; parataxic refers to experience characterized by symbols used in a private or autistic way; and syntaxic is used for

experience which one person can communicate to another, for it is conceptualized in symbols which are defined alike by each. . . .

Sullivan's *second*[4] important contribution to a theory of child development is the concept of dynamism. He defines dynamism as 'the relatively enduring patterns of energy transformation which recurrently characterize the interpersonal relations . . . which make up the distinctively human sort of being.' . . . Each . . . [human being] develops a variety of interwoven . . . patterns, in relation to the important zones of interaction with the environment (such as the oral and anal zones), and also in relation to the important needs (such as hunger and lust). These dynamisms [called "action patterns" by Kardiner[5]] are developed and patterned from early interpersonal experience and are then carried by the person into his subsequent interpersonal experience.

The interpersonal field, then, is made up of the interaction of a variety of dynamisms of two or more organisms. Some of these dynamisms are *conjunctive* (for example, the need for intimacy) and lead to an integration of a situation with a resolution or reduction of tension; others, which involve anxiety, are *disjunctive* and lead to disintegration of the situation; sometimes a dynamism can be non-operative, since there is no corresponding dynamism brought to the situation by the other person. . . .

Because my approach to psychiatry considers transformations in someikonics as participating in the processes subsuming emotional transformations, I direct special attention to Cohn's Introductory reference to the Sullivan concept of Malevolent Transformation: " . . . one of the dynamisms complicated by anxiety is the 'malevolent transformation,' in which the need for tenderness has, under the impact of anxiety, been replaced by malevolent behavior. . . ."

Since emotions are not expressible unless associated with, or even caused by concomitant bodily changes, it is not strange that this malevolent transformation idea permits an immediate swing into an elucidation of the meaning of someikonics.

Edoardo Weiss in his Introduction to *Ego Psychology and the Psychoses*[6] stated:

> Federn applied the term ego feeling only to those contents that are sensed as participating in the coherent ego unity; that is, in a distinct entity, something opposed to external reality. It is the feeling of bodily and mental relations in respect to time and content, the relation being regarded as an uninterrupted or restored unity. From an accurate study of the dreaming ego, it appears evident that mental ego and bodily ego are felt separately, but in the waking state the mental ego is [nearly] always experienced as being inside the bodily ego.
>
> . . . only when the body image [someikon] is completely vested with ego feeling does the actual feeling of bodily ego correspond to the entire body image. Conversely, the bodily ego can disappear without involving the somatic organization, which allows proper use of the body, with the unity of correctly ordered perceptions of one's own ego.
>
> . . . to account for the fluctuating intensity of the ego feeling, Federn postulated the existence of a specific ego cathexis. . . . However, . . . he never asserted that his theories could explain the actual phenomenon of the ego *Erlebnis,* the ego experience. He provided only dynamic and economic orientations which were valuable in this field of research. . . .

Weiss called attention to other important observations:

> Federn calls . . . attention to the fact that the ego is subject and object simultaneously. . . . Federn's concepts of the ego as a dynamic entity and the ego boundary as its peripheral sense organ are new . . . , [and

his] discovery that ego states can be repressed is also proved by the fact that they can be rearoused in dreams. . . .

THE BODY IMAGE

Schilder's[7] preoccupation with the body image stemmed from his neurological studies of the causes for anosognosia.[8] Schilder insisted that there is no schism between the organic nervous system and the "action patterns" that eventually establish the individual's position in space.

The wedding of someikonics with interpersonalism is revealed especially in those ikonic fragments that demonstrate a "stop or frozen motion" or a congealed stagnation or fixation of a cross section or a period (indicating by the word "period" the presence of some measure of time) of emotional development because of some traumatizing effect of the significant parent upon the maturing child. This of course alludes to an interpersonal operation between the significant parent and the child. I called attention to the most important first interpersonal relation—mother-child—in an article entitled, "The Cornelian Corner and Its Rationale,"[9] when I said:

> . . . it is frequently forgotten that at four or five months of age the [precognitive] child has not differentiated himself and his mother, the significant parent [interpersonalism]. . . . Any [maternal] restrictive activity occurring at the rectum, the urethral sphincter or at the mouth tending to regulate the operation of these areas would be construed by the child as being a part of himself operating and influencing himself. [In precognitive bowel training] a part of reality not himself but believed to be a part of himself then becomes adherent at the psychic topographical representation of the rectum, in the synthesizing body image; the 'mother' becomes adherent at the rectum, becomes adherent in the active form of rectal rigidity and restriction and spasm. In fact, in these rigid compulsive characters, there is

often an associated sphincter spasm. The 'mother' is constant and never relinquishes her grasp [somatic interpersonalism]. It is important to emphasize that, where bowel training has been prematurely enforced, the child has not yet differentiated himself from the mother; that his ego boundaries have not been restricted to his body surfaces, that his psychic body image then, as a result, contains an invagination from reality. This invagination occurring at the 'body image' of the rectum is composed of mother-child combinations.

. . . in psychic representations of the body, the invaginations and indentations of reality are interpreted as being a part of the child himself . . . the pressures in the topographical areas involved are not as yet differentiated from the outer world. At this time there was no outer world so that anything happening to the child happens to him as a manifestation of an activity of his own. . . . A part of reality becomes adherent to the superfices of the body in the body image that can never again be completely separated, . . . what belongs to the child and what does not belong to the child becomes adherent in a kind of psychic intermingling. This intermingling does not permit [complete] respective separation into that which belongs to the parent (i.e., reality), and into that which belongs to the child.

The same type of interference can be instituted at the oral level by not feeding the child when he is hungry or when he is in pain.[10] The mother absenting herself at that precise moment has an analogous effect upon the child as the mother's interference with normal anal functioning. When this occurs before homeostatic organization, it occurs at a time when the experience cannot be consciously integrated. A subcortical or reflex [or attitudinous] child is developed who remains fixed, static, stagnant and operative despite the later development of consciousness. . . . a reflex, *automatic person* comes to exist within [the] *conscious person* who is in contact with the reality situation. Two people come to live under one skin, both of them attempting to operate the organs and muscles of the body and having but one supply of energy at the command of both.

CONFIRMATION FROM HYPNOTISM

A hypnotist said to his adult subject: "When I count three you will awaken but you will be eight years old." The subject awakened and did not recognize the hypnotist. Of course, when the subject was eight years old, he had not yet met the hypnotist, but more significant, looking into the mirror the subject did not recognize his adult body, his adult identity; being eight years old he was not yet familiar with the form and character he saw reflected.

The memorial image of the body is not a simple concept. The image may be constantly changing in accordance with the contemporary changes of the body surface. But other difficulties are posed: The body image at one year of age will be different from that at two, five, or thirteen years of age. However, the development of a new body image does not wholly obliterate the old image from memory.

Anosognosia, macropsia, micropsia, instances of multiple personalities elicited by hypnosis, catatonia, *déja vu* phenomena— all indicate that a number of body images are resident in the same person. When one body image is in operation, what happens to the preceding body images? Apparently they are not cathected, are not energized. The analogy of a flashing electrical sign comes to my mind, one part of the sign being lit up, while another part remains dark. A sequence of visibility occurs. That which is dark or black can be lit up when supplied with electrical energy, and the part that had just been lit up becomes black. Perhaps the same process happens in the psyche. The memorable body images of the past that are now in darkness, i.e., forgotten, can be illuminated if energized.

DISTORTED BODY IMAGE

The sense of reality is interdigitated with the memorable picture of the body. The more normal the individual, the more the body image conforms to the actual limiting membranes of the body. The body can shrink or expand, and when this happens, a new image should form immediately. More than likely a new image does form—provided there has been no blocking of the concomitant integrated sensory registration in the psyche. The new image accommodates to the change, parallels the new body surface. This constant change is determined by the reality situation.

Actually, development of adequate memorial body images seldom occurs and the problems posited by this fact can be highlighted. For instance, a schizophrenic might feel that a leg grows out of his chest or a hand out of his head. The schizophrenic incapable of spatial relationships might lose his identity, might not know who he is, might feel that he is the "other" person—the other "significant"[11] person. The assumption is that this disturbance is brought about by the fusion of his own body image with the body image of his mother because of inadequate stimulation during infancy. Memory elements for spatial relationship between the self and mother are absent, because significant spatial relationships with the mother were in fact absent during the schizophrenic's earliest childhood.

One schizophrenic woman for many years felt as if she had two separate gastrointestinal tracts; one was the tract belonging to her adult body; the other tract, a smaller tract, commenced at her larynx and ended in her rectum. For years the extra system did not seem too real and she could banish the impression of its existence from her mind. However, on her wedding night, the husband was terribly shocked by a sudden, and incomprehensible, change in his wife's behavior. One moment she was an adult woman; the next instant she babbled like an infant, she freely passed flatus, urine, and feces into the nuptial bed. The man, instead of becoming a husband, had become a mother.

STRATIFIED PHASES OF THE SELF

The different stratifications of the body ego (occurring as the result of) the maturative process are indubitably contained in the memorial system as serial pictures of the self in some phase of the biographic relationship with the mother. The hypnotized man and the woman who became an infant on her nuptial eve demonstrated radical, shocking differences and sudden departures from the usual or expected appearance in the presentation in consciousness of the body schema. To be recognizable, however, these differences need not be so dramatically at variance with the normal. Many people, more or less vaguely, consciously appreciate defections, inconsistencies, and unrealistic characteristics in their body image. Two examples will illustrate:

A school teacher taught kindergarten for many years. She was successful and she adjusted well with her young pupils. Laughingly, she attributed her success to the belief that she was of the same emotional age as the tots that she taught. But one day she was promoted. She was made a home room teacher for seventh graders. At once she became quite disorganized. The seventh graders seemed too much larger than herself and more adult than herself. With psychoanalysis this feeling of being smaller than her charges disappeared. Today she feels that the seventh graders are but children and experiences herself as an adult— much larger, older, more competent, and more learned than her pupils.

A man, a young Apollo, six-foot three, weighing two hundred ten pounds, pictured himself as four-foot eleven inches tall and weighing in the neighborhood of eighty-five pounds. The image of his gigantic self in the mirror did not remove his sense of smallness. Despite actual measurement he could not rid himself of the feeling of being shrivelled, and physically inconspicuous. He was a schizophrenic, full of resentment and homicidal impulses. He was afraid to become aware of his great strength for fear that he would commit murder.

PRESENT-DAY PSYCHOLOGY

ANOSOGNOSIA AND ITS IMPLICATIONS

Evidences of the disturbances that occur in the memorial representation of the body are universal. Most physicians know about phantom limbs, but few seem aware of the tenacious anosognosia frequently associated with the amputation of the woman's breast. Whereas the phantom limb might eventually disappear, the anosognosia covering the breast loss may continue for a long time with undiminished intensity.[12] Sophisticated surgeons realize that in our culture women react more violently to the loss of their breasts than they do to the loss of their genitalia. In fact, they treasure their breasts even more than they treasure their limbs or any other organ or set of organs in their body.

Mrs. M. G. demonstrated in an exaggerated fashion the ego image dynamics operating behind the scene of breast amputation. She had had four children and had nursed only the second child. That her breast contained a malignant growth was established. Prior to the planned amputation she saw a young woman return from an operating room without an arm. The obsession that the doctor would cut off her left arm as well as her breast overwhelmed her. A divorcée dependent upon typing for a livelihood she feared for her future. Extension of the cancer to the arm was not suspected but her obsession terrorized the typist. When the ether mask was applied in the operating room she decided against the operation and fought furiously, preferring death from cancer[13] to losing her arm. In spite of her struggles, radical mastectomy without amputation of the arm was completed.

The surgery was followed by serious emotional disturbance. After a few emotionally sterile interviews with me, she began to castigate the various members of her family, her employer, and her associates. She charged them with abandoning her, not only during childhood, but also as the subject of a mastectomy. During childhood a young brother had robbed her of her mother, i. e., of the mother's love. Now, a "Sister," a physician, robbed her of her breast, because the doctor-sister, knowing the dangers of cancer, had not insisted over the patient's protest upon an earlier removal of the tumor. It seemed proved from future events that her mother image and her own breast image were fused in her memory. The anosognosia was intense and persistent.

Anosognosia is indicative of disturbances in the ego boundaries and the memorial body boundaries. The complicated exchangeability between breast, mother, self, and analyst were exposed in a dream of the typist: "I had a friend, a woman friend, known to me since my childhood, who had two sons. One son wore a lavender raffia shirt, the other son wore a green shirt; both shirts exuded a scent."

From free associations it was ascertained that the son covered with the lavender shirt (funeral wreath) not only represented the patient's mother (who had died of cancer some thirteen years previous to the dream) but also represented the patient's left breast that had been so recently amputated. The other son, "her breast," "her new mother," the son with the green shirt, seemed to represent the Irish therapist, who sees his patients in a room decorated in green throughout.

REVEALING DREAMS

It was necessary to cancel her next appointment. That evening she dreamed of "a woman who had no breasts at all. . . ." She awoke in a panic and telephoned me, insisting that I see her as a matter of *life* and *death*.

Not seeing me at the scheduled hour meant that she had lost me, just as earlier she had lost her mother and just as recently she had lost her substitute mother, *her own breast*. Mother—her own breast—her own analyst—all meant the same thing to her and at each loss she suffered separation anxiety.

Another dream confirmed that the patient and her mother were one and the same person. The milk-giving breast, the love-giving breast, her own breast, became her mother as well as being her own appendage. The dream catapulted her into a panic:

> I had a hang nail on my right index finger. I looked under the piece of skin and saw a worm there. I screamed and I rushed to the kitchen where I turned warm water over the finger. Worms poured out of my finger in countless numbers. They filled the sink. Then I thought I would take a knife and cut my finger off, but I knew if I did that I would bleed to death.

The day before the dream she had felt as if she were "dead and alive at the same time," and during a nervous spell had pulled the skin away from the side of the nail. That day her earlier obsession about amputation of her arm as well as her breast had been recalled to her. Three days later the terror felt in the dream still persisted, terror from an inner fear that she would need to commit suicide.

Being dead and alive represented her identification with her dead mother and with the maggots that devoured her mother. Thirteen years after her mother's death, the patient lost her own right breast, her mother. The worms in the dream represented her own teeth, her own wish to gobble up everything. This was a paranoid projection that became turned in upon herself. Her typical advance, her method of moving in on a significant host (including the analyst) was accompanied by a barrage of vitriolic, biting invectives. The biting edge of this attack included the accusation that she was being discriminated against, shabbily treated. There was a knife, a set of teeth, in most of her comments. Quite possibly her teeth, used initially to attack the denying and frustrating breast of her mother, were psychically turned against her own breast which represented the mother. They speak of cancers eating away the flesh. After this material was worked through she recalled that at four years of age she occupied herself with the phantasy of shoving pins into her mother.

The fear of bleeding to death, which would be interpreted as a castration anxiety by orthodox Freudians, must have a deeper significance. If this patient cut off her finger, ridding herself of the maggots, her teeth, she would bleed to death. When she did not exercise mastery, especially oral mastery—biting, inclusion, cannibalism—everything would be taken from her, would uncontrollably drain out of her. Helpless, without sphincters, she would be unable to dam back her world-shattering rages. She would cease to exist.

At a later visit, in evident desperation, the patient wailed: "You have disembowelled me! Your interpretations have made my past way of living life impossible. You have made me utterly dependent upon you. You have disembowelled me." She was right. In her psychic reality, at least, she *was* disembowelled, in the sense that her dependency upon me was so absolute that she had no further need for her own digestive apparatus. In the therapeutic medium, she was a fetus. The therapist was the mother (interpersonalism and parataxis) connected to her by an umbilical cord. Since the intrauterine fetus uses the digestive tract of the mother, the regression to this fetal state disembowelled her.

This woman nearly died when she was a young girl from ulcerative colitis, which subsided only when she left her mother's house. This material was represented in her dreams in a somewhat surprising way. She dreamed that a muff was attached to her vagina. As long as cream poured out of the muff,[14] she would have no more trouble with the "alley." It was clear that "trouble with the alley" meant the return of her ulcerative colitis. This colitis became more severe during negative phases of her transference.

DISPLACEMENTS AND CONFUSION

In many of her dreams she likened the scar of her mastectomy to the "scar" of the vagina. The mix-up in body image permitted the vagina to be used as a breast—and in the latest dream as a breast that gave cream. Without her penis-breast she felt empty. As an infant, as a child, as a young woman, as a physically matured woman still in possession of both breasts, she was always forlorn—always heartbroken. During a period when circumstances forced her to live in a poverty-stricken locale, she became the passive partner in a homosexual relationship. This arrangement lasted for several months but was never completely satisfying. She yearned for fulfillment, but homosexuality did not solve her problem so she terminated the arrangement.

The vagina in her waking life was considered a mutilation that prevented her giving love. If she did not give love, she would not be loved. If she were to be hated, she'd give me a good reason for hating her. She'd smear me with feces, with invectives, with her hostility. Beneath this bristling façade was a feeling of utter hopelessness and despair, weakness, worthlessness, and a great need to be loved. The interest here is in highlighting the blurring of the memorable images of her vagina and of her amputated breast; and the telescoping of the two areas—breast and vagina; both being represented at the vaginal area by the muff that gave milk. By giving milk she gave love, and because she gave love, it followed that she was lovable and that she would be loved, that her vagina would be loved.

Semantic confusions troubled the patient. To her the hollow viscus, the uterus, the vagina meant "emptiness" and the word characterized her feelings about herself. Without her breast, her mother, she felt incomplete. She sought the lost mother for the "togetherness" with the mother, which was essential for her to feel ecstatically whole, religious, complete. It may be, then, that for some women not only the culture's derogatory attitude toward the vagina[15] but also the vagina and uterus as symbols of hollowness and emptiness organize or anchor their precognitive reactionary feelings of nothingness.

SUBSTITUTION OF IMAGES

Vigorously and relentlessly this woman discouraged feelings of tenderness, attempting to make it impossible for anyone to love her or to be gentle with her. She presented the picture of *"malevolent transformation"* described by Sullivan, and also portrayed the parataxis of Sullivan and/or the mechanism of transference detailed by Freud. Her malevolent transformation of character was accomplished by substitution of one set of someikonics for an entirely different, if not antithetic set of someikonics. In serving a need for tenderness the someikonics subsuming non-masochistic passive receptivity are cathected. However, because passive reception prepares this patient for exploitation by her aggressive mother, she defended herself by attacking instead of being passive to the love object. Later she was exploited by the aggressive homosexual. The switch from an attitude of passive dependency to an attitude favoring the scurrilous excretion of barbed invectives was accompanied by a switch in cathexis from an oral someikon to an anal someikon, i.e., the switch from an oral readiness to an anal-projectile readiness is subsumed by a switch from an oral receptive psychic-somatic-psychic organization to an anal-projectile psychic-somatic-psychic organization. Giving in to her need for dependency denuded her of the accretions of action patterns that represented to her her sense of self—her sense of self that demanded out of fear of helplessness that the "conning tower" for executive functions remain continuously in her possession.

In this frame of reference the operation of the anal projectile someikon is not merely a memorable object representation of projectile activity at the anus. Actual activity at the rectum and throughout the colon (severe attacks of ulcerative colitis) took place during those times that she found it necessary to defend herself against a yearning for tenderness.

It seems obvious that this patient's traumatic neurosis from the surgery thrust upon her destroyed any feelings of confidence she may have had in the adequacy of her character structure—a structure of action patterns representing an artificial, synthetic, substitute mother. In some instances an individual develops an exaggerated independence which becomes a character construct—an action pattern. If an infantile maternal dependency is fraught with danger, unpredictability, frustration, and deprivation, the individual deserts the depriving or abandoning mother and phantasies a predictable, generous, friendly and giving mother. This new mother, although only a psychic reality, is woven into the character structure and becomes a mother of considerable magical prowess, an actual, integral part of the neurosis. However, when this psychic mother, this false character structure with the built-in maternal features, is impotent in defense against some outside danger, it disintegrates explosively, forcibly returning the person to the helpless state which immediately followed the first abandonment by the flesh-and-blood mother. This mechanism underlies the manifestations of traumatic neurosis and in relation to some of the action pattern situations he described, Kardiner[16] may have reported situations containing unreal and magical elements as well as social character constructs.

RIGIDITIES EXPLAINED

There are very few individuals living in this culture who do not in some way exhibit fixed character rigidities. These rigidities indicate total or partial failure to develop an appropriate body ego, or body schema. Some of the fixities are complex, others are subtle; but in each instance the individual has failed to arrive at memories of the self system that are distinguishable from memories of the mother system. Without exhausting the possibilities, description of a few of such rigidities will expose some of the perplexities and difficulties confronting the human being in his struggle to experience maturity.

An asthmatic patient dreamed he was in his car, which he could not move because it was straddled by a lumber-carrying machine. He awakened with asthma. From his associations the machine symbolized his mother, with the patient *in utero*. The mother was as necessary to him as the air that he breathed. In fact, in this topographic "catatonic" state, his "mother" breathed for him as she had when he was in her womb. His lungs returned to their condition of intrauterine inactivity. Such an effect is produced through the retrospective intra-psychic picture of the memorial image of the self surrounded by the memorial image of the mother. The dynamic operation of this picture, triggered by a special set of external circumstances, constituted for this patient a fixed unconscious phantasy that represented to him a psychic "reality."

A pregnant female patient dreamed that she had a tube sticking into her right foot. The tube was pulled out, leaving drainage. For many years the patient had had a weeping patch of eczema where the tube appeared in the dream. At first she considered the tube a penis. However, she was not satisfied with this interpretation. It seemed more certain to her that the tube was the umbilical cord. The same patient dreamed of an icebox that cost $5000. Upon awakening she thought the icebox contained milk and that it was in some way the analysis. As she pondered, a globus that felt like a foot developed in her throat. In her fantasies the foot turned into a penis; then she again fell asleep. In another dream she had two inguinal hernias, one on each side, and a large umbilical hernia. Awakening she thought of the inguinal hernias as testicles and the umbilical hernia as a penis. Then she remembered that there were nipples on all of the hernias. She came to the conclusion that the inguinal hernias not only were testicles but also represented breasts. The discharge or drainage from the nipple of the umbilical hernia she identified with her own breast, from which colostrum recently had appeared. The patient identified this umbilical dream with the tube dream.

TRANSPOSITIONS AND EQUATIONS

The late Dr. Lionel Blitzstein often pointed out that in psychic phantasy involving the mouth, the anus is also implied. He averred the converse to be true, as well. I have found this to be true in a study of my own cases. The umbilical cord indicates nutrition and elimination. This patterning permits the fetus to equate the mother or the mother to equate the fetus, and each can contain the other. This is demonstrated by the pregnant patient's next dream and the material derived through free association from it. In the dream, a man was being chased by police In a firing duel the man was wounded in his wrist. He proceeded to wrap his wrist with strips of blue gingham and the police stopped shooting. Her first association to blue gingham was "The Gingham Dog and the Calico Cat" and she brought the complete poem to her next session. Lines in the final verse are particularly significant:

> *Next morning, where the two had sat,*
> *They found no trace of dog or cat:*
> *And some folks think unto this day*
> *That burglars stole that pair away!*
> *But the truth about the cat and pup*
> *Is this: they ate each other up!*

Because such intermingling between the self and another person takes place before ego integration, the patient was unable to disentangle the blur of self-elements and mother-elements. Because the two individuals had not been differentiated in her mind, she felt that all elements of all systems were a part of herself. In this sector, differentiation is never complete because the time and the opportunity for distinguishing the two (mother-elements and self-elements) have passed. Such discrepancies and blurring are often revealed in body drawings.[17]

PROJECTION AND GENITALIZATION

The total or focal absence of body ego boundaries which permits psychic oozing or uncontained psychic meanderings is at times responsible for bizarre symptom patterns. Five patients were suddenly afflicted with hay fever during their analytic hours. The nasal congestions seemed totally unrelated to their free associations. The abrupt appearance of these attacks puzzled me until a medical student patient clarified the situation. A sufferer from hay fever, he directed my attention to the hollyhocks apparent through the window of the analytic room. Bumble bees laden with pollen flew in and out of the open blossoms and little time was required to establish that this sight caused the sudden onsets of hay fever. Likely the opening of the flower was to each patient a psychic projection of his mouth, a bee represented the mother entering the mouth—which devoured the mother. On another level, more nearly contemporaneous with development of the conscious ego, the vortex of the flower is conceived as the opening of the vaginal mouth and the bee with the pollen is a male organ laden with semen.[18]

This genitalization represents an evolution of the cannibalizing concept of the mouth incorporating the mother. The sneezing of a patient was a reaction formation against cannibalizing or phallic penetration. The rhinorrhea surrounding the foreign object (maternal breast or penis), was an angry liquid extension of self, and the whole intrusive object was forcibly ejected by the sneeze. George Wilson, in a private communication, likened the process to a urination against an offending foreign penetrating object. Thus conceived, there are still two aspects of the phenomenon which remain to be clarified: first, the activity occurred in the nose rather than in the mouth, and second, the activity of the bees occurred in hollyhocks at least fifteen feet away from the patients, outside a closed window. In another communication[19] I pointed out that spatial relationships are erased when traumatic experiences occur prior to the development of the conscious ego, and prior to the functioning of the integrative processes of the ego:

> The end organ (nose, eye, mouth, skin, ear) takes in a 'piece' of the mother and might interpret the piece to be the entire mother. Distances, as yet, mean nothing. The infant's powers of projection have not been effectively developed through experience. Sufficient condensation of memory traces are not available for utilization. Hence, the mother is experienced as being enveloped by or existing at the end organ. To the child, the end organ itself might become the mother.

The nose may be used for a mouth in the displacement resulting from a traumatic experience such as an actual oral frustration that occurred before the advent of ego critique:

Consequences of Maternal
Attitude Antics

Such dissociations and inconsistencies may develop lasting and serious conflicts in the older child. If the mother's voice is raucous, she may be angry, and this might trouble the child at a time when all the other senses report a situation of harmonious compatibility. The child may be thrown into conflict if his eyes see that her face is distorted with rage, and yet the other senses report serenity. Mothers have occasioned serious disorders by the wearing of false faces, by making hideous faces, or by blackening their faces. Conflicts have been produced in the unsuspecting suckling by the application of boot black or quinine to the lactating breast.

Disturbing character-conditioning reflexes may result from inconsistencies in the mother's presentation of her body to the child. Should a later traumatic event bring about a narcissistic retreat into the fixed phantasy of the original mother-child relationship, these distorted conditioned reflexes might well become activated into disturbing his existence. Their significance will defy understanding unless their biography is understood . . . .

These factors should be emphasized, because seeing, hearing, feeling, smelling, and tasting permit the incorporation of a portion of something that exists outside the body and yet in the real sense nothing irreplaceable is lost by the outer object. In being felt, heard, and seen, nothing at all is subtracted from the object. One might hypothesize that since feeling, hearing, and seeing are contemporaneously correlated with tasting, the subsequent fullness and tension in the abdomen, associated with the disappearance of the object (mother), provide the seeing, the hearing, and the feeling of the mother with a cannibalistic implication.

The ears, too, can be put to "alimentary" use. A patient "eats up" the words of the analyst, phantasying that he drains the analyst dry by listening to his interpretations. Another patient devours the analyst with his eyes and gets a "full" head. Some patients get a full feeling in their ears when the analyst talks. The noses of others become stuffy when they smell the odors associated with an analyst. Of course, this cannibalistic mastery is an illusion, however, the remembered association of physiological activities at all the sensory end organs stimulated by the mother nursing the child, permits the utilization of displacements of the eye, the nose, the skin, or the ear, for the mouth.

The frigidity or rigidity of a woman is often caused by a topographical catatonic dynamism. The dynamism is inaugurated in early childhood. The infant traumatized by one or more severe maternal affronts develops a series of self-contained, compensating, self-induced action patterns that supplant the maternal figure. The outcome of these action patterns, built out of a fear of dependency, finally is an appearance of unassailable independence, which is in fact neurotic and exaggerated. This independence becomes involved in the operation of the diacritic system.

THE WOMAN-INFANT

There is a dependency intrinsic in sexual intercourse that is not only expressive of the relationship to the sex partner, but also of the relationship to the vegetative processes involved; once initiated, the orgasm continues beyond conscious control. The woman is forced to relinquish her control, her independence, and even her personally dominated, synthetic mother. The action patterns constitute her neurotic independence of the mother; therefore they are representative of her own concept of the mother. She sets up within herself a puppet mother, controllable and predictable. For such a woman the sexual orgasm induces a limited or minor traumatic neurosis. Her helplessness during the orgasm, her inability to control or to modify it, disproves her "independence." The synthetic, self-serving mother turns out to be a myth. This is terrifying; more significant, this loss of the synthetic mother leaves the woman torn and as dependent as she was originally, when her action-patterns were first adopted, because of the real mother's abandonment.

The traumatic loss of the synthetic "mother" (created out of the constituted and instituted action patterns) reduces such a woman to helplessness and infantilism. The "infant" (woman) is in "catatonic dependency" upon the bed or is in "catatonic dependency" on her male sexual partner. During the orgasm, at least, the woman-infant is connected with the male by means of an umbilical cord represented by the penile tie. During the orgasm, the sphincters relinquish their hold. The woman-infant loses control—pours herself out. She may defecate, urinate or pass flatus in a passive way—as a fetus passively releases waste at the same time that it is nourished, warmed, and oxygenated by the mother.

Urinating, defecating or the passing of flatus during an orgasm is repugnant and humiliating to the normal mature and aesthetic aspects of the woman's ego, the portion that is adult and in contact with reality.[20] Feces, flatus, and urine are severely interdicted by this culture. No wonder a woman holds onto herself, won't let herself go, and that feminine frigidity intervenes to safeguard the woman against shame.

Genital gratification may be linked in the gestalt pattern with body pleasure, because in early life the child masturbated when deserted by the mother. The masturbation replaces the real mother with a synthetic, controllable mother of the patient's design, made up of part of the patient's own body. Therefore, genital pleasure comes to mean breast pleasure or nursing pleasure. Oral activity in this psychic setting implies anal activity—one cannot be considered without the other—and indicates regression to an early infantile period, in which liberal feeding and eliminating activities were allowed.

The analytic material of a schizophrenic woman thirty years of age exhibited the blurring that existed in her psyche between her memorial object representative for the mouth and her memorial object representative for her vagina. When frustrated she experienced many very disagreeable and frightening sensations, and because of her inordinate omnipotence needs she was nearly always frustrated. These sensations emerged from her mouth area and from her vaginal area. At one and the same time she felt like urinating, perspiring in the perineal region, swallowing, coughing, choking, and defecating. Associated with these sensations were other feelings of throat and vaginal contractions. Sexual desires of considerable intensity frequently invoked orgasms that were experienced in the buttocks as well as in the clitoris. During these orgasms aggravating pains assaulted her throat as well as her vagina.

In thinking in terms of the body image or perhaps more properly in terms of the kinesthetic aspects of the body image, one would not be too amazed to learn one spectacular thing about this schizophrenic woman. She could relieve all of her vaginal and throat sensations by smoking a cigarette, or by gorging herself on food. The gorging of herself on food was more relished and more effective if the food was surreptitiously purloined. It is true that after purloining food she experienced guilt. During analysis she came to realize that the food and the cigarettes were substitutes for the mother's breast. By smoking she could be the mother that fed the baby and she could be the baby that was fed by the mother.

In this same category belongs material from another woman patient. This woman could, by rubbing and caressing her breasts, achieve a clitoral orgasm. In my opinion, this woman because of being abandoned during infancy learned to caress herself. She took her mother's place with herself. Eventually she discovered that gratification was more concentrated in the clitoris than it was concentrated in the mouth or concentrated in any other part of the body. The fact that she was able to produce her own gratification reassured her that she need not depend upon the mother. After this narcissism was established, she clung to her dual nature (mother-baby) with hectic avidity. Surrendering this tight little narcissistic circle might expose her to the same abandonment and rejection that actually occurred during her original dependency on the mother.

Bed-wetting may belong to this dynamic category. During sleep cathexis is withdrawn from the action patterns (the synthetic, self-protective, self-gratifying "mother"). The bed then becomes the reincarnation of the first mother, with an umbilical cord attached to the bed-wetter. Satisfied by the bed-mother, the sphincters relax and urine flows into the bed and an ephemeral catatonic relationship is effected with the bed.[21]

DEPERSONALIZATION

The intense cathexis of a preconscious oral complex, involving some aspect or image of the mother or her breast, withdraws so much energy from the contemporaneous image of the person's own body that feelings of depersonalization may occur.[22] One woman portrayed a rather unusual feature of this type of depersonalization. Unconscious, reflex, cannibalistic mechanisms became a consistent part of her transference. Triggered by my presence, the reflex subconscious cannibalism operated as if there were no space intervening between her incorporating device[23] and the object of her cannibalistic intent (the therapist). At these times she felt unreal and reassured herself of her presence and my presence by becoming me, closely scrutinizing her face. Once, macropsia ushered in the phenomena and other mechanisms were condensed into the depersonalization—rage, seduction, omnipotence, and guilt.

Often, factors are involved in depersonalization which are closely allied to end-of-the-world preoccupations. Such a concept ensues when the oral regression extends backward through the historical development of the ego to the time when the individual was orally attached to the mother, a mother's breast, or a fetishistic substitute for the mother. Then there is no outside world, no ego cathexis; nothing exists but the child in a togetherness with the mother, operating through the medium of the mouth. A patient described this most adequately:

"With the recounting of one more compendious dream, I conclude the discussion of my life-long conflict, and approach the final correction which the psychiatrist made. Instead of [in]

. . . night sleep, the dream was [formed] . . . under anesthesia [for tooth extraction] . . . long ago, before my illness had struck.

I was Diana, virgin goddess of the crescent moon and of the hunt. I was rising, rising, to the top of the universe, which was imaged as a dome. When I should alight, the world would come to an end. Just as my graceful form was about to settle on the dome's peak, the dentist's voice said: 'There, Miss M——, that tooth's gone now.' . . .

The universe is dome-shaped because it is the mother's breast. The sensation of rising comes from being lifted as a toothless infant to its nipple, there to nurse; and in the nursing circuit, the mother and child become a universe to themselves . . . the outer world has come to an end. The world also ends because I am submissive . . . I am a part of her, becoming submerged, effaced, in her. Instead of total effacement, however, I merely undergo partial loss: That sharp, incisive implement which with its fellows would have enabled me to attack the sustenance-giver. My tooth . . . again my penis taken from me. My arrow as Diana; my sword, my wisdom as Minerva, that other virgin goddess and one of war as well as wisdom; my mind, my brain, my instrument with which I can equate with men.[24]

The sagacious Erasmus Darwin knew of this breast-mother importance as early as 1794-96, the period in which he wrote Zoönomia:[25]

All these various kinds of pleasure at length become associated with the form of the mother's breast; which the infant embraces with its hands, presses with its lips, and watches with its eyes; and thus acquires more accurate ideas of the form of its mother's bosom, than of the odor and flavor of warmth, which it perceives by its other senses. And hence at our maturer years, when any object of vision is presented to us, which by its waving or spiral lines bears any similitude to the form of the female bosom, whether it is found in a landscape with soft gradations of rising and descending surface, or in the forms of some antique vases, or in other works of the pencil or the chisel, we feel a general glow of delight, which seems to influence all our senses; and if the object be not too large, we experience an attraction to embrace it with our arms, and to salute it with our lips, as we did in our early infancy the bosom of our mother.[26]

SKIN DISPLACEMENTS OF INGESTIVE ORGANS

The Magic Cloak[27] referred to alimentary displacements of eye, nose, and ear rather than to the skin; I have, since, had many opportunities to observe skin displacements of alimentary function. One woman suffering during her analysis from severe pains in the bladder and frequency of micturition (which I am certain were psychologically induced and represented her attempt to wash me away with urine as a defense against her desire to be penetrated) consulted a urological surgeon. The surgeon felt that the woman was suffering from partial atresia of the ureters and they were dilated several times.

Hives developed on the inner sides of the patient's thighs, the areas touched by the surgeon and I hypothesize that the skin touched by the surgeon and the memorial picture of the surgeon himself became intermingled. A reaction formation against the skin, cannibalizing the surgeon, was evidenced by the hives. The hives were an attempt to wash away the surgeon as a defense against her wish to incorporate the analyst. Because the surgeon and her own skin were the same, the hives were tantamount to urination into her own skin. In this instance the skin became the *stoma* that ate the mother, represented by the surgeon, who also was equated with the analyst. Or, the skin represented the vagina desiring phallic penetration, reacted against by the expansion of the patient's skin in the form of a urticarial wheal.

Later, however, through fetishistic substitutes for the mother, the urinating activity took on a global expansiveness. Anything that touched the skin brought about a skin reaction, a hive. Here again, spatial relationships were obliterated. Because the whole activity had its inception in the preconscious and pregenital area of the psyche, the skin and its excitor became one without the intervention of space. The urologist and psychoanalyst were professional voyeurs who were only interested in her illness and not interested in her vagina or herself. An old friend met her one day, looked tenderly at her, made love to her, had intercourse with her, and her hives disappeared.

BREAST MEMORIES AND THEIR REACTIVATION

In this area of memory or body image of the urinary bladder, confusion is encountered in other ways. One case involved a kinetic, an action pattern. A male patient noted that whenever he suffered rather prolonged distress from enforced delay in emptying his bladder, a peculiar phenomenon materialized when voiding finally was possible: relief was sweet, and as the urine ran out he salivated so profusely that he actually drooled. The drooling and the urinating under these circumstances were connected. Relief meant gratification and he felt gratified in escaping the pain of the distended bladder. To him, this gratification was analogous to the gratification of devouring good food, hence the salivation. In this case, attention should not be directed exclusively to the confusion between the body images of the urinary bladder and the body images of the salivary glands. Relief from the distress of a distended bladder was analogous to relief from satisfying a craving for food. In fact, the patient salivated with other gratifications that were not primarily oral.

Merell P. Middlemore describes the origin of these fusions of body images in these words: "Among his new experiences are many that give him sensations allied to those he had at the breast—both sensations in the mouth and general bodily feelings; to these allied sensations, fantasies which have already been formed during suckling attach themselves directly . . . .

There the network of fantasy ends, [oral] attaching itself first to simple bodily acts and later to complicated mental processes, until in adult life there are few interests which are not in a measure influenced by it."[28]

Freud, by implication at least, discussed the same subject: "A child's first erotic object is the mother's breast that feeds him, and love in its beginnings attaches itself to the satisfaction of the need for food. To start with, the child certainly makes no distinction between the breast and his own body."[29]

A Synthetic Mother

A patient dreamed that she was eating lying down, just as at a Roman meal. While sating her appetite for food, a nurse injected a jelly-like substance into her vagina. Associations confirmed that the nurse was her mother, the mother who gave her pleasure at both ends of her body. For colic, in her infancy, her mother customarily had given her soap sticks, suppositories and even enemas. These administrations were as gratifying to her as a Roman meal. The mother, however, was inconsistent and often abandoned the baby. After a too brief period of breast feeding, she was weaned summarily. In response to, or as a reaction against this weaning, the patient had established a "mother" of her own making—a mother conjured from within her own confines. A part of her own body was allotted the task of mothering. As she experimented with ways and means of deriving pleasure she located her clitoris. To gratify herself, she masturbated—mothered herself. This was so completely satisfying that she had never permitted herself to experience an orgasm in any other way and was frigid during many heterosexual relationships.

When transference was established the patient dreamed that she "was masturbating and invited the analyst to participate in the act." This was not a sexual dream. She was merely permitting me to become fused with that side of her that played the mother rôle to herself. This ability to gratify herself immediately maintained and perpetuated the illusion of the omnipresence of the mother. However, even though the clitoris was the source of the pleasure, the clitoric façade housed a security seeking mechanism fulfilled by the narcissism. In constructing the significance of this need to be able to gratify one's self for the purpose of feeling safe, it is necessary to review the subject of masturbation.

G. P. Murdoch, Yale University anthropologist, noted that the Okinawan children did not masturbate nor suck their thumbs. In addition, I noted that the Okinawan babies and younger children also did not twiddle their noses, twist their hair between their fingers, scratch their faces, nor suck their clothing. They were not charm blanket carriers. I do not recall seeing very young children carrying around any fetishistic or toy representatives for the mother. The implication is clear. They never needed these substitutes for the mother because the mother did not abandon them during the earliest epochs of their infantile helplessness. The very young, helpless infant needs to feel that the "togetherness gestalt" with the mother is satisfied. If the mother is absent for too long intervals during a baby's infancy, a baby *may* die of moroseness, no matter how well he is fed or how appropriate the physical care.

With too frequent absences of the mother, the infant attempts to supply a substitute for her. Most often this substitute is a part of his body. He will caress himself as the mother should have caressed him; twiddle his hair and tickle his nose with fuzz as the mother should have done and suck his thumb as the mother should have provided suckle. The thumb becomes the mother's breast, he becomes the infant nursing on the breast, and he becomes the breast upon which the infant nurses. It's safe to assume that the narcissistic child will eventually discover that area of his body that will provide the greatest amount of gratification.

One little girl punished for sucking her thumb attempted to rid herself of the habit by carefully supervising herself, but despite this she would awaken at night and find her thumb in her mouth. When the parents discovered the nocturnal thumb-sucking it led to unpleasantness. She was dubbed naughty, and told that even if the parents were not present, God always knew and did not like little girls who sucked their thumbs. To prevent these undesirable events before falling asleep the girl closed her fist and locked it between her thighs. Her intent was to keep the thumb away from her mouth, however, with the fist in this position it was not long before she discovered pleasant sensations in the clitoris. Clitoris caressing then took the place of thumb sucking and the gratification became indispensable. If the mother did not supply gratification, it became incumbent upon the child to usurp the rôle vacated by the mother and to gratify herself.

The caressing of the penis or clitoris is not sexual, even though the charade is acted out on the genital stage. Caressing or self-gratification is self-mothering, self-satisfaction, a nursing upon the self as a mother. A man suddenly and unpredictably abandoned by his wife dreamed that he was sucking his own penis. He needed to replace his wife—the mother—with a part of himself—with his own breast—his own penis. A woman dreamed that a prostitute standing beside her husband was describing many affairs with men. The husband asked: "Do you always get satisfied?"

The prostitute answered: "Nearly always, but when I don't I knock off two for myself."

The patient recognized herself as the prostitute. She also realized that "knocking off two" for herself referred to masturbation and her need to be gratified. Gratification meant safety, security, and from knowledge of her material—gratification meant oral satisfaction. Sexual relations with men meant no more to her than taking a drink of milk, of whiskey, or taking a narcotic. Narcissistic persons implement their "mothering" of themselves by exploiting objects and people. These are woven into the warp and woof of their egocentric phantasies, and are utilized in the service of self-nursing.

GRATIFICATION AS SECURITY FEELING

It is evident that at times gratification rather than lust is the cipher to the activity craved or occurring at the genital zone. In this special frame of reference it is not the genital zone that preëmpts the center of the stage. It is gratification, satisfaction, that is most significant. Sexual gratification waves a magic wand, a wand that provides a sense of security. From clinical material derived in analyses of adults and from observations on children, it is ascertainable that erotic sensations occurring in the genital zones are frequently occasioned by anxieties. Thus, in some people sexual sensations are initiated by being deprived, by being threatened. In other people sexual sensations signal something being demanded of them.

In clinical psychoanalytic studies it is often noted that in some people work—the doing of something constructive—produces a feeling of being worthwhile; their mothers loved them when they were productive. When idle, even enforced idleness such as imposed by a holiday, they become depressed and develop a sense of worthlessness and retrograde feelings of going downhill or disintegrating. Each day he did not work a patient in whom these morose sensations were quite distinct masturbated repeatedly. He attempted to reassure himself that the comforting "mother" implicit in the meaning of the work pattern was not essential to his welfare. By masturbation he achieved gratification. He supplied the "togetherness with mother" schema that was contained in the "work pattern."

Another male patient always felt depressed on Sundays and holidays: He had to work to feel wanted, worthwhile, loved. When active he was a happy helmsman directing in life the course of his own operations. When idle he became a passenger on the ship of life and as a passenger he felt useless and unloved. When feeling useless he was compelled to masturbate, to give himself love. Masturbating, he was the mother who nursed the child, and he was the child nursed by the mother. He reinstituted a "togetherness" and this "togetherness" took place at the genital area. The object image of mouth and penis became fused.

Material from records of many analyses demonstrates that a man studying alone for an examination, working alone tilling the field, doing carpentry work in an empty house, or being alone at other work often experiences sexual cravings. Absence of companionship, loneliness, rather than the need to release pent-up libido, occasions the eroticism. Men have ejaculated while being hanged. As Middlemore said: ". . . in fantasies which emerge when the child feels hungry, away from breast, it is the *mother who starves him and leaves him alone.*"[30]

These phenomena are understandable when it is recalled that erotic gratification can serve as a reassurance that "all is well," that mother is here after all. The rather strange relationship of one woman with her mother is enlightening. At night, after getting into bed she would call her mother to her side. Then she would place her own right thumb into her mouth, and with her left hand she would caress her mother's hair. Usually the mother remained with her until the thumb sucker fell asleep. If the mother were absent or left the room before the daughter fell asleep, the girl continued to suck her thumb and caressed and fondled her own hair. In this quaint mixture of object relationship and narcissistic attachment to herself, she used her own body image interchangeably for the body image of her mother. In the togetherness with the mother, in the antecedent biosphere, her mother smothered her or abandoned her to such an extent that she had been unable to separate self elements from maternal elements in building her body imagery.

Another clinical illustration supports this view. After his first month of life Billie had started thumb-sucking. When he was a year old he sucked his thumb whenever picked up or approached by his mother, but his father, grandmother, and the maid could hold him and he seldom placed his thumb in his mouth. Better understanding of the mother's plight made the conundrum of Billie's thumb-sucking more comprehensible. During analysis Billie's mother was found to be schizoid and so detached that she was incapable of relating to her son. She tried to assume an artificially warm relationship with the child but Billie was not deceived. After being disappointed repeatedly by the presence of the mother which because of her detachment was really an absence, he set up a puppet mother within himself. As a mother surrogate, as a fetish, he sucked his thumb. He was the infant sucking on the mother's teat, and he was the mother's teat sucked upon by the infant. At this point the breast of the mother was not afforded an opportunity of actually becoming an external object.

Freud said, ". . . When the breast has to be separated from his body and shifted to the 'outside' because he so often finds it absent, it carries with it, now that it is an 'object,' part of the original narcissistic cathexis." For Billie the "togetherness"—the infant self and the breast of the mother—were never separated by the process of proper maturative growth. Because of selective inattention the developing cognition was not able to effect the normal schism. The body imagery contained two components—the self element, and the maternal element—the picture of the infant's own thumb that now served him as a breast. I observed this entire proceeding while I had this woman in analysis. For some two years after the baby was born, the mother actually brought the boy into her analytic sessions. The psychoanalytic situation provided an excellent opportunity to observe the operation of the communication and/or lack of it between the mother and her baby.

FOOTNOTES

[1] It is unfortunate that Sullivan ignored the work of most of the outstanding contributors (many antedating him) in his sphere of interest. But Clara Thompson, one of Sullivan's biographers, in her book "Psychoanalysis—Evolution and Development" afforded a focus in historical depth in the development of interpersonalism. Thompson said, ". . . Horney and Fromm each developed theories of the origin of character based on other premises, chiefly cultural and interpersonal . . . . a new development, formulated separately by Sullivan, Ferenczi and Rank."

[2] Harry Stack Sullivan, *The Interpersonal Theory of Psychiatry*. New York: W. W. Norton & Company, Inc., 1953.

3 Italics mine.

4 Italics mine.

5 Abraham Kardiner, M. D., *The Traumatic Neuroses of War,* Paul B. Hoeber, Inc. Medical Book Department of Harper & Bros., New York, London, 1941, p. 170.

6 Paul Federn, *Ego Psychology and the Psychoses,* Edoardo Weiss (ed.), New York: Basic Books, Inc., 1952.

7 Paul Schilder, "The Image and Appearance of the Human Body." *Psyche Monographs,* No. 4. London: Kegan Paul, Trench, Trubner & Co., Ltd., 1935. See also, W. Clifford and M. Scott, "Some Embryological, Neurological, Psychiatric and Psycho-Analytic Implications of the Body Scheme." Elaborations from a paper read at a meeting of the British Analytical Society, March 19, 1947. *International Journal of Psycho-Analysis,* 1948, vol. 3, pt. 3, 141-155.

8 Inability on the part of the patient to recognize that he is ill or disabled.

9 James Clark Moloney, "The Cornelian Corner and Its Rationale," *Problems of Early Infancy.* New York: Transactions of the First Conference, Josiah Macy, Jr. Foundation, 1947, pp. 22-23.

10 It goes without saying that there can be a similar maternal precognitive interference with urethral activity, which in turn will result in a distortion of the urethral someikon and will be accompanied by a disturbance in urethral function.

11 Significant in the sense that it was used by Harry Stack Sullivan.

12 A study of the psychic reaction of the leper to the mutilations occasioned by his disease was recorded in the chapter "Notes on Leprosy," pp. 247-257, in *The Magic Cloak.* Wakefield, Mass.: The Montrose Press, 1949.

13 Cancer is frequently said to eat away the flesh. Cancers are more frequent in the more neurotic races; it has not yet been proved that the turned-in "biting" induced by frustration does not contribute a psychological factor to the etiology of malignancy. The low incidence of malignant neoplasms among the Okinawans, although expected, was of interest. The explanation might lie in the relative absence of factors sometimes considered to be etiologically important. For example, stasis of ducts and cystic disease were not found in the mammary glands of Okinawans, and the history of these women was typically one of numerous pregnancies with prolonged lactation. The mammary glands of women past the teens appeared small and pendulous, but the glandular tissue was abundant and remained remarkably well preserved. For further information see: Commander P. E. Steiner (MC [S] USNR), *Necropsies on Okinawans,* reprinted with additions, from the *Archives of Pathology,* October, 1946, vol. 42, pp. 359-380.

14 "Muff" is referable to the jargon "muff diving"—a term used rather universally for cunnilingualism.

15 Clara Thompson, M. D., "Some Effects of the Derogatory Attitude Toward Female Sexuality." *Psychiatry,* 1950, *13,* 349-354.

16 Abram Kardiner, M. D. *The Traumatic Neurosis of War,* Paul B. Hoeber, Inc. Medical Book Department of Harper & Bros., New York, London, 1941, p. 170.

17 Karen Machover, *Personality Projection,* (Charles C. Thomas).

18 Proverbially, women are afraid of rats, mice, and snakes. The frightened rat, mouse, or snake escapes in a rush, sliding through an opening. In the presence of these animals most women hold their skirts close to

their legs. Men as a rule do not know that the gesture is made in an effort to keep the rodent or snake "out of the hair," out of the vagina. The rat rushing for a hole stirs up an intrapsychic mnemic reaction, as the bee laden with pollen pushing its way into a flower stirs up a memorial response.

[19] J. C. Moloney, *The Magic Cloak*, chapter IV, pp. 74-87. Wakefield, Mass.: The Montrose Press, 1949.

[20] "Lambs shake or wriggle their tails, at the time when they first suck, to get free of the hard excrement which had been long lodged in the bowels." Ernest Krause: *Erasmus Darwin*, New York, D. Appleton and Company, 1880. This reference was suggested by Mr. A. J. Levin.

[21] The analytic couch may come to mean a bed. Some patients kiss the couch, or fix the pillow like a breast, and often must leave the couch to urinate or defecate. One patient at times when I fed her an interpretation would leave the couch to defecate.

[22] Leo Berman. "Depersonalization and the Body Ego with Special Reference to the Genital Representation." *The Psychoanalytic Quarterly*, vol. XVII, No. 4, 1948.

[23] It was not always the mouth. See chapter IX, "Some Aspects of Success and Failure," *op. cit.*, by James Clark Moloney, M. D.

[24] Ellen MacDonald Dearborn. "Time Out for Death." *The Psychiatric Quarterly*, vol. 24, No. 1, 1950.

[25] This reference suggested by Mr. A. J. Levin, Franklin, Michigan.

[26] Erasmus Darwin, M.D.F.R.S. *Zoonomia or the Laws of Organic Life*, vol. I, The Third Edition, Corrected, London, printed for J. Johnson, in St. Paul's Churchyard, 1801.

[27] See footnote No. 12.

[28] Merell P. Middlemore, M. D. *The Nursing Couple*. London: Hamish Hamilton Medical Books, 1941, pp. 114-116.

[29] Sigmund Freud. *An Outline of Psychoanalysis*. New York: Norton, 1949, vol. 8, pp. 89-90.

[30] See footnote No. 28.

FURTHER REFERENCES

Bateson, G. and Ruesch, J. *Communication, the Social Matrix of Personality*. New York: W. W. Norton & Company, Inc., 1951.

Bychowski, G. and Despert, J. L. (editors) *Specialized Techniques in Psychotherapy*. New York: Basic Books, Inc., 1952.

Federn, P. Narcissism in the Structure of the Ego. *International Journal of Psycho-Analysis*, 1928, 9, 401.

Fenichel, O. *The Psychoanalytic Theory of Neurosis*. New York: W. W. Norton & Company, Inc., 1945.

Fromm, E. *Man for Himself*. New York: Rinehart & Co., 1947.

Fromm-Reichman, F. Recent Advances in Psychoanalytic Therapy. *A Study of Interpersonal Relations*, Patrick Mullahy (ed.). New York: Hermitage Press, Inc., 1949.

Horney, K. *Our Inner Conflicts*. New York: W. W. Norton & Co., Inc., 1945.

Masserman, J. H. *Principles of Dynamic Psychiatry*. Philadelphia: W. B. Saunders Company, 1946.

Mullahy, P. *Oedipus Myth and Complex.* New York: Hermitage Press, Inc., 1948.

Rapaport, D. *Emotions and Memory.* New York: International Universities Press, Inc., 1950.

Schilder, P. *Psychotherapy.* New York: W. W. Norton & Co., Inc., 1938.

Silverberg, W. V. *Childhood Experience and Personal Destiny.* New York: Springer Publishing Company, Inc., 1952.

Sullivan, H. S. *Conceptions of Modern Psychiatry.* The William Alanson White Psychiatric Foundation, Washington, D. C., 1947.

Thompson, C., in collaboration with Mullahy, P. *Psychoanalysis: Evolution and Development.* New York: Hermitage House, Inc., 1950.

Chapter XXXI

PRESENT-DAY PSYCHOLOGY OF SPEECH

Emil Froeschels, M.D.

Formerly Associate Professor at the University of Vienna
Chief Clinician, Speech Clinic, Beth David Hospital

EDITORIAL NOTE

In the minds of many, there is apt to be some confusion as to the relation between the psychology of language and the psychology of speech. The latter deals, of course, with the articulation of words in everyday intercourse. It is an important phase of the psychology of language, in the broadest sense, and is of special interest to us in its applied aspect, i.e., as a clinical field. Everyone is aware of such defects as stammering, stuttering, and cleft palate speech, but few realize that there are literally hundreds of possible deviations from what might be called adequate speech. The reason may be neurological, organic or psychological or a blend of the three. Speech pathology and therapy has become one of the most promising studies within the past 40 years. The term "logopedics" has been employed to designate the field of science concerned with the correction of speech and voice defects and disorders; and a logopedist is one who is especially trained to engage in such research and therapy.

Dr. Emil Froeschels who for a number of years was Professor of Physiology, Pathology, and Therapy of Speech and Voice in Vienna, and more recently has served in similar capacities either as research professor or head physician in the speech clinics of various New York hospitals, is recognized as one of the foremost speech experts of our day. He has been President of several national and international professional societies, and is the author of 24 books on anatomy, physiology, pathology, and therapy of speech and voice in German and in English, in addition to about 300 scientific papers.

Dr. Froeschels, in his ample chapter, has made an elaborate attempt to expose some of the fallacies usually associated with the physiology of speech, as a result of the older schools, and has sought to reconcile the French, Austrian and German views with the newer findings.

PRESENT-DAY PSYCHOLOGY

CLASSICAL TRENDS

This tremendous topic, almost identical with psychology as a whole, since most of the psychological processes are at least, accompanied by speech, can only be discussed here in rough outline. Fortunately, Arnold Pick[32] has torn down the walls between the medical and the non-medical branch of speech psychology in order to improve scientific insight. Nevertheless the problem might be better grasped, if the subject, including the results were first presented to the reader as if the wall were still there. Accordingly, a brief outline of the medical pre-Pickian speech psychology will be in order here. The discoveries of Broca,[6] in 1861, and of Wernicke,[36] in 1874, were so fundamental that the medical profession, first doubting, but soon affirming them, had no time to take into consideration the purely psychological approach to speech problems. And so the following medical speech psychology came into being.

THE EARLY ACCOUNT

Speech normally consists of several main parts: 1) Acoustic perception of utterances spoken by other people (in Wernicke's center in the uppermost temporal convolution). 2) A "plastic," somehow architectural procedure (in Broca's center, localized at the foot of the third frontal convolution) to stimulate the muscles, engaged in expressive speech, to perform the correct movements for repeating acoustically perceived sounds. The stimuli traveling from Wernicke's into Broca's center have to pass the island of Reil. These three areas of the brain allow of articulation but not of understanding the meaning of what was perceived acoustically. In order to bring forth understanding of what was heard (and repeated) it was assumed that there were in the brain several working pathways which connected Wernicke's center with those involved in forming ideas; e.g., when a child (or an adult learning English) hears the word "table" and is shown a table, the visual centers, and perhaps the tactile centers, too, are stimulated by that demonstration, and so there develops a collaboration of those centers with Wernicke, leading to an understanding of the word "table." All the centers participating in idea-formation have been covered (by Lichtheim) [27] by the term, "transcortical center." It is not only a theoretical assumption but one proved by clinical and anatomical facts that the pathways which serve spontaneous speech are the same as those that serve the first attempts of a baby to repeat words. That is to say, if a person wants to name a table he will remember the word by using the engrams in Wernicke's center to stimulate Broca's center via Reil's island. From there on in every speech utterance, the first word repetition as well as the spontaneous speech utterances, stimuli pass from Broca into the central convolution, thence down into the inner and external capsule, maybe (Mingazzini) [29] into some extrapyramidal pathways, to the cerebellum and finally to the muscles of the breathing mechanism, to the larynx, the pharynx, and the mouth and to mimical muscles as well as to muscles performing gestures.

Some facts must be stressed here. In righthanded people the speech centers of Broca and Wernicke are on the left side of the brain, and vice versa, although the other hemisphere seems to participate in speech (Jackson) [24] in as far as this hemisphere is used for automatically spoken words or series of words. It is well known that the conclusions drawn by Broca and by Wernicke were based on pathological observations. Since the Broca cases showed certain defects in their ability to express their ideas, to name things, to pronounce, even to repeat sounds, to write and to read, while the Wernicke patients showed lack of understanding for what they heard, and the post mortem showed lesions of certain parts of the brain, Broca, Wernicke and their followers reasoned that those parts, in normal condition, are the anatomic basis for the normal function of the respective speech process. It has been objected that physiological facts cannot be deduced from pathological observations alone. Here nonmedical psychology has been, as recently stressed by Kainz [26], of some help. On the other hand, (in the following decades), there have been reported, in the literature, thousands of cases similar to those discussed by Broca and Wernicke with analogous post-mortem findings.[1] (It is scarcely necessary to point out that, in contrast with other medical branches, the branch dealing with speech does not allow of animal experimentation which produces pathological states. The only source for pathological conditions in the science of speech is nature itself). The signs of Broca's and Wernicke's cases have been termed cortical expressive (Broca) and cortical receptive (Wernicke) aphasia, and the centers have been considered the centers for normal oral expression and acoustic perception respectively. Since reading as well as writing is—as a rule—taught so that the pupil, while he reads or writes, has to pronounce the letters, there exists in most people such a close connection between reading, writing, and talking that cortical expressive aphasia will be accompanied by alectic and agraphic signs. (Since another center is engaged in reading and writing, namely the optic center for perception and recollection of letters a lesion of that part of the brain will of course also lead to alexia and agraphia).

All the different forms of aphasia cannot be described here in detail. Suffice it to say that any damage to the parts of the transcortical center may interfere with the formation of appropriate ideas. If a person was used to stimulating oral expressions via one of the centers which together are called the transcortical center an aphasic condition might result.[30] The same holds true for an interruption of the pathways connecting "the" transcortical center with Wernicke's (and Broca's) center. The speech trouble deriving from such a lesion is called transcortical aphasia which is subdivided into a receptive and an expressive form depending upon whether the pathways from the transcortex to Wernicke's or to Broca's center are involved. (In most cases both forms are present.)

SUBCORTICAL APHASIA

There also exist—according to Wernicke, Lichtheim and others—subcortical aphasias. They are supposed to be caused by lesions of the pathways between the acoustic center in the transversal convolution of the temporal brain and Wernicke's center (subcortical receptive aphasia) and of the pathways between Broca's center and the anterior central convolution (subcortical expressive aphasia). The existence of these forms is still debatable. There are noted writers[5] who believe that the so-called subcortical receptive aphasia is just a central form of hardness of hearing. The corresponding expressive clinical picture is due to an inability of the "workmen" in the anterior central convolution to perform the work that the "architect" in Broca's center has sketched.

WHAT WE LEARN FROM LOGOPEDICS

Again without going into detail, it must be mentioned here that the logopedic reëducation of aphasic patients has contributed much to the understanding of the clinical pictures and their relationship to certain brain lesions. The logopedist who works with the patient for months, and even years, has by far the greatest opportunity to watch the speech defect, to observe the influence of certain emotional situations upon the ability to speak, (first mentioned by Hughlings Jackson at a meeting of the British Association for the Advancement of Science, 1868, in Norwich), and to study the progress and thence to draw conclusions about the very nature of aphasic conditions. Only recently logopedics has drawn attention to the peculiarities of the voice of some aphasics,[12] a field of investigation, so far almost ignored by neurology. Also the studies of Weiss[34] and of Freund[11] about cluttering have opened a new insight into some problems of aphasias. It seems also worth mentioning that the observations of the normal as well as the abnormal development of children's speech, again a logopedic area, and the comparison with the speech defects of aphasic patients could contribute to the understanding of the latter (Froeschels).[13], [19] Experimental phonetics, an important part of logopedics, has also thrown some light upon questions of speech psychology.

A few examples may illustrate the significance of logopedics for our topic. Babies start to produce sounds and syllables at an age of 4 to 6 months. These products seem not to depend on the speech of the people around the baby, since deaf children also pass through this speech period of "babbling." It is an innate force working in the baby which stimulates him to perform some acrobatics with the larynx, the pharynx, the soft palate, and the mouth. Most probably this period serves to train the muscles involved in chewing (intake of solid food) and in articulated speech which follows a little later. Now it has been observed that if the baby babbled a new sound or a new syllable he frequently repeated it over and over again with signs of enjoyment. The first production evidently was a pure motor act, while the repetitions are reproductions caused by the acoustic (in the case of the deaf child by the kinesthetic) impressions the child received from babbled sounds. These observations enabled logopedics to affirm the rôle of acoustic (and/or kinesthetic) impressions upon (motor) sound productions. The reader should recall these facts when the significance of Charcot's types is discussed later in this paper.

Another logopedic insight into the central mechanism of speech resulted from the very elaborate studies of congenitally deaf or severely hard-of-hearing children. Those patients do not learn to speak unless treated by special methods. Not so long ago, deaf mutism was considered to be the consequence of deafness *and* of a defect of the areas of the brain that normally stimulate speech. Slowly it became evident that deafness alone explains the mutism, that the acoustic impressions of speech which the normal child perceives innumerable times from the moment of birth on are the necessary stimuli for the child to produce speech. Both examples, babbling and deaf mutism, confirm the doctrine of the rôle of acoustic impressions, of their "transference" into the expressive speech area of the brain and of the impetus going from there into the central convolutions, etc., to bring forth speech. Many children do not start speaking despite sufficient hearing. If no peripheral abnormality, e.g., cleft palate, is present, they must be thought of as being either aphasic or emotionally unbalanced. Valuable findings have derived from logopedic examinations and treatment of such cases. They have helped especially to illuminate the great part which emotions play in the abnormal and normal procedures leading to speech.

WHAT HEARING INVOLVES

The writer[13] has pointed out that hearing is a very complex process consisting of the following functions: 1) The putting together and separating from each other respectively acoustic impressions according to whether or not they essentially belong together. 2) The memory that plays a part: a) in joining (and isolating) sensual impressions that do not occur simultaneously, b) in remembering the junction and separation respectively of formerly joined or separated impressions, c) the work of memory in order to join the foregoing parts of a sensual impression with the following. 3) Perception of the several degrees of loudness and an appropriate memory. 4) A constantly working function of comparing pitches which form a unity like a musical or a speech melody. The act of noticing length of duration and the degrees of loudness. 5) Analysis of tones contained in a compound. 6) Their phase-relation. 7) Experiencing of unities, namely acoustic complexes and *Gestalt*. 8) A special kind of inner experiences named in physiognomic terms, which point to essential associations of hearing with other kinds of sensual perception. 9) Localization of tones and sounds. 10) Acoustic imagination. 11) Attention.

Experimental phonetics studies all the body movements engaged in speech production chiefly by means of graphic procedures, (e.g., pneumography and X-rays), and transfers the air movements produced in speaking to graphic apparatuses (oscillographs). Phonetics also investigates the acoustic effects of sound, syllables, words, phrases. Of course, the literature is enormous. The only point to be stressed here is the result of analyses of the air either by Helmholtz' resonators or by registration of the air waves in the oscillographic way, and of some experiments to build speech sounds by mechanical or electrical means. All these experiments were made to find out of what musical sounds and of what noises the speech sounds consist.

FORMANTS

Until a short time ago the theory of Helmholtz and Stumpf[33] was almost generally accepted. According to this theory every speech sound is characterized by the so-called formants. The vibrating vocal cords deliver always a number of overtones beside the basic tone. Since every tone finds its best resonance in a cavity of specific size (a lower tone needs a larger cavity to resonate than a higher one), the basic tone and each overtone may find an opportunity to resonate in the mouth, which (instinctively) shapes itself in an appropriate way for the basic tone or for a single overtone. In this way the respective tone will become the loudest in the whole mixture. Helmholtz and Stumpf found that every speech-sound (every vowel, every consonant) is characterized by a specific loudest overtone which Stumpf called the formant. Every *ah* in the world has the formant g^2, every *ee's* formant is at the end of the fourth little octave, the formant of the consonant *m* is e^3, of *s* it is at the end of the fourth little octave (Crandall).[9]

Although as Peterson's[30] recent electro-oscillographic experiments showed the formant may wander a little up or down without interfering with the acoustic recognition of the speech sound, the fact that the loudest overtone differs from one certain speech sound to every other certain speech sound opened an important insight into the acoustic function of the brain. We do not consciously perceive the loudest overtone. However, a certain center must possess the power of analyzing the sum of tones, contained in every speech sound, and by doing so must help us to become marginally aware of the degree of loudness of tones contained in and forming the speech sound, respectively. This center is most probably Heschl's center in the transversal temporal convolution. There have been cases of those who hear single tones but do not perceive speech sounds. That the opposite may occur, namely that a person hears speech sounds better than single tones is a recent discovery made by some logopedists (see: Beebe, H. L.: [4] *A Guide to Help the Severely Hard-of-Hearing Child*).

Since logopedics also deals with missing speech sounds and correcting defective sounds in patients, extensive studies have been made on the formation of speech sounds and the muscles involved. Much has been learned about the rôle that kinesthesis plays in speech. This function has been localized in the posterior central convolution and the parietal lobe. Lip reading, which means the ability to recognize speech by observing the movements of the mouth, also taught by logopedists, has developed important insight into the rôle played by visual impressions in speech perception, another fact to be remembered when the Charcot-types are discussed.

Broca's, Wernicke's and Lichtheim's theories, only partly deduced from clinical and pathological findings, and partly developed on the basis of the theoretically constructed scheme, have been called the "classical" trend in the science of aphasia. At the beginning of this century new methods were tried to explain the clinical facts. (There were always some writers who partly or wholly opposed the classical theory. This is not the place to fully describe their arguments. However, some names, at least, should be mentioned here for they certainly did inspire the modern writers whose opinions will be discussed. Jackson, Bourneville, Bastian, Charcot, Déjerine, Freud, Monakow were contemporary critics of the "classicals").

THE CRITICS OF THE CLASSICAL THEORISTS

Before turning to the non "classical" teachings, let us first take a look at the other side of the picture. What aspect did the non-medical branch of speech psychology show in the days of Broca—Wernicke—Lichtheim? First of all, there was much opposition to the opinion that recollection means reproduction of engrams. Wm. James[25] warned against believing that "the vehicle of the same thing known must be the same recurrent state of mind." That ideas are not pictures of sensual impressions has been stressed by Ebbinghaus[10] among others.

A basic assumption of the "classical" theory was that a sentence is a sum of words or, expressed reversely, that words added to words form a sentence. Wundt[37] had already rejected this aspect. The question has been: which came first: the sentence, consisting of a sort of feeling of the speaker for the kind of matrix in which the word should be put, or the words, which added to each other finally build the sentence. It is evident that one must know first, e.g., whether one wants to ask a question or make a statement; on this knowledge depends the modulation of the voice—the words might be the same (e.g., "You are a good boy," but "You are a good boy?"). Thus it follows that the sentence has the primacy, except if one—in a contest, let us say,—has to bring words written on the blackboard into a meaningful unity, namely a sentence.[2] It has been stressed by non-medical speech psychology (as well as by some physicians, like Jackson) that every spoken word carries with it a signifying and an emotional component. (More recently this was conclusively proved by Bühler).[7]

IMAGINAL TYPES AND PSYCHOLOGICAL APPROACH

In the writer's opinion, one rather important contribution to our problems coming from medical, but chiefly from the non-medical side, has not been used sufficiently in the studies on aphasia. The writer is referring here to the imaginal types, first described by Charcot[8] as the kinesthetic, the auditory, and the visual. Most of the work on this typing has been done by non-medical psychologists. The most comprehensive discussion of the topic can be found in a book by Baerwald[2] and in one by Froeschels-Jellinek.[18] Some people learn best by reading aloud, some by silent reading, yet with articulatory movements, others by hearing, still others by reading without any accompanying speech-movements. Questionnaires (to be found in the books listed) have the examinee describe the method—many people are a mixed type—he uses in learning. He also has to keep in mind some phrases offered to him by the experimenter, and to observe whether he hears the phrases in his mind or whether he sees the words as if written, or whether he feels speech movements, although he wants to obey the demand of the experimenter, not to speak. Provided that several experiments result in the same answer one may draw some conclusions as to the type of the experimentee (kinesthetic, visual, auditory). It is important to know that frequently the results of the experimentee's self-observation (and of the experimenter's observation) are different if the sentences offered contain different topics of knowledge, (e.g. if mathematics and history are used). That already makes it probable that the way of teaching may influence the way of learning. In mathematics, e.g., most people prove to be visual, simply because this subject is taught chiefly by writing on the blackboard. Baerwald has introduced the so-called disturbance-experiment (*Störungsexperiment*). If a person described the procedures within him, *e.g.,* as auditory, a noise is produced during following experiments in order to find out whether the experimentee finds it harder, even impossible, to keep a sentence in mind. Anyhow, it so happens that all of a sudden another sense substitutes for the disturbed one. If that occurs, the conclusion is suggestive that the substituting sense is potentially the stronger one (coming into full action at the first opportunity when the formerly acting sense is eliminated!). In such cases Baerwald assumes that the now experimentally disturbed sense is the actual one while the substituting sense is the potential one, that means, that the latter was the real talent of the person and has been violated somehow by teaching, environmental influences, etc. Before justifying this whole elaborate discussion to the reader it must be stated that an important assumption underlies type-psychology. So far we have spoken only about learning and keeping in mind the sentences offered by the experimenter. The important assumption is that remembering what we were taught (reproduction) proceeds in the same way in which the subject taught "entered" the personality and in which keeping a sentence in mind proceeds. In other words, if a person has learned a subject auditorily, (and keeps a sentence in mind by way of auditory imagery), he will also remember both of them auditorily.

The writer[19] has regretted frequently that school children are not examined for their imaginal types. How are we to know which center was chiefly engaged in speaking when we do not know the type to which a person belongs? It is true that the majority of people are, as far as speech is concerned, a mixed auditory-motor type. However, there are exceptions. In a prominent auditory speech type the Wernicke center may work directly upon the anterior central convolution with no or little help from Broca. If such a case shows later a cortical expressive aphasia—and there is no way of testing the physio-psychological type in aphasic condition—how should anyone know how to localize it? Bastian[3] mentioned this insurmountable difficulty more than 50 years ago—yet nothing has been done about it to this day.

The few contributions of non-medical speech psychology which could be mentioned here may suffice to show what help some of the non "classical" aphasia investigators of the medical branch received or could have received from the other branch to find new approaches to the problems involved.

OBJECTIONS FROM DIVERSE QUARTERS

Four names are prominent among those writers who have not only criticized the "classical" trend but have developed new ways to approach the problems of aphasia: Marie, Pick, Goldstein, and Head. Marie[28] objected to the way of pressing the clinical forms of aphasia into the scheme of Wernicke-Lichtheim as well as to the types of Charcot which, in Marie's opinion, don't play any part in normal speech. There exists, according to him only *one* speech center, located in the temporal-parietal lobe. In this center no auditory word pictures (Wernicke) are localized. This center is the center of intelligence related to speech.

Speech suffers by any damage of this center; depending upon the severeness of the damage, different clinical forms result. At any rate, no auditory engram has disappeared in all these cases, but speech-intelligence is more or less reduced. Why then, asks Bonvicini[5] (p. 1613) do some of the cases of Wernicke's aphasia show "logorrhea" and paraphrasia-symptoms that can't be explained by lack of speech intelligence? Marie degraded to the rank of a dysarthria a speech trouble deriving (according to the "classics") from any lack of transference of a motor idea into the "workshop" (anterior central convolution). According to Marie it is just an inability to move the muscles correctly. Marie's famous quadrangular region reaching from a) two planes that cross vertically the anterior and the posterior poles of the island and b) from the lateral wall of the island medially to the wall of the third ventricle, is the region from which this dysarthria may derive. This area covers almost one third of the hemisphere.—Marie knows only one form of aphasia, namely Wernicke's cortical receptive aphasia. This is, in Marie's opinion, not due to a loss of the acoustic memory and perception of words but to a lack of speech intelligence. His theory is based chiefly upon "negative cases," the cases with expressive-aphasic signs but no lesion of Broca's center and cases without expressive-aphasic signs and post-mortem findings of a lesion in Broca's center. The writer again and again[19] has pointed to the fact that one is standing on very weak ground when making a diagnosis without knowing the patient's type. It therefore may be that Marie's negative cases only *seemed* to contradict Broca's teachings, while in fact they were such types as did not require motor ideas (Broca) for speaking in the premorbid phase.

PICK'S CONTRIBUTION

It is especially hard to review in brief Pick's remarkable contributions to the almost innumerable questions on aphasia. He was a living encyclopedia, mastering neurology and psychiatry as well as psychology, phonetics, and to a certain extent logopedics. Furthermore, he did not develop a new system for the understanding of aphasia, which could be described easily. He wanted to warn medical scholars in this field not to neglect other branches of speech psychology and to acquaint them with important findings deriving from those branches. Finally, he intended to shed light on some layers within the whole structure called speech. Words are only the surface, and by no means the whole. Unfortunately, the second part of his work, *Die agrammatischen Sprachstörungen,* never appeared. In the first part, he directed attention to the speed of speech, the pauses within speech, the phonetic elements ("phoneme," not letters!), to an inner formulation preceding the function of word finding, to the psychological teaching that grammatical-syntactical functions are closer to the function of thinking than the function of finding the right word, and precede the latter, that the whole form of a sentence has primacy over words (the former being the mould; the latter the small inlaid pieces of the "mosaic"), that the relationship of thinking to speaking is manifold and interwoven, that both must be studied in order to be understood. Pick furthermore directed attention to the troubles in grammar and syntax, to the essence of a sentence which consists *of the emotional attitude of the speaker* (and of the listener) to express something in a certain way plus the expression (cf. Jackson's "emotional speech!"). Pick also stresses the importance of the study of the musical qualities of speech (accent, modulation),[3] etc., for the understanding of normal and of the nature of some abnormal speech conditions. His criticism of the identity theory of thinking and speaking is fundamental. Nevertheless, he believes that loss of speech carries with it an impairment of thinking. This short, too short résumé of Pick's book should not be concluded without pointing to the important fact that Pick expects, from the enrichment of the medical by the non-medical speech psychology an insight into the central (brain) mechanism which, step by step, will lead to the dis-

covery of more and more centers that participate in the manifold functions of speaking.

THE HOLISTIC CONCEPTION

K. Goldstein, [20], [21] well known as one of the most productive writers in the field of aphasia defined language as "a means
of the individual to come to terms with the outer world and to
realize himself." This definition shows already that Goldstein
prefers a holistic (Gestalt) approach to our problems. Some
parts of the brain, to a certain extent independent of the periphery of the cortex, "point to a significance of their own,"
says Goldstein, and names them the central part of the cortex
(in accordance with some histological findings of Ramon y
Cajal).

He warns us not to localize prematurely since "we have not
or could not take into consideration all the factors which modify
the relation between the aphasic picture and the lesion." Goldstein believes with Nielsen[30a] and others that the right hemisphere in right-handed and the left in left-handed people may
partly substitute for the damaged left and right one, respectively; however, he cautions at the same time against taking
this assumption for granted since so far no definite proof has
been established for it. (Here the writer refers to his own
paper[15] in which this question has been discussed thoroughly.)
If abstract thinking is reduced by any kind (and location) of
brain damage, language will be influenced unfavorably; an
impairment of the understanding of words is the most characteristic feature of impaired abstract thinking. Concrete speech
shows a more compulsive character. The finding of "some
words, which occur easily in fluent speech," offer even under
normal conditions "difficulty in voluntary word-finding." A
patient would name colors only if they were quite pure, but
declined to extend the same name (red, blue, etc.) to shades
of those colors, for she had not used the word "red, blue, etc."
as a name for an idea (abstract thinking), "but only as a sound
pertaining to one particular object." The same patient named

a knife, if shown to her simultaneously with an apple an "apple parer," but a "bread knife" if a piece of bread was shown in conjunction with the knife. "The patients with this form of disturbance of word-finding have not lost the words but are unable to use them in a categorial sense because they cannot assume the abstract attitude." "Inequalities among different patients in the difficulty of finding words are explained . . . *by the different capacity of the patient to cover up their defect"* which depends on the pre-morbid linguistic knowledge. Cases which are not wanting in abstract thinking but in using the instrumentalities of speech show, besides difficulties in word-finding, distortion of the words (literal paraphrasia) or a substitution of another word for the correct word (verbal paraphrasia).

Goldstein is inclined, as already shown in his monograph on transcortical aphasias,[22] to explain transcortical as well as amnesic (frequent but by no means constant inability to find chiefly nouns and verbs) aphasias as the result of defects in a hypothetical central speech area. The latter is supposed to be a center to which Broca's as well as Wernicke's center is subordinated. He deals thoroughly with disturbances in finding the so-called "small" word (I, you, he, in, and, etc.) which, especially if isolated, are somehow depending on an abstract attitude. Patients with a certain form of expressive (motor) aphasia are severely handicapped in all voluntary actions, "and the defect of speaking is only the expression of this more general defect." Here again, as in Goldstein's attempt to explain some aphasic troubles as deriving from disturbed abstract thinking, we recognize one of his leading ideas. The classic school has explained all aphasic signs as *speech* defects. Goldstein's opinion is that many aphasic signs derive from a defective function which is connected with speech but is not represented by speech alone within the human personality, and has normally also other ways of utterance than speech. A whole new battery of tests has been invented by Goldstein to examine not only the verbal expressions of the patient but also his non-verbal "behavior."

Goldstein considers the type of aphasia which, according to the classical scheme, is due to a damage of the pathways between Wernicke's and Broca's center (conduction aphasia) as a result of damaged inner speech, and calls this form "central aphasia." "Inner speech is the totality of processes and experiences which occur when we are going to express our thoughts, etc., in external speech and when we perceive sounds as language." To judge the mental capacity of a patient by means of an intelligence test must be of doubtful value. The writer can affirm this statement since many cases of aphasia and of other speech troubles showed a much higher I.Q. after their speech had been improved by logopedic treatment. Goldstein offers in his books the results of profound studies of patients with disturbed reading (alexia), writing (agraphia), calculating (acalculia), gestures and pantomimic disturbances, aphasias in polyglot individuals. In the book on *Language and Language Disturbances* he thoroughly discusses speech disturbances due to impairment of the non-language mental performances. Of the many important contributions to our topic one deserves especially to be stressed here. Time and again in the history of aphasia study, there came in the foreground a trend to consider all forms of this speech trouble as signs of impaired thinking. Here Goldstein's endeavor to distinguish between a primary speech (language) trouble and a primary intelligence trouble throws light on a rather unclear question.[4]

TRANSPOSITION OF FIGURE AND GROUND

One more teaching of Goldstein must be mentioned, namely the figure-ground theory. These terms, frequently used in Gestalt psychology (first introduced by E. Rubin), designate that while at every moment something is in the focus of our thinking or perception (figure), there is always a halo around (ground) that represents innumerable former experiences and thoughts and emotions as well as less clear perceptions which accompany the figure. Goldstein explains many aphasic symptoms as resulting from an abnormal change of place between figure and ground. In such patients parts of the "halo" come into the fore, while what normally should—at a given moment—be the figure is pushed into the background. We have to restrict ourselves to those relatively few points of Goldstein's speech-psychology and have to discuss now the teachings of Head.[5]

HEAD'S VIEW

Head[23] energetically opposed the whole "classical" teaching and even refused to accept the division of aphasia into receptive and expressive forms. He introduced some valuable tests and used tests devised by other writers. These tests probe speech and speech understanding, reading and writing and other abilities, such as the understanding of a picture (with or without descriptive legend), the oral and/or written description of the picture, the understanding of pictorial commands, orientation in space, bridge playing (provided, of course, the patient did play the game previously), etc. Without any verification on the basis of a *post mortem,* Head not only rejects Broca's and Wernicke's view of aphasia; he even discounts every localization of special centers, committed to one special function. The speech function, he thinks, is a totality which can be affected in different ways by lesions of distinct parts of the brain. It is always the *whole* function of speech that is involved in the aphasic defect; only one part or several parts of this united function may be more conspicuously damaged. Therefore, no special function, e.g., the function of expressing ideas in words or the understanding of other people's speech should be considered the characteristic aphasic feature, but only symptoms pointing to the defective speech as a whole. Even that is not the be-all nor the end-all of Head's theory. Aphasia is only one expression of a defect of symbolic formulation, a basic function of man which shows in every kind of expression, speech, writing, reading, gestures, emotional expressions, drawing, painting, dancing, playing games, etc. On the other hand, all those functions may be unharmed, if not involved in speech; but they are defective in aphasics in as far as these functions are dependent on verbal expression or on speech understanding, and in as far as they are included in the complex, called speech.

Head finally divides aphasia into four groups. Three of them resemble very much the classic forms of expressive, receptive, and amnesic aphasia, while the fourth, called the semantic, is characterized by the patient's failure whenever the higher or highest meanings of a symbol (words, figures, values of cards in card games, etc.) are involved in the task the patient is facing. Thus, he can count but cannot calculate, for in this procedure, not only naming figures but their symbolic value is involved. He might find words to name things or actions but fails to form sentences out of those words because the grammatic-syntactic relationship of the words—the higher semantic level of speech—is missing.

Before summing up as far as possible what we have discussed above the reader may be reminded that one of the great American physicians, Benjamin Rush, more than a hundred years ago, devoted some of his famous letters to the psychology of speech. There is an excellent modern paper, written by F. Kainz[26] on the topic of Logopedics and Speech Psychology which offers a thorough insight into many of the problems dealt with here.[6]

RECAPITULATION

In summing up, we may say that there are three groups[7] among the medical speech psychologists, namely the localizing group, the holistic group, and one somehow in between these two.

To the first group whose first representatives were the "classics," belongs also Pick. We have seen that he warned against abandoning the localization trend and that his main purpose was to bring the medical and the non-medical branch together for the purpose of mutual fertilization. His opinion was that thus new centers may be found and that perhaps some thus far accepted centers may be replaced by others.

The second group is represented among others chiefly by

Head. He undertook a crusade against the localization psychology, to arrive finally—although at different places in the brain from those of the "classics,"—again at some centers! The writer kept hoping when first reading Head's two volumes that eventually Head would designate a center where the function of symbolization in his opinion is localized. The hope was in vain.

To the third group belong Marie and Goldstein, the latter only in a certain sense. Marie was anatomically holistic, knowing only one aphasia-center. Goldstein is holistic in so far as he considers aphasic symptoms to represent fundamentally a disturbance in the figure-ground relationship. On the other hand, he not only acknowledges the existence of different centers; he even tried in his older writings to localize the highest function which, according to him, is superimposed on the receptive and the expressive ones.

RESOLVING THE CONFLICT

Is there a possibility of deciding whether one of these trends is preferable to the other? The writer believes that he can try to answer this question first of all on the basis of his experiences as a speech therapist. There are aphasics who show relatively good understanding for spoken, occasionally also for printed and written language but who are utterly incapable of speaking spontaneously or of repeating phrases, even single words. Those cases must be treated with the optic-kinesthetic method, in other words, they must learn to speak again by looking at the mouth of the therapist and by feeling the vibrations at his throat, mouth, and nose, and the movements of the air in front of his mouth.[8] He who accepts only Wernicke's center and denies the importance of any motor-kinesthetic ideas of speech, could perhaps explain the therapeutic experiences just mentioned by saying: "Before the patient's trouble started the impetus deriving from Wernicke's center was strong enough to bring the 'expressive pathways' into action. Now Wernicke is still strong enough to do his perceptive work, but not the expressive one." (Bastian certainly would agree). Anyhow, such a discrepancy between relatively good perceptive and entirely or almost entirely missing expressive work can hardly be assumed with respect to our knowledge of the physiology (and pathology) of the speech development of the child.[13] Very soon after some speech understanding has developed the child starts talking. Not a great number of words need be understood before expressive actions start. That seems to the writer to make it improbable that the relationship between the function of understanding and the function of oral expression is such that the former normally is much greater than the latter. Therefore a still remaining relatively good speech understanding should stimulate the expressive components at least to such a degree that no complete mutism would be present. Numerous cases have been described which were literally speechless despite a not too badly disturbed understanding. From that it seems to follow that Marie's theory is not supported by clinical experience, not to speak again of the objection against this theory based on Marie's neglect of Charcot types.

The weakness of Head's final conclusions has been discussed earlier, namely, the missing anatomical clues and the lack of any attempt at localizing in the brain the function of symbolization. Pick's book, discussed in this paper, is chiefly a guide for further investigation. It seems to this writer that Pick is standing on solid ground when he discusses the medical as well as the non-medical literature on speech psychology. His suggestion also seems to be good, namely, not to throw the medical findings overboard, but to look for new centers which might serve as the anatomic basis for thus far neglected findings made by non-medical psychologists.

Goldstein does not underrate the importance of localization. However, his approach is a rather dynamic one while the classical approach has been more of the static kind. It indicates a transposition when—according to Goldstein—what should be the "figure" becomes the "ground," and vice-versa. This theory certainly represents a dynamism while the classical localization spoke of permanent, that is, of static engrams. The classic trend was in line with association-psychology, while Head, and to a certain degree also Goldstein, are closer to gestalt psychology. The human approach to nature is, as the writer[16] has pointed out, fundamentally a double one. The mind is always looking for concepts, that is to say, for definitions, a word deriving from the Latin term, *finis,* which means "limit." While we *feel* that nothing is stable, that everything is constantly changing, is in a steady flux, we nevertheless take out parts of the flowing whole, the Universe, in order to define them. In this way we are on our way to forming concepts. Many of the auditory word-engrams in Wernicke's and of the motor-kinesthetic engrams in Broca's center are names of concepts, and, taken out of the flux, of speech words—are concepts themselves. Of course, we cannot entirely escape the reality of the constant flux, we are always, or at least at times, aware of the flux, and try to express this awareness. It is easier to express it by means of art (poetry, painting, sculpture, music) than in scientific language. Scientific language, so closely adjusted to the way in which the mind thinks, has very poor means to designate the flux because to *define* (*finis*) the flux is somehow contradictory to the essence of flux, which is motion and not rest. Only rest can really be defined. If motion is defined as the change of place, it is understood that in order to change a place, that place must first be held for whatever minimum of time,—and motion really never holds a place, but moves. Therefore, every attempt at *defining* the moving unity which speech *really* is, to *define* the constantly changing personality is almost beyond the means of scientific language. That is one reason why even the non-"classics" are obliged to yield to the peculiarities of the world of definitions. Head, e.g., arrives at centers, Goldstein may face the question "*what* changes place if the ground and the figure change their rôles?" On the other hand, the "classics" spoke of association and of association-pathways. "Associate" means, according to Webster, to connect in thought. "Connect" certainly points to moving! So we see that there are not rigid but floating frontiers between the association psychology and Gestalt psychology!

At all events, it is easier to define engrams which are static than to define transitions. Transition from what to what?! The writer[17] has pointed out these facts many years ago. From these considerations the conclusion may be drawn that static descriptions of clinical signs and of their neuro-anatomic causes might more easily lead to scientific understanding than dynamic aspects. The latter are nevertheless of great importance, although in the writer's opinion their importance will chiefly lie in the rôle they may play as guides on the lookout for new centers and for what is deposited in them (engrams).

FOOTNOTES

[1] An excellent survey may be found in E. S. Henschen's *Klinische und anatomische Beiträge zur Pathologie des Gehirns,* Stockholm, 1920-1922.

[2] In a paper in press in the *American Journal of Psychology* I have pointed out that dreams, although they frequently form neologisms almost never deviate from normal grammar. That seems to prove that the "matrix" (grammar) precedes the choice of words. How else could the neologisms not interfere with normal grammar? If grammar were a "trimming" of words chosen before the grammatical matrix of the whole sentence exists the neologism at the end or in the middle of the phrase would easily cripple the grammar of the sentence!

[3] Recently stressed again by I. Pichon and S. Borel-Maisonny in: Psychophysiologie du Langage. *Folia Phoniatrica,* 7, 7, 1947, p. 39-56. The writer believes that also in this respect different types may exist. For one type inner speech may very well precede thinking, while with the other, speech is "peripheral to the thinking process," as G. A. Miller (*Language and Communication,* McGraw-Hill, New York) formulates it. However Miller believes that speech is always peripheral, which the writer considers doubtful.

[4] Valuable contributions to this question have been offered by F. Panx, G. Kandler and A. Leischer in their book *Klinische und Sprachwissenschaftliche Untersuchungen zum Agrammatismus,* Stuttgart, 1952.

[5] Readers who want to find a more extensive survey on the whole history of aphasia can find it in the writer's *Psychological Elements of Speech,* further in the outstanding book *Aphasia* by Th. Weisenberg and K. E. McBride, New York, 1935, and J. M. Nielsen's *Epitome of Agnosia, Apraxia, and Aphasia with Proposed Physiologic-Anatomic Nomenclature,* New York, 1942.

[6] Quite recently Maria Lorenz published a paper, "Language as Expressive Behavior" (*A. M. A. Archiv. of Neurol. and Psychiat.,* 70, 3, pp. 277-287) in which she points out that the general style is consistent for

each person and that grammar and syntax is partly dictated by the orientation of the speaker. This insight certainly is in line with Pick and Goldstein.

7 See also: W. Eliasberg's grouping in "Die Theorien und Methoden der Aphasieforschung." *Wiener klinische Wochenschrift*, 1922, Bd. 34.

8 Of course, the therapist will not neglect the whole personality of the patient. He will look for all signs of brain damage and approach them therapeutically. He also will not forget to take into consideration how complexly speech is interwoven with other functions. Among others Anderson[1] and Wepman[35] have stressed these necessities.

REFERENCES

1 Anderson, J. O. Aphasia and Its Treatment. In Froeschels, E. *20th Century Speech and Voice Correction,* The Philosophical Library, New York, 1948.

2 Baerwald, R. *Psychologie der Vorstellungstypen,* Berlin, 1916.

3 Bastian, H. C. Lectures in the Royal College of Physicians in London, 1897. *Lancet,* April, May, Sept., 1897.

4 Beebe, H. L. *A Guide to Help the Severely Hard of Hearing Child.* Basel, Switzerland: S. Karger A. G., 1953.

5 Bonvicini. G. *Die Störungen der Lautsprache bei Temporallappenläsionen,* Berlin-Wien, 1939, p. 1648ff., p. 1613.

6 Broca, P. A. Perte de la Parole. *Bull. de la Société Anthropol.,* Paris, 1861.

7 Bühler, K. *Sprachtheorie,* Jena, 1934.

8 Charcot, J. M. *Leçons sur les Localisations dans les Maladies du Cerveau,* Paris, 1876.

9 Crandall, J. B. The Sounds of Speech. *The Bell System Technical Journal,* B 4, 4, 1925.

10 Ebbinghaus. *Grundzüge der Psychologie,* IV Ed. edited by K. Bühler, 1919.

11 Freund, H. Studies in the Interrelationship between Stuttering and Cluttering. *Folia Phoniatica,* 4, 3, 1952, pp. 146-168.

12 Froeschels, E. Some Voice Problems In Aphasia. Logopaedie En Phoniatrie. 26, 1, April 1954, pp. 49-57.

13 Froeschels, E. *Kindersprache und Aphasie,* Berlin, Karger, 1918.

14 —— What Is Hearing? *The Nervous Child,* 9, 7, January 1951.

15 —— Ueber den zentralen Mechanismus der Sprache. *Deutsche Zeitschrift f. Nervenheilkunde,* 1915.

16 —— *The Human Race,* New York, The Philosophical Library, 1948.

17 —— *Philosophy and Aesthetic of Speech,* Boston, Mass., Expression Company, 1935, p. 176.

18 Froeschels, E. and Jellinek, A. *Practice of Voice and Speech Therapy,* Boston, Mass., 1941.

19 Froeschels, E., Dittrich, O., and Wilhelm, J. *Psychological Elements in Speech.* Boston, Mass.: Expression Company, 1932.

20 Goldstein, K. *Language and Language Disturbances,* New York, 1948.

21 —— *The Organism. A Wholistic Approach to Biology,* New York, 1939.

22 —— *Die transkortikalen Aphasien,* Jena, 1915.

23 Head, H. *Aphasia and Kindred Disorders of Speech,* Cambridge, 1926.

[24] Jackson, H. In Head, H.: Hughlings Jackson on Aphasia and Kindred Affections of Speech. *Brain,* 1915, XXXVIII, Parts 1 and 2.

[25] James, W. *Principles of Psychology,* I, 1891, p. 480ff.

[26] Kainz, F. Logopaedie und Sprachpsychologie. *Folia Phoniatrica,* 1, 3/4, 1948, pp. 178-205.

[27] Lichtheim. In H. Curschmann's *Lehrbuch der Nervenkrankheiten,* Berlin, 1906, and: Ueber Aphasie. *Deutches Archiv f. klinische Medizin,* Bd. XXXVI, 1885.

[28] Marie, P. Révision de la Question de l'Aphasie; la troisième Circonvolution frontale ne joue aucune rôle spéciale dans la Fonction du Langage. *Sem. méd.,* 1906, No. 21 et No. 42 and 48.

[29] Mingazzini, G. Ueber den heutigen Stand der Aphasielehre. *Klinische Wochenschrift,* 1925, No. 27.

[30] Nielsen, J. M. Epitome of Agnosia, Apraxia and Aphasia with Proposed Physiologic-Anatomic Nomenclature. *The Journal of Speech Disorders,* June, 1942, 7, 2, pp. 105-141.

[30a] —— Possibility of Pure Motor Aphasia. *Bull. Los Angeles Neurol. Soc., 1,* 1926.

[31] Peterson, G. E. *New Trends in Experimental Phonetics.* Lecture New York Soc. for Speech and Voice Therapy, Inc. December 12, 1952.

[32] Pick, A. *Die agrammatischen Sprachstörungen,* 1. Teil. Berlin: Springer, 1913.

[33] Stumpf, C. *Die Sprachlaute,* Berlin, 1926.

[34] Weiss, D. Der Zusammenhang zwischen Poltern und Stottern. *Folia Phoniatrica,* 2, 4, 1950, p. 252-262.

[34a] *Cluttering (Central Speech Imbalance) and its Relation to Stammering.* Lecture at the New York Society of Speech and Voice Therapy, 1950.

[35] Wepman, J. M. *Recovery from Aphasia,* New York, 1951.

[36] Wernicke, C. *Der aphasische Symptomenkomplex,* Breslau, 1874.

[37] Wundt, W. *Grundzüge der physiologischen Psychologie,* Leipzig, 1908.

Chapter XXXII

HYPNOTHERAPY

Milton V. Kline

Professor of Psychology, Long Island University
Editor, The Journal of Clinical and Experimental Hypnosis

EDITORIAL NOTE

For a long time, particularly as a result of the advent of psychoanalysis, hypnosis has been thought a dead issue in medicine and psychiatry. It still had its value as entertainment and possibly as an anaesthetic technique, or in connection with exploratory methods in states of dissociation. For this reason, theoretical interest has kept up even after the ebb in professional circles; and it was largely through the devotion of a few psychologists that we have had from time to time excellent reviews of hypnotic phenomena.

Of late, there has been an upswing of interest in the subject, and new compounds such as hypnoanalysis and hypnotherapy have been formed which goes to show the new potentialities of hypnosis in conjunction with applications of modern dynamic psychology. The days of Liébeault, Charcot, and Bernheim have gone. Modern hypnoanalysis operates with new devices; and this volume would have been more incomplete than ever without the present chapter.

Perhaps the chief promoter of this movement at the present time is Dr. Milton V. Kline, who, after his academic training at Penn State University, Columbia University, and New York University (in that order) received psychoanalytic training at the William A. White Institute. He holds a professorship of Psychology at Long Island University, and was Chief Psychologist of the Mental Hygiene Division in the Westchester County Health Department and consultant in Hypnosis at the New York University College of Engineering. He is founder and editor of The Journal of Clinical and Experimental Hypnosis, *and has written a number of articles and monographs on hypnotherapy.*

PRESENT-DAY PSYCHOLOGY

THE OLDER PERIOD

Traditionally hypnosis has always remained on the fringe of the psychological sciences as it has with relation to the other behavior sciences. Historically there have been brief though significant periods in the history of science when hypnosis has flourished as a productive experimental discipline and clinical technique in psychology and medicine.[28, 74] The historical accounts of scientific hypnosis are both interesting and enlightening as we observe the cultural, philosophical, and psychodynamic forces that have been responsible for the way in which hypnosis has been perceived and interpreted.[20, 21, 74] The scientific worker as well as the scientific historian should make reference to these variations and developmental cycles in the history of hypnosis in order to more fully observe the global meaning of hypnosis in modern psychology and our culture.

In recent times, the abandonment of hypnosis by Sigmund Freud overshadowed the productive advancements in this field by Janet,[29] Prince,[62] Sidis,[76] Binet,[3] and many other twentieth-century psychologists and physicians. Freud's abandoning of hypnosis had a profound influence beyond psychotherapy alone, since all areas of psychological hypnosis were shortly after to go into eclipse. Freud's ambivalence towards hypnosis has been well described historically and scientifically, and has had considerable influence upon psychoanalytic thinking.[20, 44] Certainly, Freud's rôle in this area, although not intentionally designed to remove all scientific interest from hypnosis, did serve this end rather well for a long time. Hypnosis remained in a relatively dormant state until the 1930's and the work of Clark Hull and his associates.[28] This is not to imply that some hypnosis work was not being done in the meantime; for it most assuredly was, and the literature reports interesting and provocative papers by a number of workers during the 20's.[27, 29, 57, 78] But it was generally isolated, sporadic, and for the greater part ignored by psychologists and psychiatrists.

Hull re-awakened interest in experimental hypnosis and his contribution to psychological hypnosis can not yet be fully evaluated. However, it would appear to be two-fold: (a) the fact that hypnosis and hypnotic phenomena are logically and empirically a part of the science of psychology and (b), the nature of experimental hypnotic phenomena bear significantly on our knowledge of the nature of human behavior. Paralleling Hull's work there was a re-awakening of clinical activity with hypnosis in psychology and medicine. Erickson's classical experimental-clinical studies stand out during this period. Erickson indicated that not only was hypnosis an effective therapeutic device within the framework of dynamic psychotherapy but that penetrating and significant insights into the motives of human behavior could be obtained in this field.[10, 11, 12, 13, 14, 15, 16, 17] Both Hull and Erickson have played a major rôle in the past two decades in developing a definitive and dynamic concept of scientific hypnosis. The emergence of hypnosis as a major technique of psychotherapy and as an area of experimental research is due largely to the work and influence of these two men.

The past decade: Since 1940 we have witnessed a significant rise in the use of hypnosis. During this contemporary period there has been a marked increase in hypnosis publications. LeCron and Bordeaux,[54] Estabrooks,[18] Brenman and Gill,[4] Wolberg, [84, 85] Watkins,[82] LeCron,[53] Schneck,[74] Rosen,[64] Kline,[33] Heron,[26] Stolzenberg,[77] Lindner,[56] Van Pelt,[81] and Gindes[23] are some who have contributed to the growing literature of contemporary hypnosis apart from the vast periodical literature.[33]

In 1948 the Society for Clinical and Experimental Hypnosis was founded. This Society, composed primarily of psychologists and psychiatrists, was created in order to promote scientific interest and communication within scientific hypnosis. The Society, in 1953 founded the first American journal devoted exclusively to scientific hypnosis. The *Journal of Clinical and Experimental Hypnosis*[30] has in the short time since its birth become the major hypnosis publication in the world. The Society also undertook the publishing of an Annual Review of Hypnosis Literature,[33] presenting comprehensive abstracts of research studies in hypnosis.

Thus the setting within which we attempt to examine contemporary orientations, concepts and techniques in hypnotherapy, is a period which may descriptively be called a renaissance in hypnosis. From the work of Hull and Erickson,[1] has emerged a vibrant and surging interest in hypnosis which at present is penetrating many areas of psychology and medicine.

Hypnotherapy, long a term of ancient and relatively static treatment by suggestion, has evolved into a therapeutic discipline within which all other techniques and devices of psychotherapy can be utilized and often enhanced with meaningful results. The nature of contemporary hypnotherapy has been dealt with rather intensively in recent textbooks and technical publications. Reference should be made to the work of Lindner,[56] Schneck,[74] Wolberg,[84] Rosen,[64] Brenman and Gill[4] and LeCron and Bordeaux[54] with respect to the techniques, concepts and management of hypnoanalysis and hypnotherapy. Perhaps as a result of this evolvement and development of treatment methods and techniques, we can at this time arrive at some definition of hypnotherapy.[2] Such a definition in the past has been rather difficult to determine primarily because hypnosis represented an eclectic psychological phenomenon being utilized in, at times, relatively unsystematized treatment techniques and procedures. Certainly we can say that hypnoanalysis, as well as contemporary hypnotherapy, as definitive therapeutic methods, did not come to maturation until much of the work of Freud in psychoanalytic theory as well as treatment technique had assumed a concrete and relatively objective status as a psychology of motivation. It is with the integration of psychoanalytic concept and technique within the broader framework of a dynamic psychology of modern times that hypnosis again appears on the scene as an effective and meaningful therapeutic device.

Traditionally some differentiation has always been made between hypnotherapy and other forms of psychotherapy that transcend the actual nature of the differences. Hypnotherapy in modern psychology is, in fact, a broadly descriptive term which designates a vast variety of therapeutic methodologies within which there is the utilization of hypnotic technique. Hypnoanalysis, which has received very strong support and recognition in recent years, is literally the utilization of psychoanalytic treatment methods within which hypnosis is employed for a variety of purposes. The major ones involve the uncovering of patterns of resistance, the elucidation of unconscious ideas and affects, and the clarification of underlying ideational and emotional material in the light of ego integration and eventual synthesis in terms of personality modification. As such, hypnoanalysis *is* psychoanalytic treatment with the utilization of hypnosis in order to facilitate the process of analysis. A great number of techniques can and have been used meaningfully in hypnoanalysis. Such techniques as artificial dream stimulation,[19, 32, 58] age regression,[2, 4, 9, 22, 24, 34, 35, 40, 50] fantasy evocation,[64] the use of hallucinatory activities for clarification,[41, 74] automatic writing,[25, 74] symptom substitution and emotional intensification[64] as well as a variety of techniques dealing with projection of imagery and other sense modalities.[42, 47, 71, 73] Clinical research with hypnoanalysis and analytic techniques has been most productive and fruitful during the past decade.[33, 74]3

A number of other psychotherapeutic methods dealing less heavily with psychoanalytic procedure, although taking into account the psychoanalytic concept of neurosis, have also made a considerable contribution to both our knowledge of the dynamics of emotional illness and the treatment of certain types of behavior disorders. Such techniques, classified broadly as hypnotherapy, range from the use of non-directive techniques[45] within an hypnotic framework to such experimental techniques as age progression,[36, 37] postural therapy,[3a] hallucinated group therapy,[42] and the modification of behavior through sensory alteration and modification.[33]

Thus in describing the nature of hypnotherapy today, we

must say that it is an approach in psychotherapy which is based upon the major concepts of modern psychodynamics within which hypnosis and hypnotic techniques are utilized as part of treatment planning and management in the light of the patient's personality organization, personality disorder, treatment needs, and, above all, the capacities and skills of the therapist. The methodologies of hypnoanalysis and hypnotherapy have been exceptionally well described in contemporary psychological and psychiatric literature. The purpose of this review is not to repeat this material but rather to emphasize and to delineate recent research and advancements in hypnotherapeutic techniques which can be incorporated into treatment methods and which reflect the growing synthesis of a general psychology of mental function in relationship to both psychodynamics and psychotherapy.

CONTEMPORARY TRENDS AND INFLUENCES

Recent advancements in hypnoanalytic and hypnotherapeutic techniques have stressed a number of factors which perhaps, by way of classification, can be grouped under a few headings. Certainly the evaluation and dealing with resistance phenomena has constituted one of the broad areas for hypnotherapeutic intervention.[64]4 The interpretation and elucidation of transference[74] phenomena through projection and projective devices with hypnosis constitutes another major area of advancement.[2, 8, 46, 48, 49, 73, 75] Dynamic or diagnostic elucidation of unconscious ideas and feelings with some clarification of them in terms of the over-all dynamic picture of the patient's personality constitute a third major area of activity.[64, 74] Specific techniques involve such methods as fantasy evocation,[64] time distortion,[7, 8] age regression and progression,[35] scene visualization,[74, 75] imagery inducement[41] and imagery therapy, postural characteristics, group therapy, symptom substitution and extensions and advancements of induction techniques. Such are the major trends, influences and advancements. There is much more to the total development of hypnotherapeutic and analytic skill than the handling of specific techniques. Perhaps it should be emphasized by paraphrasing Rosen[64] that hypnotherapy requires not less therapeutic skill than other therapies, but much greater skill. The difference between trance induction and the trance state itself has been increasingly emphasized. Nondirective trance induction techniques have been utilized and investigated and patients not infrequently are hypnotized with their implied, rather than their stated, consent. Psychotic patients are now capable of being hypnotized and in order to facilitate on one hand, treatment by electro-shock, and on the other hand, meaningful psychotherapy, such techniques appear to have their value. In one form or another, says Rosen,[33] these trends are to be found in the mid 1940's. Some can be observed earlier in rudimentary form but we would say that contemporary trends in hypnotherapeutic management and technique are essentially the result of the work done during the mid 1940's carried on and extended by a rapidly increasing number of workers during the early 1950's.

EXPERIMENTAL RESEARCH

In evaluating any advancements in hypnotherapeutic areas, some reference must be made to the advancements during the past few years in experimental areas. The vast array of recent experimental research[33] precludes any detailed analysis particularly as we are here concerned primarily with hypnotherapy. Perhaps it would be profitable to very briefly mention some of the major experimental hypnotic findings during the past decade.[33] (A) sleep-like brain waves, can be induced by suggesting sleep to hypnotic subjects. (B) some stimulus reversal can be hypnotically established. (C) emotions considered to be real can be induced by hypnosis. (D) time perception can be controlled. (E) subjects show individual differences in terms of hypnotizability and may respond differentially to different techniques of induction. (F) basal metabolic rates can be effected hypnotically. (G) temperature perception can be influenced by hypnosis. (H) certain transcendence of sense modality function can be induced through hypnotic technique although not necessarily by direct suggestion. (I) psychotic subjects, both organic and schizophrenic, can be hypnotized. Perhaps one of the major conclusions that can be reached through a review of contemporary research in experimental hypnosis, which is directly applicable to the clinical use of hypnotherapy, is that although direct suggestion is not capable of producing some of the alterations in behavior that one thinks of as being relatively definitive either by way of motivation or psychophysiological alterations, such changes can, nonetheless, be induced through the use of hypnotic techniques which rely very little upon suggestion except as the means for communication. More and more it has become clear that the hypnotic relationship, although a verbal one, is one which also involves some very fundamental changes in neuropsychological organization and perhaps more significantly in neuropsychological *accessibility* on the part of the patient or subject. Within such a framework, and interpersonal relationship, it is possible utilizing a number of recent techniques which are still largely in the investigative state to bring about major and at times radical alterations in behavior and behavior function.[36, 37, 43]

Induction and *hypnotizability*: As long as psychological practice has extended itself to hypnosis, the problem of hypnotizability has persisted. The ratio of individuals capable of being induced into a trance state and the ranges for the various "levels" of hypnosis generally have been verified from the older literature. Apparently 90 to 95 percent of all individuals are capable of some degree of hypnotizability. Apparently 10 percent are capable of a depth state within which such phenomena as complete amnesia, complete anesthesia, spontaneous amnesia, positive and negative hallucinations and post hypnotic behavior are capable of being produced easily and with long-term effectiveness.

Contemporary research in therapy with hypnosis has clearly indicated with respect to treatment procedures and in relationship to the clinical handling of psychodynamic activity, that light states of hypnosis are not only useful but often preferred. Although "deep hypnosis" has been associated with gross alterations in behavior generally, it has only recently been recognized that many highly complex and subtle changes in psychological functions can be brought about by extremely light hypnotic states. Therefore, since we are concerned here with the utilization of hypnotherapy and analysis in its broad sense, we shall be most concerned with those characteristics and forms of behavior which are not dependent upon a deeper hypnotic state. That deeper states of hypnosis are crucial for experimental work has been emphasized very distinctly by Erickson.[5] However, for much psychotherapeutic work light states offer many advantages both in terms of time and the ease of handling which the deeper states do not. The major areas within which light hypnotic states have been useful have been in the areas of projection, self reflection, increased associative functioning, imagery, psychodiagnostic testing, general psychologic productivity, fantasy evocation, somatic alteration and clarification through patient-centered activity.

A number of new techniques and modifications of technique for producing light to medium hypnotic states have been reported upon.[53] Erickson has made a substantial contribution to the understanding of variable states of hypnosis and their induction.[53]

Recent advancements in hypnotherapy have largely been based upon two distinctive trends: (1) the ability to integrate and manage psychoanalytic methods and concepts in a more productive and effective manner through the utilization of hypnosis and (2) the use of specific hypnotic techniques such as age regression, age progression, scene visualization, imagery activity and fantasy evocation within a frame of reference heavily influenced by experimental and clinical psychological processes.

Recent trends in clinical and experimental research which reflect upon theoretical and technique aspects of hypnotherapy are in themselves rather detailed and voluminous.[4, 6, 23, 56, 64,

[74, 84, 85] Some of the salient aspects of this work will be reported upon here in retrospect though the serious student should make reference to the more detailed and exacting research literature.

THE CLINICAL LITERATURE

Although Anton Mesmer's early prominence and notoriety[6] was to be found in connection with his treatment of a hysterical disorder in a youngster, little concentrated work in child psychotherapy has been reported in relation to the use of hypnosis. Ambrose[1] in England, has in recent years used hypnotherapy in the treatment of many disorders of children. He reports upon cases of anxiety reactions, asthma, enuresis, epilepsy, stammering, insomnia and various psychosomatic manifestations.

Buckley,[5] in describing the use of hypnoanalytic methods in the treatment of "post-traumatic syndrome" following head injury illustrates an effective therapy for many psychological disorders that follow physical injury and appear to be based upon body image alterations. Abreaction, ablation of time concepts, and associative methods all play a rôle in this type of therapy.

Conn,[6] in emphasizing the concept of patient-centered psychotherapy, has employed hypnotherapy as a unifying interpersonal experience. He utilizes the term hypnosynthesis to describe an approach in treatment which permits the patient to objectively experience what he is doing and to bring together in his own interpretive frame of reference the motives for his behavior.

Schneck and Kline[74, 75] have described and utilized visual imagery in the form of scene visualizations for projecting unconscious ideas and feelings through techniques involving the word association test, the TAT;* the HTP;* and direct associative activity. Visual imagery, as well as hallucinated behavior, has been utilized for purposes of unconscious productivity, clarification and abreaction.[41, 74] Rosen has developed the technique of fantasy evocation as a technique of gaining insight into primary motives of behavior.[64]

* Thematic apperception test; house-tree-person test.—*Ed.*

There has been a growing awareness that the hypnotic state is in itself a highly complex *gestalt*. Schneck in a series of provocative clinical researches has emphasized the unconscious aspects of the hypnotic relationship for the patient and has shown how this reaction is descriptive of the patient's personality dynamics and how it may be incorporated into psychotherapy.[68, 69, 70, 71]

It has largely been the recognition that in a state of hypnosis there exists a subtle, though highly complex, alteration of a patient's total neuropsychological organization that has influenced the development of contemporary hypnotherapeutic techniques and methods. For with hypnosis it has been found that total psychologic productivity, emotional accessibility, cognitive reflection, and integrated personality mechanization become not only more understandable but more manageable. To this extent contemporary hypnotherapeutic practice parallels growing insight into the essential characteristic of personality as evidenced in psychoanalysis, social psychology and other areas of dynamic psychology. It is the capacity of hypnotherapy and analysis to integrate and manipulate coexisting concepts, ideas, techniques and methods from all of the psychological sciences that has brought it to the fore among modern methods of psychotherapy.

HYPNOSIS AND PSYCHOLOGICAL TESTING

The use of hypnosis in connection with psychological testing extends the use of such devices significantly in relation to developmental and longitudinal studies of personality and personality elements. Such applications also shed considerable light on the nature and meaning of many of the test functions themselves.

HYPNOTIC AGE REGRESSION AND PROGRESSION

Two studies dealing with hypnotic age regression and hypnotic age progression are pertinent in this regard.[36, 37] In one, the Wechsler Bellevue Intelligence Scale, Form I was administered to a 22 year old female student regressed to the age of eight and at a 65 year old hypnotic age progression. The statistical variations in both the regressed and progressed states were consistent with normative variations obtained through both wide scale intelligence testing and mathematical extension of existing normative data. The results tend to indicate that age changes brought about through the use of hypnosis are more fact than artifact and they may well reflect distinct alteration in neuropsychological functions, particularly learning and perceptual mechanisms. This has marked significance for psychology in its study of the nature of personality and its organization. If the time and experience continuum of human development can validly and reliably be exposed to objective study through hypnosis, vast opportunities are opened up for longitudinal investigations of such important elements of human behavior as interest, attitudes, and temperament.

The other paper deals with the administration of the Terman-Miles Masculinity-Femininity Test in relation to age progression.[36] This test of psychological sexuality is empirical in form and would therefore be particularly hard to simulate in relation to hypnotic age changes. In this study the M-F Test was administered to a female subject first in the waking state, then one week later at a 65-year age progression under hypnosis, and finally one week following, in the waking state when the subject was told to behave "as if you are sixty-five years old." This was the simulation control. The variations in subtest patterns from the waking state to the hypnotic age progression state coincided closely with the normative data obtained by Terman and Miles in their experimental study.

These changes attributed in the original study to the expression of normal aging were induced in this study of hypnotic age progression. The simulation control failed to produce results even similar to those empirically derived. In fact, the simulation results were hardly different from the waking state results.[7]

In addition to furthering the hypnothesis that hypnotic age changes are fact and not artifact, the results obtained in this study have particular reference to wide areas of psychological concern. For if the hypnotic changes represent changes primarily in the perceptual mechanism of the individual and not in basic organic components, the whole problem of the behavioral aspects of aging may well have to be re-examined with greater emphasis upon the psychological and particularly the perceptual rôle in such changes. Aging, like other phases of human experience, has its psychological concomitants, and it is these concomitants which are rapidly assuming importance in the problem of old age adjustment. If perceptual functions play a significant rôle in age alterations, the possibility of psychological control over these changes or alterations should be considered seriously from the therapeutic point of view. The use of hypnotic age progression would seem to offer the unique possibility of empirically studying this problem further, should age progression be more definitively ascertained as emotionally synonymous with actual age change. Much work is obviously needed in age-progression studies with respect to psychological and emotional variations. This would appear to be a vast field for research in clinical psychology. Rapidly accumulating psychometric data from the various studies in gerontology and geriatrics offer unusual possibilities for correlative investigations in this field.

True, in a paper describing an experimental control in hypnotic age regression states, describes a method which he found to be effective in 82.3 per cent of the cases studied.[79] Before induction, subjects were asked to state the day of week during which certain recent events had occurred. Correct responses were given on a level no greater than chance alone would permit. Under hypnosis, subjects were regressed year by year, using significant dates as chronological landmarks. On such dates they were asked, "What day is this?", and their answers were scored against a two hundred year calendar. Correct answers to these questions were given by 82.3 per cent of the subjects. A method of this type can easily be used as an objective control for indicating the existence of an hypnotic age regression state in clinical work. As such it offers the research worker and psychotherapist alike a measure of validity for the state of hypnotic regression with which he may be working.

WORD ASSOCIATION TESTS

Diagnostically, word association tests have proven valuable instruments in the evaluation of disturbed ideational areas of personality functioning.[63] The rationale of word association techniques deals heavily with the memory aspect of associative reactions, and insights into the emotions and thought processes of the patient are usually inferred from the traces of interference rather than by any direct revelations. For therapeutic purposes, as well as for clinical investigation into the core of personality maladjustment, it is of additional value to uncover unconscious ideas as well as the defenses that are created against them. In two studies utilizing hypnosis in relation to the word association technique, this objective was explored.[49, 75]

The findings reflected alterations in both the quantitative and qualitative aspects of the test performance when hypnosis was utilized. In one study of clinic patients being seen for psychotherapy, contrasted with control college students, with both groups taking the Menninger Revised Word Association Test under hypnosis, the results reflected the following facts: (a) a marked increase in the incidence of associative alterations in the hypnotic state; (b) an increase in the percentage of fast reaction times and a decrease in slow reaction times in the hypnotic state; (c) an increase in the percentage of serious disturbance reactions for both the patient and control groups when hypnosis was used; and (d) qualitative changes in response which were meaningful for the patient group within the framework of hypnotherapy and hypnoanalysis.

Administration of the word association test under hypnosis appears to break down the defenses usually created against traumatic ideational areas with greater qualitative expression than in the usual procedure of administration. While such a technique of psychological testing will find its greatest utility in hypnotherapy, it can also be used in intensive personality investigations and in hypnodiagnostic procedures in cases where the psychotherapy which follows will not be of an hypnotic type.

Though the results of this hypnotic technique did not produce direct insights in all instances into the nature of unconscious ideation, there were indications that more image formation was involved in the hypnotic administration of this test than in the waking administration.

Visual imagery and suggested image formations have been of considerable interest in the area of psychopathology, though attempts to utilize it within a psychodiagnostic testing technique have been somewhat limited.[8] Theoretically, since most projective tests of personality involve a coördinated associative-percept formation activity, a basic component of which is the vague memory association, a method of enlarging this memory image should produce meaningful insights into the products of unconscious thought organization. In an effort to alter the one-word conceptual response to the word association test stimuli, and to replace it with an elaboration of the underlying, vague image formation assumed to be the core of the associative procedure, an hypnotic scene visualization technique was devised.[74] The test was first administered in the waking state utilizing standard directions. From the responses obtained in the association phase of the test all those scored as "not popular" were selected to be used in the hypnotic phase of the test procedure. Control words were selected randomly from among the "popular" responses. After the patient had been thoroughly trained in hypnosis and particularly in the ability to visualize scenes hypnotically, those stimulus words of the "non-popular" group were presented one by one to the patient who was not told that a scene would appear in relation to each word. The patients were also instructed to visualize scenes in relation to stimulus words resulting from "popular" responses.

Since all the patients in the study were in therapy it was possible to investigate and evaluate the validity of much of the material elicited through this combination of psychological testing and hypnotic scene visualization procedure. In general, the material obtained was consistent with the impressions contained in both the psychological and psychiatric examinations. In addition, much of the material was pertinent to the psychotherapeutic process and could be incorporated into it quite meaningfully.

Although it seems that all associative responses involve some visual imagery, two distinct types of image formations were noted. One is a correlative image in which the apperception to perception and unconscious to conscious continuum is integrated by the visual process and appears to bear a direct relationship to the elicited response words on the word association test. The other type is more of a parallel association to the stimulus word and seems unrelated to the response word. In a further study of a patient in hypnotherapy, correlative images were noted to resemble the primary visual images which are assumed in analytical psychology to be primordial in nature and arrived at through image agglutinations or condensation.[41] This type of image is then a typical basic form of an ever-recurring psychological experience in which the patient synthesizes his identificational conflicts. Associative images were found to be similar to the personal image of Jung and the secondary visual image of Prince.[31, 62] This associative formation involves no primary visual perception and is not a reproduction of a visual experience. Rather from the patient's ideas of the self and environment, factual and other, perceptions are built up which possess secondary visual imagery by association.

The nature and content of both types of image reactions are valuable in therapy,[41] since therapeutic technique can better be oriented when the constructs underlying the patient's personality experiences are clearly discerned. The technique of hypnotic scene visualization in connection with the word association test appears to be of considerable utility in this regard. In hypnotherapeutic application it was noted that frequently transition states from visualized scenes to hypnotic dreams emerge and this assists the bringing to consciousness of unconscious ideas and affects.

Rorschach Technique

Wilkins and Adams[83] report an investigation of the use of the Rorschach under hypnosis in military psychiatry. They found that such a technique was particularly useful in the inaccessible patient, cases where there is a paucity of responses, or with the fearful or combat fatigue patient. They found that the Rorschach record elicited under hypnosis shows an increase in percentage of responses to Cards VIII, IX and X. The total number of rejections is greatly reduced, generally to zero. Sum C generally was noted to decrease and M and FM to show increases. The findings from a study of this type point not only to a specialized technique for the examination of difficult patients but also to a technique for the further study and validation of projective techniques. In this connection Lane reports on a validation test of the Rorschach movement interpretations.[51] The investigation of the validity of M score interpretations involved inducing productivity and introversive mechanisms by suggestions, and noting results and changes in the M score and experience type on the Rorschach test. Rorschach tests were administered to a subject in the waking state and in a state of hypnosis *per se,* as well as in a state of hypnosis with suggestion. The results indicated that hypnosis *per se* seems to produce a slight increase of the introversive tendencies beyond the normal state, while the gross effects of hypnosis with specific suggestions intensifies the introversive tendencies far beyond the level of hypnosis per se.

In Lane's study, the qualitative analysis of the movement responses indicated that the subject was responding with movement interpretations. As a result of hypnotic excitation in addition to verifying certain constructs of the Rorschach technique, this study points up another aspect of hypnosis which has been a point of serious consideration, that is, the nature of creativity and productivity in personality as a result of hypnosis. Critics of hypnosis[21] have often labeled hypnotic behavior as "acting", and an example of non-productive psychological activity.

Schneck contradicts this point of view, and describes some distinctly productive and creative aspects of hypnotic behavior with specific reference to psychotherapeutic activity.[72] In Lane's study, the subject engaged in dream activity and verse writing, which was clearly an expression of ideational and affective productivity with pertinent relationship to definitive personality problems which were confronting the subject and which lead to some clarification. In addition to the clinical findings, the quantitative changes in the Rorschach pointed to a much more extensive use of colored areas and to improved form level. The implication was one of personal productivity of considerable degree.

Spiegel, Shor, and Fishman[9] report on an hypnotic ablation technique for the study of personality development. This study of hypnotic age regression provided for the application of the following clinical procedures in evaluating the personality changes involved: the Stanford Binet intelligence test, Kohs Block Test, Rorschach Test, conditioned reflex studies, electroencephalographs, projective drawing techniques, Thematic Apperception Test, Shor Completion Blanks, Revised Beta Intelligence tests and the Tendler Projective sheets. The regression ages studied were 1 to 6, 2, 4, 5, 5 to 9, 6, 8, 11, 12, 24, 17 and 20.

Bergman, Graham, and Leavitt[2] in their study of Rorschach changes during consecutive hypnotic chronological age level regressions of one patient found the test changes to parallel closely the clinical life data of the patient. The appearance of new interpersonal relationships which produced anxiety and unconscious hostility were noted along with the expression (psychometrically) of defense mechanisms designed to cope with these new developments and conflicts.

The possibility of employing the Rorschach as well as other techniques and instruments in clinical psychology for the longitudinal analysis of personality now exists. As such, psychological procedures of diagnostic design can be incorporated into psychotherapy and with proper management can extend both the use of psychological devices and the extent of psychotherapeutic technique. The possibility of further studying the relationship between learning theory and psychotherapy is enhanced because of the longitudinal controls which would now be available to the therapist through hypnometrics.

THEMATIC APPERCEPTION TEST

In a study of ego-defense and hypnotizability, Sarason and Rosenzweig[66] utilized the Thematic Apperception Test. The main conclusions drawn tended to confirm the quantitative findings of the earlier relationship expressed in the triadic hypothesis, which has been stated by Rosenzweig as "Hypnotizability as a personality trait is to be found in positive association with repression as a preferred mechanism of defense, and with impunitiveness as a characteristic type of immediate reaction to frustration." In analyzing the stories projected with regard to hypnosis, the dynamics of ego defense mechanisms and the needs of the individual became, united and conceptualized. On the basis of the stories produced on the TAT, it was possible to significantly differentiate hynotizable from non-hypnotizable subjects.

In a study designed to investigate the personality correlates of hypnotizability, Rosenzweig and Sarason[65] used a correlative technique to determine whether or not hypnotizability as a personality trait is to be found related to repression as a selected mechanism of defense and with "impunitiveness" as an immediate reaction to frustration. Their results would seem to validate this hypothesis in positive association, though with certain selective aspects of personality expression altering the characteristic mode of response. The correlations between suggestibility and repression were .25 and .47, and between hypnotizability and repression .66. Findings of this sort have two immediate implications: (1) a practical clinical, diagnostic technique for selecting patients likely to be workable in a hypnotherapeutic setting and (2) a means of evaluating ego defenses and the dynamics of aggression-frustration reactions.

Vocational Interests

The problem of vocational interests and personality has received considerable attention in clinical psychology and vocational guidance, and to some extent in psychoanalysis. Psychologists interested in the problem of vocational choice and personality adjustment have in recent years been placing greater stress upon the rôle of psychodynamic processes involved in occupational interests and choices. Psychometric methods for evaluation of occupational interests have become standard clinical procedures and are widely used in vocational guidance and occupational counseling settings.

In recent investigations of the origins of vocational interests and choice, an hypnotic method has been employed in studying the genesis of occupational interests and a scene visualization technique has been utilized for this purpose.[46, 73] These reports deal with patients who were seen in hypnotherapeutic and vocational analysis settings. The purpose of a technique of the scene visualization type is to further the study of the underlying personality motives and psychodynamic processes which lead to the development of occupational interests and vocational goals. In clinical application, the results proved useful not only in the therapeutic approach, but afforded insight into the unconscious factors that might become motivating elements in the development of vocational interests generally. It was found that meaningful scene visualizations could be obtained from patients in a light non-somnambulistic trance and that additional hypnotic and therapeutic techniques could be employed in interpreting and analyzing the productions from these visualizations. In many instances it was possible to undercut the conscious motivations for specific vocational plans and goals and to get directly at the unconscious origin of these patterns of behavior.[10] The findings were then utilized in the total treatment plan and led to clarification of the patient's personality difficulties. It was also noted that this hypnotic technique frequently brought to consciousness associated images which were of a non-occupational nature and which also could be incorporated with meaningfulness into the therapeutic approach.[11]

As a technique for therapeutic application and as a psychological method for further investigating the origin of vocational interests and vocational choice, the hypnotic scene visualization method would appear to have considerable value.

OTHER PROSPECTIVE METHODS

Schneck and Kline have reported upon a technique which utilized the House-Tree-Person test in measuring the effectiveness of psychotherapy. Such a method, since it is dependent upon only a light hypnotic state, can easily be utilized with almost all forms of psychotherapy.[48, 74]

Visual imagery, induced through hypnosis, has been described by Schneck,[74] Rosen,[64] Cooper and Erickson[7, 8] and Kline[41] in both psychotherapy and research investigation. Cooper and Erickson[8] have utilized imagery of an hallucinative nature in connection with time distortion and its effect upon behavior. Schneck and Kline have utilized imagery and hallucinated behavior as an integral part of hypnotherapy.[38, 42, 74]

AGE REGRESSION

Continued emphasis upon age regression has been reported in recent research. Contemporary evidence tends to confirm the validity of age regression as a neuropsychological phenomenon. A brief review of past and present status is necessary in order to fully evaluate its rôle in present-day psychological thinking.

The validity of age regression has been debated back and forth on the basis of conflicting experimental data and clinical observation. Young, in 1940, reviewed the problem and came to the conclusion that hypnotic age regression was an artifact and not a fact.[86] Since that time there have been published reports of regression investigations which both confirm and deny this position. Wolberg[85] in attempting to state contemporary authoritative attitude toward age regression states that generally it is considered to be valid. In this sense, Wolberg defined the process of hypnotic age regression as a disorientation concept with relation to person, place, and, time. Hypnotic age regression then becomes, when it is validly produced, a recapitulation of a previous stage of development with apparent amnesia for experiential activity beyond that date. In a clinical investigation, Spiegel, Shor and Fishman[12] indicate the production and use of an ablation process which was consistent with this concept and proved meaningful in psychotherapy. For a complete survey of the experimental and clinical research in this area, reference should be made to the original work.

The criteria selected for measuring the validity of age regression is critical in evaluating the phenomenon. Generally, developmental functions have been selected, and on the basis of changes or lack of significant changes an interpretation of regression validity has been made. Intelligence and intelligence test measurements have been one criterion used in many regression studies. Hakebush, Blinkovski and Foundillère[24] found that intelligence test measurements in hypnotic age regression corresponded precisely with performance at the actual chronological levels studied. They felt that it was possible to regress a subject back to infancy and possibly even to the neonatal state. Platnow[61] in addition to finding precise regression correlates also felt that clinically the behavior evidenced by the subjects when regressed was consistent with the phenomenon of chronological adaptation. In synthesizing the findings of other studies in agreement with their conclusions, Platnow[61] and Dolin[9] expressed the theoretical rationale of regression to be— "that conditioned reactions once developed do not disappear completely—but leave organic traces in the nervous system. Hypnotic stimuli may reanimate earlier conditioned response patterns."

Later experimental and clinical investigations have produced both positive and negative evidence. Studies by Leeds,[55] Mercer and Gibson,[59] True,[79] True and Stephenson,[80] and Kline and Guze[47] report results which tend to confirm the opinion that hypnotic age regression actually involves some reproduction of earlier developmental behavior.[13] Sarbin,[67] and Orne[60] present data and theoretical explanations which deny the ontogenetic reality of age regression and place such behavior on a simulation or rôle-playing basis.

In addition to studies dealing with intelligence measurements or mental functioning components, there have been some recent investigations concerning emotional and psychophysiological reactions. In one study, an experimental investigation of children's reactions to stimuli producing fear responses was repeated in hypnotic age regression with results very similar to those reported in the original study.[40] Simulation controls failed to produce similar reactions. Gidro-Frank and Buch[22] were able in hypnotic age regression to produce infantile plantar reflex reactions. On the basis of their study they concluded:

1. "It is possible to elicit an infantile plantar response in hypnotic age regression."
2. "The change in the plantar response is accompanied by changes in peripheral chronaxie."
3. "This evidence supports the authenticity of hypnotic age regression."

Kupper[50] describes a patient with a history of classical convulsive seizures of grand mal type with abnormal electro-cortical activity on the EEG. His attacks started six years before examination and were precipitated by an emotional upset. Under hypnosis, convulsive seizures were induced by discovering and suggesting the specific psychic conflict. EEG recordings could be altered by suggesting that the patient under hypnosis regress to an age prior to his first convulsion.

Brenman and Gill[4] report on a case where in the use of experimental techniques in therapy, a patient some months after being exposed to a particular situation was regressed back to that time hypnotically. This involved principally time rather than age regression, though both are related.[14] The subject spontaneously began to perspire and complain of the heat. This was rather surprising in view of the fact that this particular phase of the study took place in winter. The experimenters then recalled that on the day to which the patient was now regressed, Kansas had experienced one of its hottest summer days.

In considering the phenomena of hypnotically induced changes in age and time orientation we have in the past been concerned with a regression or a chronologically going-back problem, which involves not only the memories and recalled experiences of that time but all learned and unlearned experiential activity. The issue of experiential age activity has always been assumed as the nuclear core in age regression and has in part contributed to the difficulty in ascertaining the validity and the nature of regression. Recent evidence has pointed to time-age orientation changes in the opposite direction, namely aging.[36, 37] The term hypnotic age progression has been applied to this phenomenon. Thus in a theoretical consideration of hypnotic age regression we cannot exclude the additional concept of hypnotic age progression. In progression phenomena, the experiential component is on the surface debatable. From this factor, we may either assume (a) that regression and progression are different processes, or (b) they are the same process except that experiential conditions noted in regression reactions are not as nuclear as previously thought, or some type of substitute experiential components are to be found in progression. A theory of regression must deal with these issues.

CURRENT STATUS OF HYPNOTIC AGE REGRESSION AND PROGRESSION DATA

Three areas of psychological activity have frequently been used as criteria in regression investigations (a) intelligence and intelligence test measurements, (b) motor patterns of behavior, learned and apparently unlearned responses characteristic of specific developmental periods and, (c) affective behavior of developmental significance and in therapeutic researches, experiential recapitulations. Generally speaking, where subjects are capable of regression phenomena in one area, they are frequently capable of such activity in all areas. Regression activity appears to represent global or gestalt function rather than specificity of response formation.

1. Some investigators find positive evidence both experimentally and clinically for regression and progression phenomena in studies of mental functioning, motor behavior, and affective expressions of personality organization.

2. Some investigators find negative evidence for regression phenomena and feel that the behavior which is produced is (a) rôle-playing and/or (b) increased simulation acuity.

3. Some investigators find both positive and negative evidence for regression and progression phenomena with a general trend for subjects to either meet regression and progression criteria in several measurable respects or not at all.

Throughout the history of regression research, there has been consistent observation which reflects a high correlation between depth hypnosis and regression capacity.[52, 53] Whenever positive findings have been reported the subjects usually have been described as capable of depth hypnosis. Although existing scales for indicating the nature of hypnotic depth are of questionable validity, regression behavior has usually been classified along with the deeper trance states. Even in negative regression studies those subjects who "simulated or played a rôle better" according to objective criteria were ranked "deeper" on the hypnotic depth scale.

4. In both positive and negative studies of regression, there has been reported a high correlation between regression fact or artifact and the depth of hypnosis. Although depth of hypnosis can be evaluated to some degree by behavior and hypnotic productivity, the meaning that the various levels of trance depth may have with respect to the psychodynamics involved in the subject's achievement level is not clear. The meaning that hypnosis may have to the individual has been the subject of some study[69, 70, 71] and though there appears to be a relationship between personality structure and hypnotic capability, the psychodynamics are not definitive enough to permit localization

of specific factors or groups of factors which will accurately predict depth of hypnotic induction.

5. Personality organization as well as mental functioning components appear to be related to the depth and the meaning of hypnotic induction.

6. Depth as used conceptually with respect to hypnotic levels is somewhat ambiguous and cannot be measured with significant validity or reliability at this time.

7. Complex and subtle variations in the meaning of the hypnotic relationship may significantly change hypnotic productivity and its characteristic phenomena despite clinical similarity in subject appearance and gross hypnotic behavior.

TENTATIVE CONCLUSIONS

1. Only certain subjects appear capable of "deep" hypnosis, regardless of different concepts or criteria of depth hypnosis.

2. Within apparently similar levels as well as obviously different levels of hypnosis, some subjects develop certain reactions to the meaning and induction of hypnosis *per se,* and their behavior in hypnosis is in part a reflection of the psychodynamic correlates of this meaning.

3. Only certain subjects can regress precisely and the somnambulistic or amnesic criteria are not very predictive of this capacity though the correlation may be positive.

4. Depth hypnosis appears related to the meaning of the hypnotic transference relationship and in part, hypnotic regression and progression capacity seem linked to the psychomechanics of this transference activity.

5. Not all subjects at the same "level" or "depth" of hypnosis are involved in identical psychodynamic relationships and psychomechanical activity.

6. Some subjects capable of "depth" hypnosis will be able to regress precisely.

7. Some subjects capable of "depth" hypnosis will not be able to regress precisely.

8. Where regression activity is released, the neuro-organiza-

tional, intellectual, and affective measures of regression often reflect valid chronological changes.

9. When regression activity is resisted (inhibited), rôle-playing simulation will be evolved with invalid measures and correlates of any chronological or ontogenetic change.

HYPOTHETICAL CONSTRUCTS

Hypnotic age regression phenomena appear to involve a form of activity dependent upon the formation of a particular type of hypnotic transference relationship and its neuropsychological correlates which co-exist with "depth" hypnosis in particular personality constellations. Experimental verification of this hypothesis may involve the following requisites.

1. An investigation of the personality configurations and characteristics of subjects involved in various types of hypnotic transference relationships.

2. A study of the neuropsychological correlates of (a) each type and level of hypnotic transference activity and (b) the incidence and nature of "depth" hypnosis as found in each of these transference types.

CONTEMPORARY CONCLUSIONS

From a review of contemporary data and the use of the hypothetical constructs erected at this time the following conclusions appear theoretically tenable:

1. Valid age regression can be obtained in some instances.

2. The size of the population capable of being so involved would appear to be relatively limited within the framework of present hypnotic techniques.

3. The failure on the part of some investigators to substantiate the validity of regression phenomena through empirical measurement may be due to an inability to produce the hypnotic conditions prerequisite for regression.

4. Those investigators who have demonstrated valid regression through empirical measurement have (in part by chance) satisfied the prerequisite conditions for regression phenomena.

A Neuropsychological Theory

Experimental and clinical findings point in the direction of the validity of regression phenomena under certain conditions which appear to exist at this time in relatively limited incidences of hypnotic behavior. In the past, regression phenomena have been considered and tentatively explained on the basis of the following hypothesis:

1. a change in time organization
2. a change in space orientation (place or person)
3. a change in neuropsychological organization.

A change in neuropsychological organization would appear theoretically to include time-space continuum alterations and thus as an operational concept may be considered as a unified explanation. What are the possible justifications for considering regression as a global alteration in organizational activity rather than a specific change in chronological age status and its developmental correlates? If regression involved only the ability to go back in memory and motor time with its recapitulation of learning and spontaneous behavior it could then be seriously considered as a chronological phenomenon in terms of recall activity.

Recently, however, it has been shown that hypnotic age progression can be produced in certain subjects and that tests of mental functioning and personality characteristics show variations and changes very similar to those previously obtained in empirical studies of aging. Although much more research is needed in this area, the evidence to date supports the idea that a "valid" measure of hypnotic age progression may be obtained on the same basis as a "valid" measure of hypnotic age regression.

It would then appear that the changes noticed and measured in both regression and progression may reflect directional alterations from a central process. Thus the terms regression and progression when considered from an ontogenetic or chronological basis may represent hypnotic activity and change in a defined and directed sphere stemming from a central process which permits such change in behavioral orientation and organization.

On the surface it would seem, from an examination of the progression research data that progression does not involve recalled or recapitulated stages of development activity, since there is no apparent experiential basis for this in the organism's actual psychological or physiological growth. The possibility of phylogenetic memories and their motor correlates in possible psychobiological recapitulation activity cannot be entirely dismissed from the viewpoint of scientific theory, but there is at this stage little experimental justification for such a theoretical position.[(43)15]

At this level of theory development in hypnosis, it is possible that both regression and progression represent movement of correlated chronological reactions along developmental lines as determined by alterations in the subject's time-space continuum perception. The actual state involved in such activity is not regression, not progression, but a central state of perceptual release or space orientation for which there are either experiential antecedents or psychophysiological gradients. The organism's location in time and space, like his rotated view of the external environment is a learned and relatively fixed function. Constancy in such locations may be determined by inhibitory and other control mechanisms which condition time-space changes to external stimuli (chronological time, world time, body-object relationships and other dimensionally controlled percepts of universal similarity). The unconscious nervous system regulation of time-space perception is implemented by conscious, learned, partially volitional devices. Time-space perceptions can be disrupted by changes in neuropsychological activity, such as sleep, stuporous states, toxic states, nervous system injury, physical and emotional illnesses and hypnosis.

Thus the central induced state ("depth" hypnosis) which permits regression and progression activity may be one which breaks through learned inhibitory controls over time-space perceptual functions. Such activity deprives the organism of any secure perception of time, space, or person, unless it can effect control through transference displacement. It is the interpersonal hypnotic relationship which will permit control and regulation provided the subject is willing and capable of entering into such a relationship. Otherwise the subject's defenses against disorientation can be penetrated and his links with external controls (conditionally and associatively) may become seriously impaired.

In view of the tremendous threat which hypnotic activity implies in terms of the subject's fear of losing self control and the associated self functions which he gives particular importance to, depending on his own personality configuration, it is little wonder that subjects resist the induction of hypnosis and particularly "depth" hypnosis.[16] It is part of the organism's spontaneous defenses to resist all threats to its dynamic equilibrium.[39] This is true in the psychological universe as it is in the physical universe where dynamic equilibrium is the basis for structure, activity, change and relative stability.

In the light of this theory, resistance to hypnosis and especially to depth states involving a threat to equilibrium can involve associated equations with experiential threats like castration, death, and sexual releases. It would seem that the meaning of hypnosis (equated) and the characteristics of the subject's resistances might be determined by the subject's conditionally and associatively equated responses to total neuropsychological equilibrium. The organism's basic fear, (presumably universal and phylogenetically valid) being a fear of equilibrium loss, it would, in the communicative process, equate it with the conceptualized activity it is developmentally or experientially most concerned over controlling. Thus the emotional impulses that represent a threat to the self become incorporated into the hypnotic resistances and responses.

With respect to neuropsychological theory, in describing the hypnotic process which produces time-space disorientation, we perhaps should no longer refer to the dynamic process as regression or progression, since these two functions may involve only redirection following disorientation. Changes may be produced in any dimension of the time-space continuum depending upon the satisfaction of the prerequisite conditions for such activity. The term hypnotic retrogression would seem to be more adequate in describing the global hypnotic state within which such reorientation processes as hypnotic age regression and progression are rendered possible. In evolving a workable theory of regression and progression phenomena, we find that we are in turn faced with a more complex task, namely the nature of hypnotic retrogression. Perhaps the most significant aspect of the contemporary resurgence of hypnotherapy lies in the increasing awareness that the hypnotic state and hypnotic behavior produces profound though subtle alterations in total psychological function.[33] Modern hypnotherapy has been characterized by increasing insight into the dynamics of hypnotic reactions and their diagnostic and therapeutic implications.

SUMMARY

The past decade has witnessed a strong revival of interest and research in scientific hypnosis. A good part of this impetus has resulted in the development of more definitive and extensive forms of hypnoanalysis and hypnotherapy. Several trends in the application of hypnosis are to be noted in connection with its wider utilization in psychological and psychiatric treatment. The most significant perhaps is the emergence of the recognition of hypnosis as a psychological phenomenon with characteristic indices of validity. In this respect experimental work and clinical research have laid the basis for such an advancement. Hypnosis research has become an integral part of neuropsychology, experimental psychology, as well as the more familiar areas of psychopathology and social behavior. The continuing growth of clinical hypnosis is largely the consequence of an expanding dynamic psychology capable of perceiving human personality as a bio-social evolvement. Within this frame of reference hypnosis has proven to be a potent technique for studying such areas of behavior as learning, perception, motivation, emotion, neuro-organizational processes and response mechanisms.

Thus, concepts of unconscious ideation and affects, traumatic neuroses, repressive mechanisms and associative functions have been able to be studied and dealt with in a more effective and direct manner than heretofore. Such techniques as age regression, hallucinatory behavior and time distortion have opened the way clinically, as well as theoretically, for the systematic investigation of psychogenetic patterns of development. More than anything else, hypnosis has, in its present advancements, proven to be of significant value in elucidating, clarifying, and managing many aspects of human behavior. As Freud originally noted, hypnosis offers a way to the unraveling of the workings of the human mind.[20]

Today scientific hypnosis is a strong and vibrant area of the behavior sciences. In psychology, hypnosis is gradually being accepted, not only as a legitimate area of scientific work, but as a productive and valuable avenue to the further understanding of the mechanisms of human behavior. The prospect is good that within the next decade hypnosis will emerge not only as a respected field of psychology but also as a major area of research and clinical application with respect to all forms of psychotherapy as well as in relationship to problems of a general and experimental psychology.

FOOTNOTES

1 For a detailed account of the nature of the experimental work of Hull and Erickson, as well as their followers, reference should be made to the recent volume by A. Weitzenhoffer, *Hypnotism: an Objective Study in Suggestibility.* New York: John Wiley, 1954.

2 By definition we refer more to the designation of treatment procedure in terms of psychologic rationale than merely nomenclature.

3 It would seem that hypnoanalysis more than any other form of dynamic treatment offers the possibility of a real synthesis of psychological, neurological and cultural concepts of psychopathological theory.

3a Guze, H. Posture, Postural Reintegration and Hypnotherapy. *J. Clin. Exp. Hyp.*, 1953, *1*, 76-82.

4 Within hypnotherapy, patient resistance often becomes intensified rapidly and "acted out" either ideationally or somatically.

5 Differences in the actual level of hypnosis may account more for the differences in research results than any other aspect of the problem or experimental design. Erickson's chapter on Depth Hypnosis in LeCron, L. M. (Ed.) *Experimental Hypnosis*[53] is an excellent review of this whole problem.

6 Wydenbruck, N. *Doctor Mesmer, an Historical Study.* London: John Westhouse, 1947.

7 Additional studies utilizing projective drawings have also indicated that in hypnotic age progression there is at least increased identification with the attitudes, affects, and perceptions of aging.[47]

8 In many respects, the hypnotic use of imagery is similar to the use of projective devices like the Rorschach and Thematic Apperception Test, with increased emotional intensification, fantasy evocation and abreaction present in hypnosis.

9 *Psychosom. Med.*, 1945, vol. 5, 273-284.

10 Additional hypnotic techniques utilizing the Thematic Apperception Test and age regression have described in connection with vocational interests, their origin and their relationship to personality theory.

11 Kline, M. V. and Schneck, J. M. An Hypnotic Experimental Approach to the Genesis of Occupational Interests and Choice: I. Theoretical Orientation and the Scene Visualization Technique. *Brit. J. Med. Hypnotism*, March 1950, vol. 2, 1-10.

12 *Op. cit.*

13 In this connection, LeCron[52] reports that a conditioned response established in the waking state is present in the hypnotic state *per se*, but is lost during age regression.

14 The relationship would appear to be one involving hypnotic alteration in memory and perception.

15 Further work in this area has indicated that the possibility of a "phylogenetic regression" may well exist as a phenomenon of behavior.

16 Resistance would appear to be a normal part of hypnotic behavior. The nature of this has been described in part by M. V. Kline, "An Outline of the Nature of Some Sexual Responses to the Induction of Hypnosis." *Psychiat. Quart. Suppl.*, 1952, Part 2, *26*, 230-236.

BIBLIOGRAPHY

1 Ambrose, G. The technique and value of hypnosis in child psychotherapy. *Brit. J. Med. Hypnotism*, March, 1950, 1-8.

2 Bergman, M. S., Graham, H., and Leavitt, H. C. Rorschach exploration of consecutive hypnotic chronological age level regressions. *Psychosom. Med.*, 1947, *1*, 20.

3 Binet, A. *La Suggestibilité.* Paris: Scheicher Frères, 1900.

4 Brenman, M. and Gill, M. *Hypnotherapy, A Survey of the Literature.* New York: International Universities Press, 1947.

5 Buckley, W. The treatment of post-traumatic syndrome by hypnotic analysis. *J. N. M. D.*, Jan.-Feb., 1950, *3*, 122.

6 Conn, J. H. Hypno-synthesis, hypnosis as a unifying interpersonal experience. *J. N. M. D.*, 1949, *9*, 109.

7 Cooper, L. F. Time distortion in hypnosis. *Bull. Georgetown Univ. Med. Center,* 1948, *1,* 214-221.

8 Cooper, L. F. and Erickson, M. H. Time distortion in hypnosis, II. *Bull. Georgetown Univ. Med. Center,* 1950, *4,* 50-68.

9 Dolin, A. O. Objective investigation of the elements of individual experiences by means of experimental hypnosis. *A R K H. biol. Nauk.,* 1934, *36,* 28-52.

10 Erickson, M. H. A brief survey of hypnotism. *Med. Record,* Dec. 1934.

11 —— Hypnosis in medicine. *The Med. Clin. of North Amer.,* May 1944.

12 —— An investigation of the hypnotic subjects' apparent ability to become unaware of stimuli. *J. Gen. Psychol.,* 1944, *31,* 191-212.

13 —— A study of clinical and experimental findings on hypnotic deafness: I. Clinical experimentation and findings. *J. Gen. Psychol.,* 1938, *19,* 127-150.

14 —— A study of clinical and experimental findings on hypnotic deafness: II. Experimental findings with a conditioned response technique. *J. Gen. Psychol.,* 1938, *19,* 151-161.

15 —— The application of hypnosis to psychiatry. *Med. Record,* July 1939, 60-65.

16 —— Hypnosis: a general review. *Dis. Nerv. System.* January 1941.

17 —— Development of apparent unconsciousness during hypnotic reliving of a traumatic experience. *Arch. Neurol. Psychiat.,* 1937, *38,* 1282-1288.

18 Estabrooks, G. H. *Hypnotism.* New York: Dutton, 1943.

19 Farber, L. H. and Fisher, C. An experimental approach to dream psychology through the use of hypnosis. *Psychoanal. Quart.,* 1943, *12,* 202-215.

20 Freud, S. *Collected Papers,* vol. II. London: Hogarth Press, 1949.

21 Fromm, E. *Man for Himself, An Inquiry into the Psychology of Ethics.* New York: Rinehart, 1947.

22 Gidro-Frank, L. and Buch, M. A. A study of the plantar response in hypnotic age regression. *J. N. M. D.,* 1948, *107,* 443-448.

23 Gindes, B. C. *New Concepts of Hypnosis.* New York: Julian Press, 1951.

24 Hakebush, L., Blinkovski, S., and Foundillère, F. An attempt at a study of development of personality with the aid of hypnosis. *Trud. Inst. Psikhonevr,* Kiev, 1930, *2,* 236-272.

25 Harriman, P. L. Automatic writing as a means for investigating experimentally induced conflicts. *Personality,* 1951, *3,* 264-271.

26 Heron, W. T. *Clinical Applications of Suggestion and Hypnosis.* Springfield: Charles C. Thomas, 1950.

27 Hollander, B. *Methods and Uses of Hypnosis and Self-hypnosis.* New York: Macmillan, 1928.

28 Hull, C. L. *Hypnosis and Suggestibility—an experimental approach.* New York: D. Appleton Century, 1933.

29 Janet, P. *Major Symptoms of Hysteria.* New York: Macmillan, 1920.

30 *Journal of Clinical and Experimental Hypnosis,* vol. I. New York: Woodrow Press, 1953.

31 Jung, C. G. *Psychological Types.* New York: Harcourt Brace, 1923.

32 Klein, D. B. The experimental production of dreams under hypnosis. *Univ. Tex. Bull.*, 1930, *3001*, 1-71.

33 Kline, M. V. (Ed.) *The Annual Review of Hypnosis Literature*, vols. I and II. New York: Woodrow Press, 1953.

34 Kline, M. V. Hypnotic age regression and intelligence. *J. Gen. Psychol.*, 1950, *77*, 129-132.

35 —— Hypnotic retrogression; a neuropsychological theory of age regression and progression. *J. Clin. Exp. Hyp.*, 1953, *1*, 21-28.

36 —— Hypnosis and age progression: a case report. *J. Genet. Psychol.*, 1951, *78*, 195-205.

37 —— A measure of mental masculinity and femininity in relation to hypnotic age progression. *J. Genet. Psychol.*, 1951, *78*, 207-215.

38 Kline, M. V. and Schneck, M. An hypnotic experimental approach to the genesis of occupational interests and choice. *Brit. J. Med. Hypnotism*, Winter, 1950, 1-10.

39 Kline, M. V. Toward a theoretical understanding of the nature of resistance to the induction of hypnosis and depth hypnosis. *J. Clin. Exp. Hyp.*, 1953, *2*, 32-41.

40 —— Childhood fears in relation to hypnotic age regression: a case report. *J. Genet. Psychol.*, 1953, *82*, 137-142.

41 —— Visual imagery and a case of experimental hypnotherapy. *J. Gen. Psychol.*, 1952, *46*, 159-167.

42 —— Play hypnotherapy in psychotherapy (to be published).

43 —— A note on "primate-like" behavior induced through hypnosis: a case report. *J. Genet. Psychol.*, 1952, *81*, 125-131.

44 —— Freud and hypnosis: a critical evaluation. *Brit. J. Med. Hypnotism*, Spring, 1953, 1-10.

45 —— The application of hypnosis to non-directive psychotherapy. *J. Clin. Psychol.*, 1951, 3, 283-287.

46 Kline, M. V. and Haggerty, A. D. An hypnotic experimental approach to the genesis of occupational interests and choice: III. Hypnotic age regression and the TAT-a clinical case study in occupational identification. *J. Clin. Exp. Hyp.*, 1953, *3*, 18-31.

47 Kline, M. V. and Guze, H. The use of a projective drawing technique in the investigation of hypnotic age regression and progression. *Brit. J. Med. Hypnotism*, 1951, 10-21.

48 Kline, M. V. and Schneck, J. M. A control study relating to h-t-p testing and hypnosis. *Brit. J. Med. Hypnotism*, Autumn, 1951, 1-10.

49 —— Hypnosis in relation to the word association test. *J. Gen. Psychol.*, 1951, *44*, 129-137.

50 Kupper, H. I. Psychic concomitants in wartime injuries. *Psychosom. Med.*, 1945, 7, 15-21.

51 Lane, B. M. A validation test of the Rorschach movement interpretations. *Am. J. Orthopsychiat.*, 1948, *2*, 292.

52 LeCron, L. M. The loss during hypnotic age regression of an established conditioned reflex. *Psychiat. Quart.*, 1952, *26*, 657-662.

53 LeCron, L. M. (Ed.) *Experimental Hypnosis*. New York: Macmillan, 1952.

54 LeCron, L. M. and Bordeaux, J. *Hypnotism Today*. New York: Grune and Stratton, 1947.

55 Leeds, M. An hypnotic regression series. *Persona*, 1949, 1-14.

56 Lindner, R. M. *Rebel Without a Cause*. New York: Grune and Stratton, 1944.

[57] Lundholm, H. An experimental study of functional anesthesia as induced by suggestion in hypnosis. *J. Abnorm. Soc. Psychol.*, 1928, 338-355.

[58] Mazer, M. An experimental study of the hypnotic dream. *Psychiatry*, 1951, *14*, 265-277.

[59] Mercer, M. and Gibson, R. W. Rorschach content in hypnosis: chronological age regression. *J. Clin. Psychol.*, 1950, *4*, 352-358.

[60] Orne, M. T. The mechanisms of hypnotic age regression: an experimental study. *J. Abnorm. Soc. Psychol.*, 1951, *46*, 213-225.

[61] Platnow, K. I. On the objective proof of the experimental personality age regression. *J. Gen. Psychol.*, 1933, *9*, 190-209.

[62] Prince, M. *The Unconscious*. New York: Macmillan, 1916.

[63] Rapaport, D. *Diagnostic Psychological Testing*, vol. II. Chicago: Year Book Publishers, 1946.

[64] Rosen, H. *Hypnotherapy in Clinical Psychiatry*. New York: Julian Press, 1953.

[65] Rosenzweig, S. and Sarason, S. An experimental study of the triadic hypothesis: reaction to frustrations, ego-defense and hypnotizability: I. correlational approach. *Charact. and Personality*, 1942, *12*, 1-19.

[66] Sarason, S. and Rosenzweig, S. An experimental study of the triadic hypothesis: reaction to frustrations, ego-defense and hypnotizability: II. thematic apperception approach. *Charact. and Personality*, 1942, *12*, 150-165.

[67] Sarbin, T. R. Mental age changes in experimental regression. *J. Personality*, 1950, *19*, 221-228.

[68] Schneck, J. M. Psychosomatic reactions to the induction of hypnosis. *Dis. Nerv. Syst.*, 1950, 1-4.

[69] ———— Some aspects of homosexuality in relation to hypnosis. *Psychoanal. Rev.*, 1950, *37*, 351-357.

[70] ———— The unconscious relationship between hypnosis and death. *Psychoanal. Rev.*, 1951, *38*, 271-274.

[71] ————The elucidation of spontaneous sensory and motor phenomena during hypnoanalysis. *Psychoanal. Rev.*, 1952, *39*, 79-89.

[72] ———— A note on hypnosis and the productive orientation.

[73] ———— An hypnotic technique for the exploration of vocational interests. *J. Gen. Psychol.*

[74] Schneck, J. M. (Ed.) *Hypnosis in Modern Medicine*. Springfield: Charles C. Thomas, 1953.

[75] Schneck, J. M. and Kline, M. V. Hypnotic scene visualization and the word association test. *J. Gen. Psychol.*, 1952, *46*, 29-42.

[76] Sidis, B. *The Psychology of Suggestion*. New York: Appleton-Century, 1910.

[77] Stolzenberg, J. *Psychosomatics and Suggestion Therapy in Dentistry*. New York: Philosophical Library, 1950.

[78] Talbert, G. A., Ready, F. L. and Kuhlman, F. W. Plethysmographic and pneumographic observations made in hypnosis. *Am. J. Physiol.*, 1924, *68*, 113.

[79] True, R. M. Experimental control in hypnotic age regression states. *Science*, 1949, *110*, 583-584.

[80] True, R. M. and Stephenson, C. W. Controlled experiments correlating electro-encephalogram, pulse, and plantar reflexes with hypnotic age regression and induced emotional states. *Personality*, 1951, *1*, 252-263.

[81] Van Pelt, S. J. *Hypnotism*. London: Skeffington, 1950.

[82] Watkins, J. G. *Hypnotherapy of War Neuroses.* New York: **Ronald** Press, 1949.

[83] Wilkins, W. L. and Adams, A. J. The use of the Rorschach test under hypnosis, and under sodium amytal in military psychiatry. *J. Gen. Psychol.,* 1947, *36*, 131.

[84] Wolberg, L. R. *Hypnoanalysis.* New York: Grune and Stratton, 1945.

[85] ——*Medical Hypnosis,* vol. I. New York: Grune and Stratton, 1948.

[86] Young, P. T. Hypnotic regression, fact or artifact? *J. Abnorm. Soc. Psychol.,* 1940, *35*, 273-278.

PART IV

Methods

Chapter XXXIII

TRENDS IN STATISTICS AND PROBABILITY IN PSYCHOLOGY

Herbert Solomon, Ph.D.

Associate Professor of Education
Teachers College, Columbia University

EDITORIAL NOTE

The necessity of including a chapter on trends in statistics here requires no special pleading. Quantification has become a sine qua non in all science, although there is still a question about its application in the historical disciplines. The development of factorial analysis has been only partially responsible for the obligatory study of statistical method for graduate students in the social sciences and psychology. Regrettably, the editor took his graduate work before the statistical era, and therefore this chapter by Dr. Solomon is outside his area of competence. In the "good old days," results seem to have been more clear-cut and less open to queries, no doubt because there were fewer critics.

Dr. Solomon has covered only a few of the most recent issues and trends. It has not been his aim to present an outline of statistics, which belongs to a textbook. Factorial analysis has been taken into account in other chapters, e.g., in Prof. Pickford's paper on aesthetic appreciation. Possibly, the question as to whether measurement and quantification is applicable to all personality problems should have been treated separately.

Dr. Herbert Solomon, who received his Ph.D. at Stanford University, served as Head of the Statistics Branch of the Office of Naval Research in Washington during the years 1948 to 1952. He subsequently was appointed Associate Professor of Education at Teachers College, Columbia University, and a member of the Department of Mathematical Statistics at Columbia University.

PRESENT-DAY PSYCHOLOGY

INTRODUCTION

In recent years there has been an increasing acceleration of activity in statistics and probability. The impact of this surge on all the disciplines in the natural, engineering, and behavioral sciences has been and will continue to be considerable. It is well to remember that problems in the various content fields have been the motivation for a good part of this increased activity: the turn of the century found controversies among the physical anthropologists leading to statistical research; industry as far back as the early twenties was playing with concepts and applications which have now been formalized as quality control and sampling inspection procedures; genetics rather naturally led to probability studies and statistical inference. The last war glaringly revealed many areas needing development and provided the impetus for much important research such as Wald's sequential analysis[1] and his further work on principles for decision theory.[2]

Concomitant with these and other developments, psychology has always been in the dual position of providing problems for statistical and probabilistic research and feeding from the principles and methodology engendered by these disciplines. It is now some fifty years since Spearman made an attempt at an underlying model to explain hierarchical order in a correlation matrix derived from a battery of test scores. This mention of Spearman's single factor theory presents a good opening to express the motives of this chapter. Essentially in Spearman's endeavors we have the problems encountered in

1) probabilistic models
2) principles of statistical inference
3) statistical methodology.

These related areas of statistical and probabilistic usage in psychology were in evidence in Spearman's time and are still very much with us. Each will be touched on in varying degrees in this chapter. It would be presumptuous even to intimate that this chapter will be more than another attempt to point up what appear to be a few of the interesting issues of the day.

PROBABILISTIC MODELS

Probabilistic models, as well as deterministic models, can be classified in two ways. The dichotomy most naturally formed is: a) models which predict observable phenomena because all the interrelationships which actually explain the real process yielding the 'observables' are accounted for; b) models which predict 'observables' but fail to provide a satisfactory explanation of the process. Of course to this one can facetiously add models which do neither. It is obvious that the model-builders usually strive for (a), many times get (b), and quite often get neither. Statistical research can provide techniques to determine if at least (b) is obtained. If this is successful, resort to non-statistical research may be necessary to insure the existence of (a). For purposes of exposition, we can refer to (a) as micro models and (b) as macro models since these terms have been used in somewhat these connotations before.

To tie these remarks to a substantive area let us return to the factor analysts in connection with (1), (2) and (3). Spearman, on the basis of observed hierarchical order in a correlation matrix, postulated a single factor theory which, if it could reproduce his correlation matrix, would at least provide a macro model. If this model could also explain the physiological process that yields the observed responses to tests of mental ability, it would also be the much sought after micro model. To confirm Spearman's probabilistic model as a macro model requires statistical inferences and statistical methodology; to confirm it as a micro model certainly requires the efforts of non-statisticians, such as physiologists, surgeons, psychologists and others. The single common factor model states that the partial correlation between any two tests, removing the common factor, is zero; this can be used to demonstrate that the tetrad difference is zero. Thus, in order to decide whether a sample of observations was produced by this model it was necessary to provide information about the sampling distribution of the tetrad difference. To this day, its exact distribution remains intractable although much has been written about useful approximations to its standard error and its exact distribution.

Godfrey Thomson's model for getting at responses to tests of mental ability is quite different from Spearman's, yet mathematically they are one and the same, for both lead to correlation matrices for test scores which have rank one, i.e., the tetrad differences are zero. Thomson's "sampling of the bonds" model is quite different from Spearman's as a micro model, yet is equivalent as a macro model. The effectiveness of each as a micro model is quite out of the hands of the statistician although it appears obvious that both can never serve simultaneously as micro models and in fact neither need be correct.

The intent here is not to survey or evaluate factor analysis but to use it for illustrative purposes within the contexts mentioned for this chapter. Actually the factor analysts were early pioneers in model building. This is important to note because of the recent resurgence in popularity of this activity and the attention it is receiving at several large graduate centers. Models for measuring attitudes (e.g., latent structure analysis), various learning theory models, models depicting interaction in small groups, and others have intensified an awareness of the common statistical and mathematical problems faced by model builders in quite different disciplines of the behavioral sciences.

Now to return to factor analysis for another illustration. The Thurstone generalization of the Spearman model has enjoyed the widest usage in this country. There have been controversies, usually, however, related not to the structure of the model itself but to what one should do within the framework of the model. The framework simply states that a response is a linear function of normally distributed variables (factors). In short, this means a general acceptance of a macro model which may be shown to operate successfully since it can reproduce an observed correlation matrix but which may break down completely as a micro model. Any debate between Hotelling's principal components and Thurstone's centroid method of estimating factor loadings is academic in the macro model sense, for both use the same structure; however, there are important statistical differences. Hotelling's method is based purely on analytical considerations of reasonable statistical criteria, really also used by Thurstone, and this lends itself more readily to exact distribution theory (which is still intractable) for the estimates of factor loadings. The centroid method because of its quasi-analytic nature prohibits exact distribution theory, but this is not a serious limitation since the centroid method in the main only establishes the dimensionality of a factor space, as does the method of principal components. The method of maximum likelihood employed by Lawley is equivalent to Hotelling's method and thus the same remarks apply. A new model for factor analysis conceived by Guttman,[3] by generalizing Spearman's hypothesis in a manner different from Thurstone, will naturally create a new pile of statistical problems. The radex, as Guttman's model is called, is also a different macro model and has possibilities as a micro model in the field of test scores of mental ability.

STATISTICAL INFERENCE

The term "statistical inference" has been mentioned several times in this article; by it we mean the procedures and principles of making estimates and testing hypotheses on the basis of the incomplete evidence furnished by a sample of observations from a population. Small sample theory has been a preoccupation in recent years, but I should like to dwell on what has been termed the 'danger' in large samples because of its special relevance in psychological research. This danger applies only to the hypothesis-testing aspects of inference, for obviously the larger the sample the more potent the estimate. For this discussion let us turn again to substantive areas and choose ESP.* Here the statistical problem is resolved by testing the hypothesis that a population proportion, P, is one-fifth.

* Extrasensory perception. — *Ed.*

Psychologically, an individual with $P = 1/5$ is adjudged not to have ESP although the infinite number of alternatives $P \neq 1/5$ is not carefully marked out. In the light of present statistical techniques, it is easy to see that for extremely small samples the hypothesis $P = 1/5$ would almost always be accepted while for extremely large samples it would be rejected. As long as the true P for an individual is $1/5 + \mathcal{E}$ where $\mathcal{E} > 0$ but is as small as one pleases, extremely large samples will indicate rejection for $P = 1/5$ and of course this is the way it should be because of the manner in which the statistical machinery is constructed. Does this mean that one can control the decision by judicious (or injudicious!) use of the sample size? The answer is "Yes," but this reply should definitely not be used to indicate that the canards usually uttered about statisticians by the lay public are true. The shortcomings are both psychological and statistical. Operationally speaking how would one compare an individual with $P = .75$ to an individual with $P = .25$ in terms of ESP? It is up to the psychologist to determine how far above $P = .20$, ESP begins or to indicate that ESP is a quantitative variable increasing in some defined manner as P goes above .20. It is then up to the statistician to incorporate this knowledge in the construction of a statistical test. At present an individual with $P = .205$ would cause rejection of the non-ESP hypothesis $(P = .20)$ if the sample size were very large although it would be quite difficult to explain any operational difference between two individuals, one with $P = .20$ and the other with $P = .205$. In a recent article in Life Magazine[4] Aldous Huxley refers to an account of a card experiment in *psi* research in which the subject was remarkably gifted; for in more than 11,000 trials the subject scored so high that the odds against the results being due to chance alone were of the order of 1 to 10^{35} (one followed by 35 zeros). However it is not hard to conceive in line with our discussion that with a sample size that large, the true situation could be quite close to the situation expected by chance (operationally they could be indistinguishable) and still produce the phenomenally small probability of the observed event occurring simply by chance.

Closely related to this discussion, is the problem of optional stopping which has received little attention in statistical theory. This may be due to meager motivation in the past. Suppose for illustrative purposes *only* we return to ESP. Suppose that an individual does not have ESP but that an "unscrupulous" experimenter wishes to get an unwary statistician to reject the hypothesis that P = .2. If the sample size n has not been agreed on in advance the experimenter could adopt the technique of stopping the sampling when all the data observed to that point would indicate rejection of P = .2 if thrown into the appropriate (and correct) statistical machinery. Moreover the probability is one that the experimenter is sure to come eventually to a value of n which will cause rejection and thus he need only stop at that sample size.

How can the statistician guard against this situation? One simple way is to insist that the size of the sample be fixed in advance of the experimentation. Since such a restriction might be too rigid for practical use, the statistician might therefore content himself with setting limits on the sample size which will be flexible enough to meet the contingencies of experimentation but narrow enough to eliminate the worst effects of optional stopping. Robbins[5] has considered this problem for some specific situations and obtained an approximation which indicates that for the usual significance levels the limits on n can be quite wide.

Now to return more specifically to the questions imposed by large samples. Since many of the classical statistical techniques derive from the assumption of a sampling from normal populations, psychological researchers continually test for normality of their data in order that the usual tests of significance may be employed. If their sample sizes are of the order of 25, they will usually accept normality and confidently complete the analysis. If their samples sizes are larger than 50, they will probably reject normality and complete the analysis anyway, albeit feeling a bit embarrassed. This will occur if the chi-square goodness of fit test or any of the goodness of fit tests based on the sample cumulative distribution functions are used. Once again we have the same pattern. Rejection of normality for large sample sizes can occur often when the true distribution is approximately normal and use of the classical techniques would not be disastrous. Notice that here we are treading on more slippery ground in trying to discuss alternatives to normality (previously the alternative hypotheses to $P = .2$ could be succinctly stated) for what does the statement "approximately normal" mean? The whole question of distance between distribution functions is still nebulous although some research is under way.[6] The question of what one may do if a definite non-normality exists will be discussed shortly.

INTRA-INDIVIDUAL STATISTICS

A typical study in psychology relates to observations on two groups, an experimental and a control group, on the basis of which a decision is to be made as to whether the two groups differ. Once again if the sample sizes are large, care must be exercised. Suppose, for example, that anxiety has been induced into the individuals who will then comprise the experimental group, and then this group and a control group are subjected to the Rorschach. Assume that in the population, the mean number of total responses for each group actually differs by two. A large sample (50 or more) will usually indicate a difference between the groups, which of course is true. An article in the psychological literature will usually report a significant difference between the groups when of course, psychologically speaking, there is no operational difference. Moreover, suppose that the actual difference in means for the two groups is quite large and a drug has been used to induce anxiety. A decision that there is a difference between the group means is somewhat sterile, for it is the effect of the drug on the individual that is of interest. In treating groups we may lose some or all information on the interaction of the drug and the individual, for if in each sample half of the individuals are affected one way and the rest in a completely reverse manner the group measure will both reflect and hide this event.

All this is mentioned to demonstrate the need for statistical techniques related to decisions about individuals as contrasted with classical statistical techniques which apply only to groups. One way of getting a statistical picture of the individual is to consider him over time. Suppose for each of $2n$ individuals in the two samples we have observations for k time periods. Each set of k observations presents evidence about each of $2n$ people. The problem now is to find some way of classifying the $2n$ individuals. It is of course quite possible that a method of classification may produce two groups dichotomized by non-drug and drug application but many other configurations are possible. In looking for a classification procedure, one can draw on relevant experiences in time series analysis in other disciplines. Spectral analysis has been used on time series in economics, physics, and engineering and might find fruitful uses in studies of the individual. It has already been applied in this context.[7] The use of the spectral function (there is a unique correspondence between the distribution function of some trait in an individual over time and the spectral function) has prompted more statistical research. For instance, if we are interested in comparing two individuals and have samples of observations on each, we would like a statistical test to determine whether the resulting two sample spectral functions differ only because of sampling fluctuations. In general, we might like to test the homogeneity of several spectral functions. These questions have not been completely answered and much remains to be done about these and other aspects of the problem.

NON-PARAMETRIC STATISTICS

In a previous paragraph we discussed tests for normality and mentioned how most classical statistical techniques depend on the assumption of a normal distribution for the parent population. The problem of what to do when this assumption is not met has been the subject of many papers in recent years. Unfortunately these papers are widely scattered throughout the literature. They are classified by the term non-parametric studies. Recently, Moses[8] in an excellent article, discussed non-parametric statistics in psychological research but the state of the art is such that in the very short time since his paper was published, new and important results have appeared. One of these, by Kruskal and Wallis,[9] is a non-parametric analogue to the one-way analysis of variance. In this situation the homogeneity of the means of several groups is tested without resort to the usual assumptions of normality and homoschedasticity implicit in all analysis of variance. This technique has already proved useful in some areas of psychological research and will be used quite heavily in the future.

Though non-parametric techniques have recently mushroomed as an important special field of statistics, it is well to remember that the idea is not new. Papers related to this area were published in the nineteenth century but its first real impact was felt about fifteen to twenty years ago. The reader may well recognize the coefficient of rank correlation and the chi-square test for goodness of fit as non-parametric techniques of ancient vintage without realizing that a vast new literature has blossomed. In an extremely useful article, Savage,[10] has amassed an all inclusive bibliography of non-parametric statistics and related topics through the year 1953.

In spite of the abundance of non-parametric literature, it is difficult to provide a definition of the field. For instance, consider the classical one-way analysis of variance which leads to the F test. If we relax the assumption of equal variances but retain normality, the resulting test would not be considered non-parametric, but if we relax the normality assumption a non-parametric technique would result. Perhaps the term "distribution-free" which has been used would be more appropriate for a large class of non-parametric studies. While the basic book for use by statisticians and others is still to be written, it appears obvious that the increased research effort of recent years will certainly continue.

BIBLIOGRAPHY

The appended bibliography refers just to those publications mentioned in the text of this chapter. It contains only those articles and books which are either new or not usually met by psychologists. For instance, references for topics mentioned in the classical factor analysis are omitted.

[1] Wald, A. *Sequential Analysis,* John Wiley and Sons, 1947.

[2] —— *Statistical Decision Functions,* John Wiley and Sons, 1950.

[3] Guttman, L. A new approach to factor analysis: The Radex, In: *Mathematical Thinking in the Social Sciences* (edited by Paul F. Lazarsfeld), Free Press, 1954.

[4] Huxley, A. ESP, PK and PSI. *Life Magazine,* January 11, 1954, p. 96ff.

[5] Robbins, H. Some aspects of the sequential design of experiments, *Bulletin of the American Mathematical Society,* vol. 58, No. 5, September 1952.

[6] Birnbaum, Z. W. Distribution-free tests of fit for continuous distribution functions, *Annals of Mathematical Statistics,* vol. 24, No. 1, March 1953.

[7] Abelson, R. P. Spectral analysis and the study of individual differences, *Educational Testing Service Report,* Princeton, N. J.

[8] Moses, L. E. Non-parametric statistics for psychological research, *Psychological Bulletin,* vol. 49, No. 2, March 1952.

[9] Kruskal, W. H. and Wallis, W. A. Use of ranks in one-criterion variance analysis, *Journal of the American Statistical Association,* vol. 47, December 1952.

[10] Savage, I. R. A bibliography of non-parametric statistics and related topics. *J. of the Amer. Statis. Assoc.,* vol. 48, December 1953.

Chapter XXXIV

INTEGRATIONAL PSYCHOLOGY

Clarence Leuba, Ph.D.
Professor of Psychology, Antioch College

EDITORIAL NOTE

Since the author of this chapter has taken pains to justify his concept it is not necessary to add an introductory note, except to say that it was not easy to decide in what rubric to place the chapter. It can scarcely be considered a branch. It has not grown to that extent, for one thing. It is an over-all endeavor to fit in the various data from the different areas into an interdisciplinary clearing house; and therefore it belongs to methodology and its application to the natural, mental, and social sciences.

Dr. Clarence J. Leuba writes "Many factors have contributed to my interest in integrational psychology; several years in personnel and production work in industry where all aspects of human nature had to be taken into consideration; an M.A. in Economics at Harvard; Ph.D. work in Psychology, in which both a rigorous experimental and a broad integrative approach were stressed; and chairmanship of a small department of Psychology in a college (Antioch) which stresses a unified general education program."

Dr. Leuba has written on social psychology, systematic general psychology, and hypnosis, and there have just appeared his booklets The Natural Man *and* The Sexual Nature of Man. *A text,* Man—*a general psychology from an integrational point of view—is in press.*

Some Non-Integrational Emphases in Psychology

Within a few decades after its European origin, the science of psychology began in America to spawn an ever increasing number of specialties. Our universities no longer sought a psychologist as such, but "an animal man" or a person for tests and measurements or a child psychologist. Ambitious young Ph.D.'s were (and still are) advised to specialize further within one of the subdivisions of psychology, and to pick a specific and well delimited problem suitable for a quantitative, experimental attack, and to keep a steady stream of research articles on their specialty pouring into the psychological journals. The emphasis on objectivity, quantification, and experiments implied an analytic approach and absorption in small problems. As for integration, a psychologist might be asked occasionally to review the research literature within the general area of his specialty.

These predominantly American trends toward specialization and the rigorous, thoroughgoing application of the scientific method have brought significant advantages for psychology both as a science and in its numerous applications. An experimental concentration on specific problems has often brought rapid progress toward their solution.

Little progress of a comparable sort has occurred in Europe. Even psychology's independence from philosophy is still often incomplete there, and the degree of specialization within psychology is much less. Armchair theorizing is still acceptable. European psychologists can pride themselves, however, upon being better able to view psychology as a whole, with more perspective, and in a better balanced and integrated fashion. When attending an annual meeting of the American Psychological Association, they are likely to be impressed by the tremendous variety of research reports on disparate topics, and by the lack of papers of an integrating and unifying sort.

These American trends toward specialization and experimentation are not diminishing and probably should not diminish, but it is evident that they need to be supplemented by more comprehensive and unified approaches to an understanding of man and of the problems confronting him. At least the beginnings are now appearing of other than experimental methods for securing a knowledge of man; beginnings, also, of an integration within psychology and between psychology and the other sciences of man, both biological and social. Before describing those beginnings, let us examine more closely the present lack of a systematic, integrated knowledge of man.

THE LACK OF A UNIFIED BODY OF PSYCHOLOGICAL KNOWLEDGE

In the early days of psychology when a layman wished to inform himself about the new science of psychology, he would be likely to read a text, especially that by William James. Today he is not likely to read a text; instead he will read Freud, some case studies in clinical or abnormal psychology, the latest approach in psychotherapy, or a book on the psychological problems which happen to confront him at the moment. If he does read a text, it is as likely as not still to be William James', despite its half century. When the book editor of the *Scientific American* recently compiled, for its readers, a short list of books in psychology, it was headed by James' text; the other books were by psychiatrists.

A textbook writer usually reflects the condition of his science; in psychology he has been combining, as best he could, the increasingly vast array of experimental findings turned up by various specialists, couched often in their forbidding terminology. There were many experiments to be reported on retroactive inhibition and on experimental extinction. At that point the layman closed the text, if he had not already done so, and for good.

Though clinical psychology is itself a specialty, it has brought a new point of view which has begun to infiltrate general psychology. The good clinician inevitably must see the person as a whole, as well as from the point of view of his special complaints. The latter are interrelated and usually symptomatic of basic attitudes. The good clinician must have a synthetic, integrative point of view—though not to the exclusion of an analytical one. He must see people with perspective and as wholes, and he must get at the goals which unify seemingly disparate bits of behavior and give the latter significance.

The psychological clinician, like the physician, realizes that he is operating in an art as well as in a science; he must use disciplined observations, reflection, and hunches, as well as the results of experiments, in formulating his conceptions of human nature. If goal-directed, purposive behavior and mechanisms for protecting self-respect are significant unifying concepts, he does not omit them from consideration because of lack of experimental data. He and his client realize the value of judgments based on wide experience.

By basing its textbooks almost exclusively on the experimentally verified data furnished by its specialists, psychology won the right to call itself a science and the respect of at least those few laymen who read the texts. But for this respectful acceptance as a science, it has paid a heavy price. There has been little progress toward the development of a unified body of psychological knowledge or toward a systematic comprehensive understanding of man. A responsible scientist could write a best seller entitled *Man, the Unknown*.[1] What little integration there has been has come usually from physicians and other non-psychologists who have written out of an extensive, but none the less subjective and personal experience with people. Lacking clearly written, authoritative, integrative books by psychologists familiar with the pertinent scientific data, the public has turned to persuasively written books by authorities in other areas like well-known surgeons, biologists, and psychiatrists.

By World War II, specialization, especially in applied areas, had progressed so far that psychology was in danger of disruption. In some universities, notably Chicago and Harvard, the department of psychology was broken up so that some psychologists were affiliated not with it, but with another department or area. A business school, or a department of education or of social relations, might have its own psychologists. This happened in spite of the admonitions to the contrary from the distinguished committee which studied the place of psychology in an ideal university.[2]

Social and animal psychologists, among others, wondered whether they had anything at all in common. Special professional associations for the psychological study of social issues or for psychology in the military services sometimes claimed far greater devotion from their members than the American Psychological Association. Much of the standard training of a psychologist seemed irrelevant to success in these and other specialties.

INTEGRATION WITHIN PSYCHOLOGY

The questions—should psychologists all have a significant core of knowledge in common and should they all have a common basic graduate training as well as training in their specialty—are now being answered in the affirmative. Committees of the American Psychological Association on graduate training have been able to exert considerable pressure toward the acceptance of at least certain general standards of training. Both in subject-matter and in research methodology, most Ph.D.'s in psychology have a great deal in common.

The person who is competent only to develop an industrial testing program or to conduct market surveys is now more likely to be considered a psychological technician rather than a psychologist. The importance of this distinction between psychological technicians and psychologists is finally being recognized in drawing up laws for the licensing of psychologists. Witness, for instance, the recent Tennessee law.

That a psychologist, no matter what his specialty, should be a Ph.D. broadly trained in at least the main areas of psychology and a scientist well versed in research methodology has become widely accepted. There is still a difference of opinion, however, as to whether the increasingly numerous technical jobs in both research and applied psychology should be filled by psychotechnicians especially prepared for them, or by personnel temporarily employed while on their way to the Ph.D. The choice is not an either/or one, and the chances are that these jobs will be filled by people of both sorts.

The previous failure to distinguish clearly between psychological technicians and psychologists and the custom of calling the former, psychologists, has done immeasurable harm to the status and prestige of psychologists, both in the eyes of the general public and of such professions as medicine and psychiatry. For many in both these groups, a psychologist is still usually just a mental diagnostician.

Granted that there is now a general body of knowledge and a research methodology, which it is generally assumed should be included in the training of every psychologist, there is still little unity to that body of knowledge. The psychological curriculum, a legacy of almost exclusive emphasis on specialization, is chaotic. Courses have multiplied in various specialties with little reference to an efficient unified curriculum. The student may hear the same currently popular experiment discussed in two or three different courses.

Some years ago Dael Wolfle systematically examined the degree of overlap among textbooks in various courses and found an amazing amount of chaotic, unplanned duplication.[3] The reader has only to compare a text in general with one in educational psychology, or one in the latter with a child psychology, to get some idea of the extent of that overlap. Under Wolfle's leadership one group of psychologists has now attempted to set up an effective, integrated psychological curriculum.[3a]

The specialist who feels that he can barely keep up with the research literature in his own area needs to realize that much of his specialty is also covered by other areas. Much duplication also occurs between courses in psychology and those in the related areas of physiology, anthropology, and sociology. The endless multiplication of specialized courses and terminologies has blinded the specialist to the fact that significant, well established knowledge of human nature is not vast but minuscule. It is easily within the grasp of one person. At present we have the curious situation in which the psychologist feels overwhelmed by the vast amount of data available in just his own specialty, and the layman feels appalled by the general lack of knowledge of man. One is reminded that as psychology texts grow longer, those in physics have become shorter; as unifying principles are discovered, mountains of data can be quickly summarized.

Here and there, psychologists have crossed the arbitrary boundaries of their specialties to achieve marked successes. The conception of psychotherapy as a process of reëducation or of learning is a case in point. This conception led to the application of the facts and principles of learning to the therapeutic process, as in the penetrating writings of Mowrer[4] and Dollard and Miller.[5] At one stroke the processes of counseling and psychotherapy are no longer isolated, little understood procedures but become a part of the much studied learning process. Harlow's brilliant experiments with monkeys have illuminated the more complex and little understood aspects of learning and thinking; the actual processes involved in the hitherto vague concept of insight are becoming clearer.[5a]

There are doubtless many other areas of psychology in which exclusive emphasis on specialization and an esoteric terminology have prevented us from seeing basic similarities. For instance, if dreaming is considered as a thought process, then much of what we know about thinking might be applicable to further an understanding of dreams; hitherto, with few exceptions, dreams have been considered as a separate phenomenon, unconnected with the better understood areas of psychology and consequently a happy hunting ground for the purveyors of fantastic notions. Conversion symptoms, too, have remained almost immune to the knowledge gained over past decades regarding the circumstances under which symbols can influence behavior most markedly.

It is, of course, the Gestaltists and their successors, the field theorists, who have persistently emphasized the importance of the integrated whole. Their influence has been less than the value of their central idea would seem to merit. Gestalt enthusiasts refused to recognize any merit to analysis, and adopted questionable nativistic views of perception and a vague, mentalistic conception of learning as due to "insight." For these and other reasons, and because of the previously mentioned practical successes of the analytical approach, an integrational standpoint has been extremely slow to develop in American psychology.

Unifying principles to take the place of McDougall's instincts, or of the reflexes and conditioned responses of the early behaviorists, have not yet emerged; nor are they likely to emerge until the general psychologist is recognized as a valuable member of the psychological fraternity. There is, to be sure, a small division of the American Psychological Association known as the division of General Psychology. It has tended, however, to be a catch-all, rather than an integrative agency.

For the present, integration within psychology has consisted mainly of symposia sponsored by the American Psychological Association, on topics of current interest or of reviews of their areas by specialists. These reviews have varied from some which consist of little more than a stringing together of research items, to serious attempts of an integrational sort. The rare books on theories have usually discussed theories within subdivisions of psychology.[12, 13]

More comprehensive syntheses have been attempted by some authors of books in social psychology,[14, 15] on personality,[16, 17, 18, 19] or on the integrated functioning of the nervous system.[20, 21] Recently Cole[21a] has drawn an overall picture of general psychology, Hilgard[21b] has developed a text in which unifying concepts are stressed, and Skinner [22] has presented a stimulating view of human nature. A survey of these books, however, will indicate that, for the most part, each is a particular and partial view of man. No William James looms as yet on the horizon.

Psychology needs facts; it needs specialization and experimentation on strictly limited topics; facts are the building stones of a science. But it also needs mortar. It needs to supplement the prevailing approaches by more numerous and significant efforts of an integrating and unifying sort. Perhaps the specialists should pause at times also to become general psychologists; or perhaps we should have some respected, full-time, genuine, general psychologists, who would not need to apologize for their failure to have specialized. Perhaps the divorce from philosophy is now so old and generally accepted that we can view with equanimity the possibility of a philosophy of psychology.

Though unifying principles are not yet clearly discernible, this much is clear: they will need to consider man both as a biological organism and as a product of culture, and also both the universals of human nature and the qualities which make for the uniqueness of personality.

INTEGRATION OF PSYCHOLOGY WITH THE OTHER SCIENCES OF MAN

When psychology was the study of consciousness by means of introspection, it occupied a unique and undisputed field. No other science used introspection to analyze mental life. But when in the 20's, psychology became increasingly the objective study of behavior, it also became just one of several behavioral sciences. The biologist, in fact, is prone to consider modern psychology as but a branch of his field; and some anthropologists and sociologists feel that psychology could readily be accommodated under their roofs. In any case, it is evident that any comprehensive study of human behavior involves all of these basic sciences of man. There are other human sciences, too: economics, political science, and so on, but they are in a different category from the four previously mentioned for they deal with man under specific circumstances, as in business or government, rather than with the general principles governing his behavior everywhere.

The basic unity of the four behavioral sciences is leading to at least the beginnings of their integration in education, research, and the solution of practical problems. At Yale there is an Institute of Human Relations; at Harvard, a Department of Social Relations; at Chicago, a Department of Human Development, and at some institutions, a Division of the Life Sciences.

Each of the behavioral sciences can give but a partial view of any human problem. A comprehensive study of personality maladjustments, for instance, has physiological, psychological, and cultural aspects. The same is true for most other human problems: war, peace, crime, old age and so on. Increasingly, these problems are being attacked by teams of scientists from the various behavioral sciences. In medicine it is increasingly apparent that the physician must treat his patient as a person; this involves some appreciation of personality and culture, as well as of physiological factors. Wolff and his associates have shown what illumination can come to the dim, confused area of psychosomatics when personality studies and physiological observations are combined.[5b]

How best to integrate the behavioral sciences in general education is far from settled.[6] The early survey courses are generally discredited.[7] The faculty representatives from the various disciplines involved were disatisfied with the brief superficial surveys they were able to give of their fields. The surveys were strung together with little attempt at integration. Out of these early survey courses have sprung a number of different approaches to integration. One of these is the problems approach, as exemplified in the general education program at Michigan State College. Important everyday life situations confronting almost everybody—vocational choice, courtship and marriage, interpersonal relations, and so on—are the focal points to which contributions are made by the sciences of man. These sciences, as such, vanish from general education. The point is probably well made that most undergraduates are not interested in psychology or sociology as such, but in the contributions they can make toward enabling them to deal satisfactorily with the situations they will meet.

A somewhat similar approach is the use of case studies as developed by Berrien at Colgate[8] and now in use at Harvard.[9] Again, the student does not study one or more of the behavioral sciences as such, but the contributions they can make to an understanding of a variety of human situations in industry, family life, school, and so on. In both the problem and the case study approach, the integration springs directly from the material under consideration; this material has psychological, anthropological, and sociological aspects. In practice, this type of general education course uses mainly problems and cases to which biology can make few, if any, contributions; it is usually considered as social science, and psychologists participate in it as social scientists.

At an opposite extreme is the long established course in the biological sciences at the University of Chicago. In this course, which has been duplicated by some biologists elsewhere, the social sciences play no rôle, and psychology only a slight one. The emphasis is mainly on a unification of botany and zoölogy into a course in general biology, with considerable emphasis on human physiology.

These approaches to general education are alike in that they all split psychology. The case study or problem approach uses only—or mainly—contributions from social psychology, and, as we have seen, largely ignores biology. Its main weakness, however, is that it fails to consider the basic tools and principles which may be useful in meeting a whole variety of problems. For instance, systematic knowledge of how learning takes place, of the nature of symbols and of thinking, of the factors influencing perception, of the effects of emotion, of man's sexual nature, of the ego defenses so far devised by man, and of how he is motivated, all have widespread applications.

In a fourth approach the emphasis is on the facts of human nature, on general principles, and on techniques useful in studying man. One of the most successful courses of this sort, on the Behavioral Sciences, was prepared under the chairmanship of Kimball Young at Northwestern University.[22a] Life situations play a secondary rôle as illustrations of facts and principles or of how to use the techniques. This approach can draw contributions from biology and from all of psychology as well as from the social sciences. It can do justice to psychology both as a biological and as a social science, but it is likely to be more abstract, theoretical, and less immediately interesting to the student.

It should be possible to combine all four approaches: to have an integrated course in the behavioral sciences which deals with such vital human institutions as marriage and the family and which also provides the basic facts, principles, and tools essential to a more thorough understanding of these situations. Something of that sort has been attempted in the two year course in the behavioral sciences at Antioch College.[10, 11] Only further experience and experimentation will indicate how much emphasis to give to the various aspects of such a course and how best to present them.

It may be that the problem and case study courses will inevitably introduce sections on general principles and techniques and on problems of a more biological sort, such as health; and that the general principles courses will introduce more problems and case studies. In any case, the emphasis may well shift from courses in the conventional sciences to courses on man and on an integration of the contributions which biology, psychology, anthropology, and sociology can make toward understanding him and helping him meet life situations.

A movement toward integration within psychology and between psychology and the other behavioral sciences is but part of a general rapprochement which is occurring among the sciences. There is a powerful movement within the American Association for the Advancement of Science to make integration among the sciences one of the main purposes of that organization; and for several years the Foundation for Integrated Education has enlisted the help of distinguished philosophers and scientists to that end. For many years Stuart Chase has ably correlated data from the various social sciences;[23] and recently a group of social scientists have examined each other's fields in a book aptly called, *For a Science of Social Man.*[24]

REFERENCES

1 Carrel, A. *Man, the Unknown.* New York: Harper, 1935.

2 University Commission to Advise on the Future of Psychology at Harvard. *The Place of Psychology in an Ideal University.* Cambridge: Harvard U. Press, 1947.

3 Wolfle, D. The Sensible Organization of Courses in Psychology. *American Psychologist,* 1947, *2,* 437-445.

3a Wolfle, D. *et al. Improving Undergraduate Instruction in Psychology.* New York: Macmillan, 1952.

4 Mowrer, O. H. *Learning Theory and Personality Dynamics.* New York: Ronald, 1950.

5 Dollard, J. and Miller, N. E. *Personality and Psychotherapy.* New York: McGraw-Hill, 1950.

5a Harlow, H. Thinking, ch. 10 in Helson, H. (ed.) *Theoretical Foundations of Psychology.* New York: Van Nostrand, 1951.

5b Association for research in nervous and mental diseases. *Life Stress and Bodily Disease.* Baltimore: William and Wilkins, 1950.

6 McGrath, E. *et al. Toward General Education.* New York: Macmillan, 1948.

7 McGrath, E. *Social Science in General Education.* Dubuque, Iowa: Brown, 1948.

8 Berrien, F. K. *Comments and Cases in Human Relations.* New York: Harper, 1951.

9 Cabot, H. and Kahl, J. A. *Human Relations,* 2 vols. Cambridge: Harvard U. Press, 1953.

10 Leuba, C. and Federighi, H. A Course in the Life Sciences. *American Psychologist,* 1948, *3,* 30-34.

11 Federighi, H. and Leuba, C. The proper study of mankind is man. *J. Gen. Educa.,* 1948, *2,* 193-198.

12 Helson, H. *Theoretical Foundations of Psychology.* New York: Van Nostrand, 1951.

13 Marx, M. H. *Psychological Theory.* New York: Macmillan, 1951.

14 Asch, S. E. *Social Psychology.* New York: Prentice-Hall, 1952.

15 Queener, E. L. *An Introduction to Social Psychology.* New York: Sloane, 1951.

16 Snygg, D. and Combs, A. W. *Individual Behavior.* New York: Harper, 1949.

17 Murray, H. A. *Explorations in Personality.* New York: Oxford U. Press, 1938.

18 McClelland, D. *Personality.* New York: Dryden Press, 1951.

19 Murphy, G. *Personality.* New York: Harper, 1947.

20 Hebb, D. O. *The Organization of Behavior.* New York: Wiley, 1949.

[21] Ashby, W. R. *Design for a Brain.* New York: Wiley, 1952.

[21a] Cole, L. *Human Behavior.* Yonkers-on-Hudson: World Book Co., 1953.

[21b] Hilgard, E. *Introduction to Psychology.* New York: Harcourt, Brace, 1953.

[22] Skinner, B. F. *Science and Human Behavior.* New York: **Macmillan,** 1953.

[22a] Young, K. Some problems of interdisciplinary Courses in the Social Sciences: *J. Gen. Educ.,* 1953, 7, 201-208.

[23] Chase, S. *The Proper Study of Mankind.* New York: Harper, 1948.

[24] Gillin, J. (ed.) *For a Science of Social Man.* New York: Macmillan, 1954.

PART V

Psychological Borderlands and Humanistics

Chapter XXXV

THE PSYCHOLOGY OF LITERATURE

A. A. Roback, Ph.D.
Professor of Psychology, Emerson College

EDITORIAL NOTE

The relation between the two great fields of human endeavor is only now beginning to come to the fore. It is curious that although the same material was being viewed by the fiction writer and the psychologist, they seemed to be living in different worlds. The latter would look upon the former as a visionary who concocted situations often untrue to life, while the belles-lettrist *would regard the psychologist as restricted in his sphere of experience and unduly narrow in his interpretation because of that fact. The artist is unfettered in his imagination. He knows that life does not proceed according to rules or logic. The psychologist, on the other hand, was constantly seeking laws, and where he could not discover them readily, as in the area of the affections and motivation, he was apt to slight that whole range.*

Came Sigmund Freud and his adjutants, who gave us a new set of postulates, and opened up the vast territory which was kept sealed by the psychologists who were blind to the unconscious. That brought psychologist and littérateur closer; and now we are on the way to the cultivation of a fruitful field in more than one direction.

The writer has broached the connection between psychology and literature while still a university student. He has since shown his penchant for imaginative literature through such volumes as Curiosities of Yiddish Literature *(Cambridge, 1933)* Peretz: Psychologist of Literature *(Cambridge, 1935) and* The Story of Yiddish Literature *(New York, 1940), as well as the extensive survey of Yiddish Literature in the* Encyclopedia Americana. *He has also given seminars on The Psychology of Literature, primarily for graduate students.*

PSYCHOLOGY OF LITERATURE

It is one of the unaccountable curios that although psychology and literature deal with the same subject-matter, viz., imagery, ideas, emotions, feelings, and so on, the psychology of literature has received but scant treatment until very recently; and although there is now available an anthology under the title of *Psychology through Literature* (ed. by Shrodes, VanGundy and Husband) there is no systematic textbook or treatise which covers the growing borderland. When the present writer, as a student at Harvard, published his lecture before a Boston audience on psychology and literature[1] four decades ago, the subject seemed a novel one. Only in 1929 did the same title appear over an article by C. G. Jung, which later formed a chapter in his *Modern Man in Search of a Soul* (transl. by W. S. Dell and Cary F. Baynes), and in 1951, a book entitled *Literature and Psychology* by F. L. Lucas opened up the subject on a larger scale.

Since the advent of psychoanalysis, literature and its creators have, of course, come in for a great deal of discussion on the part of depth psychologists, and even before Freud's mono graphs and articles on artists, including *littérateurs,* stirred the intelligentsia, the serial *Grenzfragen des Nerven-und Seelenlebens* presented studies of a score or more of writers, in which various quirks of talented men were described and analyzed. It was, however, the individual and his behavior that occupied the mind of the, for the most part, psychiatrists. The literary productions were introduced only insofar as they could throw any light on the subject of the sketch. This particular type of study may be called pathography and included among others, monographs on Nietzsche, Poe, Strindberg, Maupassant, Tolstoi, von Kleist and Rousseau.

It was Freud, however, who initiated the new approach to the analysis of art (and literature) through his Leonardo da Vinci and Hölderlin monographs, which set the example for his followers to emulate him in that respect until we now possess perhaps hundreds of books and articles on authors ranging all the way from St. Paul to James Joyce. Apart, however, from the individuals, there is an ever-growing literature on the productions as interpreted by psychoanalysis. It is becoming increasingly difficult for a teacher of literature in the higher institutions to be *au courant* with his field without taking account of, let us say, Ernest Jones's *Hamlet and Oedipus* or Hanns Sachs's chapters on *The Tempest* and *Measure for Measure*. As for Dostoyevsky, psychoanalysis seems to dote on him. It will be recalled that Freud thought him the greatest master of fiction, with no exception. One may surmise the reason to be that the Oedipus complex is evident in some of his stories, chiefly the *Brothers Karamazov*.

In our survey of psychology and literature, there is to be considered a field with at least three foci. First, there is the literary proble*m per ṣe,* i.e., the interpretation of the content from a psychological angle. There is also the writer who needs analyzing, and perhaps we should consider also the reader. Indeed, the literary critic or reviewer, and even the publisher, are not altogether to be omitted; for although it is true that the latter views the Ms. only as a marketable product, we do know that there are such rare birds as prestige publishers. Furthermore, what determines a publisher or his reader to anticipate a large sale is a possible object of investigation.

PSYCHOANALYSIS TAKES OVER

Since psychoanalysis started as a form of therapy, it is only natural that the individual writer would occupy the center in that sphere rather than literature as such. Prior to Freud, the question as to why an artist should wish to create hardly made sense. In the epigrammatic literature, suggestive hints might occur now and then, but that would only be a flash in the pan. It was taken for granted, as it is mainly today, that writing for a living or for fame is a good enough reason. Naturally every one who is moved to set down his thoughts on paper thinks that bursting into print will be of advantage to him. Yet there are many who write under pseudonyms and many others who will pay to have their works published. Ordinarily it is thought that it titillates their vanity to see their brain-child worrying the brains of others. In some slight way they are affecting the world, and who knows but that even if unrecognized now—so they imagine—posterity will yet accord them their due.

As for the unmistakably gifted, it would never have entered the average man's mind that they are anything but fortunate in enjoying not only the fruits of their labors but the actual creative process. To be sure, the biography of genius is replete with sad and unhappy episodes, but these were regarded more as casual occurrences due to political events or chance relationships. It was Freud who looked for something deeper-going, and out of the unconscious he brought up the conflict which was molesting the artist who, as a result, is seeking to escape into a world of fantasy. The phrase "escape from reality" thenceforth began to take on the aspect of a spell accounting for all creative work. The artist is not a free agent but is driven by a *daimôn*, not (as Socrates thought) implanted by some supernatural power, but a demon engendered by the unconscious forces at war with one another over the heritage of infantile experiences, bound to cause misery to the nascent creator.

In connection with the artist's procedure, the function of sublimation was that of applying to social and cultural use the libido which has been playing havoc with the sensitive nature of the imaginative person and turning his pregenital fixations, whether oral, narcissistic, or anal, to good account. Freud, to use a colloquial phrase "started the ball rolling." Soon this or that disciple or co-worker would add a bit or shape it in a slightly different way, until the artist was saddled with exhibitionism and unconscious guilt feelings and fantasies compensated only in his productions.

RANK'S VOLUNTARISM

It would be instructive to examine the various interpretations of the artists by Freud, Rank and Jung. Otto Rank's conception is to be found in *Art and the Artist* (original *Der Künstler*) and *Truth and Reality,* which appeared in English before the German edition. Rank, it must be borne in mind, was the apostle of the Will, with a subtle appreciation of religious values. In the chapter "Creation and Guilt," Rank traces the genesis of willing, and makes the neurotic type out to be a willing on a lower level, practically tantamount to desiring, where external objects and obstacles are involved. A higher willing, which oscillates between a hankering for possessions and the ego-ideal or ought principle, is still fraught with guilt-feeling and can only lead to neurotic tendencies. In his early work *Der Künstler* (1908) Rank sees the artist as partaking of both the normal dreamer and the neurotic, but differing from the latter in that he turns his conflict to advantage and therefore overcomes his shortcomings through sublimation. Rank still is tied to the Freudian apron strings, and speaks of the artist as a narcissist who flaunts his fantasies upon an expectant audience. Employing such dynamisms as displacement and repression in much the same way as Freud, he may still be called a disciple.

In 1928, Rank had already more or less emancipated himself from the parental restrictions of Freud and sets up house for himself. Freud had been preoccupied with sexuality and its avowed purpose—reproduction, the creativeness of the individual but Rank stresses the productive in the universal sense. To quote the author:

> We recognize therefore in the creative impulse not only the highest form of the will affirmation of the individual, but also the most mighty will conquest, that of the individual will over the will of the species represented by sexuality. A similar victory of the individual will over generic will, as I show elsewhere, is represented in the individual love claim, whose psychological meaning lies in the fact that the individual can and will accept his generic rôle only if this is possible in an individual personal way, in the love experience. This represents, as it

were, the creativity of the average type who demands a definite individuality for himself and if necessary also creates it, an individuality that sanctions and so justifies and saves his individual will. The creative type, on the contrary, does not content himself with the creation of an individual. Instead, he creates a whole world in his own image, and then needs the whole world to say "yes" to his creation, that is, to find it good and thus justify it.[2]

Rank attributes to this going beyond the bounds of nature, which was meant for reproduction and normal sex behavior, a guilt complex arising out of the diversion of a natural instinct to a glorification of the (creative) will which, the artist fancies, makes a God out of himself—hence his punishment in the form of mental suffering.

JUNG'S COLLECTIVE UNCONSCIOUS

Just as Rank parts company with Freud on the universal *vs.* individual issue in the matter of artistic creation, so Jung objects to Freud's emphasis on the personal, really infantile, and pregenital, traits. The artist is of course a person, but his art, according to Jung, stems from the impersonal, the deeper collective layers.

In his capacity of artist he is neither auto-erotic, nor hetero-erotic, nor erotic in any sense. He is objective and impersonal—even inhuman—for as an artist he is his work, and not a human being.

Every creative person is a duality or a synthesis of contradictory aptitudes. On the one side he is a human being with a personal life, while on the other side he is an impersonal, creative process. Since as a human being he may be sound or morbid, we must look at his psychic make-up to find the determinants of his personality. But we can only understand him in his capacity of artist by looking at his creative achievement. We should make a sad mistake if we tried to explain the mode of life of an English gentleman, a Prussian officer, or a cardinal in terms of personal factors. The gentleman, the officer and the cleric function as such in an impersonal rôle, and their psychic make-up is qualified by a peculiar objectivity. We must grant that the artist does not function in an official capacity—the very opposite is nearer the truth. He nevertheless resembles the types I have named in one respect, for the specifically artistic disposition involves an overweight of collective psychic life as against the personal. Art is a kind of innate drive that seizes a human being and makes him its instrument. The artist is not a person endowed with free will who seeks his own ends, but one who allows art to realize its purposes through him. As a human being he may have moods and a will and personal aims, but as an artist he is a "man" in a higher sense—he is "collective man"— one who carries and shapes the unconscious, psychic life of mankind. To perform this difficult office it is sometimes necessary for him to sacrifice happiness and everything that makes life worth living for the ordinary human being.[3]

How does Jung explain the unhappiness of the artist? Again, it is traced to conflicts, but not the kind which Freud and Rank bring to the fore, although in the last analysis it comes to the same thing. It is curious that although Jung is generally obscure and unconvincing because of the many facets in his writing, his essay on psychology and literature, after the many learned citations and illustrations are put to one side, is a clear presentation of the common sense view, viz. that

All this being so, it is not strange that the artist is an especially interesting case for the psychologist who uses an analytical method. The artist's life cannot be otherwise than full of conflicts, for two forces are at war within him—on the one hand the common human longing for happiness, satisfaction and security in life, and on the other a ruthless passion for creation which may go so far as to override every personal desire. The lives of artists are as a rule so highly unsatisfactory—not to say tragic—because of their inferiority on the human and personal side, and not because of a sinister dispensation. There are hardly any exceptions to the rule that a person must pay dearly for the divine gift of the creative fire. It is as though each of us were endowed at birth with a certain capital of energy. The strongest force in our make-up will seize and all but monopolize this energy, leaving so little over that nothing of value can come of it. In this way the creative force can drain the human impulses to such a degree that the personal ego must develop all sorts of bad qualities—ruthlessness, selfishness and vanity (so-called "auto-erotism")—and even every kind of vice, in order to maintain the spark of life and to keep itself from being wholly bereft. The autoeroticism of artists resembles that of illegitimate or neglected children who from their tenderest years must protect themselves from the destructive influence of people who have no love to give them—who develop bad qualities for that very purpose and later maintain an invincible egocentricity by remaining all their lives infantile and helpless or by actively offending against the moral code or the law. How can we doubt that it is his art that explains the artist, and not the insufficiencies and conflicts of his personal life? These are nothing but the regrettable results of the fact that he is an artist—that is to say, a man who from his very birth has been called to a greater task than the ordinary mortal. A special ability means a heavy expenditure of energy in a particular direction, with a consequent drain from some other side of life.[4]

DAYDREAMER AND ARTIST

Hanns Sachs who had given much thought to the problems of artistic creation, took up the trend of Freud at the stage art was associated with daydreaming, but pursued it to further heights. He, too, recognizes the narcissism of the artist, nevertheless, he draws fine distinctions between the daydreamer and the poet. "The daydreamer is asocial and formless, without regard to continuity and causation, uses words and visual images indiscriminately, and groups everything around the author as the central figure."[5]

Or let us take the following delineation which shows how Sachs had almost specialized in the aesthetic problems and the artistic technique, and was able to give us a clear-cut picture of the author as compared with his daydreaming counterpart.

> The point where poetry and daydreaming disagree almost constantly is in the part allotted to the creator. The daydreamer is always his own hero, the poet never. Even when he tells his story as though it were about himself and uses a great deal of his own life and character as material, the poet does so in a sense quite different from that of the daydreamer: he is not guided by a wish for self-glorification, but for self-investigation. An author who in his own work indulges in self-flattery has not attained the standard of the artist. This form of vanity, this pleasure in looking at oneself in a beautifying mirror (narcissism) has to be sacrificed when the step is made from the asocial daydream to the work of art. It is the toll which has to be paid for the opening of the gate that leads out of isolation and to a new reunion with men.[6]

But that is not all. The narcissistic author has his heavy load of guilt-feeling which he somehow wishes to lessen, even if it cannot be entirely disposed of, and so he appeals to his audience or public for succor, for it is to their mutual advantage that he has aired out their own daydreams and presented them in such a form that they could enjoy them.

We return to the problem we left unanswered. The daydreamer uses his fantasy as a means of gaining narcissistic gratification for his own person. What happens to this narcissism when the creator has to surrender it in order to win the participation—the readiness to identification—of his audience? Form and beauty of the work appear when this transformation takes place; they make it attractive and enable it to stimulate and dominate the affects. We know that the author needs this to relieve his guilt-feeling. But he does not stop when he once has started on the quest for beauty; he is never satisfied. All the resources of his mind, all the energies of his life are spent unsparingly to achieve higher perfection in beauty for his work. What is sufficient to dazzle his audience does not satisfy his demands. We see here another force at work, one which plays between the poet and his work and is independent of the effect on the audience, even on an ideal audience. The entirely narcissistic character of this force leads to its recognition as the sacrificed narcissism of the daydreamer, reborn as the poet's desire for the beauty of his work. In other words, the form or façade which originally was but a means to an end becomes, after the transformation, a part of the end in itself; the narcissism has been replaced and shifted from the creator to his creation. In this way the poet's work becomes the essential part of his personality; since his narcissism has been transferred to it, it is generally more important than friendship or love or all the rest of life. The poet has to give up a great portion of his narcissism, probably more than average people, but his work wins back immeasurably more of it than others can hope for: acknowledged and enduring beauty, irresistible power over the minds of men, and immortality.[7]

877

Indeed Jung's demarcation between the personal and the impersonal seems to have been unwittingly made by Sachs when he tells us that

> The personality of the greatest of masters—Homer, Shakespeare—has disappeared behind their work. The operator may reserve for himself some little vanities, but the hard and long struggle, the measureless ambition, the alternation between hope and despair, all these indicate his passionate devotion to this work.

Here the line which separates the poet as artist from the hero or "leader" becomes apparent. The leader retains all his narcissism; he too wants to dominate the affects of his followers, not to relieve his guilt-feeling, since he hasn't any, but in order to use them as instruments for his own purposes, to carry out his plans for his personal aggrandizement. The artist is a leader of men, but through his work, not in his own person. He wants their affects, but without ulterior motive. For the "leader" it does not matter if the affects of his followers are shallow or spurious. All he asks is that they be useful for his purpose. Not so the artist. He cares only for those affects which are deep and genuine; but he is satisfied with the tears and laughter of his audience, and does not even think of making any further use of them. The mean between these types is kept by the author who wants to serve a definite, practical, mostly a political tendency. He certainly has in mind the further use of the affects which he has tried to arouse. But in doing this, he is a "leader" and not an "artist", and nearly always to the detriment of the artistic value of his work. With true artists sometimes the opposite happens; they set out with practical aims in view, but their genius carries them far beyond the initial narrow scope, as it happened to Cervantes when he wanted to ridicule the knight-errant novels. These works are then read and admired long after their "real" purpose has been forgotten.

The two main unconscious aims of the poet—the relief of his guilt-feeling and the replacement of his narcissism—are inseparable. One without the other would be an impossibility. But naturally they are not of equal strength in every case, and we can recognise clearly enough the preponderance of one or the other. It is feasible to make this the principle for dividing all the countless variations of literary schools and styles into two main groups with, of course, transitional forms in between.[8]

It was reserved for Edmund Bergler to come to grips with writers exclusively and plumb their unconscious more searchingly than his predecessors, and no wonder he afterwards was obliged to fight figurative duels with a whole succession of reviewers whom he classified and catalogued under not very edifying labels.

ORALITY AND MASOCHISM

In short, according to Bergler, the writer has regressed to the oral stage, or has never progressed beyond it, a stage which is characterized by psychic masochism. These people obtain pleasure out of hurts, grievances, and are collectors of injustice which they receive time and again, themselves being the instigators. The aggression displayed by the writer-masochist is not true to type; it is one which is intended by the unconscious to recoil upon oneself. Of course, it would be a curious sort of analytic interpretation, if the guilt-feeling were missing in such a state of affairs, and it certainly takes its honored place in Bergler's book, for psychic masochism which involves identification with the mother and thus by such partaking both of the mother and himself, the author is able to give and receive at the same time whatever he felt he had not gotten enough from his mother (affection, milk, tenderness) in the infant stage.

But that is not the only source of guilt-feeling. Every writer, affirms Bergler, is a voyeur, a peeping Tom. He must, in order to produce fiction or a play look into the private life of others, at least in his imagination, and that has its counterpart in exhibitionism—both tendencies, the one a reflection of the other, strong in early childhood and somehow associated with orality. Now that the relationships are more or less fixed, we can proceed to the unconscious posturings of the writer in order to exonerate himself. First, he denies he is a masochist but is ready to take the rap for another set of crimes, viz., aggression, which, as has been intimated, is not genuine but only a smoke screen. Next, the writer, who implicates his readers in his perpetration, points to them as equally guilty, and therefore he and they are equally not-guilty. He then proceeds to cover up his *voyeurism* by calling attention to his exhibitionism, for 'peeping' is something deeper-going, more regressive and more provocative of guilt-feeling e.g., spying on parents during the sex act.

Acrobatics in Psychoanalysis

It would take too much space to follow the author in all his peregrinations. Given so much latitude as turning from one extreme to the other, from posit to opposite, and leaping nimbly from one limb to another, any conclusion is possible, but Bergler is an excellent writer whose reservoir of illustrations and anecdotes never runs low, and his barbs are never blunted. Hence much of what he says possesses the charm of aphorism; and his astute observations on the editor or critic (as an inhibited or frustrated writer) are acceptable even though the psychoanalytic substructure is questionable. Bergler is not even willing to grant that the writer expresses his unconscious wishes in his stories and verse. What he contends is that the novelist or playwright brings into the open his defences against these wishes and desires. In other words, the fantasies do not appear directly but must be inferred indirectly from the reactions against them or even a further remove, the reaction to the defence against them as

shown in the literary productions. But why does Bergler not say
that the creation evidences the fight of the ego against the id,
and the resurgence of the id?

Perhaps it would be just as well to reproduce a typical passage from the author summing up his thesis.

> With slight exaggeration one could say that the sterile
> writer is the newest addition to the family of analytical
> patients. Our acquaintanceship with him is so recent, in
> fact, that clinical experiences are not even coördinated.
> The following, therefore, is not the generally accepted
> psychoanalytic opinion on writers (as yet such a uni-
> formity does not exist), and represents simply my own
> clinical experiences gathered in intensive and extensive
> "couch acquaintanceship" with thirty-six writers over a
> period of twenty years, the typical length of individual
> treatment being one and a-half to two years.

> In my opinion a writer is a person who tries to solve an
> inner conflict through the sublimatory medium of writ-
> ing. Whether the writer is successful (in the worldly
> meaning of the word) is immaterial for psychological
> evaluation.

> The writer's basic *inner* conflict pertains with amazing
> monotony to the psychic masochist's solution of his rela-
> tion to the mother image. By mother image we do not
> mean his relation to the real mother, or even the oedipal
> mother of his infancy, but to the misconceptions he built
> up in relation to that giant ogre of the nursery, the pre-
> oedipal mother. To this misconception of that "cruel,
> sadistic" mother, he (the child in the writer) became
> masochistically attached. This, in adulthood, makes the
> writer a perpetual defendant indicted before the tribunal
> of unconscious conscience. To counteract that indictment
> an alibi is instituted—the artistic creation. The inner
> alibi goes like this: "I am not masochistically attached
> to Mother; Mother does not even exist." Thus, in the

process of productivity, the writer acts both rôles: that of the "giving" mother and the "recipient" child; he gives himself, out of himself, beautiful ideas and words, thereby establishing autarchy. Whereas any other conflict needs *two* protagonists for unconscious repetitiveness, duplicating the infantile prototype, in the strange psychic economy of the writer's solution he needs but *one* person. The typical neurotic must pay psychiatric fees for his cure, but the writer, if successful, even gets paid for his "self-cure."

Having established his first alibi by achieving autarchy, the writer busily formulates his second alibi. This second alibi is an attack. Accused by his inner conscience of masochistic submission, he counters with aggression. This accounts for the seemingly constant rebellion of the writer, or, to use Elizabeth Bowen's own words? "We must have something to push against."

The third alibi, also unconsciously provided in this battle of the conscience, is a shifting of guilt; guilt rightfully pertaining to the psychic masochism is "fraudulently" entered on the balance sheet of defensive aggression.[9]

Bergler follows out this idea of oral masochism and pseudo-aggression in other literary or reading connections. Take your mystery story fan, for example. What is he but identifying with the omnipotent and omniscient detective, criminal or adventurer? But why is the aggression not real? Because, answers the author, there is the element of uncanniness in it "which is the secondary and masochistic elaboration. But even the criminal, the constant factor is based on the masochistic attempt to overcome the feeling of helplessness stemming from pre-oedipal orality" (pp. 166-167). The actual motivations of the criminal are only the outcome of rationalizations for latent unconscious motives stemming from the child-mother-father relationship and the fantasies resulting therefrom.

It must be said that this is as hard to swallow as the often-repeated thesis that a philanthropist or a humanitarian is deep down a sadist who, on the conscious level, is camouflaging his unconscious motives. It reminds us of the Jewish joke about two business acquaintances who met on a train going West. Asked one of the other where he was bound for. "On my way to Chicago" was the reply. "Listen" said his questioner. "You are telling me you're going to Chicago, so that I might suppose you are bound for Los Angeles, but you can't fool me. I feel sure you are going to Chicago, so why try to string me?"

PLAGIARISM, HACK WRITING

The guilt *motif* is heard in the analysis of the hack writer, the huckster, and the plagiarist of whom 24 varieties are listed. In all of them there is the symptom of oral regression, and they are all the victims of masochism, harking back to infant-mother relations. "Everyone would like to plagiarize" maintains Bergler "and renounces this desire . . . only on condition that others be limited likewise" (p. 208). Can we wonder at the further conclusion or scholium that "one who has never caught himself trying to plagiarize is *a priori* suspicious of plagiarizing too much?"

In passing judgment on Bergler's work, one might accept the acute observations on and analyses of the various agents in the literary set-up so long as this is done on the conscious level. When we are asked to follow the author down the labyrinthine catacombs, we are afraid that he becomes as elusive as the will-o'-the-wisp. Even if the explanation of masochistic orality is accepted, it does not seem reasonable to expect this to be at the root of literary ambitions, whodunit interest, criminal tendencies, hack writing, bluffing propensities, and plagiarism. Some writers may be criminals too, and vice versa; but surely there is no basic affinity which links the two as having come by their activities in consequence of the same experiences in infancy. Bergler applies a Freudian dynamism wholesale by following it through down the line. But that type of consistency is not in keeping with scientific procedure.

The Literary Product

Thus far we have considered the creator in the light of psychoanalysis; and as has been already stated, the depth psychologist, as a therapist, is concerned mainly with the individual, and studies the productions insofar as they help us to understand the problems of the creator and gain an insight into the solutions he has sought and partially arrived at. But the psychology of literature is something apart from its producers and must be envisaged in relation to life.

Basler has made a similar observation.

> Naturally enough, the application of Freudian theory to literature has been attempted for the most part in an endeavor to psychoanalyze the author. Beginning with Freud himself, one of the chief recreations of the psychoanalytic fraternity has been the study of the artist's personality through the application of psychoanalytic criteria to his works and to the known facts of his life . . . It is the writer's belief that, while psychoanalysis has indeed contributed much, and can contribute still more, to the understanding of individual artists as personalities, the most fruitful employment of Freudian theory by the student of literature lies in the interpretation of literature itself.[10]

Each story, each play, each poem, carries its own message and either fits into or is out of focus with the world such as we know it. It is to be feared that so much significance has been attached to the writer's unconscious that the tale receives practically no attention. It is as though we on the ground floor were so preoccupied peering through peepholes and watching the workmen puttering in the cellar that we completely neglect to observe what is happening in our very midst. Literature may be the fruit of the unconscious tree, but we have a right to examine the different species separately at closer range. There are so many diverse types of literary production even in belles-lettres alone. Is symbolism to be measured with the same unconscious yardstick as realism, and is the psychological tale in the same class as the romantic story? Is it not true that what is permissible in the one case will be decried in the other?

Depth Psychologist Slurs Psychological Fiction

One of the paradoxical features of depth psychology is that it takes little heed of the everyday psychological. In a sense, no specialist will deign to look at what he considers just ordinary. Indeed C. G. Jung surprises us by his statement that the psychologist does not find much of interest in the psychological novel. It is apparently too transparent. What he seeks is the "visionary mode of artistic creation"[11] where there is room for interpretation. It would seem as if the farther away from reality, such as we the readers can gauge, the more advantageous it is for the psychologist (read, the analytic psychologist) to make the most of his ingenuity.

From early Talmudical days, we have known the fourfold interpretation of the Scriptures, the *Pardes* i.e., the literal, the symbolic, the homiletical, and hermeneutical, which afterwards began to be applied to literature; and I daresay that is a great instrument which harmonizes with psychoanalysis, but its superiority is indicated by its keeping within the prescribed levels and not flitting from the one to the other. We can learn much from the story of Red Riding Hood or Jack the Giant Killer in regard to the folk mind or the collective unconscious, but why is Maupassant's *Boule de Suif* not grist to the psychological mill? Is Dostoyevsky greater than Tolstoi because his unconscious revealed more powerful impulses, confirming Freud's basic Oedipus doctrine?

As a reader, I can appreciate both Balzac's *Peau de Chagrin* and his *La Coméde Humaine,* but certainly the latter will strike me as the more psychological of the two. It may be that in the former and in his *Seraphita,* we catch glimpses of a Balzac we had not suspected, but as readers we are concerned with literature, not with a person. As a mystic, as a student of the occult, as an investigator of folklore, we might find much of consequence in *Seraphita*.

LITERARY PERVERSION

It is fortunate that Shakespeare, Maupassant, Balzac and Zola have lived before Freud, for his influence has been so great in literary circles that willy-nilly many writers are affected by his theories; and that cannot fail to produce a perversion of reality. Not so long ago, an indifferent fiction writer had asked me to recommend some psychoanalytic books which he said he needed for his profession. "To what purpose?" I asked. "Oh" was his simple reply, "so that I can weave into my stories the psychological [i.e. psychoanalytic] facts." I then made a fruitless endeavor to enlighten him on that point, viz., that if he gathered his material from Freud or his associates rather than from life, his fiction would not be genuine, for the imaginative elaborations would lack the experience. He would be like the professor who, when traveling with his wife through the beautiful Tyrol, could not be bothered viewing the scenery, because he was then reading a book about the Tyrol landscapes.

To a certain extent, something of the reversal in practice is due to the movies, and before this, the stage. The public would learn about court manners from the performances until the actors and actresses were actually influencing upper society. An avowed follower of Freud, A. Wormhoudt admits that "perhaps the most obvious characteristic of contemporary literature which is somehow to be correlated with Freud's influence is its obscurity, even unintelligibility to the average reader"[12] and traces this tendency back to Freud's treatment of dreams.

Wormhoudt holds apparently that there is a significant relationship between the intensity of conflict portrayed and its value as literature.

> The relatively normal person may find his sense of beauty less intense than that of the neurotic, but there is little danger that he will be totally incapable of it. The

sublimation of his libidinous and aggressive tendencies has gone far enough to permit the realization of higher values, but not far enough to disturb the psychic balance which is called normality. On the other hand it is true that precisely those works of art which have been acclaimed as the greatest show the most profound sense of inner conflict. *The Iliad, The Aeneid, The Divine Comedy,* and *Hamlet* are but a few of the major examples of this observation.[13]

Why some literature has reached the pinnacle of fame is not easy to answer. All sorts of reasons may be assigned, and one cannot be certain that it all hinges on the intensity of the conflict. Aside from circumstantial reasons—political, social, personal, and even fortuitous, we should not lose sight of such factors as the beauty of diction, the wisdom of the apophthegms, the complexity of the plot, the true characterization of the *dramatis personae.*

Indeed, it seems as if the poet sometimes prolongs (or intensifies) the conflict in order to put into the mouth of the hero or the heroine some more glittering or polished phrases. I think this is particularly true of some of the French masterpieces, *Le Cid,* in particular. A figurative pulmotor is used not to let the sentimentality of the conflict-beset maiden die before the author has had a chance to relieve himself of a plethora of observations couched in antithetic verbiage, which arouses sympathy in the reader for the victim of circumstances.

Freud has exercised a powerful hold on critics as well as writers. Even those who claim moderation and reserve and circumspection end up by capitulating to Freudian demands. Wayne Burns may serve as an illustration of a critic who makes resolutions only to break them. For he first tells us that

> More specifically, it means that we shall have to desystematize our minds—actually make an effort to clear our minds of the systematic Freudian knowledge we may have spent years in developing. Otherwise we shall in-

evitably translate rather than follow what the author as artist has written—the way a friend of mine, reading Hemingway's latest novel, the one about the big fish and the little man, translated the cramps in the little man's hand, the massaging of the fingers, etc. We simply cannot read a piece of literature in this way—as if it were merely a whetstone for our own ingenuity. If we do, we shall be writing our own poems and novels, not reading those that have been written for us. I repeat: we must try to forget our systematic Freudian knowledge. We must, because it is only by forgetting Freud's ordering of experience—so intense and powerful that it tends to overwhelm the orderings of art—that we can achieve the heightened yet unsystematized awareness art demands, preparatory to imposing its own system, its own order, upon our minds and imaginations.

All this will be difficult, yet it will, I believe, enable us to make the fullest use of our Freudian awareness without being overwhelmed by it. We will be free to exploit and control its stimulative powers, to place these powers under the direction of the artist, to do with what he will. Indeed if we can develop our new-found powers to their ultimate potential, we should be able to follow wherever the artist leads, and thus realize artistic heights and depths that were, until Freud, closed to all but the greatest and most percipient minds, that are still closed to system-bound (including Freud-bound) critics of all schools. Of course we must have a fairly active and well-balanced imagination to begin with, or Freudianism, as W. H. Auden has suggested (*The New Republic*, October 6, 1952) will stimulate us into critical foolishness, or worse. But if we possess this necessary imaginative equipment—and nearly all of us do, I believe—we can, with the help of Freudian stimulation, develop an aesthetic awareness that will, in certain instances, carry us beyond the criticism of even the most perceptive non-Freudian critics—beyond, for example, T. S. Eliot's criticism of *Hamlet,* in which he mistakes Shakespeare's psychological subtlety for inferior artistry; then on the basis of this misapprehension, pronounces Gertrude inadequate, the play a failure.[14]

But what does he do subsequently? In that very paper he proceeds to show that Emily Brontë, by using words which may have possible sexual connotation in her *Jane Eyre,* conveys to the reader the orgastic state of the heroine, when the missionary "pressed his hand firmer on my head and surrounded me with his arm, almost as if he loved me."

And how does this interpreter arrive at his conclusion?

Jane had been asked in marriage by the missionary St. John Rivers, who thought of her more as a resourceful helpmeet, than as a sweetheart turning into a loved wife. Jane stood under his spell and she relates her emotional experience. She was beginning to soften under his kindness and, she relates, "I was excited more than ever I had been." "My prayers are heard" ejaculated St. John. She heard her heart throb. She was in some sort of ecstasy which made her flesh quiver on her bones. It was a strange and startling feeling which passed at once to her head and extremities. But just as she was on the point of accepting the clergyman's proposal, she thought she heard the voice of her first love, Rochester, and, in response to his call, "Jane! Jane! Jane!" she cried "I am coming! Wait for me. Oh I will come!" Burns underlines some of the telltale words once but the more crucial ones are twice underscored, and because these latter, like "ejaculate" and "I am coming" are sometimes used in a sexual context, the author deduces that Jane is experiencing an orgasm. "In the circumstances she gives in to what she had denied herself with Rochester: her body takes over, so to speak."

The question, to my mind, is what other words Brontë might have used so as not to lay herself open to such an interpretation. Inasmuch as the very words "lay herself open" came up, would the present writer be supposed to feel himself a rival to the hero? In other words, must we look for suggestiveness and sex allusions in every expression no matter how simply and effectively it fits the situation? All authors would then be thrown into a state of bedlam, examining the possible connotations of every word and phrase, and perhaps rejecting many of the most apt and felicitous turns.

The tendency to read sexual connotations and allusions into fiction is generally prevalent among all those who have tasted of Freud's delicacies. Since analogy and metaphor are always at hand, it is the easiest thing to turn almost every noun and verb into a sex symbol. Do such interpreters ask themselves what other imagery the authors might have used in order to express their thoughts? *That* they will not do, since it would spoil their little game; for they are bent on "proving" their case. H. Slochower, e.g., observes very properly that "A striking feature of *Moby Dick* is the almost complete absence of sex"[15] yet he soon finds the novel (incidentally Jung thought it to be the greatest American literary masterpiece) shot through with sex allusions. It would take too much space to list all these metaphors and images which Slochower adduces, but the conclusion come to, viz., that Melville was mildly homosexual would require better evidence than such phrases as the latter employs, like "maidenly gentleness," "the masculine sea," "thick walls" and "interior spaciousness." One might take every sentence which one utters that is not a sheer stereotype or catchphrase and discover some possibly remote allusion to sex activity. The rabbinical interpreters of the Old Testament engaged in the same hobby, although in their case there was much greater need; for through such verbal methods were they able to establish laws, which, under a theocratic system and a credo of revelation, had to be deduced from the Biblical phraseology. Between the Talmudic *pilpul* and some of the psychoanalytic fanciful extrapolations, it would seem the former is preferable as more consistent with common sense.

Small wonder, then, that critics and teachers of literature should be divided in opinion as to the merits of the scores of articles undertaking to give us the unconscious inside story of each of the characters in well-known literary works. There are those, of course, that are prepared to accept almost every conclusion a psychoanalytic writer comes to, but there are others more critical and even skeptical. We may even grade them as to positive or negative attitude. There is, e.g., Trilling who attempts to steer a middle course, and while recognizing the value of Freudian psychology for the interpretation of literature, he is not unmindful of the vagaries of some of the psychoanalysts when they turn to literary works.[16] S. E. Hyman goes a step farther in warning against the familiar psychoanalytic method of analyzing the fossilized author and then proceeding to apply the deductions to his characters.[17] W. J. Griffin has elaborated on this objection in an exceptionally well-documented article. He finds that both critics and psychoanalysts have been at fault, for as he says

> To call the roll of literary men who have misapplied psychoanalytic theory out of half-knowledge, or a desire to be sensational, or an eagerness to make out a case, would not be enough to explain the situation. Professional psychoanalysts themselves have also frequently been undiscriminating when they have made excursions into the field of literary study. I do not here have in mind the errors into which they may fall through some lack of purely literary training. These may be charitably passed over. I refer to the failure to make reasonable distinctions, to lack of caution and a susceptibility to what are vaguely known as "excesses." In these respects the honors seem to be about even between literary men and professional psychoanalysts.[18]

Griffin pursues his topic, however, with the zeal of a logician to the disadvantage of the psychoanalyst when he observes that

> The purpose of analysis cannot be therapy. Coleridge cannot now be retrieved from his addiction to opium

nor Poe from his dipsomania; nor can the analyst help Shakespeare to resolve his "deeply rooted conflict with the mother." Yet it is apparently difficult not to adopt the tone of a diagnostician with an eye to improvement of the patient's behavior. Readers of psychoanalytic criticism are frequently irritated by what Charles Baudouin speaks of as an "air of medical superiority."
If the purpose is not control, it is just as clearly not prediction. Presumably, the intention is simply to arrive at an understanding of the author's motivations and meanings. Even conscious motivations are complex; it is unlikely that hidden ones are less so. Yet a common characteristic of psychoanalytic criticism appears to be schematic simplification. It is the besetting sin in such criticism to make overmuch of the kind of causation that might be centrally important if the end in view were therapy, overlooking the fact that when the purpose which would give certain determinants significance is altered, the significance is automatically altered. We may say that in an author's work we have a set of symptoms, but as Rudolf Eckstein has pointed out, "the symptom is really determined through an unlimited series of causes." The traditional scholar, whatever his shortcomings, cannot fail to be annoyed by readings that find *the* answer to the "riddle" of *Macbeth* in Shakespeare's fantasies of guilt about the death of his son—even if they were reactivated by the death of the barren Elizabeth.[19]

Edel is inclined to caution the critic more than the psychoanalyst, for the latter is surer of his ground and has a greater command of his tools, while the critic lacks the training and is therefore apt to project or misread. Since Edel writes rather from the philosophical than from either the literary or psychoanalytic point of view, he can afford to be neutral and dole out some sound advice to both.

How is the psychological instrument to be used? I submit

that the literary student turning psychologist for the nonce—unlike his psychological counterpart—must use his new-found tools to gain his own insight into the literary material and then he must bury the tools and write literary criticism or history or biography on his own ground and not that of the psychologist. He must convert and translate into the language of his own field. He is writing, after all, not as a psychologist but as a literary scholar and he must beware of "selling out" his own field or setting down a study that in the end is neither literary nor psychological, bulging with non-literary terminology. He need not talk about "sibling rivalries" when he can describe quite factually his subject's relationship to his brothers and sisters; he need not involve Oedipus when he wishes to discuss fear or guilt or anxiety.[20]

Edel's recent book, *The Psychological Novel 1900-1950* (1955), despite the fact that it deals only with Marcel Proust, Henry James, Dorothy Richardson, Virginia Woolf, and James Joyce, who were somehow affected by a sort of time-complex, is nevertheless illuminating in its distinctions, and replete with significant illustrations, some of which tie in with the early experiences of the writers, thus showing how things of the past keep reverberating in the minds of the authors or artists.

Taking his cue from Proust, he asks "Would all readers read such novels in the same manner?" and answers:

"Thus Proust discovered, as Henry James had done before him, that the writer of fiction can not only represent life but actually can create it . . . ."

After lingering on the commonplace that some people can get extremely excited over a book which others cannot bring themselves to read to the end, he ascribes the difference to the gap between intellectual apprehension and the intensity of feeling in the reading of a book.

Rare are the readers who can achieve a balance between intellectual apprehension of a novel and an intense feeling of it. Yet it is for the feeling as much as the intellectual apprehension that most novelists write their work.

This is particularly true of the modern psychological novel. Here the entire work by its very nature, offers us the data in higgledy-piggledy disorder. We are asked to *see into* the characters, to make deductions from such data as may be offered us—and at the same time to live for ourselves the experience with which we are confronted on the printed page.... The critical reader who intellectually apprehends a book but has achieved no particular feeling in the process usually has only a ledger-book concept of the work....

At the other extreme is the reader who has felt every page of the work, but can give us no coherent account of the data.[21]

While this is true enough, is it not simply a matter of what experiences the reader has had in the past and what aspirations he has toward the future? As for the author, would it not be safer to say that the true artist writes for himself rather than for the reader?

The most thoroughgoing discussion of the problems involved, it seems to me, is to be found in the fascinatingly-written volume, *Literature and Psychology,* by F. L. Lucas. Erudition is the hallmark of Lucas's writing, but it is also distinguished by common sense and an eye for perspective. The psychoanalytic *motif* runs through the whole book like a red thread (many of the illustrations, by the way, drawn from Stekel, whom the author wishes to accord the credit withheld from him on the part of the orthodox Freudians and followers of other depth schools) but the thread is never allowed to thicken into a cord, nor to color the rest of the material. Lucas confesses to a "deep and lasting admiration for Freud's work."[22] Indeed, he believes that "in the long run . . . mankind will have owed yet more to Freud than to Columbus, or Newton, or Darwin, or Einstein; let alone Marx, whose work suffered precisely because he remained (like many other reformers) so crude in his psychology." (page 20).

This encomium, however, does not prevent Lucas from expressing himself adversely on the endeavors of so many of the psychoanalytic writers.

To read the bound volumes of *Imago* or *The International Journal of Psycho-Analysis* for, say, the last

twenty-five years leaves an impression of great uneven-
ness and a feeling, if one dare say so, that many of the
contributors would have been no worse for a little more
scepticism. When I am told, for example, that the scene
in the *Odyssey* where Nausicaä welcomes the hero
escaped from the sea represents a birth fantasy; that the
princess represents Odysseus' mother; and that the ball
she throws to her maidens turns out to be a phallic
symbol ("I knew it would," said Alice), for such
Homeric criticism I am afraid I can find only Homeric
laughter.[23]

It would scarcely be possible within the compass of a chapter
to do more than to record the various trends, to show that
psychoanalysis has intrenched itself in the literary domain, that
willy-nilly we must examine its verdicts, although we might
appeal to the higher court of reason, if the guilt complex, the
judgment of sadism, orality regression, phallic-mother identification, etc., occur to us as preconceived and supported only
by the flimsiest circumstantiality.

FOOTNOTES

[1] Roback, A. A. Psikhologie un Literatur. *Literatur un Lebn,* vol. 1,
1915.

[2] Rank. *Truth and Reality,* (transl. by Jessie Taft). New York: Knopf,
1936, p. 134-135.

[3] Jung, C. G. *Modern Man in Search of a Soul* (transl. by W. S. Dell
and C. F. Baynes). London: Kegan Paul, 1933, p. 194-195.

[4] *Ibid.,* p. 195-196.

[5] Sachs, H. *The Creative Unconscious* (2d ed.) Cambridge: Sci-Art,
1951, p. 39.

[6] *Loc. cit.,* p. 42.

[7] *Loc. cit.,* pp. 48-49.

[8] *Loc. cit.,* 50-51.

[9] Bergler, E. *The Writer and Psychoanalysis.* New York: Doubleday,
1950, pp. 236-237.

[10] Basler, R. P. *Sex, Symbolism, and Psychology in Literature,* Rutgers
University Press, 1948, p. 11.

[11] Jung, C. G., *Loc. cit.,* p. 180.

[12] Wormhoudt, A. Freud and Literary Theory. *Am. Imago,* vol. 6, 1949,
p. 9.

[13] *Loc. cit.,* p. 7.

[14] Burns, W. "Freudianism, Criticism, and Jane Eyre". *News Letter of the Conference on Literature and Psychology* of the Modern Language Association of America, vol. 11, 1952, No. 5.

[15] Slochower, H. Freudian Motifs in "Moby Dick". *Complex*, vol. 1, 1950.

[16] Trilling, L. *The Liberal Imagination*, New York, 1951. The chapter on "Freud and Literature" had already appeared a decade earlier.

[17] Hyman, S. E. *The Armèd Vision*, New York, 1948.

[18] Griffin, W. J. The Uses and Abuses of Psychoanalysis in the Study of Literature. *News Letter of the Conference on Literature of Psychology*, vol. 1, 1951, p. 12.

[19] Griffin, W. J. *Ibid.*, pp. 14-15.

[20] *News Letter of the Conference on Literature and Psychology* of the Modern Language Association of America, vol. II, No. 5, 1952, pp. 6-7.

[20a] Lucas, F. L. *Literature and Psychology*. London: Cassell, 1951.

[20b] Lucas, F. L. *Ibid*, p. 9.

[21] Edel, L. *The Psychological Novel 1900-1950*. New York, 1955, pp. 100-101.

[22] Lucas, F. L. *Literature and Psychology*. London: Cassell, 1951, p. 9.

[23] Lucas, F. L. *Ibid.*, p. 8.

REFERENCES

Basler, R. P. *Sex, Symbolism, and Psychology in Literature*, New Brunswick, New Jersey, 1948.

Bergler, E. *The Writer and Psychoanalysis*, New York, 1950.

Bodkin, M. *Archetypal Patterns in Poetry: Psychological Studies of Imagination*, New York, 1934.

Glicksberg, C. I. "Literature and Freudianism". *Prairie Schooner*, vol. 23.

Griffin, W. J. "The Uses and Abuses of Psychoanalysis in the Study of Literature". *News Letter of the Conference on Literature of Psychology*, vol. 1, 1954.

Hyman, S. E. *The Armèd Vision*, New York, 1948.

Jung, C. G. *Modern Man in Search of a Soul* (transl. by W. S. Dell and C. F. Baynes). London, 1933.

Lucas, F. L. *Literature and Psychology*, London, 1951.

Roback, A. A. "Psikhologie un Literatur". *Literatur un Lebn.* vol. 1, 1915.

Roback, A. A. *I. L. Peretz, Psychologist of Literature*, Cambridge, 1935.

Sachs, H. *The Creative Unconscious* (2d ed.) Cambridge, Mass., 1951.

Slochower, H. Freudian Motifs in Moby Dick. *Complex*, 1950.

Trilling, L. *The Liberal Imagination*, New York, 1951.

Wormhoudt, A. Freud and Literary Theory. *American Imago*, 1949, vol. 6, No. 3.

——The Unconscious Identification of Words and Milk. *American Imago*, 1949, vol. 6, No. 1.

CHAPTER XXXVI

GLOSSODYNAMICS AND THE PRESENT STATUS OF PSYCHOLINGUISTICS

A. A. ROBACK, Ph.D.
Professor of Psychology, Emerson College

EDITORIAL NOTE

Practically in every psychology textbook, we find a paragraph or two on the psychology of language, but the information is so meager and the treatment so scant, that the student can scarcely imagine what a vast range the subject covers. There is no dearth of books on the psychology of language. They are mainly in German and French, and of an old vintage. Time was when psychology and language were almost inseparable; and the philologists and linguists were hotly debating this or that issue with psychologists. A strange aloofness has come over the two sides, although through the increasing activity of semanticists, a rapprochement *between the two is beginning to make itself felt.*

In a recent issue of Language, *we read that "the Social Science Research Council has established a Committee on Linguistics and Psychology in order to create a community of understanding among specialists in diverse fields who are concerned with problems of language behavior."*

The present writer has not aimed to cover the ground systematically. There is too great temptation to expand, so that the brief chapter is intended to whet the appetite only. He does not consider himself a linguist by training, but after a life-long avocational study of language which came to expression in numerous articles, and more recently in the publication of Destiny and Motivation in Language (*Cambridge*, 1954) *he feels that the chapter, sketchy though it be, carries its message.*

The Psychology of Language is not considered a branch. It is more a borderland or perhaps a parallel discipline, but no matter how we label it, it is of consequence to psychology, and far more to linguistics; for without it, linguistics must remain a plodding, if not sterile, collection of data.

At a time when sciences are seeking contacts with one another, and are forming alliances, such as biochemistry or astrophysics, linguistics has of late tended to part company with psychology with which it has had a good deal in common. Linguistics and philology went hand in hand when Herder and, after him, Wilhelm Humboldt sought to link the two for the benefit of the nascent science. Later we find Steinthal, a linguist and a psychologist united in the same person, joining data from both fields like hooks and eyes. Wundt, the high priest of psychology for half a century, contributed two large volumes, besides smaller publications to the problems of language. Linguistic psychology has had enthusiasts in Germany and in France, where the *Journal de Psychologie* features articles on linguistics in the light of psychology. In Holland, Van Ginneken, and in Switzerland, Séchehaye, were among the founders of psycholinguistics. One might have expected a similar understanding in the United States, but the trend seems to be just the reverse. While the older linguists did not bring themselves to recognize the basic importance of psychology in explaining linguistic phenomena, they at least made no effort to ignore it, and on occasion would call attention to the necessity of referring back verbal forms to occurrences in the mind like association and imagery. The semantic movement in linguistics made the debt to psychology even more conspicuous; for when meanings change, we must assume that experiences in the community have caused the change.

Toward Positivism

Descriptive linguistics veered from the beaten path by insisting on positivistic treatment of all the phenomena of language. Anything which would give rise to speculation or theory would be frowned upon and ignored or dismissed in a few words. Thus, glottogonics was discarded because it was held that the beginnings of language are too remote in the past to yield any but the most nebulous hypotheses which could never be verified.

Together with glottogonics went all observations on sound symbolism as altogether too subjective to be taken seriously. Nevertheless, an anthropologist and linguist like Sapir was not willing to make short shrift of such a perennial interest and on the basis of experiments arrived at a more encouraging conclusion.

PHONEMICS TAKES THE FORE

While semantics was growing as a branch of linguistics, phonology or phonemics was being built up as a bulwark of the descriptive school. Here there was little room for theory. Sounds were physical to the extent that they could be not only reproduced under all sorts of conditions but compared and measured. No wonder then that that branch for a time began to take the lead as the most reliable and scientific department of linguistics. Morphology and syntactics on a descriptive level and a comparative basis were acceptable, but care would be taken to keep them removed from psychological explanation.

With the advent of behaviorism in psychology, descriptive linguistics acquired an ally to which it now turned; and Leonard Bloomfield (1933) became the leader of the behavioristic camp in linguistics, so that words for him no longer represented thoughts or feelings or desires, but were just responses to stimuli. Our speech was considered not as symbolic of some mental content but a matter of conditioning.

INSISTENCE ON MEASUREMENT

In quest of objectivity, it was natural that linguists should turn to statistics. It was simple to say that the shorter a word, the more frequent its use, and conversely the longer word will fall into desuetude (Zipf, 1933). The frequency of words became a favorite subject of research leading to ventures in educational method (Thorndike) and quite recently to other practical moves like communication theory and its sequel, information theory.

There is no question about the value of these developments. It is only when they not only come to the forefront but usurp the whole stage and allow no access to other investigations that we can find fault. It has always been the claim of behaviorism, in its various guises, that only a stimulus-response approach is permissible in studying the organism and its functions. Hence everything which does not fit into this scheme is ruled out as unscientific. Operationism with its reinforcements or instrumental conditioning (Skinner) is only the heir of behaviorism, retaining its aggressiveness under a different name, in that it presumes to lay down the law for all investigators, even such as have other goals in view.

Psycholinguistics, if we follow behaviorism, operationism, or physicalism in the sense that what cannot be reduced to physical terminology, is non-scientific, would be non-existent. Fortunately, there are still many linguists who refuse to oversimplify and circumscribe their science, and many psychologists who will not acquiesce in the plan to dump all mental contents simply because we cannot see or touch them.

ADVANTAGE OF COMPARATIVE SEMANTICS

E. Reifler, who has made an interesting analysis of pairs of words in several languages as remote as Chinese, Hebrew, Russian, English, and Spanish, showing how apparently incompatible meanings turn out to be related in all languages cited (e.g., *contre contrée,* counter country, *gegen Gegend,* are paralleled in Chinese, as are the links between *pupil,* "a child," and "pupil of the eye") follows a line of linguistic thought which is akin to my own as presented in *Destiny and Motivation in Language.* Reifler refutes Bloomfield's arguments in connection with meaning and proceeds to say

> But whatever semantic information may be required by linguistics, if linguistics is the science of language, then no linguist can abstain from making, explicit or implicit, references to meaning. Thus, although it may be true, as Hockett says, "that general semanticists ought to know linguistics," the converse is certainly true: linguists ought to know semantics.[1]

Reifler is quite justified, even from the few illustrations he adduces, in his conclusion that comparative semantics demonstrates how common analogies and associations in various linguistic developments have been brought out by such comparisons so that what did not seem obvious or even probable to us at first blush was in point of fact obvious to those who shaped the language.

BACK TO MOTIVATION

The chief reason why we cannot go along with the descriptive linguists is that they are too narrow in scope and will not sanction any inquiry beyond their informational findings. Language is complex, especially as it evolves through the ages. Either we have to give up our search altogether, or else we must follow in the tracks of our predecessors in order to find a way out of the maze.

Let us take, as one illustration, theories as to the origin of language. Does it follow that because such have not satisfied us heretofore, nothing should be done further to seek a clue as to how words were formed? Paget, with his tongue-gesture theory, and Oehl, with his lallation theory, have blazed new trails, and I can't help but think that my own voco-sensory theory based on experiments with the consonants of the general alphabet may contain a grain of truth as to the association of meaning with sound. Since the theory has been propounded at length and illustrated in my *Destiny and Motivation in Language* by numerous examples taken from a score of languages, but particularly in connection with the semantic structure of the Hebrew root, it would, considering the space and time limit, suffice here to record the reference, and to state that the results showed a particular set of qualities attached to each consonant by the observers, and that the responses were far above the incidence of chance as computed by an educational statistician on the basis of the *chi*-square.

Weakness of Physicalistic Thesis

What has been lost sight of by the positivists in language is that motivation has been the chief factor in its evolution, and while some motives can be understood in terms of physical conditioning, the larger part, including the core, can only be reconstructed in mentalistic terms, because we move in that sphere. In examining the etymology of a word like "master," "marshal," "cattle," or "anxiety," we can trace the psychological sources in the first three, and the physiological in the last one very easily from a symbolic point of view. On a behavioristic platform, whether we bring in stimulus and response adjustment, conditioning, or reinforcement, all we could do is to state the operation formalistically in the simple abstract terms that *a* conditioned *b*, *b* conditioned *c* and so on, but the socio-historical complex with the various semantic steps would be missing, because that is all a matter of symbolic representation.

Far from dropping the purposive categories in the study of language, we must, on the contrary, be ready to deepen our interest in motivation to the extent of looking for it in every linguistic phenomenon, in every sound, every grammatical form, idiom, and syntactical construction. What about the euphemism, the phylacterism, (since this is a term not yet found in any dictionary I should explain that it signifies a protective phrase like "God forbid," "Knock on wood") the spoonerism, the doublet, the slip of the tongue, and all the variety of metaphors? They all have a purpose born of a human need. Behaviorism and its allies are prone to make it all a matter of accident: some one happened to emit a certain sound which was caught up by another and a third until it became part of the culture and transmitted to posterity.

Linguistic positivism sidesteps national characteristics in language. Just because a German can learn French, or a Frenchman German, it is supposed that there is no difference in the make-up of the two nationalities which have developed

two different linguistic patterns, and yet every divergence tells
a story and all divergences together form a coherent whole. To
say that such is the German culture and such is the French
leaves us in the dark. To refer the linguistic propria to the
general characteristics of a people is to receive enlightenment.

GLOSSODYNAMICS

Descriptive linguistics can only thrive in a mechanical sphere,
and because it is static it must necessarily remain stagnant. It
stresses the 'how,' but the 'why' in a human world is equally
important. If psycholinguistics is designated as the territory
which joins psychology and linguistics, then I should propose
the term 'glossodynamics' to represent a special strip or, better,
a stratum in that area, given over to the ascertainment of
motives in the production of linguistic phenomena. The motives
may be on the conscious level, e.g., in the use of euphemisms,
but they may also be dynamic, operating in the unconscious.
Psychoanalysis may throw considerable light on taboo words, on
the rôle of repression in the disappearance of certain vocables,
or on the emergence of metaphors, but it would be best to start
with the linguistic fact not with the psychoanalytic interpretation,
or we should be in the position of the sharpshooter who frames
the bull's eye only after he has had his random shot.

Incidentally, it is strange that both Tolman and Skinner,
leading operationists who have long since shed all mentalistic
concepts nevertheless have become reconciled to the Freudian
dynamisms, which are avowedly unconscious. Even if we should
attempt to transform these dynamisms like repression, regression,
guilt complex into physiological operations, it would not only
be contrary to the whole conception of psychoanalysis but impossible of demonstration, and thus violating the physicalistic
principle. In this instance there comes to mind the dictum of
the gospel, "straining at a gnat and swallowing a camel."

In conclusion or by way of summary, psychology has much
to offer to linguistics, and linguistic science can be of service to
psychology, but it must not be the makeshift in either case.

Both descriptive linguistics and physicalism (which includes all stages and grades of behaviorism) are fine in their restricted compass, but life deals predominantly with desires and thoughts and feelings, purposes and motives and ideals. If these are to be watered down to stimuli and responses, then our search for the facts is doomed at the very outset. We cannot make a purpose out of a reaction to a sound or a light or even a proprioceptive stimulus (any more than we can make a cube out of a square or a square out of a line).

Voco-Sensory Theory

On the basis of experiments with consonants, A. A. Roback[2] has shown that the phonemes have a symbolic value which is not subjective but bound up with the way the action of the various speech organs in different positions affects us. Thus *k* is the hardest sound because in articulating it, the air column strikes against the palate, while the soft *l,* resulting from the contact of the tongue with the moisture of the soft palate, will suggest relaxation and ease, then laxity. He has endeavored to analyze the meanings of various combinations (phonexes) like *fl-, kn-, shl-, shm-, st-,* and *ng.* The latter e.g., is the basis of hundreds of words in a score of languages signifying distress and anxiety.

According to the theory, the tightening of the vocal cords necessitated by the phonation of *ng* or *nk,* which, in turn produces tension, only parallels the emotional state of *distress, anger, stringency, anguish,* and even *hunger.* What is more, many words associated with *hanging, strangling, string,* both in the Indo-European and Semitic families of languages, contain this combination. Similarly the *st-* phonex occurs in so many words connoting rest or stopping or standing because of the "feel" in bringing the continuant *s* to a halt through slightly withdrawing the tongue. In the chapter on the "Semantic Structure of the Hebrew Root," the semantic kinship is shown to go parallel with phonetic cognateness, thus adding support to what the author calls the "voco-sensory theory" of language.

Not all facts are known through experimentation. Much is gained through experience alone, and interpreted through common sense. It has been often assumed that whatever is not operational must be speculative. This is a false dichotomy. Whether or not we are ready to accept all of the Freudian psychology we cannot dismiss much of it without laying ourselves open to dogmatism and the charge of shutting our eyes to very important occurrences. Yet the doctrine of the unconscious itself is incompatible with any behavioristic system.

To show how disparate the approach of glossodynamics is from that of descriptivism in linguistics, let us take a very minor illustration. We note that in English, which treats the names of all inanimate objects as neuter, *country, boat,* and *automobile* (occasionally an *institution*) are often referred to by the pronoun "she." Now the cultural anthropologist and descriptive linguist might make a survey of the gender of these counterparts in scores of languages, both ancient and modern, and partaking of all four or five types (isolating, agglutinative, incorporating, inflectional, and analytic) and then probably would arrive at the conclusion that it was all a matter of culture, with no special significance; perhaps originating in a fortuitous circumstance or because of a myth or legend, in which these objects were personified as women. In a radio quiz, some juvenile struck the bright idea that a boat or car was given the feminine gender because they have to be taken care of and do receive special attention on the part of the male owners. The students in a class on language seemed to agree with this adolescent observation. But it takes only a bit of mature reflection to note that all objects characterized by space, all containers or receptacles symbolize woman because of her identification with womb, or vagina, and in psychoanalysis, all dreams in which there are representations of boxes, bags, bottles, jars, pockets, etc., are veiled references to female genitalia.

That the Germans have called a woman a *Frauenzimmer* (literally 'woman's room') and then turn about and make the noun, *Weib* (wife), neuter, the same gender as *Zimmer* (room) is something which brings to light a German characteristic rather than a crucial point in grammar which must impel us to modify our above explanation.

In fine, every apparent anomaly in language requires accounting for in terms of motivation, and just as a quirk in behavior points to a certain idiosyncrasy, so a deviation from what one might consider rational in cultural development must be an indication of a social or historical hitch somewhere along the line of development, governed by the national character.

The semanticists will still have to think of meanings not in terms of mechanics, kinaesthetic imagery, or fortuitous occurrences which have become habits. Meaning is too mentalistic a thing to fit into the grooves of physiology, and even simple phonetics has come into being through some purposive objective on the part of our ancestors, who may have been inferior to the parrot in respect to articulation but they forged a language, which the parrot cannot begin to do. In the most backward Austronesian or African tribes, there is a mind which shapes the forms of utterance. Even if the Bokotudos in order to express the idea of "island" must say *land—water—middle—here is (nak—munia—pompeu—nep)* it is still more than the chimpanzee can articulate, and more than the parrot can convey. Let us concede that the difference in mentality is one of degree rather than kind, but it is still a vast difference, which no amount of mechanistic manipulation will be able to conjure away.

LINGUISTIC ASSISTANCE TO PSYCHOLOGY

What has psychology to gain from linguistics? Just this: that what we believe to be the general rule with classes or types familiar to us in our ordinary contacts need not hold everywhere. Chinese lack of grammar, for instance; the accumulation of several concrete objects to express an abstract idea, and other such oddities, from our point of view, will modify our conclusions on abstraction, even when gained in the laboratory. The circumstance that many peoples, instead of using a noun with various qualifiers like red, young, one-year-old, fat, will multiply designations so that each individual class, whether according to age, color, size, etc. will receive a different general name, as we have it in the case of 'neonate,' 'infant,' 'toddler,' 'child,' 'youngster,' 'adolescent,' 'adult,' 'oldster,' should add to the sum of our psychological knowledge.

When an incorporating language starts with the word which seems most important and takes a roundabout way in coming to the point, all the time gathering superfluities because of repeated elements, each with an additional bit of description, we must pause to ask whether there are not other modes of thinking than our own.

B. L. Whorf, for instance, has brought out much pertinent material on this head. The sentence "He invites people to a feast" is formulated in the Nootka language in one word, consisting of a core *tl'imsh* ('boiled') with five suffixes or accessories added, so that the order corresponds to our word-sequence boil-ed—eat—ers—go—for—(he) does.[3]

Similarly, although we may be certain about the functions of each of the parts of speech, the fact that some languages have as many as twenty tenses and aspects, while Hebrew is deficient in the former, and in some languages, in Hupa, e.g., verbs are used as nouns ('it comes down' means rain and 'it is tied' means bundle) and in still others, the act is expressed in the form of an epithetologue ('my seeing you' = 'I see you') should again turn our attention to the vast variety of possibilities in thinking.

The emphasis laid on pitch in speaking (whether high or low) among some of the West African languages so that it determines the favorable or unfavorable sense, while the phonetic organization is only secondary, teaches us another lesson about primitive mentality, and at the same time about ourself. We may, perhaps too, gain a slight understanding of the curious abstraction possibilities in primitives by noting the differences between our capacity to form concepts and that of South Sea Islanders through the words they use which, from our vantage point, apparently bear no relation to the objects in question. The diffuseness of thought envelops a whole sea of associations without singling out the idea which we would have dwelt on. All this could be known only through a linguistic survey on a comparative basis.

WHAT IS HAPPENING NOW?

Meanwhile general linguistics, like all sciences, has expanded, adding new twigs to its branches. Schools in linguistics have not diminished in number nor reduced their intensity, not to say vehemence, of expression. Some of the older issues have been cast overboard by the majority, although they will not sink while there are diverse types of mind in science. There is much specialization and division of labor as in psychology or sociology. The area of phonemics is greatly cultivated, and new approaches are sought. There is a good deal of activity evinced in connection with definition, nomenclature, analysis, methods and techniques. Since this is the electronic age, machines are pressed into service to determine the sequence of consonants and vowels in a variety of unrelated languages.

This autocorrelation function[3a] as it is called, showing the dependence of one phoneme upon another, may be of use in determining, under doubtful conditions, the probability that it was one sound rather than another which was employed, in a certain impaired text or relayed oral communication, but whether the game is worth the candle is a debatable point. This whole line of investigation seems to be an outgrowth of the practical phase of the communication theory, as formulated by C. E. Shannon and W. Weaver,[4] which might have some bearing on traffic control and warfare problems. A new centre of interest has formed around the information theory, which may be considered as an outlet of the communication theory, and is especially fostered by those committed to operationism as a general laboratory approach. It deals largely with the task of increasing the amount of information by reducing redundancy in expression and making for economy otherwise, through utilizing the facilities to the best advantage.[5] Statistics as to frequency plus ingenuity incidental to all efficiency goals form the groundwork of this special speech and language area.

The study of relatively unknown languages still goes on, thanks to patient plodders who will track down a fugitive phoneme, like a vanished laryngeal *h,* through space and time; and the launching of new linguistic periodicals is a sign that the quest for knowledge goes merrily on. Have we the trail blazers, the Humboldts, the Rasks, Schleichers, Grimms, Bopps, Brugmanns, Ascolis and Leskiens today? Perhaps it is too soon to answer definitely "no." There are very brilliant linguistic minds at work in several countries, not least in the United States, but it seems as if discoveries come rarer as time goes on or, differently put, the intervals become longer, and so new slants of the field as a whole are exhibited and a reshuffling of fundamentals is taking place. The *Jung-grammatiker* (younggrammarians) movement of the past century will perhaps be paralleled by a *Jung-methodiker* movement in the near future, aligning itself with logical positivism and a purely mechanistic outlook. But *pari passu,* the tendency to counteract this overemphasis of the purely descriptive is growing into a force which will carry more weight as the more or less sterile results of the mechanists are recognized as such.

FOOTNOTES

[1] Reifler, E. Linguistic Analysis, Meaning and Comparative Semantics. *Lingua,* 1953, vol. 3, p. 378.

[2] Roback, A. A. *Destiny and Motivation in Language,* Cambridge, 1954.

[3] Whorf, B. L. Languages and Logic. *Technology Rev.,* 1941, vol. 43 p. 19, included in his *Four Articles on Metalinguistics,* Washington, 1950.

[3a] Newman, E. B. The Pattern of Vowels and Consonants in Various Languages. *Amer. Jour. of Psychol.,* 1951, vol. 64.

[4] Shannon, C. E. and Weaver, W. *The Mathematical Theory of Communication,* 1949.

[5] Miller, G. A. *Language and Communication,* 1951.

REFERENCES

Bloomfield, L. *The Study of Language,* New York, 1933; (rev. ed.), 1950.
Bonfante, G. The Neolinguistic Position. *Language,* 1947, vol. 23.

Bull, W. E. Natural Frequency and Word Counts; the Fallacy of Frequencies. *Classical Journal,* 1948, vol. 44.

Kantor, J. R. *An Objective Psychology of Grammar.* Bloomington: Indiana University Publ., 1936.

Newman, E. B. The Pattern of Vowels and Consonants in Various Languages. *American Journal of Psychology,* 1951, vol. 64, pp. 369-379.

Paget, R. *Human Speech,* London, 1930.

Pronko, N. H. Language and Psycholinguistics. *Psychological Bulletin,* 1946, vol. 43.

Reifler, E. Linguistic Analysis, Meaning and Comparative Semantics. *Lingua,* 1953, vol. 3, pp. 378, 379.

Roback, A. A. *Destiny and Motivation in Language,* Cambridge, Mass., 1954. (Sci Art).

Shannon, C. E. and Weaver, W. *The Mathematical Theory of Communication.* Urbana: University of Illinois Press, 1949.

Skinner, B. F. *Verbal Behavior* (William James Lectures), Harvard University, 1947. (These lectures are as yet unpublished).

Stein, L. *The Infancy of Speech and the Speech of Infancy,* London, 1949, XIV, 209 pp.

Sturtevant, E. H. *Linguistic Change,* Chicago, 1917.

Trager, G. L. *The Field of Linguistics.* Norman, Okla.: Battenburg Press, 1949, p. 8. (Studies in Linguistics, Occasional Papers, No. 1.)

Whorf, B. L. Languages and Logic, in *Four Articles on Metalinguistics,* Washington, 1950.

Zipf, G. K. *The Psycho-Biology of Language,* Boston, 1933.

Chapter XXXVII

FACTORIAL STUDIES OF
AESTHETIC JUDGMENTS*

R. W. Pickford, Ph.D., D.Litt.

Head of Psychology Department, Glasgow University, Scotland

EDITORIAL NOTE

Experimental aesthetics dates from G. T. Fechner's work about eighty years ago. It started on a quantitative basis (Golden Section) and therefore one should have expected great progress in that sphere. Perhaps there is cause for disappointment, although the reasons are not altogether clear, and it would take too much space to attempt to analyze the source of the lag.

It is good, therefore, to be able to report some advances made in the direction of measuring art appreciation through factorial methods, and especially is the present chapter to be welcomed because it represents British technique.

Dr. Ralph William Pickford studied biology and psychology at Cambridge University between 1923 and 1927. He was an exhibitioner, honorary senior scholar and honorary internal research student of Emmanuel College, and carried out research in the Cambridge Psychological Laboratory until 1930. He is an M.A. and Ph.D. of Emmanuel College. In 1930, he moved to Glasgow University, Scotland, where he became Senior Lecturer in Psychology and Head of the Department, and is a D.Litt. of Glasgow University. He has published many papers on experimental, social, and clinical psychology, and is author of The Psychology of Cultural Change in Painting (1943), Individual Differences in Colour Vision (1951) *and* The Analysis of an Obsessional. *He has been Chairman and is now retiring Secretary of the Scottish Branch of the British Psychological Society, and was first President of the Experimental Psychology Group. He is a psychotherapist at the Notre Dame Child Guidance Clinic, and an analyst at the Davidson Clinic, Glasgow.*

INTRODUCTION

There are a number of approaches to the psychology of art and of aesthetic judgments. They are, in the main, experimental, psycho-analytic, biographical and historical avenues. The experimental approach was first made by Fechner, and has been utilized in the present century by such workers as Bullough (1908, 1921; see also 1912, 1919a, 1919b), Langfeld (1920), Valentine (1922), Myers (1925), Spearman (1930), Burt (1933), Lowenfeld (1939), Révész (1950, 1953), Stapleton (1953) and Lindsey (1953). The psychoanalytic or psychiatric avenue has been explored by many workers, such as Freud (1932), Jones (1923), Fairbairn (1938a, 1938b), Barwell (1937), Guttmann and Maclay (1937, 1941), Guttmann, Maclay and Mayer-Gross (1937), Pickford (1939, 1942), Macquisten and Pickford, dealing with a fairy tale (1942), Rickman (1940, 1948), Sharpe (1950), Reitman (1950, 1954), and Kris (1953). The biographical approach has been made by Harding (1942) and the historical approach by Pickford (1943). The study of child art has also been valuable (Oldham, 1940; Viola, 1942; McIntosh and Pickford, 1943). For the purpose of complete insight into the psychology of art and of aesthetic judgments all these approaches are necessary. A widely based approach has been made by Huisman (1954). The present chapter, however, will confine itself to certain experimental studies of aesthetic judgments which form an interesting but little known group of researches.

By way of introduction it will be useful to give a brief résumé of the work, which consisted of experimental studies of aesthetic judgments and preferences by the methods of factorial analysis. First came tests, problems of the selection of pupils for art schools and the question of the existence of a general factor corresponding to the capacity for artistic training and the appreciation of art. This led to a fuller study and comparison of tests of aesthetic judgments by empirical methods, and to the discovery of a bipolar factor tending to divide aesthetic preferences, the persons making them, and therefore also kinds of art, into two classes corresponding to introverted and extraverted types of temperament. Literature and applied art were dealt with as well as pure pictorial art. An important question arose about the degree of universality of the general factor governing aesthetic preferences. Some workers, such as Eysenck, considered it truly universal, while others, like McElroy, feel convinced that the embodiment and expression of aesthetic taste and judgment are much influenced by racial and cultural differences. Questions about the psychological laws of pictorial composition were studied and hypotheses were tested experimentally, while factorial analysis of aesthetic qualities rather than of tests or persons yielded results of interest in respect of the psychological nature of art and of aesthetic responses. The whole series of factorial researches on aesthetic judgments forms an interesting development of the psychology of art, and the brief review of it to be given in the following pages will suggest further problems and lines of approach for the thoughtful reader.

EARLY TESTS AND THE GENERAL FACTOR

The studies to be discussed began with Burt's work on the selection of pupils for the London County Council Schools of Art, particularly St. Martin's School of Art in Charing Cross Road. The results of the tests he devised were reported in the Annual Reports of the London County Council Psychologist, but are no longer available and would not now be of any particular interest. The chief conclusion of the tests was evidence for the existence of a general factor of artistic ability. This Burt mentions as the fourth in his list of the special capacities which he set out as being well established, in the memorandum he was asked to draft for the Report of the Consultative Committee of the Board of Education on "Psychological Tests of Educable Capacity." This was published as Chapter I of the Report (Burt, 1924, p. 20), and was the first mention of such a factor.

Subsequently he was invited to start a Department for Vocational Guidance and Selection in the National Institute of

Industrial Psychology opened in London by C. S. Myers. His Assistant, Violet Pelling, was specially interested in the psychology of art, and they worked out a number of tests of artistic ability for people of an age slightly older than the children for whom his earlier tests had been designed. Of these he considers that the most useful was the "Picture Postcard Test" described in a chapter in "How the Mind Works," (Burt, 1933). In this very interesting chapter he reviews the whole problem of the psychology of art in a readable and philosophically insightful way, and it is well worth attention as an introduction to the subject.

The test in question was one in which the examinees were asked to rank certain picture postcards in order of preference. Free use was made of the method of factorizing correlations between persons in dealing with the results, a method up till then little or perhaps never used. This technique revealed bipolar factors for specific types of artistic appreciation, which seemed to be related to the temperamental differences between the subjects tested. This aspect of the whole problem was subsequently taken up by Eysenck. The main results of Burt and Pelling's work were summarized in the second part of a paper which he published in *Character and Personality* (Burt, 1939).

Work by Bulley, Dewar and Others

Burt had also worked with Margaret Bulley in Liverpool, as far back as 1910, and in London later they used series of paired designs which, for the purposes of a talk broadcast by him in 1933, were printed in *The Listener*. Views on the subject of the psychology of art judgment were invited from those who heard the broadcast, and a vast amount of material was collected, from all sorts and conditions of men and women, ranging from dock laborers to the Earl Russell. The test material included various types of applied art, such as furniture, dress materials, vases, china, and so on; and the experiments were described in *The Listener*, (Burt and Bulley, 1933). An account of this work is also given by Margaret Bulley in two publications (1933 and 1934); and, in her recent book, *Art and Everyman* (1951), she has included an interesting series of pairs of pictorial reproductions of artistic objects and materials which may be used as a test to measure the conformity of the subject's artistic taste with the standards she has adopted on general aesthetic grounds, which are fully explained in the book.

An elaborate factorial study of artistic tests was made by Heather Dewar, and in her report on this (Dewar, 1938), she says that four tests were used:—the Maier-Seashore test of Art Judgment; the McAdory test of appreciation of form, color and distribution of light and shade; an extended version of Burt and Bulley's tests used in the broadcast experiments; and a modified form of Burt and Pelling's Picture Postcard Test. A single general factor was revealed by statistical analysis, as being mainly responsible for the orders of preference given in the tests, and some evidence was found for specific factors, which were suggestive of types of artistic appreciation related to those previously described by Bullough (1908). Specific factors tended to be swamped by the general factor, and a small correlation was found between artistic appreciation and intelligence.

Amongst other devices the method of correlating persons and factorizing the resulting tables of intercorrelations was again used, and at first it evoked strong criticisms from Stephenson, who served as a subject in Dewar's tests, and tried out her test material on some extra-mural classes. He published the results of his experiments, together with those of other work, by way of illustrating what he called the 'Q-technique' of investigation (Dewar, 1938, p. 40, footnote 1). The highest of Dewar's reliability coefficients on a repetition of the tests was gained by the Picture Postcard Test as a group test in a private school, and it amounted to 0.93, which is very high for a test of this kind.

In 1938, E. D. Williams, L. Winter and J. M. Woods published a paper reporting studies of literary appreciation comparable with those of the appreciation of pictorial art just mentioned, (Williams, Winter and Woods, 1938). In this work they were able to show, in the appreciation of poetry, a general factor similar to that found by Burt, Pelling and Dewar, and a bipolar factor which contrasted romantic with classical styles of writing. From the comments made by subjects who took part in their research they claimed that, as age increases, appreciation becomes more and more dependent upon the "specific literary merits" of the poetry, and less and less upon its "irrelevant" features, in which they include emotional appeal and subject-matter. They add that the power of logical thinking is more important in the appreciation of literary than in that of the more concrete forms of art. If logical thinking were involved in literary appreciation, it is possible that the subject-matter might influence appreciation to some extent, and this was confirmed by Gunn (1951).

LAWS OF AESTHETIC COMPOSITION

Burt was interested in the laws of artistic composition as well as in the problem of the determination of the factors and testing of the capacities involved in appreciation. The laws of composition seemed to be very largely special applications of the laws of attention or of apperception. Speculations along these lines are to be found in his chapter on "The Psychology of Art" (Burt, 1933). J. B. Parry and H. J. Eysenck became interested in these problems, and Parry completed a thesis on the laws of artistic composition, as yet unpublished (Parry). In this work the general psychological theory of attention and of apperception in relation to art is considered, taking music into account as well as pictorial art, and numerous experiments are described in which sets of picture material were used. The method of factorial analysis of intercorrelations between persons was freely exploited.

Interesting work was also done by E. A. Peel (1945, 1946). He carried out a series of tests of which he selected two for discussion: the Landscapes Test and the Still-Life Test. The Landscapes Test consisted of 31 items of picture postcard size, being reproductions of landscapes by a wide variety of classical and modern artists. The Still-Life Test consisted of 31 varied water-color representations of a still-life subject composed of a coffee pot, a glass decanter, a cloth, a plate with cheese and tomatoes upon it and two books. Care was taken that the judgments on these items used in the statistical analysis should fall into line with an approximately normal distribution. Twelve persons, including art specialists and non-expert adults, arranged the items of these tests in order of liking. A team of art experts were also asked to arrange the items in accordance with certain criteria: for the Landscapes Test these criteria were detailed naturalism, composition and atmospheric light; for the Still-Life Test they were realism, technique and spontaneity. Study of the intercorrelations between the persons' orders of aesthetic preference and the selected criteria provided a basis for calculating the estimate of the persons' liking in terms of the artistic qualities of items, and for estimating factors characterizing the group of persons and the criteria. The results tended to emphasize the qualities of the work of art rather than the temperamental qualities of the person, but were complementary to those of earlier researches in which emphasis was placed on aesthetic types. Realism and technique overlapped to a large extent, and spontaneity was bipolar to both.

RACE, CULTURE AND THE GENERAL FACTOR

Eysenck took up the subject of aesthetic judgments and the study of the general and bipolar factors underlying them, and treated the whole matter with some thoroughness, (Eysenck, 1939, 1940, 1941a, 1941b, 1941c, 1942, 1948). It would hardly be possible in this short review to give a detailed account of his work in this field, but it may be said that he tried to meet Burt's own criticism of earlier work that a given picture in the Picture Postcard Test, for example, may have been placed in a position of higher preference than another simply because it had greater conventional value in a certain cultural environment, namely, in this case our own culture. He tried to use material for his researches which would be free from such "irrelevant associations." He required three essential conditions governing the selection of the material to be presented to the subject for ranking:—no traditional tendency should single out a given picture as superior to any other; no differences in clarity or representational accuracy should exist between the pictures in a given set; and the content of no picture should be more familiar to the subject than that of any other. He believed that he had established, by the analysis of the results of numerous experiments, that there is a general factor, which he called *"T,"* or the factor of "good taste," which is independent of age, sex, artistic sophistication, race or nationality. He also claimed to have established the existence of a bipolar factor which was a "type"-factor, called *"K,"* which divided the population into two groups, the one preferring modern, colorful, and the other preferring older and more formal kinds of art. The color-form test which he used appeared to be correlated with extraversion-introversion tests, and the functioning of the *K* factor was due in his view to the presence in the populations tested of these different types of temperament.

Eysenck clearly supports the interpretation of the general or good taste factor that it is due to the operation of "some fundamental biological" tendency which is determined innately, but, as W. A. McElroy has pointed out (1952), such an interpretation may be criticised on several counts. Eysenck did not include subjects from radically different racial stocks or patterns of culture. Anthropologists, however, report widely differing standards of aesthetic taste in various groups, as we see in the change from European to Asiatic or African traditional art, or in that from the representational accuracy of traditional academic painting in Europe in the nineteenth century to the work of the Impressionists, Post-Impressionists, Surrealists and others. Oriental art is often unsatisfying aesthetically for European judges. Nevertheless, the general factor might be expressed in the tendency which operates in respect of whatever artistic material happens to be culturally established in a given group. The essence of beauty does not lie in the characteristics of any one of its particular manifestations, any more than the essence of morality lies in a particular type of behavior as such. This interpretation of the general factor, however, would probably not be acceptable to Eysenck.

In a very well-planned and executed series of experiments, McElroy (1952) tested aborigines of Arnhem Land in Australia and also Australian Whites in Sydney, with ten art judgment tests in each of which the subjects were asked to arrange sets of pictures in order of aesthetic preference. The material was chosen carefully to accord with Eysenck's fundamental requirements. Statistical analysis of the data showed little or no evidence of the existence of a general factor representing interracial "good taste," based on inherited predispositions. There was, however, much evidence in favor of the view that the aesthetic valuation of visually presented objects is almost entirely determined by the cultural conditioning of perception. It is evident that many more experiments should be done in order to compare the aesthetic judgments of different cultural and racial groups about the same sets of material, and also in order to compare the judgments of the same groups about works of art of different origin and period. Miss Aydin Cancardas, who is working in Istanbul, has been using some of Burt's tests to demonstrate the differences between the aesthetic judgments of peoples of different cultures and racial stocks.

ANALYSIS OF AESTHETIC QUALITIES

In a closely related group of researches Pickford (1948, 1948a), and others took up the problem of the factorial analysis of intercorrelations between aesthetic qualities rather than between subjects or tests. The qualities chosen were usually such attributes as liking, representational accuracy, emotional expressiveness, harmony of design, and sentimentality. Sets of pictures were rated on a five- or seven-point scale, or ranked in order for these and other qualities, by various groups of subjects. The analysis of the intercorrelation tables tended to show in every experiment the existence of a large general factor which was usually dominated by emotional expressiveness and by harmony of design. This was called the "aesthetic" factor because it showed the fundamental nature of aesthetic judgments from a psychological point of view. Art was good if it successfully manipulated feeling and design in an integrated way. In the analyses there followed a bipolar factor, usually dividing the qualities into contrasted groups such as rhythm, sentimentality and representational accuracy on the one hand and impressionistic effect, colorfulness and expressive distortion on the other. This was called the "technical" factor, because it showed contrasted modes of handling of the essential aesthetic problems. Experiments with recorded music, which Dorothy Lawson carried out with the help of P. E. Vernon and the writer, gave the same kind of result (Pickford, 1948).

EXPERIMENTS WITH ACTUAL ART WORKS

Since most of the work on pictorial appreciation hitherto reported had been carried out with postcards and small-sized or sometimes larger reproductions, Pickford, (1948), arranged to take a group of students to an art exhibition in Glasgow and to make ratings for a selected set of the actual pictures in the exhibition. This experiment confirmed the earlier results, and met to some extent the criticisms of people who considered that some experiments had been vitiated by the inadequacy of small reproductions of the original works of art. An experiment was also carried out with a representative selection of 22 of the works of van Gogh in the Exhibition of his paintings held in the Kelvingrove Art Gallery, Glasgow, in 1948, and it was hoped that this would be the first of a series of similar experiments with the works of individual artists. It was found that the general factor was most heavily loaded with emotional expressiveness, harmony of design, harmony of coloring and dynamic expression. The first bipolar (or second) factor sharply contrasted expressive distortion, harmony of coloring, emotional expressiveness, and dynamic expression against photographic accuracy, impressionistic effect and liking by the subject. There was a second bipolar (or third) factor, which contrasted photographic accuracy and harmony of design with expressive distortion and impressionistic effect.

These experiments with actual pictures were done with the kind permission of Dr. T. J. Honeyman, then Director of the Glasgow Art Galleries, and a further experiment by McElroy (1950a, 1950b) was also carried out with his permission. In this last the responses to modern and to traditional sculpture of groups of school children were studied in the "Sculpture in the Open Air" Exhibition in the Kelvingrove Park, Glasgow, in 1949. The primary aim of this research was to discover whether there was any relationship between the hedonic tone of a piece of sculpture and its readiness of recall. A secondary aim was to analyse and classify the verbal responses made by the children to the sculptures, and a third aim was to factorize a matrix of intercorrelations between nine aesthetic qualities of the pieces of sculpture. In general, pleasant items were recalled more readily than unpleasant ones. The analysis of verbal responses gave no less than twelve different types, which need not be detailed here. In the factorial analysis a large general factor appeared, which probably corresponded to Burt's general factor, although three of the qualities had negative loadings: distortion, abstraction and vagueness, which were particularly characteristic of modern sculptures. McElroy says that these qualities were probably so strong in modern sculptures that they rendered the works less meaningful, and masked other aesthetic qualities. Factorizing intercorrelations between sculptures supported this, and it seems that some modern works appeal to aesthetic good taste only after the adoption of a mental set different from that usually adopted by the viewer. This again supports the doubts about the universality of the general factor of good taste.

EXPERIMENTS WITH POETRY

Following up the work of Williams, Winter and Woods, and that of Pickford, D. G. Gunn, (1951, 1952), carried out an experiment on the factorial analysis of aesthetic qualities in the appreciation of poetry, by three Forms of schoolboys and a Class of University students. The results for each group were treated separately and compared. In general the factorial analysis supported the previous findings of a general or aesthetic factor, here dominated by emotional effect, mode of expression, and appeal of the subject-matter, and a bipolar technical factor which contrasted rhyme, word music, and rhythm with emotional effect, appeal of the subject-matter, comprehension and mental imagery. It is probable that the aesthetic and technical factors in these experiments are complementary throughout to the general and bipolar factors of Burt, Pelling, Dewar, and others, since they deal with aesthetic qualities rather than with persons' judgments.

CONCLUSION

In conclusion, it is evident that a very interesting series of experiments on the psychology of art were initiated by Burt's original work. Further studies of aesthetic judgments and qualities by similar methods should be carried out, most particularly in order to discover how much variety and conformity of aesthetic judgments exists the world over, among different races and cultures, and between various types and styles of artistic product, wherever possible using the actual aesthetic objects rather than reproductions.

The value of researches of this kind might be said to lie in the fact that they enable us to draw conclusions from empirical data, but this would ordinarily be taken to mean that the methods used are contrasted with methods which enable us to draw conclusions from pure theories or from allegedly authoritative sources. Many modern art critics, however, would say that they do base their judgments on empirical data, namely the paintings or works of art which they actually study at first hand. The contrast lies therefore not between what is empirical and what is nonempirical, but rather between relatively objective methods of analysis as contrasted with subjective, individual or impressionistic inferences. The estimates used in these researches are based on the observations of many people, instead of being individual impressions of a single critic, and this applies even where the judgments of experts have been used to set up criteria.

Finally it may be said that it is now well established that there is a general factor of aesthetic capacity, which is educable and leads to uniformity of artistic productions and valuations within cultural patterns and groups. It is not likely that the general factor would lead rigidly to interracial and intercultural uniformities, any more than the existence of a general principle of morality in human social life leads to absolute uniformity of moral behavior. The general aesthetic factor usually involves the presence in artistic works of emotional expressiveness with harmony of form, design and coloring as its main influence. The laws of composition and form in pictorial and other arts and music are expressions of the psychological principles underlying attention, perception and apperception. In addition to the general factor, all kinds of pictorial art, music, and literature studied reveal a bipolar factor. This contrasts the more colorful, emotionally expressive, impressionistic or expressively distorted kinds of art with those which are more subdued, more accurate in representation and less colorful. The first group are generally liked by extraverted and the second group by introverted people, and often the contrast lies between the more modern and less modern, or between the romantic and the classical in artistic productions and in aesthetic attitudes and valuations.

FOOTNOTE

* The writer is grateful to Professor Burt for the generous help he gave with this chapter, and for the notes he supplied about the early phases of the work.

REFERENCES

Barwell, J. S. The Nature of Ugliness. *Brit. J. Med. Psychol.*, 1937, *17*, 119-127.
Bulley, M. *Have You Good Taste?* London: Methuen, 1933.

——An Inquiry into Aesthetic Judgments of Children. *Brit. Educ. Psychol.,* 1934, *4,* 162-182.

——*Art and Everyman.* London: Batsford, 1951.

Bullough, E. The Perceptive Problem in the Aesthetic Appreciation of Single Colours. *Brit. J. Psychol.,* 1908, *2,* 406-468.

——Psychical Distance. *Brit. J. Psychol.,* 1912, *5,* 87.

——The Relation of Aesthetics to Psychology. *Brit. J. Psychol.,* 1919a, *10,* 43-50.

——Mind and Medium in Art. *Brit. J. Psychol.,* 1919b, *11,* 26-46.

——Recent Work in Experimental Aesthetics. *Brit. J. Psychol.,* 1921, *12,* 76-99.

Burt, C. Psychological Tests of Educable Capacity, Chapter I in *Report of the Consultative Committee of the Board of Education,* London, 1924.

——The Psychology of Art, Chapter 15 in *How the Mind Works,* Ed. by Cyril Burt. London: Allen and Unwin, 1933.

——The Factorial Analysis of Emotional Traits. *Character and Personality,* 1939, *7,* especially pp. 291-299.

Burt, C. and M. Bulley. *The Listener,* B. B. C., *London; 9*; 8th. Jan., 8th. Feb. and 27th Dec. 1933.

Dewar, H. A Comparison of Tests of Aesthetic Appreciation. *Brit. J. Educ. Psychol.,* 1938, *8,* 29-49.

Eysenck, H. J. The Validity of Judgments as a Function of the Number of Judges. *J. Exp. Psychol.,* 1939, *25,* 650.

——The General Factor in Aesthetic Judgements. *Brit. J. Psychol.,* 1940, *31,* 94-102.

——'Type'-Factors in Aesthetic Judgements. *Brit. J. Psychol.,* 1941a, *31,* 262-270.

——A Critical and Experimental Study of Color Preferences. *Amer. J. Psychol.,* 1941b, *54,* 383.

——The Empirical Determination of an Aesthetic Formula. *Psychol. Rev.,* 1941c, *48,* 83.

——The Experimental Study of "Good Gestalt". *Psychol. Rev.,* 1942, *49,* 344.

——*The Dimensions of Personality.* London: Routledge and Kegan Paul, 1948, 202-205.

Fairbairn, W. R. D. Prolegomena to a Psychology of Art. *Brit. J. Psychol.,* 1938a, *28,* 288-303.

——The Ultimate Basis of Aesthetic Experience. *Brit. J. Psychol.,* 1938b, *29,* 167.

Freud, S. *Leonardo da Vinci.* New York: Dodd, Mead, 1932.

Gunn, D. G. Factors in the Appreciation of Poetry. *Brit. J. Educ. Psychol.,* 1951, *21,* 96-104.

——Further Observations on Factors in the Appreciation of Poetry. *Quart. Bull. Brit. Psychol. Soc.,* 1952, *3, 15,* 24-26.

Guttmann, E. and Maclay, W. W. Clinical Observations on Schizophrenic Drawings. *Brit. J. Psychol.,* 1937, *16,* 184-205.

——Mescalin Hallucinations in Artists. *Arch. Neurol. Psychiat.,* 1941, *45,* 130.

Guttmann, E., W. W. Maclay and W. Mayer-Gross. Spontaneous Drawings as an Approach to Some Problems in Psychopathology. *Proc. Roy. Soc. Med.,* 1937, *31,* 1337-1350.

Harding, R. E. M. *An Anatomy of Inspiration.* Cambridge: Heffer, 2nd Ed., 1942.

Huisman, D. *L'Esthétique.* Paris: P. V. F., 1954.

Jones, E. *Essays on Applied Psycho-Analysis.* London: Hogarth, 1923.

Kris, E. *Psychoanalytic Explorations in Art.* London: Allen and Unwin, 1953.

Langfeld, H. S. *The Aesthetic Attitude.* New York: Harcourt Brace, 1920.

Lindsey, D. *The Psychological Factors involved in Aesthetic Reactions to Form.* Ph.D. Thesis, Liverpool University, 1953 (unpublished).

Lowenfeld, V. *The Nature of Creative Activity.* London: Kegan Paul, 1939.

Macquisten, A. S., and R. W. Pickford. The Fantasy of Snow White and the Seven Dwarfs. *Psychoanalytic Rev.,* 1942, 29, 233-252.

McElroy, W. A. Responses to Traditional and Modern Sculpture, and the Factors Influencing its Recall. *Quart. Bull. Brit. Psychol. Soc.,* 1950a, *1, 8,* 310-331.

——The Appreciation of Sculpture. *Scottish Art Rev.,* 1950b, *3, 2,* 11-15.

——Aesthetic Appreciation of Aborigines of Arnhem Land: A Comparative and Experimental Study. *Oceania,* 1952, *23, 2,* 81-94.

McIntosh, J. R. and R. W. Pickford. Some Clinical and Artistic Aspects of a Child's Drawings. *Brit. J. Med. Psychol.,* 1943, *19,* 342-362.

Myers, C. S. *An Introduction to Experimental Psychology.* Cambridge U. P., 3rd Ed., 1925.

Oldham, H. W. *Child Expression in Colour and Form.* London: The Bodley Head, 1940.

Parry, J. B. *The Role of Attention in Aesthetic Experience.* Ph.D. Thesis, University College, London, (unpublished).

Peel, E. A. On Identifying Aesthetic Types. *Brit. J. Psychol.,* 1945, *35,* 61-69.

——A New Method for Analyzing Aesthetic Preferences: Some Theoretical Considerations. *Psychometrika,* 1948, *11, 2,* 129-137.

Pickford, R. W. Some Interpretations of a Painting Called 'Abstraction'. *Brit. J. Med. Psychol.,* 1939, *18,* 219-249.

——Rossetti's 'Sudden Light' as an Experience of Déjà Vu. *Brit. J. Med. Psychol.,* 1942, *19,* 192-200.

——The Psychology of Cultural Change in Painting. *Brit. J. Psychol. Monog. Supp.,* 1943, No. 26.

——'Aesthetic' and 'Technical' Factors in Artistic Appreciation. *Brit. J. Psychol.,* 1948, *38,* 135-144.

——Form and Expression in Art. *Scottish Art Rev.,* 1948a, *2, 1,* 7-11.

——*An Experiment with van Gogh's Paintings* (unpublished), 1954.

Reitman, F. *Psychotic Art.* London: Routledge and Kegan Paul, 1950.

——*Insanity, Art and Culture.* Bristol: Wright, 1954.

Révész, G. *Psychology and Art of the Blind.* London: Longmans, 1950.

——*Introduction to the Psychology of Music.* London: Longmans, 1953.

Rickman, J. On the Nature of Ugliness and the Creative Impulse. *Int. J. Psycho-Anal.,* 1940, 22.

——The Nature of Ugliness and the Creative Impulse. *Int. J. Psycho-Anal.,* 1948, *29.*

Sharpe, E. *Collected Papers on Psycho-Analysis.* London: Hogarth, 1950.

Spearman, C. *Creative Mind.* London: Nisbet, and Cambridge U. P., 1930.

Stapleton, J. H. *A Study of the Significance of Color and Form in Neurotic Patients' Free Paintings and Drawings.* M. A. Thesis, Bristol University, 1953 (unpublished).

Valentine, C. W. *An Introduction to the Experimental Psychology of Beauty.* London: Jack, 1922.

Viola, W. *Child Art.* London: U. P., 1942.

Williams, E. D., L. Winter and J. M. Woods. Tests of Literary Appreciation. *Brit. J. Educ. Psychol.*, 1938, *8*, 265-284.

CHAPTER XXXVIII

PSYCHOLOGY OF ART

H. G. SCHRICKEL, Ph.D.

Assistant Professor of Psychology, University of Nebraska

EDITORIAL NOTE

The psychology of art has not received its rightful place in psychology. It is often thought to be synonymous with aesthetics and relegated to philosophy. While there are many courses in the various branches of psychology (abnormal, social, comparative, etc.) on the curriculum of most colleges, the psychology of art is still regarded as a luxury; and the number of textbooks on the subject are few and far between. The consequence is that the average student graduates from college sophisticated in clinical psychology or social psychology but blissfully ignorant of the principles of art psychology, although as an appreciator of paintings, sculpture, music, the theatre and dance, he should definitely know something about their motivation and psychological interrelations.

Dr. H. G. Schrickel has gone into some of the salient issues involved without, however, spreading out. An adequate chapter on this subject would require a good deal more space than a comprehensive volume can afford.

While Dr. Schrickel has not devoted himself exclusively to this field, he has accomplished much here, as is evidenced by the fact that at one time he was lecturer in musicology at the Cincinnati Conservatory of Music and was co-editor of an encyclopedia of the Arts, as well as Managing Editor of the Journal of Aesthetics and Art Criticism. *He is also co-author of* Understanding the World *and* Personality: Development and Assessment. *After teaching at the University of Cincinnati, Carnegie Institute of Technology, and Brooklyn College, he was awarded a Faculty Fellowship on the Foundation for the Advancement of Education at Harvard University. He is at present on the Faculty of the University of Nebraska.*

PRESENT-DAY PSYCHOLOGY

Sources

In 1876 Fechner published his *Vorschule der Aesthetik*. This event is generally regarded as marking the beginning of modern experimental aesthetics. The history of this field of inquiry up to 1935 has been competently recorded by Chandler.[3] An excellent survey of psychological aesthetics in Austria, Italy and Germany up to 1935 is to be found in Munro.[10] More inclusive but philosophically oriented is the work of Gilbert and Kuhn[5] which begins with the ancient Greeks. For the growth of psychology of art since 1935 the best single reference is the article by Morgan[9] in the *Journal of Aesthetics and Art Criticism* where also one may find annual bibliographies of current articles on art criticism and general aesthetics. Less frequent but important references are also to be found in *Psychological Abstracts*. The sources cited provide extensive bibliographies. In brief, what has been done in psychology of art has been adequately recorded although there is much which has not yet been translated into English; a fact which accounts *in part* for the almost total ignoring of European research in this area by American psychologists.

Types of Approach

Study of available sources reveals that modern psychology of art began in the psychophysical laboratory. Here an abstractly simple subject-matter was investigated in a manner more to satisfy what has become almost a compulsion to quantify than to develop an adequate understanding of aesthetic processes. Although some investigators such as R. M. Ogden[11] and Max Dessoir[4]—as well as others—have soundly criticized this premature urge to mathematize the aesthetic, the need persists among many American psychologists of art, especially those of "behavioristic" and "neo-behavioristic" theoretical persuasion. Parallel with the laboratory approach during these early years were numerous writings which sought to explain artistic and appreciative activities in terms of play, empathy, or psychical distance.

As Morgan points out, these three once central ideas no longer play an effective rôle in most aesthetic theorizing today. He suggests that in addition to the continuing experimental (now "behavioristic") tradition there are at least two other movements going on in America, England and Italy. One of these is the *psychoanalytic,* which draws from a tradition including Plato, Schopenhauer and Nietzsche, as well as Freud. Perhaps Charles Baudouin[2] and Harry B. Lee[7] have formulated as well as any the central ideas in this approach. The former is concerned primarily with the psychoanalytic aspects of appreciation, while the latter uses clinical materials and symbolic interpretations of art works with a view toward understanding artistic creation and differential aesthetic responses. The need for symbolic expression of conscious and unconscious needs (some erotic) is the central idea of the psychoanalytic approach.

The Gestaltists, on the other hand, regard as central the perceptual organizing processes (fundamentally neural) which tend to produce patterns or wholes; these processes are used to account for both creative and appreciative aesthetic activities. Arnheim[1] has presented the Gestaltist point of view with suggestions for an extension of the concept of equilibrium to account for artistic motivation. Excellent applications of Gestaltist analysis to specific works of art are to be found in Pepper.[12]

EVALUATION

Only superficial examination of these views would permit the suggestion that each complements the other, that if all is not well in psychology of art today it will be so soon; that together these developments constitute the beginnings and sufficient conditions of what will eventually become a fundamentally adequate science of the aesthetic. Leaving matters to history has always been an easy solution and one which would readily be adopted in this instance by the many American psychologists who have shown little or no inclination to investigate aesthetic problems. It would be more accurate to say that in at least one respect psychology of art has been one of the many victims of the overspecialization which has taken hold of psychology as a science. Growing recognition that this fragmentation has gone far enough is evidenced in new types of research which cross over the traditional fields of inquiry. Perceptual and motivational processes, learning and socialization are being viewed as they actually occur, inextricably interwoven and interrelated with personality systems—themselves functioning in social and cultural systems. Old barriers between research areas, too long taken consciously and unconsciously as based on material differences are now being seen for what they really are: methodological conveniences to be or not be employed as dictated by the problems under investigation. These new areas of research implicating all the fields of psychology as well as psychiatry, cultural anthropology, sociology and semiotics are developing new concepts and orientations and methods appropriate to their implementation in research. Stimulus-response ideology is seen to be as inappropriate to these new research areas as the classical mechanics theory which inspired it is inadequate to current investigations in nuclear physics. Kluckhohn, the anthropologist, voices this view when he says, "Our studies have convinced us beyond question that the basic model upon which the behaviorists and positivists and many others have acted in the past—the model of common sense—is inadequate . . . Human beings always react to stimuli as interpreted, not to the stimuli as they exist in the external world." ("The special character of integration in an individual culture," *Main Currents in Modern Thought*, 1950, vol. 7, No. 4, 102-107). The implications of these and similar critical observations on theory and methods in current psychological science constitute a large area of concern within the philosophy of science, an area which can only be hinted at here. For present purposes it is enough to note that crucial years are ahead for psychology as a science; that, involved in and contributory to these developments, could be a new psychology of art based upon the concepts and methods emerging from current interdisciplinary research.

Admittedly, accomplishment has been relatively meager in psychology of art. Some of the methodological and theoretical reasons for this have been very briefly suggested. Other factors working against the development of a psychology of the aesthetic are not difficult to discern. What psychologists of art have done in the past has too frequently antagonized the very individuals with whom they need to work in the closest coöperation; viz., artists and aestheticians. The rush to quantify, to measure before achieving adequate sophistication regarding the qualitative complexity of their subject matter, has led to a kind of brashness in art psychologists which, even if unintended, has strained their relations with those in the arts upon whom they must depend for so much. Friendly coöperation will have to be developed. Again, psychology today centers in the United States where aesthetic values play a minor rôle in the life-way provided by the culture pattern. And unfortunately, in some respects, psychologists have tended to restrict themselves to those processes and events which dominate the American scene. Thus, learning psychology has strongly emphasized the learning of instrumental acts and values because of the plentitude of such processes in our highly competitive society. The scientific explication of learning of ends has yet to be done. When one considers that the learning of aesthetic values is preëminently a learning of ends and of end-activities, it is not difficult to see why American learning psychology has contributed so little to our understanding of the aesthetic. Further, there are numerous instances today wherein the arts are running ahead of the appreciative capabilities of a great many people—just as theoretical physics has gone beyond the ken of many relatively well-educated persons. And where there is no significant experience one cannot begin a scientific investigation. These are only a few of the possible reasons for the unsatisfactory state of psychology of art today. Now let us consider some of the implications of what has been said regarding the development of a more adequate psychology of art.

PRESENT-DAY PSYCHOLOGY

A New Approach

It is now clear that the early modern psychologists of art who carried on their investigations in terms of an anonymous sensing subject responding to isolated colors and tones were dealing with an abstractly simplified subject matter in order to conform to the demands of a pseudo-physical methodology. It is to be expected that their findings often turned out to be irrelevant and inconsequential to an understanding of aesthetic processes. Such processes occur in their most fully developed forms in individual personalities living in and interacting with the particular societies and cultures in which they are participants. Further, to the degree that aesthetic processes are functions of personality dynamics in society and culture they are also semiotic (sign and symbol) processes. The basic concepts of the psychologist of art, the fundamental ideas in his central frame of reference, must be *personality, society, culture,* and *semiotic* rather than sense datum and stimulus. The psychologist of art will draw upon the growing sciences of personality, of unified social and humanistic studies, and of a general semiotics. [14] Rather than wait upon the full development of these interdisciplinary forms of research he would do well to pose his own problems, develop his own theory and methods, and thus contribute to the growth of integrated social and humanistic research. What are some of these problems which heretofore have received practically no attention?

Some Problem Areas

At least three fundamental problem areas for psychology of art are suggested by the approach outlined above: the personality dynamics of the artist with special reference to his aesthetic creative processes; the nature of the psychological processes involved in the aesthetic enjoyment of the individual appreciator; and the rôle of the arts in society and culture. These three areas overlap and between them they do not exhaust the field of inquiry.

937

Regarding the first we need to know more about the personal and social motivation of the artist. The artist, as he has been more or less abstractly considered by past psychologists of art, is remote from what most artists actually are in our time—the more or less commercial artists who fit into the interstices of our economic life as best they can. They do what they are hired to do, what will pay their employers to pay them, because it provides what the public wants. And the public wants art to relieve it of the fear and anxiety that burden modern existence.[13] Thus, we should inquire about the status personality as well as about the personal dynamics of an individual artist; and such inquiry should view the artist as participant in his society and culture.

Only by means of such an approach can we hope to understand better the personal and socio-cultural factors involved in aesthetic creativity and in such matters as style. What *rôles* does an artist play in our time and how does he manage these while being an artist? What cognitive (factual) and valuative judgments does the artist share with members of his cultural and subcultural groups and how do these function in his artistic activities? Very frequently it has been said that the artist expresses himself, communicates with others. By what sign and symbol processes does he achieve these results and what are the relations of these artistic semiotic events to other communicative processes in his particular society and culture? If the artist communicates, *what* does he communicate? Is he duplicating what is communicated in the culture by other media?

The enjoyment of something for its own sake is the generically aesthetic. Forms of play in early life, before socialization has had a good start, have some of the characteristics of such enjoyment. Becoming a human being involves among other things the learning of ever more subtle and more varied forms of aesthetic sensitivity and subsequent enjoyment. What is the psychology of this development of taste? How do aesthetic appreciative processes function in the adjustive and integrative behavior and experience of the individual personality in his particular socio-cultural environment? Where do aesthetic values fall in the distinctive value patterns of different basic personality types and of individuals? What differences exist in aesthetic value orientation between individuals and their cultures? What are the loci of aesthetic satisfactions or reinforcements? Which personality factors are most determinative of the range and intensity of aesthetic enjoyments? Are these determinative factors the same for all cultures?

In the third area suggested investigation becomes most broadly cultural but nonetheless psychological in nature. Malraux's recent work[18] and that of Kallen[6] are written from a perspective broad enough for this type of inquiry but their observations too frequently do not lend themselves to scientific research design. Chief concern in this problem area is with inter-and intra-cultural and individual aesthetic values and the relations of these to each other. Typical questions are: What values (moral, religious, epistemic—as well as aesthetic) of the particular culture are conveyed to and preserved for its members by what art media? Or, how does society employ the arts to socialize its members and perpetuate its culture? Here intercultural analyses of aesthetic experiences and behavior are also undertaken. Intra-cultural investigation would include studies of the aesthetic as employed in educational practices, advertising and propaganda as means to essentially non-aesthetic ends. Also, are there particular classbound aesthetic values and are these comparable from culture to culture? But again, only intimations can be given regarding a host of problems which have not heretofore been subjected to scientifically oriented study.

THE ARTIST TODAY

Every culture, in its simplest terms, is a way of life. Since the eighteenth century we have been developing a culture in which natural science has been intellectually preëminent and in which an industrialized technology has increasingly monopolized the waking hours of ever larger numbers of individuals. Our way of life has developed in such manner as to relegate to lesser and lesser significance the artist and his works. Certainly this rôle of the artist and his works must be investigated by any psychology of art seeking understanding of aesthetic values as they occur in our time. In a very important sense we need to study the status personality of the artist, what rôles are expected of him, and to what degree his living these rôles affects his creative activities. From culture study we thus move to examination of personality processes and their interrelations in the particular artist. Too frequently in the past psychologists of art have entered into such personality studies with the current popular evaluation of the artist and his works as different in some radical ways from other human beings and their activities. Fundamentally, all men are involved in the processes of interpreting and transforming their environment with the view toward increasing their freedom and happiness. In this sense the artist and the next man are the same person, though called by different names according to the field they work in, the kind of materials and tools they use, and the sort of problems they prefer. Happily, in art the promotion and celebration of ends become fused; means and ends become the same throughout. In this the psychology of the artist's personality could give cues to all of us on how to achieve that integration and fullness of living which we hint at in our vague conceivings of happiness.

ART AND SCIENCE

The more conspicuous interpretations and transformations of experience made by scientists and artists focalize in a quest for more significant form; they seek to understand and to cultivate the order and significance which give more form to life and more life to form. But this is what all men do within the limitations of their potentialities and the economic and social restrictions that are set upon them by their culture. Thus, while it would be well for psychologists of art to orient their inquiry in terms of the unique personality dynamics of the particular artist it is equally advisable that they regard the aesthetic as universal, natural and fundamental to human adjustive and integrative behavior and experience. Viewed this way, the aesthetic ceases to be regarded as the functioning of special talents and dynamisms restricted to a few and becomes instead one of the criteria of humanness.

Centuries ago, Plato said in effect that we must seek conceptions that will carve reality at its joints. Both scientists and artists, each in their various ways, do this most consciously and most conspicuously. There are, however, some basic differences in the conceivings of scientists and artists. Whereas both begin with the common sense interpretations of experience current in their day, the former soon depart from this type of experience to a realm of postulated forms, relations and entities which they hope will, in their abstraction from the concrete, be adequate to describing specific universes of phenomena. The scientist uses discursive types of symbolism—technical languages, including mathematics—to symbolize the significant forms he finds in what Northrop (*The Logic of the Sciences and the Humanities,* 1947) has called the "theoretic component" of reality. The artist, on the other hand, begins with the common sense world but conceptualizes only that within it which is immediately apprehendable. He creates objects which will more adequately embody and infuse the forms which he has developed out of immediate apprehension. His forms are sensuous both in intuition and execution; the artist's meanings are intrinsic to his experience and to the experience of the capable appreciator of the art object which the artist produces.

The significant forms of aesthetic experience are understood only in terms of the immediately apprehended which they inform. Such aesthetically informed experiences cannot literally be symbolized by discursive symbols or languages but must be signified by the presentational types of symbolism which characterize the various forms of art. Thus, while it may eventually be possible to speak of the "language of art" to the degree that the presentational symbols which constitute the arts occur in some type of order or system, we cannot understand by "language" in this phrase what we mean when we refer to presently known systems of discursive symbols as languages.

These differences in *what* science and art symbolize and in *how* they symbolize must not be lost sight of. It is the main reason why art criticism and commentary can only suggest in discursive symbolism what is only adequately symbolized by the presentational symbolism of the particular art involved. In short, we can at best roughly correlate the forms of science with those of art. Such occurs when an artist conveys analogically by means of immediately experienceable materials, the postulated, non-sensous, theoretic component of reality which is literally expressible only in the technical language of science. What is important to note, however, is that the aesthetic component of reality—its sensed-felt aspect which is the concern of the artist, and the theoretic component of reality which occupies the scientist, are never identical and each yields forms which are basic to human understanding yet irreducible to each other. Without one or the other the understanding of life is incomplete, unbalanced and poor.

ART AND SIGNS

Such considerations as these show us that the psychologist of art must needs concern himself with meanings, with signs and symbols, with semiotics. The significant form or meaning of an art object as symbol is not primarily referential or indexical. As an aesthetic symbol the adequacy of the art object must be judged in terms of the degree to which it facilitates self-contained, intrinsically significant perception. This is the primary function of art: to render sensuously by colors, tones, textures and other media of the arts, meanings which cannot be signified by such discursive symbolisms as language and mathematics. There is nothing mystical in this. We all experience feelings, tensions, subtle sensations and ideas which we cannot adequately verbalize but recognize as symbolized in a musical composition, a painting, or piece of sculpture. In fact, it is to the arts that men have long gone to learn what it means really to live, to strive, to love, to die. But the creative artist who is free does more than symbolize the significance of unspeakable actualities. He frees his fellow men to pursue ideal possibilities which he alone can suggest via the symbols he creates. The psychologist of art has yet to realize fully the implications of such facts. He has yet to devise techniques for studying the non-discursive logic of artistic symbolism, of the creative artist's ways of conceptualizing experience—his ways of carving reality at its joints.

AESTHETIC ENJOYMENT

Turning now to consideration of the appreciator other problems are suggested by the newly oriented psychology of art. Quite simply, the enjoyment of something for its own sake may be taken as the generically aesthetic. Becoming a human being involves among other things the learning of ever more subtle and more varied forms of aesthetic sensitivity and enjoyment. What is the psychology of this development of taste? How is it related to the emerging modes of satisfaction in phylogenesis of the species and in ontogenesis of the individual human being? While it may be said that the most developed forms of the aesthetic are possible only as symbolistic activities emerge, the aesthetic also involves processes more characteristic of lower levels of living. To understand aesthetic enjoyment we need to apply semiotic analysis, but we need also to apply whatever we find useful to our purposes in these studies which investigate the lower levels; e.g., psychosomatics. At so complex a level as personality-in-culture, determination of the point at which any kind of satisfaction occurs—or what the psychologist would call "the locus of reinforcement"—becomes extremely difficult. For example, at what point on the various levels of the dynamic-structural evolution does food become satisfying? At sight? In the mouth? In the stomach? In the cells of the body? And in the last case, are we in any way conscious of cellular satisfaction? The raising of similar questions regarding the locus of reinforcement in aesthetic enjoyment should dispel once and for all any notions of completely understanding such experiences through semiotic analysis alone. What is involved in answering such questions is nothing less than a unified socio-humanistic science. But again, it should be pointed out that such a science will not adequately develop without the contributions of a growing psychology of art. Let us not fall into a misconception analogous to that held by some psychologists to the effect that their science must wait upon the perfection of neurophysiology.

METHODOLOGY

The suggestions presented here are hardly a basis for recommending a systematic methodology for psychology of art; the theoretical orientation will have to be worked out in greater detail first. As Darwin once observed, there is nothing so foolish as entering a laboratory to perform an experiment just for the sake of performing an experiment. To develop such a methodology, one might be tempted to exploit existing techniques used for other purposes. Rorschach ink blots, for example, ordinarily used in psychodiagnostics, present intriguing possibilities to an aesthetician interested in various form-color perceptual processes. The open-end type of interview offers a possible approach to new techniques of assessing aesthetic sensitivity. The method of content-analysis developed by White (*Value Analysis: The Nature and Use of the Method,* 1951) for the study of values might be applied to the literature of art criticism and aesthetics. Cross-cultural methods of the Yale group and techniques being developed by the Social Relations group at Harvard in their study of values in various cultures might be adaptable to the purposes of the psychologists of art. It seems more likely, however, that some radical departures in methodology will be necessary to develop techniques adequate to the problems posed by the theoretical reorientation we have suggested. It is also more likely that these new techniques will be primarily, but not exclusively, intensive rather than extensive, more personality-oriented than statistically collective of data regarding anonymous "subjects," qualitative rather than quantitative, more unstructured than structured in research design, more frequently of the field than of the laboratory.

CURRENT EXPERIMENTS

In line with the general problem of developing new techniques it might be in order to report briefly on some experimentation currently under way. Not too long ago there came to the writer's attention the work of B. J. Kouwer (*Colors and Their Character*, 1949) in the Netherlands dealing with word-color relationships. His results interested me but it was the possibilities I saw in his technique which instigated the present study. He had his subjects sort a number of word-cards into slots labeled with color-names. The sorting was urged to a fast tempo so that the subjects had little opportunity to treat the task as a rational problem but had to choose impulsively. Also, once a card was dropped into a slot it could not be recovered for reconsideration. Using a similar technique with ten slots labeled yellow, orange, red, purple, blue, green, brown, white, black and gray, Mr. Eugene Gloye, one of my graduate students, had 25 subjects sort out 159 cards bearing various words, placing each word with the most appropriate color available. It was made clear to the subjects that they had complete freedom of choice, that this was not a "test" in any sense, and that they need only sort the words as quickly as possible. Included were such words as: action, death, defeat, goodness, passion, soul, religion, festivity, jealousy, morals, crime, faith and others. After the sorting is finished the subject is asked to express in order his preferences regarding the ten colors. He is then asked to select from several color samples of each color that one which is closest to his own image of a color as elicited by its name. The next step consists in confronting the subject with the word-cards he has selected for each color, asking him in each case to comment on his choices. It is at this point that many subjects are stimulated to respond orally and otherwise in ways that are quite revealing of thoughts and feelings which under most circumstances are relatively inaccessible.

There are some points that should be made regarding this investigation. It started out as an inquiry into the validity of certain traditional assertions regarding the expressive significance of colors. As the project went on some depth materials became available which gave some insight into the personality dynamics of the subjects. A traditionally-oriented experimental psychologist would more frequently than not ignore such materials as irrelevant to the problem at hand. It is my suggestion that such personality data are of first-order relevance; that color meanings are something more personal than conventions; that the psychologist of art must therefore be a personality psychologist rather than a student of laboratory-isolated variables. Support for such views is to be found in such a situation as has been briefly described. There are undoubtedly similar situations occurring every day; instances where techniques of inquiry are being applied with no cognizance of their potential value to a personality-in-culture orientation to psychology of art. It may be hoped then, that several existing methods of investigation may be found to be adaptable to the new perspective.

Another point worth mentioning here is the reciprocal relation possible between two apparently different areas of research. In the instance just described it is psychology of art and psychology of personality. The communication network here works both ways; each area contributes to the other. Similar mutualities are possible and desirable in other problem areas. Currently I am interested in another project involving an analysis of styles and the use of projective and other psychological techniques along with anthropological and sociological methods of describing the basic personality type of a particular cultural group with a view toward determining what of the values of that group may be symbolized in its art styles. This will necessitate the coöperation of an artist-aesthetician along with psychologists, semioticians, anthropologists, and sociologists. In this case the complexity of the problems is recognized at the outset and appropriate methods will be devised to fit this complexity rather than oversimplify to distorted proportions the object of our investigations so that a popular methodology will fit it.

Many other aspects of this color project could be touched upon if time permitted. What impresses most at this juncture is the need for coöperation among artists and scientists if the new psychology of art is to achieve the goals it has set for itself. The ultimate end of aesthetic inquiry is better understanding of the artist and his works, his rôles in contemporary society, the place of the values he knows best in better living for all. Such understanding will not be easy to come by under any circumstances and least of all is it apt to be achieved by artist or scientist working alone.

SELECTED BIBLIOGRAPHY

[1] Arnheim, R. Agenda for the Psychology of Art. *Journ. of Aesthetics and Art Criticism,* vol. X, No. 4, June, 1952.

[2] Baudouin, C. *Psychoanalysis and Aesthetics* (tr. by Paul, New York, 1924).

[3] Chandler, A. R. *Beauty and Human Nature,* Appleton-Century, 1934.

[4] Dessoir, M. *Aesthetik und allgemeine Kunstwissenschaft,* Stuttgart, 1923.

[5] Gilbert, K. E. and Kuhn, H. *A History of Esthetics,* Macmillan, 1940.

[6] Kallen, H. M. *Art and Freedom,* Duell, Sloan and Pearce, 1942.

[7] Lee, H. B. On the Esthetic State of Mind. *Psychiatry,* 1947, pp. 281-306, and other articles.

[8] Malraux, A. *The Psychology of Art* (tr. by Stuart Gilbert), Pantheon Press, New York, 1949.

[9] Morgan, D. N. Psychology and Art Today; A Summary and Critique. *Journ. of Aesthetics and Art Criticism,* vol. IX, No. 2, Dec., 1950.

[10] Munro, T. M. Methods in the Psychology of Art. *Journ. of Aesthetics and Art Criticism,* vol. VI, No. 3, March, 1948.

[11] Ogden, R. M. *The Psychology of Art,* Scribner, 1938.

[12] Pepper, S. C. *Principles of Art Appreciation,* Harcourt, Brace, 1949.

[13] Schoen, M., Schrickel, H. G., and Ames, V. M. *Understanding the World,* Harpers, 1947.

[14] Schrickel, H. G. A Psycho-Anthropological Approach to Problems in Aesthetics. *Journ. of Aesthetics and Art Criticism,* vol. IX, No. 4, June, 1952.

Chapter XXXIX

RECENT TRENDS IN THE PSYCHOLOGY OF VALUES

ROBERT F. CREEGAN, Ph.D.

*Professor of Philosophy, State University of New York,
at Albany*

EDITORIAL NOTE

Operationists and positivists may frown upon the introduction of values into a general survey of psychology, but unless we are willing to restrict ourselves to experimental data only, the values must figure in a symposium of this sort; for if they are out of bounds to the psychologist, we ought to know the reason why, other than that they are not operationally manageable. In the brief chapter before us, we have at least a peg for discussion. If we continue to dismiss the values from our midst as of no psychological import, we can never hope to discover the means of handling them empirically. Psychology, after all, should at least make an effort to interpret the values from its own angle.

Dr. Robert F. Creegan has received his M.A. and Ph.D. degrees at Duke University. He was at various times Assistant Professor of Psychology at Bucknell University, and at Carleton College, and also Assistant Professor of Philosophy at Ohio University. He is now Chairman of the Philosophy Department at the State University of New York, State College, Albany. He wrote a number of articles in psychology and philosophy, and has just brought out a book entitled The Shock of Existence *(Cambridge, Mass. 1954).*

ENTANGLEMENTS

At no time in the history of psychology has a substantial amount of work been devoted exclusively to the psychology of values. Some of the most explicit work in that field, like E. Spranger's classical *Lebensformen* (transl. as *Types of Men*), could be classified under the heading of characterology with equal propriety.

Other works of importance, like Helge Lundholm's *The Aesthetic Sentiment,* has been concerned with one kind of values only. William Stern's monumental writings on personalistic psychology and philosophy contain many incidental insights on the value orientation of the person, but the chief interest is at all times the structure of personality. W. Köhler's challenging study, *The Place of Value in a World of Facts,* is actually a Gestalt theory of perception, including a systematic treatment of the relationship between the field of experience and the brain field. Thus, it is no exaggeration to say that an encyclopedic study of the psychology of values would have to concern itself in the main with the implications of investigations which were oriented equally, and in most cases primarily, towards other problems.

At the beginning of his last year of teaching at Duke University, William McDougall commenced a graduate course on the psychology of values, and had intended to publish a book on the topic. The course was never completed.

A considerable portion of the psychology of values, as it has been developed in recent American research and theoretical writing, is virtually identical with the psychology of motivation. Under this heading we may include all the work on attitudes and their formation, and the work on the measurement of public opinion. The classical questions about nature and nurture could be asked concerning value attitudes, and the genesis of individual differences and group differences could be appraised. The present chapter, however, will avoid repeating, even in a somewhat different perspective what others have written on collateral topics. We shall use freely the resources of contemporary phenomenological and existential thinking. The conceptual scheme to be offered will have a certain novelty.

The Rôle of Shock

The philosopher, George Santayana, somewhere noted that the experience of shock is of great interest to the theorist of knowledge because it usually conveys a perception of an ill-defined but oppressive presence. Psychologically speaking, the

951

shock experience helps us realize that the objects of our experience are by no means products of our own logical expectations. Theodore Reik, the psychoanalyst, made a parallel observation when he noted that the exploration of a strange personality is surprising because it arouses unexpected reverberations in the psychologist who is learning about himself even as he explores the alien mentality. Jean Paul Sartre's theory that "the glance of the other," especially if it catches the sacred self in an embarrassing situation, is a psychological basis for transcending pure solipsism or subjectivism, illustrates the same line of thought. These and many other theoretical leads would tend to justify the assertion that there is an intimate relationship between the psychology of values and the psychology of surprise, shock, and astonishment. The pivotal importance of the attitude of wonder in personal development as portrayed by many writers of the Romanticist school, including Goethe, himself, must also be mentioned here. This essay will explore some of the implications of this orientation to the psychology of values.

The functional psychologist might state that if wish-directed behavior were immune to surprising consequences, there would be no need for standards of value. The classical distinction between "what is desired" and "what ought to be desired" may be psychologically grounded in the discovery that wishes frequently prove deceptive. Certain wishes must be subordinated, as a psychological defense measure, to normative standards of conduct. The theory of values must be a theory of standards since on any other terms momentary satisfaction and authentic celebration of value would be identical. John Dewey, the functional psychologist and instrumentalist philosopher, was among those who recognized that there is a factor of judgment in even the most direct perceptions of values.

Some of the most deeply cherished wishes have proven to be unrealistic in the sense that it was impossible to fulfill them. This reminds us rather forcibly of the philosophical debate as to whether this is "the best of all possible worlds." If the world is "good," then some of the most cherished human wishes must be "bad," in some sense of the term, since it is impossible to fulfill many of these wishes. It is to be noted that advances in science and technology do make it possible to establish some of the conditions of "the good life" which in previous ages evaded human constructive efforts. Reflective persons and groups may find it difficult to agree upon which wishes are in principle unfulfillable. Fantasy and scientific achievement at times are closely allied. At other times, the two are flatly opposed to each other. The chief point for the development of our thinking about the psychology of values is simply that the "stubborn resistance," of the world in relation to the cherished wishes of the self proves rather a surprise to the immature individual, and may even make a moral philosopher of him, certain other conditions having been met. There is no doubt that the witty Voltaire won a decided victory on the journalistic level over the contention of the metaphysician, Leibniz, that this is, after all, the "best of all possible worlds." It may be, however, that the metaphysician's theory of possibility was a bit more complicated and, perhaps, grim than Voltaire was able to recognize.

Sigmund Freud and the other depth psychologists have demonstrated amply enough that some wishes prove to be unrealistic in a more subtle way. The situational fulfillment of some wishes simply fails to provide the expected satisfactions. The individual may discover that conditions or relationships which had seemed to promise the greatest happiness are in fact productive only of anxiety or boredom, disgust or remorse, or some other unsatisfactory subjective state. Conversely, the most thrilling gratifications sometimes prove to be associated with conditions or with relationships the very possibility of which had been ignored, or even had been avoided by every device at the disposal of the individual. Disillusioned individuals complain that life is a much meaner thing than they had been taught at the mother's knee to expect. Romantically surprised individuals, on the other hand, have been heard to exclaim that even the most ordinary-seeming situations may swarm with secret promise.

Literary psychology is quite familiar with the naive types of individual, the disillusioned types of individual, and the so romantically re-illusioned types. Actually, of course, a complex individual may exemplify all three attitudes, depending upon what type of value is under consideration. Sensitive men seem continually to be surprised at how "good" or how "bad" the various features of the human scene can be. The most hardened cynic at times may be vulnerable to re-illusioning "charms."

THE NEED FOR SURPRISE

The point that we were trying to make, however, was the much simpler one that the human need for standards of value answers to the human capacity to be surprised or, perhaps we should say, to stay surprised. Doubtless, the frustrations of the higher subhuman organisms, too, are compounded by any failure of complex anticipatory behavior to be completed in the appropriate type of overtly consummatory behavior. The behavioristic psychologists have had nothing to say about those consummations which exceed the structure of anticipations, and are more liberating and gratifying than had been thought possible. A purely cognitive frustration may be involved even in such cases.

The high level of symbolic responses of which socialized man is capable make possible that well-articulated and lasting apprehension of astonishing incongruity whence emerge both the comic and the tragic views of life, no less than the attitudes of nihilistic despair or of mystical exultation. All taking of attitudes toward life in general, or toward the whole matrix of life is, we dare say, a product of this experience of astonishing incongruity. There is always an element of frustration in it, but there are what may be called sweet shocks, and sublime incongruities. The frustration may be more cognitive than directly emotive, the "goodness" of things transcending all rational expectation. In other cases, the very sweep of disaster may have such pronounced dramatic qualities that the emotion of loss is swallowed up in an inexplicable sense of belonging to something which is boundless in energy, if scarcely sociable in the warm, chummy sense. The phenomenology of these personality-transforming experiences of the incongruous is never completed, since ever new subclasses of this type of experience may be discovered. Immanuel Kant was aware of this challenge, and in his theory of "the sublime" he described one type of semantic confusion which could have productive consequences.

AESTHETIC DEFENSE REACTIONS

How has man defended himself against misleading wishes and wishful expectations? As a first step toward a theory of the dynamics of value standards, we may be permitted to construct a theory of types. First, let us glance at the Puritan.

The Puritan defends himself against misleading wishes and expectations by trying to reduce many of his ambitions to a minimum, and by trying to simplify and consolidate the routines of his behavior. Puritanical standards minimize the chances of unfavorable surprise by minimizing risk-taking in general. Of course, when we speak of the Puritan we are dealing with an ideal construct, not a description, a limiting fiction, grounded in observation (direct or indirect) but transcending it in the Platonic sense. The value of the construct would be related to its functioning in our attempt to understand the psychodynamics of evaluative standards in general. All persons who are capable of any sort of self-frustration in the interest of an ideal have some resemblance to our "detestable" Puritan.

In the field of morals, the Puritan is a legalist in the ancient Hebraic sense of the term, or perhaps he is a duty theorist of the ilk of the above-mentioned German pietist, Kant. In aesthetics, the Puritan is a primitivist like Emily Dickinson, or a classicist like T. S. Eliot. In theory of knowledge, the Puritan is in all cases a doctrinaire. He may find "the Word" in some favored teacher, after the manner of the Fundamentalist Christians or the revolutionary Communists, or he may find it in some favored science after the manner of the Logical Positivists and other "physicalistic" philosophers. In order to avoid confusing thoughts, the intellectual Puritan tests all other teachers and all other sciences in terms of the criteria established by the one loved teacher or science. There is strict "monogamy" here.

LIMITATIONS OF LIBERTINISM

Most revolts against Puritanical standards of value are likely to be in favor of limitless sensual indulgence, or limitless artistic experimentation, or limitless intellectual speculation. The ancient Hebrew Prophets were realistic when they warned against the pursuit of strange gods, yet Puritanism and Legalism do, at times, overshoot the mark. If, having been burned once, man had erected a taboo against the observation of fire, he never would have mastered it. The world which at times is much less comfortable or flattering than the primitive or the child might have wished also is capable of rewarding boldness. There are constructive possibilities which are no less unknown to the primitive man or to the child than many of the perils of the world are unknown. The boldly questing hero discovers original beauty through accepting dreaded encounters. Thus does the Promethean ideal counterbalance the ideal of the Puritan. Psychologically mature standards of value, it would seem, must be designed not only to defend persons against destructive risks, but equally to facilitate and encourage constructive wish-fulfillment and risk-taking to that end.

The scientific method, for example, warns against the conceits of ungrounded speculation, but not, as the Positivists imagine, against speculation in general. The canons of aesthetic form warn against the conceits of unshaped fantasy but not, as the Classicists imagine, against Romance in general. The ethic of loyalty warns against trusting the stranger initially, but not, as McCarthyism implies, against the quest for universal brotherhood. Every form of the ethics of restraint or of security is a peril to man's quest for self-transcendence.

THE REWARDS OF DARING

Experimentalism is the royal road to the discovery of unknown constructive possibilities. Experimentalism, however, could continue only while self-control and social regulation reconcile one experimental activity with other experimental activities. Cultural survival depends upon a systematic, continuous experimentalism and those who identify the experimental way of life with moral anarchy are enemies of both survival and the quest for self-transcendence.

Systematic rationalism is empirical. Systematic empiricism is rational. Man controls more and more of nature only through learning more and more levels of methodological discipline. Man's conquest of values is a self conquest, fulfilling, rather than defying, pre-given conditions for more generous order. The most original individual exemplifies the most intricate lawfulness of life process, and in originality is fullness of life. Lunacy is impoverished life because it is impoverished order in life, and in relatedness.

Man's very potentialities "exist" only so far as he is a questing being willing to face up to dreaded incongruities, and willing to risk his definition of self and of the good life. The initial expression of astonishment in the face of a widened view of nature or of human nature is poetical. The language of strict definition grows from that of poetical similitude, and the language of strict correlation grows from that of tragic involvement. That is why thinkers as diverse as the poet, Walt Whitman, and the philosopher, Martin Heidegger, have attributed prophetic significance to the great artists.

The major historical crises in standards of conduct follow from dread-producing recognitions of the vast power or the vast intricacy of nature, far transcending traditional concepts of the human situation. Each such crisis seems to portend the onset of cultural chaos, intellectual and moral, until some prophet of the epoch utters the liberating word. Perhaps this liberator does no more than find symbols to express human concern for the incongruity between the anticipated and the actual revelations of history. Perhaps no other victory is necessary. By giving dread a name, and a stage on which to play its historic part, he releases other constructive powers.

Now we are in a position with confidence to restate the initial claim that there is an intimate relationship between the psychology of values, and the psychology of surprise, shock, and astonishment. Only through intellectual confrontation of once dreaded facts are the unsuspected creative powers of a life or of an epoch liberated for their redemptive work. We conclude with the observation that to understand the psychology of values is to understand the psychology of religion also.

In all candor it must be said in this context that such themes of universal destiny, not to speak of such a conclusion, have been denied any importance by certain self-styled "tough-minded" thinkers in psychology and other fields. We are able to say, however, that equally tough-minded psychologists believe that the substructure of all decisions for practical action is constituted by both "conscious" and "unconscious" self-definitions, including human attitudes towards singular and universal destiny. Decision-making is still a very obscure psychological process, even though it ought to be one of the most important chapters in the psychology of values.

Directional Constants

The process of decision-making is receiving increased attention as a psychological topic at mid-century, but not so much in academic psychology, proper, as in collateral fields, including "Human Relations" and "Group Dynamics." Sooner or later, the more rigorous experimental and mathematical methods must be mobilized to clarify and to correlate some of the qualitative findings of those collateral fields. For the philosopher, the concept of enlightened decisions is no less important than the concept of truth, because the quest for truth and other values depends upon decision-making processes of various types. This very quest implies that while, perhaps, no theory is perfect, there is still a basis for absolutely rejecting certain alternatives in a decision-making situation. There are no absolutes, but there are directional constants. The fact that we do learn is the point of departure for all our philosophizing. Animals learn, but man

958

discovers learning and becomes a philosopher. The initial human astonishment involves some knowledge, even in its recognition of a vast ignorance.

Persons who have been honored with trustee authority make many decisions for institutional groups and for total communities. Only an informed electorate is able to pass enlightened judgments upon the decisions of its leaders. At all levels of delegated power, psychology could perform the function of unmasking obsessive attitudes and self-definitions, so that those engaged in decision-making processes might continue thinking and feeling in terms of an open field of growing, reconcilable powers and configurations of power.

CULTURE AS VALUE

Culture is a crystallization of past decisions, including the pivotal self-defining decisions. In some measure, at least, human culture is amenable to modification by future decisions. The horrors which mankind faces at the dawn of the Atomic Age are symptoms rather of human pathology and immaturity than of an unanswerable fate. What was American "isolation," other than immaturity, and American boasting than pathology?

Our concluding thought was, however, that the psychology of religion is the crux of the psychology of values. Perhaps at its highest level the religious attitude could be defined as the attitude of creative acceptance. We control certain factors in nature only by accepting real correlations. We learn satisfying uses of power only by accepting facts of interpersonal similitude and involvement. Universal Man shall celebrate the intimate in the stranger or in the strange, no less than questing to discover the stranger beneath the intimate surface of selfhood. Universal Man will be man, awakened from national "dreams."

This far-reaching ideal is only the completion of the working processes of science and democracy, which are processes of creative acceptance in an experimental way of life. Since the transcendence of renewal over loss is only a special case of the transcendence of likeness over difference, it is true that love, by

959

conquering hate, conquers despair, also. But that is not easy. Only through ordeals of self-discovery, involving the destruction of every egocentric and ethnocentric myth, could an élite of freedom learn consistently to love the way of creative acceptance, thereby discovering something of what transcendence means, not as concept, only, but as work, or as artistry in which devotion and recreation are wholly one.

REFERENCES

Boas, G. Habit, Fact & Value. *J. of Philos.* 1939.
Bryn-Jones, D. *The Dilemma of the Idealist,* 1950.
Creegan, R. F. *The Shock of Existence,* 1954.
Dewey, John, Theory of Valuation. *Intern Encyclop. of Unif. Sci.,* vol. II, No. 3.
Eaton, H. O. *The Austrian Philosophy of Values,* 1930.
Freed, L. *Social Pragmatism,* 1948 (Watts).
Köhler, W. *The Place of Value in a World of Fact,* 1938.
Laird, John, *The Idea of Value,* 1929.
Lossky, N. O. *Value and Existence,* 1935.
Perry, R. B. *The General Theory of Value,* 1926.
Roback, A. A. Character and the Values in *The Psychology of Character,* (3d ed.) 1952.
——The Concept of Character in a Dictator-Ridden World in *The Psychology of Common Sense,* 1939.
Santayana, G. *Dominations and Powers,* 1951.
Urban, W. M. *Valuation,* 1909.
——Science & Value; Fact & Value in the Social Sciences, *Ethics,* 1914.
——The Present Situation in Axiology. *Rev. Intern. de Philos.,* 1939.

Chapter XL

THE PSYCHOLOGY OF RELIGION

Vergilius Ferm, Ph.D.
Professor of Philosophy, The College of Wooster

961

EDITORIAL NOTE

While the psychology of religion in years gone by had its specialists in men like Emile Durkheim (largely sociological), William James, James Leuba, and Edwin Starbuck, it has fallen on lean days within the last 25 years. There is a feeling in psychological departments that it belongs elsewhere. Even the addition of pastoral psychology in the general area of counseling has not added to its prestige, while best sellers, like The Return to Religion, Peace of Mind *and* Peace of Soul, *only tended to turn the average academic psychologist against considering it as pabulum for science.*

In keeping, however, with the general plan of this volume, a brief chapter on religion was thought desirable, and Dr. Vergilius Ferm was kind enough to write it. Dr. Ferm, who received his doctorate at Yale, had been a clergyman in earlier years, but subsequently became a teacher of philosophy. He is at present Compton Professor of Philosophy at The College of Wooster. Dr. Ferm has been the editor of several large collective volumes and reference works, such as An Encyclopedia of Religion (1945), Religion in the Twentieth Century (1948), *and a* History of Philosophical Systems (1950) *and has brought out* The Collected Writings of Jonathan Edwards. *He is also author of* First Adventures in Philosophy (1936), First Chapters in Religious Philosophy (1937), A Protestant Dictionary (1951), Pastoral Psychology (1955) *and other volumes.*

DAWN OF RELIGION

Man's observations of the characteristic human elements in religious ideas and behavior are, of course, as old as critical reflection. Guesses were made as to how religious people operate as they think and behave religiously. Eastern religions developed psychological techniques from practical observation and self-analysis as to how persons might come into intimate terms with the most Real in the Universe and attain bliss. Religious psychology grew up under the guiding and comforting wings of philosophy and theology. Mysticism was, probably, the most fertile soil for the development of what we would now call the psychology of religion; for mysticism is the expression of intimacy and personal appropriation in religion.

In Western Christian thought and practice, religious psychology became entwined with Biblicism so that, it was thought, there was a special Biblical psychology which would explain the human responses in religious aspirations. As late as the end of the nineteenth century, books were published to point out the lessons which "revealed truth" had to offer to the understanding of religious man and his mental framework.

At the turn of the century, a scientific psychology of religion was being developed which aimed to turn aside from theological and philosophical presuppositions and to set its roots in the soil of psychology itself. The hope was to understand religious man not from the point of view of religion but from the securer vantage point of "secular" psychology. Pioneers in this movement were Edwin D. Starbuck (*The Psychology of Religion*, 1899), George A. Coe (*The Spiritual Life*, 1900, *The Psychology of Religion*, 1916), James H. Leuba (*A Psychological Study of Religion*, 1912), G. Stanley Hall (*Adolescence*, 2 vols., 1905), William James (*The Varieties of Religious Experience*, 1902), James B. Pratt (*The Psychology of Religious Belief*, 1907, *The Religious Consciousness*, 1920) and others who followed their leadership. It was in America that the scientific psychology of religion had its initial flourish.

EARLY METHODS

When psychology itself—a daughter of philosophy—set up her own housekeeping as a scientific discipline, it was natural that a methodology to ascertain facts must be critically scrutinized and followed. The crudest laboratory techniques were set up, with only partial success. It was difficult to extricate the subject from a type of psychology predisposed to certain theories of mind such as that of analytic psychology which viewed mind as an area to be mapped out into relations amenable to analysis and synthesis. The American pioneers of the psychology of religion grasped the question-answer method to establish a technique which they thought sure to lead to sound scientific conclusions.

Starbuck's pioneer book on *The Psychology of Religion* was a study of a limited area of religion: that of conversion. By the questionnaire method, he believed he had applied certain laws of physiological psychology to illuminate religious behavior: that religious decisions followed a definite pattern of the physiological maturing process. Hailed as a revolutionary approach (even William James depended upon Starbuck's methods and conclusions in his own monumental work *The Varieties of Religious Experience*) the questionnaire method (employed also by Coe, Leuba, Pratt and others) soon revealed its limitations. Starbuck's work was clearly channelled to the river-bed of an evangelistic theology which prescribed an adolescent crisis-experience. A definite correlation between physiological maturation and a Methodist revival directed to a certain age-level may well have been a shocking revelation of the human element in religion, but it had little bearing on those areas of religion where such crisis-expectancy was not held to be necessary or normative for a wholesome religion. In other words, the early studies of conversion were studies in the psychological reactions to ideological motivations and moved within the framework of group-expectancy as represented by a school of orthodoxy.

BIOGRAPHICAL AND ANTHROPOLOGICAL APPROACHES

There were other methods of promise. William James took to the study of biography and autobiography which offered the directness of testimony. But, as his critics were fond of pointing out, the James study provided a study of striking, and even abnormal rather than normal, types of religious response. Perhaps the most promising and significant method was that of the study of anthropology, because it opened up the wider vistas of religious psychology as opposed to a more parochial study of circumscribed religion and because it emphasized rightly the tremendous rôle of social psychology operating in religious areas. The anthropological approach produced some classics in the field: E. B. Tylor, *Primitive Culture* (5th ed., 2 vols., 1913), J. G. Frazer, *The Golden Bough* (abd. ed., 1923), M. Jastrow, *The Study of Religion* (1921), E. Durkheim, *Les Formes élementaires de la Vie réligieuse* (1912), Eng. trans. 1915, and the early classic and perennially significant volume by Edward S. Ames, *The Psychology of Religious Experience* (1910).

SOCIOLOGICAL DEVELOPMENT

The anthropological approach developed into what, in more recent years, has become known as the sociology of religion. Stress upon cultural influences—economic, geographic, political, industrial—in setting their stamp upon religious beliefs and practices has, of course, broadened the field of the psychology of religion and to be shared by students of sociology. It is considered axiomatic now to view man in his interrelations with others of his particular society. For man is never isolated from a particular group. Religion itself is a cultural phenomenon with powerful group pressures upon the individual to fashion for him his religious thinking and to mold him into the pattern of the social heritage. Institutionalism, a commonplace in any group solidification, from tribal to the most advanced form of community life, continues to transmit the frozen beliefs and the behaviors of the long preceding generations. The church may claim divine sanction for its being, but its *raison d'être* is nourished in the same matrix of group psychology as any other institutional expression (fraternities, nationalistic loyalties, political parties, and the like). Religious psychology includes a folk psychology and thus overflows into the sociological field. Early classics in the social emphasis upon religious beliefs and behavior were W. G. Sumner: *Folkways* (1906), Wilhelm Wundt: *Elements of Folk Psychology* (Eng. tr., 1916), Max Weber: *Gesammelte Aufsätze zur Religionssoziologie* (1920), E. W. Hopkins: *The Origin and Evolution of Religion* (1923)—to name but a few. More recent books, typical of the emphasis, are A. E. Haydon: *The Quest of the Ages* (1929), H. L. Fries and H. W. Schneider: *Religion in Various Cultures* (1932) and, in the field of Christian theology, notably, G. B. Foster: *The Function of Religion in Man's Struggle for Existence* (1909), E. Troeltsch: *Gesammelte Schriften* (4 vols., 1912-1925), S. J. Case: *Experience with the Supernatural in Early Christian Times* (1929), Shailer Mathews: *The Growth of the Idea of God* (1931) and other of his many pioneer publications.

MECHANO-BIOLOGICAL PROBES

When psychologists began to take seriously the study of animal psychology under the spell of the functional school (which in turn had its setting in the evolutionary emphasis) much of the wind was taken out of the sails for students of religious psychology. Behavioristic psychology with its magical S-R (Stimulus-Response) bond closed in and took over the field of psychology, thus squeezing out, for a long period of time, any claim to respectability on the part of studies come by any other method. The religious type of response could not easily conform to the limits set by mere animal behavior and to S-R methods even though man is genetically related to lower organic forms.

One very signal attempt to reorientate the whole field of the psychology of religion into the pattern of the genetic emphasis in psychology came in the form of a book by J. Cyril Flower,

An Approach to the Psychology of Religion (1927), a book which did not have the influence it rightly deserved. Its thesis was that all organisms, from the simplest to the most complex, make adjustments to their environment with nature furnishing the tools. The simpler the tools, the more restricted the environment. Man is nature's greatest outreach to date: the human mind is capable of awareness of an environment of far-flung areas. Tools to control this wider environment successfully constitute knowledge. Tools of partial control over that in the environment which remains baffling and frustrating are those ideological symbols which are typically religious and by which religions are nourished. Man becomes religious in so far as he is aware of an environment for which he is unprepared to cope with in the day-to-day responses. Religion itself is thus the outgrowth of a genetic development of wider awareness and is not something apart from its natural setting in evolutionary history.

THE FREUDIAN POSSIBILITIES

The field of the psychology of religion became barren with the years of the rule of behaviorism in general psychology. Only by the bankruptcy of this orthodox school of psychologists and the rise of the more speculative schools led by Freud and others could a revival occur. Stimulations which brought about fresh interests came from the struggles and frustrations of war. Scientific psychology seemed remotely encased in laboratories with their experimentations upon animal subjects. Men came home from wars with minds bruised and full of maladjustments. In England a school of religious psychologists grew up with the express purpose of attempting therapeutic aid to the stricken soldiers. Freud's continued probing of the unconscious mind furnished the key for the hopeful understanding of frustrations and phobias and all other forms of maladjustments. The new Dynamic School of British psychologists poured forth a flood of books dealing with the psychology of religion, scientific in their claim by reason of specific case-studies of shell-shock victims and their return to normal stature by the concrete aid of both religion and psychology.

Prominent among the books issued by this school was J. A. Hadfield's *Psychology and Morals* (1926) and, to a less degree, T. W. Pym's *Psychology and the Christian Life* (1922). Although more or less restricted to an Anglican circle and to more or less conventional Christian concepts this dynamic school did pioneer work in the therapeutic phase of religious psychology. Many conventional ideas were made reasonable by reinterpretation: such concepts as original sin, moral disease, religious sentiment, faith, regeneration, the God-idea, miracles, conversion, personal salvation, the so-called Christian virtues, and the like.

REACTION TO FREUD

It was the beginning of the day when psychologists were fond of such terms as complexes, repressions, free association, instincts, redirection, integration, and the like. Great stir was created in religious and theological circles by the rediscovered fact of auto-suggestion, the stir of fear lest religion would be thought to be a merely creative expression of the human mind without ontological significance beyond man himself. A flood of theological and philosophical books came to the defence of a realistic theology in reaction against the temper of subjectivism which psychoanalysis had seemed to foster. Both philosophical phenomenalism (in its unique way) and theological existentialism developed to offset the trend.

Religious psychology continued to center upon and to probe the depth of man's fears, frustrations and inner conflicts. Psychology itself became more human and realistic in dealing with personality problems, many of which became accentuated by recurrent wars, depressions, instability, and the conflicts brought on by the swiftly changing modes of living (technological advances in all areas). Para-Freudianism continued to flourish with modifications of what Freud had regarded as the deepest urge in man (sex), some holding the basic unconscious drive to be the feeling of inferiority (Adler) while others holding it to be a dominating egocentricity. The present vogue of depth psychology with its flood of books among theologians wishing to defend traditional ideas of sin in the garb of Freudian insights is but an elaboration of Para-Freudianism. Man as a characteristically sick soul rather than as a normally healthy-minded personality (borrowing James's term) has captured the interests of many present-day students of religious psychology, particularly among those operating in the circle of neo-orthodoxy in theology. This development is an elaboration of a school rather than a unique contribution to the development of the psychology of religion, although the widespread current interest seems to give the contrary impression.

Popular interest in the whole field of personality adjustment and its relation to religion is evidenced by the widespread acceptance of such books as H. C. Link's *The Return to Religion* (1936), J. L. Liebman's *Peace of Mind,* (1946) F. Sheen's *Peace of Soul* (1949), and Leslie D. Weatherhead's *Psychology, Religion and Healing* (1952). Clergymen have become overtaken with interest in the psychological field, in "the art of ministering to the sick," in family adjustments, sex education, gerontology and in the whole area of counseling. A magazine directed to these interests has appeared under the title *Pastoral Psychology* (in its fifth year, 1954).

THE CRUX OF THE PROBLEM

What has made the development of the field of the psychology of religion difficult and scientifically disappointing—a field so important to the understanding of both man and his religion—has been the chasm that continues to exist between those who are trained psychologists and those disciplined in the field of religion. Many psychologists are first to admit their incompetence to deal with religion (a highly complex phenomenon) and are cautiously silent while many theologians who follow the groove of their predecessors seem to develop aspects of a psychological fashion (or school) to support the framework of their conventional religious patterns.

Religion itself is a term which has different meanings to different students. In many cases, it is normatively conceived in terms of a particular brand rather than descriptively as a universal phenomenon. Psychology of religion fundamentally deals with the whole area of religion, not with one particular faith. Furthermore, there is no religious psychology *per se*. Men do not take on a nature that is different when they affirm and give loyalty to religious ideas or when they behave in a manner that is characteristically religious. Man is all of one psychological piece whatever the interests may be at the time, whether in art, in community living, in educational enterprise, in a commitment to a destiny (which is religion) or in just the plain business of getting on. It is to the scientific psychologist that religious psychology must turn for its moorings. There is, of course, the deeper difficulty of attempting to develop the field of the psychology of religion in the face of the diffusion into schools which psychology itself has engendered in the growing pains of its own discipline.

PSYCHOSOMATICS AND RELIGION

A most promising area of inquiry into the field has developed, it must be admitted, in the now commonplace stress of psychosomatic medicine, of the interplay of the body and the mind in human behavior (in sickness or in health). Personalities are seen to have deep physiological roots of explanation while both organic health and disturbances are equally motivated and nourished by psychic activities. Religion as man's total response to the totality of life or that which gives ultimate meaning and for man his destiny is seen to be of vital significance both to health and illness. There is a present-day ontological emphasis given to religious ideas, such as God, faith, petitional prayer, which are taken to be of enormous medical significance to personality-balance, an emphasis which was absent among scientifically trained medical specialists decades ago. Both psychology and a religion-with-objective-reference are now seen to be a part of a normal life pattern and not as distinct from each other or both apart from nature. Certainly, religion is not viewed as something alien or superimposed upon normal living. Ideas, such as the soul, may need revision but the realism to which such religious terms point still registers on the sensitive plate that life presents.

A LOOK TOWARD THE FUTURE

The psychology of religion is hampered by provincial tendencies to regard all religious behavior after the pattern of one faith. The coming *rapprochement* of Western and Eastern religions will correct in time this deficiency. Easterners have given the philosophical rather than the psychological emphasis to religious studies, this because of a long tradition; while Westerners have now taken to religious psychology with far too little attention to the broader aspects of religion.

The future course of the psychology of religion lies, it would seem, in a profound conviction—a conviction that is part and parcel of the scientific spirit—that all life is of one piece and that there are fundamental and universal experiences and expressions which undergird all differences of symbols and behavior patterns. Human beings are fundamentally the same psychologically as they are physiologically. But environments differ with their bag full of tricks and influences now to bring out one phase and now another until men seem altogether different both psychologically and religiously. The greatest contribution which the serious study of the psychology of religion can offer, and will no doubt offer, is the increasing realization of the wholesome truth that though religions differ and though faiths separate they have common elements because men everywhere are fundamentally the same, because nature is fundamentally one (a postulate of the scientific approach itself) and that religious phenomena *commonly* reflect man's grasping of his total environment which is so infinitely larger than himself. To understand this is to become tolerant of the variety of religious expressions and to appreciate the singleness of living. Religious psychology is a perennial testimony of man's getting on with the *total* business of life in a world that is fundamentally a unity both as to structure and function. As such, the serious student of the psychology of religion as a scientific discipline contributes an antidote to religious provincialism, the tempting sin of religious philosophers and theologians.

BIBLIOGRAPHY

(Supplementary to Titles mentioned in the Text)

Stratton, G. M. *Psychology of the Religious Life,* 1911.
Leuba, J. H. *The Belief in God and Immortality,* 2nd ed., 1921.
——*The Psychology of Religious Mysticism,* 1925.
Josey, C. C. *The Psychology of Religion,* 1927.
Roback, A. A. *The Psychology of Character,* 1927.
Uren, A. R. *Recent Religious Psychology,* 1928.
Coe, G. A. *Motives of Men,* 1928.
Clark, E. T. *The Psychology of Religious Awakening,* 1929.
Conklin, E. S. *The Psychology of Religious Adjustment,* 1929.
Selbie, W. B. *The Psychology of Religion,* 1929.
Dunlap, K. *Mysticism, Freudianism and Scientific Psychology,* 1920.
——*Religion, Its Functions in Human Life,* 1946.
Wieman, H. N. and Wieman, R. W. *Normative Psychology of Religion,* 1935.
Thouless, R. H. *Introduction to the Psychology of Religion,* 1936.
Jones, W. L. *Psychological Study of Religious Conversion,* 1937.
Ferm, V., ed., *Religion in Transition,* 1937.
——*Pastoral Psychology,* 1955.
Thorpe, L. P. *Psychological Foundations of Personality,* 1938.
Cutten, G. B. *Instincts and Religion,* 1940.
Allport, G. W. *The Individual and his Religion,* 1950.

INDEX

Abbot, F. K., 624
Abelson, R. P., 848
Abraham, K., 574, 588
Abramson, D. L., 608, 609, 622
Abt, L. T., 548, 556, 559, 677
Ackerman, N. W., 390, 391, 399
Adams, A. J., 814, 834
Ades, H. W., 13, 15, 30, 31
Adler, Alexandra, 731
Adler, Alfred, 193, 247, 249, 250
  251, 503, 564, 606, 608, 622,
  649, 656, 660, 667, 673, 676,
  699, 705, 707, 712, 713, 714,
  718, 719, 720, 728, 729, 730,
  969
Adler, H. M., 622
Adorno, T., 388, 389, 391, 399
Adrian, 36
Aeschylos, 686
Aichhorn, A., 707
Alexander, Franz, 233, 579, 582,
  586, 588, 592, 600, 610, 622, 648,
  650, 656, 658, 660, 661, 662, 663,
  676
Allee, 351
Allen, Frederick H., 692, 707
Allen, Robert M., 634, 642
Allerhand, Melvin E., 614, 622
Allport, Floyd L., 332
Allport, Gordon W., 193, 214, 218,
  219, 237, 242, 257, 332, 384, 388,
  399, 494, 514, 542, 640, 641, 642,
  972
Almy, T. P., 600, 624, 626
Alper, T. G., 130

Altschule, M. D., 22, 29, 600-607,
  609-614, 622
Amark, C., 607, 625
Amatruda, C. S., 708
Ambrose, G., 830
Amerongen, F. K., 19, 30
Ames, A., 67, 74, 85, 87
Ames, Edward S., 965
Ames, V. M., 947
Ammons, R. B., 560
Anand, B. K., 18, 29
Anders, P., 542
Anderson, G. L., 542, 556, 559
Anderson, H. H., 542, 556, 559
Anderson, J. O., 795
Angell, J. R., 493, 608, 622
Angell, R., 642
Anrep, G. V., 90, 101
Angyal, Andras, 237
Appel, Jesse, 625
Appel, Kenneth, 673
Aquinas, Thomas, 496, 499
Aristotle, 369, 491, 496, 498, 499,
  538, 685, 713
Arnheim, R., 542, 934, 947
Arnold, Magda B., 139, 154, 156,
  157, 172, 183, 184, 186
Arnold, Matthew, 365
d'Arpentigny, C. St., 542
Asch, S. E., 346, 347, 353, 386,
  393, 399, 400, 862
Ascoli, 910
Ash, Philip, 354
Ashby, W. R., 863
Auden, W. H., 888

Ruch, T. C., 43, 44, 45, 50, 54, 55, 114, 133
Ruckmick, C. A., 185, 188
Ruesch, J., 768
Ruilmann, C. J., 624
Rulon, P. J., 466
Rush, Benjamin, 492, 790
Rush, James, 493
Russell, Earl, 917
Russell, R. W., 341, 353
Russell, W. R., 133
Ruyer, 503
Rylander, Gosta, 157, 188
Rytand, D. A., 615, 625

Sachs, B., 709
Sachs, Hanns, 590, 870, 876, 878, 894, 895
Sacks, J. M., 560
Sanctis, Sante De, 705, 708
Sand, A., 53, 56
Sandiford, P., 304, 319
Sanford, F. H., 543
Sanford, R. N., 386, 401, 543, 549, 561, 640, 643
Santayana, George, 951
Sapir, E., 900
Sarason, S. B., 694, 709, 816, 833
Sarbin, T. R., 820, 833
Sargent, H., 555, 561
Sartre, Jean-Paul, 139, 174-178, 188, 952
Saslow, G., 594
Sattler, T. H., 606, 607, 625
Saudek, Robert, 192, 543
Saul, Leon J., 590, 597, 599, 600, 620, 624, 625, 658
Savage, I. R., 847, 848
Scarisbrick, R., 608, 624
Schachtel, E. G., 133, 553, 561
Schachter, J., 101
Schacter, S., 400
Schafer, R., 75

Schelling, 670
Schilder, Paul, 671, 672, 678, 734, 738, 767, 769
Schiller, Friedrich, 592
Schkloven, N., 622
Schleicher, 910
Schmeidler, G., 484, 486
Schmideberg, M., 590
Schmideberg, Walther, 585
Schneck, J. M., 800, 801, 807, 808, 815, 818, 830, 832, 833
Schneider, H. W., 966
Schneider, R. A., 604, 607, 625
Schneiders, Alexander A., 284, 296
Schneirla, T. C., 342, 346, 349, 352-354
Schoen, M., 947
Scholz, L., 707, 709
Schopenhauer, 934
Schou, H. I., 604, 613, 625
Schreber, 551
Schreiner, L. H., 30
Schrickel, H. .G., 947
Schroeder, P., 709
Schumann, 118, 962
Schweiker, R. F., 466
Schweitzer, Albert, 213
Schweiz, 608, 625
Scott, J. P., 353, 354
Scott, M., 767
Scott, R. C., 626
Sears, R. R., 238
Séchehaye, M. A., 669, 676, 678, 899
Seeleman, V., 543
Seidenfeld, Morton, 701
Selbie, W. B., 972
Selling, L. S., 616, 625
Selye, H., 590
Semmelweiss, 565
Semmes, Josephine, 347, 354
Senders, V. L., 42, 54
Senn, 582